SMITHSONIAN

TIMELINES

OF THE

ANCIENT WORLD

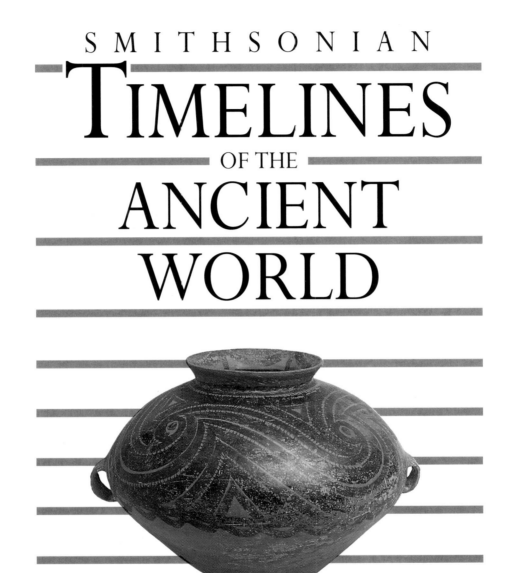

SMITHSONIAN
TIMELINES
OF THE
ANCIENT
WORLD

CHRIS SCARRE

SMITHSONIAN INSTITUTION

A DORLING KINDERSLEY BOOK

Project Editor Corinne Roberts **Senior Art Editor** Neville Graham

Art Editor Karen Ward

Editors

Roddy Craig, Louise Abbott, Claire Le Bas, Jeanette Mall

Designer

Steve Painter

Editorial Direction

Daphne Razazan

Managing Art Editor

Carole Ash

Production

Rosalind Priestley

SMITHSONIAN INSTITUTION PRESS BOOK DEVELOPMENT DIVISION STAFF

Executive Editor Caroline Newman **Senior Picture Editor** Paula Dailey

Editor Heidi M. Lumberg

First American edition, 1993

2 4 6 8 10 9 7 5 3 .

Published in the United States by Dorling Kindersley, Inc., 232 Madison Avenue, New York 10016

Library of Congress Cataloging-in-Publication Data

Smithsonian timelines of the ancient world: a visual chronology from
the origins of life to AD 1500 / editor-in-chief, Chris Scarre. --
1st American ed.
p.   cm.
Includes bibliographical reference and index.
ISBN 1-56458-305-8
1. History, Ancient--Chronology. 2. History, Ancient--Pictorial
works. 3. Middle Ages--History--Chronology. 4. Middle Ages--
History--Pictorial works. I. Scarre, Christopher.
II. Smithsonian Institution.
D54.5.S65 1993
930'.02'02--dc20   93-1840
                                                          CIP

Reproduced by Colourscan, Singapore
Printed and bound in Italy by A. Mondadori Editore, Verona

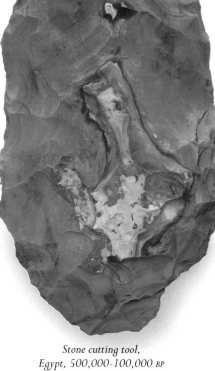

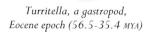

Dalmanites, a trilobite,
Silurian period (440-410 MYA)

Turritella, a gastropod,
Eocene epoch (56.5-35.4 MYA)

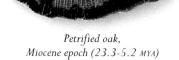

Petrified oak,
Miocene epoch (23.3-5.2 MYA)

Stone cutting tool,
Egypt, 500,000-100,000 BP

Laurel-leaf-shaped flint point,
Volgu, France 19,000-16,000 BP

Obsidian, Melos, Greece,
contemporary example

Shell-and-bone bead necklace,
Mugharet el-Kebara, Israel, c.10,000 BC

Clovis stone point,
Colorado, 9200-8900 BC

CONTENTS

*Terra-cotta figurine,
Greece, 7th millennium BC*

*Azurite, a mineral yielding a
blue pigment used by rock artists*

*Marble Cycladic figurine,
Greece, 2700-2400 BC*

*Chert projectile point,
North America, c.1800 BC*

*Bronze ritual vessel,
China, c.1500 BC*

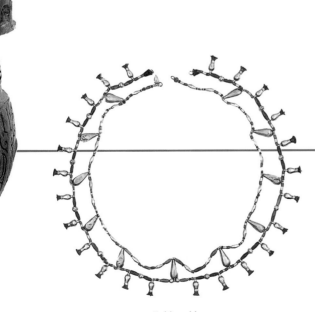

*Gold necklace,
Egypt, 1400-1200 BC*

*Canopic jar,
Egypt, 1000-500 BC*

*Bronze figurines,
Sardinia, 1000-800 BC*

FOREWORD

To this very day there are old men in the tents of Arabia who can recite the history of their ancestors for forty generations, and if in their recital they stray but a jot from the facts, others within hearing will immediately correct them, or supply forgotten details.
Nelson Glueck, *The River Jordan* (1946).

Mayan stelae, inscriptions on Egyptian mummy sarcophagi, petroglyphs in the American southwest, and ancient monumental architecture in many areas of the world all testify to the human desire to communicate something of who we are to subsequent generations. The human instinct to acquire, preserve, and transmit knowledge about our past seems to be equally compelling. Why this is so remains something of an enigma, but it must certainly be related to the learning process, which enables us to understand and express more completely our humanity. Because of our early learning experience, many of us sense, if only intuitively, that knowledge is crucial to our existence, that we become fully human as we learn from those who have lived before us, and that we are most completely part of the human odyssey as we pass information on to those who follow us.

Human beings, for at least the past several thousand years, have had an intense interest in who their ancestors were and what they did. Epic histories were memorized by members of many communities who, having been taught the origins and traditions of that society, then passed this information to the next generation – often with remarkable accuracy. With the advent of writing, the transmission of history and tradition to subsequent generations became less dependent on memory, and the potential for an enriched understanding of the human past was greatly increased.

Bronze jingle for war horse harness,
China, 8th century BC

Gold ear ornament,
Peru, 7th century BC

Olmec ceremonial ax head carved
with dragon god, Mexico, c. 900 BC

Pottery amphora for storing wine
or olive oil, Roman Empire, c. 200 BC

In a world in which the barriers of space and culture are constantly being lowered, particularly by the revolutions seen this century in transportation, communication, and a globally linked economy, it becomes ever more crucial for us to be aware of those lines of history that provide the foundation for human society today.

Science and scholarship do not exist in an isolated cultural vacuum. Those who occupy this realm of human endeavor need to communicate the substance of what they do to others. Knowledge that is not broadly shared contributes little to the human odyssey in which we are all participants. There are many barriers to achieving this objective, including the often esoteric and arcane language of the scholarly specialist. Also facts of history or prehistory rarely make sense outside the context of theory and integrating ideas that may be complex and difficult to understand.

Nevertheless, the effort to share knowledge through writing is a worthy objective that is the contemporary expression of a remarkable tradition extending back in time many thousands of years. All those who contributed to the development of *Smithsonian Timelines of the Ancient World* share the hope that each reader will find both interesting information and new meaning in the remarkable achievements of our ancestors.

Donald J. Ortner,
Curator of Anthropology,
National Museum of Natural History,
Smithsonian Institution

Terra-cotta tomb model of a watchtower,
Later Han period (206 BC-AD 220), China

Stone Buddha, Gandhara,
Pakistan, 2nd century AD

Bronze coin with inscription in Greek,
Axum, Ethiopia, 4th century AD

Roman silver spoons, Mildenhall, England,
4th century AD

INTRODUCTION

From earliest times, humankind has sought to explain the mystery of the dawn of time and human origins through myth and legend. Our ancient forebears would no doubt have been as surprised as many 19th-century people were to have learned the full story of human evolution.

Until the mid-19th century, the prevailing view of the past among western scholars was that set out in the Bible: the divine creation of Adam and Eve, followed by the new start for humanity in the aftermath of the Flood. Fossil evidence of extinct animals – including the massive bones of dinosaurs – was dismissed as the remains of biblical giants or of creatures that had lived before the Flood and perished in it. Even the great ages given in the Bible to such early figures as Noah (950 years) and Methuselah (969 years) were widely believed. In 1650, James Usher, Archbishop of Armagh in Northern Ireland, used these ages to calculate that the Creation had occurred 4,004 years before the birth of Christ.

It was not until the early 19th century that the Biblical version of events was scientifically challenged by the developing sciences of geology and evolutionary theory.

The great antiquity of geological deposits came slowly to be accepted, and the discovery of stone tools of human manufacture embedded in ancient deposits showed that humankind must be much older than the 6,000 years that had been proposed. Then, in 1859, the naturalist Charles Darwin published his *Origin of Species*, in which he showed that the diversity of living things in the world today can be explained by gradual change and extinction under the pressures of competition, both between species and between individual members of a species. Three years earlier, a skull fragment found in Germany's Neander Valley – the first discovery of Neanderthal remains – had shown that earlier kinds of humans had once existed. It was but a short step to the conclusion that the human race had also undergone hundreds

Glass drinking horn,
Lombardy, Italy, 6th century AD

Gold earrings, Shilla kingdom,
Korea, 6th century AD

Wheeled toy, Tres Zapotes,
Mexico, c. AD 500

Mayan ceremonial incense burner,
Chiapas, Mexico, AD 600-800

of thousands of years of natural selection, and that somewhere back along the line we have a shared ancestry with our closest living relatives, the great apes.

It would have been impossible for these theories to be formulated and developed without the work of archaeologists, and it is archaeological excavation and study that provides an account of the early human past – with evidence of how people lived, what they ate and drank, and the tools and technologies that they used in their everyday tasks.

Excavation itself has a long history. Clay tablets found in Mesopotamia tell how Nabonidus, king of Babylon in the 6th century BC, dug down into the foundations of the ziggurat at Ur in order to discover its original form, which he proposed to restore. Furthermore, both the Romans and the Chinese believed there had been successive "ages" of stone, bronze, and iron in the human past, a sequence that archaeologists have since shown to be broadly correct.

Yet none of these early investigations or ideas resulted in a clear view of the early human past, nor in a systematic attempt to uncover and understand ancient remains. The first scientifically conducted archaeological excavation was instigated in 1784 by Thomas Jefferson, third president of the United States, in a prehistoric burial mound on his Virginia estate. Techniques of excavation were steadily refined during the 19th and 20th centuries, the important principle being that of stratigraphy – that older remains are overlain by more recent remains. Another key principle is typology, which holds that many types of object undergo changes in form and decoration as fashions change or design is improved. Once the archaeologist has established a typological sequence – whether for bronze swords, bone combs, or pottery figurines – each new discovery can be slotted into its proper place in the sequence, and so given a relative age.

Seal and ring recording a land grant, Gujarat, India, 7th century AD

Silver cross, Sudan, 8th century AD

Carved wooden mask, Zambia, contemporary example

Mayan ceramic vessel, El Salvador, AD 800

Stratigraphy and typology, supported by estimates of geological age, were virtually the only ways of dating ancient objects available to archaeologists until the mid-20th century. Since then, a battery of new methods has become available, largely as a by-product of research in nuclear physics. The most revolutionary is radiocarbon dating, still one of the key methods used by archaeologists today. It is based on the fact that all living things contain carbon, a known proportion of which is radioactive. As soon as the organism dies, it stops taking in radioactive carbon and the amount remaining in the tissues begins to decay. By measuring the radioactive carbon that is left, and comparing it with the amount of non-radioactive carbon, it is possible to say when a particular organism died. Bones, shells, seeds, timbers, and even fragments of charcoal can be dated in this way.

However, after 50,000 years have passed, so little radioactive carbon is left that it is almost impossible to measure it. But similar kinds of techniques have been discovered that can trace the human story back to its origins many millions of years ago. These methods become increasingly imprecise the further back in time one goes. An artifact 3,500 years old can be dated to within 150 years or so, but for one that is 35,000 years old the margin of error may be as large as 4,000 years. It is for this reason that, in the pages that follow, the BC (before Christ) dating convention is not used for dates prior to 35,000 years ago; the 2,000-year difference between BC and BP (before present), relative to the vast time spans being discussed, becomes insignificant.

One important consequence of the new scientific dating methods has been to document the course of events in regions such as Africa, Australia, and large parts of the

Ceramic bird-effigy vessel, Panama, c. AD 1100

Bronze statue of the Hindu god Shiva, Chola period (9th–12th centuries AD), India

Sinu gold chest ornament, Colombia, c. AD 1300

Inlaid sitar, India, contemporary example

Americas that have been without any datable historical records until recent times. This allows us to give these regions their due prominence in the global story and to develop a fully multiethnic view of the human past.

Our knowledge of recent periods is greatly improved once written texts become available. In conventional terms, this is where "prehistory" ends and "history" starts. Archaeology does not stop here, however: all human societies, including our own, leave remains for archaeologists to study. We must also remember that writing is a relatively recent innovation in most parts of the world: although the earliest texts date back no more than 5,500 years, it is only during the last few centuries that literacy has become widespread. Furthermore, archaeology tells us about aspects of human life that are often passed over by written records, particularly in societies where the oral tradition is still strong. It is the archaeological record that enables a seamless view of the past to be presented, uninterrupted by the introduction of writing and the beginning of "history" in any particular region.

The aim of *Smithsonian Timelines of the Ancient World* is to present a tapestry of the human story from the earliest times to AD 1500, covering all parts of the world and all kinds of society in a series of timecharts, special "feature" pages, and maps. Making full use of archaeological evidence, it seeks to emphasize the great richness and variety of ways of life. Each timechart shows at a glance the full range of human diversity in a given time period, highlighting both change and continuity. For however distant the world of our ancestors seems to us today, one human characteristic never changes: the past continues to intrigue and fascinate modern generations as it did our forebears.

Chris Scarre, Editor-in-Chief
University of Cambridge

*No theatrical mask,
Japan, 14th century AD*

*Glass mosque lamp,
Syria, c. AD 1000*

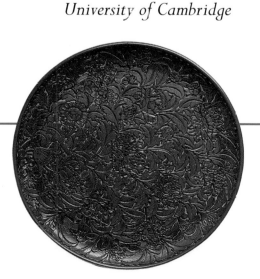

*Lacquer tray with floral motif,
Ming Dynasty (AD 1368-1644), China*

*Cat figurine, Key Marco,
Florida, 15th century AD*

HOW THIS BOOK WORKS

Smithsonian Timelines of the Ancient World starts with the origins of life on earth and ends at AD 1500.
The timespan of the book is divided into 18 chapters, with information presented in a series of specially
devised large-scale timecharts supported by introductory, map, and feature spreads.

TIMECHARTS

Each chapter is built around a sequence of timecharts, each of which deals with a segment of the time period covered by the chapter. The timecharts highlight change and continuity in different societies, pinpointing significant events and developments. The five regions – Americas; East Asia & Australasia; Middle East & South Asia; Europe; and Africa – are examined under four themes: *Food & Environment* covers such

fundamentals as diet, food gathering, farming, and medicine; *Shelter & Architecture* features buildings throughout history, from grass shelters and mud-brick huts to ornate palaces and temples; *Technology & Innovation* focuses on such pivotal developments as the first stone tools, experiments with metallurgy, or the invention of the first banknote; *Art & Ritual* embraces belief systems, burial practices, art, and cultural developments.

Heading indicates time span of each timechart within a chapter

Timeline pinpoints time span of timechart

Artwork reconstructs building of the period

Grid structure presents information by geographical region and by theme

Each geographical region is color-coded throughout

Theme illustrated with specially photographed artifact of the period

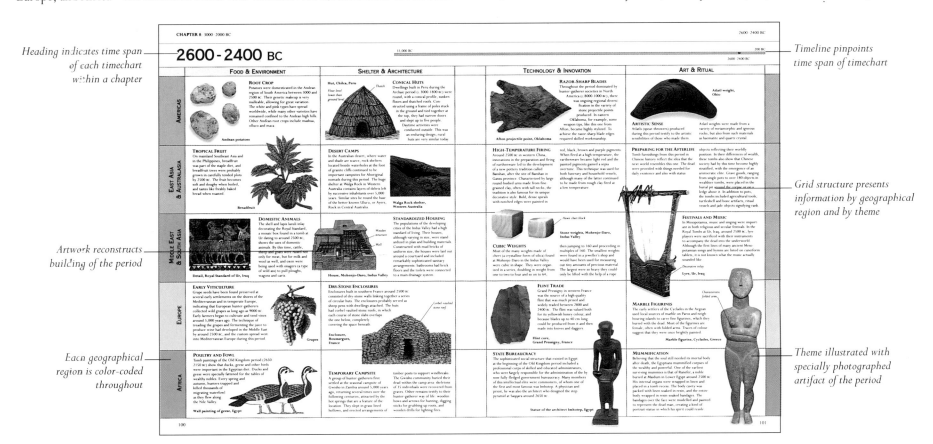

INTRODUCTORY SPREADS

Each chapter opens with an intro-duction that sets the period under discussion in its historical context. A panel of "Key Dates" highlights some of the most significant events of the period. The introductory text leads into a series of five maps, each with its own explan-atory text. Each map focuses on a different part of the world, illustrating in detail a topic of particular significance to the time period covered by the chapter.

Topics covered by the maps include ecological and climatic change, territorial expansion, the rise and fall of empires, the migration of peoples, cultural influences, and the spread of trading contacts. Where appropriate, the maps show the coastline and rivers of the period where they differ from those of today. The maps also carry comprehensive keys, where necessary, either to symbols pinpointing sites specific to the map's theme, or to shaded areas highlighting such elements as extent of territories or spheres of influence.

Key Dates panel pinpoints significant events of the period

Key explains symbols used on map

Timeline

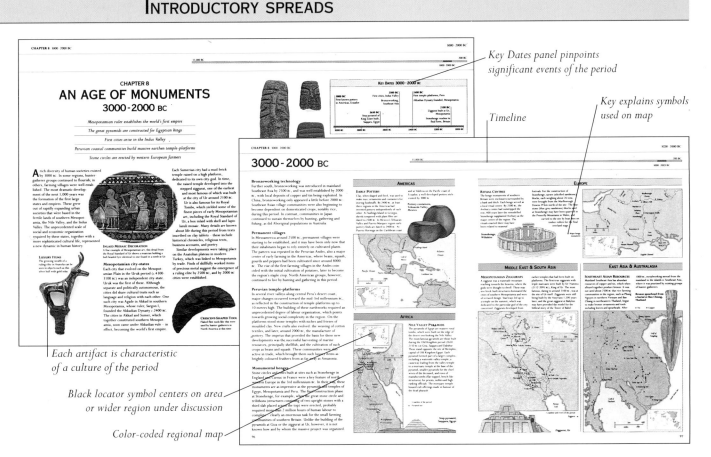

Each artifact is characteristic of a culture of the period

Black locator symbol centers on area or wider region under discussion

Color-coded regional map

FEATURES

In each chapter a topic of particular significance is explored in more detail in special feature pages. Some features are specific to a region or culture, such as the Olmec of Mexico (*pages 140-41*), Alpine Lake Villages (*pages 114-15*) or The Neanderthals (*pages 48-49*); some are more global, such as The Ice Age Cycle (*pages 40-41*); others explore distinct issues or themes, such as East African Trade (*pages 226-27*) and Origins of Food Production (*pages 80-81*).

Features such as The Pyramids at Giza (*pages 104-05, right*) focus on spectacular architectural constructions, describing the purpose for which they were built, the beliefs that surrounded them and the society of which they are emblematic. A location map pinpoints the appropriate region, and artists' reconstructions recreate buildings as they once were, using archaeologists' evidence and original plans where available.

Artist's reconstruction based on archaeologists' and historians' plans and drawings

Timeline

Subsidiary theme, explored in greater detail

Location map shows key sites, features, and boundaries

Cutaway illustrations and enlarged details reveal more about skills and technology

Artifacts are characteristic of the period and location

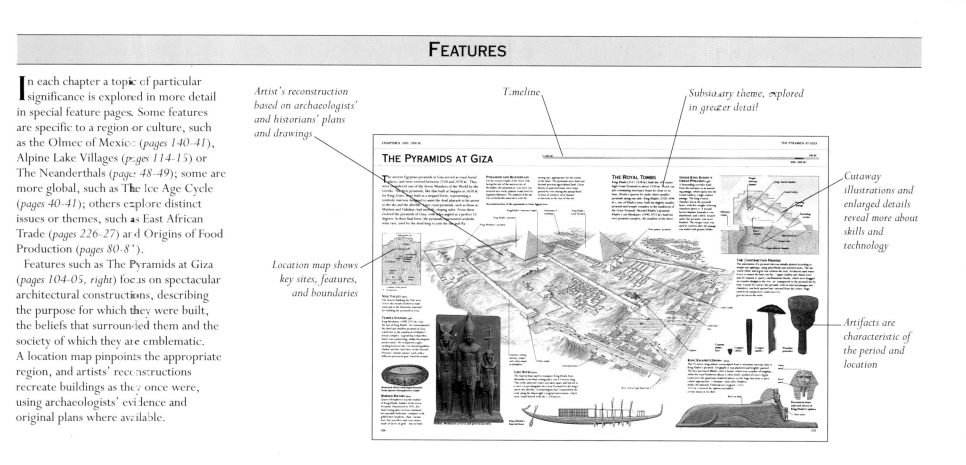

GEOGRAPHICAL DEFINITIONS

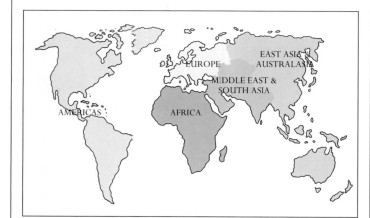

☐ **AMERICAS**

☐ **EAST ASIA & AUSTRALASIA**: China, Japan, Korea, Southeast Asia, Malaysia, Australasia, and the Pacific islands.

☐ **MIDDLE EAST & SOUTH ASIA**: Turkey, Syria, Lebanon, Israel, Jordan, the Caucasus Republics (Azerbaijan, Armenia, and Georgia), Arabian Peninsula, Iran, Iraq, Central Asia, and the Indian subcontinent.

☐ **EUROPE**: the continent of Europe to the Ural Mountains.

☐ **AFRICA**

Throughout *Smithsonian Timelines of the Ancient World*, locations have been set within the historical context of the time period under discussion, with modern equivalent place names given where necessary. Within the five broad divisions above, there exist many regions, which may be defined by either political, topographical, or cultural boundaries. Definitions are given here (*right*) for those most commonly used in this book. For additional reference, pages 244-48 comprise larger-scale maps of the five broad regions described above, featuring sites of historical and/or archaeological interest placed within the context of modern geographical boundaries.

AMERICAS
Caribbean islands: *Cuba, the Dominican Republic and Haiti, Jamaica, Puerto Rico, Trinidad and Tobago, and adjacent island groups.*
Central America: *the republics of Guatemala, Honduras, El Salvador, Nicaragua, Costa Rica, and Panama.*
Great Basin: *natural basin and mountainous region in Nevada and Utah.*
Great Lakes: *the region of Lakes Superior, Michigan, Huron, Erie, and Ontario in central North America.*
Great Plains: *the central part of North America, extending from the Rocky Mountains in the west to the Mississippi River valley in the east.*
Mesoamerica: *the pre-Hispanic cultural area comprising central and southern Mexico, all of Guatemala, Belize, and El Salvador, and parts of northern Costa Rica, Nicaragua and Honduras.*
North America: *Canada, Greenland, the continental United States, Mexico, Central America, and the Caribbean.*
Midwestern North America: *the region south of the Great Lakes, including much of the central United States.*
Southeastern North America: *the southern United States from the Mississippi River valley to the Atlantic Ocean.*
Southwestern North America: *all of Arizona and portions of Nevada, Utah, Colorado, New Mexico, and northern Mexico.*

EAST ASIA & AUSTRALASIA
Australasia: *islands of the South Pacific, including Australia, New Zealand, New Guinea, and adjacent islands.*

Island Asia: *Indonesia (except for Irian Jaya), Brunei, Malaysian states of Sabah and Sarawak, and the Philippines.*
Melanesia: *island groups of the Bismarck Archipelago, Solomon Islands, Vanuatu, New Caledonia, and Fiji.*
Micronesia: *the Mariana Islands, Marshall Islands, Caroline Islands, and Gilbert Islands.*
Polynesia: *the Hawaiian Islands, Line Islands, Phoenix Islands, Tuvalu, Samoa, Tonga, Tokelau, Cook Islands, Tubuai, Tuamotu, Society Islands, Marquesas Islands, and Easter Island.*
Southeast Asia: *Burma, Thailand, Cambodia, Laos, Vietnam, and peninsular Malaysia.*

MIDDLE EAST & SOUTH ASIA
Anatolia: *Asian peninsula between the Black, Aegean, and Mediterranean Seas, comprising most of modern Turkey. Also called Asia Minor.*
Central Asian steppes: *region of grasslands lying north and northeast of the Caspian Sea, ranging from the basin of the River Don eastward through Kazakhstan to the mountain ranges of Altai and Tien Shan.*
Deccan: *triangular plateau covering most of peninsular India south of the Narmada River.*
Fertile Crescent: *broad arc of, historically, agriculturally rich territory curving from the head of the Persian Gulf around the northern edge of the Syrian Desert to coastal Israel and the borders of Egypt.*
Levant: *the coastal strip of Syria, Lebanon, and Israel.*
Mesopotamia: *ancient region of southwestern Asia around the lower Tigris and Euphrates rivers in modern Iraq*

South Asia: *subcontinental mass of India, Pakistan, Nepal, Bhutan, Bangladesh, and Sri Lanka.*

EUROPE
Balkan Peninsula: *region of southeastern Europe between the Adriatic, Ionian, Mediterranean, Aegean, and Black Seas. The lower Danube river is generally taken as the northern limit.*
Caucasus: *mountainous region lying between the Caspian and Black Seas, including the southernmost part of Russia and the modern states of Armenia, Azerbaijan, and Georgia.*

AFRICA
East African Lakes: *group of freshwater lakes extending from Lake Nyasa in the south to Lake Turkana (Rudolf) in the north, including Lake Victoria and the Rift Valley lakes of Tanganyika, Edward, and Albert.*
Maghreb: *countries of northwestern Africa including Morocco, Algeria, and Tunisia.*
Nubia: *historical region of the middle Nile straddling, in modern terms, the southern part of Egypt and the northern part of Sudan, mostly consisting of desert.*
Rift Valley: *natural depression extending from Syria through East Africa to Mozambique.*
Sahel: *vaguely defined region immediately south of the Sahara, running through the modern states of Senegal, Mauritania, Mali, Burkina, Niger, and Chad.*
Sudan: *the largest country in modern Africa extending from Egypt and the Middle Nile south to Zaire, Uganda, and the Sudd swamps. Historically, the term referred to the lands lying immediately south of the Sahara (the modern Sahel, above).*

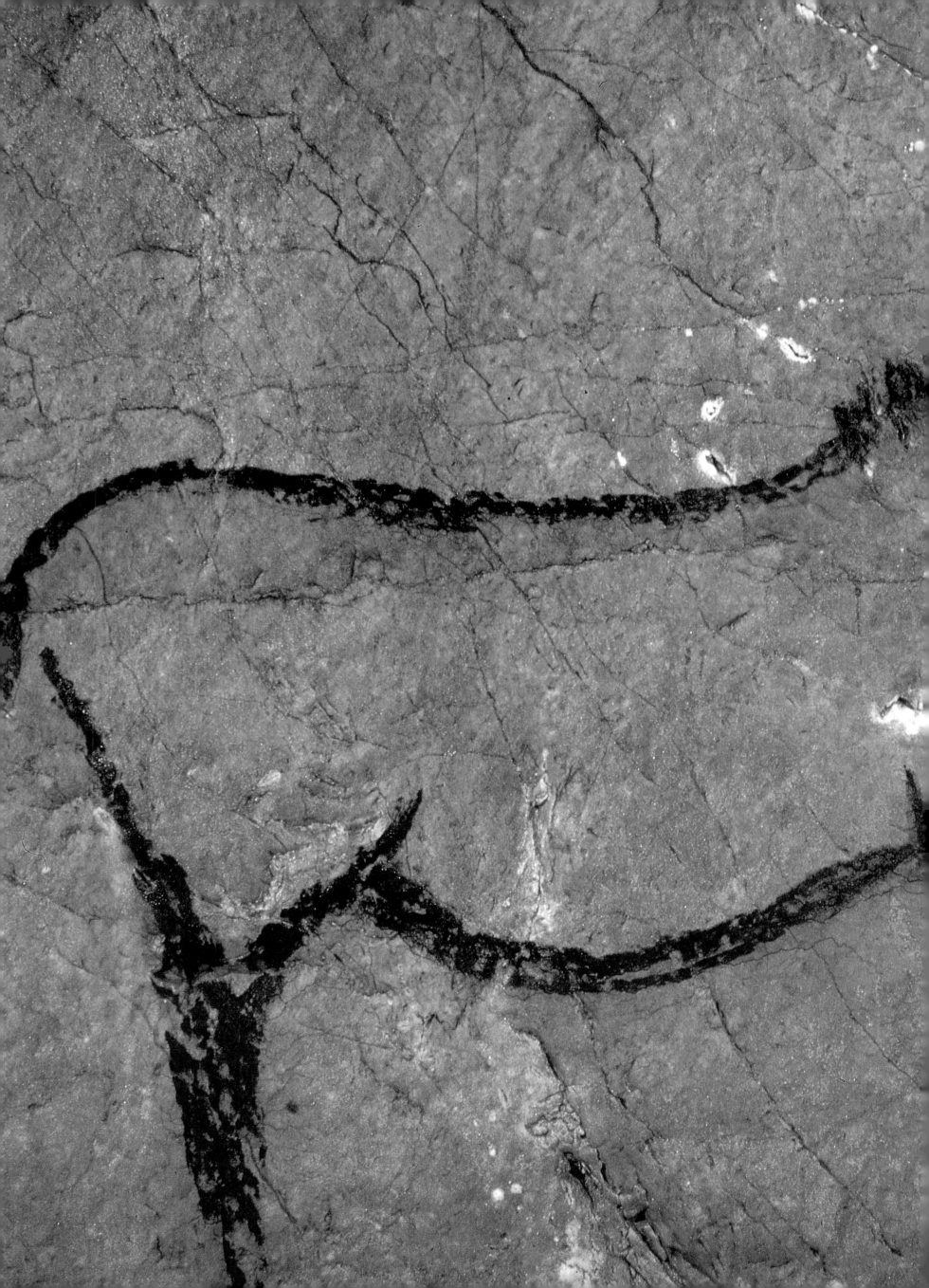

PART ONE

4,600
MILLION YEARS AGO
— TO —
5000 BC

This is the period of prehistory, before written records began. It is the geological record that tells the story, with fossils providing evidence of the earliest life forms, which slowly evolved giving rise to the dinosaurs and the first small warm-blooded mammals. Humankind made a relatively late appearance, spreading over the globe during the rigors of the Ice Age and developing into diverse societies of skillful hunters and gatherers.

Outline of a horse sketched in charcoal on a cave wall, Niaux, France, c. 3,000 BC.

CHAPTER 1
FIRST LIFE ON EARTH
4,600-1 MILLION YEARS AGO

Chemicals combine to create DNA, the genetic blueprint for all life

Single-celled organisms are the only life on earth for almost 3,000 million years

First vertebrates emerge from the sea to colonize the land

Mass extinction of dinosaurs clears the way for mammals

Larger brain gives early hominids advantage over rival species

When the earth came into being some 4,600 million years ago, its atmosphere consisted of volcanic gases with little oxygen, making it hostile to life. The emergence of the first primitive life forms, around 3,500 million years ago, was due to the existence of chemicals that could combine and replicate. Gradually, oxygen levels rose, creating conditions that were favorable to a wider range of life forms. Simple organisms – single-celled creatures similar to modern algae – dominated life on earth for almost 3,000 million years, until around 570 million years ago, when more complex organisms began to evolve.

Fossil evidence

A vast expansion in the variety of life forms over the past 570 million years is recorded in fossils. The first vertebrates appeared some 500 million years ago; the first plants around 430 million years ago; the earliest land animals approximately 400 million years ago. Between 200 and 65 million years ago the earth was populated by the dinosaurs, ranging in length from a few feet to over 130 feet.

Why the reign of the dinosaurs came to its sudden end is not known for certain. One theory suggests that a great meteorite struck the earth, possibly in the region of the present-day Gulf of Mexico, shrouding the world in dust and causing widespread destruction and death. Whatever the cause, the disappearance of these huge beasts opened the way for other kinds of animals, notably mammals. By 50 million years ago a variety of mammals roamed the earth, including recognizable ancestors of many modern animals such as monkeys, horses, elephants, and felines.

Apes and humans

The story of apes and early humans begins some 25 million years ago with *Proconsul*, an early species of ape that lived in the forests of East Africa. By around 4 million years ago, the lineages of humans and of modern apes (gorillas and chimpanzees) had diverged. The first species to belong indisputably to the human line were the australopithecines, differing from apes in being bipedal (able to walk on two legs). Although australopithecines may have used rocks and bones as crude tools, the first deliberately made stone tools were produced by a later and more developed species, *Homo habilis* ("handy man"), some 2.5 million years ago. The success of *Homo habilis* was due, in part, to the development of a larger brain.

FORESTED EOCENE SWAMPLANDS
Giant palms and flowering grasses proliferated in the warm, humid conditions of the Eocene epoch, an age in which mammals flourished and diversified.

COLONIZING THE OCEAN FLOOR
Tiny colony-forming organisms such as this bryozoan were among the earth's first multicellular creatures and still survive today, most spectacularly as coral reefs.

GEOLOGICAL TIME 570-1 MILLION YEARS AGO

The Precambrian era (4,600-570 million years ago) covers the time before complex life evolved on earth. The last 570 million years, when increasingly complex forms of life proliferated, are divided into three eras: the Paleozoic (old life, from the Greek *palaios,* "old" and *zoos,* "life"), Mesozoic (middle life, from the Greek *mesos,* "middle"), and Cenozoic (recent life, from the Greek *cenos,* "recent"). These are subdivided into timebands, known as periods in the Paleozoic and Mesozoic eras and epochs in the Cenozoic era.

Cambrian 570-510 MYA	Ordovician 510-440 MYA	Silurian 440-410 MYA	Devonian 410-360 MYA	Carboniferous 360-290 MYA	Permian 290-245 MYA	Triassic 245-208 MYA	Jurassic 208-146 MYA	Cretaceous 146-65 MYA	Paleocene 65-56.5 MYA	Eocene 56.5-35.4 MYA	Oligocene 35.4-23.3 MYA	Miocene 23.3-5.2 MYA	Pliocene 5.2-1.6 MYA
PALEOZOIC ERA						MESOZOIC ERA			CENOZOIC ERA				

570 MYA	500 MYA	450 MYA	400 MYA	350 MYA	300 MYA	250 MYA	200 MYA	150 MYA	100 MYA	50 MYA	1 MYA

Increased brain size

A still larger-brained hominid, *Homo erectus,* developed in Africa around 1.7 million years ago. It took its name from the fact that it habitually stood and walked fully upright. The development of a larger brain is the most significant feature of the human lineage. Eventually, in modern humans, the brain increased in capacity to become three times larger in relation to body size than that of our closest living relatives, the chimpanzees.

PARASAUROLOPHUS SKULL
A large plant-eating dinosaur, *Parasaurolophus* could tear and grind tough vegetation in its powerful beak and jaws.

Hollow crest probably functioned as a resonator to amplify calls

Horny beak gave the name "duckbills" to this group of dinosaurs

Teeth for grinding plant matter

Dependence on adults allows long learning period for infant primates

PRIMATE FAMILY
Our earliest fossil evidence of ancestors of the living apes, such as this gibbon, is *Proconsul,* found in Africa. Today's apes live in both Africa and Asia.

Skills and strategies

Increased brain capacity enabled the development of advanced foraging strategies and skills. A larger brain was dependent on a high protein intake, however, and the adoption of a meat-eating diet may have been crucial. But early human ancestors were not heroic hunters. *Homo habilis* was small in stature and would have been at risk from predators. The safest way to obtain meat was by scavenging from carcasses, and for this task, tools were necessary. *Homo erectus* had skills that enabled it to adapt to an increasing range of environments. *H. erectus* fossils discovered on Java, which date to before 1 million years ago, are among the earliest evidence of an expansion of hominid settlement that has dominated the human story for hundreds of thousands of years.

Brow ridge developing even in a child

Braincase

HOMINID SKULL
Homo erectus spread from Africa to reach Java in Southeast Asia over a million years ago. This skull of a *Homo erectus* child was found at Mojokerto in Java.

19

4,600-410 MILLION YEARS AGO

MICROBES

The Precambrian world was once thought to be lifeless, but some Precambrian rocks have been found to contain tiny fossils of single-celled organisms. The fossil record shows prokaryotes (cells without nuclei) up to 3,500 million years old, and eukaryotes (cells with nuclei) dating back to 1,750 million years ago.

PRECAMBRIAN (4,600-570 MYA)
About 2,000 million years ago, rising levels of oxygen in the atmosphere provided an environment in which eukaryotes flourished. The earliest fossilized plant spores date to late Ordovician times, but primitive algae may have colonized damp environments during the Precambrian.

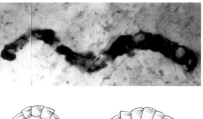

3,500 million years old
Less than 0.1 mm long, this prokaryote is preserved in a section of rock found in western Australia.

2,300 million years old
Formed in columns, these stromatolite fossils were colonies of sediment-trapping microbes.

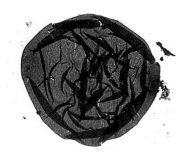

800 million years old
This tiny eukaryotic algal cell fossil, *Valeria*, lived in the plankton of a late Precambrian ocean.

LAND AND FRESHWATER ANIMALS

There is no evidence of terrestrial animals until the Silurian period, when centipedes and other arthropods (animals with jointed external skeletons) appeared.

MARINE ANIMALS

Multicellular animals appeared in the sea only in the very late Precambrian. During the Cambrian, invertebrates with hard, fossilizable skeletons increased in number and variety. Fish, the first vertebrates, date to the Ordovician but are far outnumbered in the fossil record by corals and other invertebrates that inhabited the sea bed.

PRECAMBRIAN (4,600-570 MYA)
Tribrachidium, a fossil less than 1 inch in diameter with a peculiar trifold symmetry, is a member of the late Precambrian Ediacara Fauna, first discovered in South Australia, which consists of the impressions in sandstone of jellyfish and other animals lacking hard skeletons.

Tribrachidium
Complex animals made of many cells, like this *Tribrachidium*, appeared at the end of the Precambrian.

CAMBRIAN (570-510 MYA)
Invertebrates with hard external skeletons, such as mollusks and trilobites (arthropods which grew by molting their old skeletons to form new ones), diversified during the Cambrian. Most of the earliest fossils with hard skeletons were composed of calcium phosphate, but forms with skeletons of calcium carbonate minerals later became dominant.

Porous skeleton

Central cavity

Metaldetes
Archaeocyathans – extinct sponges including *Metaldetes* – flourished briefly during the Cambrian. Some lived as colonies, constructing reefs on the sea bed.

Burgess Shale worm
Animals like this worm can be found preserved in the shale deposits of British Columbia in Canada.

ORDOVICIAN (510-440 MYA)
A great variety of marine life is fossilized in Ordovician rocks. Invertebrates proliferated during this period, many living on the sea bed and feeding on plankton. Their shells accumulated to form thick beds of limestone.

Serrations housed individuals in colonies

Didymograptus
This colony of tiny individuals floated on the surface of late Ordovician oceans. Dead colonies sank to the sea bed and became entombed in mud.

Stenaster
Fossilized starfish like this tiny *Stenaster* are rare. Their skeletons fragmented quickly, making fossilization difficult.

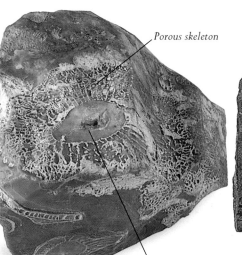

Lower surface of starfish

Beak of larger valve

Convex ribbed shell

Platystrophia *above*
Invertebrates with shells consisting of a larger and smaller valve, brachiopods like *Platystrophia* are common Ordovician fossils.

Chasmatopora *above right*
Growing on the sea bed, *Chasmatopora* was a bryozoan (an entire colony of microscopic creatures, each with tentacles for catching plankton) that became fragmented during burial.

Short, flexible tail

Cothurnocystis
The Ordovician *Cothurnocystis* may be related either to starfish or to primitive vertebrates. It probably used its tail to move around on the sea bed.

4,600 - 410 MYA

LAND PLANTS

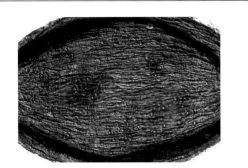

675 million years old
Toward the close of the Precambrian, larger and more complex eukaryotes, such as this one, began to evolve.

SILURIAN (440-410 MYA)

It is probable that most of the earth's surface was devoid of vegetation during Silurian times. Any land plants that did exist may have inhabited damp areas, such as tidal mud flats. Primitive vascular plants like *Cooksonia*, whose tissues conducted water and nutrients, lived alongside hornworts, mosses, and liverworts.

Stem tip with spore capsule

Cooksonia
This tiny plant grew less than an inch tall. Round structures at the tips of its slender stems contained the spores used in asexual reproduction.

Branching stem

Shelly mudstone

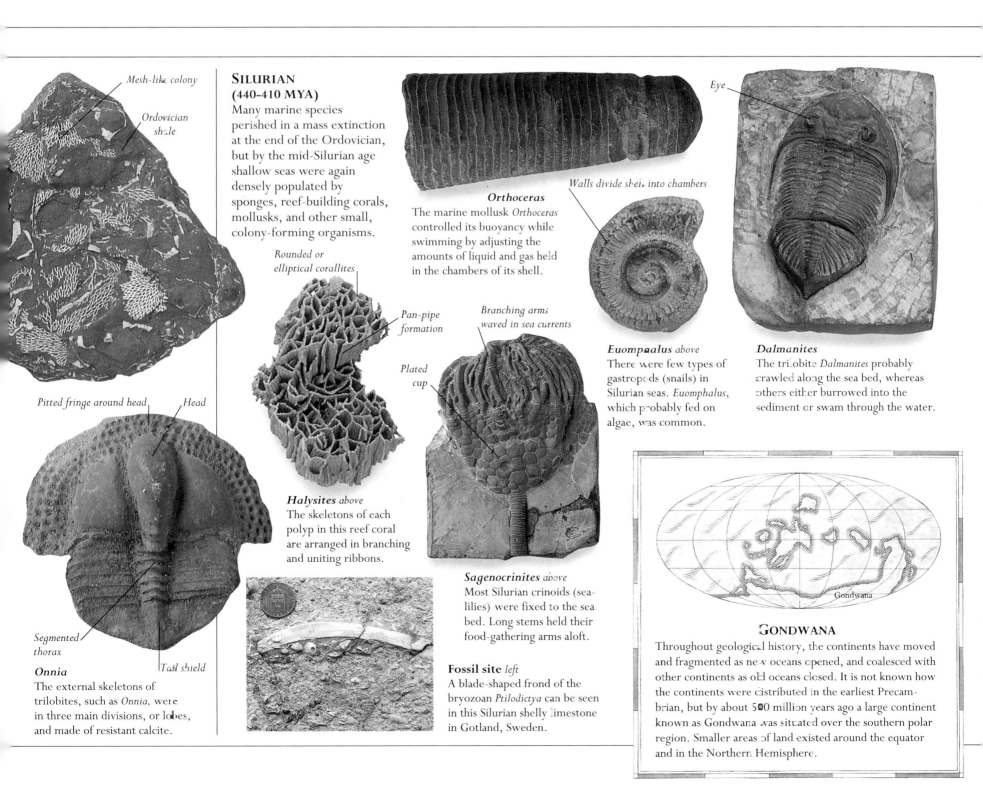

Mesh-like colony

Ordovician shale

SILURIAN (440-410 MYA)

Many marine species perished in a mass extinction at the end of the Ordovician, but by the mid-Silurian age shallow seas were again densely populated by sponges, reef-building corals, mollusks, and other small, colony-forming organisms.

Rounded or elliptical corallites

Pan-pipe formation

Plated cup

Branching arms waved in sea currents

Orthoceras
The marine mollusk *Orthoceras* controlled its buoyancy while swimming by adjusting the amounts of liquid and gas held in the chambers of its shell.

Walls divide shell into chambers

Eye

Euomphalus above
There were few types of gastropods (snails) in Silurian seas. *Euomphalus*, which probably fed on algae, was common.

Dalmanites
The trilobite *Dalmanites* probably crawled along the sea bed, whereas others either burrowed into the sediment or swam through the water.

Pitted fringe around head   *Head*

Halysites above
The skeletons of each polyp in this reef coral are arranged in branching and uniting ribbons.

Sagenocrinites above
Most Silurian crinoids (sea-lilies) were fixed to the sea bed. Long stems held their food-gathering arms aloft.

Segmented thorax   *Tail shield*

Onnia
The external skeletons of trilobites, such as *Onnia,* were in three main divisions, or lobes, and made of resistant calcite.

Fossil site *left*
A blade-shaped frond of the bryozoan *Ptilodictya* can be seen in this Silurian shelly limestone in Gotland, Sweden.

Gondwana

GONDWANA

Throughout geological history, the continents have moved and fragmented as new oceans opened, and coalesced with other continents as old oceans closed. It is not known how the continents were distributed in the earliest Precambrian, but by about 500 million years ago a large continent known as Gondwana was situated over the southern polar region. Smaller areas of land existed around the equator and in the Northern Hemisphere.

410-245 MILLION YEARS AGO

LAND PLANTS

In the Late Paleozoic (410-245 MYA), primitive spore-bearing plants such as clubmosses and horsetails, and a few seed plants, were dominant. By Carboniferous times, forests of trees over 135 feet tall had appeared. In the freshwater swamps beneath the canopy, dead vegetation accumulated as peat, later turning to coal.

Archaeopteris

DEVONIAN (410-360 MYA)
Many plant species emerged during the Devonian period, covering the land with a dense layer of vegetation. The majority were spore-bearing plants. Gymnosperms (plants that protect their seeds in a cone) appeared only in the very late Devonian. A forerunner was a progymnosperm called *Archaeopteris*, which grew up to 60 feet tall.

CARBONIFEROUS (360-290 MYA)
During the Carboniferous period, which lasted 70 million years, many diverse species of clubmosses and horsetails evolved. Their sizes differed greatly, but both groups included species that grew as trees. This period derives its name from the plant remains deposited in the coal measures, a series of layers of coal-bearing rock.

Horsetail
The narrow leaves of horsetails grow in concentric rings around the stem. One horsetail survives today; varieties were much more numerous during the Carboniferous.

Fossilized impression

Modern horsetail

LAND AND FRESHWATER ANIMALS

Amphibians were the first vertebrates to colonize the land in the Devonian period of the Late Paleozoic. They were accompanied by insects, including cockroaches and dragonflies. Reptiles were better adapted for terrestrial life. They appeared in the Carboniferous and diversified in the Permian, when fish and mollusks also flourished.

DEVONIAN (410-360 MYA)
Primitive fish like *Pteraspis* lived in freshwater habitats. These jawless fish are related to modern lampreys and hagfish.

Pteraspis

CARBONIFEROUS (360-290 MYA)
The first flying insects appeared during the Carboniferous, including dragonflies, some with huge wingspans of nearly 20 inches. The amphibians and reptiles that inhabited the freshwater swamps spent most of their time in the water. The amphibians were bulky creatures quite unlike the frogs and newts living today.

Graephonus above
Early spiders, like modern species, had spinnerets for weaving webs to trap prey.

Carbonicola below
Bivalve mollusks such as *Carbonicola* lived on the muddy bottoms of freshwater and brackish swamps.

Growth lines on shell

MARINE ANIMALS

Fishes first appeared in the Ordovician, but the Devonian saw a great increase in their variety and abundance. Shelled invertebrates continued to diversify. About 95 percent of marine species disappeared toward the end of the Permian period. Some scientists attribute this mass extinction to climatic warming.

DEVONIAN (410-360 MYA)
Marine life in the Devonian included many invertebrates, such as corals, which lived on the sea bed. Swimming predators were fish and sea scorpions. Many species became extinct toward the end of the period.

Modern African lungfish

Chirodipterus below
Whereas modern lungfish live in freshwater environments, the Devonian lungfish *Chirodipterus* inhabited shallow marine environments. Lungfish are close relatives of the earliest terrestrial vertebrates.

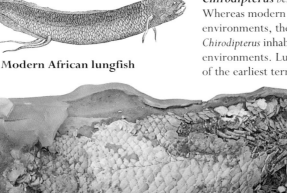

Thick scales

Armored head

CARBONIFEROUS (360-290 MYA)
Sharks first became common in the Carboniferous, joining the squid-like cephalopod mollusks as swimming predators. Brachiopods (bivalve, or two-shelled, creatures that usually lived permanently attached to the sea floor), bryozoans (colonies of tentacled creatures), sea lilies, and mollusks continued to prosper on the seabed. Corals and sponges, although numerous, seldom built reefs.

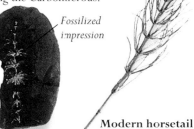

Tubina
This loosely coiled shell belongs to a bellerophontid, one of an extinct group of snail-like mollusks.

Loosely coiled shell

Bothriolepis left
The fish-like vertebrate *Bothriolepis* was heavily armored with a head shield and a body shield. Its hinged "arms" may have been used in movement across the sea bed.

Hinged "arm"

Spirifer
Brachiopods, including *Spirifer,* characteristically have two articulated valves joined together along a straight hinge line. The valves gaped open to allow planktonic food to be sucked inside.

Deep fold

Convex shell

Hinge line

Lepidodendron
This characteristic clubmoss tree of the coal measure swamps grew up to 150 feet tall. Its tall trunk supported a small, open crown of branches.

Impression of bark in sandstone

Lepidostrobus
The cones borne by *Lepidodendron* have their own name because they were originally found in isolation from the rest of the tree.

Cross section through cigar-shaped cone

PERMIAN (290-245 MYA)
The land surface became more arid in the Permian period. Seed-bearing plants became dominant, surpassing the spore-bearing plants that had flourished in the wetter environments of the Carboniferous. *Psaronius* is a Permian tree fern. Modern tree ferns are only found in the tropics and Southern Hemisphere.

Psaronius

Polished section

PERMIAN (290-245 MYA)
Reptiles less dependent on water flourished in the drier climate of the Permian. Their eggs contained amniotic fluid and could be laid on dry land. One group of reptiles, the sail-backed pelycosaurs, were probably the largest land animals in the early Permian.

Eryops
This amphibian was 6 feet in length and had the sharp teeth of a carnivore. The robust limb bones suggest that *Eryops* was fully capable of moving on land.

Thick skull bones

Sturdy legs

Small sharp teeth

Bony spine from dorsal sail

Edaphosaurus
The "sails" on the back of the herbivorous pelycosaur *Edaphosaurus* are thought to have been covered by a thin layer of skin rich in blood vessels, enabling the creature to regulate its body temperature.

Dagger-like teeth

Dimetrodon
The pelycosaur *Dimetrodon* was carnivorous. Pelycosaurs had a sprawling gait compared to the upright gaits of dinosaurs.

Fossil site
The stems of dead crinoids (sea lilies) accumulated on the Carboniferous sea bed, forming crinoidal limestones, as shown here at Clitheroe in northern England.

Archimedes *below*
In the distinctive bryozoan *Archimedes*, a screw-shaped central skeleton supported a twisted lacy frond comprising the plankton-feeding individuals of the colony.

PERMIAN (290-245 MYA)
Marine life in the Permian continued the pattern set in the Carboniferous. However, there is evidence of a slow decline in the diversity of marine life before the mass extinction at the end of this period. As the continents coalesced, the shallow seas around them gradually dried up, eliminating environments inhabited by marine animals.

Heavy scales

Large eye

Paleoniscus
The primitive bony fish *Paleoniscus* belonged to the group *Chondrostei*, of which the sturgeon is one of only a few forms still living.

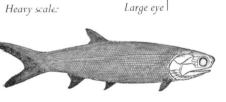

Reconstruction of *Paleoniscus*

Hard spiral of solid calcite

Goniatites *left*
A type of cephalopod mollusk, *Goniatites* probably employed jet propulsion for swimming, just like modern cephalopods.

Polygonal corallites

Lonsdaleia
Solitary corals, and those that grew in colonies, were common in the Carboniferous. The colonial coral *Lonsdaleia* was made up of polygonal (many-sided) individuals, or corallites, with central protuberances.

Actinocrinites
The robust cup of *Actinocrinites* fossilizes more readily than most crinoids (sea lilies). The heavy polygonal plates of the cup may have formed a defense against predators.

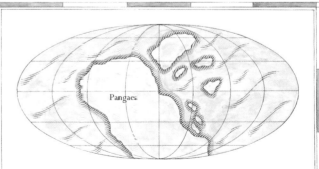

Pangaea

SUPERCONTINENT
By Devonian times, a grouping of smaller continents straddling the equator formed the Old Red Sandstone Continent. This was separated by an ocean from the mass of Gondwana to the south. The supercontinent Pangaea came into existence during the Carboniferous when Gondwana and the Old Red Sandstone Continent collided. Pangaea grew more during the Permian when it fused with the once-separate Siberian continent.

245-65 MILLION YEARS AGO

LAND PLANTS

Gymnosperms, plants that protect their seeds in cones, flourished in the Triassic and Jurassic, and included cycads (palmlike trees), conifers, and ginkgos. Angiosperms, flowering plants that protect their seeds in a fruit, evolved during the Cretaceous. Flowers co-evolved with the insects that pollinated them.

Dicroidium

TRIASSIC (245-208 MYA)
Rocks of Triassic age contain the earliest representatives of ginkgos and araucariaceans (monkey puzzle trees). Ferns were probably the most common plants during the Triassic. The seed fern *Dicroidium* (*left*) possibly grew as a shrub or a small tree.

JURASSIC (208-146 MYA)
Land plants of the Jurassic were similar to those of the Triassic. Cycads, conifers, and ginkgos multiplied, forming evergreen forests. The absence of polar ice enabled trees to grow at very high latitudes, although photosynthesis ceased during winter.

Todites below
The leaves of Jurassic *Todites* are almost identical to ferns today.

Ginkgo *above*
Ginkgos flourished in the Jurassic but only one, the maidenhair tree, survives today.

LAND AND FRESHWATER ANIMALS

Of all the reptiles of the Mesozoic (245-65 MYA), the dinosaurs are the most familiar, but mammal-like therapsids, flying pterosaurs, and early lizards and crocodiles also evolved. Mammals and birds first appeared in the Triassic and Jurassic respectively. Dinosaurs died out in the mass extinction at the end of the Cretaceous.

TRIASSIC (245-208 MYA)
Vertebrates such as mammals, dinosaurs, crocodiles, and frogs flourished in the Triassic. Pterosaurs, the first flying vertebrates, evolved during this period, pre-dating birds.

Eye socket

Nostril

Benthosuchus skull
The amphibian *Benthosuchus* probably resembled a crocodile. It inhabited fresh water and fed on fish.

Eye socket

Opening for jaw muscle

Riojasuchus skull *above*
The predator *Riojasuchus* belonged to a group of reptiles called thecodonts, which may have been ancestors of dinosaurs.

JURASSIC (208-146 MYA)
Herbivorous and carnivorous dinosaurs flourished in the Jurassic and reached enormous sizes. Sauropod dinosaurs such as *Diplodocus* and *Apatosaurus*, with small heads, long necks, and tails, existed at this time, as did bony-plated dinosaurs like *Stegosaurus* and primitive mammals.

Defensive tail spines

MARINE ANIMALS

Predators such as crabs and bony fishes diversified during the Mesozoic. Their prey was bivalve mollusks (with shells made up of two hinged valves), which responded by evolving thicker shells and burrowing lifestyles. Large swimming reptiles perished before or during the Cretaceous mass extinction.

TRIASSIC (245-208 MYA)
New life forms began to emerge after the Permian mass extinction. Mollusks, corals, and sea lilies diversified, and the first turtles and ichthyosaurs (fish-like reptiles) date to this period.

The sea lily Encrinus

JURASSIC (208-146 MYA)
Marine life flourished in the Jurassic as it had before the Permian extinction: bivalve mollusks and echinoids (sea urchins) lived on the sea bed; cephalopod mollusks (with tentacles and eyes) and fishes lived in the waters above.

Cylindroteuthis below
The extinct squid-like mollusk *Cylindroteuthis* had a long conical body that contained gas- and liquid-filled chambers, which functioned as a buoyancy control. The bullet-shaped guard (a kind of internal shell) counterbalanced the head and tentacles.

Apex

Guard

Crushed conical body

Pleurotomaria *above*
A Jurassic gastropod, *Pleurotomaria* is almost identical to modern slit shells. Unlike the predatory snails that first appeared in the Cretaceous, *Pleurotomaria* was a herbivore.

Gryphaea below
The bivalve mollusk *Gryphaea* had a large convex valve that rested in sediment on the sea bed; the smaller lid-like valve opened to feed.

Plankton-catching arms

Cup

Stem

Long root

Plesiosaur tooth
Marine reptiles with a long neck and tail, the carnivorous plesiosaurs had four paddle-like limbs that helped propel them through the water.

Ring of bones surrounding eye socket

Very sharp teeth

Ichthyosaur skull *above*
The streamlined, predatory ichthyosaur used its powerful tail to swim fast like a shark.

Reconstruction of an ichthyosaur

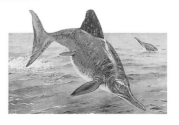

Araucaria

Monkey puzzle trees are primitive conifers with tightly packed, leathery leaves. They survive today in Australia, New Zealand, and the forests of the Andes, but were much more abundant in Jurassic times. This petrified cone has been preserved in great detail, as this cross-section shows.

Seeds within cone

CRETACEOUS (146-65 MYA)

Cycadeoids, a group of plants similar to the surviving cycads, died out during the Cretaceous, but plants belonging to many other groups flourished, including sycamores, palms, and magnolias. The dominant plants of the early Cretaceous were conifers.

Flat palmlike leaves

Fossilized cycadeoid leaves

Modern cycad

Polished section

Conifer wood
Even after the advent of angiosperms, conifers continued to be the dominant trees in the colder, high-latitude environments of the Cretaceous.

Growth rings

Stegosaurus skeleton

Over 18 feet long, *Stegosaurus* was native to North America. Bony plates on its back were probably used in temperature regulation.

Bony plates

Small head

Turanophlebia
The delicate body of this Jurassic dragonfly was preserved in stagnant mud.

Phascolotherium jaw
A shrew-like Jurassic mammal, *Phascolotherium* was probably nocturnal and fed mainly on insects.

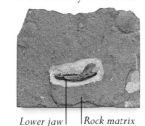

Lower jaw | *Rock matrix*

CRETACEOUS (146-65 MYA)

Until the mass extinction at the end of this period, dinosaurs continued as the dominant large land vertebrates. Duck-billed and horned dinosaurs evolved during the Cretaceous, as did *Iguanodon* and *Tyrannosaurus*. Snakes also evolved, while frogs, salamanders, and lizards diversified. Birds and pterosaurs competed for dominance in the air.

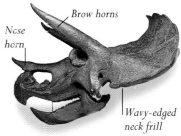

Brow horns

Nose horn

Wavy-edged neck frill

Triceratops skull
The late Cretaceous plant-eater *Triceratops* was one of the last surviving dinosaurs. It probably weighed more than 5 tons.

CRETACEOUS (146-65 MYA)

Marine life diversified further during the Cretaceous. The ancestors of many modern groups can be traced back to this period. Mosasaurs (giant lizards), rudists (coral-shaped bivalves), and other exotic animals inhabited Cretaceous seas.

Sediment between the corallites

Thecosmilia *above*
A coral composed of individuals living as a colony, *Thecosmilia* inhabited small reefs.

Central body

Brittlestars
Fossilized brittlestars are rare because their delicate skeletal plates usually fall apart soon after death.

Club-shaped defensive spine

Tylocidaris *right*
Primitive regular echinoids (sea urchins), such as *Tylocidaris*, continued to flourish on the sea bed. Irregular echinoids, such as heart urchins, also became common.

Position of mouth

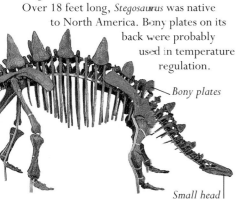

Bony fish
Bony fish proliferated in the Cretaceous. Today they are the most abundant group of freshwater and marine fish, including salmon, cod, herring, plaice, and pike.

Ptychodus tooth
The strong teeth of the fish *Ptychodus* were apparently used in feeding to crush the shells of mollusks.

Concentric growth lines on shell

Fossil site *above*
Shells of bivalve mollusks such as *Inoceramus* are abundant in chalky Cretaceous deposits, such as this site in northern France.

Turtle shell
Turtles nearly 12 feet long are known from the Cretaceous but most species were similar in size to living species.

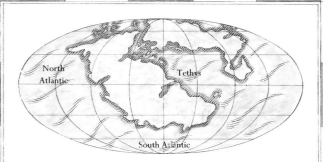

North Atlantic | *Tethys*

South Atlantic

NEW OCEANS

Pangaea broke up during the Mesozoic, due to the growth of the ocean Tethys. Stretching from the modern Mediterranean Sea to the present position of the Himalayas, Tethys separated the northern from the southern continents. Later North America and Eurasia were split apart with the opening of the North Atlantic Ocean. The southern continents also fragmented as the South Atlantic and other new oceans began to develop.

65-1 MILLION YEARS AGO

LAND PLANTS

Plant life during the Cenozoic (65-1.6 MYA) was similar to that of today; however, it was not until the later Cenozoic, around 15 million years ago, that grasses and other herbaceous plants became abundant. They were better adapted than woody vegetation to the cooler, drier, and more seasonal climate of this time.

EOCENE (56.5-35.4 MYA)
During the Eocene, angiosperms (flowering plants that protect their seeds in a fruit) formed the dominant group of land plants. Many angiosperm species thrive today, including roses. Grasses first evolved in the earliest Eocene, but grasslands appeared much later.

Seed base

***Ficus* seed**
This fossilized angiosperm seed was once surrounded by a fleshy fruit, which perished before it could be fossilized.

Sabal palm
Palms are not often fossilized, although there are some early examples dating to the Cretaceous.

Palm leaf

LAND AND FRESHWATER ANIMALS

Mammals evolved dramatically during the Cenozoic era. This has been attributed to the extinction of dinosaurs at the end of the Cretaceous, about 65 MYA, which opened up new ecological opportunities for mammals. Most significantly for the human story, apes, forerunners of the early hominids and hence of humankind, appeared.

EOCENE (56.5-35.4 MYA)
The majority of modern mammals had evolved by the Eocene, including primates, rodents, carnivores, and bats. However, other groups of mammals became extinct at the end of the Eocene, during a period of global cooling and initial growth of the Antarctic icecap.

***Planorbina* left**
Snails like *Planorbina* had lungs and needed to come to the water surface in order to breathe.

Prophaethon
Probably a sea bird, *Prophaethon* is a rare fossil. Wading shore birds are more common Eocene fossils.

Long gull-like bill

OLIGOCENE (35.4-23.3 MYA)
Mammals that survived the late Eocene extinction evolved significantly during the Oligocene. Huge rhino were abundant, including *Indricotherium,* which stood over 15 feet tall and weighed as much as four elephants.

Abliguritor
Insects and spiders like *Abliguritor* occur in Oligocene amber (fossilized resin) from the Baltic.

MARINE ANIMALS

The Cenozoic saw a great increase in marine species, several of which survive today. Many of these species were peculiar to the new geographical provinces that had developed. The cooler climates and glaciations that occurred in the late Cenozoic had relatively little effect on marine life.

EOCENE (56.5-35.4 MYA)
Large, primitive whales evolved in the Eocene. Squid flourished, but were seldom fossilized. There was diversification among gastropod (snail-like) mollusks and bivalves (those with a shell made up of two hinged valves).

High-spired shell

Rock concretion

Claw

Homarus
Lobsters, such as this Eocene specimen of *Homarus,* are rare fossils, because their shells tend to disintegrate quickly after death.

***Trionyx* above**
The skulls and shells of turtles are only rarely found fossilized together. This carapace is from the Eocene turtle *Trionyx.*

Muscle scar

Aperture

Turritella
Gastropods are common fossils in shallow marine rocks of the Eocene. *Turritella* could burrow beneath the sand and mud; however, most gastropods lived on the surface of the sea bed.

***Venericardia* left**
A large proportion of Eocene bivalves, including *Venericardia,* were burrowers, often using long siphons to filter food particles from the water above.

Bony skeleton

Dorsal fin

***Sparnodus* left**
The bony fish *Sparnodus* is closely related to the modern porgy or sea bream. By Eocene times, bony fish had become the overwhelmingly dominant group among fish.

Limestone

OLIGOCENE (35.4–23.3 MYA)

About half the angiosperm species of the Oligocene period survive today. Grasses grew in swamps and woodlands but did not form open prairies. Microscopic spores, pollen and seeds, such as those of *Mastixia*, were most commonly fossilized in Oligocene rocks.

Mastixia seeds

MIOCENE (23.3–5.2 MYA)

During the Miocene, the number of grass species increased dramatically. About 10,000 species still survive today. Another angiosperm family, *Compositae* (of which 13,000 species, including dandelions and lettuces, survive) also flourished.

Populus **(Poplar)**
This leaf of a Miocene poplar hardly differs from that of the modern tree.

Quercus **(Oak)**
A polished slice of petrified oak reveals seasonal growth rings, the narrower bands denoting periods of poor growth.

Heartwood shows growth rings

Diplocynodon **right**
Alligators, including the Oligocene *Diplocynodon*, have a long fossil history as semiaquatic predators. However, they have varied relatively little in shape over time.

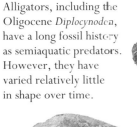

Eye socket

Hoplophoneus **left**
Several extinct cats, including *Hoplophoneus,* evolved large canine teeth to stab their prey – hence the term "saber-tooth."

MIOCENE (23.3–5.2 MYA)

Mammals continued to diversify during the Miocene. They included species of deer, antelope, cattle, and sheep. Songbirds, snakes, and rodents became more common as spreading grasslands provided suitable habitats. The development of *Proconsul* and its fellow primates set the scene for the first hominids to appear (*see pages 28-31*).

Orycteropus
This skull belongs to the Miocene aardvark *Orycteropus*, a pig-like animal with a long snout and tongue adapted for feeding on termites.

Proconsul
Many species of ape, including *Proconsul*, flourished during the Miocene. Only chimps, gibbons, orangutans, and gorillas survive.

MIOCENE (23.3–5.2 MYA)

By the Miocene, dolphins and almost all families of modern whales had appeared. Living on the sea bed were bivalves, gastropods, reef corals, bryozoans (colonies of tiny tentacled creatures), and echinoids (sea urchins with tube feet and external skeletons), including *Clypeaster*.

Five-rayed symmetry

Clypeaster

Fossil site
Some Pliocene marine deposits containing many bivalve and gastropod shells formed "shell gravels," as at this locality in Florida.

Engraving of *Carcharadon*

Carcharadon **tooth**
Teeth of the shark *Carcharadon* can be 4 inches long, which suggests that some Pliocene sharks may have been over 39 feet long.

PLIOCENE (5.2–1.6 MYA)

Pliocene marine animals were similar to those of the present day, with a large number of species still surviving, especially among sea bed dwellers such as bivalves and gastropods.

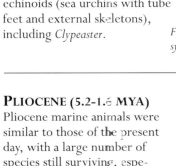

Individual coral

Stephanophyllia
The corallum (skeleton) of the solitary Pliocene coral *Stephanophyllia* was made of hardened secretions. It used stinging cells on its tentacles to stun prey.

Schizoretepora
Colonies of *Schizoretepora*, a bryozoan, often broke into fragments that drifted in the currents before being buried and fossilized.

Pecten
The bivalve scallop *Pecten* has a fan-shaped shell and a long fossil history.

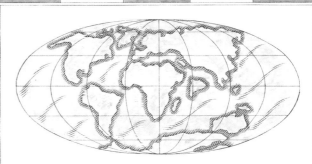

RECOGNIZABLE WORLD

The continents and oceans became more recognizable during the Cenozoic. The northward movement of Africa toward Europe gradually closed the Tethys Ocean, as did the collision of India and Asia, which pushed up the Himalayan Mountains. Meanwhile the Atlantic opened wider, further separating the Americas from Europe and Africa. The Isthmus of Panama developed as a land bridge linking the Americas about 3.4 million years ago.

HUMAN ANCESTRY: THE PRIMATES

The human story begins with that of the apes. Apes are primates, an ancient group of animals that also includes, among others, monkeys and humans. Early primate fossils, dating to about 55 million years ago, are of creatures resembling today's small nocturnal primates, such as galagos. By 36 million years ago, primitive ancestors of monkeys and apes had appeared. The first apes, emerging around 25 million years ago, established the primate superfamily Hominoidea, which today includes humans, gorillas, chimps, orangutans, and gibbons. For 10 million years the early apes were confined to Africa. By around 15 million years ago, apes had reached Turkey; then, around 12 million years ago, India and Pakistan. Over the next 6 or 7 million years the first hominids were to evolve through the natural process of diversification and development among the apes.

Capuchin

Both eyes at front of head allow 3-dimensional vision

Gorilla

Forelimbs set at sides of body, not front

Opposable thumb and fingernails instead of claws aid dexterity

The monkeys
Fossil monkeys date to around 19 million years ago. Light, agile tree-dwellers, today's monkeys are divided into two groups: those living in Africa (the group Cercopithecoidea) and those, like this capuchin, in South America (Ceboidea).

The apes
Whether fossil or living, apes, like humans, belong to the group Hominoidea. Some of the larger apes, such as the gorilla, spend more time on the ground than in the trees. The forelimbs are left free to perform tasks such as grooming.

PROCONSUL

The earliest known ape belonged to the group known as *Proconsul* and lived in East Africa 25 million years ago. Early finds were only fragmentary but this skull, found by the distinguished archaeologist Dr. Mary Leakey in 1948, comes from later deposits in Kenya and is just under 18 million years old. At that time, there were several species of *Proconsul* living in East Africa. Although it was an ancestor of the later apes, *Proconsul* would have looked more like a monkey than any of its descendants. Its primitive teeth were ideally suited to a diet of soft fruit, suggesting that *Proconsul* was a forest dweller.

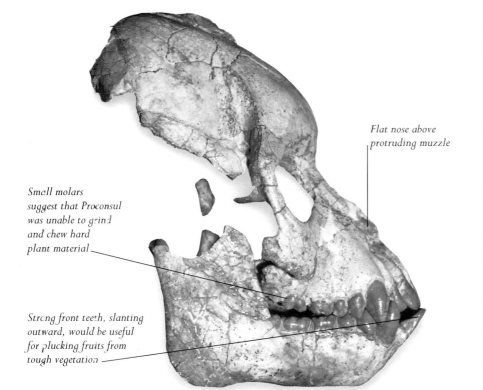

Flat nose above protruding muzzle

Small molars suggest that Proconsul was unable to grind and chew hard plant material

Strong front teeth, slanting outward, would be useful for plucking fruits from tough vegetation

KENYAPITHECUS

The appearance of *Kenyapithecus* in East Africa around 15 million years ago marked the first major shift in the course of ape evolution. Thick tooth enamel enabled *Kenyapithecus* to eat hard fruits and thus move into more seasonal and varied habitats. The development of thick enamel had begun about 17 million years ago in *Afropithecus*, a possible ancestor of *Kenyapithecus*, in Africa. Thick-enameled teeth appear in *Griphopithecus*, another possible descendant of *Afropithecus* first found in Turkey. These 14-million-year-old *Kenyapithecus* jaw fragments were found at Fort Ternan, Kenya.

Overlapping canines suggest Kenyapithecus jaws moved like those of modern chimps when chewing — up and down, not side to side as in humans

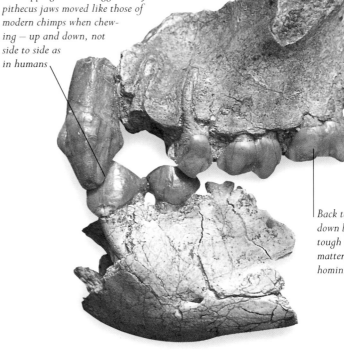

Back teeth, worn down by chewing tough vegetable matter, resemble hominid molars

The living apes
While gorillas, chimpanzees, and orangutans are sometimes referred to as the great apes, gibbons, smallest of all the apes, are often called the lesser apes. There are at least six species of gibbon living in Asia today. Long, powerful arms assist the gibbon with its highly specialized form of locomotion through tree limbs, known as brachiation.

Gibbon

The African apes
There are three living species of African apes: gorillas, chimpanzees, and pygmy chimpanzees. Today's chimps live in large groups and are generally gregarious. Genetically they are the closest of all apes to humankind. Indeed, it could be argued (though few would do so) that in terms of "genetic distance," chimps and humans could be classified within the same genus.

Chimpanzee

THE LINKS OF EVOLUTION

The divergence of the earliest human ancestors from the lineage leading to modern apes began between 8 million years ago, a time that has yielded such fossil evidence as the ape *Sivapithecus* (below), and 4 million years ago, the date of the earliest hominid fossils (*see overleaf*). The dearth of fossil finds from this period inhibits our understanding of the human story and makes it difficult to trace the ancestral patterns of all of today's higher primates. The fragmentary discoveries that have been made give rise to many questions. While it is possible to chart the chronological stages in development from early primate to modern human over the millennia, the links between the stages cannot be firmly established until more evidence comes to light.

Early primate

Modern human

Proconsul

Homo habilis

Australopithecine

Homo erectus

Neanderthal

SIVAPITHECUS

Possibly a descendant of *Kenyapithecus*, dating to 11-7 million years ago, the ape *Sivapithecus*, found in India and Pakistan, also had thick-enameled teeth. Its skull already shows many of the specializations of the modern orangutan, so it is probably one of its ancestors. Found in an 8-million-year-old deposit in Potwar, Pakistan, this skull is the most complete specimen of its period.

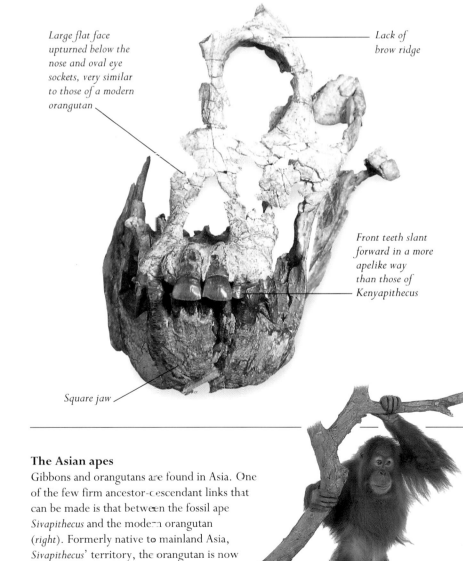

Large flat face upturned below the nose and oval eye sockets, very similar to those of a modern orangutan

Lack of brow ridge

Front teeth slant forward in a more apelike way than those of Kenyapithecus

Square jaw

The Asian apes

Gibbons and orangutans are found in Asia. One of the few firm ancestor-descendant links that can be made is that between the fossil ape *Sivapithecus* and the modern orangutan (*right*). Formerly native to mainland Asia, *Sivapithecus*' territory, the orangutan is now found only in Borneo and Sumatra. A large ape with distinctive orange body hair, it lives a rather solitary life in the tropical forests.

MUZZLE COMPARISONS

Modern and fossil muzzle lengths have been used to support and refute many evolutionary theories. For example, it could be postulated that from a common ancestor, *Kenyapithecus*, a lineage leading to modern humans produced a flat face, while the chimpanzee developed a longer and stronger muzzle, enabling it to survive, when necessary, on the toughest and driest savanna vegetation.

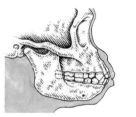

Kenyapithecus
Medium muzzle, with large incisor and canine teeth.

Chimpanzee
Longer muzzle, large overlapping canines, chews up and down.

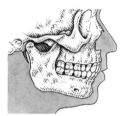

Modern human
Short muzzle (flat face), small canines, chews side to side.

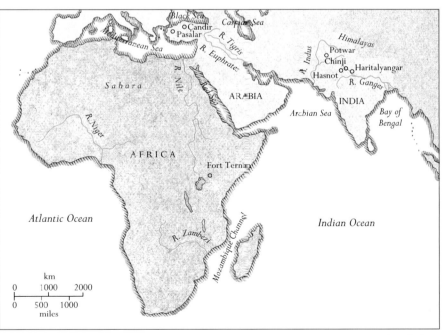

○ Fossil ape find site

DISTRIBUTION OF FOSSIL APE DISCOVERIES

Apes are now found only in tropical Africa and Asia, but fossil ape finds indicate that at one time apes were common not only in the tropical regions of today, but also in parts of southern Europe, the Middle East, and Pakistan. The development of thick-enameled teeth, enabling a more varied diet, was crucial to the early migration of apes from Africa.

HUMAN ANCESTRY: THE HOMINIDS

By 4 million years ago, fossil evidence shows without doubt that the human evolutionary line had become distinct from those of the other primates. Hominid development between 4 and 1 million years ago falls into what can be called a "pre-human" (*Australopithecus*) and a human (*Homo habilis* and *H. erectus*) stage. *Australopithecus* was the name coined for a new fossil find in South Africa: an apelike child's skull with human-looking teeth. Its discoverer, anatomist Raymond Dart, believed that *Australopithecus* represented an early stage of human evolution, but it took many more discoveries of australopithecines and members of the *Homo* species before his views were taken seriously. We do not know exactly how *Australopithecus*, *Homo habilis*, and *Homo erectus* were related to each other, but they may be taken to represent successive stages in human development.

Ape skull (modern gorilla)

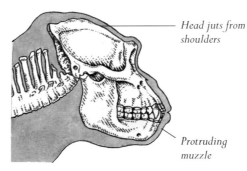

Head juts from shoulders

Protruding muzzle

Skull of a modern human

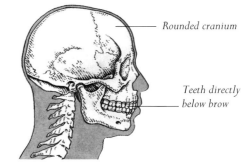

Rounded cranium

Teeth directly below brow

Comparison of skull shapes
The key feature that *Homo habilis* and *Homo erectus* share with modern humans is a larger brain capacity, for their size, than that of the apes. The human cranium, or vault of the skull, is fully rounded. The human skull sits atop the spine, indicating an upright stance, whereas apes, although they can stand upright, cannot do so for long. Human teeth are directly below the brow, rather than protruding in front, possibly a result of a change to gathering food by hand rather than with the teeth.

AUSTRALOPITHECUS

At least three forms of australopithecine are thought to have existed. The earliest was *Australopithecus afarensis*, first discovered in the region of Afar in Ethiopia; the nickname Lucy was given to this partial skeleton of a young female, who lived about 3 million years ago. The two distinct later forms were gracile, with smaller teeth; and robust, with massive teeth. The long-suspected fact that the australopithecines could stand and walk upright was dramatically confirmed by the discovery, in 1978, of footprints preserved in hardened ash from a then active East African volcano. The prints showed that one day around 3.6 million years ago, three australopithecines had walked across the ash.

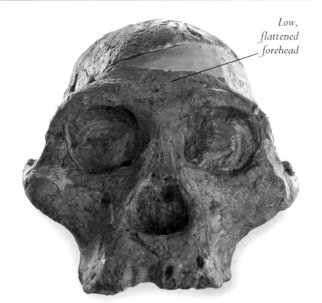

Low, flattened forehead

Australopithecus africanus
The first gracile australopithecine, *A. africanus*, was discovered at Taung, South Africa. It has been proposed that *A. africanus* is the closest form of australopithecine to later humans, although there is much less certainty about this theory today.

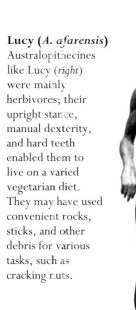

Lucy (*A. afarensis*)
Australopithecines like Lucy (*right*) were mainly herbivores; their upright stance, manual dexterity, and hard teeth enabled them to live on a varied vegetarian diet. They may have used convenient rocks, sticks, and other debris for various tasks, such as cracking nuts.

Model of Lucy

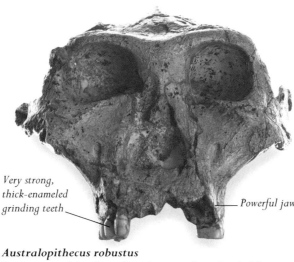

Very strong, thick-enameled grinding teeth

Powerful jaw

Australopithecus robustus
Discoveries of *A. robustus* have been made in South African caves. A similar form, *A. boisei*, lived in East Africa at about the same time. Both were well-adapted to a hard vegetarian diet: their powerful jaws required strong chewing muscles, which were attached to a bony crest along the top of the skull similar to that seen in modern gorillas.

HOMO HABILIS

The first habilines (*Homo habilis*) lived around 2 million years ago. There are many reasons for supposing that *Homo habilis*, or "handy man" (so called because of its dexterity and toolmaking ability), was an intermediary between australopithecines and later humans. *Homo habilis* had a relatively large brain and possessed new skills, including the ability to make stone tools.

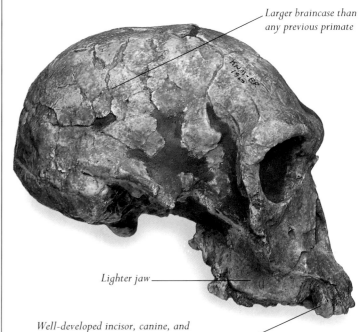

Larger braincase than any previous primate

Lighter jaw

Well-developed incisor, canine, and molar teeth suggest an omnivorous diet in which food was both torn and chewed

Handy man
Homo habilis used tools to make tools, a crucial innovation. It was also probably the first hominid to eat meat regularly. The two developments went hand in hand: stone tools were essential to detach meat from animal carcasses. The slightly built habilines were largely scavengers rather than hunters who killed their prey.

COMPARISON OF BRAINCASES

Fossil hominid braincases record the increasing size of the brains that they contained. While hominid body size and weight were also increasing, the accompanying increases in brain size exceed what can be expected from a simple incremental progression.

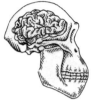

Australopithecus
The skull capacity of the australopithecines was 21-37 cu in.

Homo erectus
The skull capacity of *H. erectus* averaged bet-ween 43 and 76 cu in.

Modern human
Homo sapiens sapiens skull capacity is in the range of 73-98 cu in.

HOMO ERECTUS

About 1.7 million years ago, while the last of the habilines and robust australopithecines still lived in Africa, a new species appeared – *Homo erectus*, or "upright man." This new kind of human walked fully erect and was larger-brained, with a tall, long-legged, narrow-hipped physique. Compared with earlier forms, the skull of *Homo erectus* was quite distinctive: longer and thicker-walled, it had a strong brow ridge of bone jutting out over the eyes. By around 1 million years ago, *Homo erectus* had spread from Africa to Asia, Southeast Asia, and probably to Europe as well. This skull was found at Trinil on the Solo River in Java (an area which was then part of the Southeast Asian mainland).

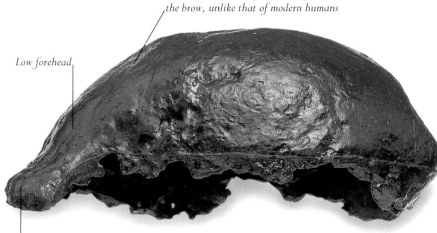

Skull still slopes away backward from the brow, unlike that of modern humans

Low forehead

Brow ridge was possibly a protective shield or shock-absorbing bar to take the stresses of chewing tough material

Upright man
With a brain twice the size of an australo-pithecine's, *H. erectus* was skilful and enterprising, making innovations that were to enable hominids to migrate from their tropical homelands. They invented the hand ax, which was to be the most versatile and most widely used tool for the following million years, and by 1 million years ago may already have made one of the greatest human discoveries – how to make and control fire.

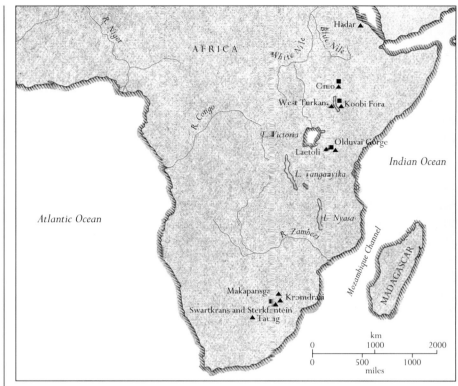

▲ *Australopithecine find site*　■ *Homo habilis find site*

DISTRIBUTION OF AUSTRALOPITHECINE AND HABILINE FINDS

All the important discoveries of the various types of *Australopithecus* have been made in two areas of Africa: the South African caves and scattered sites in the Eastern Rift Valley of Tanzania, Kenya, and Ethiopia. Although claims have been made on the basis of artifacts found elsewhere, the most complete fossil evidence for *Homo habilis* is found in East Africa. One of the richest sites is Olduvai Gorge in northern Tanzania (see page 32-3), where *H. habilis* and *Australopithecus boisei* were first found. These and many other significant fossil discoveries were made by Mary and Louis Leakey, the archaeologists whose names are inseparable from that of Olduvai.

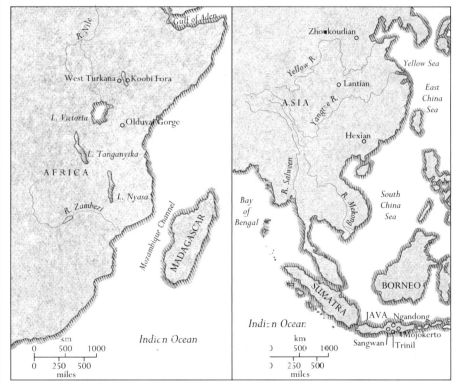

○ *Homo erectus find site*

DISTRIBUTION OF *HOMO ERECTUS* FINDS

Fossil finds have been used to suggest that as early as 1.5 million years ago scattered groups of hominids moved north into the Levant (coastal Syria, Lebanon, and Israel), then across the then-tropical wooded landscape of Arabia and Iran. *Homo erectus* probably evolved in Africa and soon began to migrate: by 1 million years ago, capable of surviving a cooler climate, they are found in Europe and throughout Asia from the Caucasus to China and Java. Among the most extensive Javanese evidence of *Homo erectus* is the collection of skullcaps and other bones found on the Solo River on Java.

OLDUVAI GORGE

One of the most important places in the world for the study of human evolution is Olduvai Gorge, a canyon carved by erosion in the Serengeti Plain of northern Tanzania. Once a lake environment surrounded by lush vegetation, it was a magnet for animals and for hominids – the early australopithecines, and later members of the *Homo* genus, *H. habilis* and *H. erectus*. Crucial deductions have been made from the rich deposits of fossil bones and human artifacts at the site. The oldest type of deliberately made stone tools, Oldowan, takes its name from the gorge, where the first examples were found. The pioneering work of archaeologists Mary and Louis Leakey at Olduvai established Africa as the home of our oldest human ancestors. Their discoveries proved not only that more than one hominid lineage was apparent as early as 2 million years ago, but also that the stages of evolving hominids did not replace one another, but coexisted for many millennia.

COMPETING FOR FOOD *below*
Early hominids were resourceful foragers, adding meat to a varied plant diet. Finds at Olduvai and elsewhere in Africa indicate a degree of organized activity in the food-gathering process. At Olduvai, hominids are known to have repeatedly carried parts of animal carcasses, tools, and rocks to certain sites on the lake edge; finds of these accumulations of tools, fossil bones, and other butchering debris provide the oldest evidence of hominids collecting resources from different places. Sources of rocks used in toolmaking are up to 6 miles away from the butchering sites. These sites seem simply to have been areas of activity, rather than settlement.

A REVEALING LANDSCAPE
Olduvai Gorge was largely created when the old lake basin was uplifted and cut by streams. The combined geological forces of erosion and earth movements along fault lines have brought to the surface many rock layers containing fossils and human artifacts that provide clues about past environments. These strata are often visible on the canyon's slopes. Erupted debris from nearby volcanoes is sandwiched between the layers. Since volcanic ash contains radioactive potassium, it can be dated accurately. Excavations have also helped to determine and date the precise layers in which remains from many phases of the human story are preserved.

Many animal bones show gnaw marks made by hunting and scavenging carnivores

Vultures, hyenas, and other carrion-eaters competed with hominids for food

Early toolmakers used quartzite from hills some distance from the lake

Lakeside woods offered shade, safety, and possibly a place to scavenge fresh animal kills

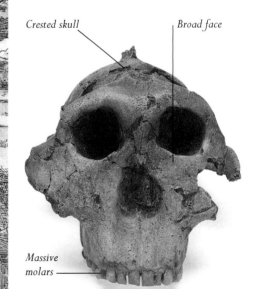

Crested skull

Broad face

Massive molars

ZINJ SKULL
In 1959 Dr. Mary Leakey discovered the first hominid of great antiquity – 1.75 million years old – to be found in East Africa and named it *Zinjanthropus*. Once later discoveries had established and defined *Australopithecus*, "Zinj" was classified as a robust australopithecine, and renamed *A. boisei* after the Leakeys' sponsor, Charles Boise.

Toolmakers brought lumps of suitable stone to these sites to be worked into choppers

Sharp stone flakes produced during toolmaking were often the most effective knives

Scavenging hominids carried legs and other parts from dead animals to the tool sites for further butchering

4,600 - 1 MILLION YEARS AGO

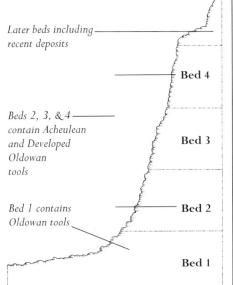

Later beds including recent deposits

Bed 4

Beds 2, 3, & 4 contain Acheulean and Developed Oldowan tools

Bed 3

Bed 1 contains Oldowan tools

Bed 2

Bed 1

ANATOMY OF A GORGE *above*

The distinct layers, or beds, identified at Olduvai (through the work of geologist Richard Hay) record periods of deposition, erosion, landscape change, and hominid and animal life over the past 2 million years.

Beds I and II (c.1.9 to 1.2 million years old) were deposited on the floor of the old lake basin, which was formed by an extensive lava flow. The lake is known to have fluctuated in size. These beds are of crucial interest to paleontologists. Oldowan tools and remains of *Homo habilis* and *Australopithecus boisei* have been discovered in Bed I. Remains of *Homo erectus*, early Acheulean tools (the stoneworking technology associated with *H. erectus*, of which the classic tool is the teardrop-shaped hand ax) and Developed Oldowan tools (slightly later Oldowan artifacts that include crude hand axes) have been excavated from Bed II.

Beds III and IV (c.1.2 million to 700,000 years old) were deposited mainly by streams once earth movements and an increasingly arid climate had permanently eliminated the lake. Stone tools and animal fossils have been unearthed from these beds but finds of hominid bones are rare. Later beds (c. 700,000 years old to present) are of more recent deposition; some contain bones of animals extant today.

OLDOWAN TOOLS

These simple stone tools were used for butchering meat and preparing plant foods. They reflect an ongoing process of experimentation with striking stone against stone. Scrapers, choppers, and other useful items were formed in the process of making sharp-edged flakes, of cutting or crushing, or as a result of wear and tear.

Lava chopper

Stones were flaked by striking the edge with another rock

Scars indicate repeated flaking around the edge

Diskoid chipped on a lava cobble

Pits made by crushing pods and nuts, or by breaking bones with a hammerstone

Stone anvil pitted by use

Scars indicate where sharp slivers were struck (knapped) from the core

Ulna   Tibia   Femur   Femur   Pelvic bone   Pelvic bone

Scapula   Humerus   Mandible   Scapula   Humerus   ● Stone tool debris

Elephas recki

Antelope mandible

Teeth and their wear patterns help identify the animal and its diet

Cracks made by weathering help determine how long bones lay exposed on the ground before being buried by sediments

Antelope leg bone

MAPPING FOSSIL FINDS *left*

As an excavation proceeds, the positions in which objects are found are meticulously recorded. This site plan, based on one made by Dr. Mary Leakey, provides a graphic illustration of Oldowan activity. It shows the fossil skeleton of an extinct type of elephant (*below*) found in Bed I, surrounded by other animal bones and Oldowan tools. Marks on these bones indicate that toolmakers cut meat from them. Small creatures may have been hunted, but the hominids were probably only able to scavenge the larger animals. Some Oldowan bones show tool cuts overlaying carnivore gnaw marks, suggesting that cautious hominids may only have picked over the carcass once the predator that killed the beast had left.

FOSSIL ANIMAL BONES

Species preserved in Beds I and II include antelopes, zebras, pigs, monkeys, giraffes, hippopotamuses, and rhinoceroses, identified chiefly from fossilized jaws and skulls. Recovery and study of animal bones has provided valuable information about the variety of animals encountered by early hominids and their foraging and meat-eating opportunities. Although plants were probably important, bones are all that remain of hominid meals.

UNDER THE MICROSCOPE

The SEM (scanning electron microscope) has helped to identify the causes of damage seen on fossil bones found at Olduvai Gorge. Non-fossilized bones damaged experimentally in different ways in the laboratory, then viewed by SEM, have revealed that cut marks made by tools, animal teeth, and damage from excavation all look distinctly different under high magnification. The sequence (*right*) shows this process stage by stage.

Antelope bone from Olduvai displays a groove that may be a tool cut or bite mark

Experimental mark made with a hyena's tooth produces smooth, rounded grooves

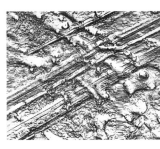

Experimental cuts with a lava flake leave tiny parallel lines in and around the grooves

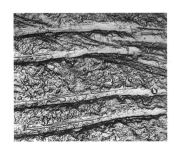

Under SEM, the Oldowan fossil bone displays the tiny lines that indicate tool use

CHAPTER 2
SURVIVING THE ICE AGES
1 MILLION - 100,000 YEARS AGO

Ice Age cycle creates a new landscape

Animal and plant life adapts to a changing climate

Hominids colonize cooler northern latitudes using shelter, clothing, and fire

Skilled stoneworking produces more efficient tools and new hunting weapons

Homo sapiens — "thinking man" — evolves from early hominids

Few species of animal have achieved the success of humans, who have colonized virtually every area of the globe. By 1 million years ago, *Homo erectus* spread throughout its African homeland and beyond to the Levant (the coastal strip of Syria, Lebanon, and Israel), Arabia and Iran, China, and mainland and island Southeast Asia. In Europe, evidence from the Vallonnet Cave on the Mediterranean coast of France indicates that it was occupied by hominids as early as 950,000 years ago.

Fluctuating temperatures
The success of early hominids in spreading beyond the tropical zone is all the more remarkable because it took place during a successive cycle of glacial episodes and warmer interglacial periods, which began over 2 million years ago. During the glacial episodes, or Ice Ages, which have occurred approximately every 100,000 years, ice sheets advanced from the north to cover much of Eurasia and North America. During the interglacial periods, which typically lasted for around 20,000 years, temperatures were similar to, or warmer than, those of today. Within the glacial episodes themselves, there were also occasional warmer phases. Plants and animals responded to these fluctuating temperatures by spreading northward during milder periods but retreating south again when the glaciers advanced.

Shelter and clothing
The early hominids probably followed the advance and retreat of plants and animals. The quest for food was rivaled only by the constant necessity to keep warm, a key problem of the early hominids who migrated from the tropics to less hospitable regions. The cold was combated not by slow adaptation to the new environment through biological changes, but by the peculiarly human urge to experiment with materials to find out about their characteristics, and by the ability to make things, notably shelters and clothing.

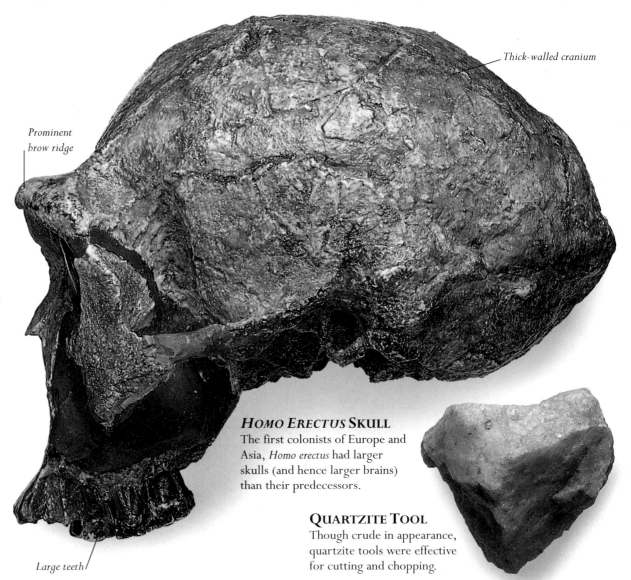

Thick-walled cranium

Prominent brow ridge

HOMO ERECTUS SKULL
The first colonists of Europe and Asia, *Homo erectus* had larger skulls (and hence larger brains) than their predecessors.

Large teeth

QUARTZITE TOOL
Though crude in appearance, quartzite tools were effective for cutting and chopping.

Control of fire

Possibly more important than shelter and clothing was the control of fire. The earliest hominids were familiar with fires that occurred naturally, but only within the last million years did they master this powerful force and use it for their own benefit. In many areas of the world it is impossible to know when fire was first used, but evidence from the Zhoukoudian caves in northern China shows that their occupants controlled fire around 460,000 years ago.

Fire not only gave warmth, it offered protection from predators. It could also be used for cooking, making food easier to chew and digest. Fire could defrost meat preserved by burial in the frozen soil. The use of stored food suggests a sharing of resources and the emergence of social cohesion. A fire, requiring constant tending, would also have provided a community focus for groups gathered within a cave or shelter.

Some parts of Europe and Asia offered convenient caves for shelter, but elsewhere hominids built windbreaks with stones or made simple shelters of wooden poles, probably covered with leafy branches or animal hides. Because groups were nomadic, often on the move in search of food, the campsites were temporary, although favored locations were returned to year after year. At these sites, huge quantities of stone tools and other debris would accumulate, as at Olorgesailie in East Africa.

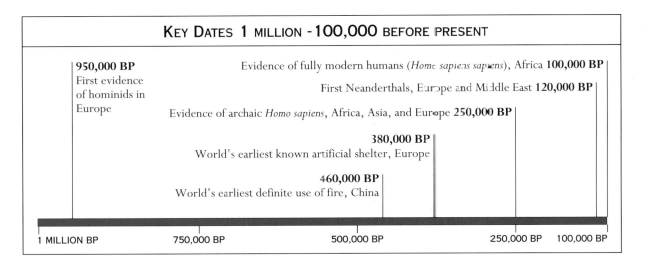

KEY DATES 1 MILLION - 100,000 BEFORE PRESENT

950,000 BP First evidence of hominids in Europe

Evidence of fully modern humans (*Homo sapiens sapiens*), Africa **100,000 BP**

First Neanderthals, Europe and Middle East **120,000 BP**

Evidence of archaic *Homo sapiens*, Africa, Asia, and Europe **250,000 BP**

380,000 BP World's earliest known artificial shelter, Europe

460,000 BP World's earliest definite use of fire, China

1 MILLION BP — 750,000 BP — 500,000 BP — 250,000 BP — 100,000 BP

Irregular shape characteristic of earlier chopper

Rough cutting edge

Size reduced due to sharpening action

Sharp cutting edge

HAND AXES

First seen 1.3 million years ago, stone hand axes developed from crudely worked choppers to carefully shaped tools. These examples are 300,000-70,000 years old.

Thick skull cap

Gap left by missing fragment

HOMO SAPIENS SKULL FRAGMENT

Some 225,000 years old, this skull found at Swanscombe in Kent, England, belongs to an early type of our own species, *Homo sapiens*. It is viewed here from the top.

Early technology

The story of human achievement over many thousands of years is told by these accumulations of debris and by fossil bones, both human and animal. Carefully shaped stone hand axes testify to the toolmaking skills of *Homo erectus*. These tools were probably used for butchering carcasses, working with hides, cutting branches, and preparing plant foods. Wooden implements must also have been used, but since wood is perishable, little evidence has survived. A willow plank from Israel and a sharpened yew point from Clacton-on-Sea in England are remarkable finds. In East Asia, bamboo, an ideal raw material, was probably carved to make sharp tools and spears.

In crafting spears and other weapons, hominids used new hunting methods that revolutionized the way meat was obtained. Humans may have begun to track and hunt larger animals for the first time. Although these hominids did not possess a complex language, animals today show that only coded sounds and gestures are necessary to coordinate complicated hunting maneuvers. Hominids hunted small or weak animals with such weapons as wooden spears with fire-hardened tips and also created a variety of pits and traps for larger animals. There is evidence that marine resources such as shellfish and seals became part of their diet.

Emergence of "thinking man"

By around 250,000 years ago, humans were very different from their early ancestors. Although physical forms varied, their intellectual advancement grouped them as a new species, *Homo sapiens*, or "thinking man." By 100,000 years ago, these archaic humans had developed into two groups: the Neanderthals of Europe and the Middle East, and fully modern humans like ourselves (*H. sapiens sapiens*).

1 MILLION - 500,000 YEARS AGO

	FOOD & ENVIRONMENT	SHELTER & ARCHITECTURE

AMERICAS

No evidence of human habitation found to date.

No evidence of human habitation found to date.

EAST ASIA & AUSTRALASIA

VARIED LANDSCAPE
The landscape inhabited by the first hominids in northern China was quite varied. Remains of at least 95 species of mammal have been identified at some of the earliest occupation sites. These included water-loving animals like water buffalo, woodland species such as macaque and boar, and grassland animals like horse, gazelle, and the giant Chinese deer. Some of these may have been hunted or scavenged.

Giant Chinese deer

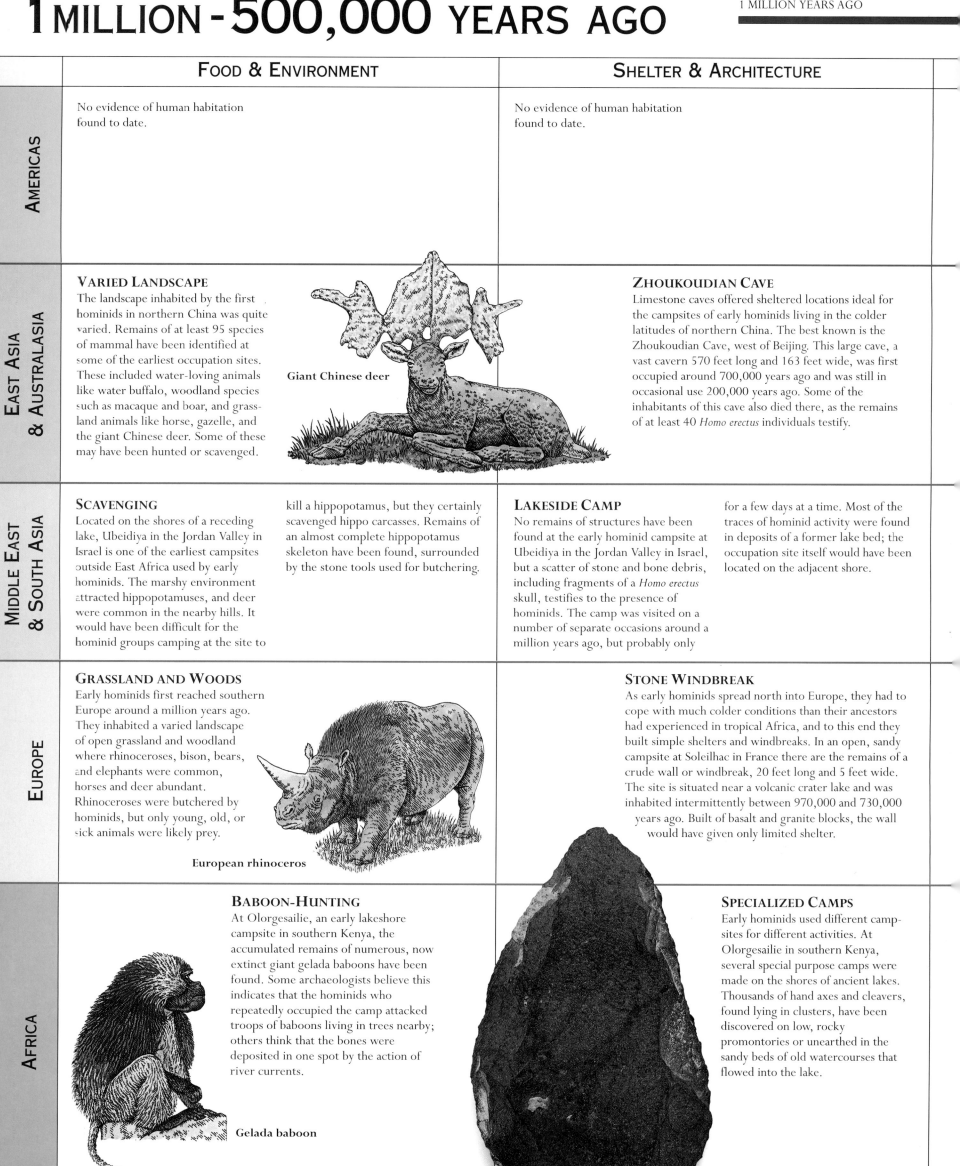

ZHOUKOUDIAN CAVE
Limestone caves offered sheltered locations ideal for the campsites of early hominids living in the colder latitudes of northern China. The best known is the Zhoukoudian Cave, west of Beijing. This large cave, a vast cavern 570 feet long and 163 feet wide, was first occupied around 700,000 years ago and was still in occasional use 200,000 years ago. Some of the inhabitants of this cave also died there, as the remains of at least 40 *Homo erectus* individuals testify.

MIDDLE EAST & SOUTH ASIA

SCAVENGING
Located on the shores of a receding lake, Ubeidiya in the Jordan Valley in Israel is one of the earliest campsites outside East Africa used by early hominids. The marshy environment attracted hippopotamuses, and deer were common in the nearby hills. It would have been difficult for the hominid groups camping at the site to kill a hippopotamus, but they certainly scavenged hippo carcasses. Remains of an almost complete hippopotamus skeleton have been found, surrounded by the stone tools used for butchering.

LAKESIDE CAMP
No remains of structures have been found at the early hominid campsite at Ubeidiya in the Jordan Valley in Israel, but a scatter of stone and bone debris, including fragments of a *Homo erectus* skull, testifies to the presence of hominids. The camp was visited on a number of separate occasions around a million years ago, but probably only for a few days at a time. Most of the traces of hominid activity were found in deposits of a former lake bed; the occupation site itself would have been located on the adjacent shore.

EUROPE

GRASSLAND AND WOODS
Early hominids first reached southern Europe around a million years ago. They inhabited a varied landscape of open grassland and woodland where rhinoceroses, bison, bears, and elephants were common, horses and deer abundant. Rhinoceroses were butchered by hominids, but only young, old, or sick animals were likely prey.

European rhinoceros

STONE WINDBREAK
As early hominids spread north into Europe, they had to cope with much colder conditions than their ancestors had experienced in tropical Africa, and to this end they built simple shelters and windbreaks. In an open, sandy campsite at Soleilhac in France there are the remains of a crude wall or windbreak, 20 feet long and 5 feet wide. The site is situated near a volcanic crater lake and was inhabited intermittently between 970,000 and 730,000 years ago. Built of basalt and granite blocks, the wall would have given only limited shelter.

AFRICA

BABOON-HUNTING
At Olorgesailie, an early lakeshore campsite in southern Kenya, the accumulated remains of numerous, now extinct giant gelada baboons have been found. Some archaeologists believe this indicates that the hominids who repeatedly occupied the camp attacked troops of baboons living in trees nearby; others think that the bones were deposited in one spot by the action of river currents.

Gelada baboon

SPECIALIZED CAMPS
Early hominids used different campsites for different activities. At Olorgesailie in southern Kenya, several special purpose camps were made on the shores of ancient lakes. Thousands of hand axes and cleavers, found lying in clusters, have been discovered on low, rocky promontories or unearthed in the sandy beds of old watercourses that flowed into the lake.

Hand ax, Olorgesailie, Kenya

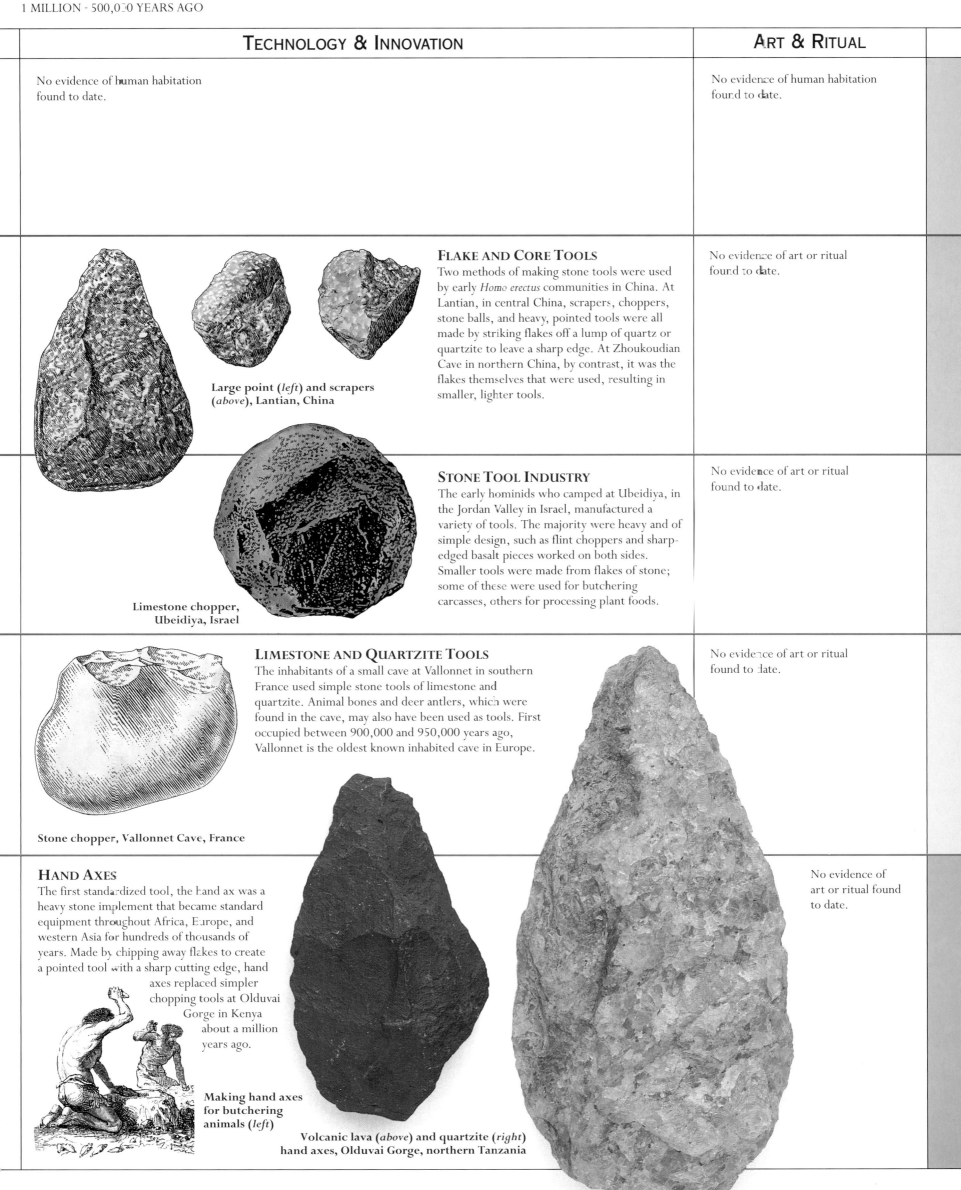

TECHNOLOGY & INNOVATION	ART & RITUAL	
No evidence of human habitation found to date.	No evidence of human habitation found to date.	

FLAKE AND CORE TOOLS

Two methods of making stone tools were used by early *Homo erectus* communities in China. At Lantian, in central China, scrapers, choppers, stone balls, and heavy, pointed tools were all made by striking flakes off a lump of quartz or quartzite to leave a sharp edge. At Zhoukoudian Cave in northern China, by contrast, it was the flakes themselves that were used, resulting in smaller, lighter tools.

No evidence of art or ritual found to date.

Large point (*left*) and scrapers (*above*), Lantian, China

STONE TOOL INDUSTRY

The early hominids who camped at Ubeidiya, in the Jordan Valley in Israel, manufactured a variety of tools. The majority were heavy and of simple design, such as flint choppers and sharp-edged basalt pieces worked on both sides. Smaller tools were made from flakes of stone; some of these were used for butchering carcasses, others for processing plant foods.

No evidence of art or ritual found to date.

Limestone chopper, Ubeidiya, Israel

LIMESTONE AND QUARTZITE TOOLS

The inhabitants of a small cave at Vallonnet in southern France used simple stone tools of limestone and quartzite. Animal bones and deer antlers, which were found in the cave, may also have been used as tools. First occupied between 900,000 and 950,000 years ago, Vallonnet is the oldest known inhabited cave in Europe.

No evidence of art or ritual found to date.

Stone chopper, Vallonnet Cave, France

HAND AXES

The first standardized tool, the hand ax was a heavy stone implement that became standard equipment throughout Africa, Europe, and western Asia for hundreds of thousands of years. Made by chipping away flakes to create a pointed tool with a sharp cutting edge, hand axes replaced simpler chopping tools at Olduvai Gorge in Kenya about a million years ago.

No evidence of art or ritual found to date.

Making hand axes for butchering animals (*left*)

Volcanic lava (*above*) and quartzite (*right*) hand axes, Olduvai Gorge, northern Tanzania

37

500,000 - 100,000 YEARS AGO

	FOOD & ENVIRONMENT	SHELTER & ARCHITECTURE	

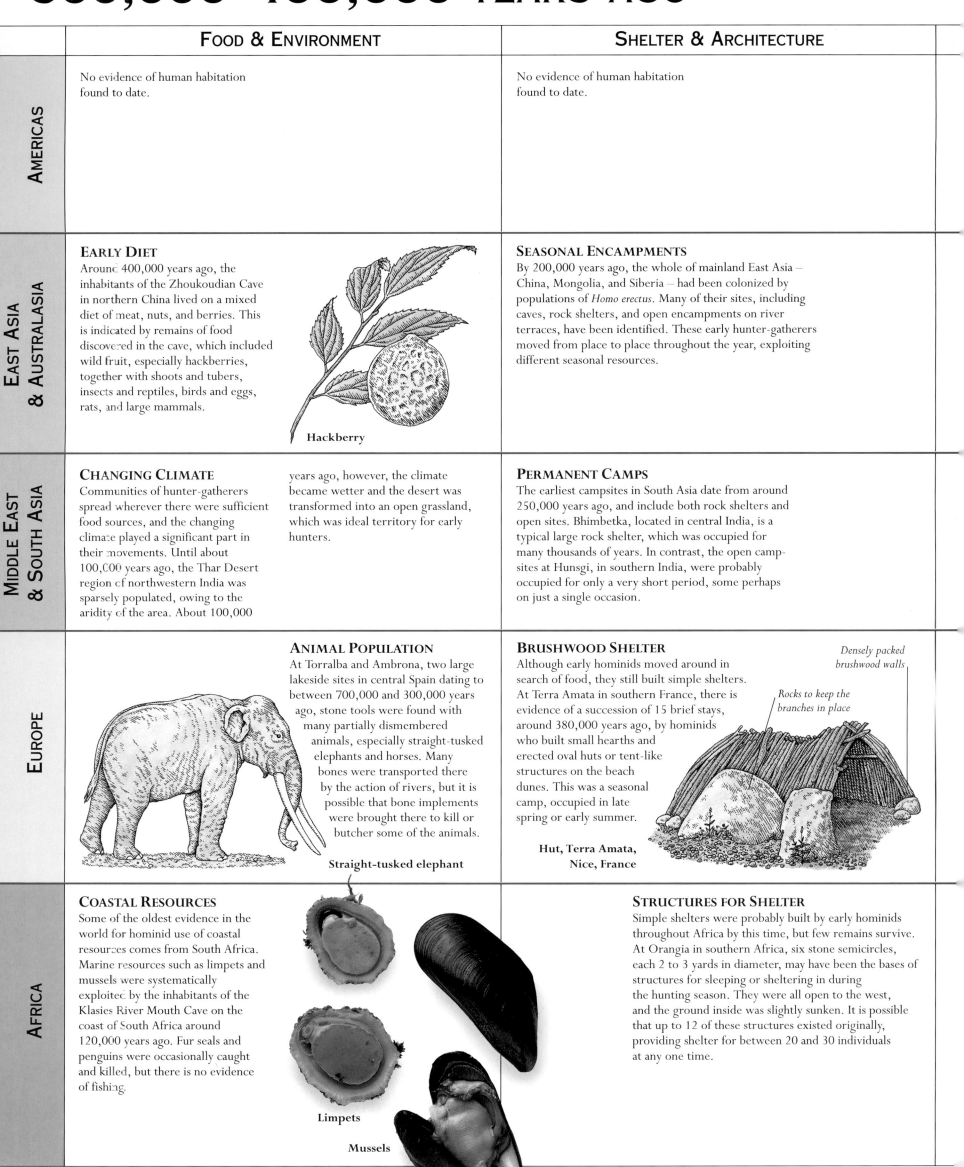

AMERICAS

FOOD & ENVIRONMENT

No evidence of human habitation found to date.

SHELTER & ARCHITECTURE

No evidence of human habitation found to date.

EAST ASIA & AUSTRALASIA

EARLY DIET
Around 400,000 years ago, the inhabitants of the Zhoukoudian Cave in northern China lived on a mixed diet of meat, nuts, and berries. This is indicated by remains of food discovered in the cave, which included wild fruit, especially hackberries, together with shoots and tubers, insects and reptiles, birds and eggs, rats, and large mammals.

Hackberry

SEASONAL ENCAMPMENTS
By 200,000 years ago, the whole of mainland East Asia – China, Mongolia, and Siberia – had been colonized by populations of *Homo erectus*. Many of their sites, including caves, rock shelters, and open encampments on river terraces, have been identified. These early hunter-gatherers moved from place to place throughout the year, exploiting different seasonal resources.

MIDDLE EAST & SOUTH ASIA

CHANGING CLIMATE
Communities of hunter-gatherers spread wherever there were sufficient food sources, and the changing climate played a significant part in their movements. Until about 100,000 years ago, the Thar Desert region of northwestern India was sparsely populated, owing to the aridity of the area. About 100,000 years ago, however, the climate became wetter and the desert was transformed into an open grassland, which was ideal territory for early hunters.

PERMANENT CAMPS
The earliest campsites in South Asia date from around 250,000 years ago, and include both rock shelters and open sites. Bhimbetka, located in central India, is a typical large rock shelter, which was occupied for many thousands of years. In contrast, the open camp-sites at Hunsgi, in southern India, were probably occupied for only a very short period, some perhaps on just a single occasion.

EUROPE

ANIMAL POPULATION
At Torralba and Ambrona, two large lakeside sites in central Spain dating to between 700,000 and 300,000 years ago, stone tools were found with many partially dismembered animals, especially straight-tusked elephants and horses. Many bones were transported there by the action of rivers, but it is possible that bone implements were brought there to kill or butcher some of the animals.

Straight-tusked elephant

BRUSHWOOD SHELTER
Although early hominids moved around in search of food, they still built simple shelters. At Terra Amata in southern France, there is evidence of a succession of 15 brief stays, around 380,000 years ago, by hominids who built small hearths and erected oval huts or tent-like structures on the beach dunes. This was a seasonal camp, occupied in late spring or early summer.

Densely packed brushwood walls

Rocks to keep the branches in place

Hut, Terra Amata, Nice, France

AFRICA

COASTAL RESOURCES
Some of the oldest evidence in the world for hominid use of coastal resources comes from South Africa. Marine resources such as limpets and mussels were systematically exploited by the inhabitants of the Klasies River Mouth Cave on the coast of South Africa around 120,000 years ago. Fur seals and penguins were occasionally caught and killed, but there is no evidence of fishing.

Limpets

Mussels

STRUCTURES FOR SHELTER
Simple shelters were probably built by early hominids throughout Africa by this time, but few remains survive. At Orangia in southern Africa, six stone semicircles, each 2 to 3 yards in diameter, may have been the bases of structures for sleeping or sheltering in during the hunting season. They were all open to the west, and the ground inside was slightly sunken. It is possible that up to 12 of these structures existed originally, providing shelter for between 20 and 30 individuals at any one time.

TECHNOLOGY & INNOVATION	ART & RITUAL

No evidence of human habitation found to date.

No evidence of human habitation found to date.

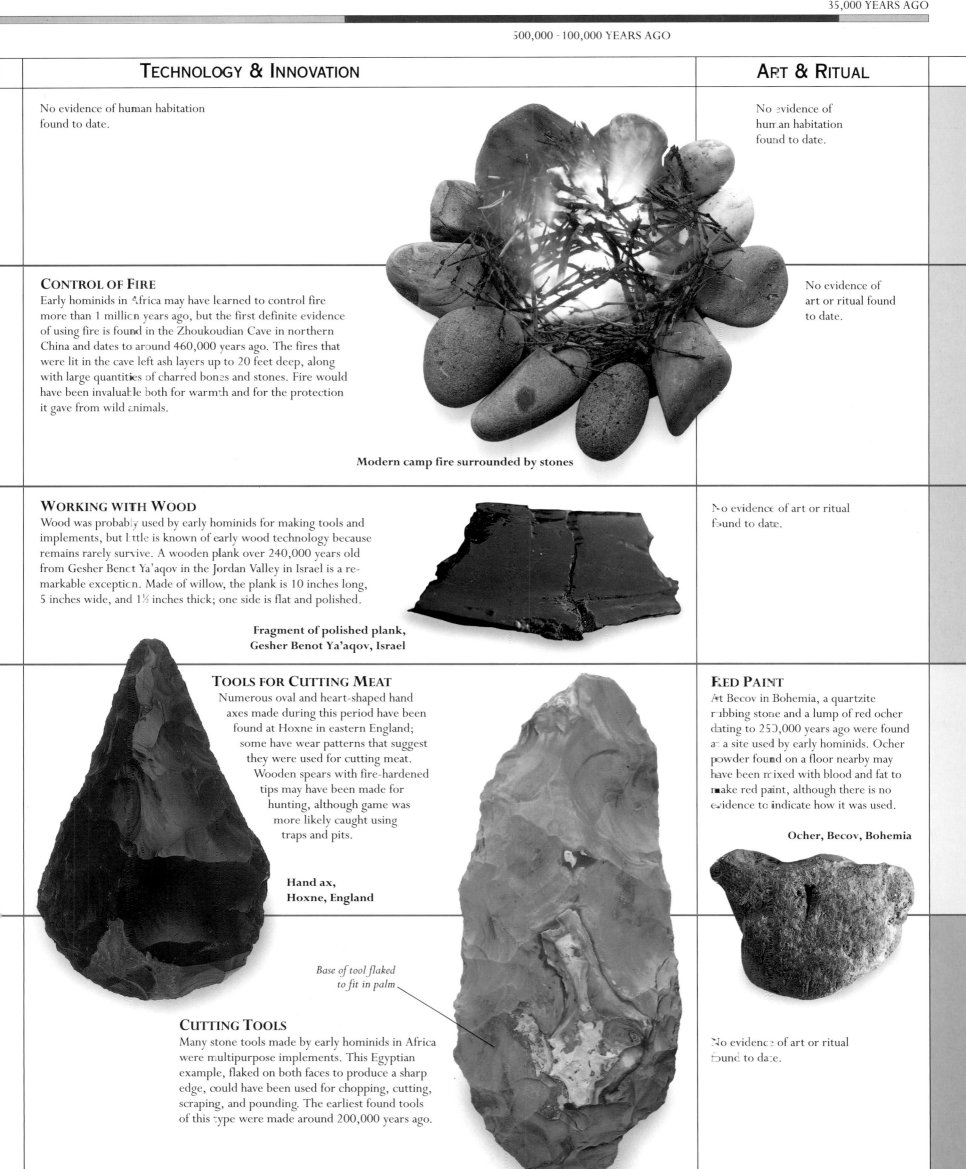

CONTROL OF FIRE

Early hominids in Africa may have learned to control fire more than 1 million years ago, but the first definite evidence of using fire is found in the Zhoukoudian Cave in northern China and dates to around 460,000 years ago. The fires that were lit in the cave left ash layers up to 20 feet deep, along with large quantities of charred bones and stones. Fire would have been invaluable both for warmth and for the protection it gave from wild animals.

No evidence of art or ritual found to date.

Modern camp fire surrounded by stones

WORKING WITH WOOD

Wood was probably used by early hominids for making tools and implements, but little is known of early wood technology because remains rarely survive. A wooden plank over 240,000 years old from Gesher Benot Ya'aqov in the Jordan Valley in Israel is a remarkable exception. Made of willow, the plank is 10 inches long, 5 inches wide, and 1½ inches thick; one side is flat and polished.

No evidence of art or ritual found to date.

Fragment of polished plank, Gesher Benot Ya'aqov, Israel

TOOLS FOR CUTTING MEAT

Numerous oval and heart-shaped hand axes made during this period have been found at Hoxne in eastern England; some have wear patterns that suggest they were used for cutting meat. Wooden spears with fire-hardened tips may have been made for hunting, although game was more likely caught using traps and pits.

Hand ax, Hoxne, England

RED PAINT

At Becov in Bohemia, a quartzite rubbing stone and a lump of red ocher dating to 250,000 years ago were found at a site used by early hominids. Ocher powder found on a floor nearby may have been mixed with blood and fat to make red paint, although there is no evidence to indicate how it was used.

Ocher, Becov, Bohemia

Base of tool flaked to fit in palm

CUTTING TOOLS

Many stone tools made by early hominids in Africa were multipurpose implements. This Egyptian example, flaked on both faces to produce a sharp edge, could have been used for chopping, cutting, scraping, and pounding. The earliest found tools of this type were made around 200,000 years ago.

No evidence of art or ritual found to date.

Cutting tool, Egypt

THE ICE-AGE CYCLE

Today, the polar ice caps cover one-tenth of the earth's surface, yet a drop of only 8 degrees Fahrenheit in the world's average temperature would result in one-third of the globe being covered in ice. Such regular climatic changes have been occurring at intervals for at least the last 2.5 million years, resulting in the cycle known as the Ice Ages. The advance and retreat of glaciers and ice sheets has had profound effects on the earth's surface. Erosion caused by glaciation diversifies the landscape, creating deep valleys and lakes, jagged peaks, and mountain ridges. As the ice melts, rivers and waterfalls form, and the drowning of glacial valleys creates fjords and deep-cut estuarine inlets. Glaciation depletes the amount of available water on earth, resulting in falling sea levels and reduced rainfall; the reverse occurs during an interglacial episode. The alternate locking up and release of vast quantities of water has had far-reaching implications for earth's flora and fauna – including humankind.

|||| Ice sheets *c.*20,000 BP   ▦ Ice sheets *c.*8000 BP   -- Coastline *c.*20,000 BP

EXTENT OF GLACIATION *above*
At the height of the last Ice Age, ice covered huge areas of Europe, Asia, and North America. A drop of more than 330 feet in sea levels exposed newly dry land around the world's coastlines and uncovered bridges between landmasses formerly separated by water. The Bering land bridge between Siberia and Alaska was over 620 miles wide; Australia, Tasmania, and New Guinea were one huge continent; Britain was joined to Europe; and Indonesia was all part of mainland Southeast Asia.

CHANGING CLIMATE *right*
The cycle of repeated glaciation began around 2.5 million years ago. Warmer periods, known as interglacials, have punctuated the Ice Ages, but have rarely lasted more than 20,000 years. The last Ice Age began about 110,000 years ago. Its climatic fluctuations have been traced through evidence from sediments and pollen on land, and from geological core samples drilled from the ocean bed, as shown (*right*). At the height of the last Ice Age, between around 25,000 and 15,000 years ago, global temperatures reached their lowest levels, ice sheets were at their maximum extent, and sea levels were dramatically lower than they are now. The latest interglacial began about 10,000 years ago and continues today.

Depth of core (ft)	Estimated ages (BP) Before Present
0	13,000
	32,000
	64,000
	75,000
	128,000
10	195,000
	251,000
	297,000
	347,000
20	367,000
	440,000
	472,000
	502,000
	542,000
30	592,000
	627,000
	647,000
	688,000
40	700,000

☐ Cold stages   ☐ Warm stages

GLACIER LANDSCAPE *right*
When snow falls faster than it can melt, the resulting compacted ice will eventually, under its own weight, begin to travel, forming a glacier, or "river of ice," and producing dramatic effects on the landscape. The rate at which glaciers move varies from a few inches to 15 feet a day. Underlying rock is scoured and polished by ice and by rocks dragged along under the glacier, and valleys are eroded. Glacial valleys are typically U-shaped – deep basins with steep sides – whereas those carved by rivers are V-shaped. Moraines (masses of debris carried by the ice) are laid down at the limits of the glacier, forming ridges and mounds.

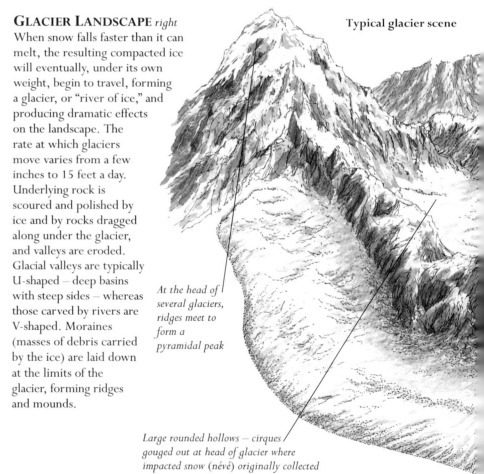

Typical glacier scene

At the head of several glaciers, ridges meet to form a pyramidal peak

Large rounded hollows – cirques gouged out at head of glacier where impacted snow (névé) originally collected

ICE-AGE ANIMALS *below*
In northern latitudes bulky, thick-coated, cold-tolerant animals such as the woolly mammoth and woolly rhinoceros prevailed during the glacial periods. In tundra areas, where wood was scarce, mammoth bones were used for the framework and supports of skin-covered huts. At the end of the last Ice Age, deprived of their natural environment and habitat, many of these species became extinct.

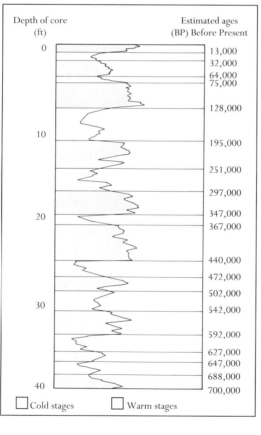

Frozen baby mammoth being lifted from excavations, Siberia

ANIMAL MIGRATIONS
As temperatures dropped during a glacial episode, the ice sheets advanced and forests were replaced by open vegetation. Animals either became extinct, adapted their diet and way of life, or followed the retreating wooded areas. Animals from cold latitudes, such as the musk ox and reindeer, spread into what are now very warm areas of Europe. Reindeer even lived in northern Spain, as shown in Ice-Age rock art such as this engraving in a Basque cave.

Engraved reindeer and fox, Altxerri cave, Spain

DESERTIFICATION *below*

Glacial episodes were also very dry, because so much less water was available to fall as rain. Deserts became even more arid than they are today and covered larger areas. Fossil sand dunes discovered in the Sahel of north-central Africa show that the Sahara once extended much farther south, and the Zaire rainforest was much smaller. The release of water at the end of a glacial period was not the only encouragement to new vegetation; huge quantities of rock dust, shattered and ground by the ice, combined with impacted earth to produce loess, a fertile, loamy soil more amenable to plant growth.

Southern edge of Tassili Massif, Algeria

VEGETATION *below*

The geographical distribution of plants and animals alters with changes in the climate. The advance of the ice sheets displaced the world's vegetational zones so that tundra replaced forest in northern latitudes, and coniferous trees mixed with species that tolerate colder climes, like birch and willow, spread farther south over much of Europe.

Silver birch

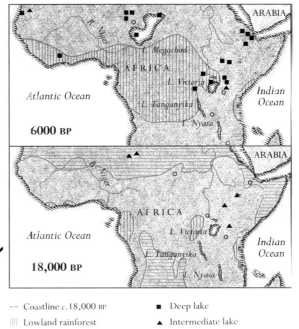

6000 BP

18,000 BP

-- Coastline *c*.18,000 BP
||| Lowland rainforest
≡ Desert
■ Deep lake
▲ Intermediate lake
○ Shallow lake

CHANGES IN THE LANDSCAPE *above*

The dramatic landscape changes of the Ice Ages in the tropics can be seen in Africa, where lake levels and fossil pollen show fluctuations in the distribution of forest, savanna, and desert during the last glacial cycle. When the last Ice Age was at its coldest (*map 18,000 BP*), rainforests and lakes contracted while deserts reached their maximum extent. Once the Ice Age was over, lakes and forests expanded again, and were in fact more extensive 6,000 years ago (*map 6000 BP*) than today.

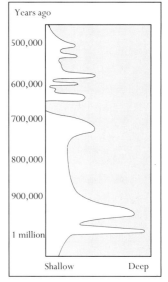

Years ago

500,000
600,000
700,000
800,000
900,000
1 million

Shallow   Deep

LAKE LEVELS AT OLORGESAILIE *above*

At Olorgesailie in Kenya, the fossil record of tiny lake organisms and evidence of changing shorelines over the past million years reveal that lake levels oscillated widely. The accompanying shifts in vegetation and the landscape probably affected the survival of early humans and other species. The end of the last Ice Age affected lake levels in every continent: the Great Lakes of North America, for example, were created by meltwater.

Arête (sharp ridge between glaciers)

Lateral moraines consist of rocky debris rubbed off and picked up from valley sides. Glaciers always move faster in the center than at the sides

Tundra landscape

Where two glaciers meet at the base of an arête, their lateral moraines combine to form a medial moraine

Boulders and other material deposited at the base of a glacier form the terminal moraine. Foreign rocks that have been carried and then deposited great distances from their origins are known as glacial erratics

CHAPTER 3
THE FIRST MODERN HUMANS
100,000 - 35,000 YEARS AGO

Ice Age tests resilience of Neanderthals and fully modern humans

First human burials mark the beginnings of ritual

First sea crossing made from Asia to Australia

Humans find creative expression in rock carving, painting, and engraving

Homo sapiens sapiens — "man the doubly wise" — becomes the single human race

The period from 100,000 to 35,000 years ago was a testing time for the resilience of early humankind. Despite the bitterly cold conditions of the Ice Age, *Homo sapiens* not only survived, but migrated into previously uninhabited regions, including Australia, where the world's earliest known rock art was the first sign of an emerging creative impulse.

Two subspecies of humans

Among the several variations of *Homo sapiens* that occurred around the world as hominid populations evolved, two distinct types dominate the fossil record from 100,000 years ago. The two subspecies were *Homo sapiens neanderthalensis* (the Neanderthals), in Europe and the Middle East, and *Homo sapiens sapiens*, "man the doubly wise" (fully modern humans), who may have originated in Africa.

Natural white crust on original rock surface

Carefully shaped cutting edge

WORKING TOOL
Probably designed for preparing animal hides, this Neanderthal flint scraper has been carefully chipped along one side to give a regular, curved working edge.

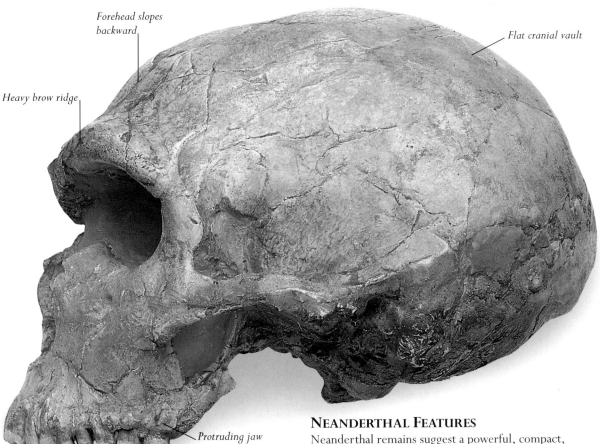

Forehead slopes backward

Flat cranial vault

Heavy brow ridge

Protruding jaw

NEANDERTHAL FEATURES
Neanderthal remains suggest a powerful, compact, heavy build, well-equipped to withstand the cold.

The Neanderthals, so called because the first skull cap of their type was recognized in the Neander Valley in Germany, lived in Europe and the Middle East from around 120,000 years ago. Although in physical appearance the archetypal "caveman" of popular imagination, they had brains at least the size of those of modern humans and were far from brutish, with a way of life that may have included cultural rituals and expression. Like modern human groups at Qafzeh in Israel and other sites,

Neanderthals sometimes buried the dead, decorating their graves. Meat and tools found in Neanderthal graves suggest belief in an afterlife. One man buried at Shanidar Cave in Iraq some 60,000 years ago had been badly injured at some point in his life; he had lost an arm and probably an eye and was crippled in both legs. To have survived until his comparatively advanced age of 40, he must have been supported by his community, suggesting a degree of social solidarity in Neanderthal groups.

Stone neck has been formed, around which to tie a thong

Decorative grooves

PERSONAL ORNAMENT
This European pendant is around 35,000 years old. The natural shape of the stone has been refined and patterned.

Emergence of modern humans

The earliest fossil remains of fully modern humans are found in Africa and date to a little over 100,000 years ago. Modern humans appeared very soon afterward in Israel, around 100,000 years ago. Here they were in direct contact with Neanderthal groups. Forced to develop new strategies to move into cooler territory, modern humans became clever, skillful hunters, equipped with improved tools and weapons – smaller blades and points set into handles of wood or bone. Composite tools were more efficient than heavier, single-piece tools: they could be made in a wider range of shapes, permitting a variety of increasingly specialized tasks.

Language and abstract expression

Although the Neanderthals may have behaved like fully modern humans in certain respects, their language skills were probably not as highly developed. A command of language would have enabled fully modern humans to talk about the past, and to plan ahead – which gave them a formidable advantage over the Neanderthals. Fully modern humans also possessed a new capacity for abstract expression. Fragments of engraved animal bone and traces of red ocher (a natural pigment) testify to emergent artistic activity in many regions.

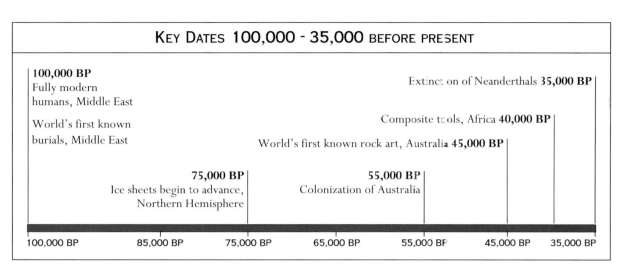

KEY DATES 100,000 - 35,000 BEFORE PRESENT

100,000 BP
Fully modern humans, Middle East

World's first known burials, Middle East

Extinction of Neanderthals **35,000 BP**

Composite tools, Africa **40,000 BP**

World's first known rock art, Australia **45,000 BP**

75,000 BP
Ice sheets begin to advance, Northern Hemisphere

55,000 BP
Colonization of Australia

100,000 BP	85,000 BP	75,000 BP	65,000 BP	55,000 BP	45,000 BP	35,000 BP

Impetus for colonization

By 60,000 years ago fully modern humans must also have been established in Southeast Asia. Armed with the capacity to plan and the ability to coordinate activities, they began to colonize areas that had previously been beyond human reach. Seagoing boats were needed to make the crossing from Southeast Asia to Australia, as there would have been at least 37 miles of open sea to cross at any given time. Yet by 55,000 years ago the first human settlements had been established in northern Australia. It is here that some of the oldest human creative expressions are seen. The petroglyphs (rock engravings) found at Panaramitee, around 45,000 years old, are the earliest known examples of rock art in the world.

Neanderthal extinction

Between 45,000 and 35,000 years ago, fully modern humans also spread throughout Europe. Contact with the indigenous Neanderthals is evident from the way the newcomers' improved toolmaking techniques influenced the Neanderthals' tool industry. But ultimately the Neanderthals would not benefit from this contact. By 35,000 years ago, for reasons that are still unclear, modern humans completely replaced the Neanderthals. In contrast to the hundreds of millennia during which early hominid types had coexisted, the transition was swift and decisive. As temperatures fell still further and the Ice Age entered its coldest phase, *Homo sapiens sapiens* was the only human species left in an increasingly hostile environment.

Flake

Chopper

Hand ax for general cutting and chopping

Sidescraper, possibly for preparing hides

Diskoid

Point

Endscraper

Blade (top), backed blade (center), and burin (bottom)

NEANDERTHAL TOOLKIT
Whereas *Homo erectus* made tools largely as necessary, *H. sapiens* made a range of implements for a variety of specialized tasks, as shown by this early "toolkit."

43

100,000-50,000 YEARS AGO

FOOD & ENVIRONMENT	SHELTER & ARCHITECTURE	

AMERICAS

No evidence of human habitation found to date.

No evidence of human habitation found to date.

EAST ASIA & AUSTRALASIA

GIANT MARSUPIALS

When modern humans first reached Australia about 55,000 years ago, the continent was inhabited by a variety of large marsupials, including giant kangaroos and wallabies and the wombat-like diprotodon, a plant-eater that weighed up to 2 tons. These animals became extinct mainly because they were hunted by humans.

Diprotodon

ROCK SHELTERS

The oldest campsites in Australia are the sandstone rock shelters at Malakunanja and Malangangerr. These lie at the foot of the Arnhem Land plateau, near the northern coast of the continent. The modern humans who set up camp here around 55,000 years ago were probably the near descendants of the first humans to cross the open sea to Australia from Southeast Asia.

MIDDLE EAST & SOUTH ASIA

WILD GOATS

The bezoar goat, the wild ancestor of the modern goat, was one of the staple resources exploited by modern human groups living around 50,000 years ago in the mountains of western Asia. Like most wild goats, it was probably hunted most effectively by ambushing the herds or by driving them into natural cul-de-sacs for slaughter.

Bezoar goat

LIMESTONE CAVE

The limestone cave at Kebara in Israel was occupied by Neanderthals around 60,000 years ago. Hearths and layers of ash show that it was used as a dwelling. Caves were particularly favored as shelters in which to survive the rigors of the last Ice Age. Where caves were not available, groups of humans may have built shelters of wooden frames covered in animal hides.

Kebara Cave, Israel

EUROPE

EFFICIENT HUNTING

The appearance of specialized open-air slaughter camps in southern France indicates the development of more effective hunting methods. At these camps, large animals such as the steppe bison and the aurochs (wild ox) were killed and butchered en masse. In a camp at Mauran, in the Pyrenees, thousands of bone fragments from over 100 animals were found, representing hundreds of tons of meat.

European steppe bison

CAVE-MOUTH STRUCTURE

Cave dwellings during this period were sometimes improved by building structures at the entrance to give added protection from bad weather. These windbreaks or fences were probably supported by stakes driven into the ground. A small hole at the mouth of a cave at Combe-Grenal in France may have held a stake that supported one of these structures: a cast taken of the hole was shaped like the pointed end of a stake.

**Cast of posthole,
Combe-Grenal, France**

AFRICA

ELAND AND BUFFALO

Around 60,000 years ago, the eland was abundant in what is now Cape Province, South Africa. A natural herd animal, it was probably killed in mass drives. The ferocious Cape buffalo was more difficult to kill, and only the most vulnerable individuals would have been hunted. Meat must have been scavenged from animals that were already dead. Eland and buffalo bones have been found in South African caves that were occupied during this period.

Eland

SEASONAL CAMPS

The huge cave at Haua Fteah, on the Libyan coast of North Africa, was occupied continuously from at least 60,000 years ago. It was probably a seasonal camp used by people exploiting coastal resources during the dry summer months. During the wet winter season, the occupants moved inland to areas of open grassland where there were abundant equine animals and gazelles.

TECHNOLOGY & INNOVATION	ART & RITUAL

No evidence of human habitation found to date.

No evidence of human habitation found to date.

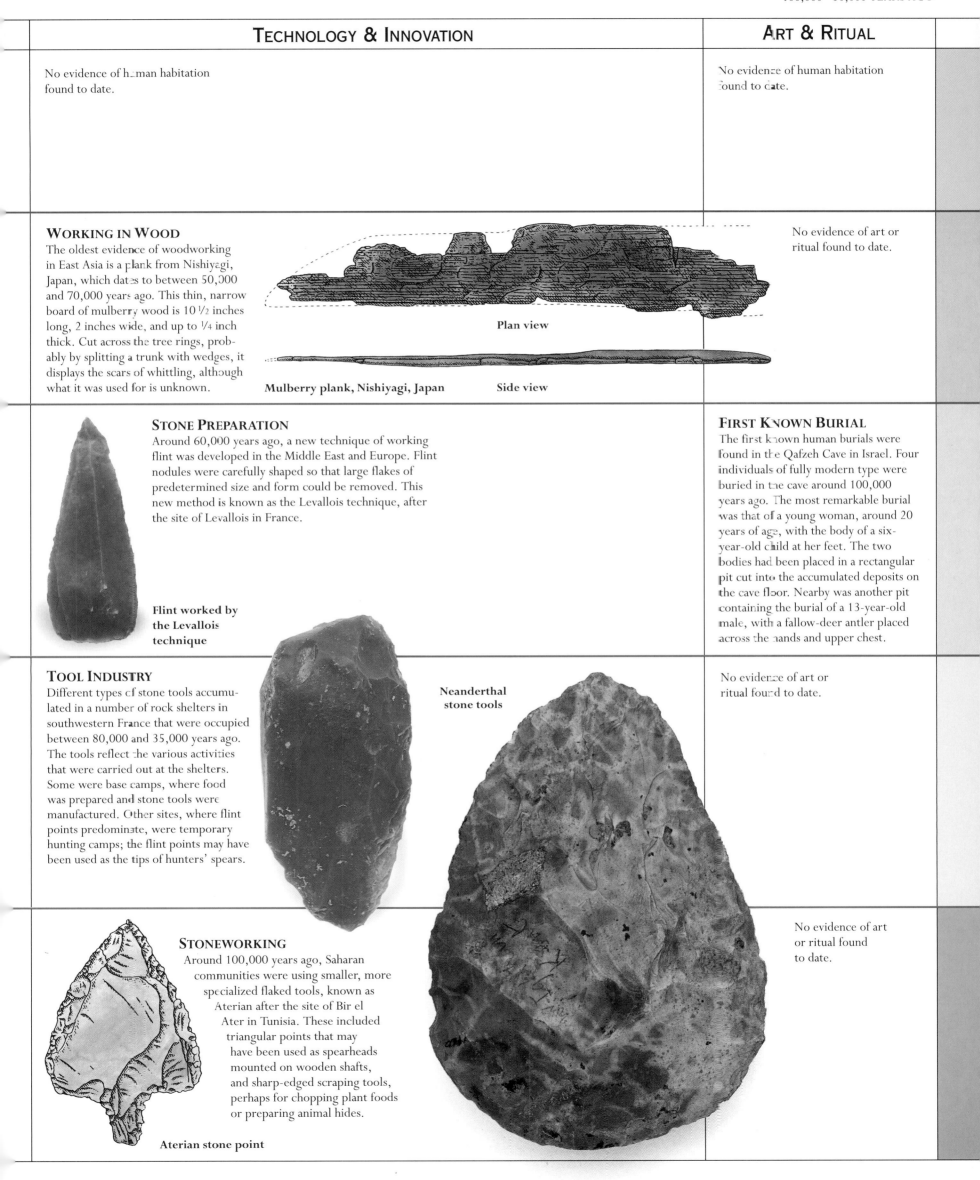

WORKING IN WOOD

The oldest evidence of woodworking in East Asia is a plank from Nishiyagi, Japan, which dates to between 50,000 and 70,000 years ago. This thin, narrow board of mulberry wood is 10 ½ inches long, 2 inches wide, and up to ¼ inch thick. Cut across the tree rings, probably by splitting a trunk with wedges, it displays the scars of whittling, although what it was used for is unknown.

Plan view

Mulberry plank, Nishiyagi, Japan   **Side view**

No evidence of art or ritual found to date.

STONE PREPARATION

Around 60,000 years ago, a new technique of working flint was developed in the Middle East and Europe. Flint nodules were carefully shaped so that large flakes of predetermined size and form could be removed. This new method is known as the Levallois technique, after the site of Levallois in France.

Flint worked by the Levallois technique

FIRST KNOWN BURIAL

The first known human burials were found in the Qafzeh Cave in Israel. Four individuals of fully modern type were buried in the cave around 100,000 years ago. The most remarkable burial was that of a young woman, around 20 years of age, with the body of a six-year-old child at her feet. The two bodies had been placed in a rectangular pit cut into the accumulated deposits on the cave floor. Nearby was another pit containing the burial of a 13-year-old male, with a fallow-deer antler placed across the hands and upper chest.

TOOL INDUSTRY

Different types of stone tools accumulated in a number of rock shelters in southwestern France that were occupied between 80,000 and 35,000 years ago. The tools reflect the various activities that were carried out at the shelters. Some were base camps, where food was prepared and stone tools were manufactured. Other sites, where flint points predominate, were temporary hunting camps; the flint points may have been used as the tips of hunters' spears.

Neanderthal stone tools

No evidence of art or ritual found to date.

STONEWORKING

Around 100,000 years ago, Saharan communities were using smaller, more specialized flaked tools, known as Aterian after the site of Bir el Ater in Tunisia. These included triangular points that may have been used as spearheads mounted on wooden shafts, and sharp-edged scraping tools, perhaps for chopping plant foods or preparing animal hides.

Aterian stone point

No evidence of art or ritual found to date.

50,000-35,000 YEARS AGO

	FOOD & ENVIRONMENT	SHELTER & ARCHITECTURE	
AMERICAS	No evidence of human habitation found to date.	No evidence of human habitation found to date.	

EAST ASIA & AUSTRALASIA

CARNIVOROUS MARSUPIALS

Among the few carnivorous predators encountered by Australia's first settlers was the Tasmanian tiger, a marsupial that became extinct on the mainland around 3,000 years ago owing to competition from the more efficient dingo. The Tasmanian tiger survived until much more recently in Tasmania, where there were no dingoes.

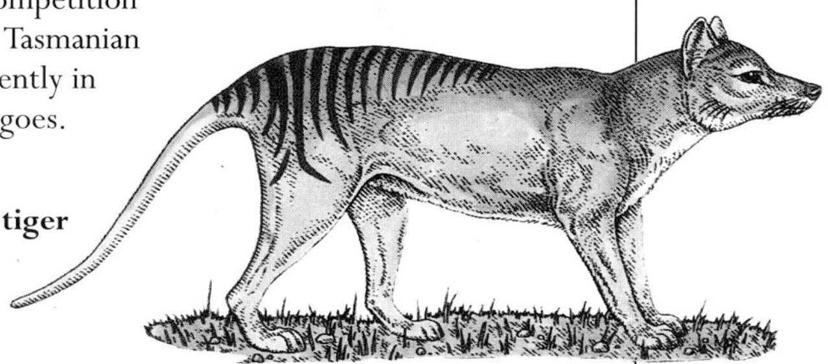

Tasmanian tiger

LIMESTONE CAVES

A network of huge limestone caves at Niah in Sarawak, Borneo, has the longest record of human occupation on any island in Southeast Asia. The Great Cave, an enormous cavern 800 feet wide at the mouth and nearly 200 feet high inside, is the most important. Its floor area covers approximately 64 acres. This splendid natural shelter was first occupied by modern humans around 40,000 years ago.

MIDDLE EAST & SOUTH ASIA

FLOWERING PLANTS

Pollen found in Shanidar Cave in northern Iraq shows that the climate around 50,000 years ago was much as it is now. Plants existing at that time still grow in the area today: yarrow, St. John's wort, hollyhocks, St. Barnaby's thistle, groundsel, grape hyacinth, and woody horsetail. Some have medicinal properties, but whether they were used medicinally at this date is unknown.

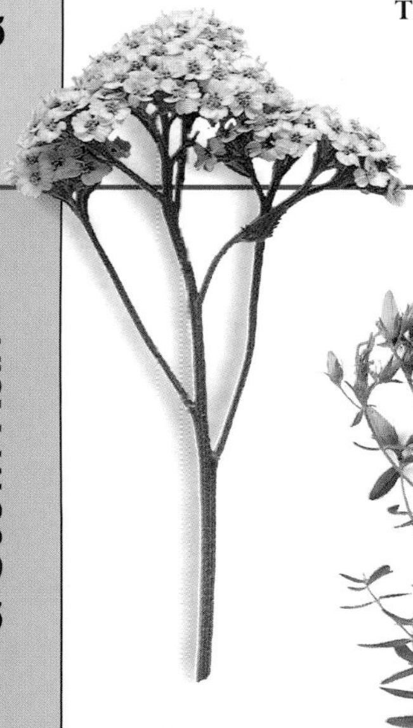

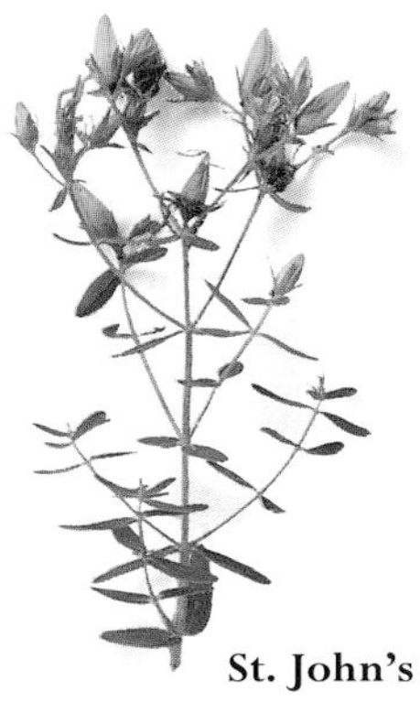

Yarrow   **St. John's wort**

SEASONAL BASES

Shanidar Cave was occupied around 50,000 years ago by a group of Neanderthals. Located in the foothills of the Zagros mountains, in Anatolia (modern Turkey), the cave was used as a seasonal base from which to hunt bezoar goats in the surrounding mountains, and to gather local food plants. The occupants probably spent the rest of the year in lower terrain.

EUROPE

HIBERNATING BEARS

The cave bear, which is now extinct, was so named because it hibernated in caves and often died there. It was a huge animal, twice the size of a brown bear. Its teeth and the chemistry of its bones show that it was a vegetarian. Cave bear bones are often found in caves mixed with stone tools and other traces of human settlement. Some archaeologists believe that humans hunted the bears.

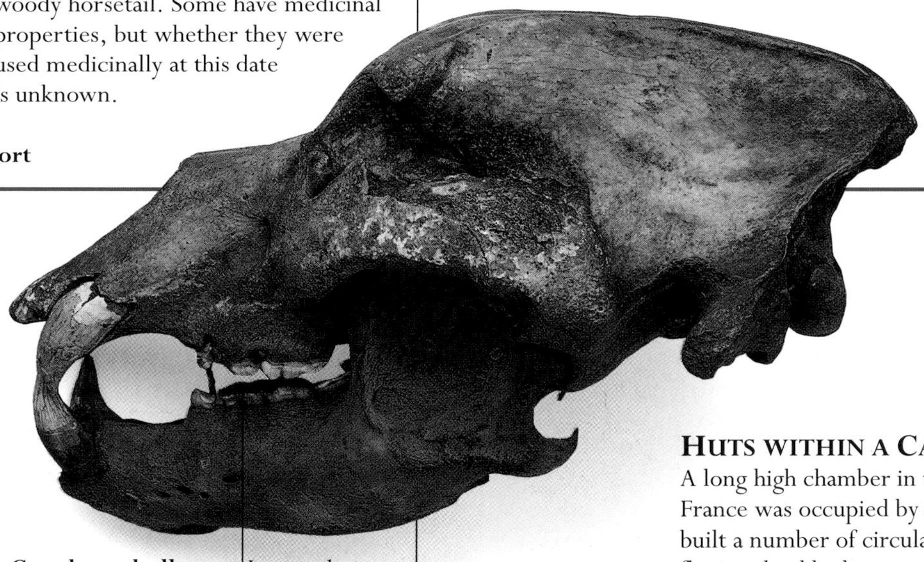

Cave bear skull, Germany   *Large molars for grinding vegetation*

HUTS WITHIN A CAVE

A long high chamber in the Grotte du Renne in northern France was occupied by a group of Neanderthals who built a number of circular huts within it. These had floors edged by limestone slabs and mammoth tusks set upright in postholes. There were also several small hearths containing burned lumps of ocher.

AFRICA

CHANGING CLIMATE

Some 45,000 years ago, the Sahara was much wetter than it is today, with types of Mediterranean-like evergreen vegetation in the highlands, and rivers crossing the dry grassland plains below. At Bir Tarfawi in southwestern Egypt, settlers on the shore of a shallow lake were able to hunt gazelles, warthogs, and ostriches. This way of life changed around 38,000 years ago when the Sahara entered an arid phase, and human communities were forced to withdraw to its margins.

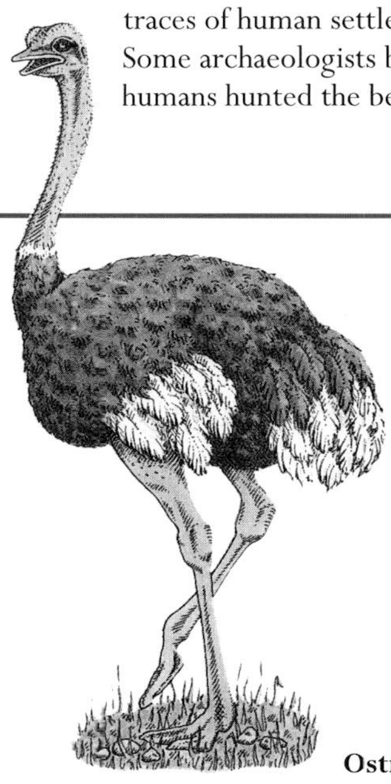

Ostrich

STOPOVER SITES

Rock shelters provided convenient temporary camps for early African hunter-gatherers. Many of these shelters would have been used as stopovers by small groups moving about the landscape collecting wild fruit and hunting game. Some, such as Sehonghong in Lesotho and Kalemba in Zambia, were first occupied over 35,000 years ago.

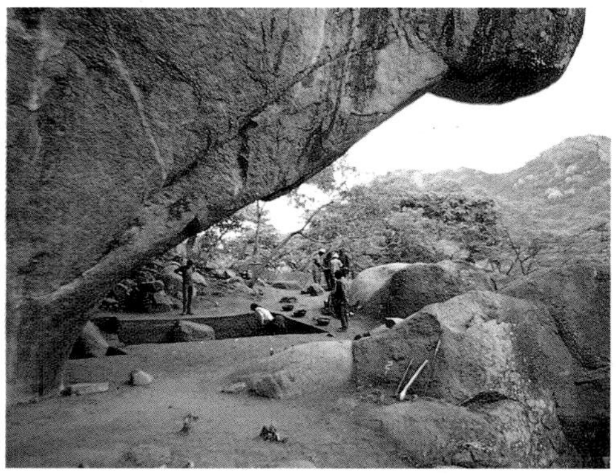

Kalemba rock shelter, eastern Zambia

TECHNOLOGY & INNOVATION

No evidence of human habitation found to date.

AXES WITH HANDLES

Heavy stone axes with flaked cutting edges are among the earliest traces of human presence on the island of New Guinea. These axes had notches cut into either side, creating a narrow waist where a wooden handle would have been attached. On the Huon Peninsula in northeastern New Guinea, such waisted axes were in use 40,000 years ago.

Waisted ax, Huon Peninsula, New Guinea

SMALLER TOOLS

Around 45,000 years ago, human communities in the Middle East began to produce smaller flint tools, which were suitable for setting into wooden or bone handles. Many tools of this kind have been found in the Mount Carmel Caves on the coast of Israel. Known as Aurignacian, the new technology was later adopted by communities across the whole of southern Europe.

Aurignacian tools, Israel

CHATELPERRONIAN FLINTS

The last Neanderthals in western Europe produced flint tools similar to those of contemporary groups of modern humans further east. The tools were smaller than any previously known and were set into handles. This style, known as Châtelperronian because the first examples were found at Châtel-perron in France, is exemplified by small flint points that were probably set obliquely into handles of bone or wood.

Châtelperronian point

DABBAN TOOLS

As the Sahara became increasingly dry with the onset of an arid phase around 38,000 years ago, new types of settlements and tools developed. Dabban tools, named after the site of ed Dabba in Libya, are characterized by smaller flint blades mounted in wooden or bone hafts. They are restricted to coastal North Africa, because the interior was by then too dry for permanent habitation.

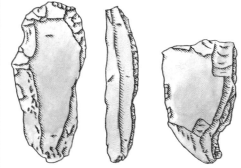

Dabban tools, Haua Fteah Cave, Libya

ART & RITUAL

No evidence of human habitation found to date.

ROCK ENGRAVINGS

The oldest rock engravings in the world are simple non-figurative designs that were etched into rocks in Australia from around 45,000 years ago. These engravings are known as Panaramitee petroglyphs, named after a site in South Australia, and come in a variety of patterns: mazes, circles, dots, and arcs. They represent the earliest stage in a long and varied tradition of Australian rock art.

Petroglyphs, Panaramitee, Australia

BURIAL RITES

Like the Neanderthals who occupied Kebara Cave in Israel some 10,000 years before, the Neanderthals living in Shanidar Cave in northern Iraq around 50,000 years ago buried their dead. Remains of at least nine individuals were found in the cave. Some may have been victims of a rock fall, but others were intentionally buried. Remains of pollen suggest that one adult may have been laid on a bed of woody branches with a variety of small, brightly colored flowers placed around the body.

Engraved bone, Bacho Kiro, Bulgaria

ENGRAVED PATTERNS

In Europe, the decoration of bones may have begun around 50,000 years ago. A bone fragment from a cave at Bacho Kiro in central Bulgaria bears zigzag markings that seem to be deliberate engravings rather than the result of damage caused by chopping strokes.

COUNTING DEVICE

Rudimentary counting devices may have been made in Africa as long as 37,000 years ago. Among engraved pieces of wood and bone from Border Cave in South Africa was a baboon fibula with 29 parallel incised notches. This resembles the wooden calendar sticks that are still used today by some Bushman clans in southwestern Africa.

Incised notch _____

Baboon fibula, Border Cave, South Africa

THE NEANDERTHALS

Fully modern humans – *Homo sapiens sapiens* – can be defined as hominids whose skeletal form and mental potential bear no significant difference from humans today. It is certain that from 35,000 years ago, when the last Neanderthal lived in Europe, there has been no other hominid species in existence but our own. But how do we compare with the humans that preceded us? And is it now proven that older, indigenous populations around the world – such as the Neanderthals – were swept aside by fully modern humans who originated in Africa? Just as Darwin's theories stated that we shared common ancestors with the apes – and not that we descended from them, as is popularly assumed – so recent evidence increasingly suggests that the Neanderthals were not our forebears, but ancient cousins, our common ancestor being *Homo erectus*.

▲ Neanderthal remains find site

DISTRIBUTION OF NEANDERTHAL POPULATIONS
Neanderthal remains have been found as far apart as western Germany, Iraq, the Levant, and Uzbekistan. During the coldest phase of the Ice Age, ice sheets would have isolated the Neanderthals of Europe from those of the Middle East.

PEOPLE OF THE ICE AGE

Homo sapiens neanderthalensis lived in Europe and the Middle East from around 120,000 years ago, surviving until around 35,000 years ago in western Europe. Despite many similarities, the Neanderthals were significantly different in skeleton and physique from fully modern humans – heavily muscled, with great physical strength and a compact body shape, ideally adapted to a harsh, cold environment. The Neanderthal way of life, however, may have been very similar to that of our own species. Possession of a fully developed language seems to be the main area in which *Homo sapiens sapiens* had the edge.

Low and sloping forehead

Large nose warmed the cold inhaled air

Strong jaw muscles were attached to bony processes

TOOL TECHNOLOGY *below*
The Neanderthals revolutionized toolmaking with the prepared core technique, in which several sharp flakes were split from a single flint. Their simple but effective implements included scrapers and piercing tools to make warm clothing from hides. Tools made by fully modern humans – single-edged knives and leaf-shaped blades – show more refined stoneworking techniques.

Sharp flake split lengthwise from prepared flint

Neanderthal flake tool

NEANDERTHAL SKULL
This classic example reconstructed from fragmented remains dates to around 36,000 years ago and was discovered at a rock shelter in St. Césaire in France. It is probably that of one of the last Neanderthals, suggesting that in western Europe physical characteristics changed little, some even becoming more pronounced as the Ice Age progressed. Interestingly, modern human-style tools were found in association with this skull, implying that late Neanderthals were modifying toolmaking techniques, perhaps through contact with communities of modern humans.

BURIAL CEREMONIES *above*
Some Neanderthals buried their dead, marking and seemingly mourning the loss of a community member – a characteristic that they shared with fully modern humans. Evidence of ceremonies has been found in both Europe and the Middle East. Some graves appear to contain items to equip the deceased for an afterlife. At some sites, burned or charred bones, showing evidence of butchering, suggest that cooked joints of meat were placed in the grave. At Shanidar in Iraq, flowers seem to have been placed in one grave. Children's burials were often a focus for such activity. At La Ferrassie in France, an infant's skull was found beneath a patterned slab in what appears to have been a family cemetery in a rock shelter.

RUDIMENTARY ART *right*
There is no comparison between the simple, non-utilitarian markings that distinguish the few Neanderthal art objects that have been discovered and the mass of art – engravings, rock paintings, figures – that is found at the later *Homo sapiens sapiens* sites. Nevertheless, the existing Neanderthal objects – burial slabs, engraved bones, or the very early objects from Hungary (*right*) – testify to an emerging appreciation of decorative artifacts that may have had some symbolic function.

Carved and polished mammoth molar

Line scratched across natural crack to make a cross

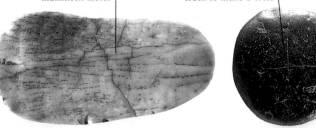

Mammoth ivory plaque, Tata, Hungary

Engraved fossil, Tata, Hungary

COMPARISON OF BONE STRUCTURE

Neanderthals were stocky and extremely powerfully built, with stout, sometimes bowed limb bones. Their skulls have a low, flattened crown with a bulging bun at the back. The neck muscles that attached here helped brace the head against any force generated in using the strong jaw. The face is large and forward-thrusting, with large teeth, no chin, a large nose, and characteristic brow ridges. The modern human skeleton is taller and less powerful, with a higher skull crown, smaller teeth, a prominent chin, a shorter and flatter face, and almost no brow ridge.

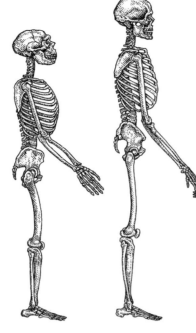

Neanderthal   **Modern human**

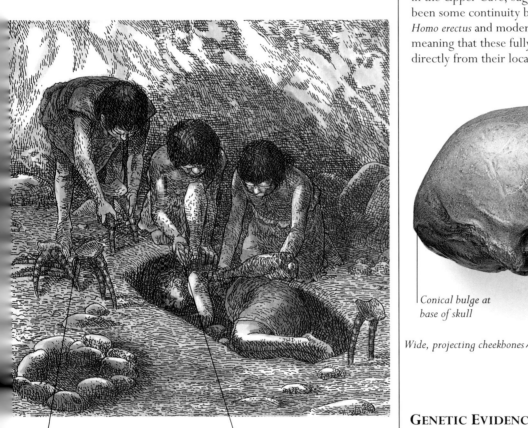

Possible ritual items, such as stone slabs and rings of animal horns, sometimes surround the head

Tools and food may have been buried with the deceased, perhaps to equip him in an afterlife

Cupules (shallow circular hollows)

Neanderthal slab covering cave burial, La Ferrassie, France

DEBATING THE EVIDENCE

The still unresolved fate of the Neanderthals has long been the focus of debate surrounding the origins of modern humans. Should *Homo sapiens neanderthalensis* be included among our ancestors, or did fully modern humans with their origins in Africa simply sweep them aside – perhaps by being more successful at gathering food, by violence, or by carrying diseases to which the Neanderthals had no resistance? Archaeological discoveries and other evidence are used to support the theory that modern humans evolved in Africa, although the "Multiregionalists," who favor the notion of parallel development in many areas of the world, can claim other evidence that seems to suggest local lineages stretching back from *Homo sapiens sapiens* through such forms as the Neanderthals to *Homo erectus*.

ZHOUKOUDIAN SKULL *below*

Evidence from China is used to support multiregionalism, the theory of parallel human development. The Lower Cave at Zhoukoudian near Peking is famous as the home of a *Homo erectus* community some 450,000 years ago. The skulls of these *H. erectus* individuals are somewhat different from those found in Africa and other regions. Some of these differences are claimed to reappear in a modern human skull (*below*) found in the Upper Cave, suggesting that there may have been some continuity between ancient indigenous *Homo erectus* and modern populations in China – meaning that these fully modern humans evolved directly from their local predecessors.

QAFZEH SKULL *below*

The theory that modern humans emerged from Africa and gradually supplanted other human groups is supported by fossil evidence from Africa and the Middle East. This skull from Qafzeh, Israel, would seem to belong to a modern-type individual and has been dated to 100,000 years ago. Although Neanderthal remains in Israel such as those at Tabun date back to 120,000 years ago, we know that Neanderthals were still present in the region, at sites such as Kebara, only 60,000 years ago. The co-existence of these two physically dissimilar groups is used as evidence that there is no clear ancestor-descendant relationship between them.

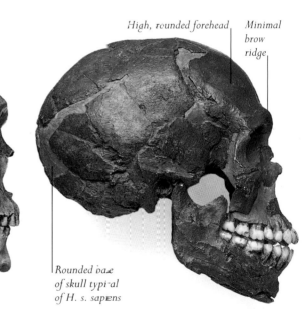

High, rounded forehead   *Minimal brow ridge*

Conical bulge at base of skull

Wide, projecting cheekbones

Heavy jaw

Rounded base of skull typical of H. s. sapiens

GENETIC EVIDENCE

Genes, which determine inheritance, are composed of DNA (deoxyribonucleic acid). Genetic evidence increasingly suggests that Africa was the birthplace of modern humans. Africans have the greatest genetic diversity, implying that they also have a long lineage, while strong genetic similarities in non-African peoples point to a common center of origin. It has also been suggested that modern human populations arose in parallel in different regions of the world, because early modern humans retain characteristics found in *Homo erectus* groups.

Model, DNA double helix

DARWINISM

The discovery of a Neanderthal skull in 1856 provided crucial evidence for the theory of human evolution that scientists were beginning to piece together. At the time when the skull was found, many people still interpreted the Bible as saying that modern humans similar to ourselves had been created by a special act of God less than 6,000 years ago. The Neanderthal skull, however, showed clearly that other types of hominids had once existed and had since become extinct. The discovery gave scientific support to Darwin's *Origin of Species,* published in 1859, which claimed that all living things today are the result of millions of years of evolution.

Charles Darwin (1809-82)

49

CHAPTER 4
CROSSING TO AMERICA
33,000 - 13,000 BC

(From 35,000 years ago [33,000 BC], the BC/AD dating system conventionally comes into operation)

The coldest phase of the last Ice Age tests human ingenuity

Siberian hunters migrate to North America across the Bering land bridge

Microliths: a technological breakthrough in Africa

Wild grain is harvested and ground in the Middle East

At the coldest point of the last Ice Age, around 20,000 years ago, global temperatures were as much as 59° Fahrenheit lower than today. So much water was trapped in the ice sheets that sea levels were 325 feet lower than they are today, exposing land bridges and linking continents previously separated by the oceans. Since less water was available in the atmosphere to fall as rain, large areas of the tropics became arid. In northern Eurasia and North America, huge ice sheets advanced across the landscape, generating strong arctic winds. Plants, animals, and humans all had to adapt to these extreme environmental conditions.

Strategies for survival

By this time, *Homo sapiens sapiens* was the sole surviving human species. Physically less robust than the Neanderthals who had inhabited northerly latitudes, these fully modern humans had to use their skills and ingenuity to combat the increasing cold. Resourceful and inventive, they used natural materials fully, employing not only stone but also bone, hide, and antler in new ways. Innovations included weapons that could be thrown or aimed accurately over long distances – spear-throwers, bows and arrows, boomerangs, and barbed harpoons; improved clothing technology – thong-softeners, toggles, and needles with eyes; and sturdier shelters to protect them from the harsh climate.

Substantial shelters

Larger, more durable shelters were built at this time in many regions of the world: traces have been found at Central European sites such as Dolni Vestonice in the Czech Republic, and at Middle Eastern sites such as Ohalo in Israel. The most common form was a superstructure of wooden posts covered with animal hides.

Some of these huts had sunken floors and hearths. Most notable were the mammoth-bone dwellings known to have been built in eastern Europe, which demonstrate an ability to use whatever materials available for building. Meanwhile, caves continued to provide convenient, ready-made shelters in many regions of the world.

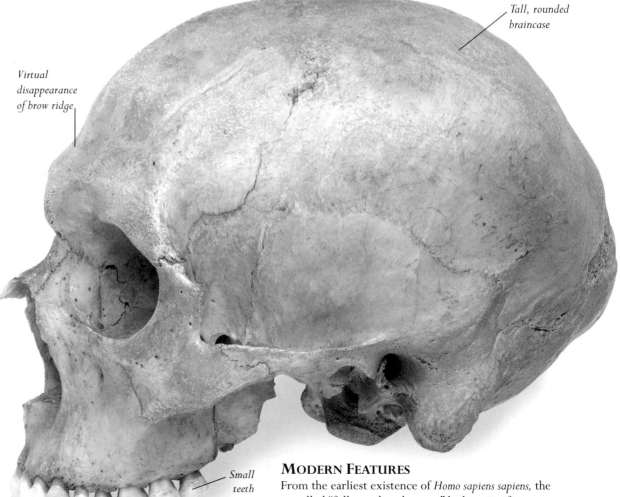

Tall, rounded braincase

Virtual disappearance of brow ridge

Small teeth

MODERN FEATURES
From the earliest existence of *Homo sapiens sapiens*, the so-called "fully modern humans" had no significant anatomical differences from humans today.

13,000 BC
Earliest evidence of colonization, North America

World's earliest known clay figurines, Europe **23,000 BC**

17,000 BC
Wild grain gathering,
Middle East

First rock paintings, Africa **24,000 BC**

25,000 BC
Last Ice Age enters
coldest phase

18,000 BC
Coldest point of
last Ice Age

| 33,000 BC | 30,000 BC | 25,000 BC | 20,000 BC | 13,000 BC |

ANIMAL SKETCHES
Outline drawings of animals such as these
from a cave at Santimamiñe, northern Spain,
were the most common form of European
cave art during this period.

Hunting territories

In the harsh Ice Age conditions, the
resilience of modern humans was fully
tested. Scattered groups of hunter-
gatherers managed to survive, and some
even migrated northward into the frozen
steppes of Siberia. Superior hunting skills,
improved weaponry, and a command of
language – combined with a detailed
knowledge of the habits, diet, and
movements of animals – resulted in
a search for fresh hunting territory.

Colonization of the Americas

It is not known exactly when the first
settlers arrived in the Americas. Most
archaeologists think that the first people
to cross the Bering land bridge, which
connected the North American mainland
to the Siberian landmass, did so around
15,000 years ago. Claims that certain rock
shelters in Brazil were already occupied up
to 40,000 years ago have not generally
been accepted. The earliest secure
evidence for the arrival of hunter-gatherer
groups in the western Yukon region of
Canada supports the later date. Two huge
North American ice sheets were major
obstacles blocking their migration
southward to the rest of the American
continent: the Cordilleran, centered in
the northern Rockies and extending to
the west coast, and the Laurentide around
the Hudson Bay area.

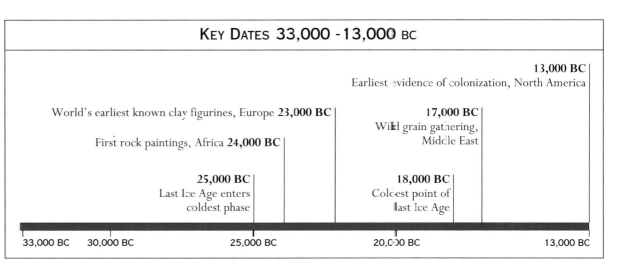

Eye

Tusk

**ICE-AGE
MASTERPIECE**
Stylized mammoth
follows the natural
shape of the bone.

*Exaggerated
female
characteristics*

*Rounded
form*

FERTILITY SYMBOLS
Female figurines were produced across Europe from
Spain to Russia around 25,000 years ago. Some, like this
one from Lespugue, France, portray pregnant women or
are characterized by exaggerated breasts and buttocks.

Cultural expression

With the crossing to America, well-
organized groups, supported by efficient
hunting and gathering techniques, were
established in every continent of the
world. Yet this was not only a period of
migration, but also of new cultural
expression, which is seen most vividly
in the rock paintings of Africa, Europe,
and Australia.

Examples in Africa and Europe were
being produced at least 25,000 years ago.
In Australia, the first rock paintings, as
opposed to the earlier petroglyphs (rock
engravings), are more than 18,000 years
old. The rich tradition of African rock art
began to take shape during this period;
some of the oldest examples can be seen in
the Apollo II Cave in Namibia. The most
famous European sites of polychrome rock
art dating to this period are in caves at
Lascaux and Pech-Merle in France and
Altamira in Spain. Simple outline drawings
of animals were more common, however.

33,000 - 13,000 BC

Ritual and tradition

In many parts of the world, human communities were producing sculpted forms and engraved objects in bone, stone, and ivory, and fired clay figurines. The few examples that survive only hint at a wealth of artistic and symbolic expression that may well have taken many other forms, including decoration on perishable materials such as wood, animal hides, and the human body. Oral traditions such as myth and storytelling may also have existed. Burial was common to many groups during this period, although the beliefs held about death are unknown. The earliest known cremation, near ancient Lake Mungo in southeastern Australia, dates to around 26,000 years ago. Together with sophisticated rock painting and engraving, it testifies to the complexity of Aboriginal ceremonial life.

Tool technology

Advanced tool traditions developed in different parts of the world, characterized by ever-smaller stone points and blades, and by the first extensive use of bone and antler. The development of microliths in Africa around 35,000 years ago was a critical improvement. These tiny stone blades could be mounted in wooden or bone handles to produce tools whose damaged blades could be replaced. New, more refined toolmaking techniques also became the standard technology throughout Europe and the Middle East.

New uses for tools

In the Middle East, two important tool traditions were the Baradostian (c.32,000-18,000 BC), named after caves in the Baradost Mountains in southern Kurdistan, and the Kebaran (c.18,000-12,500 BC), named after the Kebara Cave in Israel. The latter industry included flint microliths, which were probably used in implements such as reaping knives, and a variety of grinding stones, since the hunter-gatherer groups who developed the Kebaran tradition also gathered wild grains and other seeds as part of their diet. These people were the predecessors of Natufian communities (named after the site of Wadi en-Natuf in Israel) who, by the end of this period, are known to have been harvesting wild grains intensively in the Levant – the coastal strip of Syria, Lebanon, and Israel.

Retreating ice sheets

By 13,000 BC, the worst of the Ice Age was over, and communities throughout the inhabited world began to consolidate their gains. The total human population was still sparse, but well adapted to a variety of environments. The skills and adaptability built up in climatic adversity would soon prevail in the more clement conditions following the retreat of the northern ice sheets. As the milder climate precipitated an expansion of new vegetation on fertile soils, the grain-gatherers of the Middle East pioneered the next major development in the human story.

AMERICAS

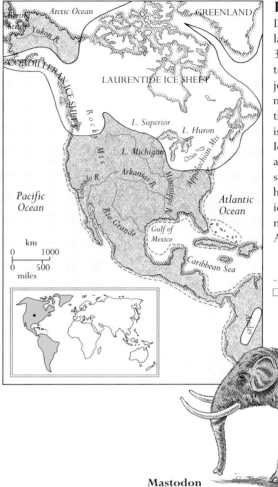

Mastodon

ICE-AGE MIGRATION

During the coldest phase of the last Ice Age, when sea levels were 330 feet lower than they are today, a land bridge was exposed joining Siberia to Alaska and northwestern Canada – the area that is today the Bering Strait. It is likely that humans and some Ice-Age fauna migrated into this area, but further movement southward into America would have been blocked by the massive ice fronts presented by the merging of the two major North American glacial masses.

-- Coastline of the period
☐ Approximate extent of ice sheet

AFRICA

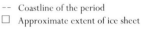

CAVE ART

At Kisese in central Tanzania, ocher fragments and ocher-stained palettes dating back 29,000 years have been found in decorated rock shelters. Painted stone slabs discovered in Namibia may be as much as 26,000 years old. Finds of art objects include terra-cotta figurines from Afalou Bou Rhummel in Algeria, incised and engraved objects from the Border Cave in South Africa, and a perforated stone from Zaire (*below*), which is decorated with incised lines and dates to around 20,000 years ago.

-- Coastline of the period
■ Rock art site

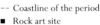

Fragment of perforated stone, Matupi Cave, Zaire

EUROPE

PORTABLE ART

Among the thousands of carved objects that date to the height of the last Ice Age in Europe (around 25,000-15,000 years ago), one of the most remarkable is a curved piece of mammoth tusk from a cave at Oblazowa in Poland. It is about 23,000 years old and thought to be the oldest boomerang in the world. Its flattened ends and span of 27 inches would have made it a formidable hunting weapon, which could be thrown accurately up to a distance of 650 feet,

much farther than a spear. Together with the carved antler spear-throwers found in southwestern France at sites such as Mas d'Azil and Bruniquel, and other finds of portable art in Europe, they testify to the ingenuity and sophistication of the Ice-Age hunter-gatherer communities.

Coastline of the period --
Approximate extent of ice sheet ☐
Ice Age portable art find site ▲

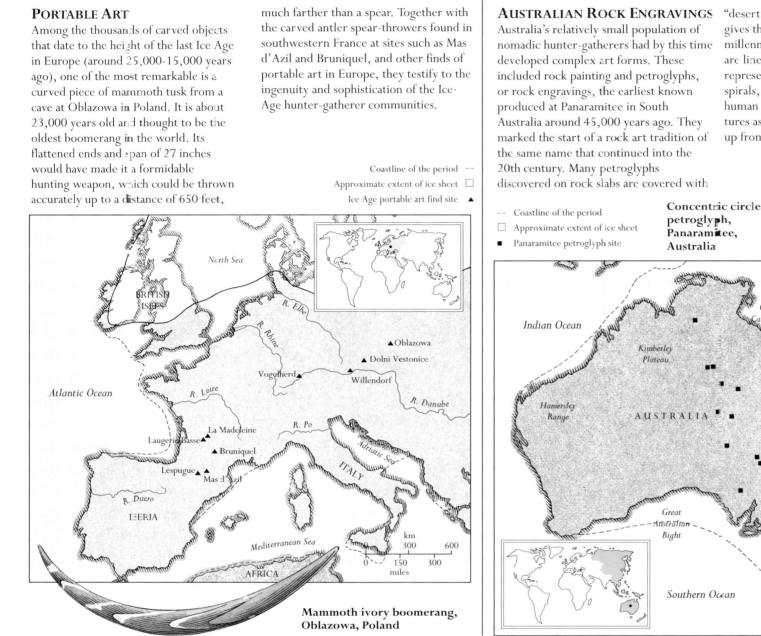

Mammoth ivory boomerang, Oblazowa, Poland

EAST ASIA & AUSTRALASIA

AUSTRALIAN ROCK ENGRAVINGS

Australia's relatively small population of nomadic hunter-gatherers had by this time developed complex art forms. These included rock painting and petroglyphs, or rock engravings, the earliest known produced at Panaramitee in South Australia around 45,000 years ago. They marked the start of a rock art tradition of the same name that continued into the 20th century. Many petroglyphs discovered on rock slabs are covered with

"desert varnish," a natural coating that gives them a dark sheen and takes many millennia to build up. Petroglyph motifs are linear and abstract in design, often representing kangaroo tracks, bird tracks, spirals, crescents, and circles. Tracks and human footprints may symbolize creatures as seen by an imaginary eye looking up from beneath the earth's surface.

-- Coastline of the period
☐ Approximate extent of ice sheet
■ Panaramitee petroglyph site

Concentric circle petroglyph, Panaramitee, Australia

MIDDLE EAST & SOUTH ASIA

ARTISTIC ACTIVITY

Rock art in central Arabia and at Bhimbetka, India, was probably first produced during the coldest phase of the last Ice Age. Rare finds of "portable" art include an engraved pebble from Urkan e-Rub, Israel, an engraved ostrich eggshell from Patne in central India, and a carved limestone pebble from Aq Kupruk, Afghanistan, showing a human head. This last item, which may be 20,000 years old, is 2¼ inches tall, has circles for eyes, a concave nose, an ear, and a strangely shaped mouth. Such pieces are evidence of artistic activity throughout the region during this period.

Coastline of the period --
Approximate extent of ice sheet ☐
Ice Age portable art site ■

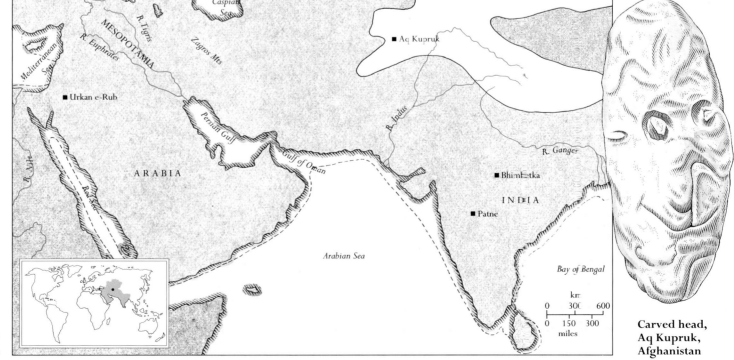

Carved head, Aq Kupruk, Afghanistan

33,000 - 18,000 BC

	FOOD & ENVIRONMENT	SHELTER & ARCHITECTURE	

AMERICAS

No evidence of human habitation found to date.

No evidence of human habitation found to date.

EAST ASIA & AUSTRALASIA

SHELLFISH SUPPLIES
The Willandra Lakes, located in an arid part of New South Wales, Australia, were frequented by Aboriginal groups. Their dietary staple was shellfish, including mussels. On the shores of one of these lakes, substantial middens (mounds of discarded shells) were created by such groups between 36,000 and 31,000 years ago.

Shellfish midden, New South Wales, Australia

CAMPSITES
The campsites on the shores of Lake Mungo, one of the Willandra Lakes in New South Wales, Australia, were used repeatedly by Aboriginal groups for several thousand years. The clearest remains are of hearths containing fish, bird, and mammal bones. In addition to the hearths, shallow scoops in the ground have been identified at some of the campsites. Heated lumps of clay may have been placed in these scoops to cook food. The Aboriginal groups spent the remainder of the year at other sites with different kinds of resources.

MIDDLE EAST & SOUTH ASIA

LAKESIDE LIVING
At Pushkar in northwestern India, a series of lakes in an otherwise arid region attracted groups of hunter-gatherers who first settled there around 30,000 years ago. Increasingly dry conditions from this time onward made these lakes a vital source of water and game, such as the spotted deer. Campsites, marked by scatters of stone tools and debris, were clustered around the shores of the lakes.

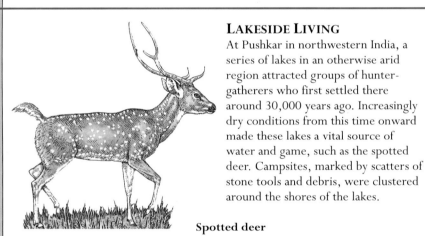

Spotted deer

HUNTERS' SHELTERS
The caves at Mount Carmel on the coast of Israel have been occupied frequently for over 100,000 years. Around 34,000 years ago, the El Wad Cave provided shelter for a group of modern humans who hunted fallow deer on the hills above. These people probably spent several months each year at the site, moving inland during the winter.

El Wad Cave, Mount Carmel, Israel

EUROPE

HORSE MEAT
The horses that abounded in Europe at this time resembled the modern Przewalski or Mongolian wild horse. Living in areas of open grassland, these horses were of great importance to prehistoric people as a source of meat. Their bones are commonly found at habitation sites, and horses were frequently depicted in the rock art of the period.

Przewalski's horse

CLAY AND LIMESTONE HUTS
By 24,000 BC, European hunter-gatherers were adept at building permanent dwellings. One of the huts at Dolni Vestonice in Moravia had a low outer wall of clay and limestone, and a few shallow postholes that would have supported a basic timber superstructure with a skin and brushwood roof. In the center of the hut was a hearth modeled from clay and stone.

Skin and brushwood roof

Clay and stone oven

Cross-section of hut, Dolni Vestonice, Moravia

AFRICA

FLORA AND FAUNA
At caves in South Africa, traces of charcoal and pollen show that the local environment at this time was made up of shrubs and grass, with few fruits. The fauna was dominated by grazing animals such as giant species of buffalo, horse, and hartebeest. These species later became extinct as the climate and vegetation changed. The horse was only reintroduced into South Africa in the 17th century AD.

Hartebeest

CONVENIENT BASES
In South Africa, few caves were permanently inhabited. Most were used only occasionally as convenient bases for specific activities such as tool manufacture or, at coastal sites, collecting shellfish. Some caves like Boomplaas in South Africa, located near open grasslands rich in game, were occupied repeatedly throughout this period, and until relatively recent times.

Boomplaas Cave, South Africa

TECHNOLOGY & INNOVATION	ART & RITUAL

No evidence of human habitation found to date.

No evidence of human habitation found to date.

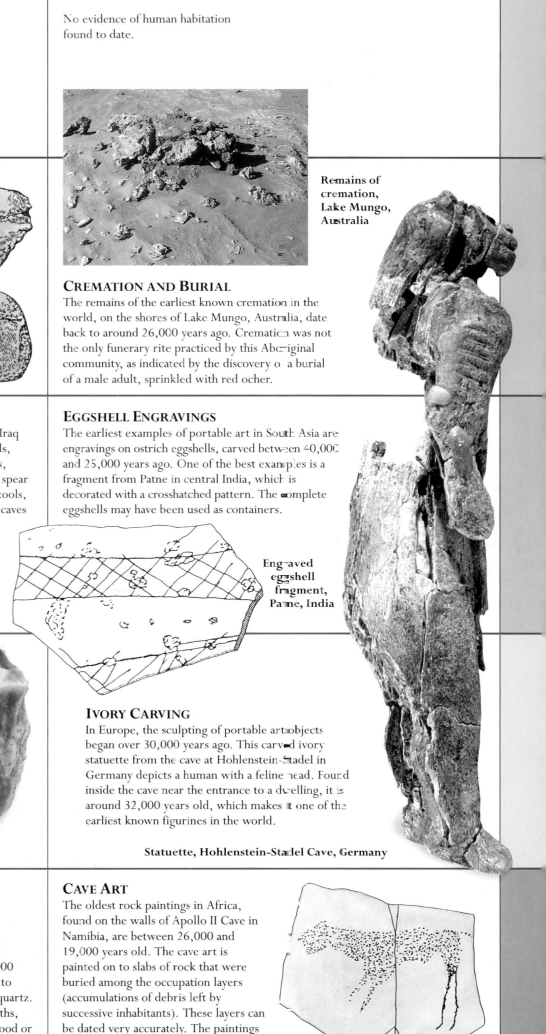

Remains of cremation, Lake Mungo, Australia

EDGE-GROUND AXES

Aboriginal stoneworkers in Australia developed the technique of grinding the edges of stones to make axes over 30,000 years ago. Edge-ground axes, like these from Kakadu in northern Australia, were often traded over hundreds of miles and were probably used for cutting branches off trees. The oldest known edge-ground ax, from Sandy Creek in Queensland, dates to over 32,000 years ago.

Edge-ground axes, Kakadu, Australia

CREMATION AND BURIAL

The remains of the earliest known cremation in the world, on the shores of Lake Mungo, Australia, date back to around 26,000 years ago. Cremation was not the only funerary rite practiced by this Aboriginal community, as indicated by the discovery of a burial of a male adult, sprinkled with red ocher.

BLADE-MAKING

Between 32,000 and 18,000 BC, human groups in Iraq and Iran began to broaden their range of stone tools, making slender leaf-shaped points, which may have been used as spear points. These smaller, finer tools, called Baradostian after the caves in Mount Baradost in southern Kurdistan, are part of a trend also occurring in Africa and Europe at this time.

Baradostian industry stone tools, Shanidar, Iraq

EGGSHELL ENGRAVINGS

The earliest examples of portable art in South Asia are engravings on ostrich eggshells, carved between 40,000 and 25,000 years ago. One of the best examples is a fragment from Patne in central India, which is decorated with a crosshatched pattern. The complete eggshells may have been used as containers.

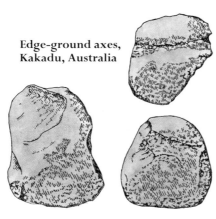

Engraved eggshell fragment, Patne, India

NEW TOOL INDUSTRIES

The stone tools made by human groups in western Europe between 32,000 and 19,000 years ago are known as Aurignacian, after the site of Aurignac in southern France. The tool tradition includes flint blades, smaller and more finely worked than those of the Neanderthals, as well as bone and antler tools, particularly split-based bone points.

Aurignacian stone chopper, Belgium

IVORY CARVING

In Europe, the sculpting of portable art objects began over 30,000 years ago. This carved ivory statuette from the cave at Hohlenstein-Stadel in Germany depicts a human with a feline head. Found inside the cave near the entrance to a dwelling, it is around 32,000 years old, which makes it one of the earliest known figurines in the world.

Statuette, Hohlenstein-Stadel Cave, Germany

QUARTZ MICROLITHS

In northeastern Zaire around 35,000 years ago, hunter-gatherers began to make tiny stone blades from local quartz. These blades are known as microliths, and were mounted in handles of wood or bone to make composite tools. Often of standardized shapes, microliths later became widespread in Africa, Europe, western Asia, and China.

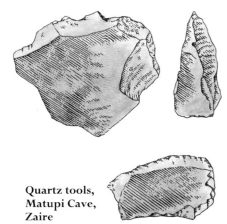

Quartz tools, Matupi Cave, Zaire

CAVE ART

The oldest rock paintings in Africa, found on the walls of Apollo II Cave in Namibia, are between 26,000 and 19,000 years old. The cave art is painted on to slabs of rock that were buried among the occupation layers (accumulations of debris left by successive inhabitants). These layers can be dated very accurately. The paintings are in black or red and include figures of animals such as a black rhinoceros and zebras.

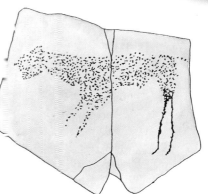

Painted plaque, Apollo II Cave, Namibia

18,000 - 13,000 BC

FOOD & ENVIRONMENT	SHELTER & ARCHITECTURE

AMERICAS

TUNDRA HUNTERS' PREY

At the coldest phase of the last Ice Age, around 20,000 years ago, the North American mainland was connected to the Siberian landmass by the Bering land bridge. Groups of hunters from Siberia settled the land bridge itself, and arrived on the North American mainland around 15,000 years ago. These were tundra hunters, who relied on larger animals such as mammoths, bison, caribou, and camels for their survival.

YUKON CAVES

The first tundra hunters to arrive in mainland North America around 15,000 years ago sheltered from the harsh arctic climate in caves. Stone and bone artifacts, similar to those found in Siberia, along with the remains of Ice Age animals dating to this time, together testify to the occupation by tundra hunter groups of the Bluefish Caves in the western Yukon territory of Canada.

EAST ASIA & AUSTRALASIA

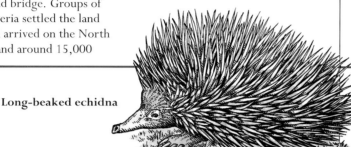

Long-beaked echidna

CHANGING COASTLINE

Evidence for the changing coastline of Australia is provided by rock paintings located near what is now the continent's northern coast. The paintings, some of which are over 18,000 years old, are the earliest examples of their kind in Australia. The fact that they depict only land animals such as the now extinct long-beaked echidna suggests that the coastline was much farther north than it is today.

SOUTHERNMOST SITE

The world's southernmost Ice Age dwelling site is a huge cave at Kutikina in southwestern Tasmania, which extends more than 550 feet back into the limestone cliff. The cave is situated near the banks of the lower reaches of the Franklin River, in a remote and heavily forested part of the island. It has extraordinarily rich remains sealed beneath a stalagmite layer. The cave was occupied by 20 to 30 people for a few weeks each year between 20,000 and 15,000 years ago. These people were highly specialized hunters whose principal prey was the wallaby. Hearths were built on the cave floor, and openings in the roof of the cave provided patches of light. Below each of these openings was a mass of debris left from the manufacture of stone tools, such as scrapers, choppers, and blades.

MIDDLE EAST & SOUTH ASIA

HARVESTING WILD GRAINS

The earliest evidence for the harvesting of wild grains comes from Ohalo, a large winter base camp on the shores of Lake Galilee in Israel. Wild barley and wheat grains dating to around 19,000 years ago were found there. The camp inhabitants also relied heavily on fish, fruit, and other plant foods.

Wild wheat

WINTER CAMP

The winter base camp at Ohalo on the shores of Lake Galilee covered roughly 1,800 square yards. The remains of a hut, two other structures, a cooking area, a circle of stones, and hearths have been found there. The hut, built of wood, was 15 feet wide and was occupied during at least three distinct periods.

EUROPE

REINDEER HUNTING

For many hunter-gatherer communities in Europe at this time, reindeer were an important resource. Their very presence in southern Europe indicates how the Ice Age conditions forced northern species to migrate southward. Reindeer were hunted not only for meat, but also for their hides, sinews, bones, and antlers, which were important raw materials used for making tools, clothing, and portable art objects.

Reindeer

Mammoth bone hut, Mezhirich, Ukraine

MAMMOTH BONE HUTS

In areas of central and eastern Europe where wood was scarce, hunter-gatherer groups used mammoth bones and tusks to construct huts. Those at Mezhirich in the Ukraine, the remains of which are between 18,000 and 12,000 years old, were 13 to 26 feet in diameter, and were probably covered in animal hides.

Stone hearth

Tusks forming walls and roof arch

AFRICA

CHANGING CONDITIONS

Around 15,000 years ago, rising sea levels began to submerge coastal areas of Africa. When the sea was still 7 miles away, the cave dwellers at Nelson Bay and Eland's Bay in South Africa mainly exploited the large game animals, such as the Cape buffalo, which grazed the open grasslands nearby. As the sea encroached and the grasslands were submerged, buffalo became extremely rare and marine foods became the cave dwellers' dietary staples.

Cape buffalo

COASTAL CAVE

Eland's Bay Cave, on the southwestern coast of South Africa, had been abandoned for thousands of years before it was reoccupied by groups of hunter-gatherers some 20,000 years ago. Although the cave was probably used for only a few weeks or months each year, occupation debris accumulated to a depth of 10 feet.

TECHNOLOGY & INNOVATION

YUKON TOOLS

The stone tools found in the Bluefish Caves in western Yukon included microliths (tiny stone blades), a wedge-shaped core, and other tools. These tools would have been used for hunting, and for the processing of animal carcasses and hides.

BONE NEEDLE

In Australia, bone tools were used for working animal hides and plant fibers. Among the tools found at Cave Bay Cave, on an island off the coast of Tasmania, was a small, sharp bone point 3 ½ inches long that is around 18,550 years old. It was made from the shin bone of a wallaby and was probably used as an awl for making fur clothing or as a needle for making nets and baskets.

Bone points, Cave Bay Cave, Tasmania

KEBARAN INDUSTRY

Dating to between 20,000 and 14,500 years ago, what is known as the Kebaran tool technology was practised by nomadic hunter-gatherers who occupied the Kebara Cave in Israel and other nearby sites. The tools of the industry are characterized by flint microliths (tiny blades) and ground stone tools such as mortars and pestles.

Kebaran industry stone tools, Lebanon

PRECISION STONEWORKING

In western Europe between 19,000 and 16,000 BC, the Solutrean tool tradition was developed, named after Solutré in eastern France. This technique involved the knapping of tiny flakes off a flint core, which was sometimes heated to make the final flaking more precise. Tools made in this way included elegant laurel-leaf points, carefully worked on both faces.

Solutrean laurel-leaf point, Volgu, France

BONE TOOLS

At Ishango, on the shores of Lake Edward in Zaire, a mound of accumulated debris dating to around 20,000 years ago contains evidence of a long sequence of settlement by hunter-gatherer groups. Together with fish and animal remains, the debris includes crude quartz microliths (tiny blades), and an abundance of bone implements, notably harpoon heads. The earlier harpoons were barbed on both sides, later ones were barbed on one side only.

ART & RITUAL

No evidence of art or ritual found to date.

HAND STENCILS

Some of the silhouettes of hands on the walls of the Wargata Mina Cave in southwestern Tasmania are 15,000 years old. There are 16 stencils of the left and right hands of five people, made by blowing a spray of powdered pigment mixed with water over the hands. Located in the pitch-black interior of the cave, the stencils might have been associated with initiation rituals or visits by initiates and elders.

Hand stencil, Wargata Mina Cave, Tasmania

ENGRAVING

Around 15,000 years ago, the hunter-gatherer communities of the Levant (the coastal strip of Syria, Lebanon, and Israel) produced few decorative objects that have survived. Only one portable object, an engraved limestone pebble with "ladder" motifs and parallel lines carved into it, has been found. It comes from Urkan e-Rub in Israel. These hunter-gatherer communities buried their dead as burials found beneath the floors of cave dwellings and artificial shelters indicate.

Engraved pebble, Urkan e-Rub, Israel

Hind leg   Eye

Ivory reindeer, Bruniquel, France

IVORY CARVING

By 20,000 years ago, hunter-gatherer communities in western Europe were producing a wide range of portable art objects, from simple engravings on stone slabs or plaques, to carved ivory sculptures like these reindeer from Bruniquel in southwestern France. The reindeer was one of the most common subjects depicted in portable art.

TERRA-COTTA FIGURINES

Evidence for the beginnings of portable art in Africa is provided by finds in the north of simple terra-cotta figurines, such as this small hand-modeled head of a horned animal from Afalou Bou Rhummel in eastern Algeria, which is around 15,000 years old.

Terra-cotta head, Afalou Bou Rhummel, Algeria

DECORATED CAVES

Some of the most striking records of human achievement during the last Ice Age are provided by the decorated sites of Europe. The vast majority are caves and rock shelters, although open-air surfaces were sometimes decorated. Between 35,000 and 20,000 years ago, most decoration was limited to areas exposed to daylight, and much of the detail has therefore weathered away. Most surviving cave art dates to between 20,000 and 10,000 years ago, when the darker depths of large caves were decorated. It encompasses an astonishing variety of subjects and techniques, from hand stencils, outline drawings, and polychrome paintings to engravings, bas-relief sculptures, and clay figures. The artists applied pigments with fingers, brushes of animal hair, pads (perhaps of animal fur), or spitting techniques. Some of the art is clearly visible, while some is carefully hidden in crevices, possibly indicating that the act of producing an image, rather than the image itself, was the important factor. Early attempts at interpretation involved notions of artistic expression, hunting magic, or fertility magic. It is now generally accepted that complex religious beliefs underlie the content and distribution of cave art.

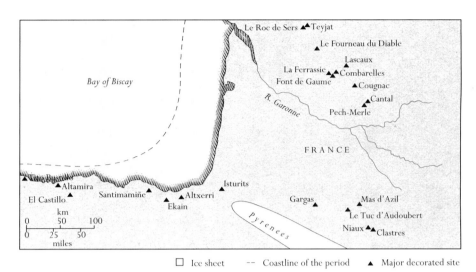

ICE-AGE ART SITES
The rich legacy of the decorated sites of southwestern France and northern Spain provides a glimpse into the cultural life of human communities in the last Ice Age. Large animals, such as horse, bison, and deer, are the most common images.

☐ Ice sheet　-- Coastline of the period　▲ Major decorated site

ARTISTS AT WORK *right*
Horse, bison, and wild cattle dominate the cave walls, but non-figurative signs such as dots, rectangles, and lines often appear to be of equal importance. In some caves, wooden scaffolding was used to enable the artists to reach high walls and ceilings — in the Lascaux Cave in France the sockets for a platform of posts survive in one passage. The interior of the caves would have been lit by burning animal fat placed on flat or dished stones. Cave paintings by adults are in some cases accompanied by finger-tracings and simple figures that may be the work of children. Most footprints in caves appear to be those of children.

Cave-painting scene

Brush made of animal hair or of crushed or chewed vegetable fiber

Lamps burning animal fat, with plant material as wicks, shed a dim, trembling light

Mortar and pestle for crushing pigment

Fire for heating pigments to make different hues, as well as for lighting and warmth

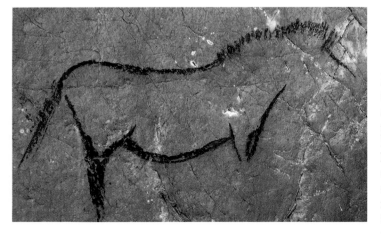

SUBTLE TONES
Most painted figures were simple outlines like this charcoal sketch of a horse on the walls of a cave at Niaux in the French Pyrenees. In some cases figures were filled in either wholly or in part — a painted frieze in a cave at Pech-Merle in France has horses with bodies filled with dots. The polychrome paintings of animals at Lascaux in France and Altamira in Spain, which are among the best known cave paintings, are in fact very unusual.

MAKING PIGMENTS
Cave artists made pigments from a variety of minerals ground to a powder, then mixed with water. Red pigment was produced from hematite (iron oxide, or red ocher), white came from kaolin or chalk, while black was either manganese dioxide or charcoal. Some communities heated minerals to produce new colors. Most minerals used for pigments were readily available and could be collected locally, although some must have been mined. In Africa, ocher mines have been discovered that were first worked around 42,000 years ago.

Kaolin

Hematite

Charcoal

33,000-13,000 BC

PERSONAL IMAGES

Stencils of hands are quite common and sometimes dominate certain areas of a cave. They were produced by placing the hand flat on the wall and spraying or spitting pigment at it. In some caves, particularly at Gargas in France (*left*), the hands are incomplete, with various combinations of fingers or finger segments missing. It is unclear whether the joints had actually been lost through frostbite or some other condition, or whether the fingers were bent in some kind of signaling system.

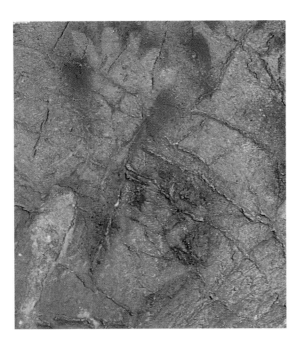

CAVE SCULPTURES

Cave art is by no means restricted to the painted figures of Lascaux or Altamira. Engraving was by far the most common means of creating images on cave walls. The artists were also highly skilled at working in three dimensions, incorporating natural rock shapes ingeniously into their compositions to give them volume, or carving bas-relief sculptures and clay statues.

Head-to-head clash between two ibex

CARVED LIMESTONE *above*

Bas-relief sculpture is limited to western and central France, where the local limestone was easy to carve. Such work is always found in areas exposed to daylight, and many of the earliest sculptures were on large blocks rather than on walls. These ibex are from a number of images carved into blocks that had been arranged in a semicircle at the back of a rock shelter at Le Roc de Sers. Most sculptures were also painted, but few traces of pigment survive.

WALL ENGRAVING *left*

From deeply carved lines to very fine incisions, like this bull's head from Teyjat in France, engraving encompasses a variety of forms. Almost any sharp flint could be used for such work. Fine engravings are almost invisible when lit from the front, so cave artists must have positioned their light source to one side while they worked, to prevent the shadows of their hands from falling on the image.

Wooden platform gives access to high walls and ceilings

Children may have produced finger tracings and simple figures

Stencils made by blowing pigment over the hand

LIGHTING THE CAVES

Only 300 lamps have been identified dating to the 25,000 years of cave art production. Beautifully carved lamps, like this one from Lascaux, are extremely rare. The most common sources of illumination for the cave artist were probably flaming torches and simple lamps made from flat stones holding burning lumps of animal fat.

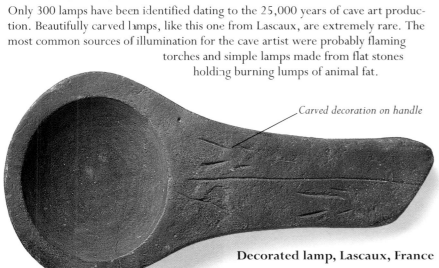

Carved decoration on handle

Decorated lamp, Lascaux, France

WORKING WITH CLAY

The finest examples of clay sculpture dating to the last Ice Age are these two bison from Le Tuc d'Audoubert in France. About one-sixth life-size, they were propped up against rocks at the center of a distant, low-ceilinged chamber. The artists seem to have made a single visit to this remote spot, cleared up after their work was done, and never returned. Work in clay has been discovered only in the French Pyrenees.

CHAPTER 5
THE ICE THAWS
13,000 - 8000 BC

Ice sheets begin to melt and retreat as temperatures rise

Modern continents gradually take shape as rising seas submerge land

Hunter-gatherers reach the southern tip of the Americas

First farmers harvest wild grains in the Middle East

Japanese hunter-gatherers produce the world's first pottery

As the ice sheets began to retreat from Eurasia and North America 15,000 years ago, the world was transformed radically. Global temperatures, which had been rising since the coldest point of the last Ice Age (around 20,000 years ago) had almost reached their present level by 8000 BC. As the ice sheets melted, trapped water was released, causing sea levels to rise by around 325 feet. This inundated what had previously been dry lowland areas such as the Bering land bridge, the Gulf of Siam, the North Sea, and the Sahul Shelf (between Australia and New Guinea). More water was available to fall as rain, so the extensive deserts that had formed in parts of the tropics began to shrink.

Population increase
Although gradual, these climatic changes offered new opportunities to the human populations whose survival strategies became so highly developed under the harsh conditions of the Ice Age. As the climate improved, plants and animals colonized larger areas of the world, including previously uninhabitable parts of Africa, Europe, and North America. The abundant resources in these territories more than compensated for the lands lost beneath the rising seas. Indeed, the availability of new food supplies catalyzed a steady growth in human populations, which has continued almost unbroken to the present day.

During these more benign climatic conditions, the Americas were fully colonized. Groups of hunter-gatherers penetrated south of the retreating ice sheets and began to establish themselves throughout North America. By 11,000 BC, humans were present in South America, as shown by a well-established settlement at Monte Verde in central Chile, where remains of hearths and shelters have been found. By at least 9000 BC, they had reached Patagonia, at the continent's southern tip.

Big-game hunting
The first North Americans, isolated from their Siberian homeland by the Bering Sea, ventured south in search of new hunting grounds. Traveling in small bands, they followed game over vast expanses of new territory. These scattered groups developed a common stoneworking technology. Although stone points from the Monte Verde site attest to earlier styles, the best known of the Paleoindian (earliest people in the Americas) weapon types was the large Clovis point, capable of piercing mammoth hide; the later Folsom points were used to kill bison. Both technologies are named after towns in New Mexico where the first examples were found. The wide distribution of tools indicates that band territories incorporated vast areas.

Serrated edge

Surface shows flakes have been removed

PALEOINDIAN TOOLS
Thin, sharp blades for tools would have been flaked off a blade core (*above left*). Bone tools (*above right*) were used for scraping the flesh off animal hides.

HUNTERS' PREY
The North American Plains supported herds of big game such as bison and mammoths (*above*). The latter became extinct in the region around 9000 BC.

Obsidian blade

KEY DATES 13,000 - 8000 BC

13,000 BC Rising sea levels progressively submerge lowlands	**10,500 BC** World's first known pottery vessels, Japan
11,000 BC World's first known domesticated dogs, Middle East	**8000 BC** Large farming settlements, Middle East
First datable evidence of human populations in South America	**9000 BC** Beginnings of farming, Middle East
	Mammoths extinct, North America

13,000 BC	12,000 BC	11,000 BC	10,000 BC	9000 BC	8000 BC

MICROLITH TECHNOLOGY

By c.13,000 BC, microlith tool skills had spread throughout most of Africa, later reaching Europe and Asia. These microliths are from Gamble's Cave, Kenya.

Environmental changes

The success of the early hunters may have played a part in the extinction, in North America, of the mammoth and other Ice Age fauna, which coincided with the end of the Clovis epoch. However, much debate surrounds this subject: changes in climate and vegetation patterns were probably equally important. By 8000 BC, regional environments similar to those of the present day existed throughout North America. Groups began to settle and specialize in hunting the animals that characterized various habitats — caribou in the north; deer in the eastern woodlands; fish and sea mammals in coastal, lake, and riverine territory; small game in the scrublands and arid mountains of the southwest; and, on the Great Plains, the bison.

Flourishing cultures

In the southern continents of Africa and Australasia, the wetter climate at the end of the last Ice Age turned some desert areas to grassland, making them more attractive to hunter-gatherers. In resource-rich areas of Africa such as the Nile Valley, groups began burying their dead in cemeteries, sometimes consisting of many dozens of graves. In both Africa and Australia the tradition of rock art established in previous centuries continued to flourish. Rock art provides insights into everyday activities in South Asia during this period; the scenes that depict hunting and fishing in the rock shelters at Bhimbetka in central India are particularly vivid.

HAND STENCILING

A form of rock art widespread in Australia, hand stencils were made by blowing pigment around an outstretched hand, perhaps using a tube.

Early farming methods

It was in the Middle East that the most significant changes of this period occurred. Wild wheat and barley were native to the uplands of southern Turkey and the Fertile Crescent, a broad arc stretching from the southern Levant (coastal Israel) to the Zagros Mountains south of the Caspian Sea. People in the Levant had been gathering these wild grains since around 17,000 BC and had developed grinding stones to crush the grains into flour. By 13,000 BC, their successors, the people of the Natufian communities (named after the site of Wadi en-Natuf in Israel) were harvesting wild grains even more intensively. From this point, it was only one further step to the intentional planting of some grains.

By this simple process, farming began in the Middle East around 9000 BC. The long-term implications were enormous: whole communities could be supported by cultivated crops, and storage of grain throughout the year made it easier for people to live in fixed settlements. The nomadic life of hunter-gatherer groups, their moving from place to place in order to use seasonal resources, gradually became more settled as dependence on different cultivated plants increased.

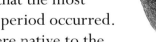

GRINDING GRAIN

Common implements among early farming communities in the Middle East, mortars and pestles were used to grind hard cereal grains into flour to make bread or beer.

61

13,000 - 8000 BC

Expanding settlements

The shift to more permanent settlements can be most clearly seen at Jericho in the Jordan Valley, where a natural spring provided a well-watered area of fertile soil ideal for growing grain. By 8000 BC the people farming this land had established a flourishing settlement covering six acres: tiny by modern standards, but vast in comparison with anything that had gone before.

Disappearing habitats

The retreat of the ice sheets altered the Eurasian environment dramatically. Mammoths and woolly rhinoceroses became extinct around 10,000 BC, although dwarf mammoths may have survived until some 4,000 years ago on Wrangel Island, off the coast of Siberia. The cause of their extinction was most probably a combination of overhunting by humans and the gradual disappearance of their native habitat. Deciduous forests, which had been restricted to temperate areas in southernmost Europe, now spread northward, and with them came red deer, wild boar, and aurochs (wild ox).

New dietary staples

Throughout Eurasia, human communities responded to the warmer conditions by increasing the range of plants and animals in their diet, notably seafood such as fish and shellfish. Large shell middens (mounds of discarded debris) found along the coast of northwestern Europe mark the campsites used by small groups of hunter-gatherers.

Seafood also played a major role in the diet of hunter-gatherers in East and Southeast Asia during this period. In Japan, the hunter-gatherer people of the Jomon culture exploited the abundant fish stocks along the east coast of Honshu island during spring and early summer. The Jomon people were the first in the world to produce pottery vessels, their culture being named after the *jomon* ("cord-marked") decorative patterns that characterize the pottery they made during the 10th millennium BC.

Plants were also an important resource. Although evidence of particular species rarely survives, the remains of 22 plant types were found at the Spirit Cave in Thailand. The remains included some plants from which poison could have been extracted for use on arrows.

Fundamental change

Farming, already established in the Fertile Crescent, was soon to develop in China, Southeast Asia, Europe, and the Americas. It eventually became the mainstay of human existence, and remains so today. Whether the move away from the hunter-gatherer way of life was, in the long run, a good thing for humanity is, of course, debatable. But whatever the disadvantages of the farming way of life — such as the increased exposure to infectious diseases that was the corollary of a sedentary agricultural existence — there was no going back.

AMERICAS

SOUTHERN MIGRATION

It is likely that tundra hunters migrated south into the plains of North America only when an ice-free corridor of land existed between the Cordilleran and Laurentide ice masses. Alternatively, when this corridor was blocked, it is possible that humans ventured south along the Pacific coast in boats. The earliest possible human habitation sites in the Americas are known as Pre-Clovis sites, but these are not accepted by all archaeologists. The first sites that archaeologists agree were definitely inhabited by humans are those that have yielded finds of Clovis stone tool technology — for example, Murray Springs and Blackwater Draw.

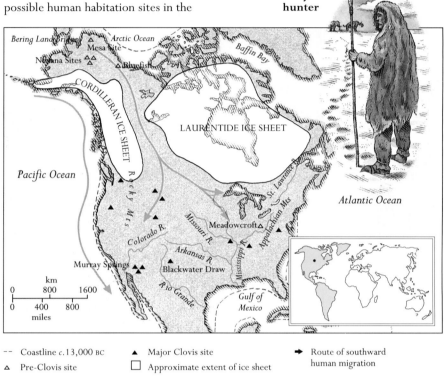

Early hunter

-- Coastline c.13,000 BC
△ Pre-Clovis site
▲ Major Clovis site
☐ Approximate extent of ice sheet
➡ Route of southward human migration

GATHERING PLANTS

Wild plant remains found at Monte Verde, in the Andean region of central Chile, include tubers and sugarcane. These were gathered from distant areas and brought back to the settlement for processing.

Herbal remedies made from such plants are still used by indigenous Andeans today. This knowledge of the medicinal properties of plants could only have evolved over many years of experimentation and familiarity with their sources, which suggests a well-established human occupation of the area by 11,000 BC.

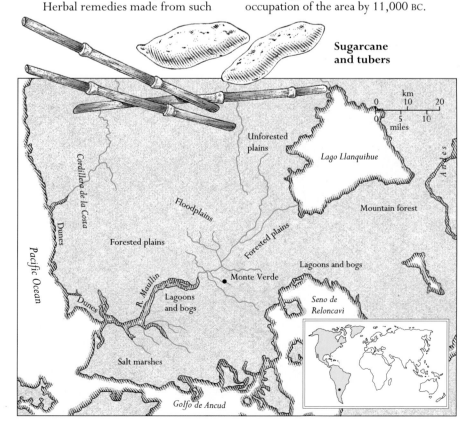

Sugarcane and tubers

AFRICA

HUNTER-GATHERERS

In the Nile and Niger river valleys, African hunter-gatherers spent much of the year in permanent base camps, living on fish, wild grains, and tubers. The Saharan highlands were home to highly mobile hunter-gatherers, whose staple diet included gazelles. The forest regions of western and central Africa supported foraging groups who relied on plants and small tree-living game, including monkeys. Nomadic hunter-gatherers also lived in the savanna and semiarid lands of eastern and southern Africa, including the modern Kalahari Desert, hunting and foraging for seasonal plants.

≡ Approximate extent of tropical forest
∭ Approximate extent of desert
■ Hunter-gatherer site

Hunter-gatherer brush shelter, Kalahari region, southern Africa

EUROPE

FOREST RESOURCES

Toward the end of the last Ice Age, the milder climate and abundant deciduous forests provided an excellent environment for small groups of hunter-gatherers, who set up base camps in lowland valleys and on lake edges. These localities were often marshy, rich in edible roots and tubers; game and fish were plentiful, providing the impetus for the development of new hunting and fishing techniques and tools. The settlers at Star Carr, on the shores of ancient Lake Pickering in Yorkshire, England, were particularly adept at hunting red deer, aurochs (wild ox), elk, and wild boar, making barbed points and harpoons of red-deer antler.

Antler harpoons, Star Carr, Yorkshire, England

≡ Approximate extent of deciduous forest
■ Hunter-gatherer base camp
-- Coastline c.13,000 BC

EAST ASIA & AUSTRALASIA

SOUTHEAST ASIAN SEA LEVELS

As sea levels continued to rise toward the end of the last Ice Age (around 10,000 years ago), large areas of coastal lowland were inundated in Southeast Asia. The islands of Borneo, Java, and Sumatra emerged. As temperatures rose, forest vegetation became denser, creating new opportunities for hunter-gatherer communities. Coasts and estuaries — around the Gulf of Tongking in modern Vietnam, for example — were good food sources, and occupation sites of the period can be identified from shell middens (mounds of discarded debris). Other groups of hunter-gatherers occupied upland caves and rock shelters. Mainland occupation sites are characterized by finds of flaked cobble tools, called Hoabinhian after the cave at Hoa Binh in Vietnam. Island sites are characterized by finds of blades or flaked tools made of chert (a crystalline form of silica) or obsidian (black volcanic glass)

▲ Hoabinhian tool site
△ Flake and blade site
-- Coastline c.12,000 BC

Hoabinhian chipped quartzite river cobble tool, Vietnam

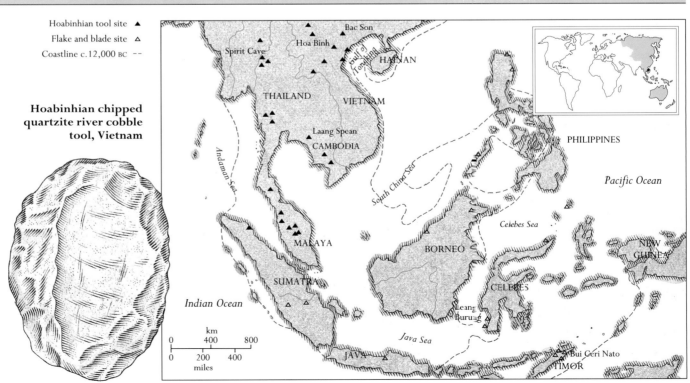

63

13,000 - 10,000 BC

| FOOD & ENVIRONMENT | SHELTER & ARCHITECTURE |

AMERICAS

BUTCHERING TOOLS
Throughout the Americas, finds of butchering tools dating to this period are widespread, confirming that meat was an important dietary staple. This quartzite knife from Colorado is typical of those found in big-game kill sites. Made from large, thin flint flakes, the knives were used to butcher the carcasses efficiently.

Flint butchering knife, Colorado

WOODEN DWELLINGS
The earliest evidence for constructed dwellings in the Americas is from the site of Monte Verde in Chile, which dates to the 12th millennium BC. The remains of 10 huts were found. They were originally joined together in two parallel rows. Each dwelling consisted of a square wooden frame covered with animal skins. Small clay-lined pits located inside the dwellings were used for cooking or heating; the large hearths outside the huts suggest a high degree of group cooperation.

Pit used for cooking

Dwellings, Monte Verde, Chile

EAST ASIA & AUSTRALASIA

FISHING AND HUNTING
The earliest populations of Japan survived on seafood and the hunting of forest animals such as deer and wild pigs. Those living near the coast gathered shellfish. Favored locations along the east coast of Honshu, where fish and other marine resources proliferated in the warm Pacific currents during spring and early summer, were probably visited each year. Large middens (mounds of discarded fish bones and shell debris) built up at these seasonal campsites. Inland resources were important in the autumn; hunters used stone arrowheads to kill their prey and stone scrapers for working the hides.

CAVE DWELLINGS
In Japan, caves were popular dwellings for hunter-gatherer groups, and some were occupied for many thousands of years. The earliest occupation of the Fukui Cave, near Nagasaki in southern Japan, began around 13,000 years ago and remains from this period include some of the earliest pottery in the world. The cave was probably used by groups exploiting the resources of the coastal lowlands nearby, but only for short periods at specific times of the year.

MIDDLE EAST & SOUTH ASIA

DOMESTICATED DOGS
Dogs were the first animals to be domesticated. Their wild ancestors were probably wolves rather than jackals. The earliest evidence for domesticated dogs in the world comes from Israel and dates to around 11,000 BC, but it is possible that wolves were tamed and trained at an earlier date to help in hunting.

Wolf, the wild ancestor of dogs

ROUND HUTS
Around 12,000 years ago, round, stone-walled, sunken huts became common in the Levant (the coastal strip of Syria, Lebanon, and Israel). The inhabitants gathered wild grains that could be stored easily, so they could settle in one place all year round.

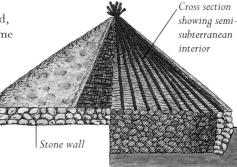

Cross section showing semi-subterranean interior

Stone wall

Round hut, Ain Mallaha, Israel

EUROPE

MAMMOTH EXTINCTION
In Europe the period between the coldest point of the last Ice Age (around 20,000 years ago) and 10,000 BC was marked by the gradual extinction of the large mammals that had previously flourished on the tundra. Among these were the woolly mammoth (an ancestor of the modern elephant that was protected against the harsh climate by a thick, warm coat), the woolly rhinoceros, and the giant deer. Changes in climate and forest cover were partly responsible for their extinction, but many were tracked down and killed by human hunters with improved skills and hunting equipment.

Crudely stitched seam

Wood frame

TENTS FOR THE SUMMER
In the summer months, late Ice Age hunters lived in wood-framed tents covered in animal hides. All that survives of those erected at a campsite at Pincevent, France, is a scattering of food remains, the ashes of a hearth, a few discarded flint tools, and a ring of stones that held the base of a tent in place.

Hunter's tent, Pincevent, France

AFRICA

TROPICAL FRUIT
Edible plant foods became increasingly important in tropical Africa in the period leading up to the end of the Ice Age. The bauhinia tree was favored by hunter-gatherers for its fruit and roots, especially during the summer. It is still a staple today for the San people of southern Africa and many other hunter-gatherer groups.

Branch of bauhinia tree

HABITABLE SITES
Caves and rock shelters, many of which looked out over wide plains rich in game, continued to be important habitation sites for African hunter-gatherers during this period. They offered protection from lions and other predators and shelter in wet weather. Most groups used convenient shelters for short periods of the year, returning for generations to the same location – perhaps when local plants were ripe or shellfish abundant. The coast of southeastern Africa was home to many hunter-gatherers who used caves as base camps for hunting game and sea mammals for several months of the year. One of the inhabited caves was at Klasies River Mouth in South Africa. First occupied 120,000 years ago, it was used as a shelter by visiting groups until 1,000 years ago.

TECHNOLOGY & INNOVATION

STONE TECHNOLOGY
Stone points chipped on both faces have been found at Monte Verde in Chile; they date to 11,000 BC. This bifacial technology is also known from sites over 20,000 years old in northeastern Asia – evidence for a technological link between Asia and the first Americans.

Stone projectile points, Monte Verde, Chile

FIRST POTTERY
The earliest pottery vessels in the world were produced by hunter-gatherers in Japan over 12,000 years ago. These round-based vessels, like this one from Nasunahara, are called Incipient Jomon, because they were the forerunners of the *jomon* (meaning cord-marked) vessels made in the 10th millennium BC.

Round-based pot, Nasunahara, Japan

GRINDING STONES
By 12,000 years ago, people living in the hilly regions of the Fertile Crescent were relying increasingly on gathering wild grains and other seeds for their food. For harvesting, they may have used composite tools such as sickles made with microliths (tiny stone blades) set into wooden or bone handles. To grind the seeds into flour, a new technology of grindstones, mortars, and pestles gradually developed.

IMPROVING MATERIALS
High-quality stone for tool-making was of vital importance to human communities throughout the world at this time. One of the best materials was obsidian (black volcanic glass), which produced a razor-sharp edge when flaked. As early as 11,000 BC, the inhabitants of the Franchthi Cave in southern Greece were sailing over 80 miles in simple boats to gather obsidian from the Cycladic island of Melos in the Aegean Sea.

Obsidian, Melos, Greece

STONE-TIPPED SPEARS
Sharp obsidian tip

For tens of thousands of years, African hunters relied on stone-tipped spears. The tips were microliths (tiny blades), often of obsidian (black volcanic glass), which were mounted in wooden shafts. Such blades were in use in central and western Africa 35,000 years ago, but appeared in the eastern Rift Valley only 13,000 years ago.

Obsidian microliths, Gamble's Cave, Kenya

ART & RITUAL

CULTURAL LINK
Red ocher, a powder pigment derived from grinding iron ores such as haematite, was used by early North Americans in a variety of ways: to make red paint to protect the skin from insects and sunburn; in the processing of animal hides; and for ceremonial purposes. Its use is considered to be a cultural link between the earliest Americans and Eurasia (and indeed Australia), where similar evidence is commonly found.

Haematite ore

Red ocher stain

Iron ore nodule

Sandstone grinder

ENGRAVED ANTLER
The earliest known portable art object from China dates to around 13,000 years ago. Found at Longgu Cave, it is a red deer antler engraved with three distinct patterns: a wavy line, several long, parallel grooves, and regularly spaced oblique strokes. The antler was originally coated with red ocher pigment and the precision of the engraving is impressive.

Engraved antler, Longgu Cave, China

Shell and bone bead necklace, Mugharet el-Kebara, Israel

BURIALS AND BEADS
From 60,000 years ago onward, human burials have been found throughout Europe and Asia, but they are rare. By 10,000 BC in the Middle East, burials under the floors of huts and in cemeteries were common. Personal ornaments such as necklaces, bracelets, and anklets were often buried with the dead.

ANNUAL CALENDAR
Early rituals may have depended on observation of the seasons and measuring the passage of time. Found at the Grotte du Tai in France, a piece of bone about 4 inches long, dating to around 10,000 BC, may be the oldest known solar calendar. Each of more than 1,000 marks engraved on it may represent a day. The arrangement of the marks suggests they are grouped into years.

Bone plaque, Grotte du Tai, France

JEWELRY
Ostrich eggshell was an invaluable raw material for making beads. Small pieces of shell were carefully pierced through the center with a fine, stone-tipped drill. The perforated fragments were then strung on a suitable fiber or thong, and ground into uniform, round beads that were used to make necklaces and amulets. Sometimes the shell beads were used to adorn caps or skins, or were worn in the hair. Fragmentary remains of such decorated ostrich eggshell have been found in graves at a rock shelter in Taforalt, Algeria, and date to around 12,000 years ago.

10,000-8000 BC

| | FOOD & ENVIRONMENT | SHELTER & ARCHITECTURE |

AMERICAS

EARLY DOMESTICATION

Although dogs were first domesticated in the Middle East and Europe, they are known to have accompanied the first settlers of North America. Dogs may have been used as pack animals and for pulling sleds. The earliest remains of a dog found in North America date to around 8000 BC and were found at the Jones-Miller site, a bison kill site in Colorado, which suggests that dogs may also have been used for hunting.

Dog jawbone fragments, Colorado

ANIMAL HIDE SHELTERS

The earliest evidence for built shelters in North America is identified by postholes. At the Hell Gap site in Wyoming, a small circular outline of postholes represents the remains of tents, which would have been covered either by animal hides or brushwood. The small size of the tents suggests that they were occupied by single families. In contrast, at the Thunderbird site in Virginia, posthole patterns appear to outline a large rectangular shelter, which was built as a dwelling for several families.

EAST ASIA & AUSTRALASIA

FOREST RESOURCES

The forests of Southeast Asia provided abundant food resources for small bands of hunter-gatherers, such as the group that occupied the Spirit Cave in Thailand around 10,000 BC. They collected fish and shellfish from a nearby stream, as well as almonds and butternuts from the surrounding forest. The sap of poisonous plants was applied to arrowheads for hunting gibbons, macaques, and squirrels.

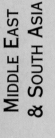

Almonds

SKIN AND BONE TENTS

Skins stretched over bone framework

Hunters living in Siberia, where wood was scarce, built tents made from a framework of large animal bones covered with skins. These simple structures enabled them to survive the harsh climate and are similar in construction to the earlier mammoth-bone huts of the Ukraine. This indicates an eastward diffusion of tent-building techniques.

Skin and bone tent, Siberia

MIDDLE EAST & SOUTH ASIA

CULTIVATING FOODS

Around 9000 BC, after millennia of harvesting wild grains and hunting, the inhabitants of the Middle East began cultivating wheat and barley and domesticating livestock. At first, the Asiatic mouflon and bezoar goat (the wild ancestors of sheep and goats) were simply herded. Later, they were bred selectively and changes in their size occurred. These changes have been observed in bones discovered at archaeological sites.

Similarly, through selective harvesting and planting, new varieties of grains evolved. This change from hunting and gathering to farming ensured a supply of food throughout the year, and made it possible for people to develop a new, settled way of life in farming villages. This served as the basis from which all later civilizations would arise.

GROWING SETTLEMENTS

Early farming villages in the Middle East had at most a few hundred inhabitants. Jericho, however, may have had a population of more than 1,000. As early as 8000 BC, a ditch and stone wall about 2,100 feet long surrounded it. Inside the wall was a semi-circular tower 33 feet wide and at least 33 feet high.

Internal staircase *Stone wall*

Cross section of stone tower, Jericho, Israel

Ditch

EUROPE

HUNTING

The remains of animals occasionally bear the evidence of the work of early human hunters. The skeleton of an aurochs (wild ox) found in Denmark dating to this period had three flint arrowheads embedded in its chest. It must have been attacked on two occasions because the earlier wound had healed. The hunters might have been helped by trained domesticated dogs. The earliest skeletal evidence for the use of dogs in Europe dates to around 8500 BC.

Aurochs

SEASONAL CAMPS

A typical European lowland settlement, Star Carr, situated on the shores of ancient Lake Pickering in Yorkshire, England, was a winter camp used by a group of hunter-gatherers. The inhabitants laid down birch brushwood to make dry platforms where they may have built simple shelters. The camp was probably one of several occupied by this particular group at various times of the year, as they moved from place to place exploiting different natural resources.

AFRICA

RIVERS, LAKES, AND SEA

From 10,000 BC, African hunting and foraging methods became increasingly sophisticated, as more lightweight and specialized weaponry was developed. Many groups of people settled near rivers and lakes, exploiting their rich resources of fish and mollusks, while sea mammals were of greater importance for coastal settlements. The ability to extract these resources from rivers, lakes, and the sea enabled many groups to remain in the same place for most of the year. At this time, much of the Sahara was covered with semiarid grassland and shallow lakes, which attracted small groups of hunters as they ranged over large hunting territories. Elsewhere, Africans became increasingly localized, living off the abundant resources that were available within limited areas.

FISHERMEN'S HUTS

Framework of sticks *Grass and reeds woven through sticks*

The quantity of fish in the Nile River is greatest in the autumn, when the annual floods recede. The fishing communities that settled on the river banks at this time lived in temporary huts made of grass and matting. These were abandoned when rising waters forced the people to higher ground.

Grass shelter, Nile Valley, Egypt

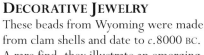
TECHNOLOGY & INNOVATION

ART & RITUAL

WEAPONS FOR HUNTING

Hunters in North America during the Clovis and Folsom periods (*c.*9200-8900 BC) used projectile points with fluted bases. Clovis points have been found at mammoth kill sites, while smaller Folsom points were used to hunt bison. The sources of stone are widespread, indicating that early North Americans were highly mobile.

**Folsom point (*right*) and
Clovis point (*far right*), Colorado**

DECORATIVE JEWELRY

These beads from Wyoming were made from clam shells and date to *c.*8000 BC. A rare find, they illustrate an emerging appreciation of decorative items. Sharp-tipped stone drills were used to pierce the shells, which were then strung on fine sinew cords to make necklaces. Earlier engraved bones and pebbles have been found, but they too are rare.

**Shell beads, Wyoming (*above*),
and engraved bone disks, Colorado (*far right*)**

VERSATILE TOOLS

In mainland Southeast Asia around 8000 BC, hunter-gatherers used simple tools made from beach or river pebbles, which were flaked along one side or all over to produce cutting edges. The tools were used for a wide range of tasks including butchering animals. Axes were made from larger stones, their regular, sharp cutting edges achieved by polishing. In addition to stone tools, bone points were used, probably for stitching animal hides.

CORDED POTTERY

The *jomon* (meaning cord-marked) pottery vessels produced during the 10th millennium BC in Japan had pointed bases and were made by building up coils of clay into the desired shape. The cord-marked patterns that decorated the vessels were often complex. The vessels may have been intended for ritual or funerary use rather than for everyday purposes.

Pointed-base *jomon* pot, Japan

BONE IMPLEMENTS

The people of the Natufian culture, named after the site of Wadi en-Natuf in Israel, had lived in villages in the Levant (the coastal strip of Syria, Lebanon, and Israel) since around 13,000 BC. They continued to manufacture a wide variety of tools made from bone. These included awls and needles for working animal hides, fish hooks, spatulae, and reaping knives with grooves into which small flint cutting blades were set. Some of these implements were decorated with incised geometric patterns. The handles of reaping knives were occasionally carved into the form of animal heads, such as deer heads.

CONTINUING TRADITION

The tradition of rock painting in the shelters at Bhimbetka in central India began well before 11,000 BC and was still flourishing at this time. Some of the paintings are abstract outlines, others are colorfully filled in. They depict animals (such as deer, antelope, and bison), fishermen, hunters, expeditions to gather honey, scenes of family life, and dances.

**Rock painting of a bison,
Bhimbetka, India**

ORGANIC MATERIALS

As well as stone, the early inhabitants of northern Europe made extensive use of organic materials, such as bone, antler, wood, and plant fibers, to make tools and equipment. The winter camp at Star Carr in England yielded a wide range of organic artifacts, such as wooden mattocks and barbed points of elk or deer antler. A wooden paddle indicates that canoes were in use.

Side view

Plan view

Wooden paddle, Star Carr, England

ANTLER HEADDRESS

Little is known of the religious practices of early societies in northern Europe, but at Star Carr in England a group of red deer frontlets (antlers still attached to the skull) were found. These may have been worn as headdresses in hunting or fertility rituals.

Holes for attaching straps

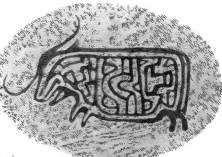

Red deer frontlet, Star Carr, England

MICROLITHIC TOOLS

By 8000 BC, microliths (tiny stone blades), which had first appeared in Zaire around 35,000 years ago, were being produced throughout most of the African continent. Hunter-gatherer groups developed tools for specific tasks, such as scrapers for woodworking and preparing animal hide cloaks that were worn by women when plant foraging.

**Stone scraper,
Gamble's Cave,
Kenya**

REPRESENTATIONAL ART

In North Africa around 8000 BC, hunter-gatherer groups represented humans and animals in a variety of media. In the rock shelter at Taforalt in Algeria, for example, there is a crude engraving of male and female genitalia.

Other finds from the region include ostrich eggshells carved with intricate designs incorporating animal figures, and pebbles engraved with elephants. Stone pendants carved with human masks and phallic symbols have also been found.

THE BIG-GAME HUNTERS

The first Americans were descendants of the big-game hunters of the Siberian Arctic, possessing survival skills developed during the last Ice Age. As the Ice Age drew to a close, they ventured south beyond the retreating ice sheets in search of new hunting territories. Finding grassy plains rich in game, these groups, armed with expertly made weapons, hunted mammoths, bison, and other North American animals such as the native camel and horse that had not developed a natural fear of humans. By 9000 BC the days of the large Ice-Age mammals such as the mammoth were over, and the groups turned to other prey. The hunters of the vast American Plains were to focus their superb hunting and tracking skills on the bison.

BUFFALO COUNTRY
Like the bison on the Medano ranch in Colorado today, prehistoric bison congregated at ponds and lakes that dotted the landscape. Hunters of the Folsom age (from around 8900 BC) commonly ambushed the animals as they gathered around water, using spears tipped with fluted points, similar to Clovis spear points but much smaller.

EXPERT STONEWORKERS *below*
The earliest American tool technology is known as Clovis, named after the site in New Mexico where it was first found. Clovis toolmakers took great care when selecting raw materials, preferring fine-grained, durable, and colorful stones such as agates and chert. They traveled and traded over great distances to obtain desirable stone. At a quarry, quantities of "blanks" would be made – thin, oval stones made by removing chips from two faces. Stones were inspected before leaving the quarry and were lighter to carry over long distances. The blanks were carried around until a spearhead or other tool was needed, then a stone would be carefully worked into the item required.

MAMMOTH KILL SITE *below*
A mammoth kill provided enough meat to feed a group for several months, plus hide, tusks, and bones that became tools, shelters, and clothing. These huge beasts must have been extremely dangerous and difficult to kill outright in an attack. Instead, they were ambushed and wounded with spears or darts. These may have been coated with poison and were thrown using an atlatl, or spear-thrower. The hunters then followed the wounded mammoth, perhaps for many days, as it sought a watering hole at which to rest. When opportunities availed, more darts were launched. Once the animal came to rest, some of the hunters would wait for it to die, while others returned to their camp to bring help for butchering and carrying meat back to the camp.

1 *Experimental archaeologist Errett Callahan has recreated the technique used to make a Clovis point. First, large flakes were detached, using an antler hammer, from both sides of the blank until it was thin enough for a spearhead.*

2 *Using a pad of leather to protect the palm, the fine shaping of the edges of the blank was accomplished by using the tip of an antler to pry off narrow flakes in sequence.*

3 *To remove the characteristic large flute flake at the base where the point was hafted, the blank was securely held in a vise, and a specially prepared striking platform located in the center of the base was struck with an antler hammer.*

Modern point made by recreating the Clovis method, mounted on a shaft

Finely worked edge, sharp enough to cut mammoth hide

Sinew wrappings bind the point securely to the shaft

Mammoth kill site

More darts are thrown to hasten the animal's death

Dying mammoth rests at a watering hole

Well dug by hunters at the bottom of a dried pond to attract wounded animals

Waiting for the mammoth to die, hunters rest and repair their equipment

13,000 - 8000 BC

Butchering site | *Leg bones were saved for their rich marrow* | *Workers stretch and scrape the hides as they dry* | *Butchering is known to have followed a methodical sequence* | *The hunters replace their broken spear points after a kill*

HUNTERS' CAMP *above*

The scenes of activity that ensued when a small herd of bison was killed can be reconstructed from evidence at sites such as Stewart's Cattle Guard in Colorado. The group set up camp near the kill and systematically extracted everything of use from the carcasses. Work teams were formed and skilled butchers distributed the jointed meat for further processing: meat was dried and pounded up with fat and berries to make trail food and marrow was extracted from bones. Leather and rawhide were made from the skins, and broken tools repaired or replaced. The camp may have been occupied only as long as it took to repair tool kits and prepare provisions to support the group as it moved on in search of the next kill.

CLOVIS POINTS *right*

These complete points were found in the remains of a mammoth in Arizona. Points would normally have been retrieved during butchering; it seems probable that this animal escaped its pursuers.

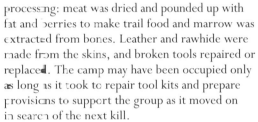

Eight Clovis points

Bones and tusks from dead mammoths

EXTINCT ANIMALS *below*

By 8000 BC, climatic changes and overhunting probably contributed to the extinction not only of large Ice-Age mammals like the mammoth, but also many other indigenous American species.

Ice-Age bison

Native camel **Native horse**

BISON KILL SITE *above*

The technique of "driving" animals towards a trap was made possible by an intimate knowledge of their habits and movements. The remains of nearly 300 bison found at the Jones-Miller site in Colorado attest to its efficiency. The animals were skillfully driven either into steep gullies or into a constructed corral where they were killed. After this, a winter base camp was set up in a nearby river valley. The processed meat would have lasted until early summer.

CHAPTER 6
FARMERS & HUNTER-GATHERERS
8000 - 5000 BC

Growing populations increase the need for reliable food supplies

Farmers begin to cultivate millet in the Yellow River Valley, China

Earliest small-scale cultivation in the Americas begins at seasonal campsites in Mexico

Middle Eastern farmers enhance land's potential with irrigation systems

Decorating pottery with mineral pigments leads to early experiments in metallurgy

An analysis of the world some 10,000 years ago would have shown that while farming was becoming established in parts of the Middle East, hunting and gathering was the most widespread way of life in the world as a whole. The same was true 3,000 years later, but by this time communities in China, the Americas, and perhaps also the Nile Valley and the Sahara had, independently of each other, adopted plant cultivation. Farming techniques spread to Europe from the Middle East, possibly along trade routes. In Australia, on the other hand, the hunter-gatherer way of life continued to flourish. Aboriginal rock art at open-air sites and on the walls of rock shelters, as at Ingaladdi in the Northern Territory, depicts the flora and fauna that were the basis of the local diet.

New sources of food
The increased demand for food, created by an expanding human population, was an important factor in the development of farming. After the end of the last Ice Age around 10,000 years ago, abundant plant and animal resources enabled communities to grow rapidly, requiring careful management of resources. Domestication of suitable wild species of plants and animals was the natural step toward securing reliable food sources, first on a small scale, then more intensively as communities grew too large to be supported by hunting and gathering alone.

Asian villages
In South Asia, farming began around 6500 BC at Mehrgarh, a village settlement in the hills west of the Indus Valley. The main crops, wheat and barley, were grown initially to supplement hunting and gathering. Sheep, goats, and cattle were also herded. The trade networks of the

Incised decoration may represent clothing

TERRA-COTTA FIGURINES
Early farming communities of eastern Europe used clay to model stylized figurines of humans as well as to make containers. Once shaped, the clay was fired.

people of Mehrgarh are revealed by their burial goods of turquoise and lapis lazuli from Central Asia and Afghanistan.

The story of farming in China begins in the fertile Yellow River Valley in the north around 6000 BC. Here, the farmers lived in villages of small round or square houses, sometimes surrounded by a timber stockade. They grew millet and raised pigs, dogs, and chickens. Rice was cultivated in southern and central China, and the practice spread northward to reach the Yellow River Valley around 5000 BC.

Seasonal farming villages
Cultivation in the Americas began in a similar way, with one or two crops grown as an adjunct to hunting and gathering. In Mexico, chilies, squash, and avocados were cultivated at seasonal campsites from around 5500 BC, over 1,000 years before

CULTIVATED SQUASH
People in the Tehuacan Valley in Mexico experimented with cultivating several plants, including squash, one of the first plants to be domesticated in Mesoamerica.

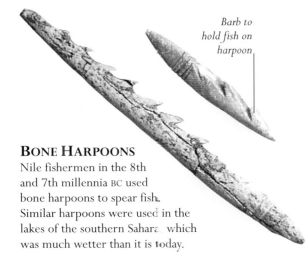

BONE HARPOONS
Nile fishermen in the 8th and 7th millennia BC used bone harpoons to spear fish. Similar harpoons were used in the lakes of the southern Sahara, which was much wetter than it is today.

Barb to hold fish on harpoon

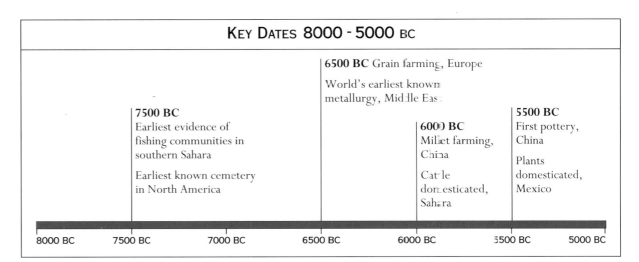

KEY DATES 8000 - 5000 BC				
		6500 BC Grain farming, Europe		
		World's earliest known metallurgy, Middle East		**5500 BC**
	7500 BC		**6000 BC**	First pottery, China
	Earliest evidence of fishing communities in southern Sahara		Millet farming, China	Plants domesticated, Mexico
	Earliest known cemetery in North America		Cattle domesticated, Sahara	

8000 BC	7500 BC	7000 BC	6500 BC	6000 BC	5500 BC	5000 BC

maize, which was to become the most important crop, came into regular cultivation. In large areas of the Americas, hunting and gathering continued to provide the everyday foods, with human communities adapting to changes in the food supply. Thus, when bison began to leave the western part of the Great Plains of North America around 5000 BC, human groups responded by moving with them.

Irrigation techniques

New farming practices developed during this period in the Middle East. The first farming villages appeared where rainfall alone provided water for the crops.

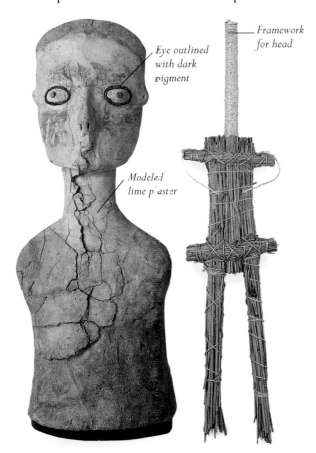

Eye outlined with dark pigment

Framework for head

Modeled lime plaster

LIME PLASTER SCULPTURE
The earliest sizable sculptures of human forms are from Ain Ghazal in Jordan. Made of lime plaster over a reed framework (*right*), they include busts and whole figures.

ANIMAL PAINTINGS
The best-preserved Australian rock art dates to after the last Ice Age. It portrays painted animals, such as this one at a rock shelter at Ingaladdi in the Northern Territory.

In Mesopotamia, irrigation techniques enabled better use of fertile soils. An ample supply of water was available from the Tigris and Euphrates rivers and their tributaries. Toward the end of the 7th millennium BC, farmers constructed canal systems to bring water to the fields. These were developed further by the farmers of the Ubaid period (c. 5900-4300 BC), named after the site of Tell al-Ubaid in southern Mesopotamia. Ultimately, it was efficient irrigation systems that provided the economic basis for the first Mesopotamian cities.

Settled farming communities

The early farming villages of the Middle East were linked together by social ties, marriage alliances, and trade. The clearest evidence of trade at this period is provided by finds of obsidian (black volcanic glass), which was ideal for making sharp tools and

was traded over extensive distances from sources in eastern Turkey. Trading contact between early Anatolian farmers and communities in southeastern Europe led to the adoption of farming in Europe around 6500 BC.

The adoption of a settled way of life in Europe and Asia was accompanied by an important innovation: the widespread production of pottery containers for functional purposes. The first pottery containers were made by a community of hunter-gatherers in Japan more than 12,000 years ago, but the technique did not spread. It was not until the 7th millennium BC that communities in Africa, the Middle East, Europe, and South Asia independently developed the technique of using fired clay to produce containers. The spread of farming techniques throughout Europe was accompanied by a variety of decorated pottery styles. Terra-cotta figurines, probably used in cults or rituals, were also made, while in the Middle East, human figures were sculpted from lime plaster.

8000-5000 BC

33,000 BC

Functional pottery vessels

Heavy and fragile, pottery containers were useful only to peoples who remained in one place for long periods of time. Pottery containers dating to around 7000 BC from hunting and fishing communities in the Nile Valley and the southern Sahara demonstrate that the people in these regions had adopted a relatively settled life. Other fishing communities thrived by lakes in the Rift Valley of Kenya and Tanzania.

Middle Eastern metallurgy

The earliest experiments with smelting copper took place in the Middle East in around 6500 BC. Although the first metallurgy was a milestone in human development, it did not revolutionize everyday activities to the same extent as the new food production methods had done. In its early stages, the use of metal was limited to making simple objects of copper, gold, and lead. These are all soft, easily worked metals that melt at relatively low temperatures. Beads and trinkets of copper and lead were being made by the inhabitants of Çatal Hüyük in Turkey by 6000 BC, and 1,000 years later the farming communities of southeastern Europe were also experimenting with copper and gold.

Although copper was used to make axes and knives, it is likely that most early copper objects were intended to be impressive decorative items indicating the status of the owner rather than implements for daily use. Certainly, heavy tasks such as felling trees and woodworking became easier with the development of harder copper alloys such as bronze. Meanwhile, stone axes were also still used for woodworking.

Experiments in pottery decoration

The first inkling that minerals could be transformed by heat into something with different properties probably came indirectly, from pottery production – perhaps through experiments with painted decoration. Early potters used a variety of ground minerals as pigments to make paint for their pots. They may have been attracted to brightly colored copper ores such as malachite or azurite as a source of pigment, only to find that the material with which they painted their vessels produced, when fired, not a blue or green coloring, but a few shiny droplets of copper.

Effects of agriculture

The most far-reaching development of this period was the establishment of farming villages in many parts of the world. However, wild food remained a significant part of the human diet, and the hunter-gatherer way of life survived not only in areas where the land was not suited to agriculture – the arctic wastes and arid deserts – but even in regions where the land could have been cultivated, but was not. The permanent settlements that resulted from the adoption of farming led to the building of large communal projects, such as irrigation systems. These in turn created larger, complex communities – the forerunners of all later civilizations.

AMERICAS

CLIMATE ON THE GREAT PLAINS

A period of reduced rainfall and warmer temperatures, which began before 5000 BC, dominated much of the Great Plains of North America for the following 3,000 years. Grazing resources for bison declined and the herds moved eastward. Hunters dependent on bison for their survival were forced to follow the herds, leaving large regions thinly populated. The close relationship between humans and bison characterized life on the Great Plains for thousands of years, perhaps becoming even more intense after the introduction of the horse in the AD 1600s.

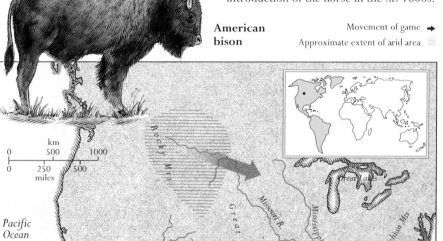

American bison

Movement of game ➡
Approximate extent of arid area

km 500 1000
0 250 500 miles

Pacific Ocean

Rocky Mts
Great Plains
Missouri R.
Mississippi R.
Great Lakes
Appalachian Mts
Colorado R.
Arkansas R.

AFRICA

SAHARAN ROCK ART

Between 8000 and 5000 BC, the wooded massifs, semiarid grasslands, and shallow lakes of what is now the Sahara Desert supported sparse bands of hunter-gatherers, whose staples were lake fish, edible plants, and such game as aurochs (wild oxen) and gazelles. After 6000 BC, the Sahara gradually dried up. Drought forced humans and animals toward permanent but shrinking lakes and springs. Hunters domesticated wild cattle, then dispersed over their former hunting grounds as herders. This change is documented in Saharan rock art – that dating to before 6000 BC depicts only wild animals; after 6000 BC, domesticated cattle were also portrayed. As the Sahara became drier, so the cattle herders withdrew to its margins where there were permanent water sources.

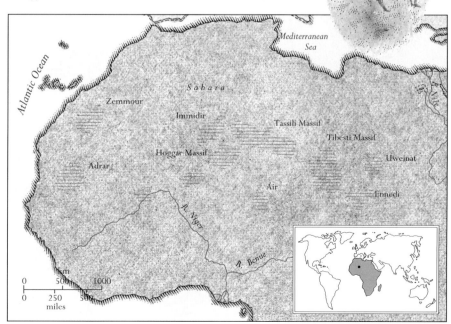

Rock art depicting gazelles, Tassili Massif, Sahara

-- Coastline of the period
≡ Approximate area of Saharan rock art

Atlantic Ocean
Mediterranean Sea
Sahara
Zemmour
Immidir
Tassili Massif
Tibesti Massif
Hoggar Massif
Uweinat
Adrar
Aïr
Ennedi
R. Niger
R. Benue

km 500 1000
0 250 500 miles

EUROPE

SPREAD OF FARMING

Farming practices and pottery manufacture were first adopted in the Balkans shortly after 6500 BC, through contact with farmers in Anatolia (modern Turkey). The new way of life, in permanent village settlements, spread through most of the rest of the continent, reaching the south of France and the Netherlands by 5000 BC, although hunter-gatherer societies persisted in many areas. In the Mediterranean, plants, animals, and pottery were probably passed on and adopted by hunter-gatherer groups through contact with local sailors and fishermen. Typical early pottery from the Mediterranean is known as Cardial, after its distinctive *cardium* or "cockleshell" decoration. North of the Alps, farming was carried rapidly across Central Europe by groups of migrating Hungarian farmers, who developed the *Bandkeramik* pottery style, characterized by incised linear decoration. The distribution of Anatolian painted pottery also charts the locations of early farming communities.

Bandkeramik decorated vessel,
Langweiler, Germany

Coastline of the period --	Early farming settlement ■	Distribution of Cardial pottery ▨
Spread of farming ➡	Distribution of *Bandkeramik* pottery ▥	Distribution of Anatolian pottery ▤

MIDDLE EAST & SOUTH ASIA

MIDDLE EASTERN TRADE

Obsidian (black volcanic glass) was highly valued by the early farming communities of the Middle East for the sharp-edged cutting blades that could be made from obsidian flakes. Since the chemical composition of obsidian varies according to its origin, the sources of the obsidian found at settlement sites can be traced; these chart the contemporary trade routes along which it passed. The widespread distribution indicates that these trade routes were extensive, and that the early farming communities in the region were in regular contact with one another. The most highly prized, and therefore the most important, sources of obsidian were the extinct volcanoes of central and eastern Anatolia (modern Turkey). The unique chemical composition of this obsidian made it particularly good for creating the sharpest possible blades.

Unworked obsidian

-- Coastline of the period
■ Early farming settlement
• ▤ Distribution of volcanic obsidian from Acigöl
• ▥ Distribution of volcanic obsidian from Çiftlik
• ▨ Distribution of volcanic obsidian from Nemrut Dag

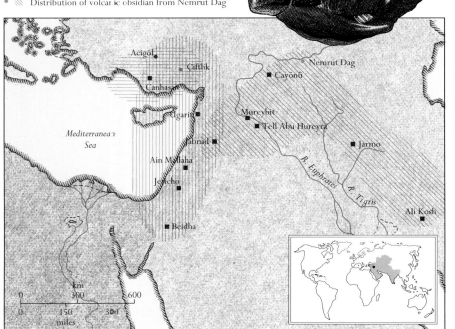

EAST ASIA & AUSTRALASIA

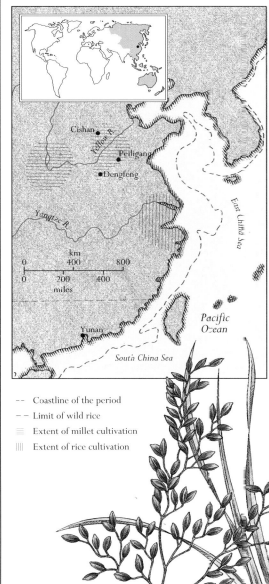

-- Coastline of the period
- - Limit of wild rice
▤ Extent of millet cultivation
▥ Extent of rice cultivation

CROPS IN CHINA

There were at least two centers of early plant domestication in East Asia, based on different types of grain. The earliest, dating to around 6000 BC, was on the North China Plain, around the Yellow River and its tributaries, where the main domesticated plants were broomcorn and foxtail millet. In southern and central China, the crucial early domesticated plant was rice. Rice grew wild across a broad belt of territory stretching from northern India to the mountains of mainland Southeast Asia and into southern China. Rice cultivation was initially practiced by groups of hunter-gatherers, gradually spreading northward from one settlement to another. By around 5000 BC, it was well established in the Yangtze River delta region.

Wild rice grains

Wild rice plant

8000 - 7000 BC

FOOD & ENVIRONMENT

SHELTER & ARCHITECTURE

AMERICAS

ACORNS AS FOOD
Deciduous forests, dominated by oaks and hickories, expanded across many areas of eastern North America during the climatic warming that followed the end of the last Ice Age (around 10,000 years ago). High in starch and easily stored for later consumption, various species of acorn became an important food source for many thousands of years.

Acorns

STONEWORKER'S HUT
Located near a stone quarry in New Mexico, a shallow circular depression, ringed with a semi-circle of stones 6½ feet in diameter, outlines a hut used by a stoneworker. Broken tools at various stages of manufacture were found in the hut along with manufacturing equipment and discarded, worn-out tools.

Stoneworker's hut, New Mexico

Frame of small poles
Walls of dried grass
Ring of stones around base

EAST ASIA & AUSTRALASIA

WILD RICE
Hunter-gatherers in East and Southeast Asia relied on a range of wild plant and animal foods, including rice. Early remains of rice grains suggest that wild rice was native to Southeast Asia, southern China, and northern India. Carbonized grains of rice, broken husks and straws, and their imprints in clay have been found in coastal areas of southern China.

Wild rice

WINDBREAKS
In the Central Australian desert, the scarcity of building materials and food resources meant that nomadic groups moved frequently. In the absence of large trees or rock shelters, these groups erected simple windbreaks made with branches, which provided both privacy and shade. At night, when temperatures dropped below freezing, small fires were kept burning nearby, and people would huddle against dogs for warmth.

Modern brushwood shelter, Australia

MIDDLE EAST & SOUTH ASIA

PIGS AND CATTLE
The wild ancestors of pigs and cattle, the boar and the now extinct aurochs (wild ox), were domesticated after sheep and goats. Wild boar and aurochs were native to most of Europe and Asia. They were probably first domesticated in southern Turkey, and it is possible that they were domesticated independently in different regions. Pigs proved very useful, since they acted as scavengers in human settlements. It is difficult to see the benefits offered by domesticating cattle, however, as the animals were fierce and dangerous, and it was only later that they were kept for milk and as beasts of burden.

BUILDING MATERIALS
Mud is an exceptionally good material for building in dry climates; it has good structural and thermal qualities and is readily available wherever agriculture is practiced. Mud bricks had been invented in the 9th millennium BC: the mud was molded by hand and dried in the sun, then built into walls using mud mortar. After 8000 BC, mud bricks were mass-produced using wooden molds.

Mud brick, Jericho, Israel

Fingerprint made in molding process

EUROPE

Oyster shells

PROTEIN FROM THE SEA
Oysters and other shellfish were an important source of protein for European coastal dwellers after the end of the last Ice Age around 10,000 years ago. Large shell middens (mounds of discarded debris) survive on Atlantic coasts from Iberia to Denmark, marking locations to which groups of hunter-gatherers returned year after year at certain seasons to gather and eat shellfish.

WOOD AND REED
The earliest known houses in the British Isles were built about 7500 BC by a small community of hunter-gatherers on a low rise overlooking the Bann River in Northern Ireland. Flexible poles were sunk into the ground to form a circle, then bent inward to join at the center, creating a domed hut. Gaps were filled in with smaller branches and reeds. The huts were probably temporary shelters and were not intended to stand for long periods, although the site itself was reoccupied on several occasions over a period of 500 years.

AFRICA

LIVING OFF THE RIVER
The inhabitants of the Nile Valley relied heavily on river fish for their livelihood. Thousands of fish were stranded in the shallows when the Nile retreated after flooding each year in late summer. Nets made of reed and papyrus were used to trap fish throughout the year.

Reed and papyrus twine fishing net, Egypt

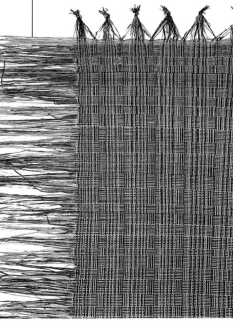

VERSATILE MATTING
Africans have always used versatile local materials to build houses. From prehistoric times to the present day, they have employed matting woven from palm fronds and other fibrous materials. Sometimes richly decorated, these mats served not only as beds, but also as thin, airy walls for houses in hot climates. They could be easily removed or replaced as needed.

Matting, Africa

TECHNOLOGY & INNOVATION

MULTIPURPOSE WEAPONRY

Versatile weapons that could be adapted for use as tools were developed by hunters in North America. Weapon tips of chert (a crystalline form of silica) were mounted on a foreshaft (short handle) and then hafted to a spear shaft. The spear was thrown with an atlatl, or spear-thrower, and when it was retrieved after a kill, the foreshaft and point could be removed and used simply as a hafted knife to butcher the animal.

Hell Gap point, Jones-Miller bison kill site, Colorado

HUNTING WEAPONS

Stone tools are all that remain of the equipment used by hunter-gatherers in China. In the north, microliths (tiny stone blades) continued to be made as they had been for the last 4,000 years. In the south, people may have relied on larger tools and, in the south-west, on sharpened bamboo.

Stone spear- and arrowheads, China

WHITE WARE VESSELS

Before the development of pottery, vessels were made of unbaked, sun-dried mud or of white ware. White ware vessels, made from a mixture of lime and gray ash, were built up around a basket, which was removed just before firing. This kind of vessel was made and used at several villages in the Levant (the coastal strip of Syria, Lebanon, and Israel) and southern Turkey for several centuries around 7000 BC.

White ware vessel, Abu Hureyra, Syria

STANDARDIZED BLADES

Flint microliths (tiny blades) are the hallmark of the European Mesolithic, the period between the end of the Ice Age (around 10,000 years ago) and the beginnings of farming (around 6500 BC). The blades were produced to standardized shapes and mounted on wooden hafts to form knives, spears, and arrowheads.

Broad blade flint microliths, Sheffield, England

HUNTING TECHNOLOGY

The African hunter depended on lightweight, composite spears and bows and arrows. These weapons had sharp points of bone or wood, often fitted with tiny stone barbs and smeared with poison. The head was mounted on a foreshaft (short handle), which broke off when the weapon struck an animal. Hunters carried quivers of spare points to replace heads that snapped off during the hunt.

Arrowhead, Egypt

ART & RITUAL

GRAVE GOODS

The Sloan burial site in Arkansas, dating to 7500 BC, is the earliest known cemetery in North America. Caches of unused projectile points, unfinished points, and other unused tools may have been placed as offerings in graves, hinting at a ritualized ceremony and a belief in an afterlife.

Dalton projectile points, Sloan site, Arkansas

BONE ORNAMENTS

In northern China and Manchuria, the first personal ornaments were made around 7500 BC. The hunters who made them worked the bones of tigers, leopards, bears, and deer into needles and picks, and engraved designs on antler pieces. The teeth of badgers and other game were perforated and strung together to make necklaces, pendants, or earrings.

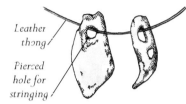
Leather thong
Pierced hole for stringing
Pierced teeth, Zhoukoudian Cave, China

ANCESTOR WORSHIP

Graves beneath the floors of houses in farming villages in the Levant often contained headless skeletons. The skulls may have been displayed in the houses or in a special hut. They sometimes had flesh modeled in plaster and shells in the eye sockets: it is thought that this was associated with ancestor worship.

Cowrie shells stuck in eye sockets

Plastered skull, Jericho, Israel

ANIMAL FIGURINES

In Denmark and southern Sweden, carvings of animals were first made around 7000 BC. Most attractive are small figurines of amber (a natural fossil resin), including an elk's head and a bear or wild boar. As well as these figurines, there are engravings on tools and other objects of bone and antler, including several stylized humans and a detailed depiction of a red deer.

Amber figurine, Denmark

PAINTING WITH PIGMENTS

A natural pigment, red ocher can be derived from any iron-bearing mineral, including brown clay. It was used as a paint by African hunters to adorn their bodies with intricate designs. In powdered form, it was scattered on the dead in their graves. Artists in southern Africa continued to use red ocher to paint animals and human figures on the walls of caves and rock shelters.

Lumps of brown clay

7000 - 6000 BC

FOOD & ENVIRONMENT

SHELTER & ARCHITECTURE

AMERICAS

VITAMINS AND OILS
Chilies and avocados added important variety to the Mesoamerican diet from as early as 7000 BC. While squash, maize, and beans provided the staple complex carbohydrates and protein, chilies added flavoring and essential vitamins, and avocados provided oils necessary for the breakdown of other nutrients.

Avocado and chili

TEMPORARY SETTLEMENTS
Early hunter-gatherers in eastern North America occupied small settlements for short periods during a particular season, often returning to the same place year after year. They built temporary shelters, often in river valleys, with a light frame of wood covered in grass and an outdoor hearth. The huts were renewed each time the site was revisited.

Hut, Icehouse Bottom, Tennessee

EAST ASIA & AUSTRALASIA

DRAINAGE FOR FARMLAND
Throughout Southeast Asia, the adoption of farming was a gradual process based on such indigenous plants as wild rice and the root crop taro, which were first domesticated in small plots adjacent to settlements. A similar process of gradual adoption and small-scale cultivation took place in New Guinea; as long ago as 7000 BC, local people endeavored to drain a marshy valley floor in the highlands of the island so that it could be cultivated. They dug a channel to carry off excess water and created a system of tributary gutters draining into it. This was replaced by an even more extensive network of drains 1,000 years later. The prepared land was probably planted with taro, and the scale of the drainage shows that, although it grew wild in New Guinea, taro also became an important cultivated dietary staple.

WEATHERPROOF SHELTER
Rock shelters were sometimes occupied for thousands of years; the one at Ingaladdi in the Northern Territory of Australia, for example, was inhabited continuously from before 7000 BC until this century. It provided welcome shade and protection from tropical downpours in the hot, wet summer.

MIDDLE EAST & SOUTH ASIA

FARMING COMMUNITY
Mehrgarh, in the hill country west of the Indus Valley, began as a seasonally occupied village of hunters and herders. Around 6500 BC the people began to farm, cultivating wheat and barley, and raising sheep, goats, and cattle. The cattle (zebu) were probably indigenous to the area, but the grain and small stock may have originated elsewhere.

Indian zebu

Settlement, Çatal Hüyük, Turkey

Ladder for access to ground from roof

LARGE VILLAGE
Çatal Hüyük in southern Anatolia was perhaps the most spectacular of all early farming villages. It was one of the largest settlements of the 7th millennium BC, covering some 32 acres. Mud-brick houses and shrines were built against each other, with occasional open yards but no intervening streets. Access was across flat rooftops, with ladders leading down into the buildings.

EUROPE

FARMING REACHES EUROPE
Farming was first practiced in Europe in about 6500 BC, and was initially confined to the extreme southeast of the continent – Greece and the Balkans. These parts of Europe are closest to the Middle East, where farming had already been established for over 1,000 years, and it is clear that the early European farmers adopted the ideas and techniques of their Middle Eastern neighbors. These first European farmers grew barley and two varieties of wheat (emmer and einkorn), both of Middle Eastern origin; they herded sheep, goats, and cattle. Once established in the southeast, the new way of life soon began to spread north and west to adjacent parts of Europe.

Thatched roof *Sturdy timber supports*

Thick walls covered with clay

FARM HOUSES
The houses of the first farmers in southeastern Europe were small square or rectangular structures with walls of wattle and daub (interwoven twigs and sticks covered with clay), and a roof of reeds or thatch. The houses had only a single room, often with a raised hearth and a baking oven, and sometimes a clay storage bin to hold grain or flour.

House, Nea Nikomedeia, Greece

AFRICA

PLANTING YAMS
The borders of Africa's rainforests support an exceptionally diverse population of edible plants. Among them is the wild African yam, which sustained people for millennia. Many groups exploited yams intensively, cutting off the tops and planting them so they would regerminate in the damp soil. Such a simple form of deliberate cultivation, sometimes called vegeculture, probably began thousands of years ago in some areas, and may be as old or older than the cultivation of wheat and barley in Europe and western Asia. Vegeculture was an effective and logical way to increase food supplies and is practiced to this day.

SUNKEN HUTS
Around 6500 BC, the first settlers at Nabta Playa, a village in semiarid grasslands to the east of the Nile Valley, lived in oval huts that were dug into the ground and roofed with animal hides sometimes mixed with grass. This structure gave some protection during extremely hot days and bitterly cold nights and was widespread in northeastern Africa for many centuries.

Gap in roof allowed smoke to filter out

Oval house, Nabta Playa, Egypt

TECHNOLOGY & INNOVATION

WOODWORKING TOOLS

The early hunting societies of North America learned to adapt to the expansion of the forests that followed the end of the last Ice Age (around 10,000 years ago). Woodworking became important to these communities, and while wooden objects from this period are rarely preserved, the tools used are commonly found; stone adzes with distinctive curved cutting edges are evidence of this type of craftsmanship.

Adze, Advance Lowland, Missouri

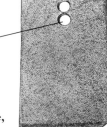

Holes for attaching handle

Stone spade, Shandong, China

STONE SPADES

In coastal regions of China, early cultivation of tubers like taro and yam was accompanied by the appearance of more sophisticated implements for digging and planting. This spade, for example, has two holes drilled through one end, where a wooden handle may have been attached. Taro and yam fibers were used to make fishing lines and nets, and for caulking canoes.

EARLY TECHNOLOGIES

Pottery first came into widespread use in the Middle East after 7000 BC. The earliest vessels were crudely shaped and poorly fired, but progress was rapid; within 1,000 years finely made pottery with elaborate painted and incised designs was being produced at village settlements from western Iran to Anatolia. In northern Mesopotamia, large domed kilns 6 feet in diameter generated high enough temperatures to fire exceptionally fine painted pottery, known as Hassuna ware after the site of Hassuna in central Mesopotamia. These kilns were also suited to the melting and smelting of copper, and it is no coincidence that the first experiments in copper metallurgy were made in northern Mesopotamia at this time.

PAINTED POTTERY

The first European farmers were also the first people in Europe to produce pottery. Like farming, this was an innovation that had been developed in the Middle East, from where it spread to Europe. Early pottery in southeastern Europe was handmade without a potter's wheel, but was well-finished and painted with geometric designs in red or black.

Painted pottery

WAVY-LINE POTTERY

In Africa around 7000 BC, the first pottery was manufactured by groups of hunters and fishermen living across a broad stretch of the southern Sahara, from Mali in the west to Khartoum in the Nile Valley to the east. The pottery was decorated with parallel wavy lines. In the Nile Valley, the pattern was made by dragging the spine of a fish across the clay while it was still soft; in the west, similar effects were achieved using wooden or bone points.

Fragments of wavy-line pottery, Egypt

ART & RITUAL

CLAY FIGURINES

In North America, early unfired clay figurines of humans were incised with stylized decoration, but had no details to indicate their gender. Complete figurines lack any facial features, although some fragments have noses formed by pinching a ridge, and holes for eyes. Their function is unknown, but they are found with objects that might have belonged to individuals rather than to a social group.

Figurine, Cowboy Cave, Utah

Engraved bird tracks, Yiwarlarlay, Australia

ROCK ENGRAVINGS

A fragment of sandstone found in deposits dating to before 6000 BC at the Ingaladdi rock shelter in the Northern Territory of Australia is engraved with bird tracks and parallel lines. Similar marks appear on the walls of this and other shelters like Yiwarlarlay, and may have been symbols used in Aboriginal hunting magic.

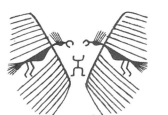

Wall painting of birds, Çatal Hüyük, Turkey

SHRINES AND RITUALS

One-third of the buildings at Çatal Hüyük in southern Anatolia were decorated with wall paintings and figures of leopards, bulls' heads and horns, and female figures. These buildings have been identified as shrines. One wall painting that depicts scavenging birds attacking headless corpses may represent the practice of excarnation, or exposure of the dead.

TERRA-COTTA FIGURINES

The production of terra-cotta figurines was another activity that the earliest farming communities of southeastern Europe copied from their neighbors in the Middle East. Female figurines with prominent buttocks are the most common type, and two were found together in a building at Nea Nikomedeia in Greece, which has been identified as a shrine.

Terra-cotta figurine, Nea Nikomedeia, Greece

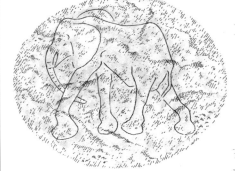

ROCK ARTISTS

Rock paintings of the Saharan plateaus reveal much about the life of the hunters who roamed these areas before 6000 BC. Paintings on the walls of caves and rock shelters depict wild animals long extinct in the region: *Bubalus antiquus* (an extinct buffalo), giraffe, elephant, rhinoceros, and hippopotamus. Only after 6000 BC were domestic cattle portrayed.

Rock painting, Tassili Massif, Sahara

6000 - 5000 BC

33,000 BC

FOOD & ENVIRONMENT

SHELTER & ARCHITECTURE

AMERICAS

CENTURY PLANT
The American agave, or maguey, blooms once in 10 to 30 years. It was formerly thought to flower only every 100 years, which explains why it is also known as the century plant. A tropical plant native to Mesoamerica, it was put to a variety of uses from earliest times. An important source of food and drink (some species can be used to make intoxicating beverages), it also provided a fibrous material for making cords and clothing in the colder highland regions of Mexico and Guatemala.

Agave

CAVE SETTLEMENTS
Although global temperatures had risen virtually to present-day levels by 8000 BC, the high plateau of the Andes in South America remained cold, and hunter-gatherers lived in caves and rock shelters. Junin, a settlement high

in Peru's central sierra over 13,000 feet above sea level, was one of the first places to domesticate llama and alpaca. Several caves were found to have been occupied continuously between 10,000 and 4000 BC. They contain highly stylized depictions of llamas and alpacas, and hunting scenes.

EAST ASIA & AUSTRALASIA

CULTIVATING THE LAND
Cultivation of millet began just before 6000 BC in the Yellow River Valley on the North China Plain, and was fully established after 6000 BC. The area was ideal for agriculture: light rainfall meant that the forest was thin and easy to clear, while annual river floods enriched the soil. Grain was stored in pits and ground into flour.

Clay covering wattle frame

Central pit for fire   *Entrance*

Early wooden house, Banpo, Shaanxi, China

WOODEN HUTS
The early farmers of the North China Plain built semipermanent settlements, moving on when they needed new land, and returning when the soil had regained its fertility. Their houses were round or square with walls of wattle and daub (interwoven twigs and sticks covered with clay), and thatched roofs made of layers of millet stalks, reeds, and clay supported on beams.

MIDDLE EAST & SOUTH ASIA

DATE PALMS
The date palm played an important role in the life of the earliest farming communities in southern Mesopotamia. Every part of the palm was used: the nutritious fruits were easily stored and transported, while the trunk and fronds provided valuable building materials. The fibers were twisted to make string and rope, and the leaves woven into mats and baskets.

Date palms

UBAID TEMPLES
By about 5900 BC, a culture known as Ubaid (named after the site of Tell al-Ubaid) was flourishing in southern Mesopotamia; 500 years later it had spread to the whole of Mesopotamia, replacing the Halaf culture, which had dominated the north. Eridu, one of the earliest Ubaid settlements, had a series of temples, each built on the remains of the last. The oldest one consisted of a single mud-brick room with an altar and an offering table.

Offering table

Altar

Plan of temple, Eridu, Mesopotamia

EUROPE

SPREAD OF FARMING
In 6000 BC, farming in Europe was still restricted to Greece and the Balkans; 1,000 years later it had spread as far as Iberia, where remains of cultivated grains have been found at cave settlements such as Coveta de l'Or on the southern coast of Spain. In the Mediterranean, the concept of plant and animal domestication – which formed the basis of the new economy – passed from one community to the next, eventually

reaching Portugal. In Central Europe, however, groups of colonizing farmers advanced westward along the valley of the river Danube to the Rhineland and the Paris basin. These pioneer farmers preferred to plant their crops in the lighter soils that flanked the rivers, growing them in small fields or garden plots close to their dwellings.

TIMBER LONGHOUSES
The earliest farmers of Central Europe lived in a forested environment and were able to build substantial timber houses up to 150 feet long. A framework of load-bearing posts provided the basic structure. The outer walls

were of wattle and daub (interwoven twigs and sticks covered with clay), and the roof, steeply pitched to keep out rain and snow, was thatched with reeds or straw. Each longhouse accommodated one or more families, plus their livestock and grain stores.

Timber longhouse, Bylany, Moravia, Czech Republic

Timber supports   *Brushwood rafters*   *Thatched roof*

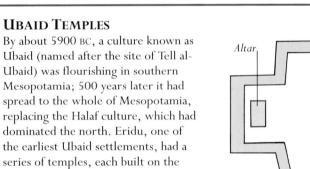

AFRICA

DOMESTICATED LIVESTOCK
Cattle were first domesticated in the Sahara around 6000 BC and in the Nile Valley slightly later. It is not clear whether the idea developed independently, or as a result of influences from the Middle East. Cattle herding assumed great importance throughout the Sahara and the Sudan until the area became desert after 4000 BC.

African cattle

WINDBREAKS
Hunter-gatherers living on the edges of the great rainforests of Central Africa did not need permanent dwellings, because they were constantly on the move in search of game and wild plant foods, and there was ample timber and brush for temporary shelters. They built low structures using branches and leaves, often tied together with long fibers, to house a family and provide shelter from wind and rain. Vegetable fibers were woven into clothing and matting for bedding and screens.

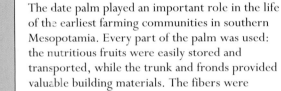

TECHNOLOGY & INNOVATION

ADAPTABLE TECHNOLOGY
As human populations increased after the end of the last Ice Age (around 10,000 years ago), people living in the mountains and deserts of southern California found new ways of coping with their changing environment, including making a wider variety of tools to prepare foods in new ways. Stones for grinding nuts and seeds became more important as areas of forest increased.

Grinding stone, Buena Vista Lake, California

INCISED POTTERY
The earliest pottery in China was crafted in fishing settlements along the southern coast. Creamy-buff and brown bowls and large globular jars were made from a thick gritty clay. The surface of the vessels, except for the rim, was decorated with marks made by fiber cords or stone knives.

Wavy lines made with a cord

Cord-marked and incised shards, Ta-p'en-keng, Taiwan

STAMP SEALS
In the Middle East, the first impressions of stamp seals on clay date to after 6000 BC, and are thought to indicate ownership, suggesting the development of administrative practices and perhaps private property. No impressions have been found of earlier seals. The first seals had simple geometric designs; later ones had images of people and animals.

Stamp seal, Tepe Giyan, Iran

Incised lines in curving bands

Pottery with banded decoration

DECORATED POTTERY
Pottery-making spread with farming along the Danube and the Rhine. The earliest pottery vessels of Central Europe, known as *Bandkeramik*, were decorated with incised lines infilled with dots or cross-hatching. Such pottery is found from France to Hungary and the Ukraine.

FISHING WITH HARPOONS
Fishing implements are common finds at early settlement sites close to the shallows of the Nile and East African lakes, which supported vast populations of catfish and other sluggish, bottom-dwelling fish. The settlers who lived by such waters developed barbed bone harpoons and points mounted on wooden shafts to spear the fish, which were then dried.

Barbed bone harpoons, Egypt

ART & RITUAL

AMAZONIAN ART
Throughout the northern Amazon region of South America, groups of people carved thousands of images into rock outcrops. Some show animals and the weapons and tools used in hunting and fishing. Others, like the one shown here, are simple renderings of the human form along with symbols that may relate to the natural environment.

Rock engraving, Venezuela

JADE IMPORTS
In China, pure nephrite, the only jade known at the time, was imported as early as the 6th millennium BC from Central Asia or Lake Baikal in Siberia by people living in northern Manchuria. This indicates the existence of highly developed societies able to trade and support skilled craftsmen. From the earliest times, jade was associated with ritual or sacrifice, and its qualities of purity, hardness, luminescence, and varying color symbolized ideal virtues.

Being too hard to be cut even with steel, jade must be worked with abrasives: it appeared indestructible and was therefore linked with immortality. Jade objects were buried with the dead and used in rituals as a means of communicating with the spirits.

FUNERAL GIFTS
Burials dating to between 6000 and 5000 BC at Mehrgarh, in the hills west of the Indus Valley, show that the deceased were placed in pits beside mud-brick walls, together with funerary offerings. Among the offerings, the presence of beads of turquoise from Central Asia and lapis lazuli from Afghanistan suggests trade over long distances. A figurine reminiscent of those from the Zagros Mountains in Iran attests to contacts even farther afield. Even infants were sometimes buried with rich grave goods, which indicates that they inherited social status from their parents.

RIVER GOD
At Lepenski Vir on the banks of the Danube in Serbia, a flourishing community of hunters, fishers, and gatherers, who had not yet adopted settled farming, developed a distinctive style of stone carving. Their artistry is best represented by the fish sculptures placed next to the hearths in their houses, which may be representations of a local river deity.

Fish sculpture, Lepenski Vir, Serbia

SAHARAN PAINTING
Herds of domesticated humped cattle were featured prominently in Saharan rock art between 6000 and 4000 BC. Many scenes show long- and short-horned beasts, often accompanied by their herders and milkers. The people who painted these naturalistic scenes also produced startling depictions of supernatural beings and magical religious subjects.

Cattle rock painting, Jabbaren, Sahara

79

ORIGINS OF FOOD PRODUCTION

33,000 BC

Nearly 10,000 years ago in the Middle East, a combination of environmental, biological, and cultural factors resulted in a dramatic change in the way people obtained food – a change that transformed the relationship between humans and the world around them. The Fertile Crescent, an arc of land extending from the Zagros Mountains of Iran to the southern Levant (southern Israel and Jordan), was the region where plants and animals were first domesticated and the home of the first food-producing communities. Domestication involves control of the reproduction of a plant or animal to increase the yield of a resource produced by that species. Reliance on farming and herding need not immediately follow the initial domestication of plants and animals, however. In the Middle East, different species were domesticated in different places at different times, and fully-fledged farming communities were not established until more than 1,000 years after the first domesticates appeared.

PLANT DOMESTICATION

Domestication often changes the physiology of a plant species, making it more attractive to humans and more dependent on them for its propagation. Cultivation also results in the spread of domestic plants into areas unsuitable for their wild progenitors. Wild wheat and barley have brittle stalks that ensure the seed head breaks on impact, allowing grains to reseed themselves, but making it difficult to harvest and transport ripe grain. Domestic grains have larger, plumper seeds and tough stalks, making them easier to harvest and carry from the fields for processing or storage.

PATHWAYS TO FOOD PRODUCTION *below*

From around 20,000 years ago, people in the rolling hills of the Levant relied increasingly on wild grains, and, by around 8000 BC, on domestic crops. Hunting of wild game, especially gazelles, persisted until about 7000 BC, when domestic sheep and goats first appear in the archaeological record. In the rugged Zagros Mountains, wild grains were restricted to less prolific varieties, and gazelles were less plentiful. Between 20,000 and 10,000 years ago, plants seem to have played a more limited role in the diet of people living in the region, and wild sheep and goats, which were more abundant than in the Levant, a more prominent one. Domestication of sheep and goats may have preceded the domestication of grains in this region, and is certain to have occurred by 7500 BC, when the earliest evidence for domestic grains in the Zagros is found.

LEVANT
Ain Mallaha Large semipermanent camp (*c.*8000 BC) with evidence of grain storage and processing, burials, and art objects.
Tell Aswad Earliest evidence of fully domesticated emmer wheat, *c.*7800 BC, indicating domestication had already occurred.
Beidha Evidence for management of wild herds of goats *c.*7000 BC. Structures change from small round self-contained houses in the Early Neolithic (*c.*7000 BC) to larger rectangular structures at a later date (*c.*6500 BC) with signs of repeated remodeling and expansion.
Jericho Early evidence of domestic goats *c.*7000 BC. Large stone tower, storage facilities, and wall on western perimeter of site indicate increasing level of communal activity.
Ain Ghazal Early village occupied *c.*7000-5500 BC, evidence of flowering and collapse of mixed farming and pastoral way of life. Large cache of plaster figures in later levels* indicates more elaborate forms of art and ritual.
Abu Hureyra Early levels (*c.*10,000 BC) show heavy dependence on wild grains and hunted gazelles and onagers (wild ass). Later levels (*c.*7000 BC) show a shift to agricultural and pastoral economy.
Mureybit Late Natufian (*see page* 67) through Early Neolithic village site (*c.*9000-7500 BC) showing heavy dependence on wild grain collecting and hunting gazelles and onagers.
Bougras Late pre-Pottery Neolithic village (*c.*6500 BC) with both domestic grains and domestic goats and, especially, domestic sheep.

ANATOLIA
Çayönü Neolithic village (*c.*7000 BC) with domestic grains and possibly domestic sheep.
Çatal Hüyük Large settlement (*c.*6500-5500 BC) heavily involved in obsidian exploitation and trade, with evidence of cattle veneration and domestication of cattle.

Wild einkorn (*Triticum boeticum*)

Domestic einkorn (*Triticum monococcum*)

Grains of wild einkorn

EARLY WHEAT
Wild einkorn, the progenitor of one of the earliest forms of domestic wheat, is still found throughout the Middle East. Domestic einkorn is distinguished by its larger seeds and tough stalk, which requires threshing for seed dispersal.

Wild emmer (*Triticum dicoccum*)

EARLY EMMER
Like einkorn, emmer (another early domestic wheat) differs from its wild ancestral form in its plumper seeds and non-shattering stalk. Unlike einkorn, its distribution is largely restricted to the Levant where, even today, it can be found in dense stands.

Grains of domestic emmer

Domestic emmer (*Triticum dicoccoides*)

-- Coastline of the period

Vegetation zones of the period

≡ Forest   ▨ Steppe grassland

▨ Subtropical woodland   ▥ Desert grassland

Map text: *Level = layer of debris left by successive occupants

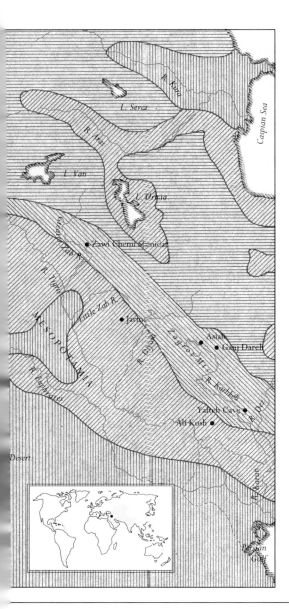

Skull of modern wild goat (Capra aegargus) from Iran

Large, sharp-keeled horn core

ZAGROS

Yafteh Cave Upper Paleolithic (c.18,000 BC) cave occupation with evidence of heavy dependence on wild sheep and goats.

Zawi Chemi Shanidar Open-air site (c.10,000 BC) with evidence of plant processing and heavy dependence on wild sheep and goats, with possible evidence of early management of sheep.

Asiab Open-air site (c.8000 BC) with evidence of heavy reliance on adult male goats.

Ganj Dareh Early levels* (c.7500 BC) suggest a transitory highland encampment with evidence of domestic grains and focus on exploitation of wild goats. Later levels may represent a permanent agricultural village, with heavy emphasis on herding domestic goats.

Ali Kosh Early levels (c.7500 BC) suggest a lowland encampment with evidence of cultivation of domestic grains and heavy emphasis on goats at a transitional stage between wild and domestic forms. Later levels (c.6700 BC) indicate a permanent village exploiting domestic grains and fully domestic goats and sheep, although wild hunted game continue to play a major role.

Jarmo Village (c.6000 BC) with domestic grains, domestic sheep and goats, and early evidence of pig domestication.

Today's landscape in southern Mesopotamia

DAMAGING EFFECTS *left*
Irreversible environmental changes accompanied the initial success and eventual collapse of farming and herding in fragile Middle Eastern environments. Irrigation and an increasing reliance on pastoral products dramatically reduced biological diversity, changing the face of the landscape forever.

Plaster sculpture, Ain Ghazal, Jordan

CULTURAL CONSEQUENCES *left*
Reliance on stored food that could be both shared and hoarded brought about profound social changes. Art forms such as this plaster sculpture from Ain Ghazal may be tied to new forms of social relations, family organization, or ritual in these sedentary communities.

ANIMAL DOMESTICATION

The earliest changes in the bodies and bones of domesticated animal species may have been side-effects of human selection — both conscious and unconscious — for certain behavioral characteristics, or the result of adaptations to the new conditions under which animals were kept. Sheep, goats, pigs, and cattle all show a reduction in size from the wild forms to the domestic — probably as a result of having a poorer diet, but also due to the selection of more docile, tractable, and smaller individuals for herding. In sheep, goats, and cattle, controlled breeding eliminated the need for the massive horns used in the wild for sexual display and combat, resulting in changes in horn size and shape.

Smaller, twisted, and flattened horn core

Skull of modern domestic goat (Capra hircus) from Iran

EFFECTS OF DOMESTICATION

The wild male bezoar goat has long, curved horns, which attract mates and fend off competitors. In domesticated herds, males did not need to compete for females, so animals with shorter, twisted horns were able to reproduce. This resulted in much smaller, flattened, and twisted horns. Changes such as these help archaeologists distinguish the remains of wild animals from domesticates.

BONE STRUCTURE *below*

The bones of the now extinct aurochs (wild ox) are larger than those of its domestic descendants. The diminutive size of the second phalanx (toe bone) of domestic cattle from the 5th millennium BC in northeastern Syria can be compared to that of wild cattle from the same region. The aurochs was hunted at the same time as this domestic specimen was being exploited for its milk, meat, or for use as a draft animal.

Second phalanx of wild Syrian cattle (Bos primagenius)   **Second phalanx of domestic Syrian cattle (Bos taurus)**

PART TWO

5000 BC
— TO —
500 BC

*New ways of life began to emerge as human populations
grew and diversified in different parts of the world. In some
regions, hunting and gathering gave way to farming — the
cultivation of plants and the raising of livestock.
The growth of the first cities was coupled with new types of
political organization — states and empires — and new
forms of cultural expression, notably the construction of
large ceremonial structures and richly furnished tombs.*

*Wall painting depicting a nobleman hunting birds on the Nile River,
accompanied by his wife and daughter. Egypt, c.1400 BC*

CHAPTER 7
FROM VILLAGE TO CITY
5000 - 3000 BC

Earliest city-states develop on the fertile Mesopotamian Plain

Mesopotamian traders and accountants invent a writing system

King Narmer creates a united Egypt and becomes the first pharaoh

Settlers from Mexico migrate to the Caribbean islands in dug-out canoes

Western European farmers construct large, stone chamber tombs

By 5000 BC the physical outline of the world had reached its present general form, and temperatures were as high as those of today, if not higher. Hunting and gathering were still the mainstay of life in many parts of the world, but farming villages had existed in northern China, the Middle East, Europe, the Nile Valley, and the hill country west of the Indus Valley for 1,000 years or more. Agriculture was also important in Central and South America. After 5000 BC a number of factors, including changes in social life, organization of craft production, and more efficient food production, caused farming villages in Mesopotamia, Egypt, and the Indus Valley region to develop into more complex societies, culminating in the birth of cities and, ultimately, in states and empires.

Urban development

In Mesopotamia, farming communities grew increasingly complex during the Late Ubaid period (c.5400-4300 BC), so called after the site of Tell al-Ubaid in southern Mesopotamia. The real urban revolution occurred during the Uruk period (c.4300-3100 BC), named after Uruk, one of the first (perhaps the very first) city-states in Mesopotamia. The growth of this and other city-states was made possible by the exploitation of the natural fertility of the Mesopotamian Plain, larger areas of which were gradually brought into cultivation

with more extensive canal systems. These transported water to the fields from the Tigris and Euphrates rivers. Tens of thousands of city-dwellers could then be supported on the abundant grain yields. The Mesopotamian Plain was deficient in many raw materials, however, including

SAHARAN SPIRIT-BEINGS
The abundant rock art of the Tassili Massif in the central Sahara includes mystical beings and fantastic animals. Little is known of the beliefs that lay behind them.

timber for building, hard stone for tools and weapons, and metals. These had to be imported from the upland regions of Lebanon, southern Anatolia in modern Turkey, and the western edge of the Iranian plateau. Extensive trading networks were established to carry these materials to the nascent Mesopotamian cities. Among the cities themselves, a system of accounting was developed to administer the lively trade in food and products, and this led to the invention of a pictographic system of writing around 3300 BC.

Mass production was another development, and everyday objects such as beveled-rim bowls were made in large numbers to a highly standardized pattern. Temples played a major role in city life, acting as economic as well as religious institutions. Built of mud brick and colorfully decorated, they were raised on platforms that overlooked the cities, symbolizing the protective role of the deity or deities specific to each city.

Developments in Mesopotamia were paralleled in other parts of the world, where ample natural resources fueled population growth and the consequent development of modest farming villages into walled towns and cities. This was especially true in the Nile Valley, where farming settlements first arose after the adoption of Middle Eastern wheat and barley in around 5000 BC, and in the hill country west of the Indus Valley.

KEY DATES 5000 - 3000 BC

5000 BC
Grain farming, Egypt

Copperworking, southeastern Europe

4500 BC
Megalithic tombs,
western Europe

4300 BC
Cotton
cultivation,
Mexico

4000 BC
First temple-pyramids, Peru

Introduction of plow,
Europe and Middle East

3300 BC
Invention of writing, Mesopotamia

3100 BC
Narmer becomes first pharaoh of Egypt

| 5000 BC | 4500 BC | 4000 BC | 3500 BC | 3000 BC |

DECORATED POTTERY
Early pottery from the Ukraine was often of high quality, and by 4000 BC large urns were sometimes decorated with elaborate painted patterns, such as this red geometric design.

Complex Asian societies
The farming communities in the hills west of the Indus Valley were forerunners of the cities that arose in the Indus Valley itself in the centuries that followed. In these village settlements, skilled crafts people manufactured fine painted pottery and copper artifacts from the 5th millennium BC. The size and prosperity of these communities increased from around 4000 BC, as harvests improved because of the introduction of irrigation techniques.

Sign possibly meaning first day

Sign for barley

Sign for bowl or food

Crescents possibly represent numbers

ADMINISTRATIVE RECORDS
The pictographs on this Mesopotamian clay tablet, which dates to before 3000 BC, represent the earliest known stage in the invention of writing. They may record crop yields.

HUNTERS' TOOL
The atlatl (spear-thrower) provided leverage to increase the speed and force with which a spear could be thrown.

Farther north in East Asia, agriculture was slowly adopted by a growing number of communities, gradually becoming the mainstay of life throughout most of the region. In northern China, one of the earliest regions of grain cultivation, farmers experimented with different varieties of wild grains. Larger and more sophisticated societies were developing in this area; they were skilled in jade carving and the manufacture of finely decorated pottery vessels. Their villages were built to a more orderly plan than earlier ones, with distinct residential, workshop, and

Prismatic flakes of obsidian

Obsidian core

RAZOR-SHARP TOOLS
A natural volcanic glass, obsidian can be flaked to give a razor-sharp edge. It was the favored material for tools in Mexico.

burial areas. These were socially complex societies, in which differences in individual wealth and status were reflected by the objects placed in graves – those of important individuals contain intricate jade carvings, beads, and cups. Careful attention was paid to the alignment of the deceased in relation to the four cardinal points, as this was believed to ensure an easy passage into the next world.

Unification of Egypt
In Egypt, a group of walled towns in the south (Upper Egypt) formed the core, in the 4th millennium BC, of a small state that grew in prosperity and power as the centuries passed. In around 3100 BC the ruler of this southern state, King Narmer, successfully attacked and conquered the Nile Delta region in the north (Lower Egypt), creating a unified kingdom and becoming Egypt's first pharaoh. This marked the end of the Predynastic period (c.5000–3100 BC).

5000 - 3000 BC

Hunters and cattle herders

The Sahara was too dry to allow the establishment of villages and towns, but groups of hunters and cattle herders roamed the semiarid grasslands around the high central Saharan plateaus and those of the Sahel strip bordering the southern edge of the desert. On the plateaus, these nomadic groups continued to leave a record of their presence in rock paintings. In certain areas, notably the wind-sculpted rock formations of the Sefar region, the subjects of the paintings included not only herds of cattle, but also white-painted depictions of mystical and fantastic creatures, perhaps spirits or demons. Spirit-beings were also a common subject in the Australian figurative rock art that proliferated throughout that continent after the end of the last Ice Age.

American communities

Farming became gradually more important in the life of Andean and Mesoamerican communities, although it was practiced only at seasonal camps; permanent villages did not appear until the 3rd millennium BC. Most communities in other regions of America continued to rely wholly or in part on hunting and gathering. Copper was used in a limited way by North American groups living in the Great Lakes region by 3000 BC, but it was only later that knowledge of metallurgy was acquired in Central and South America. In the north, complex communities arose in previously unoccupied regions of northern Labrador, tapping the rich resources of land and sea mammals. Meanwhile, in the tropics, migrating groups from the mainland set out in log canoes to colonize the Caribbean islands.

Innovations in Europe

In eastern Europe, farming villages of rectangular houses remained the most common type of settlement, although increasingly they were enclosed by protective ditches or wooden barriers. Pottery became more sophisticated and was often decorated with painted designs, sometimes in two or three colors. At the same time, eastern European communities began to use Balkan copper to make tools and ornaments. Around 4000 BC, the introduction of the plow made farming methods more efficient and so helped to increase the amount of agricultural land that could be worked.

In western Europe, the most distinctive remains of the period are stone-built burial chambers, most of which were originally covered by mounds of earth or rubble. Many incorporated megaliths (large stones, from the Greek *megas*, "big," and *lithos*, "stone"), some of which were engraved with decorative patterns. These tombs were often used as burial places for dozens or even hundreds of bodies. Skulls and other bones may have been removed from the chambers for use in ceremonies outside, but there is little direct evidence of the beliefs that lay behind such rituals. Elsewhere in Europe other burial traditions were followed, including individual burials in cemeteries.

AMERICAS

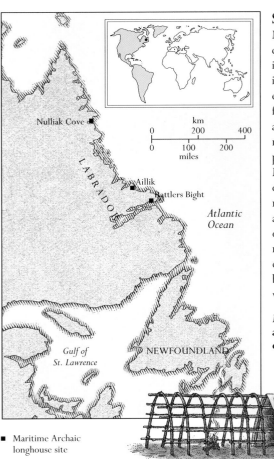

■ Maritime Archaic longhouse site

SUBARCTIC LONGHOUSES

Maritime Archaic Indian cultures spread north from what is now the Gulf of St. Lawrence into northern Labrador, at the edge of the expanding coniferous forest. The rich resources of the area, such as caribou, sea mammals, fish, and sea birds, provided abundant food. Maritime Archaic Indian cultures developed technologies for making harpoons, large boats, and burial mounds. They traded over long distances from settlements of communal longhouses, each of which had rooms for between 8 and 30 families and were up to 300 feet long.

Maritime Archaic longhouse and section showing construction, Labrador, Canada

CARIBBEAN MIGRATION

The colonization of the Caribbean islands began between 5000 BC and 4000 BC. Settlers probably came from the Yucatán peninsula, crossing the sea in dug-out canoes. Stone tools at the Levisa rock shelter in Cuba and the Barrera-Mordan site in the Dominican Republic indicate the presence of a hunter-gatherer society, but there is no evidence of permanent architecture from this period. Some Caribbean settlers used a wide variety of stone tools called Casimiran after one find site. Such tools have only been found on the larger of the Greater Antilles (Cuba, Jamaica, Hispaniola, and Puerto Rico).

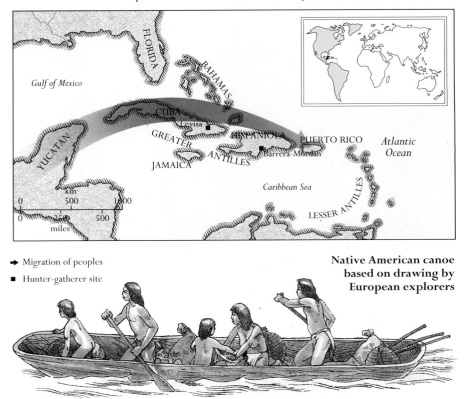

→ Migration of peoples
■ Hunter-gatherer site

Native American canoe based on drawing by European explorers

AFRICA

FARMING ON THE NILE FLOODPLAIN

During the Predynastic period in Egypt (c.5000-3100 BC), early farming communities like that at Nekhen, known for its distinctive pottery, flourished on the edges of the Nile floodplain as far as the First Cataract, including the Faiyum Basin. These villages gradually came together into increasingly large confederations headed by local rulers. At the same time, trading activity up and down the Nile increased. One confederation of villages was centered in Hieraconpolis in Upper Egypt, whose rulers prospered from trade, possibly mining gold deposits in the Eastern Desert. In around 3250 BC, the first walled towns were built at Hieraconpolis and Naqada. One of the rulers of this region, Narmer, unified Upper and Lower Egypt into a single kingdom in around 3100 BC, establishing a new capital at Memphis. This heralded the start of the Early Dynastic period (3100-2685 BC).

Predynastic pottery burial urn, Nekhen, Upper Egypt

-- Coastline of the period
▫ Walled town
≡ Area of fertile floodplain
■ Early farming community

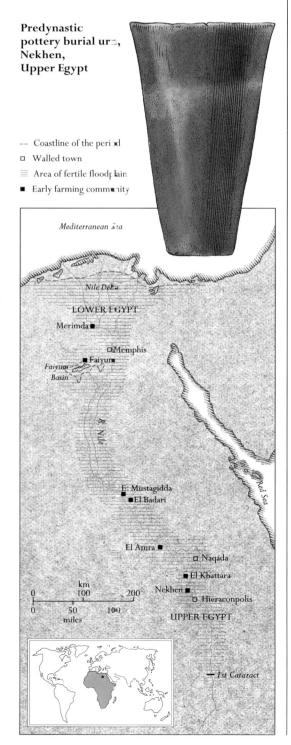

EUROPE

MEGALITHIC TOMBS

Substantial chamber tombs were built by agricultural communities in northern and western Europe around 4500 BC. Bodies were placed together in the chambers, indicating that the tombs were designed as communal burial places, and the dynamics of the work required for tomb construction suggest increasing social organization. The most elaborate, such as Newgrange in Ireland, were decorated with complex designs engraved on the stones of the chamber or passage that led to it, or on the curb around the mound.

Major chamber tomb site ■
Distribution of megalithic chamber tombs ≡

Megalithic chamber tomb, Poulnabrone, County Clare, Ireland

EAST ASIA & AUSTRALASIA

AUSTRALIAN ROCK ART

Australian rock art after the end of the last Ice Age (around 10,000 years ago) is distinguished by the development of a figurative style and greater regional diversity. Simple figurative paintings and petroglyphs (rock engravings) are characterized by outline or filled-in silhouettes of animals and humans. The prolific petroglyphs of the Pilbara include dynamic scenes of hunting, fighting, and lovemaking. The complex figurative style concentrated more on decoration, using fine polychrome linework. The so-called "X-ray" paintings in Arnhem Land depict the internal organs or bones of fish and other creatures. The Wandjina cloud-spirits in the Kimberley are portrayed with haloed heads, eyes, and noses, but no mouths.

≡ Area of rock art sites
△ Simple figurative style
○ Complex figurative style
▫ Both simple and complex style

Simple figurative rock art, Magnificent Shelter, Quinkan, Australia

5000-4000 BC

FOOD & ENVIRONMENT

SHELTER & ARCHITECTURE

AMERICAS

MAIZE DOMESTICATION
The earliest cultivation of maize occurred in Mexico between 4500 and 3500 BC. The domesticated plant was derived from teosinte, a native wild grass. Numerous and widespread archaeological finds indicate that several varieties of maize were experimented with and improved around this time throughout Mesoamerica.

Maize cob fragment, enlarged to show kernels

GROUPED PITHOUSES
Hunter-gatherers in northeastern California built small clusters of semi-subterranean dwellings, or pithouses, each with a single room and hearth. The superstructure consisted of a framework of poles covered with brush and a layer of soil.

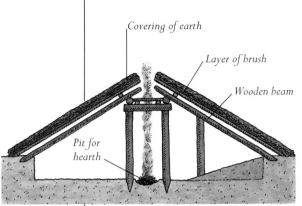

Covering of earth
Layer of brush
Wooden beam
Pit for hearth

Cross-section of pithouse, Surprise Valley, California

EAST ASIA & AUSTRALASIA

WET RICE FARMING
In China, rice cultivation was well established in the Yangtze River delta by 5000 BC. Large quantities of cultivated rice and bone tilling tools have been found at Hemudu in the delta. Rice was ideally suited to Monsoon Asia, and with time became the staple crop throughout the area.

As well as being highly nutritious, rice is self-fertilizing, producing up to three crops a year. Wet rice farming, so called because the rice is grown in submerged paddy fields, had a decisive influence on rural society: the work was labor-intensive, but the need to build dykes, dams, and canals for irrigation led to organized cooperation on a scale unknown in other types of agricultural or pastoral societies.

SHELTER FROM THE RAINS
The large, shady rock shelter at Garnawala in the Northern Territory of Australia was used by family groups who camped there during the wet season and decorated the walls with paintings of ancestors from the mythical past. The dry interior and soft earth floor made it ideal for use as sleeping quarters. Many stone tools for chopping, cutting, scraping, and engraving were manufactured just outside the shelter.

Wall paintings, Garnawala, Australia

MIDDLE EAST & SOUTH ASIA

AGRICULTURAL INNOVATIONS
At Mehrgarh, in the hill country west of the Indus Valley, a number of innovations in cultivation occurred during this period. Western Asiatic emmer wheat was crossed with local goatsface grass to produce bread-wheat, and Indian dwarf wheat was also cultivated. Other domesticated crops at Mehrgarh included dates. Evidence of cotton plants suggests the beginnings of textile production.

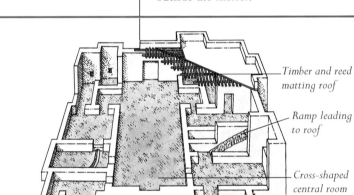

Timber and reed matting roof
Ramp leading to roof
Cross-shaped central room

TRIPARTITE HOUSES
Throughout Mesopotamia during the Late Ubaid period (c. 5400-4300 BC) mud-brick houses were arranged in a tripartite plan. A large rectangular or cross-shaped room ran the full width of the house, with rows of smaller rooms on each side. The house illustrated here stood at the center of Tell Madhhur, a village of about a dozen houses.

Cutaway of tripartite house, Tell Madhhur, Iraq

EUROPE

FOREST CLEARANCE
In the temperate regions of Europe, the early agriculturalists were forest-dwellers who cleared the forest or selected areas of open ground to cultivate their crops. Rings were cut through the bark and into the wood of trees that were too large to fell, such as oak or elm. This killed the tree, allowing light to reach crops underneath. Smaller trees and scrub were cleared by hand, using polished axes of flint or specially selected hard stone from upland regions such as the Alps and the English Lake District. These were some distance from the prime lowland farming areas, and a lively trade in axes developed from uplands to lowlands. In addition to its utilitarian role in forest clearance and woodworking, the axe became an important status symbol, and many examples were carefully finished to serve as attractive prestige goods.

PASSAGE GRAVES
The early farmers of western Europe developed a distinctive burial tradition involving the construction of megalithic (large standing stone) or dry-stone chambered tombs covered by a mound. The most famous of these are the passage graves, where a burial chamber within the mound was reached by a passage, allowing other corpses to be interred or bones from earlier burials to be removed, possibly for ceremonies outside the tomb.

Entrance to passage grave

Burial mound, Dissignac, France

AFRICA

CROP DOMESTICATION
Wheat and barley were first cultivated in the eastern Sahara and the Nile Valley around 5000 BC. The new food source soon assumed great importance along the Nile, where domesticated crops quickly became a staple. Distinctive grindstones were used to prepare grain. These developed from earlier types of grindstones made for the processing of wild seeds.

Upper and lower grindstones, Egypt

TEMPORARY DWELLINGS
From around 5000 BC nomadic cattle herders began to range widely over the semiarid grasslands of the Sahara, Sahel, and Nubia, grazing their herds over enormous areas. They lived with their herds in small camps of dome-shaped huts protected by a thorn fence to keep out lions. The huts were made with a light framework of saplings and thatched with long grass. They were never permanent dwellings and were made from whatever materials were at hand, since the herders were constantly on the move, rotating their herds from one grazing ground to another, and making sure they were watered regularly.

TECHNOLOGY & INNOVATION

FISHING TECHNIQUES

The rivers of northwestern North America were fished intensively. Fishermen caught salmon and other migrating fish in gill nets (nets suspended vertically in the water) or speared them from platforms above rapids. River pebbles were chipped so that they could be more easily bound to the gill nets to weight them.

River pebble net weight, Hood River, Oregon

POTTERY TECHNOLOGY

The production of pottery became increasingly specialized in China during this period. Finely decorated wares were made for ritual purposes such as funerary offerings. Household pots like the self-filling water jar reflect sophisticated technology; when submerged in running water by a rope pulled through the handles, it automatically adjusted its own angle, allowing continuous filling.

Self-filling water jar, Banpo, China

PAINTED POTTERY

Baskets with a waterproof lining of bitumen were replaced by pottery vessels at Mehrgarh by 5000 BC. Over the next 1,000 years, fine plain and painted wares were produced at Mehrgarh and at other sites nearby.

Pottery vessel, Mehrgarh, Indus Valley

EARLY METALLURGY

Metallurgy was discovered in southeastern Europe soon after 5000 BC. Copper and gold were the first metals to be worked, and soon copper was being cast in molds to produce beads, daggers, and heavy tools such as axes with a shafthole for a wooden handle. Deposits of these metals were easily accessible in rivers and streams which flowed from the Balkan Mountains. Once these were exhausted, new supplies were sought, and by 4500 BC, mining for metals had begun.

BURNISHED POTTERY

The Badarian people (c. 5000-4500 BC) of the Nile Valley are known for their finely made, semicircular polished bowls. Some are red or black, while others, fired with their rims buried in sand, are red with black rims. Many were decorated with ripples produced by dragging a comb over the surface of the soft clay, and most were also highly burnished to give a smooth, polished surface.

Badarian pot, Egypt

ART & RITUAL

TEMPLE PYRAMID

Temples and monuments for ritual purposes were constructed in the Andean region of South America around 4000 BC. El Aspero, located in the Supe Valley on the north central coast of Peru, is one of the oldest religious structures in the Americas. Standing on a raised platform, it consists of a pyramid in which human burials and many buried offerings such as dogs and guinea pigs have been found. The building faces the sea, and may have been dedicated to some form of worship associated with the sea.

ORIENTATION OF BURIALS

The Chinese believed that earthly well-being depended on achieving harmony with the heavenly sphere. From earliest times, the four cardinal points were symbolized by mythical creatures with supernatural powers. To ensure an easy passage into the next world, the corpse of the deceased had to be properly aligned; in one grave of this period the corpse was placed on a north-south axis flanked by a stone dragon (symbol of the east) and a stone tiger (symbol of the west).

HUMAN FIGURINES

During the Late Ubaid period in Mesopotamia, baked clay figurines of human forms were sometimes deposited in graves. Although their heads appear reptilian, this seems to have been a stylistic convention rather than an attempt to portray hybrid beings. There is no indication that they were intended as images of deities, but the presence of offerings in the graves suggests belief in an afterlife.

"Lizard-headed" figurine, Ur, Iraq

EARLY ICONS

Baked clay figurines are one of the few sources of information about the beliefs of the early farmers of eastern Europe. Most of the figurines are of the female form, but this striking figure from Szegvár-Tusköves in Hungary is clearly male. The sickle that he carries over his shoulder may be a mark of social status or the symbol of a particular deity.

Seated figurine, Szegvár-Tusköves, Hungary

BIRD DEITY

This clay figurine of a female deity with a birdlike face may be a forerunner of the vulture goddess Nekhbet, protective deity of the Predynastic peoples (c. 5000-3100 BC) of Lower Egypt.

Female figurine, Egypt

4000-3000 BC

33,000 BC

	FOOD & ENVIRONMENT	SHELTER & ARCHITECTURE

AMERICAS

CULTIVATED COTTON

There are two species of domesticated cotton in the Americas, each with a different origin. One, *Gossypium hirsutum*, was domesticated in the Tehuacan Valley, Mexico, by *c.*4300 BC, and was later traded north into southwestern North America. The other, *G. barbadense*, was domesticated in Peru and Ecuador *c.*3300-3100 BC.

Burst cotton boll

BRUSH AND GRASS HUTS

Small huts were built many times a year by hunter-gatherers in south-western North America. These may have been domed or conical dwellings, with brush and grass tied to a lattice framework. Camps often consisted of a pair of small huts, only 3 to 6 feet apart, with a shared outdoor area that sometimes included a single hearth.

Branches tied together
Walls covered in layers of grass

Small hut, New Mexico

EAST ASIA & AUSTRALASIA

FRUIT GROWING

Different species of wild seeds found in storage pots on the North China Plain suggest that local settlers were conducting experiments to improve their domesticated grain crop. Meanwhile, in the east, farmers supplemented their diet by growing tubers and fruit trees – remains of peaches, watermelons, water chestnuts, and possibly beans have been found.

Branch of peach tree

VILLAGE PLANNING

The villages occupied by farming communities in northern China around 4000 BC were laid out according to a plan, with residential districts separated from workshop and burial areas. In the large village of Banpo in Shaanxi province, which covered over 12 acres, the central dwelling area was enclosed by a ditch 16 to 20 feet deep and wide. Within this area were storage pits, animal pens, and small and medium-sized houses of a fairly permanent nature clustered around a central longhouse. Outside the ditch to the east were pottery kilns and workshops. The adult graveyard lay to the north, while infants and children were buried in pottery vessels between the dwellings.

MIDDLE EAST & SOUTH ASIA

IRRIGATION METHODS

Agriculture in the arid Indo-Iranian borderlands took a great step forward around 4000 BC with the development of garaband dams. These were designed to catch and store rainwater runoff from the mountains for use in simple irrigation. Settlements in the region grew in size and complexity, and monumental architecture developed at some sites, notably at Mundigak in Afghanistan.

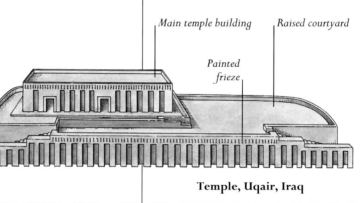

Main temple building
Raised courtyard
Painted frieze

Temple, Uqair, Iraq

DECORATED TEMPLES

In Mesopotamia during the Uruk period (*c.*4300-3100 BC) temples often followed the tripartite plan of houses from the Late Ubaid period (*c.*5400-4300 BC), but with much more elaborate wall decoration. The temples had complicated buttresses and niches and were raised on platforms. The labor invested in their construction and maintenance suggests that religion was a powerful force in the organization of society.

EUROPE

SIMPLE PLOW

Early European farmers relied on the hoe to till and weed their fields, but much greater efficiency was achieved when the simple ox-drawn plow, or ard, was introduced in about 4000 BC. This new tool made it easier to work heavy soil, and therefore opened up new areas for cultivation. Marks in the ground, preserved beneath later burial mounds, show that the ard made only a narrow, shallow furrow, and cross-plowing was necessary to break up the soil effectively. Wheat and barley were the staple crops, and legumes such as peas and beans were also grown, but wild nuts and fruits still formed a significant part of the diet.

Frame of oak timbers
Walls of daubed clay
Raised wooden floor

House, Hornstaad-Hornle, Germany

TIMBER STRUCTURES

Farmers in Europe lived in timber houses, which had to be rebuilt frequently. In one village in Germany, tree rings in the timbers reveal that the first houses were built of mature oaks in 3586 BC. Forty years later they were rebuilt, but only small oaks around 40 years old were available. For the final phase of building in 3507 BC, large oaks were brought in from farther away, indicating that local supplies were now exhausted.

AFRICA

ANTELOPE-HUNTING

Farmers living by the Nile River supplemented their diet by fishing in the river and hunting on the dry grasslands and water-courses of the desert margin. Among the animals hunted was the antelope, as shown by this box of the Gerzean culture, which was based in Upper Egypt around 3400-3100 BC.

Gerzean pottery box, Egypt

SMALL VILLAGES

Farmers of the Gerzean culture cultivated the floodplain of the Nile River in Upper Egypt, building small villages on the high ground that overlooked the river. The houses had walls of wattle and daub (interwoven twigs and sticks covered with clay), which thickened towards the base. The roofs were made of mud and thatch, and doors and windows had beams of timber.

Model of Gerzean house, Egypt

200 BC

4000 - 3000 BC

TECHNOLOGY & INNOVATION

IMPROVING WEAPONS

Weights made of ground bone or stone were attached to the handles of atlatls (spear-throwers) to increase their efficiency. The mechanical advantage of the added weight caused spears to travel faster and farther, and to hit the target with greater impact than a simple hand-thrown spear.

**Stone atlatl weights,
Indian Knoll site, Kentucky**

SPECIALIZED TOOLS

A significant change occurred around 3000 BC in Australian tools. Earlier tools were large, hand-held, multipurpose implements. Specialized small tools suddenly appeared without obvious precursors, so the technology may have spread from Asia. They included carefully flaked microliths (tiny stone blades) resembling penknives. Some were hafted onto a handle using resin and were used for cutting and engraving; others were mounted as barbs on spears.

EARLIEST WRITING

Writing was invented during the 4th millennium BC in Mesopotamia. These clay tablets from Syria, which date to around 3300 BC, may belong to the earliest phase. The circles represent the number 10, and the pictographs show animals: a goat and possibly a sheep. Tablets found at Uruk in southern Mesopotamia may be from a later stage: they bear impressions of just the heads of animals, suggesting that pictographs were becoming more stylized.

Circle represents the number 10

Clay tablets, Tell Brak, Syria

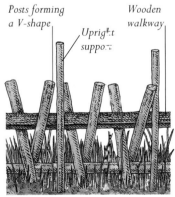

Posts forming a V-shape *Wooden walkway*

Upright support

CONNECTING PATHWAYS

In wet and marshy lowlands, European farmers built timber trackways to link areas of drier ground. The oldest of these, built in the winter of 3807-3806 BC, is the Sweet Track in southwestern England, a raised walkway across 5,900 feet of reed swamp from the edge of the Somerset Levels to Westhay Island.

Sweet Track, Somerset, England

CEREMONIAL WEAPONS

During the Predynastic period (c.5000-3100 BC) Egyptians were expert stoneworkers who fashioned superb ceremonial knives and daggers. Large flint flakes formed the blanks from which these delicate, flat-sided artifacts, often with subtle curves, were fashioned. Many were mounted in bone or ivory handles, which were themselves engraved with animal figures representing the family group of the owner and other symbolic motifs.

Handle

**Flint knife,
Naqada, Egypt**

ART & RITUAL

ANIMAL ART

The making of split-twig figurines, using a technique similar to basketry, was a characteristic craft of southwestern North America around 3500-1500 BC. The figurines usually represented four-legged animals, probably deer. They are often found near hunting equipment in dry cave deposits in upland areas, and are rarely found in domestic settings.

**Split-twig figurine,
Coconino County, Arizona**

CREATORS OF THE LANDSCAPE

The Aborigines believed that rainbow serpents (mythical snakelike beings) created the landscape along their "dreaming track" as they writhed inland from the sea. The first rock paintings of rainbow serpents date to around 6,000 years ago, when the serpent Gorrondolmi and his wife are said to have "painted themselves on the wall" at Wirlin-gunyang at the end of their dreaming track.

**Rainbow serpents,
Wirlin-gunyang, Australia**

LOST-WAX CASTING

The distribution of luxury goods was controlled by the ruling elite, both in the cities of Mesopotamia and in the less hierarchical societies in Israel, Lebanon, and Syria. The hoard of prestige objects from Nahal Mishmar in Israel was cast from pure copper, or an alloy of copper and other metals, using the lost-wax technique. A prototype was modeled in wax and covered with clay; the wax was then melted away, leaving the clay mold ready for molten metal.

Status objects, Nahal Mishmar, Israel

MEGALITHIC TOMB ART

In some parts of western Europe megalithic tombs were decorated with carved designs, sometimes of axes or female breasts, but most often abstract. At Newgrange in Ireland the stones of the burial chamber and of the curb around the mound were decorated with elaborate designs of concentric spirals, chevrons, and labyrinths.

**Decorated stone,
Newgrange,
Ireland**

SYMBOLS OF POWER

This palette, carved on both faces, was a symbol of power and may record the unification of Upper and Lower Egypt by King Narmer in around 3100 BC. The pharaoh, wearing the crown of Upper Egypt, is smiting his enemies, while the falcon symbol of the god Horus, holds the people of Lower Egypt captive by a nose ring.

Detail and palette of Narmer, Egypt

THE URUK CIVILIZATION

33,000 BC

Uruk in southern Mesopotamia was already an unusually large settlement by around 3500 BC, but the centuries that followed brought a truly spectacular development. Expanding to cover 1,000 acres, six times its previous size, Uruk may well have been the first city in the world. An unprecedented concentration of people gave rise to a completely new way of life. Despite the fertility of the alluvial soil around the city and an extensive system of irrigation canals, it became necessary to import food from farther afield. Trade was essential for the city's survival, and the impact of developments at Uruk spread along trade routes into northern Syria and eastward into Iran. By 3000 BC, the city stood at the heart of a network of interlinked Middle Eastern communities.

-- Coastline and rivers of the period

MESOPOTAMIAN SETTLEMENTS
Following the rise of Uruk in southern Mesopotamia, other settlements, and later cities, evolved throughout the Middle East. Evidence of early clay tablets, beveled-rim bowls, and cone mosaics has been found in these later cities.

CONE MOSAIC COURT *below*
The city of Uruk grew up around two religious complexes: Kullaba, devoted to the worship of the supreme sun god, An, and, about a quarter mile to the east, Eanna, where Inanna (later called Ishtar), the goddess of love and war, was worshiped. The buildings that formed the Eanna complex were constructed in accordance with complicated plans. Like the Cone Mosaic Court, these buildings were elaborately decorated with cone mosaics and intricate niches. The prestige of the city's ruler was expressed in the temple architecture and in the exotic, rare materials, precious metals, and gems that were brought to the temple from distant regions.

DOMESTIC ARTIFACTS *below*
One of the most characteristic domestic artifacts of the Uruk culture was the beveled-rim bowl, a vessel for everyday use made of straw-tempered clay and mass-produced in molds. The bowls were widely traded throughout the Middle East.

Beveled rim

Rough finish shows hasty production method

Naked servants bring offerings for the temple

NATURALISM AND VITALITY IN ART *below*
This fragment of a small stone cup only 5 inches high shows two bearded figures; one is wrestling with two bulls. The wrestling scene is sometimes interpreted as a symbolic victory of humans over the forces of nature. The scene recurs in later Mesopotamian art, where it has been identified with an epic about Gilgamesh, one of the kings of Uruk. This epic, a masterpiece of early Mesopotamian literature, tells of Gilgamesh's journey from Uruk in search of eternal life, and the hazards he overcomes on the way.

Sheep, goats, and crops created Uruk's wealth

Bearded figure

Bearded figure wrestling

Bull's head

GODS AND RULERS
Art was used as a political device to reinforce the authority of the ruler. At the top of this stone vase (*above*), found in the temple area of Uruk, the ruler of the city is shown in front of the goddess of love and war, Inanna. The close association of the ruler with one of the city's two principal deities reinforces his position of authority over the lower levels in Uruk society.

Reconstruction of Cone Mosaic Court, Uruk

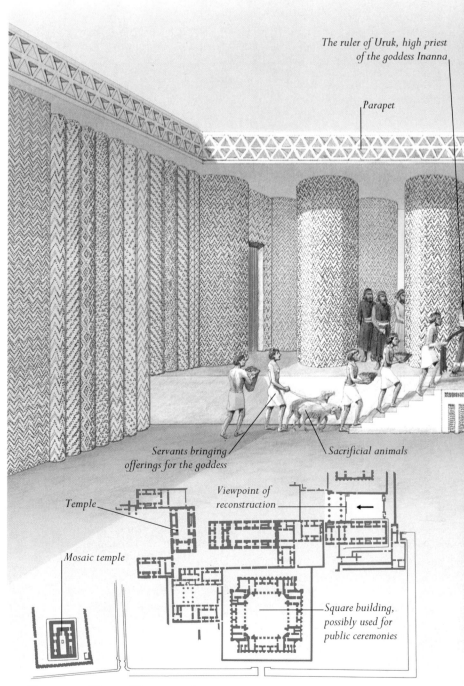

The ruler of Uruk, high priest of the goddess Inanna

Parapet

Servants bringing offerings for the goddess

Sacrificial animals

Temple

Viewpoint of reconstruction

Mosaic temple

Square building, possibly used for public ceremonies

PLAN OF URUK TEMPLE AREA
The Cone Mosaic Court was part of a sacred precinct. Beyond it were several buildings, which have been identified as temples.

MESOPOTAMIAN WRITING

The earliest writing in Mesopotamia took the form of simple marks scratched onto the surface of a hollow clay ball. Small clay tokens that represented commodities such as sheep, goats, or jars of oil were placed inside the clay ball as a record of a commercial transaction. Marks were scratched onto the surface of the clay ball as a record of its contents. At first, the tokens themselves represented the commodities – the notation on the exterior of the container was simply a label of the contents. The tokens themselves became redundant once the notation came into general use. The clay ball then evolved into a flatter clay tablet, and the scratched notations formed the basis of the earliest writing system in the world.

OFFICIAL INSCRIPTIONS

The inscriptions on the Blau monuments, named after a previous owner, Dr. A. Blau, are in an early form of cuneiform script (*see below*). The circles and broad lines are metrological measures. Like all early writing tablets and pictographs, the Blau monuments were probably official documents.

Pictographic accounting sign

EARLY PICTOGRAPHS *right*

A pictographic writing system was used by temple bureaucrats and merchants to keep a record of revenues and transactions. The deep circles impressed in the clay are numerals. This clay tablet is probably an accounting text, but scholars have yet to find the key to its translation.

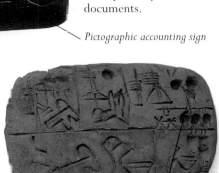

Head and bow sign　　*Pictographic numeral*

CUNEIFORM SCRIPTS

Clay was the most affordable and readily available writing material in Mesopotamia. Since it is difficult to scratch signs onto baked clay, scribes learned instead to impress wet clay, using a rectangular-ended stylus. This created the cuneiform script (called after its wedge-shaped marks) that developed over the centuries, until the pictographic origin of the script was no longer recognizable. Most of the signs used were derived from identifiable pictures of real objects.

PICTOGRAPHIC SIGN c.3100 BC						
INTERPRETATION	Star	Stream	Barley	Bull's head	Bowl	Head and bowl
EARLY CUNEIFORM SIGN c.2400 BC						
LATER CUNEIFORM SIGN c.700 BC						
MEANING	God, sky	Water, seed, son	Barley	Ox	Food, bread	To eat

---

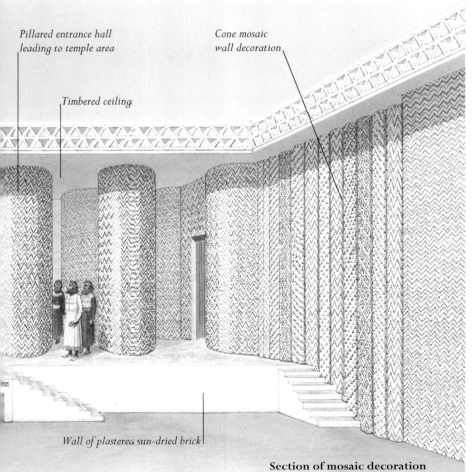

Pillared entrance hall leading to temple area

Cone mosaic wall decoration

Timbered ceiling

Wall of plastered sun-dried brick

CONE MOSAICS

A new form of decoration, developed in Uruk, used colored cones made of stone or baked clay. These were pressed into the wet plaster surface of a wall; in temples they were grouped to create regular patterns. Baked-clay cones have been found in other settlements throughout the Middle East, indicating the widespread influence of this innovative technique.

Clay cone

Section of mosaic decoration

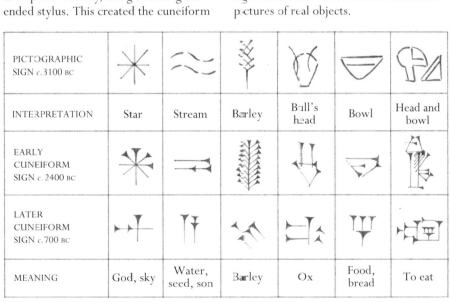

Color painted on flat end of cone　　*Wet plaster into which clay cone is pushed*

SEALS AND DESIGNS *below*

Around 3400 BC, temple bureaucrats in southern Mesopotamia invented a new cylinder seal that replaced the simple stamp seal. It was easy to roll over soft clay to produce a continuous design and could be applied to larger areas such as sealed doors. Cylinder seals represented specific themes but were not inscribed. They may have been used in an official, rather than a personal, capacity.

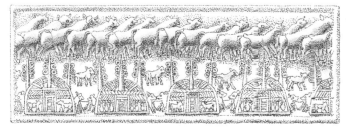

Roll-out impression of cylinder seal　　　　**Cylinder seal**

CHAPTER 8
AN AGE OF MONUMENTS
3000-2000 BC

Mesopotamian ruler establishes the world's first empire

The great pyramids are constructed for Egyptian kings

First cities arise in the Indus Valley

Peruvian coastal communities build massive earthen temple-platforms

Stone circles are erected by western European farmers

A rich diversity of human societies existed by 3000 BC. In some regions, hunter-gatherer groups continued to flourish; in others, farming villages were well established. The most dramatic development of the next 1,000 years was the formation of the first large states and empires. These grew out of rapidly expanding urban societies that were based in the fertile lands of southern Mesopotamia, the Nile Valley, and the Indus Valley. The unprecedented scale of social and economic organization required by these states, together with a more sophisticated cultural life, represented a new dynamic in human history.

INLAID MOSAIC DECORATION
A fine example of Mesopotamian art, this detail from the Royal Standard of Ur shows a musician holding a bull-headed lyre identical to one found in a tomb at Ur.

Mesopotamian city-states

Each city that evolved on the Mesopotamian Plain in the Uruk period (*c.*4300-3100 BC) was an independent city-state. Uruk was the first of these. Although separate and politically autonomous, the cities did share cultural traits such as language and religion with each other. One such city was Agade in Akkad in southern Mesopotamia, whose ruler, Sargon I, founded the Akkadian Dynasty *c.*2400 BC. The cities in Akkad and Sumer, which together constituted southern Mesopotamia, soon came under Akkadian rule – in effect, becoming the world's first empire.

Each Sumerian city had a mud-brick temple raised on a high platform, dedicated to its own city-god. In time, the raised temple developed into the stepped ziggurat, one of the earliest and most famous of which was built at the city of Ur around 2100 BC. Ur is also famous for its Royal Tombs, which yielded some of the finest pieces of early Mesopotamian art, including the Royal Standard of Ur, a box inlaid with shell and lapis-lazuli mosaic. Many details are known about life during this period from texts inscribed on clay tablets – these include historical chronicles, religious texts, business accounts, and poetry.

Similar developments were taking place on the Anatolian plateau in modern Turkey, which was linked to Mesopotamia by trade. Finds of skillfully worked items of precious metal suggest the emergence of a ruling elite by 2500 BC, and by 2000 BC cities were established.

LUXURY ITEMS
The growing wealth of a ruling elite in Anatolia can be seen in objects such as this silver bull with gold inlay.

CRESCENT-SHAPED TOOL
Flaked flint tools like this were used by hunter-gatherers in North America at this time.

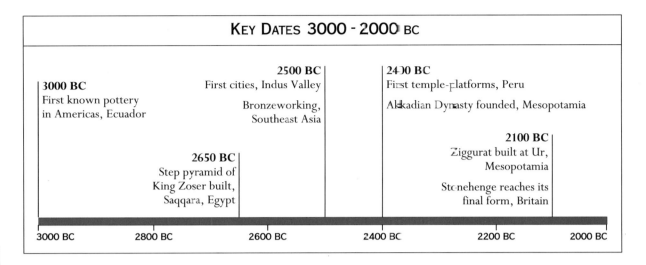

3000 BC
First known pottery
in Americas, Ecuador

2500 BC
First cities, Indus Valley

Bronzeworking,
Southeast Asia

2400 BC
First temple-platforms, Peru

Akkadian Dynasty founded, Mesopotamia

2650 BC
Step pyramid of
King Zoser built,
Saqqara, Egypt

2100 BC
Ziggurat built at Ur,
Mesopotamia

Stonehenge reaches its
final form, Britain

| 3000 BC | 2800 BC | 2600 BC | 2400 BC | 2200 BC | 2000 BC |

HUMAN REPRESENTATIONS

The earliest known representations of humans in the
Americas are highly stylized stone figurines from
Valdivia, Ecuador, which date to around 3000 BC.

Early Egyptian cities

The farmland of the Nile Valley floodplain
provided economic support for the early
civilization, which gathered momentum
soon after the unification of Egypt around
3100 BC. The development of writing was
linked to the growth of the first cities; the
need for administrative records provided
the stimulus that led to the development
of hieroglyphic writing.

The tombs of the elite, including the
pyramids, were built at a distance from
habitable areas. The pyramids required
the mobilization of the entire Egyptian
state for their construction. The fact
that the major Egyptian monuments
of this period are tombs illustrates
the importance placed on proper
provision for the afterlife. The
survival of the physical body was
considered essential and led to the
first attempts at mummification.
Wealthy individuals also furnished
their tombs with painted models
and statues of themselves. These
were standardized in terms of color
– yellow for women and red for
men – and in the poses of the
individuals portrayed.

Indus Valley cities

The third civilization that developed
during this period was located in the Indus
Valley. The fertile soils of the valley were
crucial to the development and expansion
of cities around 2500 BC. Among the
largest and best known were Mohenjo-
Daro and Harappa, each covering about
148 acres, with a population of as many as
40,000 people. It is still unclear whether
each Indus city was an autonomous city-
state, as in Mesopotamia, or whether the
whole valley was united under one ruler,

HETEPHERES AND KATEP

Statues of affluent Egyptians were painted in
standard colors, the paler shade denoting that
wealthy women did not work outdoors.

Handle

*Characteristic
spiral decoration*

BURIAL URNS

In western China around 2500 BC, vessels like this
one from Gansu province were decorated with
swirling painted patterns and buried with the dead.

as in Egypt, but there certainly were
many shared cultural features,
including a standardized system of
weights and measures.

Asian crafts

Chinese farming communities
continued to develop new skills in
this period, including the raising of
silkworms and the production of silk
thread. Craftsmen of the Longshan
culture, named after the site of
Longshan on China's east coast,
invented the potter's wheel and soon
became expert at making eggshell-
thin pottery vessels and drinking
cups. Less delicate, but equally
striking, are painted burial urns from
western China, which date to around
2500 BC. In addition to these refined
pottery styles, advanced stoneworking techniques were also well
established, notably in the production
of ritual objects fashioned from jade
and other types of hard stone.

3000 - 2000 BC

Bronzeworking technology

Farther south, bronzeworking was introduced in mainland Southeast Asia by 2500 BC, and was well established by 2000 BC, with local deposits of copper and tin being developed. In China, bronzeworking only appeared a little before 2000 BC. Southeast Asian village communities were also becoming dependent on domesticated crops, notably rice, during this period. In contrast, communities in Japan continued to sustain themselves by hunting, gathering, and fishing, as did Aboriginal populations in Australia.

Permanent villages

In Mesoamerica around 2500 BC, permanent villages were starting to be established, and it may have been only at this time that their inhabitants began to rely entirely on cultivated plants. The pattern was repeated in the Peruvian Andes, also a major center of early farming in the Americas, where beans, squash, gourds, and peppers had been cultivated since around 8000 BC. The rise of the first farming villages in the Andes coincided with the initial cultivation of potatoes, later to become the region's staple crop. North American groups, however, continued to live by hunting and gathering in this period.

Peruvian temple-platforms

In several river valleys along central Peru's desert coast, major changes occurred toward the mid-3rd millennium BC, as shown by the construction of temple-platforms up to 33 feet high. The building of these earthworks required an unprecedented degree of labor organization, which points toward growing social complexity in the region. On the platforms stood stone temples with niches and friezes of molded clay. New crafts also evolved: the weaving of cotton textiles, and later, around 2000 BC, the manufacture of pottery. The impetus that provided the basis for these new developments was the successful harvesting of marine resources, principally shellfish, and the cultivation of such crops as beans and squash. These communities were also active in trade, which brought them such luxury items as brightly colored feathers from as far away as Amazonia.

Monumental henges

Stone circles and rows built at sites such as Stonehenge in England and Carnac in France were a key feature of north-western Europe in the 3rd millennium BC. In their way, these monuments are as impressive as the pyramids and temples of Egypt, Mesopotamia, and Peru. The final construction phase at Stonehenge, for example, when the great stone circle and trilithons (structures consisting of two upright stones with a third slab placed across the top) were erected, probably required more than 2 million hours of human labor to complete – clearly an enormous task for the small farming communities of southern Britain. Unlike the building of the pyramids at Giza or the ziggurat at Ur, however, it is not known how and by whom the massive project was organized.

AMERICAS

EARLY POTTERY

Clay, when shaped and fired, was used to make ornaments, toys, and containers for foodstuffs. By 2400 BC, at least three regions in the Americas had invented pottery independently of each other. At Stallings Island in Georgia, sherds tempered with plant fiber are dated to 2500 BC. In Mexico's Tehuacán Valley and Puerto Marquez region, early pottery finds are dated at 2400 BC. At Puerto Hormiga on the Caribbean coast and Valdivia on the Pacific coast of Ecuador, a well-developed pottery style existed by 3000 BC.

Pottery containers, Tehuacán Valley, Mexico

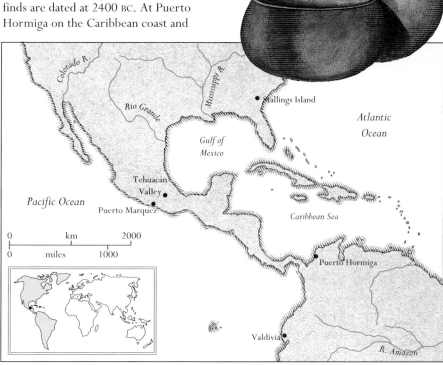

AFRICA

NILE VALLEY PYRAMIDS

The pyramids of Egypt are massive royal tombs that were built on the edge of the Western Desert overlooking the Nile Valley. The most famous pyramids are those built during the Old Kingdom period (2650-2150 BC) at Giza, Saqqara, and Dahshur. These stand opposite the site of Memphis, capital of Old Kingdom Egypt. Each pyramid formed part of a larger complex, including a waterside valley temple, a causeway leading from the valley temple to a mortuary temple at the base of the pyramid, smaller pyramids for the chief wives of the deceased, and rows of mastaba tombs (flat-topped, benchlike structures) for priests, nobles, and high-ranking officials. The mortuary temple housed cult offerings made in honor of the dead pharaoh.

-- Coastline of the period
▲ Pyramid site

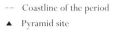

Step pyramid, Saqqara, Egypt

EUROPE

RITUAL CENTERS

The henge monuments of southern Britain were enclosures surrounded by a bank and ditch. Each henge served as a local ritual center. By 2500 BC, the Avebury center had outstripped the rest; 400 years later the remodeled Stonehenge supplanted Avebury as the major center of the region. The rituals enacted there may have been related to seasonal festivals.

For the construction of Stonehenge, sarsen (silicified sandstone) blocks, each weighing about 26 tons, were brought from the Marlborough Downs, 18 miles north of the site. The bluestone (bluegray sandstone) blocks used at Stonehenge may have been quarried in the Prescelly Mountains in Wales and carried to the site by boat, then transported on timber rollers for the final overland stage.

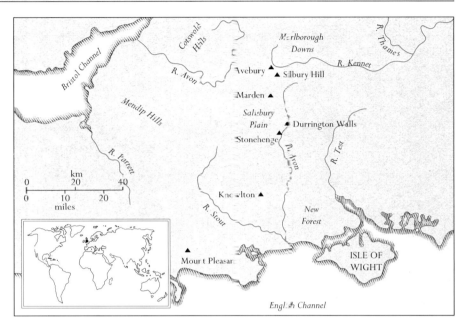

Stonehenge, Wiltshire, England

▲ Major henge monument

MIDDLE EAST & SOUTH ASIA

MESOPOTAMIAN ZIGGURATS

A ziggurat was an artificial mountain reaching toward the heavens, where the gods were thought to dwell. These massive brick-built structures dominated the cities of southern Mesopotamia and were of terraced design. Stairways led up to a temple on the summit, which was dedicated to a city's particular god. Ziggurats developed from earlier temples that had been built on platforms. The first true ziggurats with triple staircases were built by Ur-Nammu (2112-2095 BC), King of Ur. The most famous, dating to around 2100 BC, was at the site of Ur itself. Ziggurats were still being built by the Assyrians 1,500 years later, and the great ziggurat at Babylon may have provided the model for the biblical story of the Tower of Babel.

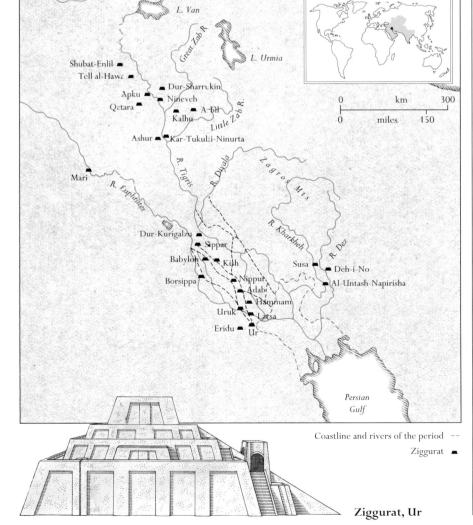

Coastline and rivers of the period --
Ziggurat ▲

Ziggurat, Ur

EAST ASIA & AUSTRALASIA

SOUTHEAST ASIAN RESOURCES

Mainland Southeast Asia has abundant resources of copper and tin, which when alloyed together produce bronze. It was not until about 2500 BC that rice-farming communities in the region, such as Phung Nguyen in northern Vietnam and Ban Chiang in northeastern Thailand, began to make bronze ornaments and tools including knives and spearheads. After 1000 BC, metalworking spread from the mainland to the islands of Southeast Asia, where it was practiced by existing groups of hunter-gatherers.

Bronze spearhead from a burial at Ban Chiang, Thailand

□ Tin   ■ Copper

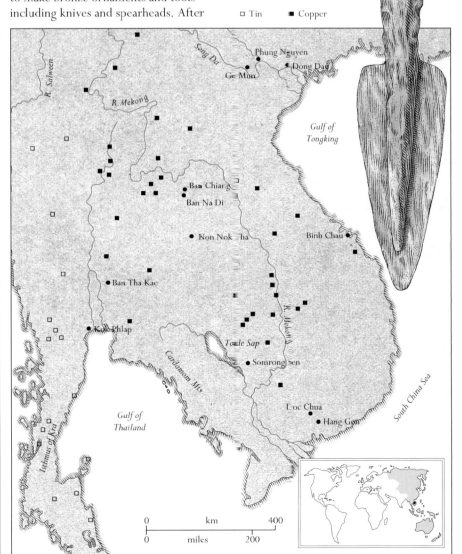

3000 - 2600 BC

FOOD & ENVIRONMENT	SHELTER & ARCHITECTURE

AMERICAS

RITUAL CROP

At lower elevations throughout the Andean region, coca was cultivated for use in rituals but was also used routinely by a large segment of the population. The mild effect produced by chewing the leaves, especially when taken with a small amount of lime, warded off hunger and fatigue from working at high altitude – often over 12,000 feet above sea level. Coca leaves are also rich in vitamin C and calcium.

Coca leaves

VILLAGE SOCIETIES

In the valleys of Peru's Pacific coast, populations organized themselves into hamlets and villages, practicing horticulture and textile crafts on a community basis. The Asia village site, on the central coast of Peru, is a typical example of this kind of small village society, with an economy based on fishing and horticulture.

EAST ASIA & AUSTRALASIA

ORIGINS OF SERICULTURE

In Chinese legend, farming and sericulture (the raising of silkworms for the production of silk) are inextricably connected. Both are attributed to the mythical hero-rulers of antiquity. Remains of half-cut cocoons and stone and pottery spindle whorls from Chinese settlements indicate that early farmers knew how to raise silkworms and utilize their thread by around 2700 BC.

Silkworm in mulberry leaves

COMMUNITY CENTERS

In China, large meeting houses were built in open areas in the middle of villages. This one, at Banpo in the north of the country, was about 66 feet long and 41 feet wide. The open area was encircled by small houses, their doors facing the center.

Thatched roof
Timber beams
Entrance tunnel
Rammed earth foundations

Large meeting house, Banpo, China

MIDDLE EAST & SOUTH ASIA

CROP SURPLUS

So successful were farmers in southern Mesopotamia that a substantial crop surplus was produced. Grain and textiles may have been traded in exchange for valuable goods from the mountains of Iran, such as gold, silver, lapis lazuli, and carnelian, and vessels of green or gray chlorite (a soft mineral rock) from southern Iran, like this one decorated with a snake deity.

Chlorite vessel, southern Iran

FLOOD-PROOF SETTLEMENTS

The fertile plains of the Indus Valley may have been difficult for farmers to settle at first, because of the risk of extensive river flooding. By the early 3rd millennium BC, however, pioneers had conquered the problem by building planned settlements with thick mud-brick walls that fortified them well against flood waters. Such early sites include Kot Diji and probably Mohenjo-Daro in the Indus Valley itself, and Kalibangan in the plains east of the valley.

EUROPE

FOODS FROM THE WILD

Food remains from Skara Brae, a coastal settlement on the Orkney islands off the northern tip of Scotland, illustrate the continued importance of wild foods in the diet of some farming settlements, especially those in harsh and inhospitable environments. Alongside bones of domestic cattle and sheep were abundant fishbones and numerous limpet shells. The limpets were probably collected as bait for fishing, and may have been kept alive in small stone sinks found in the houses. These could have held water when their joints were sealed with mud. Crab, venison, and birds' eggs were also part of the diet at Skara Brae, while plant foods included wheat, barley, and hazelnuts.

DRY-STONE HOUSES

The settlers at Skara Brae on the Orkney islands built a cluster of dry-stone houses connected by narrow passages. The houses were buried within a mound of sand and domestic rubbish as protection against the harsh climate. Wood was scarce, so hearths, sinks, and other furnishings were all made of stone.

Stone slab dresser
Flagstone
Bed base

House, Skara Brae, Orkney, Scotland

AFRICA

DOMESTICATED ASSES

The Egyptians relied heavily on domesticated asses for the transportation of grain and other commodities between villages, as Egyptian farmers do today. The wild ass was tamed in the Nile Valley as early as 3000 BC and was important in long-distance trade until the domestication of the camel in later times.

Domesticated ass, Egypt

RURAL DWELLINGS

From 3000 BC onward the majority of Egyptians lived in small farming villages on the floodplain or in the delta of the Nile River. Their houses, usually containing several rooms, were made of sun-dried bricks, with thick walls and small, high windows to keep out the sun. The thatch and mud roofs were flat, supported by palm beams, and strong enough for people to sleep on in hot weather. Most rural people lived in small communities among their fields, on higher ground that was not inundated during the annual Nile flood. Very similar houses are built in rural Egypt to this day.

TECHNOLOGY & INNOVATION

CERAMIC FIGURINES

The Valdivia culture of coastal Ecuador produced the earliest known ceramic human figurines that have been discovered in the Americas. The simplicity with which the nude body is depicted contrasts dramatically with the elaborate individuality of the hairstyles. The majority of these early figurines are female; the faces were usually left unpainted, while the body and shaved portions of the head are a polished red color.

Ceramic figurine, Valdivia, Ecuador

POTTER'S WHEEL

The development of the potter's wheel in China took place around 3000 BC during a formative phase of the Longshan culture, named after the site of Longshan in northeastern China. The wheel enabled artisans to produce more sophisticated forms and made the mass production of vessels possible. It was later developed, probably independently, in southern and western Africa.

Reconstruction of sledge from a royal tomb, Ur, Iraq

TRANSPORT

Sledges are represented by pictographs on tablets from Uruk in southern Mesopotamia dating to around 3200 BC, and the first wheeled vehicles were indicated by the addition of circles beneath later pictographs. It is unlikely, however, that the wheel was invented in Mesopotamia. Sledges and wheeled carts were buried in the tombs of the rulers of Ur and Kish, which date from around 2700 BC to 2400 BC.

Lead boat model, Naxos, Cyclades, Greece

AEGEAN SEAFARING

Boats must have played an important part in the increasing prosperity of the islands of the Aegean during the 3rd millennium BC. Judging from the lead models found on the island of Naxos in the Cyclades, which date to this time, these boats were relatively simple craft. They were probably constructed from a dug-out log base with planks added to raise the sides of the hull.

JEWELRY DESIGN

Egyptian goldsmiths were highly skilled in the design and manufacture of fine jewelry, masterfully setting turquoise and other semiprecious stones in gold imported from gold-rich areas in Nubia and the Sinai Desert. Such personal ornaments were important indications of wealth and social status; four bracelets of gold and precious stones were found on the mummified arm of a queen buried in a tomb at Abydos in Upper Egypt around 2800 BC.

Gold and turquoise bead necklace, Egypt

Gold falcon amulet

ART & RITUAL

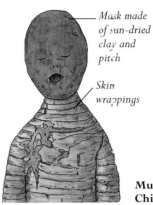

Mask made of sun-dried clay and pitch

Skin wrappings

EARLY MUMMIFICATION

The earliest evidence for the practice of mummification in South America comes from Chinchorros in northern Chile, where a variety of human burials display a ritualized treatment of the bodies. In evident concern for the deceased in an afterlife, an attempt was made to reconstitute the physical body by wrapping strips of skin around the skeleton. Facial features were sometimes recreated with sun-dried clay and pitch masks.

Mummified human remains, Chinchorros, Chile

SYMBOL OF HEAVEN

According to the Chinese, heaven was round and the earth square. Perforated disks made of jade and hardstone to symbolize heaven were used in ritual human sacrifices to the heavens until the early 20th century. Such disks, reserved for use by the ruling classes, were often placed on the sacrificial corpse for protection in the afterlife.

Hardstone disks, eastern China

ETERNAL PRAYER

Temples dominated life in the cities of southern Mesopotamia. As well as meeting the religious needs of the population, they possessed great wealth, extensive estates, and abundant herds. Small statues of worshippers were brought to temple sanctuaries and dedicated by both men and women. The statues were intended to pray perpetually on behalf of the donors for their well-being.

Statue of a female worshipper, Iraq

SCHIST PLAQUES

Portuguese tombs from 3000-2500 BC frequently contained plaques of schist (a stone similar to slate) decorated with engraved designs. The lower parts of the plaques carry geometric patterns, which probably indicate multicolored clothing; at the top is a pair of circular eyes that may represent a spirit-being or deity. Geometric decoration is also found on stone hooks, or croziers. These objects may have been associated with a ritual of the dead.

COMMEMORATIVE ART

Abydos in Upper Egypt was a royal Egyptian burial place from 3100-2650 BC. The early pharaohs were buried in brick-built subterranean tombs with flat roofs. Commemorative stelae, upright slabs of stone decorated with figures or inscriptions relating to the life of the deceased, were also set up for the rulers' descendants to revere.

Gray granite stela commemorating King Peribsen, Abydos, Egypt

2600 - 2400 BC

FOOD & ENVIRONMENT

SHELTER & ARCHITECTURE

AMERICAS

ROOT CROPS

Potatoes were domesticated in the Andean region of South America between 3000 and 2500 BC. Their genetic makeup is very malleable, allowing for great variation. The white and pink types have spread worldwide, while many other varieties have remained confined to the Andean high hills. Other Andean root crops include mashua, olluco, and maca.

Andean potatoes

Hut, Chilca, Peru

Floor level lower than ground level

Thatch

CONICAL HUTS

Dwellings built in Peru during the Archaic period (c. 3000-1800 BC) were round, with a conical profile, sunken floors, and thatched roofs. Constructed using a frame of poles stuck in the ground and tied together at the top, they had narrow doors and slept up to five people. Daytime activities were conducted outside. This was an enduring design; rural huts are very similar today.

EAST ASIA & AUSTRALASIA

TROPICAL FRUIT

On mainland Southeast Asia and in the Philippines, breadfruit was part of the staple diet, and breadfruit trees were probably grown in carefully tended plots by 2500 BC. The fruit becomes soft and doughy when boiled, and tastes like freshly baked bread when roasted.

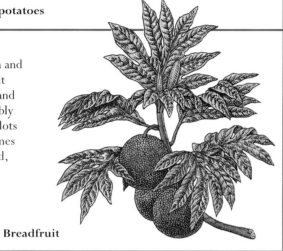

Breadfruit

DESERT CAMPS

In the Australian desert, where water and shade are scarce, rock shelters located beside waterholes at the foot of granite cliffs continued to be important campsites for Aboriginal nomads during this period. The huge shelter at Walga Rock in Western Australia contains layers of debris left by successive inhabitants over 5,000 years. Similar sites lie around the base of the better known Uluru, or Ayers, Rock in Central Australia.

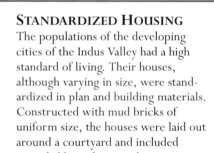

Walga Rock shelter, Western Australia

MIDDLE EAST & SOUTH ASIA

DOMESTIC ANIMALS

The shell and lapis lazuli inlay decorating the Royal Standard, a mosaic box found in a tomb at Ur dating to around 2500 BC, shows the uses of domestic animals. By this time, cattle, sheep, and goats were raised not only for meat, but for milk and wool as well, and oxen were being used with onagers (a type of wild ass) to pull plows, wagons, and carts.

Detail, Royal Standard of Ur, Iraq

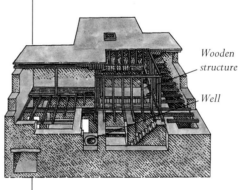

Wooden structure

Well

STANDARDIZED HOUSING

The populations of the developing cities of the Indus Valley had a high standard of living. Their houses, although varying in size, were standardized in plan and building materials. Constructed with mud bricks of uniform size, the houses were laid out around a courtyard and included remarkably sophisticated sanitary arrangements: bathrooms had brick floors and the toilets were connected to a central drainage system.

House, Mohenjo-Daro, Indus Valley

EUROPE

EARLY VITICULTURE

Grape seeds have been found preserved at several early settlements on the shores of the Mediterranean and in temperate Europe, indicating that European hunter-gatherers collected wild grapes as long ago as 9000 BC. Early farmers began to cultivate and tend vines around 5,000 years ago. The technique of treading the grapes and fermenting the juice to produce wine had developed in the Middle East by around 2500 BC, and the custom spread west into Mediterranean Europe during this period.

Grapes

DRY-STONE ENCLOSURES

Enclosures built in southern France around 2500 BC consisted of dry-stone walls linking together a series of circular huts. The enclosures probably served as sheep pens with dwellings attached. The huts had corbel-vaulted stone roofs, in which each course of stone slabs overlaps the one below, completely covering the space beneath.

Corbel-vaulted stone roof

Enclosure, Boussargues, France

AFRICA

POULTRY AND FOWL

Tomb paintings of the Old Kingdom period (2650-2150 BC) show that ducks, geese, and other birds were important in the Egyptian diet. Ducks and geese were specially fattened for the tables of wealthy nobles. Every spring and autumn, hunters trapped and killed thousands of migrating waterfowl as they flew along the Nile Valley.

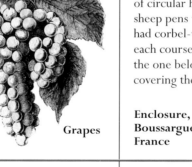

Wall painting of geese, Egypt

TEMPORARY CAMPSITE

A group of hunter-gatherers first settled at the seasonal campsite of Gwisho in Zambia around 5,000 years ago, returning several times over the following centuries, attracted by the hot springs that are a feature of the location. They slept in grass-lined hollows and erected arrangements of timber posts to support windbreaks. The Gwisho community buried their dead within the camp area: skeletons of 35 individuals were recovered from graves. Other remains testify to their hunter-gatherer way of life: wooden bows and arrows for hunting, digging sticks for grubbing up roots, and wooden drills for lighting fires.

TECHNOLOGY & INNOVATION

ART & RITUAL

RAZOR-SHARP BLADES

Throughout the period dominated by hunter-gatherer societies in North America (c.8000-1000 BC), there was ongoing regional diversification in the variety of stone projectile points produced. In eastern Oklahoma, for example, some weapon tips, like this one from Afton, became highly stylized. To achieve the razor-sharp blade edges required skilled workmanship.

Afton projectile point, Oklahoma

Atlatl weight, Ohio

ARTISTIC SENSE

Atlatls (spear-throwers) produced during this period testify to the artistic sensibilities of those who made them.

A-latl weights were made from a variety of metamorphic and igneous rocks, but also from such materials as hematite and quartz crystal.

HIGH-TEMPERATURE FIRING

Around 2500 BC in western China, innovations in the preparation and firing of earthenware led to the development of a new pottery tradition called Banshan, after the site of Banshan in Gansu province. Characterized by large round-bodied urns made from fine-grained clay, often with tall necks, the tradition is also famous for its unique decorative style. Bold, dense spirals with notched edges were painted in red, black, brown, and purple pigments. When fired at a high temperature, the earthenware became light red and the painted pigments gained a sepia overtone. This technique was used for both funerary and household vessels, although many of the latter continued to be made from rough clay fired at a low temperature.

PREPARING FOR THE AFTERLIFE

Tomb furnishings from this period in Chinese history reflect the idea that the next world resembles this one. The dead were provided with things needed for daily existence and also with status objects reflecting their worldly position. In their differences of wealth, these tombs also show that Chinese society had by this time become highly stratified, with the emergence of an aristocratic elite. Grave goods, ranging from single pots to over 180 objects in wealthier tombs, were placed in the burial pit around the corpse or on a ledge above it. In addition to pots, the tombs included agricultural tools, turtleshell and bone artifacts, ritual vessels, and jade objects signifying rank.

Hewn chert block

Stone weights, Mohenjo-Daro, Indus Valley

CUBIC WEIGHTS

Most of the many weights made of chert (a crystalline form of silica) found at Mohenjo-Daro in the Indus Valley were cubic in shape. They were organized in a series, doubling in weight from one to two to four and so on to 64; then jumping to 160 and proceeding in multiples of 160. The smallest weights were found in a jeweler's shop and would have been used for measuring out tiny amounts of precious material. The largest were so heavy they could only be lifted with the help of a rope.

FESTIVALS AND MUSIC

In Mesopotamia, music and singing were important in both religious and secular festivals. In the Royal Tombs at Ur, Iraq, around 2500 BC, lyre players were sacrificed with their instruments to accompany the dead into the underworld. Although the first lines of many ancient Mesopotamian songs and hymns are listed on cuneiform tablets, it is not known what the music actually sounded like

Decorative inlay

Lyre, Ur, Iraq

FLINT TRADE

Grand Pressigny in western France was the source of a high quality flint that was much prized and widely traded between 2800 and 2400 BC. The flint was valued both for its yellowish honey color, and because blades up to 16 inches long could be produced from it and then made into knives and daggers.

Flint core, Grand Pressigny, France

MARBLE FIGURINES

The early settlers of the Cyclades in the Aegean used local sources of marble on Paros and neighboring islands to carve fine figurines, which they buried with the dead. Most of the figurines are female, often with folded arms. Traces of color suggest that they were once brightly painted.

Characteristic folded arms

Marble figurine, Cyclades, Greece

STATE BUREAUCRACY

The sophisticated social structure that existed in Egypt at the beginning of the Old Kingdom period included a professional corps of skilled and educated administrators. They were largely responsible for the administration of the by now fully fledged government bureaucracy. Many members of this intellectual elite were commoners, of whom one of the first and most famous was Imhotep. A physician and priest, he was also the architect who designed the step pyramid at Saqqara around 2650 BC.

Statue of the architect Imhotep, Egypt

MUMMIFICATION

Believing that the soul still needed its mortal body after death, the Egyptians mummified corpses of the wealthy and powerful. One of the earliest surviving mummies is that of Ranefer, a noble buried at Maidum in Lower Egypt around 2500 BC. His internal organs were wrapped in linen and placed in a tomb recess. The body cavity was packed with linen soaked in resin, and the entire body was wrapped in resin-soaked bandages. The bandages over the face were modeled and painted to represent the dead man, creating a kind of portrait-statue in which his spirit could reside.

2400 - 2000 BC

FOOD & ENVIRONMENT	SHELTER & ARCHITECTURE

AMERICAS

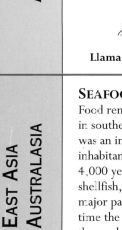

Tassels

Llama

CAMELID DOMESTICATION
The llama and alpaca, two of the four camelid species native to the Andes, were domesticated between 4000 and 2000 BC. They provided meat and wool and were also used for transport. The herders pierced the ears of their animals and strung colored yarn through the holes. Two other species, the vicuña and the guanaco, have never been domesticated.

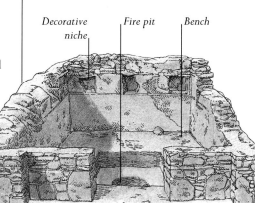

Decorative niche *Fire pit* *Bench*

MONUMENTAL CENTER
La Galgada in Peru, a monumental temple built c.2300 BC, was used for burials and agricultural rituals. The walls of the temple were made of stone and mud, then plastered and painted. Commoners were buried outside the temple, while the tombs within were reserved for an elite.

Temple chamber, La Galgada, Peru

EAST ASIA & AUSTRALASIA

SEAFOOD AND WILD RICE
Food remains from Kok Phanom Di in southern Thailand show that rice was an important food for the inhabitants of this early village some 4,000 years ago. Seafood such as fish, shellfish, turtles, and crabs was also a major part of the diet, since at the time the settlement was not far from the seashore. The rice was harvested locally in the surrounding area, where it grew wild. It is not known exactly when the first attempts were made to cultivate rice in Southeast Asia, although it had already been under cultivation in China since around 5000 BC. The fact that rice grew wild in many parts of Southeast Asia may have removed the need for its intentional cultivation until larger communities developed.

FISHING VILLAGES
In Japan, the remains of fishing villages with pit dwellings and ground-level houses have been found dating to this period. The circular or rectangular timber and thatch houses were built around a central hearth, with evenly spaced posts supporting the roof. Stone altars were found on the northwest side of some houses.

Opening for smoke
Layers of thatch

Circular house, Honshu, Japan

MIDDLE EAST & SOUTH ASIA

INDUS PROSPERITY
The cities of the Indus Valley, such as Harappa and Mohenjo-Daro, owed their prosperity to the fertile, arable lands of the Indus River floodplain. The river flooded each year, depositing rich layers of silt and providing valuable water that could be held in ponds for the dry season. Wheat and barley were the major crops, and domestic animals included zebu (humped cattle), sheep, goats, elephants, boars, and camels.

Bull seal (*above*) and impression (*above right*), Mohenjo-Daro, Indus Valley

ROOFING MATERIALS
The traditional form of roof in the Middle East by now was flat and consisted of timber beams covered with layers of earth and mud plaster. In regions without good supplies of wood, however, vaults of mud brick were constructed. Such vaults had been used in underground tombs from as early as 4000 BC. Two thousand years later, brick vaults were commonly used above ground in large buildings such as temples and palaces. For the most prestigious buildings in lowland Mesopotamia, massive timber beams were imported from the mountains of Lebanon (home of the famous cedars), the Amanos Mountains in southern Turkey, and western Iran.

EUROPE

POTTERY BEAKERS
The beaker was a standardized type of pottery drinking vessel that became widely used in western Europe around 2400 BC. Its popularity may have owed something to the drink it contained: one beaker vessel found in Scotland still held traces of a deposit that may have been mead or a similar honey-sweetened brew.

Beaker vessel, Barnack, Cambridgeshire, England

DEFENSIVE ENCLOSURES
Early European farming societies had been relatively peaceful. In Britain, however, this situation changed around 2200 BC, when independent communities began competing for territory and resources. This caused the first defensive enclosures to be built. One enclosure, at Mount Pleasant in Dorset, had a sturdy gate framed by massive timber posts 5 feet in diameter.

East gate, Mount Pleasant, Dorset, England

AFRICA

HUNTER-GATHERERS
While Egypt supported an agricultural economy, sub-Saharan Africans developed new skills in hunting and foraging. The population of hunter-gatherers in Africa c.2000 BC numbered around 200,000, having roughly doubled over the preceding 8,000 years. Local groups became increasingly specialized in their hunting or foraging activities, becoming expert at pursuing sea mammals, collecting shellfish, catching sluggish fish from the shallows, or foraging for edible plants. Even in lean years when the supply of staple provisions had diminished, most groups had ample alternative animal and plant foods.

TEMPLE OBELISK
Several rulers of the 5th Dynasty (2465-2323 BC) in Egypt built massive temples to the sun-god Ra. The most famous, built at Abu Ghurab around 2400 BC, was dominated by a huge masonry obelisk erected in a large, open courtyard.

Temple of Ra, Abu Ghurab, Egypt

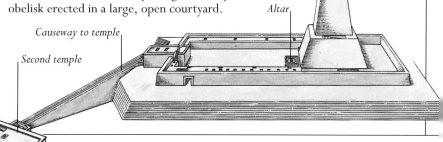

Obelisk
Altar
Causeway to temple
Second temple

TECHNOLOGY & INNOVATION

TRAPPING FISH

Along the east coast of North America, early Americans built fish weirs in river mouths, using the estuarine tides to catch fish. Weirs comprised a fence of stakes and brushwood or netting placed across an estuary. At high tide fish could swim upstream over the weir, but would then be trapped at low tide, when they could be speared or netted.

Watercolor of fish weir, Virginia

EARLY BRONZEWORKING

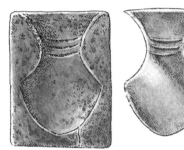

Some of the earliest Chinese artifacts made of copper alloyed with zinc and lead are two awls from northeastern China dating to c.2000 BC. In northeastern Thailand, tools of true bronze, an alloy of copper and tin, were made at Ban Chiang and Non Nok Tha, using small sandstone molds.

Mold and bronze ax head (above), Thailand

ROYAL REFORMS

A series of administrative reforms was undertaken by Shulgi, a king of the 3rd Dynasty of Ur (2095-2047 BC) in southern Mesopotamia. Among these was the introduction of a new taxation system with different tax levies for the central core and for the peripheral regions of his empire. Shulgi also introduced a new calendar, composed the earliest surviving code of laws, started scribal schools, and reformed the system of weights and measures.

CREATING ALLOYS

Bronze, an alloy of copper and tin, was initially costly to make, and in Europe many of the earliest bronze objects were designed to display wealth and power. Bronze was harder than copper and could be cast in a greater range of tools and weapons. It came into widespread use in Europe around 2000 BC.

Head of bronze halberd, Germany

MASONRY TOOLS

During the later stages of the Old Kingdom period (2650-2150 BC) Egyptian stoneworkers became increasingly skilled in the construction of impressive monuments such as the pyramids and associated temples, although they used only the simplest tools. Among them were heavy hardstone pounders, like this dolerite example, which were used as chisels in conjunction with wooden mallets for hewing granite blocks.

Dolerite pounder, Egypt

ART & RITUAL

ENGRAVED PENDANTS

Early coastal dwellers on the Labrador peninsula in northeastern Canada wore soapstone pendants as charms. Found in burials and the remains of longhouses, many are engraved with skeletal or branching designs, and in shape are thought to represent the top of a cleft-peak mountain known as the Bishop's Mitre, home to an important local deity.

Decoration

Engraved pendants, Labrador, Canada

EGGSHELL-THIN POTTERY

The Longshan culture (named after the site of Longshan on China's eastern coast) was at its artistic zenith at 2500-2000 BC. Artisans produced jade objects and distinctive black earthenware pottery, which was wheel-thrown and only a half-inch thick. Of particular beauty were elegant vases, polished and incised with simple, unpainted decoration before firing.

Longshan black earthenware vase, Weifang, Shandong, China

DIVINE KINGSHIP

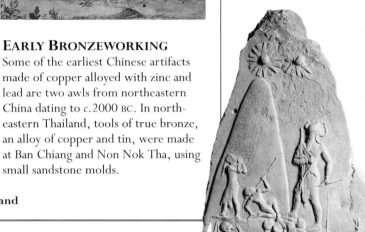

King Naram-Sin (c.2255-2218 BC) of the Akkadian Dynasty, which controlled the whole of southern Mesopotamia from 2334-2154 BC, was the first Middle Eastern king to call himself divine in his own lifetime. This victory stela of Naram-Sin, probably from Sippar in modern Iraq, was later taken to Susa, in western Iran, as booty; it shows the king trampling his enemies and wearing a horned headdress, a prerogative of the gods.

Stela of Naram-Sin, Susa, Iran

STANDING STONES

In southern France and Corsica, a series of standing stones carved with representations of the human form dates to this time. Emphasis was given to the eyes, sometimes framed above and on either side by geometric patterns representing long hair. Those on the mainland often wear a necklace and a belt around the waist, and female breasts are sometimes indicated. In Corsica all the stones depict males, often equipped with knives or daggers.

MORTUARY SCULPTURE

Nenkhefta was an Egyptian noble who lived some time during the 5th Dynasty. This red-painted statue from his tomb at Deshasha portrays him standing in a pose typical of mortuary sculpture — left foot forward, arms by his sides, his hand clutching a bolt of cloth, a symbol of authority. The color red was conventionally used for statues of men. The statue partook symbolically of food offerings made to the dead.

Painted limestone statue of Nenkhefta, Deshasha, Egypt

THE PYRAMIDS AT GIZA

33,000 BC

The ancient Egyptian pyramids at Giza served as royal burial places and were erected between 2550 and 2470 BC. They were considered one of the Seven Wonders of the World by the Greeks. The first pyramids, like that built at Saqqara in 2650 BC for King Zoser, were built in a stepped form, representing a symbolic stairway designed to assist the dead pharaoh in his ascent to the sky and the afterlife. Later royal pyramids, such as those at Maidum and Dahshur, had smooth, sloping sides. From these evolved the pyramids of Giza, with sides angled at a perfect 52 degrees. In their final form, the pyramids represented symbolic solar rays, used by the dead king to join the sun-god Ra.

PYRAMIDS AND FLOODPLAIN
On the western bank of the Nile River, facing the site of the ancient city of Memphis, the pyramids at Giza were constructed on a rocky plateau made level by Egyptian laborers. The position of the site was symbolically associated with the setting sun, appropriate for the tombs of the dead. The pyramids were built just beyond precious agricultural land. Great blocks of quarried stone were transported on the river during the annual flooding. Armies of workers were housed in barracks at the rear of the site.

Reconstruction of the pyramids at Giza, Egypt *below*

King Khafre's mortuary temple

King Khafre's pyramid

King Menkaure's pyramid

Storerooms or workshops

King Khufu's Great Pyramid

Causeway linking mortuary temple with valley temple on floodplain

Valley temple

Cultivated land

-- Coastline of the period
▲ Pyramid site

NILE VALLEY *above*
The deserts flanking the Nile were rich in the metals needed to make tools, and in the limestone essential for building the pyramids at Giza.

TEMPLE STATUES *right*
King Menkaure (2490-2472 BC) was the son of King Khafre. He commissioned the third and smallest pyramid at Giza, which lies to the southwest of Khafre's burial complex. Legend has it that Menkaure was a pious king, unlike his despotic predecessors. He is depicted (*right*) striding between the cow-horned goddess Hathor and the chief deity of the Seventh Province. Similar statues, each with a different provincial god, lined his temple.

Restored silver-and-lapis bracelet from Queen Hetepheres' tomb

BURIED RICHES *above*
Queen Hetepheres was the mother of King Khufu, builder of the Great Pyramid. Discovered in 1925, her final resting place at Giza contained her portable bedroom, complete with gilded bed, headrest, chair, curtain box, fine jewelry, and even razors made of layers of gold – but no body.

Hathor, Menkaure (*center*), and provincial deity

LAST RITES *below*
The funeral boat used to transport King Khufu from Memphis to his final resting place was 141 feet long. This richly adorned vessel was taken apart and buried in a rock-cut pit alongside the Great Pyramid for the king's use in the afterlife. Archaeologists have reassembled the craft using the shipwright's original instructions, which were found buried with the 1,220 pieces.

King Khufu's funeral boat

THE ROYAL TOMBS

King Khufu (2551-2528 BC) built the 482-foot-high Great Pyramid in about 2550 BC. Rock-cut pits containing mortuary boats lie close to its base; Khufu's queens lie under three smaller pyramids along one side. King Khafre (2520-2494 BC), one of Khufu's sons, built his slightly smaller pyramid and temple complex to the southwest of the Great Pyramid. Beyond Khafre's pyramid, Khafre's son Menkaure (2490-2472 BC) built his own pyramid complex, the smallest of the three.

INSIDE KING KHUFU'S GREAT PYRAMID *right*

A descending corridor leads from the entrance to an ascending passage, which opens into the Grand Gallery, a high vaulted passage. The king's burial chamber lies at the pyramid's center, with five weight-relieving chambers above it. A second burial chamber beneath it was abandoned, and a third, located under the pyramid, was never finished. The escape route was used by workers after the passage was sealed with granite blocks.

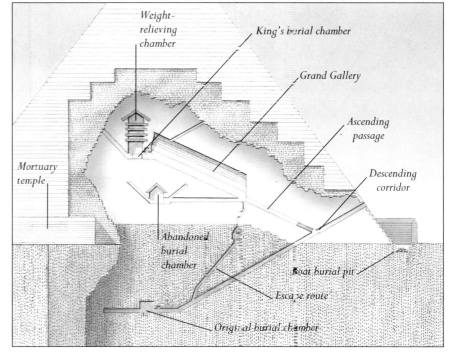

Weight-relieving chamber
King's burial chamber
Grand Gallery
Ascending passage
Mortuary temple
Descending corridor
Abandoned burial chamber
Boat burial pit
Escape route
Original burial chamber

THE CONSTRUCTION PROCESS

The orientation of a pyramid site was initially plotted according to simple star sightings, using plumb bobs and notched sticks. The site was leveled and a grid was cut into the rock. Architects used water levels to ensure the base was flat. Copper mallets and chisels were used by masons to quarry vast limestone blocks, which were dragged on wooden sledges to the river and transported to the pyramid site by boat. Course by course, the pyramid — with its internal passages and chambers — was built upward and outward from the center. Huge mud-brick ramps were constructed to give access to the work.

Copper plumb bob
Copper chisel
Copper mallet
Wooden pounder

Three queens' pyramids

Nobles' tombs

Cultivated land

Sphinx

Nile River at high flood tide

KING KHAFRE'S SPHINX *below*

The 240-foot-long sphinx was sculpted from a limestone outcrop close to King Khafre's pyramid. Originally it was plastered and brightly painted. The face portrayed Khafre, with a beard, which was a symbol of kingship, while the royal headdress shows a cobra motif, symbol of Lower Egypt. Lions were the guardians of sacred places, so the huge lion body is particularly appropriate. A thousand years after Khafre's death, the pharaoh Tuthmosis IV (reigned c.1425-1417 BC) restored the sphinx and added a royal statue at its chest.

Cobra motif

Royal beard

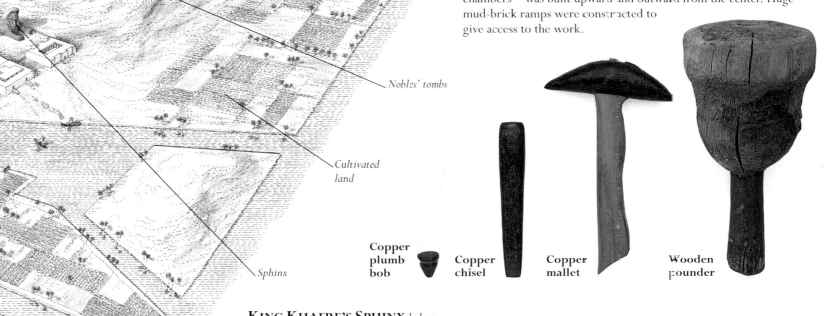

Rock-cut body

Reconstructions (*left* and *above*) of **King Khafre's sphinx**

Chest statue

CHAPTER 9
DIVERGING CULTURES
2000 - 1600 BC

Palace-centered states arise in Minoan Crete

Warring city-states dominate the political landscape of the Middle East

Farmers of coastal Peru develop irrigation agriculture

The great cities of the Indus Valley slowly decline and are abandoned

Walled urban centers arise and flourish on the North China Plain

Archaeology and early written records together testify to the continuing development of human societies around the world in the early 2nd millennium BC. In Europe, Africa, and the Americas, small-scale societies predominated, each with its own distinctive way of life. New urban communities emerged in northern China and the eastern Mediterranean, while existing urbanized societies of Egypt and Mesopotamia continued to flourish.

Bronze Age Europe

In Europe north of the Alps, the 2nd millennium BC was a period of technological innovation and social change. Soon after the start of the Early Bronze Age (c. 2300-1800 BC) European bronze-workers had attained a remarkable mastery of the new material, producing skillfully crafted swords and daggers for the use of an emerging local elite. The growing power of this elite is also evident from the large burial mounds that were constructed in many regions of Europe. Under these mounds, chambers of timber or stone held the remains of powerful individuals, probably local leaders, who were interred with ornaments and weapons of gold and bronze. Further changes in agricultural society are shown in the creation of field systems in parts of western Europe. These indicate that land was in short supply, and that ownership of land was taking on a new importance.

Minoan Crete

On the Mediterranean island of Crete, socio-political developments in the village settlements that had grown up in the 3rd millennium BC resulted in the emergence of small palace-centered states in the early 2nd millennium. The earliest palace was built c. 2000 BC at Knossos and is associated with the legendary King Minos, after whom the Minoan civilization is named.

BRONZE WEAPONRY
This decorated metal-hilted dagger from Italy was intended for display as well as use.

MARTIAL POSE
Figures of gods in warlike stances were a feature of Syrian religions in the 2nd millennium BC.

Other palaces followed at Phaistos, Mallia, and Zakros. All were built at strategic locations, well connected to the rich rural interior and sea-trading routes; the Minoans had extensive trade contacts as far away as Egypt and the Levant (the coastal strip of Syria, Lebanon, and Israel) and mainland Greece. Around 1700 BC, the early palaces were destroyed, possibly by earthquakes, but they were rebuilt in the centuries that followed.

Political alliances

The Middle East during this period was a land of warring city-states, each striving for military and political supremacy over the others and locked into complicated alliances and diplomatic exchanges. The machinery of government is well documented by the archives of clay tablets found in the ruins of royal palaces at Mari in northern Mesopotamia and Ebla in western Syria. The tablets record tariffs and taxes, numbers of slaves and artisans, and relations with neighboring cities. Political federations were common, with the kings of Babylon, Larsa, Eshnunna, and Qatna each commanding the allegiance of up to 15 lesser kings. The major historical figure of the age was Hammurabi, king of Babylon (1792-1750 BC), who gained temporary control over almost all of Mesopotamia. He issued a unique code of laws covering a wide range of matters such as trade deals, marriage, and land disputes.

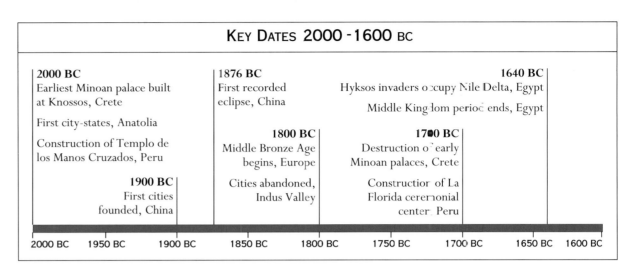

2000 BC
Earliest Minoan palace built
at Knossos, Crete

First city-states, Anatolia

Construction of Templo de
los Manos Cruzados, Peru

1900 BC
First cities
founded, China

1876 BC
First recorded
eclipse, China

1800 BC
Middle Bronze Age
begins, Europe

Cities abandoned,
Indus Valley

1640 BC
Hyksos invaders occupy Nile Delta, Egypt

Middle Kingdom period ends, Egypt

1700 BC
Destruction of early
Minoan palaces, Crete

Construction of La
Florida ceremonial
center, Peru

2000 BC 1950 BC 1900 BC 1850 BC 1800 BC 1750 BC 1700 BC 1650 BC 1600 BC

Aswan Granite
Pink-speckled granite from Aswan was a favorite
medium for stylized statues of Egyptian kings like
this one of King Sobkemsaf I (c.1642-1626 BC).

Trade contacts
The palace-centered economies
of Mesopotamia and Syria had
extensive trade links with Anatolia
(modern Turkey) to the north,
where city-states first appeared
around 2000 BC. Details of these
contacts are provided by clay tablets
from Kanesh, an Anatolian center where
merchants from the Assyrian city of Ashur

in Mesopotamia established a trading
colony in around 1950 BC. What attracted
these merchants was Anatolia's gold and
silver, which were exchanged for Mesopotamian textiles. Strong trade links also
existed between the cities of southern
Mesopotamia, those of the Indus Valley
(until around 1800 BC), and the flourishing
communities on the islands of Failaka and
Bahrain in the Persian Gulf.

Middle Kingdom Egypt
Egypt at the beginning of this period was
recovering from a century or so of unrest.
Order was restored and power consolidated under the pharaohs of the Middle
Kingdom period (2040-1640 BC). The
frontier was extended into Nubia as far as
the Third Nile Cataract, and a series of
forts were built, perhaps
in order to gain

Cutting edge

COPPER KNIFE
The source of cop-
per for tools like this
knife was the Great Lakes
region of North America.

TRANSLUCENT STONE
Points of chert (a crystalline
form of silica) were traded
in northeastern North
America around 2000 BC.

control of Nubia's extensive gold deposits
and lucrative trading routes. Egypt's
strength did not endure, however, and
during the 17th century BC it again entered
a period of weakness. Around 1640 BC a
dynasty of chieftains from the Levant, the
Hyksos, seized control of the Nile Delta
region and forced the whole of Egypt to
recognize their sovereignty. Shortly
afterward, a native kingdom rose to
dominance in Nubia, making the town of
Kerma its center.

Developments in the Americas
In the Americas, many societies still
depended on hunting and gathering. The
exceptions were in Mesoamerica and the
Andes of Peru, where farming villages had
appeared from 2500 BC, and the central
coast of Peru, where farming
villages that relied on
irrigation had begun to
emerge by 2000 BC.
Around 1700 BC in Peru a new departure
was heralded by the construction, at La
Florida, of a ceremonial center on an
unprecedented scale. This major undertaking required the cooperation of several
communities, marking the beginnings of
state formation in South America. In
North America, there were two major
developments in the early 2nd millennium BC. Plants including sunflowers,
chenopods, marsh elder, and gourds
were being cultivated by 1800 BC in
the east. In the northeast, long-
distance trade networks emerged,
bringing copper and a kind of
crystalline silica known as Ramah
chert to regions where these
materials were not found naturally.

2000 - 1600 BC

Regional variations

Throughout Mesoamerica, the use of ceramic vessels, particularly rounded neckless jars and flat-bottomed bowls, was well established by 2000 BC. Along with the emergence of permanent farming villages in the area, regional variations in the style and decoration of ceramics developed between 2000 and 1600 BC, reflecting the growing diversification and sophistication of these communities.

Decline in the Indus Valley

The great cities of the Indus civilization, including Harappa and Mohenjo-Daro, declined gradually from 2000 BC and were ultimately abandoned by 1800 BC. Why exactly this happened is unknown; the most plausible theory attributes their decline to the drying up of a local river system, which led to the collapse of the intensive agriculture on which the region depended. Warfare and epidemic disease may also have played a part. After 1800 BC, people living in the Indus Valley returned to dwelling in smaller and more scattered settlements. No settlements on the scale of the Indus cities were to be seen in South Asia for the next 1,000 years.

Origins of urban China

The story of urbanization in China started before 2000 BC in northern regions such as Henan and the Shandong peninsula, where walled settlements began to appear. The first known city was founded around 1900 BC at Erlitou on the Yellow River. This settlement was unprecedented in size, with a palace platform over 300 feet square. There is also evidence of crafts of the kind usually associated with urban societies: bronze tools, weapons, and vessels, finely carved jades, and pottery. Erlitou may have been one of the capitals of the Xia Dynasty which, according to tradition, ruled this part of China until the rise of the Shang state around 1600 BC.

Wild and cultivated foods

Urban civilizations still covered only a small part of the habitable world in the 2nd millennium BC. Other kinds of communities, many of which continued to live by hunting and gathering or by small-scale agriculture, continued to flourish. The Jomon people of Japan, named after the *jomon* ("cord-marked") decorated pottery found at their sites, by now lived in settled villages but still survived by hunting and gathering. In Africa south of the Sahara, small-scale societies of farmers and herders who lived in traditional hut villages now existed, as well as other groups that continued to rely wholly on hunting and gathering, a way of life that predominated in the south of the continent.

Wild plant foods continued to be important in the diet of Southeast Asian villages, despite the fact that rice farming was by now well established. In Europe, Alpine lake village communities also relied on a mixture of farming and gathering – a combination that has remained important in many parts of the world up to the present day.

AMERICAS

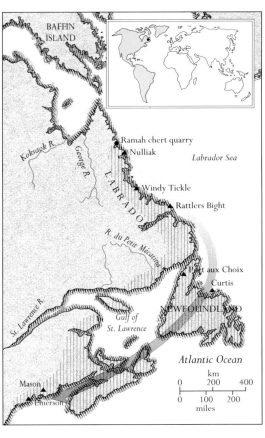

RAMAH CHERT TRADE

Early communities on the coast of North America, from Maine to northern Labrador, buried their dead in large cemeteries. These "red paint" cemeteries contain graves with large deposits of red ocher and decorated tools. Many offerings were made from such exotic raw materials as Ramah chert (a beautiful translucent stone obtained from quarries in northern Labrador), copper, greenstone, and birch bark, which were preserved in the burials. Despite the cost of obtaining these materials through long-distance trade, grave goods were routinely "killed" at the time of burial by being snapped in half. The released spirits of the tools could then accompany the soul of the deceased.

➡ Ramah chert trade route

||| Distribution of Ramah chert

▲ Habitation and burial site

Ramah chert tool "killed" for burial, Rattlers Bight, Canada

PERUVIAN IRRIGATION

By 2000 BC plant cultivation had reached an important early stage of development on the southern Pacific coast of Peru. This is an area of arid desert traversed by rivers fed by rain and mountain streams. The inhabitants of the area constructed complex networks of irrigation channels, which increased the amount of arable land available. An enormous variety of plants was then cultivated. In association with the channels, U-shaped temples were built, such as that at La Florida in the Rímac Valley.

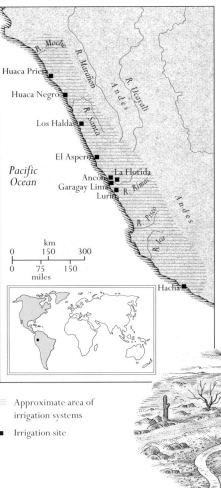

≡ Approximate area of irrigation systems

■ Irrigation site

Irrigation systems, Rímac Valley, Peru

MIDDLE EAST & SOUTH ASIA

MARITIME TRADE LINKS

Trading contacts between the cities of Sumer and the ancient countries of Dilmun, Magan, and Meluhha are recorded on cuneiform texts dating from 2450 BC to around 1800 BC, which were found at sites in southern Mesopotamia. Dilmun is identified with the Barbar culture of Failaka and Bahrain in the Persian Gulf. Stamp seals probably made in Dilmun have been found in both Mesopotamia (Iraq) and India. Magan probably occupied modern Oman; Meluhha is identified

with the Indus civilization. Indus seals inscriptions, and carnelian beads have been found in Oman, Mesopotamia, Bahrain, and Failaka. Mesopotamian commodities included silver, oil, textiles, and barley, which were traded for copper from Oman, timber and precious stones from India, and pearls from the Gulf. The demise of this trading network coincided with that of the Indus civilization in around 1800 BC. Many southern Mesopotamian cities were also abandoned around 1740 BC.

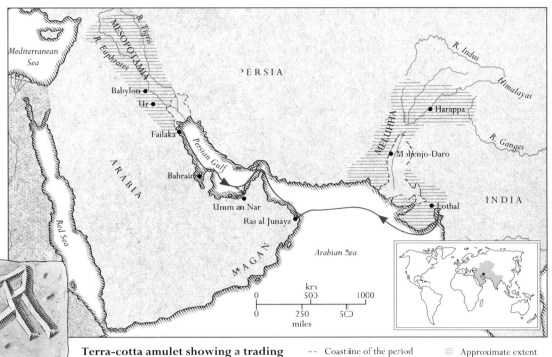

Terra-cotta amulet showing a trading ship, Mohenjo-Daro, Indus Valley

-- Coastline of the period
➔ Trade route
≡ Approximate extent of cultivated land

AFRICA

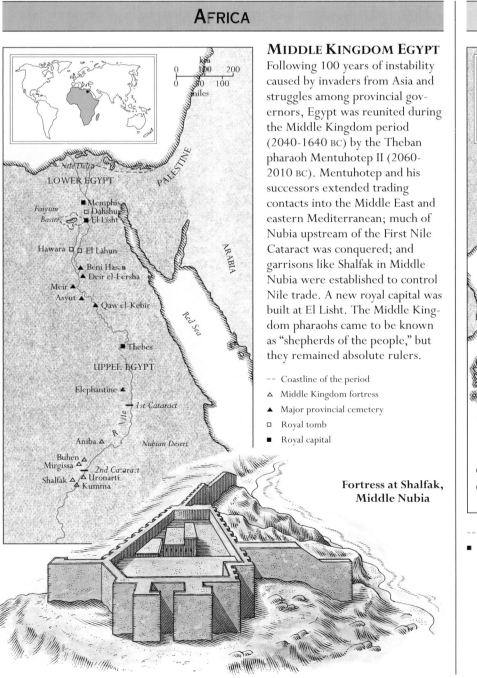

MIDDLE KINGDOM EGYPT

Following 100 years of instability caused by invaders from Asia and struggles among provincial governors, Egypt was reunited during the Middle Kingdom period (2040-1640 BC) by the Theban pharaoh Mentuhotep II (2060-2010 BC). Mentuhotep and his successors extended trading contacts into the Middle East and eastern Mediterranean; much of Nubia upstream of the First Nile Cataract was conquered; and garrisons like Shalfak in Middle Nubia were established to control Nile trade. A new royal capital was built at El Lisht. The Middle Kingdom pharaohs came to be known as "shepherds of the people," but they remained absolute rulers.

-- Coastline of the period
△ Middle Kingdom fortress
▲ Major provincial cemetery
□ Royal tomb
■ Royal capital

Fortress at Shalfak, Middle Nubia

EAST ASIA & AUSTRALASIA

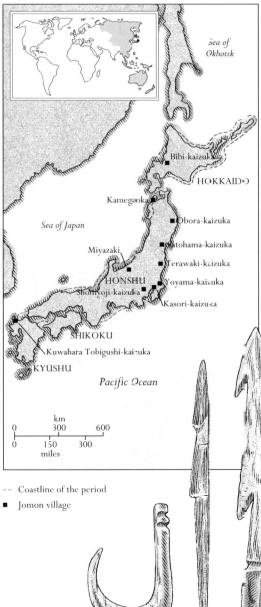

-- Coastline of the period
■ Jomon village

JAPANESE FISHING SITES

The people of Japan continued to live by hunting, gathering, and fishing during this period, long after rice farming had been adopted in adjacent parts of China. One reason for this was the richness of the offshore fishing grounds on the eastern coast of Japan, especially around Honshu, where most of the early Japanese villages of the Jomon culture were located. Bone fishhooks are common at these sites. Fishing was most rewarding during the spring and early summer, when tuna and other deep-sea species migrated to these waters. In the autumn, Jomon villagers turned their attention inland to gather fruits, nuts, and seeds, which they stored in underground pits until the spring.

Jomon bone fishhooks, Japan

2000-1800 BC

FOOD & ENVIRONMENT	SHELTER & ARCHITECTURE

AMERICAS

PROTEIN SOURCE

By 2000 BC the guinea pig, or *cuy*, was a common domesticated animal in several regions of South America, including the central Andean high plateaus of Peru and the western Andean range of Colombia. It was and still is a major source of dietary protein.

Guinea pig

RITUAL BUILDING

At Huaricoto in the mountains of northern Peru, the building of a shrine, or ritual chamber, began in around 2100 BC. The most important feature, dating to around 2000 BC, is a ceremonial sunken fire pit for burning offerings. The hearth and floor of the shrine were plastered, and the walls were of wattle and daub (interwoven twigs and sticks covered with clay).

Sunken fire pit, Huaricoto, Peru

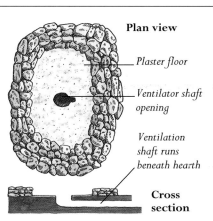

Plan view

Plaster floor

Ventilator shaft opening

Ventilation shaft runs beneath hearth

Cross section

EAST ASIA & AUSTRALASIA

VARIED DIET

Coastal villages in Japan around 2000 BC still relied entirely on fishing, hunting, and gathering. Fish such as tuna and shellfish, including cockles and winkles, were staples, but the villagers also hunted deer and pigs and collected walnuts, chestnuts, acorns, lily bulbs, seeds, and fruits. They extracted starch from vegetables and made tools to scoop the marrow out of bones.

Winkles

Cockles

RAMMED EARTH

From earliest times until today, a distinctive feature of Chinese architecture has been the use of *hangtu* (the rammed-earth technique) for constructing damp-proof foundations and walls. Within a framework of wooden planks, soil was pounded into a succession of thin layers between 3 and 4 inches thick, using stones attached to long handles. By around 2000 BC, people in northern China were building walled settlements using this method.

MIDDLE EAST & SOUTH ASIA

CHANGE AND DECAY

While the city-states of Mesopotamia continued to prosper and vie with each other for political dominance, the Indus civilization to the east was in rapid decline. Although Indo-Aryan warriors from Central Asia may have been active in the Indus area, they cannot be held responsible for its dramatic collapse. A major reason was probably the drying up of the Saraswati River system, which ran parallel to the Indus. Another reason may have been the development of rice cultivation and the introduction of several millet species from Africa, which opened the rest of India to agriculture. Urban decline is evident from the shanty dwellings in cities like Mohenjo-Daro, where the dead were buried in the ruins of former mansions. Skeletal remains testify to illness, particularly from malaria.

TEMPLE DECORATION

The walls of temples in Mesopotamia were traditionally decorated with intricate niches and recesses. These decorations became more elaborate after 2000 BC, when temple facades were embellished with columns in the shape of barley-sugar twists or palm trunks, and made with specially shaped mud bricks.

Spiral column, Tell Rimah, Iraq

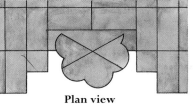

Plan view

Front view

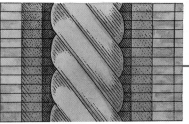

EUROPE

DOMESTICATION OF HORSES

Horses were first domesticated on the steppes of the Ukraine about 6,000 years ago, but it was some time before they became common in eastern Europe and began to spread west. Horses were used for pulling carts and wagons, as this harness cheekpiece from Romania illustrates, but by 2000 BC they were also proving their value as mounts, giving a crucial advantage in warfare.

Hole for strap

Horse harness cheekpiece, Vattina, Romania

MODEST TEMPLES

Shrines and temples in eastern Europe around 2000 BC were fairly simple, judging from the remains of an example at Salacea in Romania. This was a rectangular building of wattle and daub, differing from an ordinary dwelling house only in having two raised altars on either side of the door. Found within the shrine were clay figurines, miniature cart models, a clay boat model, and a model altar. Outside the door was a pit containing the bones of a child, who may have been placed there as a sacrifice. The temple stood within a fortified settlement and was probably the ritual center for the whole community.

AFRICA

VINTAGE WINES

The Egyptians valued grapes for making wine. Wine jars preserved in the tombs of nobility bear labels that distinguish different vintages, and even identify Syrian wine makers who practiced their craft in Egypt. By 1900 BC, wine may also have been imported from Crete. Egyptian wines probably had a strong resin flavor, because resin was added as a preservative.

Wall painting of grape-picking, Egypt

FARMING VILLAGES

Seasonal flooding makes the area around Lake Chad in northern Nigeria extremely fertile. The first substantial settlements on the edges of the lake basin date to around 4,000 years ago. The oldest of these, known as Bornu 38, was probably occupied by a group of farmers and herders for several centuries from around 2000 BC. The settlement consists of a mound of clay and debris, including pottery, groundstone axes, bone points, and grindstones. The mound, 10 feet high, is made up of successive layers of hard clay, which had been the floors of huts.

TECHNOLOGY & INNOVATION

WORKING WITH COPPER

In the Great Lakes region of North America, where natural deposits of copper are found, the metal was commonly used for making such utilitarian items as spear points. Farther away from the source, copper artifacts are less common and tend to be personal ornaments rather than working tools. Large, open pit mines cover Isle Royale in Lake Superior, testifying to the intense use of its native copper deposits throughout prehistory.

Copper spear point, Wisconsin

ASTRONOMICAL RECORDS

Early Chinese chroniclers kept careful records of astronomical events like eclipses, relating them to the reigning years of their monarchs. This allows ancient Chinese history to be dated very accurately. The earliest recorded eclipse took place in the fifth year of the reign of one King Zhong Kong, fourth king of the Xia Dynasty ruling in the north. The eclipse took place on the first day of the last month of autumn (roughly equivalent to October) and is reported as having caused fear and confusion. So precise are the records that the exact date of the event can be calculated to October 16, 1876 BC.

LETTERS AND ENVELOPES

Scribes in the Middle East encased clay tablets in clay envelopes for safekeeping. Early examples come from Kanesh in southern Anatolia, home to a colony of merchants from Ashur in Assyria. A copy or summary of the document was written on the envelope, and this could be compared with the original inside. Seals were employed as an extra safeguard.

Letter and envelope bearing cuneiform script, Kanesh, Anatolia

Bronze ax head, River Vecker, Hungary

BRONZE WEAPONS

The skills of European bronzeworkers in the Early Bronze Age (c.2300-1800 BC) are apparent in the weapons produced in Hungary around 2000 BC. These included swords with engraved decoration — intended as much to impress others as to be used in combat — and simpler items such as this ax head, found in a dry river bed.

IMITATION TURQUOISE

The Egyptians prized turquoise for making ornamental items, but its scarcity led them to develop an imitation — faïence. A glassy substance with a quartz or crystal base, it was made into beads, amulets, and small figurines. These were coated with a high-gloss glaze made of a compound of calcium silicates. By 1800 BC, whole vessels were made of faïence, and the technology had spread to Lebanon and Crete.

Molded faïence hippopotamus, Egypt

ART & RITUAL

Rough stone construction

Crossed hands modeled in plaster

Ruins of the Manos Cruzados temple, Huanaco Valley, Peru

EARLIEST TEMPLES

One of the sacred precincts at Kotosh, the earliest and most important ritual center in the Huanaco Valley of central Peru, is the Manos Cruzados (Crossed Hands) temple. The name is derived from the two crossed hands found fashioned in bas-relief above a portal. Dating to around 2000 BC, the walls were originally plastered and painted.

BURIAL GOODS

The practice of burying funeral gifts with the dead was widespread in Southeast Asia by this time. A cemetery at Ban Kao in southeastern Thailand contained 44 graves in which the bodies were buried with fine pottery vessels, animal bones, and stone adzes. The red and black vessels may have originally contained food for the deceased.

Funerary vessel, Ban Kao, Thailand

RULING BY DIVINE RIGHT

According to Mesopotamian tradition, the right to rule descended from heaven on to a particular city, giving it dominion over all neighboring city-states until the gods once again transferred their favor. Rulers could thus legitimize their sovereignty as divinely inspired. This copy of an earlier list of kings made at Isin in Sumer, southern Mesopotamia, around 1820 BC indicates that this tradition was still powerful in the 19th century BC.

Copy of the Sumerian king list, Isin, Iraq

BURIAL MOUNDS

Powerful leaders in central and western Europe in the Early Bronze Age were buried in timber graves beneath large mounds. In this grave in Germany, bronze axes, daggers, and gold ornaments were buried with the deceased male, as was a younger female.

Male skeleton

Female skeleton

Cutaway, burial mound, Leubingen, Germany

SYMBOLIC SUBSTITUTES

In Egypt, statues of the deceased were placed in tombs of wealthy nobles. These were intended to act as symbolic substitutes in case the deceased's mummified body was destroyed. By the Middle Kingdom period (2040-1640 BC) a statue of the deceased was also often set up in a local temple, so that food offerings could be brought there without the need for a lengthy journey to the tomb itself. This statue of Ankhreku, a noble and official, dates to around 1850 BC.

Seated statue of Ankhreku, Egypt

1800 - 1600 BC

FOOD & ENVIRONMENT	SHELTER & ARCHITECTURE

AMERICAS

WINTER FOOD SOURCE

Chenopod seeds

Sunflower seeds

Chenopods and sunflowers, which are both native to North America, were domesticated in eastern North America by c.1800-1600 BC, making this region an independent center of plant cultivation and marking a critical change in the way of life of North American societies. The seeds were important to many communities, since they could be stored for use as food in late winter.

PYRAMID SHRINE

The building of monumental structures was well established in the Andes by c.1800 BC. An example built in this period is the Huaca (burial mound) de Los Idolos at El Aspero, on Peru's central coast. It consists of a series of quadrangular enclosures built on a pyramid. The platforms are made of stone and molded adobe.

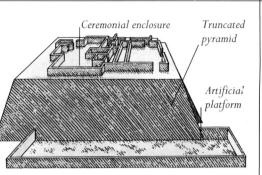

Ceremonial enclosure

Truncated pyramid

Artificial platform

Huaca de Los Idolos, Peru

EAST ASIA & AUSTRALASIA

WILD AND FARMED FOODS

Southeast Asian villages of this period typically relied on a mixture of wild and domesticated food sources. The village site of Ban Na Di in central Thailand, for example, was situated close to good rice-growing land near the confluence of two small streams. In addition to cultivating rice, the inhabitants kept cattle and pigs for meat and collected fish and shellfish during the rainy season when the streams were well stocked. The fish could have been salted or turned into paste for use during the long dry season. Small clay pellets were found in large numbers, and these may have been used as ammunition for hunting wildfowl, but the evidence indicates that birds did not form an important part of the diet.

Shell midden, Murramarang, southeastern Australia

ABORIGINAL CAMPSITES

In Australia, shell middens (mounds of discarded shell debris) are common features of Aboriginal campsites. Shelter would have been provided by huts made from large sheets of bark, or simple windbreaks made of branches. Evidence from this shell midden at Murramarang on the southeastern coast indicates that the place has been used regularly as a campsite over the past 4,000 years.

MIDDLE EAST & SOUTH ASIA

IMPORTED CLOVES

The cities of the Indus Valley were abandoned by 1800 BC, and there is no evidence that trade between Mesopotamia and South Asia continued after 1740 BC. In southeastern Syria, however, a jar containing cloves dating to around 1700 BC has been found; since cloves were native only to the East Indies, they must have been brought almost 5,000 miles — a journey unparalleled in length by any other import of this period.

Cloves

ROYAL PALACE

The palace at Mari by the river Euphrates in northern Mesopotamia took several centuries to build, and covered 35 acres. With more than 260 rooms, it housed the ceremonial and residential quarters of the royal family as well as the civil service and workers producing goods for court use and trade. It was destroyed by the Babylonians in 1757 BC.

Courtyard

Throne room

Royal palace, Mari, Syria

EUROPE

FIELD BOUNDARIES

Farmers of the Middle Bronze Age (c.1800-1400 BC) in Europe fenced or hedged their fields to prevent wild animals from eating the crops, but few traces of these boundaries have been found. The oldest surviving examples are those in southern Britain, covering several square miles. Farmers used dry-stone walls to divide the landscape into fields and pastures. In the fields, which were small and square, but large enough to be worked by ard (a simple plow), wheat, barley, peas, and beans were grown. Each harvest was followed by a fallow period during which the soil could recover its fertility.

Wooden shingles

Tiny windows to keep out the elements

Bronze Age houses, Sissach, Switzerland

ALPINE CABINS

Houses in the Alps in the Middle Bronze Age were built to withstand the harsh climate. At Sissach, Switzerland, sturdy log dwellings were erected on stone bases. Their roofs were made of shingles, or wooden slates, firmly fixed in place and weighted down by heavy stones.

AFRICA

GRINDING GRAIN

Every Egyptian household made its own flour by pounding grain with mortars on dish-shaped grindstones. The flour was then mixed with water to make dough and baked into bread, which was either eaten or used in the brewing of beer. This tomb model shows a male member of an Egyptian household kneading dough.

Tomb model of a man kneading dough, Egypt

FARMING VILLAGES

The earliest remains of houses in West Africa come from sites of the Kintampo group in modern Ghana. The houses, dating to around the 18th century BC, were permanent rectangular structures built of wattle and daub (interwoven twigs and sticks covered with clay), roofed with thatch. Some of the woodwork was decorated with carved moldings. These were farming villages, with remains of domestic goats and cattle as well as oil palm nuts and yam graters. Most had only a handful of houses, although some spread over a wider area. The remains at Ntereso, one of the largest villages, cover almost two acres, but how much of this area was occupied at one time remains uncertain.

TECHNOLOGY & INNOVATION

FOREST-CLEARING TOOLS

As eastern North American societies shifted toward greater reliance on cultivated crops, they needed field areas for planting. The manufacture of grooved axes, like this example found in Ohio, consequently became more important. These tools were used for clearing land and cutting down trees, and would have been attached to a handle at the groove.

Grooved ax, Ohio

BRONZEWORKING

Alloys of copper and zinc or lead had come into use in East Asia shortly before 2000 BC, and true bronze, which is an alloy of copper and tin, was in widespread use by 1800 BC. The first bronze ritual vessels were made at the city-state of Erlitou in northern China, which had been founded in around 1900 BC. These ritual vessels were to become one of the most sophisticated products of Chinese metalworkers. Great advances were made in the centuries that followed, with bronze being used to make not only ritual equipment, including vessels designed to contain food and wine, but also large numbers of tools and weapons.

BABYLONIAN SCIENCES

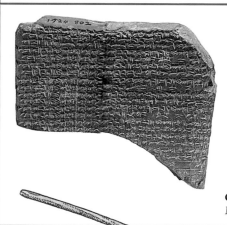

The Babylonians were famous for their expertise in astronomy, astrology, and mathematics. Systematic planetary observations were recorded and used to predict the future. Those made at the city of Kish of the rising and setting of the planet Venus are accurate enough to be used to establish the exact dates of the early Mesopotamian kings.

Copy of the Venus Tablet, Kish, Mesopotamia

WOODEN PLOW

Although the horse- or ox-drawn ard, or simple plow, had been in use in Europe since around 4000 BC, the oldest preserved plow in Europe is this crook ard found at Hvorslev in Denmark. The design could hardly be simpler, with the arm and the coulter, or cutting point, made from a single forked branch of a tree.

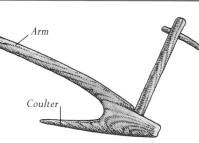
Arm
Coulter

Crook ard, Hvorslev, Denmark

ARMY EQUIPMENT

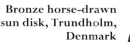

Soldiers in Egypt were equipped with hide shields and bronze spears; they wore short linen skirts and leather helmets, but were barefoot. The army relied heavily on mercenaries from neighboring regions, like this archer from Nubia. A major innovation in around 1700 BC was the introduction of the horse-drawn chariot. Chariots could operate only on level terrain, however, and in most military operations infantry remained crucial.

Nubian archer

ART & RITUAL

HARVESTING RITES

One of the earliest sacred enclosures at Kotosh, in the Huanaco Valley of central Peru, is the Templo de Los Nichitos (Temple of the Little Niches). The temple was the ritual center of an egalitarian small-village society, and was associated with planting and harvesting ceremonies. The enclosure itself was a low-walled, quadrangular structure made of stone, aligned north to south.

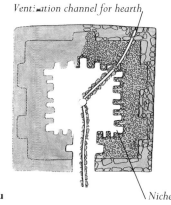
Ventilation channel for hearth
Niche

Plan view, Los Nichitos temple, Kotosh, Peru

STATUS BURIAL

In a small chamber in a cemetery at Roonka, beside the Murray River in South Australia, an Aboriginal man and child of high status were buried around 4,000 years ago. The man wore a headband of notched wallaby teeth and a feather-fringed skin cloak fastened with bone pins. Earlier skulls found in New South Wales show that the top two front teeth had been forcibly removed, probably as part of a male initiation ritual.

Skull with headband, Roonka, South Australia

NATURE OF THE GODS

Mesopotamian religion boasted a multitude of deities; one Babylonian list records the names of over 2,000. Most took human form, but there were various good and evil beings with animal features. Some were associated with particular places, or represented natural forces or abstract qualities, and others were deified rulers. Over the centuries the characters of the gods evolved and often the attributes of one were synthesized with those of another. Originally An, the sun-god of Uruk, was king of the gods, but during the 3rd millenium BC he was succeeded by Enlil, the god of the city of Nippur.

Bronze horse-drawn sun disk, Trundholm, Denmark

SUN WORSHIP

This bronze wheeled model of a sun disk pulled by a horse, found at Trundholm in Denmark, suggests that sun worship was common in Scandinavia during the Middle Bronze Age. One side of the disk was covered with gold leaf to represent the sun, while the other was blank, perhaps representing night.

KING OF THE UNDERWORLD

Hieroglyphic texts painted on Egyptian coffins in the 18th century BC show that the myth of Osiris, god of the underworld, had become the basis for the dominant afterlife belief. Slain by his brother Set, Osiris was resurrected by the goddesses Isis and Nephthys. He thus became a symbol of rebirth after death, and it was widely believed that the deceased would dwell for all eternity in a netherworld ruled by him.

Osiris figurine, Egypt

ALPINE LAKE VILLAGES

33,000 BC

The prehistoric lake villages of Europe's Alpine region are famous because of their exceptionally well-preserved remains. These were first revealed in Switzerland in 1853-54, when severe wintry conditions followed a prolonged drought that dried up rivers and lakes. Clusters of wooden posts, which proved to be the remains of Neolithic and Bronze Age houses, were exposed to view. The wood had stayed intact in the waterlogged lake beds, where destructive bacteria could not thrive, and even perishable foods were preserved. The wealth of remains made it possible to reconstruct a vivid picture of daily life in an Alpine lake village.

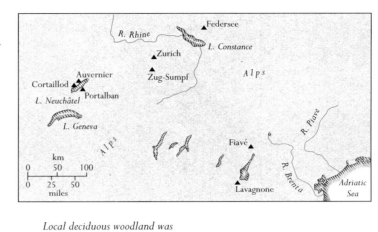

ALPINE EUROPE *left*
The sites of several hundred lake villages have been identified in the Alpine region of Europe (covering eastern France, Switzerland, northern Italy, and Austria). They are located mostly around the shores of Lake Constance, Lake Zurich, and Lake Neuchâtel in Switzerland.

▲ Lake village site

Local deciduous woodland was the source of timber supply

Alpine lake village

Fields of grain on lower slopes

Livestock kept on dry pasture outside the settlement

Reed-thatched roofs

Gap beneath roof allowing smoke out

Animal brought into compound to be slaughtered

Racks for drying fish

CULTIVATED CROPS
Alpine villagers farmed the dry ground near the lakeshore, cultivating grains such as wheat and barley. Beans, peas, and lentils, and flax for making linen, were also grown. The abundant wild plant foods were gathered, notably nuts, berries, and apples. Livestock included cattle, pigs, and sheep, and fish were a dietary staple.

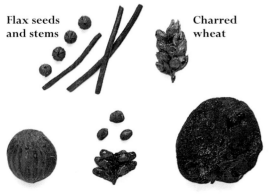

Flax seeds and stems

Charred wheat

Hazelnut   **Charred barley**   **Charred apple**

TOOL TECHNOLOGY
The Alpine slopes were covered by thick forests when the lake villages were occupied. At first, stone axes and adzes were used by the villagers to clear land for fields and fell trees for building houses and fences. These were replaced by harder, more durable bronze axes around 2000 BC. Both stone and bronze axes were originally mounted on handles made of beechwood or ash.

Smaller tools, including composite tools made by wedging stone blades into sleeves of antler, were used for lighter tasks such as cutting reeds for making baskets and thatching. By the Late Bronze Age (c.1400-800 BC), bronze had replaced stone even for utilitarian tools such as sickles.

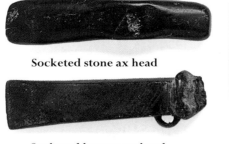

Socketed stone ax head

Socketed bronze ax head

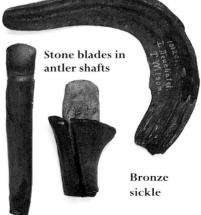

Stone blades in antler shafts

Bronze sickle

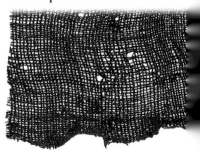

Bronze pin

WOVEN TEXTILES
Fragments of textiles are some of the most delicate preserved remains from the Alpine lake villages. Textiles were woven on looms either from locally grown flax (to make linen cloth) or from wool, and some were dyed with brightly colored patterns, using dyes derived from plants.

SECURE LOCATIONS *below*

Some Alpine lake villages were located on the lakeshore, others were built on platforms raised on piles above shallow water at lake edges, perhaps for security reasons. A typical feature of lakeshore villages was a timber fence surrounding the settlement. Villages consisted of some 10 to 20 rectangular timber-framed houses with walls of timber planks and pitched roofs of reed thatch. Pathways over marshy ground were made by placing split logs side by side and pegging them down. Analysis of tree rings in timbers has revealed how settlements grew from a handful of dwellings to maximum size within a decade. Settlements were typically occupied for 30 or 40 years, because any wood that was continuously damp and exposed to the air soon began to decay.

Coniferous forests at higher altitudes

Fishing on lake

Reed beds at lake edges provided material for thatching and basketry

Timber piles supporting houses over marshy ground

Split-log pathway

Timber plank walls

Timber fence surrounding settlement

TOGGLES AND PINS

Fragments of clothing were rarely preserved, even in the waterlogged environment of the Alpine lake settlements, but decorated clothing fasteners are common remains. These fall into two categories: buttons and toggles of bone or antler; and bronze pins Pins were used to fix capes or cloaks at the shoulder; they have been found near the shoulders of bodies in graves, although the clothing itself was not usually preserved in burials. Toggles were used to fasten coats or tunics, although some may have been elements of horse harnesses.

Woven textile fragment

Perforated deer-horn toggle

Perforated bone amulet

Engraved decoration

Decorated pottery jug

Incised geometric decoration

DECORATED CONTAINERS

The inhabitants of the Alpine lake communities made extensive use of pottery vessels for cooking and storage. The finer vessels were well made and often decorated with incised geometric designs. Other remains indicate that these people did not rely on pottery alone but also used baskets and containers of carved wood.

Wide-rimmed pottery vessel

CHAPTER 10
EXPANSION & CONSOLIDATION
1600 - 1000 BC

Settlers colonize the Pacific islands and Arctic North America

Hittites, Egyptians, and Mitannians struggle for supremacy in the Levant

Mycenaeans of mainland Greece take control of Crete and the Aegean

The Olmec of Mesoamerica begin to build massive ceremonial centers

The Shang state assumes control in China

Toward the middle of the 2nd millennium BC, urban civilizations and well-established farming communities flourished in the temperate and tropical latitudes of Eurasia and the Americas. Beyond the Arctic Circle, the ancestors of the Inuit people were learning to cope with the harshness of the climate; in the Pacific, intrepid sailors began to colonize far-flung islands, a process that took 2,000 years to complete.

Resourceful colonizers
The colonization of the Pacific islands began around 1600 BC, with settlers migrating from Southeast Asia. Although initially they reached only the westernmost Pacific islands, the colonists had spread as far east as Tonga and Samoa by 1000 BC. Taking with them pottery, livestock, and cultivated plants, they soon adapted to their new island environments, but continued to make long sea voyages to other islands to obtain commodities such as basalt and obsidian (black volcanic glass) for making tools. These colonists are known as the people of the Lapita culture, after a site of the same name on the Pacific island of New Caledonia. The culture is characterized by elaborately decorated pottery known as Lapita ware.

An equally remarkable colonization was also taking place far to the north, on the edge of the Arctic Circle. From the coasts of Alaska, groups of Arctic seal hunters

migrated eastward to settle the Hudson Bay area in around 1600 BC, ultimately reaching as far as Greenland. These settlers soon adapted to the freezing climate, aided by the development of a

Royal headdress

EGYPTIAN QUEEN
One of the finest works of art in New Kingdom Egypt, this painted head portrays Nefertiti, queen of Egypt during the reign of the pharaoh Akhenaten (1353-1335 BC).

distinctive technology known as the Arctic Small Tool Tradition, in which small stone blades were used to form the cutting edges of knives.

Warfare and diplomacy
The Egyptian civilization was at its height during the New Kingdom period (1550-1070 BC), while the Hittite Empire dominated Anatolia (what is now Turkey), and the kingdom of Mitanni held sway over the upper reaches of the Euphrates River. Alternating between diplomacy and warfare, these three states vied for control of the Levant (the coastal strip of Syria, Lebanon, and Israel). Cities were besieged and battles were fought in open country between bodies of infantry supported by elite forces equipped with the new, light-framed, two-wheeled chariot. For most of this period the cities of southern Mesopotamia were under the rule of the Kassite dynasty of kings (1415-1155 BC), who had their capital at Babylon. They played little part in the Levantine wars, but there was a constant flow of diplomatic correspondence between them and the other Middle Eastern courts. The common language used in this diplomacy was the Akkadian language of Mesopotamia, written in the script known from its wedge-shaped marks as cuneiform. The Kassites also introduced the *kudurru*, a kind of boundary stone used to record allocations of land.

GOLD NECKLACE
Fine gold jewelry, such as this necklace from Anatolia, testifies to the wealth of the rulers of the Middle East.

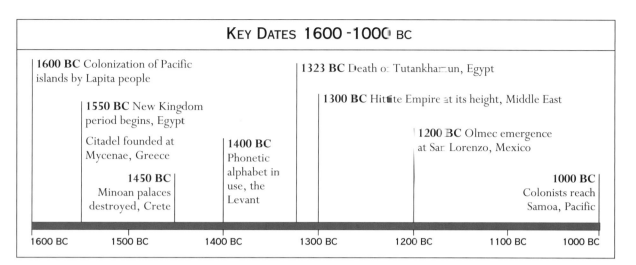

KEY DATES 1600 -1000 BC		
1600 BC Colonization of Pacific islands by Lapita people		**1323 BC** Death of Tutankhamun, Egypt
1550 BC New Kingdom period begins, Egypt		**1300 BC** Hittite Empire at its height, Middle East
Citadel founded at Mycenae, Greece	**1400 BC** Phonetic alphabet in use, the Levant	**1200 BC** Olmec emergence at San Lorenzo, Mexico
1450 BC Minoan palaces destroyed, Crete		**1000 BC** Colonists reach Samoa, Pacific

1600 BC   1500 BC   1400 BC   1300 BC   1200 BC   1100 BC   1000 BC

Wealth of Egypt

In Egypt, despite the strain of war in the Levant, funds were still available for major building works at home. Most of the great temple of Karnak, with its many courts and pylons (gateway towers), was built in this period. So too were the vast seated statues known as the Colossi of Memnon, and the rock-cut temple at Abu Simbel. So great was pharaonic wealth that even a minor king such as Tutankhamun (reigned 1333-1323 BC) was buried with amazing treasures. This was also an age of powerful queens, including Hatshepsut and Nefertiti.

Mycenaean civilization

Named after a site in the eastern Peloponnese, the Mycenaean civilization developed on the Greek mainland in around 1600 BC. The Mycenaeans were warriors and traders and soon dominated the Aegean. Their power spread to Minoan Crete around 1450 BC. There they borrowed the Linear A script, which had been developed for the purposes of Minoan administration, and adapted it to make a new script, Linear B, for recording their own language.

Ear spool   *Spout*

EFFIGY JARS
Ceramic effigy jars from Ecuador often depict humans with congenital abnormalities, including dwarfs.

Complex societies

In North America, impressive earthworks began to be built at sites like Poverty Point, Louisiana. These served primarily as ceremonial centers and were the work of small communities that were gradually growing in social complexity.

The major development in Mesoamerica was the birth of the Olmec culture and the building of its great ceremonial centers on low hills above the coastal plain of the Gulf of Mexico. This was one of the most fertile agricultural regions in Mesoamerica, with the potential to support a large population. Toward 1000 BC a similar development took place in the central Andes, with the rise of a ceremonial center at Chavín de Huantar and the birth of the Chavín decorative style, evident in architecture, ceramics, and art. The style is characterized by dramatic representations of mythical and real animals and snarling human faces.

Animals symbolizing various deities

Stylized cuttlefish motif

Creamy color characteristic of Mycenaean pottery

Contract inscribed in cuneiform text

SYMBOLIC REPRESENTATIONS
Boundary stones were used in Mesopotamia to record land grants and tax concessions. The gods, represented here by symbolic motifs, act as witnesses to the contract.

DECORATED POTTERY
Mycenaean pottery was widely traded in the eastern Mediterranean from 1500 to 1100 BC. This vessel is decorated with a typical stylized cuttlefish motif.

1600 - 1000 BC

Spread of bronze in Europe

In about 1200 BC the Mycenaean palaces in mainland Greece were abandoned, the Hittite Empire fragmented, and even the Egyptian state was struggling against the onslaught of neighboring peoples. Yet in Europe beyond the Aegean, this was a time of increasing prosperity; the use of bronze for tools and weapons became widespread and even regions without sources of copper and tin, such as Denmark, produced refined bronzework with imported raw materials.

There were also cultural changes, indicated by the spread of urnfield burials from Central Europe to the south and west. This burial custom involved cremating the dead and placing their ashes in pottery urns, which were then buried in cemeteries known as urnfields. New metal tools, weapons, and vessels spread with the burial rite, giving large areas of Europe a more homogeneous cultural identity.

Rise of Shang China

In East Asia the period following 1600 BC was also one of progress under the Shang Dynasty (c.1600-1027 BC), which assumed control of northern China. Extensive cities arose; and royal graves at the later Shang capital, Anyang, testify to the skill of Shang bronzeworkers, who created exquisite ritual vessels, many in the form of animals. Animals were important in Shang mythology as messengers through which the rulers could communicate with their ancestors. The new skill of writing developed, as seen on the oracle bones used to interrogate divine forces and foretell the future.

In contrast to the refinement of courtly life, the ordinary Shang farmer had to make do with tools of wood and stone to cultivate crops of millet, rice, and soy beans. Yet it was these farmers who were the backbone of the Shang economy.

Eastward shift to the Ganges Valley

In South Asia the pattern of events during this period is less clear. Indo-Aryan groups came to dominate northern India, as recounted in the *Rigveda*, a later Indian religious epic. After the demise of the Indus civilization to the west, the main cultural and political focus gradually shifted further east, where farmers were slowly taming the heavy soils and dense vegetation of the fertile Ganges Valley. It was here that the foundations of classical Indian civilization were laid.

Cattle herders

Around 1200 BC, groups of cattle herders from the Nile Valley became established in the Great Lakes region of East Africa. In addition to herding, they gathered wild plant foods and probably engaged in some small-scale cultivation. They also made decorated wood and pottery containers as well as carved stone bowls. Some groups practiced cremation, whereas others buried their dead under stone cairns or in rock crevices. They were still pursuing their traditional way of life when the first Bantu-speaking groups arrived in the region from West Africa in the last few centuries BC.

AMERICAS

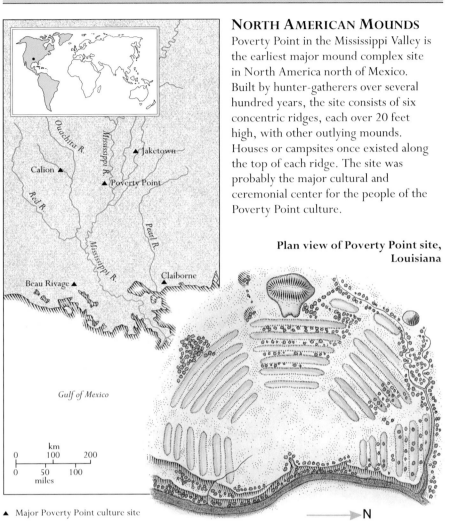

▲ Major Poverty Point culture site

NORTH AMERICAN MOUNDS

Poverty Point in the Mississippi Valley is the earliest major mound complex site in North America north of Mexico. Built by hunter-gatherers over several hundred years, the site consists of six concentric ridges, each over 20 feet high, with other outlying mounds. Houses or campsites once existed along the top of each ridge. The site was probably the major cultural and ceremonial center for the people of the Poverty Point culture.

Plan view of Poverty Point site, Louisiana

CEREMONIAL CENTERS

While monumental structures had existed in South America since around 2400 BC, a new phase of building temples and other structures for communal use on top of earthen mounds began around 1600 BC. Monumental architecture at centers of ceremonial and civic importance marks the beginning of complex societies in South America and Mesoamerica. While there are similarities in artistic and ceramic traditions, people in these regions started building ceremonial centers independently. The engravings shown here adorn a wall at Cerro Sechin, a ceremonial center in Peru's Casma Valley. They depict warriors and their mutilated victims.

■ Settlement site

Engravings, Cerro Sechin, Casma Valley, Peru

EUROPE

MYCENAEAN GREECE

During the Mycenaean Age (16th-12th centuries BC), the Greek mainland was divided into small kingdoms governed from fortified citadels and royal palaces. Good examples are known at Mycenae, Thebes, Orchomenos, Tiryns, and Pylos. Despite the warlike nature of their society – illustrated in Homer's epic poems, the *Iliad* and *Odyssey*, which describe the war against Troy – some Mycenaeans became successful traders. During the 14th and 13th centuries BC, their decorated pottery vessels were exported throughout the Aegean and eastern and central Mediterranean, in exchange for copper from Cyprus and Sardinia, ivory from Syria, and gold from Egypt.

Mycenaean decorated vessel, Greece

Coastline of the period --
Major administrative center ■
Major settlement □

AFRICA

NEW KINGDOM EGYPT

The New Kingdom period in Egypt (1550-1070 BC) began when the Theban pharaoh Ahmose I, "the Liberator," finally expelled the Hyksos, chariot-riding soldiers and traders from the Middle East who had invaded and ruled most of Lower Egypt for more than 100 years. Five centuries of prosperity followed. Egypt became an imperial power under such rulers as Amenhotep III (1391-1353 BC); giant twin statues of his image – the 69-feet-high Colossi of Memnon – were erected at his mortuary temple near the Valley of the Kings.

Coastline of the period --
Extent of New Kingdom Egypt ▦
Temple ▲
Royal tomb site ■
Royal capital □

Colossi of Memnon, Egypt

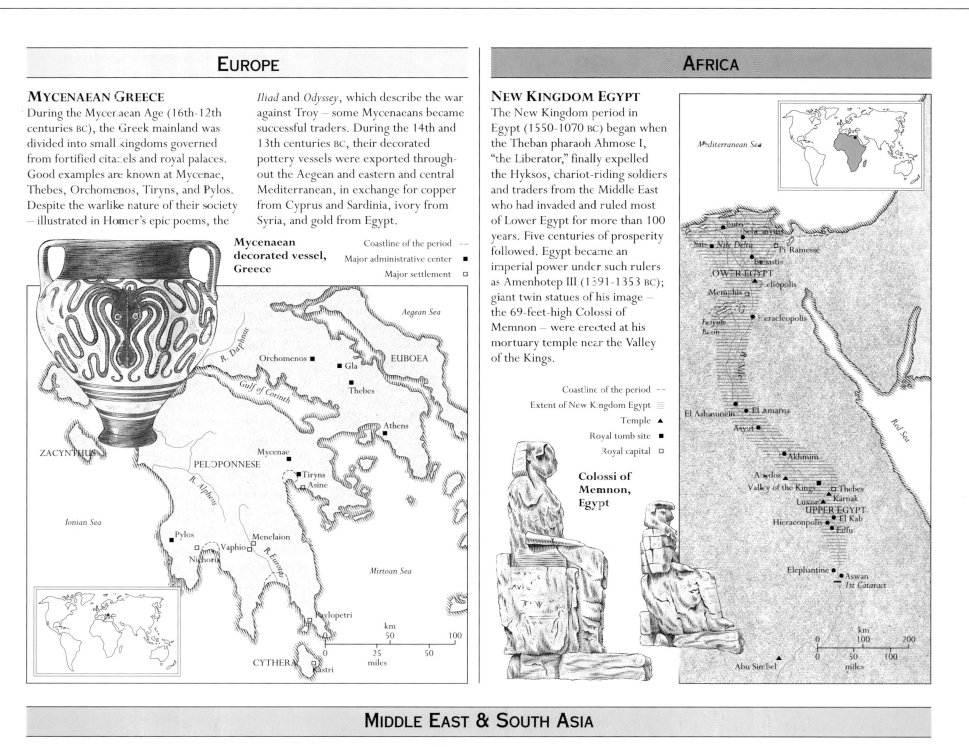

MIDDLE EAST & SOUTH ASIA

HITTITE EMPIRE

The Hittites, who spoke an Indo-European language, gained control of most of the Anatolian Plateau, in modern Turkey, during the 14th century BC, with their capital at Hattushash (modern Bogazköy). They struggled with Egypt and the rulers of the kingdom of Mitanni in northern Mesopotamia for control of the Levant (the coastal strip of Syria, Lebanon, and Israel). After the inconclusive Battle of Qadesh in 1285 BC, the Hittites signed a peace treaty with the Egyptians, which left them in control of the northern Levant. In the west the Hittites were in contact with the country of Ahhiyawa on the Aegean coast of Turkey, sometimes identified with the Achaeans who fought in the Trojan War. The Hittite Empire was destroyed early in the 12th century BC, perhaps by invaders who came across the Bosphorus from the northwest.

Heartland of Hittite Empire ▦
Greatest extent of Hittite Empire ▥

Seal impression of a Hittite king, Hattushash

1600 - 1400 BC

33,000 BC

FOOD & ENVIRONMENT	SHELTER & ARCHITECTURE

AMERICAS

KEY ROOT CROP

Finds of specialized ceramic griddles in the Orinoco River delta and elsewhere in the American tropics and the Caribbean, including Puerto Rico, indicate the widespread consumption of the root crop manioc by 1500 BC. Griddles were used to cook cakes of grated manioc, which is still an important crop in Central and South America today.

Griddle, Puerto Rico

SMALL VILLAGES

By 1500 BC, small indigenous communities had grown up throughout the river valleys of eastern North America. At Iddins, Tennessee, the remains of a circular house about 10 feet across, made of wooden poles covered with a layer of thatching, were found. A number of pits used to store food and supplies were located nearby.

Layers of thatch

Fish-smoking rack

Iddins village scene, Tennessee

EAST ASIA & AUSTRALASIA

FOOD FROM THE SEA

The oceangoing colonists from Southeast Asia who gradually began to settle the islands of the western Pacific as far as Tonga and Samoa around 1600 BC were accomplished fishermen, whose diet included fish, porpoises, and turtles. They also gathered shellfish in shallow coastal waters, which is evident from the many middens (mounds of discarded shell debris and fishbones) littering their campsites. Shells were also used to fashion fish hooks, like this later example from the Marquesas Islands.

Shell fish hook, Marquesas Islands, South Pacific

PLANNED CITIES

The Shang state (1600-1027 BC) in China was, at this early stage, made up of individual walled cities with gate towers. Before a city was built, oracles would be consulted, and the city was then constructed according to a plan with clearly defined areas for different social groups and occupations. For example, Zhengzhou, a city on the Yellow River in northern China founded around 1400 BC, was roughly square in plan, and enclosed by a rammed-earth perimeter wall over 4 miles long and 33 feet high. Within the wall to the north were a palace and an earthen altar; to the south were dwellings, storage pits for grain, pottery, and oracle bones, and burial pits containing human sacrifices. Outside the wall were separate industrial areas for bone workshops, pottery kilns, and bronze foundries.

MIDDLE EAST & SOUTH ASIA

DOMESTICATED CHICKENS

First domesticated in China around 6000 BC, chickens were common in the Indus Valley by 2000 BC, and by 1500 BC they were widespread in the Middle East. Chickens were often represented on works of art, and their bones have been discovered at many archaeological sites. Described as "birds that lay eggs every day," chickens were included in tribute paid by the Syrians to the Egyptian pharaoh Tuthmosis III (1479-1425 BC).

SMALLER SETTLEMENTS

Characteristic wall niches

Mud-brick wall

Entrance

Plan view of a mud-brick house, Pirak, Indus Valley

After the demise of the cities of the Indus civilization, the people of northwestern India and Pakistan returned to living in smaller settlements. One of the largest was Pirak, a town of solidly built mud-brick houses covering 22 acres, which flourished around 1500 BC. Although large for the period, it was less than a quarter of the size of major Indus Valley cities such as Harappa and Mohenjo-Daro. The substantial size of the houses and grain storage silos at Pirak indicates that it was a prosperous agricultural community.

EUROPE

FOOD STORAGE

Olive oil, wine, grain, and other agricultural produce were delivered to the palaces of Minoan Crete, including Knossos, by farmers in the rural interior by way of tax or tribute. The produce was stored in rows of huge pottery jars in the palace larders. Most of it was used to support the palace communities – ruling elite, servants, and craftsmen – but some was destined for overseas export.

Storage jar, Knossos, Crete

FRESCOED PALACE

The Minoan palace of Knossos in Crete, rebuilt during this period, was a complex structure containing workshops, larders, shrines, reception rooms, and royal apartments, arranged around a paved central courtyard. The building itself was of limestone and up to four stories high, with painted wooden columns and walls covered with frescoes.

Painted wooden columns

Frescoed wall

Cross section, Knossos palace, Crete

AFRICA

PLOWING THE LAND

Egyptian farmers used wooden-bladed plows pulled by a pair of oxen to work the damp, fertile soil of the Nile floodplain. The same type of plow is still used in the Nile Valley today.

Plow, Egypt

FRONTIER FORTRESS

The great fortress at Buhen by the Second Cataract of the Nile River lay hundreds of miles to the south of the southernmost towns of Egypt proper. It was reoccupied and restored by the Egyptians around 1500 BC as they regained control over this region in the early part of the New Kingdom period (1550-1070 BC). It defended Egypt's southern frontier and protected the lucrative river trade, especially the passage of gold from Nubia. Imposing rectangular brick foundations enclosed a governor's palace, temples, houses, and barracks.

Fortified walls *Main gateway*

Fortress, Buhen, Egypt

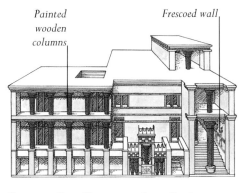

TECHNOLOGY & INNOVATION

EARLY CERAMICS

The site of Ocós, near Chiapas on the border of Mexico and Guatemala, has yielded some of the earliest ceramics in Mesoamerica. The pottery is shell-marked and stamped (a decorative style typical of this period), or impressed with cord and fabric marks. In later phases, it was occasionally decorated with iridescent paint. The pottery has been found throughout southern Mesoamerica and may be related to the Chorrera ceramic tradition of Ecuador.

Grooves made with shells

Pottery fragments, Ocós, Guatemala

MASS-PRODUCED BRONZES

The quantity of bronzes surviving from the Shang period in China indicates a very high degree of organization and specialization in their production. Using techniques derived from ceramic production, bronzes were made in multi-piece ceramic molds with incised decoration, which were assembled before firing. This system enabled the Chinese to mass-produce vessels of a complexity and size unknown elsewhere at this period.

Bronze vessel, Erligang, China

GLASS AND GLAZE

In the Middle East from around 1600 BC, glass was molded to form objects and vessels, and was used as a glaze applied to pottery. Glass also served as a substitute for semiprecious stones. An earlier technique of glazing stones and objects of quartz paste, which had been used since around 5000 BC, continued to be practiced.

Molded glass plaque representing a naked female, Lachish, Israel

LINEAR B SCRIPT

Some of the clay tablets found at Knossos are inscribed with a script known as Linear B. This was developed from Linear A script for use by the mainland Greeks who took control of Crete around 1450 BC. Linear A had been designed for the purposes of Minoan administration and was in use in Crete and parts of the Cyclades by 1650 BC. In contrast with Linear B, Linear A has yet to be deciphered.

Linear B tablet, Knossos, Crete

Each symbol represents a syllable

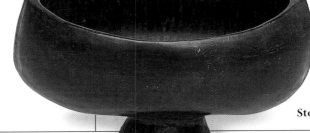

RAISING WATER

A device known as a *shaduf* was introduced around 1500 BC in Egypt. It enabled farmers to lift water from rivers, streams and irrigation canals to water their fields. The original *shaduf* was a weighted lever holding a clay, leather, or wooden bucket; it took more than one day to water an acre.

ART & RITUAL

SHAFT TOMBS

Shaft-and-chamber tombs are a distinctive feature of the early cultures of western Mexico. Consisting of a vertical shaft leading to one or more beehive-shaped chambers, some tombs contained the remains of up to 10 people. The gathering and stacking of bones also suggests that the tombs were reopened for later burials. The tombs at El Opeño, Michoacán, contained ceramics dating to 1450 BC.

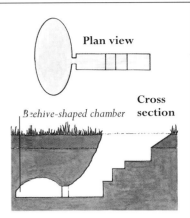

Plan view

Beehive-shaped chamber

Cross section

Shaft-and-chamber tomb, El Opeño, Michoacán, Mexico

SACRIFICIAL VICTIMS

Human sacrifice was common during ceremonies for the ancestors, at funerals and during the construction of city walls or temples during the Shang period in China. The victims, many of whom were beheaded, included men with weapons and dogs, women, children, prisoners of war, and shackled convicts. Some were buried in massive royal grave pits; others, in smaller pit graves outside royal tombs, were clearly distinguished by rank – their burials range from single interments with grave goods to multiple interments without offerings. Humans, oxen, sheep, and pigs were also buried in the foundations of walls.

INDO-ARYAN BURIALS

Indo-Aryan groups may have moved into the Indian subcontinent around 1800 BC, introducing new languages and the horse, but there is little clear archaeological evidence of their arrival. In the centuries following, signs of change are clearest in the Gandhara region of northwestern Pakistan, where a new kind of burial was adopted around 1600 BC — the stone-lined pit-grave, in which a body was laid in a chamber sealed over with substantial stone slabs.

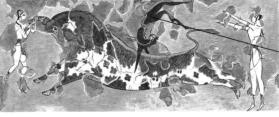

Acrobat vaults over bull's back

Fresco, Knossos, Crete

RELIGION AND RITUAL

Frescoes and figurines indicate the nature of Cretan religion at this time. One of the principal deities was a goddess, portrayed bare-breasted and wearing a long robe; in one depiction she clutches a snake in each hand. One fresco shows a hazardous bull-leaping ritual, in which acrobats seized the horns of a charging bull and vaulted over its back. There were shrines in the palaces and towns, but other important sanctuaries were located on mountaintops some distance away, where people gathered to celebrate seasonal religious festivals.

STONE BOWL CULTURE

Cattle herding spread southward from the semiarid fringes of the Sahara as the region became increasingly desertified after 4000 BC. Herder groups from the Nile Valley also moved southward into areas free of the tsetse fly, reaching the East African grasslands about 2,500 years later. Their most substantial possessions were heavy, elegantly crafted stone bowls like this example from Kenya.

Stone bowl, Kenya

121

1400 - 1200 BC

FOOD & ENVIRONMENT

SHELTER & ARCHITECTURE

AMERICAS

DUCK HUNTING

The duck decoys discovered in Lovelock Cave, Nevada, were stored some time after 1500 BC. Together with other caches of bone fish hooks, often on setlines, which have many hooks on a single line, they show the importance of lake-side resources to early residents of the cave.

Feathers tucked under twine that held reeds together

Duck decoys, Lovelock Cave, Nevada

CEREMONIAL COMPLEX

The most significant early culture in Mesoamerica was that of the Olmec (c.1500-400 BC). San Lorenzo, near the Coatzacoalcos River on Mexico's Gulf Coast, is the earliest known, most important Olmec ceremonial center, first occupied around 1500 BC. By 1200 BC, the inhabitants had altered a natural hill formation by building up high ridges and carving

out deep ravines, then building a series of earthen, flat-topped ceremonial mounds on the leveled hilltops. Surrounding these mounds were 20 artificial ponds, fed and drained by a system of covered stone water conduits, the earliest known in the Americas. Around the center of San Lorenzo some 200 house mounds have been found, indicating a population of perhaps 1,000 people.

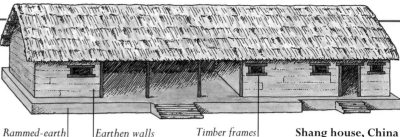

Rammed-earth foundations *Earthen walls* *Timber frames* **Shang house, China**

EAST ASIA & AUSTRALASIA

DOMESTICATED ANIMALS

Farmers living in village communities in northern China at the height of the Shang civilization, from around 1400 BC, supplemented grain crops by large-scale breeding of domestic animals such as dogs, cattle, water

buffalo, pigs, and sheep. These animals satisfied the demand both for meat, skin, and bones, and for ritual sacrifices in which up to 1,000 cattle were slaughtered at a time. Remains of dogs have also been found buried in tombs alongside human sacrifices.

WOODEN-FRAMED HOUSES

The large houses of the Shang period (c.1600-1027 BC) in China were built on rammed-earth foundations, which

supported a superstructure of wooden beams covered with thatch. This building technique remained a permanent feature of Chinese architecture.

MIDDLE EAST & SOUTH ASIA

FLOURISHING FARMS

Small farming villages had flourished in peninsular India while the Indus civilization was at its peak, and they continued to grow in prosperity after its demise (around 1800 BC) through the 2nd millennium BC. Barley was the main crop, along with millet and rice introduced from East Asia. At the site of Inamgaon, a massive rubble and mud-mortar embankment was built to protect against flooding, as was a water channel that may have been used for irrigation. Cattle, sheep, and goats were important, and fishing provided a further source of protein for many communities. Farming villages were also flourishing in the Ganges Valley in northeastern India by this time.

Sculpted stone lion *Gate tower*

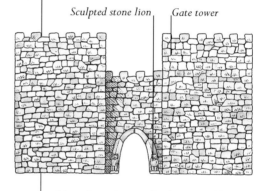

Lion Gate, Hattushash, Anatolia

FORTIFIED GATES

By 1300 BC the Hittites controlled an empire stretching from Anatolia to northern Mesopotamia. The capital at Hattushash (modern Bogazköy), Anatolia, was located on a promontory formed by the junction of two branches of the Budakozu River. The city's stone fortifications were 4 miles in perimeter. Massive gates were decorated with sculptures of gods, sphinxes, or animals, perhaps inspired by contact with Egyptian architecture.

EUROPE

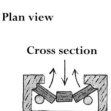

Plan view

Cross section

Wooden animal trap, Nisset Norremose, Denmark

HUNTING AND TRAPPING

In large areas of northern Europe, hunting and trapping continued to be important long after farming was introduced, especially where marshes, poor soil, or harsh climate made agriculture impossible. This wooden animal trap from Nisset Norremose in Denmark was a sophisticated device, with beechwood springs that activated a pair of oak flaps. It may have been designed to trap forest game such as wild boar and deer.

BORROWED STYLE

The Mycenaeans of mainland Greece borrowed many architectural features from Minoan Crete, including brightly painted frescoes to decorate walls and timber columns to support upper stories. In the palace at Pylos, the main reception room floor was painted with colored squares and had a large decorated central hearth.

Ceremonial hearth

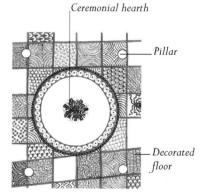

Pillar

Decorated floor

Plan view of main palace reception room, Pylos, Greece

AFRICA

HARVESTING PLANTS

Evidence for early cultivation in the forest zone of West Africa may date to this period or earlier. At Iwo Eleru, a rock shelter in southwestern Nigeria, new implements were adopted around the middle of the 2nd millennium BC. These were tiny blades of chalcedony, probably mounted in a bone or wooden handle to form a kind of sickle. They were used for cutting plant stalks, perhaps to harvest cultivated grains or to cut reeds for thatching.

COLUMNED HALLS

Egyptian architects used closely spaced columns to support the stone cross beams of high temple roofs. These were known as hypostyle halls (from a Greek term for a room with many columns). The hypostyle hall at Karnak, with its 134 relief-carved columns, is an architectural masterpiece that dates to around 1280 BC.

Model of hypostyle hall, Karnak, Upper Egypt

TECHNOLOGY & INNOVATION

FISHING EQUIPMENT

Objects as mundane as plummets (fishing-line weights) were often imbued with considerable beauty by their makers. This plummet, found in Ohio, is made of hematite (a type of iron ore), and would have been in daily use as fishing equipment.

Groove for attachment to fishing line

Hematite plummet, Ohio

Inscribed oracle bone fragments, China

CHINESE WRITING

In China around 1200 BC, a writing system based on pictographs developed from the early use of distinctive marks on pots to denote numbers or clan names. Shang rulers recorded events on wooden or bamboo slips (the origin of writing in vertical lines). Inscriptions on oracle bones and bronzes include at least 2,000 characters, many of which are related to those in use today.

PHONETIC ALPHABET

By 1400 BC, a phonetic alphabet that used symbols to represent the sounds of individual letters — instead of syllables or words — was being widely used in the Levant (the coastal strip of Syria, Lebanon, and Israel). It was invented by the Canaanites, a Semitic people, who based their alphabet on Egyptian hieroglyphs. A version in the cuneiform script (named after its wedge-shaped marks) was invented for writing on clay tablets in Ugarit, a town on the coast of Syria. The alphabet was used by the Phoenicians in northwestern Syria and was passed from them to the Greeks.

WOVEN WOOL

Weaving must have been a major activity in Bronze Age societies in Europe, but remains are rare. A woven tunic and a short corded skirt, both of wool, were preserved in the Egtved burial mound on the island of Jutland in Denmark. Unsuitable for daily wear in a cold northern climate, the skirt may have been worn on ritual occasions.

Bronze buckle

Woolen clothing, Egtved, Denmark

GOLD JEWELRY

The Egyptians employed their finest craftsmen for working in gold, using the ore from over 100 mines in Nubia. Slaves broke up the rock, crushed it in huge mortars, ground it to a powder, and finally washed it to separate the gold. Goldsmiths fashioned ornaments that were important symbols of rank and prestige, including necklaces in intricate combinations of gold strung together with semiprecious stones.

Coral

Gold necklace, Egypt

Lapis lazuli

ART & RITUAL

Hole for attachment to cord

Sandal-sole shape

Shell gorget, Wisconsin

IMPORTED ORNAMENTS

In North America, long-distance exchange of shell, copper, and other raw materials increased during this period.

In the Great Lakes region, marine shell from the Gulf of Mexico was made into large "sandal-sole" gorgets, which were worn as neck ornaments.

ANIMAL DECORATION

Bronze ritual vessels made during the Shang period in China were decorated with stylized animals such as tigers, birds, or cattle. Animals were believed to possess powers of communication with spirits, and their presence on these vessels was intended to facilitate contact with the ancestors. Stylized decoration was achieved using multi-piece clay molds incised with elaborate motifs.

Incised decoration

Fragments of ceramic piece molds, China

EXCHANGE OF GIFTS

In the 15th century BC, the rulers of Egypt, Mitanni, Hatti, Assyria, Babylonia, Elam, and Anatolia corresponded with each other and exchanged gifts and brides. One letter records that a statue of the Mesopotamian goddess Ishtar was sent from Assyria to the ailing pharaoh of Egypt in the hope that she would cure him; another that a sculptor was sent as a present by the king of Babylon to the king of the Hittites. This gold figurine of a Hittite king, dating to around 1400 BC, was found in western Anatolia.

Gold figurine of a Hittite king, western Anatolia

VOTIVE FIGURINES

The Mycenaeans produced terra-cotta figurines that are often found among the ruins of shrines and sanctuaries. Models of animals are common, but many others represent humans with arms upraised.

Votive figurine, Mycenae, Greece

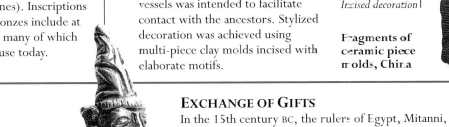

Papyrus from *Book of the Dead*, Egypt

JUDGMENT DAY

During the New Kingdom period (1550-1070 BC), wealthy Egyptians were buried with a *Book of the Dead*, a collection of spells that, it was believed, would help them attain eternal life. Papyruses depict the deceased appearing before the gods to claim that they are worthy of the gift of eternal life. The heart of the deceased was then weighed on the scales of justice, and if the verdict was favorable, the deceased would finally be led into the presence of Osiris, god of the underworld.

1200 - 1000 BC

FOOD & ENVIRONMENT	SHELTER & ARCHITECTURE

AMERICAS

HILLSIDE TERRACING

The Andean region of South America is precipitous, with steep slopes and valleys. Farmers in Peru wishing to increase their lands to feed an expanding population overcame the problems of steep slopes and erosion by building cultivation terraces and ridged fields. Such terracing, which included irrigation channels, was first built around 1200 BC.

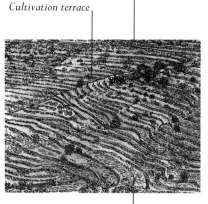

Cultivation terrace

Agricultural terraces, Andes region, Peru

MONUMENTAL COMPLEX

Among the monumental constructions at Moxeke in the Casma Valley on the northern coast of Peru, Pampa de las Llamas stands out as the largest and most complex series of enclosures. These were rectangular compounds, made of stone and molded adobe (mud and straw), and were intended for public use. The site dates to 1200 BC, and was possibly the residence of the elite of Moxeke, but may also have been the bureaucratic center of the region.

EAST ASIA & AUSTRALASIA

Soybeans

SOYBEANS

The soybean was introduced throughout China from its native Manchuria in around 1200 BC during the late Shang period (c.1600-1027 BC). It proved crucial in times of famine, since the crop could withstand both drought and flood. Soybean cultivation spread throughout East Asia, and its by-products, such as oil, bean curd, and soy sauce, became major sources of protein.

RAISED HOUSES

The early inhabitants of the western Pacific islands built settlements along the shoreline, their houses being raised on wooden stilts over the shallow coastal waters. A number of wooden posts — the remains of a house built around 1100 BC — have been found on Eloaua Island in the Bismarck archipelago off the coast of New Guinea. Large quantities of food remains and other debris had fallen from the house into the water, where they were preserved. The house was built early in the life of the settlement, but the village itself was occupied for another 700 years.

MIDDLE EAST & SOUTH ASIA

LAND TENURE

Land in Mesopotamia was owned by kings, temples, and private individuals; it could also be rented. The sale or gift of land was recorded on clay tablets, and by 1200 BC it had become common practice to record royal land grants on a *kudurru* (boundary stone), which was carved with motifs symbolizing the gods and preserved in city temples.

Scorpion motif, detail from a boundary stone, Babylon, Iraq

Grain storage basket

House, Inamgaon, India

Storage jars in pit

HOUSE DESIGN

Inamgaon, an important farming site in peninsular India, continued to flourish during this period. The layout of the town and differences in the size and complexity of its houses suggest the emergence of a social hierarchy. The houses contained cooking fire-pits, sunken storage chambers lined with lime for keeping barley, and round, mud platforms that supported enormous wheat baskets.

EUROPE

SCENES OF FARMING

In a few locations in the high valleys of the Alps and in parts of southern Sweden, notably Bohuslan, carvings on rock faces depict scenes from daily life in the Late Bronze Age (c.1400-800 BC). One scene found in both areas shows a man plowing with an ard, or simple plow, pulled by a pair of oxen. In the Alps, there are also what seem to be plans of fields, some showing the positions of individual trees. The plowing scenes may have been connected with ceremonies of a religion associated with agricultural fertility, and the sites themselves may have been open-air sanctuaries.

Wasserburg village, Germany   *Single-room log houses*   *Raised walkway*

ISLAND VILLAGE

Warfare in Europe during the Late Bronze Age led to an increase in fortified settlements like the Wasserburg in Germany, located on a small island in the Federsee. A timber palisade supported a walkway along the water's edge, and bridges connected this to the dry ground of the island.

AFRICA

HUNTING

This detail from a tomb wall painting indicates that it was common for Egyptian nobles to go hunting in the papyrus marshes along the Nile. Accompanied by his family, this nobleman is using a snake-shaped throw stick and holds up three herons as decoys to disguise his approach. The painting also shows the rich variety of birdlife in the area.

Detail of wall painting, Egypt

VALLEY TOMBS

A vast barren valley to the west of the Nile and the city of Thebes, known as the Valley of the Kings, became the burial place of Egyptian pharaohs during the New Kingdom period (1550-1070 BC). One of the largest tombs is that of Ramasses IX (1131-1112 BC), a great series of rock-cut corridors and halls hewn 262 feet back into the hillside. Within the tomb an architect's plan of the tomb was carefully marked out in red lines on a limestone slab.

TECHNOLOGY & INNOVATION

VERSATILE MATTING

Tule reeds, willows, and cattails were common materials used by nomadic hunter-gatherers in western North America to make lightweight woven matting. Mats could easily be carried and tied to new hut frames with each move. Mats were also used for seating or sleeping areas.

Fragment of reed matting, Lovelock Cave, Nevada

TRADE IN BRONZE

Bronzeworking spread from the Caucasus (the mountainous region between the Black Sea and the Caspian Sea) via Central Asia to southern Siberia, where by 1200 BC a flourishing bronze industry had developed. Ornaments, daggers, and socketed axes were produced, some of which were traded south across the Gobi Desert to China, even though the Chinese were mass-producing their own bronzes.

Bronze socketed ax, Siberia

Socket for handle

IRONWORKING

In India, the first experiments in ironworking took place before 1000 BC. Since most of peninsular India has relatively restricted supplies of copper ore, although iron ore is abundant, ironworking soon took over from copper and bronzeworking. At first, crude daggers and ax heads with iron cross-bands (for attachment to handles) were produced.

MUSICAL INSTRUMENTS

The ceremonial lures (horns) made during the Late Bronze Age in Denmark are magnificent examples of highly skilled bronzeworking. They were made in segments using the lost-wax technique, in which a wax model was used to shape a clay mold; when the clay was fired, the wax melted, and molten metal could be poured in.

Mouthpiece

Bronze lures (horns), Brudevaelte, Denmark

ORIGINS OF THE HARP

The Egyptians' enjoyment of music and revelry is shown in the many wall paintings depicting parties. They also had public festivals at which people were entertained by singers and dancers. Music was played on lyres, flutes, harps, and castanets, often by small orchestras of women. Harps originated in Egypt and varied in size — some were as tall as the player. The number of strings also varied, from four to over 20.

Woman playing a harp; detail of a wall painting, Egypt

ART & RITUAL

BURIAL GOODS

At Tlatilco in the Valley of Mexico several hundred burials were found beneath the floors of houses. The occupation of the site began around 1200 BC and continued until 500 BC. The social class of the deceased can be distinguished by the type and number of objects buried with them. Small figurines like the one shown here are known as Pretty Ladies.

Ceramic figurine, Tlatilco, Mexico

DECORATED POTTERY

The red-slipped pottery vessels made by the early inhabitants of western Pacific islands (islands east of, and including, Tonga and Samoa) were elaborately decorated with patterns incised or stamped on the vessels before firing. Most of the designs were geometric, but stylized human eye and face motifs were also used.

Eye

Pottery shard with human face motif, Santa Cruz Islands

PANTHEISM

Each of the culturally distinct peoples of the Middle East — the Sumerians and Akkadians of Mesopotamia and, to the north and west, the Kassites, Amorites, Hurrians, Hittites, Elamites, and Canaanites — had their own pantheon of deities. Each deity looked after a particular aspect of life and was venerated according to the customs of each people. However, early Middle Eastern religions were not exclusive, and adherence to one did not preclude worship of the gods of other peoples. Gods were readily identified across cultures — thus the weather gods of the Hittites, Babylonians, and Elamites were deemed to be different manifestations of the same god.

CREMATION

Around 1200 BC, the people of Central Europe abandoned their traditional custom of burying the dead. They began instead to cremate the bodies and place the ashes in pottery urns, which were buried in cemeteries known as urnfields. Urnfields are striking for their uniformity, with rich and poor being disposed of in a very similar way. The custom, which may have been linked to new religious beliefs, eventually spread to western and southern Europe.

Funerary urn, northeastern France

ROCK GONGS

In many parts of Nigeria, projecting pieces of rock have been used for thousands of years as "rock gongs," producing a ringing note when struck with another stone. Some of these gongs are capable of giving out as many as 13 different notes, and have been used in recent times during initiation ceremonies. At Dutsen Habude in the Kano region of northern Nigeria, a passage leads from a rock shelter to a narrow cleft in which a slab of granite has been wedged upright. Marks show that it was used as a gong. Excavations in the rock shelter itself yielded a number of hammerstones dating to the 2nd millennium BC, which may have been discarded after being used to strike the gong.

THE SHANG STATE IN CHINA

Named after the Shang Dynasty of kings who ruled China from *c.*1600 to 1027 BC, the Shang state was one of several contemporary Bronze Age states in China, with successive capitals at Erlitou, Zhengzhou, and Anyang. The use of cowrie shells for currency and the movement of raw materials such as jade show that long-distance trade and commerce were well established between these states. The Shang period was characterized by highly developed ceremonial and ritual systems, and by exquisite bronzework. The state was centered in a king who, through his ancestors, was the sole link with the high god. The social hierarchy was highly stratified: hereditary craftsmen used the earliest known mass-production techniques, and tens of thousands of laborers and slaves were mobilized to build defensive city walls, royal palaces, and tombs.

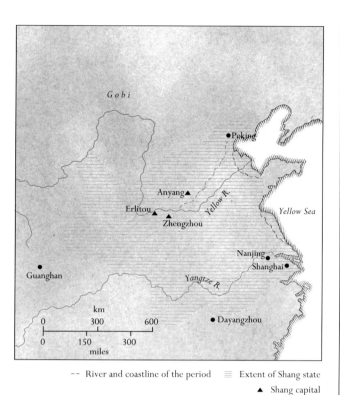

-- River and coastline of the period   ≡ Extent of Shang state

▲ Shang capital

SHANG CHINA *above*
The Shang state included cities in the Yellow River Valley and the North China Plain. Evidence points to other contemporary states around Peking to the northwest, Nanjing and Shanghai to the southwest, at Guanghan in Sichuan, and at Dayangzhou in Yunnan, near the Vietnamese border.

RITUAL BRONZES

Many bronze vessels were used in China for ritual sacrifices to the ancestors and associated ceremonies. Ritual bronze vessels were used in sets. The quantity, type, and size of vessel depended on the owner's wealth and social status. Strict traditionalism was observed in the rites, and each vessel had its own shape and function. Some were used for wine, others for food.

BRONZE FOOD VESSEL *below*
This type of *fang ding* (four-legged food vessel) evolved from the earlier three-legged variety. The raised-knob and double-bodied-snake decoration was common throughout the Shang period.

EARLY PALACE COMPLEX *below*
At its height the Shang state consisted of over 1,000 walled cities linked to the royal capital and palace at Anyang. The palace complex included official halls and offices from which the king ran the administration and army. A prototype Shang palace or temple building at Erlitou, the earliest capital, dates to around 1500 BC. It consisted of a large, south-facing rectangular hall in a courtyard surrounded by galleries, and a gateway on the southern side – a pattern that persisted throughout the Shang period and in Chinese imperial architecture until the 20th century.

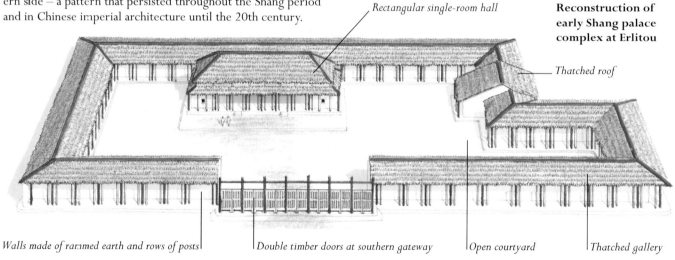

Rectangular single-room hall

Reconstruction of early Shang palace complex at Erlitou

Thatched roof

Walls made of rammed earth and rows of posts | *Double timber doors at southern gateway* | *Open courtyard* | *Thatched gallery*

MEANS OF DIVINATION
Over 100,000 oracle bones made from cattle bones and tortoiseshell were found in storage pits in palace and temple areas at Anyang. These were a means of divination and were used by the king to consult his ancestors. Engraved with questions, the bones were then heated, and the resulting cracks interpreted as positive or negative answers. The answers, and their verification or otherwise by future events, were also recorded on the bones, which were then stored in royal archives. Oracle bones reveal much about Shang society, recording sacrifices, rituals, and events such as military campaigns, hunting expeditions, and official appointments.

Engraved oracle bones

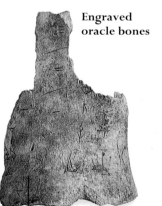

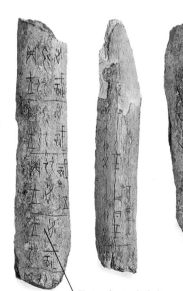

Oracle bone texts reveal the date, inquirer's name, the question, and its verification

Texts also included questions about state matters, the weather, harvest, and health

Bronze vessel with ram's head decoration

ANIMAL MOTIFS *above*
Since the Chinese thought that animals were able to communicate with the ancestors in the spirit world, vessels were decorated with the stylized heads of animals, including tigers and rams.

WINE VESSEL *above*
This three-legged wine vessel could be placed over a fire and then be removed using the raised knobs.

WEALTHY ELITE
The wealth of the Shang elite was dramatically revealed by the discovery at Anyang in 1976 of the unplundered tomb of Fu Hao, one of the three main wives of the Shang king Wuding (1324-1266 BC). According to inscriptions recorded on oracle bones, Fu Hao was a military commander and landowner in her own right, and was responsible for certain sacrificial rites. Although smaller than most royal burials, her tomb contained over 1,600 bronze ritual vessels and other artifacts.

FU HAO'S SHAFT TOMB *right*
The tomb consisted of a 25-foot-deep pit with walls sloping slightly inward. At the base of the pit was a timber chamber housing Fu Hao's coffin. Unlike larger tombs, Fu Hao's tomb had no access ramps, although the entrance was covered by a sacrificial hall at ground level. Grave goods were found within the burial chamber itself and in the earthen fill between the shaft walls.

BURIAL GOODS
One of a pair of food vessels was among the most refined bronzes found in Fu Hao's tomb. Unlike those of ordinary four-legged vessels, the legs are not straight but represent standing dragons. The decoration on the sides of the vessel consists of double animal masks. Fu Hao's name is inscribed inside.

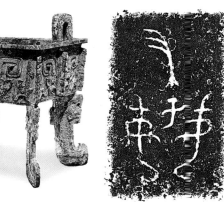

Food vessel inscribed with Fu Hao's name

COMMUNING WITH SPIRITS
The 590 jade items found in Fu Hao's tomb include many representations of animals and birds, exquisitely and naturalistically carved.

Cowries

Jade bird

MONEY COWRIES
Cowrie shells were imported from Southeast Asia to Shang China, where they were exchanged as a form of currency. Over 7,000 cowrie shells were found in Fu Hao's tomb.

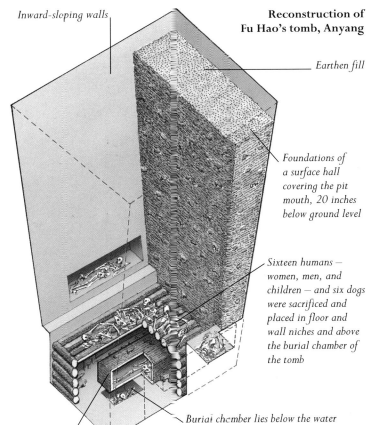

Reconstruction of Fu Hao's tomb, Anyang

Inward-sloping walls

Earthen fill

Foundations of a surface hall covering the pit mouth, 20 inches below ground level

Sixteen humans — women, men, and children — and six dogs were sacrificed and placed in floor and wall niches and above the burial chamber of the tomb

Fu Hao's coffin

Burial chamber lies below the water table; timber walls have disintegrated

ROYAL INSCRIPTION
Over 80 artifacts discovered in Fu Hao's tomb at Anyang were inscribed with her name or various titles, making hers the earliest tomb in China whose occupant is historically identifiable. She was already known as a royal personage from contemporary oracle bone records.

Rubbing of inscription of Fu Hao's name

IVORY *right*
Ivory objects dating to the Shang period are rare, so one of the surprising finds from Fu Hao's tomb was a pair of ivory beakers inlaid with turquoise. This one has a handle resembling a bird of prey. The decorative animal and mask patterns are similar to those on bronze ritual vessels, suggesting that the beakers also had a ceremonial purpose.

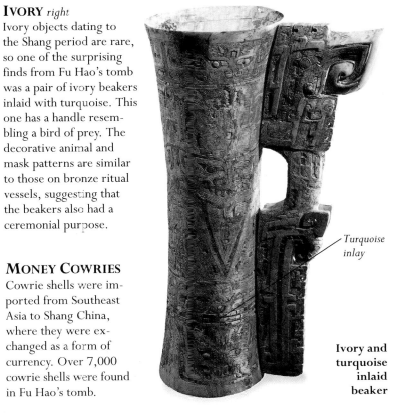

Turquoise inlay

Ivory and turquoise inlaid beaker

CHAPTER 11
RISE & FALL OF EMPIRES
1000 - 500 BC

Olmec culture thrives in the Mesoamerican lowlands

Ironworking adopted in the Middle East, Europe, India, and China

Assyrian, Babylonian, then Persian hegemony in the Middle East

Epic poetry and the classical arts flower in an age of Greek prosperity

China fragments after the fall of the Zhou Dynasty

The period 1000 BC to 500 BC witnessed the development of major cultural traditions in several regions of the world, in societies as diverse as the Nok of northern Nigeria, the Adena of North America, and the Assyrians of Mesopotamia.

Cultures and traditions

By 1000 BC the Olmec civilization, centered at San Lorenzo in Veracruz, Mexico, had constructed an impressive complex of monuments, including giant basalt heads that possibly represent Olmec rulers. After 900 BC, however, owing to religious iconoclasm or political upheaval, San Lorenzo was abandoned and a new capital was founded at La Venta. Here the Olmec developed a unique jade-working tradition, which influenced countless subsequent cultures.

In the Andean region of South America, the Chavín style, an artistic tradition centered in the site of Chavín de Huantar in central coastal Peru, was dominant during this period, and influenced Peruvian art for many centuries. Some regional art styles in northern South America suggest contact with Mesoamerica; for example, certain designs and decorative techniques of Chorrera ceramics from the central coast of Ecuador appear to be Mesoamerican in origin.

In parts of midwestern and eastern North America, earthen mounds began to be built specifically for burial purposes from 1000 BC. The first of these were the work of the Adena people, who lived along the banks of the Ohio River. Plant cultivation also became widespread in these areas. Throughout the Canadian Arctic, populations expanded as advanced techniques for large-scale hunting of marine mammals were developed.

Revolutionary raw material

In Europe and Asia, hunting and farming were revolutionized by a new material: iron. Iron has two main advantages over bronze: iron ore is relatively common, while the copper and tin needed to make bronze are less widespread; and when iron is mixed with carbon, it becomes, through a process called carburization, much harder than bronze. The first ironworking experiments were made in the Middle East before 2000 BC, but for centuries the use of iron was limited. By 1000 BC it was common in the Aegean and the western Levant, and had reached Europe, India, and China by 700 BC.

Characteristic downturned mouth

MASTER STONEWORKERS
This 3-inch-high ritual mask dating to 900 BC is made from serpentine, a highly prized green stone, and illustrates the expertise of Olmec stoneworkers.

EARLY AMERICAN GOLDWORKING
The first gold artifacts made in the Americas were Peruvian, in the Chavín style. This gold crown, dating to around 750 BC, was found near Chiclayo in Peru.

TRAPPINGS OF THE TOMB
Canopic jars, in which the internal organs of the deceased were stored in the tomb, were essential to the Egyptian mummification process. They came in sets of four.

Jackal head represents one of the four sons of the god Horus

Empire building

This was an age of powerful empires in the Middle East. During the 9th century BC, the Assyrians began to expand from northern Mesopotamia until they controlled the whole region, and by 700 BC the Assyrian Empire stretched from the eastern shores of the Mediterranean to the edge of the Iranian plateau. Assyrian rulers adorned their capital cities with temples dedicated to their many deities – such as that to Ninurta, goddess of love, at Nimrud – and with massive palaces from which they administered their extensive territories. However, Assyrian dominance was not to last, and a coalition of their enemies sacked the royal cities in 612 BC, making way for a new Middle Eastern empire centered in the city of Babylon. This in turn was overthrown in 539 BC by yet another power,

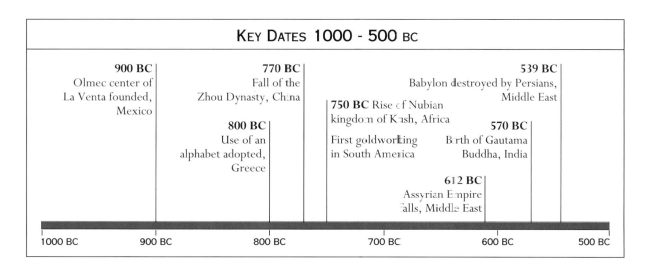

KEY DATES 1000 - 500 BC

900 BC Olmec center of La Venta founded, Mexico	**770 BC** Fall of the Zhou Dynasty, China		**539 BC** Babylon destroyed by Persians, Middle East
	800 BC Use of an alphabet adopted, Greece	**750 BC** Rise of Nubian kingdom of Kush, Africa / First goldworking in South America	**570 BC** Birth of Gautama Buddha, India
		612 BC Assyrian Empire falls, Middle East	

1000 BC   900 BC   800 BC   700 BC   600 BC   500 BC

that of the Persians, who by the end of the century had established an empire larger than any the world had yet seen. Their domain extended from Egypt and the Aegean Sea in the west to the borders of India in the east.

Alphabetic script

A major development of this period was the adoption of an alphabetic script in the Levant (the coastal strip of Syria, Lebanon, and Israel) and the Greek-speaking lands to the west. The first alphabet originated in the 2nd millennium BC and was transmitted to other parts of the Mediterranean by Phoenician traders and colonists after 1000 BC. The new script, in which each sign stood for a single sound, was much simpler than earlier syllabic or pictographic writing systems, and ultimately made writing accessible to many more people.

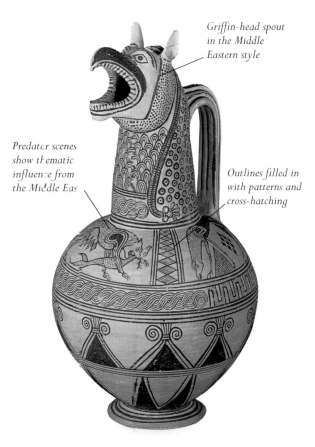

Griffin-head spout in the Middle Eastern style

Predator scenes show thematic influence from the Middle East

Outlines filled in with patterns and cross-hatching

DECORATIVE WARE
Greek potters drew inspiration for the decoration of painted vessels from designs and ideas current in the Middle East.

Blue color typical of Assyrian decorative ware

ASSYRIAN DEITY
This decorative tile from the Assyrian capital of Nimrud depicts Ninurta, goddess of love.

The alphabet was adopted in Greece around 800 BC and was adapted to the Greek language, with far-reaching consequences. One of the earliest uses of the Greek alphabet was to record Homer's epic poems, the *Iliad* and *Odyssey*, and by the 5th century BC a genuinely popular literary culture had developed – the first in Europe. The spread of a literate, Greek-speaking population was accompanied by the emergence of classical art and architecture during the 6th century BC, particularly in such prosperous cities of Aegean Turkey as Ephesus and Miletus.

1000-500 BC

Early coinage

Coinage made its first appearance in these centuries. The earliest coins were issued by the kings of Lydia, a state of western Anatolia (modern Turkey), around 600 BC. The advantages of the new money were soon recognized by Greek cities, which derived much of their wealth from trade, and by 560 BC both Greeks and Lydians were minting silver coins. The invention of coinage firmly established precious metals as the enduring measure of value in Europe.

Developments in Africa

The northeast of Africa was still dominated by the Egyptian state, although this was no longer as powerful as in previous centuries. The impact of Egyptian culture remained considerable, however, and many traditional features of the Egyptian way of life continued unchanged. The early rulers of the developing kingdom of Nubia (also known as Kush), in what is now northern Sudan, adopted the pyramid for their own burial monuments and used Egyptian hieroglyphs for their inscriptions. Nubia was no mere satellite of Egypt, but an independent state. The kingdom was at first centered in Napata, near the Fourth Nile Cataract, but in around 600 BC the capital moved south to Meroë.

The Phoenicians (after the Greek *phoenikes*, or "purple men," due to their trade in dyed cloth from Tyre) from the eastern Mediterranean founded a series of cities along the North African coast in the 9th century BC. Among them was Carthage, which soon became a major Mediterranean power. South of the Sahara, Nok farming communities in northern Nigeria began making, towards 500 BC, terra-cotta sculptures that are among the most striking examples of African art.

Continuing traditions

The demise of the Shang Dynasty in the 11th century BC at first had little effect on Chinese culture. Although the Zhou Dynasty (1027-770 BC) was now in power, ancient craft and architectural traditions were little changed. After Zhou rule ended in the 8th century BC, China was split into a series of small states, which were engaged in constant warfare over the next 500 years. In response to the unsettled conditions, much of the population sought refuge in newly built, fortified cities.

Elsewhere in Asia, the early 1st millennium BC was a time both of continuity and development. In Japan, although hunting and gathering remained the basis of daily subsistence for most communities, domesticated rice began to be grown in the south around 500 BC. In Southeast Asia and Australasia, traditional ways of life continued more or less unchanged. The rich diversity of natural resources available in these regions was skillfully exploited by the inhabitants, although Southeast Asian communities were increasingly relying on the cultivation of crops such as rice, yams, and taro. Meanwhile, in Polynesia, communities were well established on the islands of Tonga and Samoa, and distinctive Polynesian cultural traditions were being formed.

AMERICAS

ADENA CULTURE

Based along the Ohio River, the people of the Adena culture (1000-100 BC) subsisted by hunting, gathering, and limited plant cultivation. They were the first in the North American Midwest to build large earthen mounds in which the elite were buried. The Adena Mound (after which the culture is named) near Chillicothe, Ohio, was built in two stages: the first level contained a large, bark-lined tomb and other log-lined tombs with interred and cremated remains; the second contained burials but no tombs.

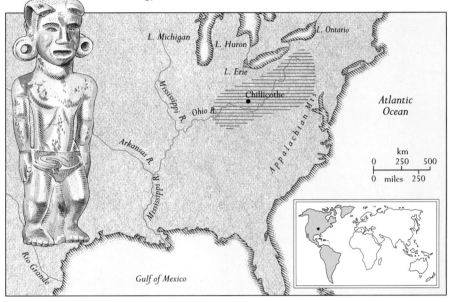

Adena effigy, Adena Mound, Ohio · Approximate extent of Adena culture ≡

AFRICA

MEROITIC KINGDOM

A native state had arisen in Nubia by 750 BC. Centered in Napata, it was known as Kush until around 600 BC, when the capital was transferred to the city of Meroë. Situated in an area of fertile land, Meroë was able to support a large urban population, and its proximity to sources of iron ore made it a major early ironworking center. Camel caravans imported luxury goods from Arabia via trading ports on the Red Sea coast and from the Mediterranean, while Meroë exported gold, ivory, and other raw materials in return. For centuries the Meroitic kingdom thrived at the edge of the classical world – too distant even for the Romans to attempt to conquer. Major Meroitic sites included the temples of Jebel Barkal and Musawarat es-Sofra.

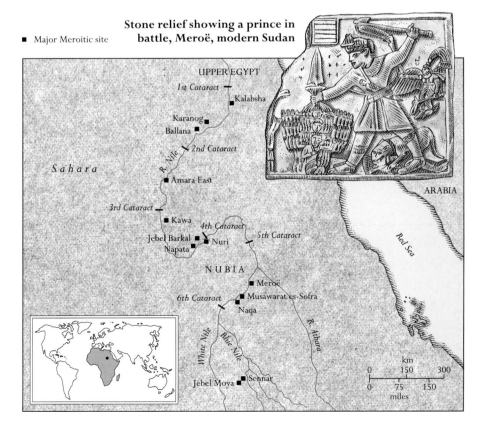

■ Major Meroitic site

Stone relief showing a prince in battle, Meroë, modern Sudan

EUROPE

GREEK COLONIES

After the Mycenaean Age, Greece remained fairly poor and isolated from the 12th to the 8th centuries BC until a Greek revival led to a remarkable period of colonization. Opportunists and those simply seeking to escape political or economic difficulties set out from their home cities to found new settlements around the shores of the Mediterranean and the Black Sea. Many of these settlements sprang up at the sites of good natural harbors and became hubs of trade by land and sea with Greek and non-Greek peoples. By the end of the 7th century BC, the network of Greek colonies stretched from Hemeroscopium (in modern Spain) in the west to Trapezus on the far side of the Black Sea in the east.

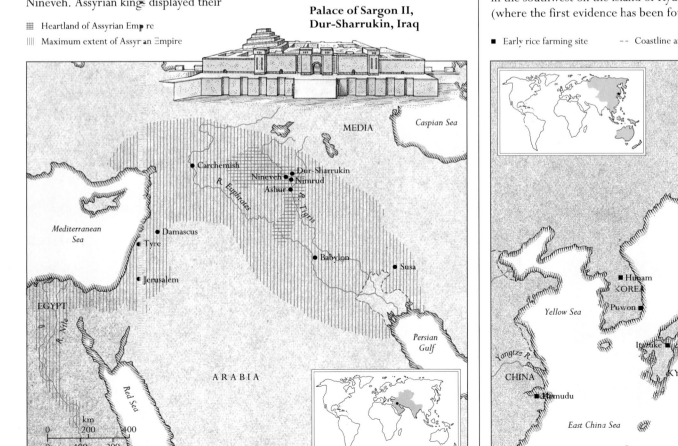

Greek merchant ship

Greek colony ▲
Greek city △

MIDDLE EAST & SOUTH ASIA

ASSYRIAN EMPIRE

From the 9th to the 7th centuries BC, the Assyrians dominated the Middle East from their heartland in modern northern Iraq, under powerful kings such as Sargon II (reigned 722-705 BC) and Ashurbanipal (668-627 BC), under whom the empire reached its fullest extent. Successive capitals were at Ashur, Nimrud, Dur-Sharrukin (modern Khorsabad), and Nineveh. Assyrian kings displayed their power in the construction of magnificent palace and temple complexes. Through military campaigns (which were recorded in the royal annals), diplomacy, and effective administration, the Assyrians extended their hegemony over most of the peoples of the Middle East, even conquering Egypt. The Assyrians were defeated, and Nineveh sacked, by the Babylonians and the Medes in 612 BC.

Palace of Sargon II, Dur-Sharrukin, Iraq

▦ Heartland of Assyrian Empire

▥ Maximum extent of Assyrian Empire

EAST ASIA & AUSTRALASIA

RICE FARMING

One of the most important staple foods in the world today, rice was being grown by Chinese farmers over 7,000 years ago. It was several millennia, however, before rice farming was adopted in Korea and Japan. Indeed, rice farming did not begin in Korea until the middle of the 2nd millennium BC, and a further 1,000 years passed before it reached Japan, beginning in the southwest on the island of Kyushu (where the first evidence has been found at the Itazuke site) and gradually spreading northward to Shikoku and Honshu. This delay in the adoption of rice farming is testimony to the continuing success of the fishing and hunter-gatherer way of life in these regions.

Cultivated rice

■ Early rice farming site   -- Coastline and rivers of the period

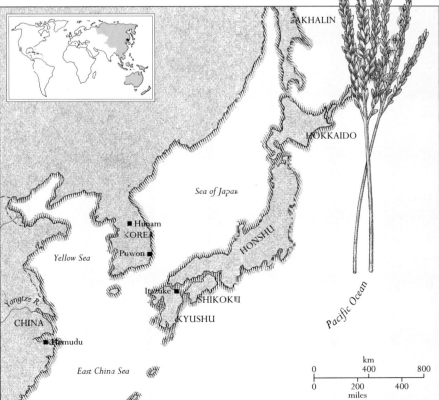

1000-800 BC

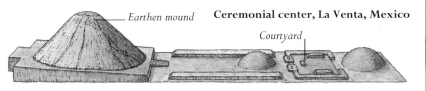

FOOD & ENVIRONMENT	SHELTER & ARCHITECTURE

AMERICAS

BEANS AND SQUASH
As hunter-gatherer populations expanded in southwestern North America, plants began to be cultivated to make food resources more reliable, rather than to increase food quantities. Over the next few centuries, beans and squash, along with maize, became staple crops for many societies in this region.

Beans and squash, New Mexico

CEREMONIAL CENTER
The early Olmec capital, San Lorenzo, was ritually destroyed and eventually abandoned. It was replaced in importance by a new center founded at La Venta, in a swampy region near the Tonalá River in southern Mexico.

— *Earthen mound*

Construction of many of the ritual buildings began around 900 BC. The central structure was a conical mound 98 feet high, possibly representing a volcano. Colossal sculpted basalt heads, characteristic of the Olmec civilization, were found nearby.

Ceremonial center, La Venta, Mexico

Courtyard

EAST ASIA & AUSTRALASIA

WINE DRINKING
Wine was an essential ingredient in sacrificial offerings made to the ancestors in China. Many bronze ritual vessels were made for storing or mixing wine, and different shapes were used for the clear and milky white varieties. Both types of wine were made from fermented grain, usually millet. Although white wine could be made overnight, clear wine took months to prepare. Drinking to excess was discouraged, and the use of modest wooden or bronze ladles, instead of larger vessels, was praised as a sign of moderation.

ROCK SHELTERS
At Fromm's Landing, on the Murray River in southeastern Australia, a series of limestone rock shelters was regularly used as a campsite by groups of Aboriginal hunter-gatherers for at least 5,000 years. These groups used the rich food resources of the river valley, but would have spent much of the year elsewhere, perhaps on the coast.

MIDDLE EAST & SOUTH ASIA

COOKING METHODS
Mesopotamian texts and recipes record 20 kinds of cheese, 100 varieties of soup, and over 300 types of bread. Meat was cooked over an open flame, while other food was boiled or baked. Much of the food was saturated in fat and oil.

Assyrian stone relief showing food preparation

DOORS AND GATES
In the Middle East, the earliest doors were not fixed on hinges but pivoted on posts, the bases of which rested on a socket stone. The massive doors of the palace at Balawat, Iraq, built by the Assyrian ruler Shalmaneser III (reigned 858-824 BC) worked on this principle. Temple and palace doors were often elaborately decorated with bronze cladding.

Details from bronze cladding, Balawat Gates, Iraq

EUROPE

FARMING TECHNIQUES
In northern Europe, farming tools developed slowly. The crook ard, a curved plow fashioned from a single block of wood, remained the standard implement for cultivation, as it had been for the previous 1,000 years. Farmers continued to cultivate a range of staple crops including wheat, barley, beans, and peas, but cattle herding remained important on the poorer soils. In coastal regions, the diet could be supplemented from the shoals of sea fish common in northern waters, such as cod, flounder, and haddock. The typical farmhouse was a long building of timber and thatch with stalls at one end where livestock could be kept during the winter months.

Hut urn, Italy

SIMPLE DWELLINGS
During the early Iron Age in Italy, people lived in huts built of wattle and daub, with wooden posts supporting a thatched roof. The huts are best known from terra-cotta models made as funerary urns. The earliest settlement at Rome, founded in the 10th or 9th century BC, was a village of dwellings like these.

AFRICA

Castor oil beans

MEDICINAL PLANTS
Egyptian physicians used a wide range of plants to treat their patients. Castor oil, for example, was believed to prevent baldness, and was also combined with beer as a laxative. Stomachaches were treated by eating bread made with lotus, while a mixture of elderberry and honey soothed headaches and eyestrain. The onset of gray hair was thought to be delayed by the application of a mixture of balsam and bird blood.

Elderberries

CAVE HOUSES
In the drier parts of East Africa and the savanna grasslands, caves and rocky overhangs continued to serve as convenient stopping places in which herders built temporary shelters. Construction involved a framework of twigs and branches covered with dry grasses. The herders would bring their animals under cover for the night to protect them from attack by lions and other marauding predators. These dwellings were never intended to be permanent; they were used to provide shelter only when livestock were moved from one pasture to another according to the different seasons of the year, and depending on the location of water. Rocky overhangs provided natural protection and a fire was built to deter unwelcome visitors. This traditional herder lifestyle continues in much of the Sudan and other parts of Africa to this day.

TECHNOLOGY & INNOVATION

CERAMIC STAMPS

Incised curvilinear motif

Handle for rolling seal

Seal and stamp, Tlatilco, Mexico

Cylinder seals and ceramic stamps have been found in burials at Tlatilco, an early village in Mexico's central valley. The presence of the stamps, as well as pyrite mirrors, necklaces, celts (small axlike objects), and ornaments, shows that the deceased were of high rank. The stamps were used to decorate textiles and the skin. Many motifs are Olmec in style, the result of trading between the two cultures.

BRONZE CASTING

This continued to be one of the great periods of bronzeworking in China. The bronze was a mixture of 90 percent copper and 10 percent tin, melted in a crucible inside a charcoal-fired oven. By tapping a small hole at the base of the crucible, the molten metal was channeled through the oven wall and into molds. The resulting ingots were remelted to make bronze objects.

Casting channel *Gas and smoke outlet* *Crucible*

Bronze-casting furnace, China

METROLOGY

Detail, Rassam Obelisk, Nimrud, Iraq

An accurate system of weights was essential for commerce in Mesopotamia, because payment was usually made by measuring out silver or copper. Weights were calculated according to the sexagesimal (multiples of 60) system. An obelisk found at Nimrud, Iraq, shows tribute being weighed before the Assyrian king Ashurnasirpal II (reigned 883-859 BC).

SPREAD OF IRONWORKING

The use of iron to fashion a wide variety of tools and weapons originated in the Middle East around 2000 BC, but it was many centuries before it spread to Europe. Iron tools and weapons made their first regular appearance around 1000 BC in Greece, where they were occasionally placed in graves with other burial goods accompanying the deceased. This emergent use of iron played an important part in the revival of Greek civilization and the subsequent

rise to power of the classical city-states. The advantage of using iron rather than copper and bronze was primarily its availability: iron is one of the most common metal ores. Properly worked, it could also give a very hard, durable cutting edge. Higher temperatures, however, were required in order to extract it from the ore.

PAPYRUS MANUFACTURE

Cyperus papyrus is a marsh reed that grows by the Nile. Ancient Egyptian papermakers peeled the bark off the reeds and cut the inner stems into strips approximately 20 inches long. These were then laid out on cloth in perpendicular layers and pounded, then pressed with weights, until they merged together to become one solid sheet. The resulting leaves of papyrus paper were dried and often glued together using a flour paste.

Papyrus reeds

Chopped stem

ART & RITUAL

STYLIZED POTTERY

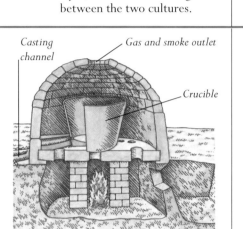

Chorrera ceramic vessel, Manabi, Ecuador

Pottery vessels in the Chorrera style (named after a site in Ecuador) were traded widely in the northern regions of South America, where they have been found at a variety of sites. The shape of this vessel, with its straight sides and flat bottom, is Mesoamerican. The incised geometric decoration is also reminiscent of Olmec motifs and suggests that even at this early date there may have been contact between Central and South America.

BRONZE INSCRIPTIONS

Chinese bronze vessels were considered to be representations of status and power in Chinese society. They were no longer designed only for the ritual use of the ruler, however, but were engraved with inscriptions that record relationships between the ruler and his dependents. Some allude to important events in the owner's life, describing, for example, official appointments, military victories, and transfers of land or slaves. They reflect a growing belief that supreme power rested on a moral rather than a divine principle, and that successful government depended on a system of reciprocal duties and rewards that was recognized by everyone.

COMMEMORATIVE ART

The Babylonian king Nabu-apla-iddina (reigned *c.* 887-855 BC) left this stone tablet to commemorate the erection of a statue of the sun-god Shamash. According to the text, the new statue was based on a clay image that had been discovered by chance. The style of carving is anachronistic, resembling that used in Babylonia 1,000 years earlier.

Stone tablet, Temple of Shamash, Sippar, Iraq

BRONZE FIGURINES

The island of Sardinia, to the west of Italy, was home to a flourishing bronzeworking industry in the 9th century BC. Among its most distinctive products were small figurines representing warriors and chiefs who inhabited *nuraghi*, powerful stone fortresses with high walls and towers, each fortress being the seat of a local ruler or clan.

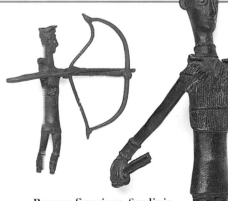

Bronze figurines, Sardinia

RELIGIOUS SYMBOLISM

Many bracelets and ornaments buried with the kings of the 21st Dynasty (1085-945 BC) at Tanis in the Nile Delta carry the sacred hieroglyph known as the *ankh*, the symbol of both physical and eternal life. It was depicted in the form of a cross with a loop at the top, often carried by gods as a way of representing eternity. The *ankh* had enormous significance in the cults surrounding Egyptian rulers.

Ankh, Egypt

800-700 BC

FOOD & ENVIRONMENT

SHELTER & ARCHITECTURE

AMERICAS

COOKING TECHNIQUES
Among the more unusual legacies of the Poverty Point culture of the Mississippi Valley (c.1500-700 BC) were thousands of small clay objects. Shaped into hundreds of different styles, these clay objects made it possible to cook the contents of a skin bag without damaging the bag. The bag was filled with water and food, and the clay objects, red-hot from the fire, were dropped inside.

Clay cooking objects, Louisiana

CIRCULAR HOUSES
The Adena people (1000-100 BC) of the Ohio River valley built circular houses ranging from 13 to 32 feet in diameter. The walls were formed by closely spaced vertical posts, indicating a wicker-work type of paneling. Posts supported the conical roof, and a hearth was set in the center of the building.

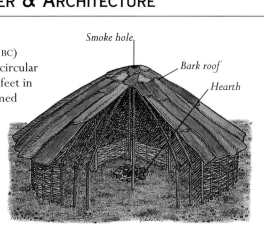
Smoke hole
Bark roof
Hearth

Adena house, Kentucky

EAST ASIA & AUSTRALASIA

SPECIAL FOODS
Chinese delight in good food was well established, and a poem written in the 8th century BC gives a list of succulent dishes that were the height of luxury. The basic Chinese principle of dividing food into grain, such as rice, wheat, or millet, and "dishes" to add flavor to the grain, spread throughout the East. The remarkably varied Chinese food tradition has its basis in early culinary experimentation combined with a thorough knowledge of wild plants and fruits, and a wide range of ingredients, which included fish from the Chinese coast, game from the northern hunters, and agricultural produce from the central plains.

ROOF TILES
Baked clay tiles, later to become a permanent feature of housing in central and northern China, began to replace thatch in the 8th century BC. Roofs were made from interlocking convex tiles with a row of rounded tiles, often decorated with animals for luck, along the eaves.

Round eave tile, Shaanxi, China

MIDDLE EAST & SOUTH ASIA

Seal impression showing a sick man being treated, Iraq

MEDICAL TREATMENT
Doctors and surgeons in the Middle East treated symptoms with remedies drawn from wild or cultivated plants. Hundreds of different diseases were recognized, each with its own prescribed remedy. Other healing practitioners in Mesopotamia were the exorcists who, believing that illness was caused by the actions of gods or demons, treated their patients through magical rituals.

HILLTOP FORTRESSES
The Urartians, whose kingdom of the 9th-7th century BC covered what is now eastern Turkey, Armenia, and northwestern Iran, were masters at fortifying their hilltop strongholds. Massive stone walls survive at many sites, and contemporary models reveal the extent of the battlements and turrets.

Bronze model of the royal Urartian fortress, Toprakkale, Turkey

EUROPE

DETERIORATING CLIMATE
Plant and animal remains from Biskupin in Poland illustrate the diet of northern Europeans during the 8th century BC. Wheat and barley had been the staple crops for over 1,000 years, but spelt replaced emmer as the principal wheat variety as the climate became wetter and cooler – part of a general climatic change affecting the whole of Europe at this time. Cattle were the dominant livestock, providing both meat and dairy produce.

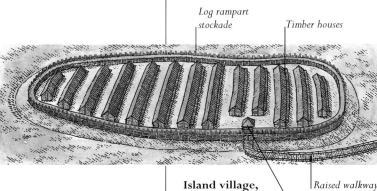
Log rampart stockade
Timber houses
Island village, Biskupin, Poland
Raised walkway
Gate tower

LAKE DWELLERS
Fortifications were an important consideration in the building of northern European villages such as Biskupin, a heavily fortified island village in a lake in northern Poland. Tens of thousands of oak and pine trees were felled in order to build the settlement, with its breakwater, rampart, and roads made of tree trunks laid side by side. Within these defenses, 13 rows of terraced houses were ranged along parallel streets.

AFRICA

MONKEY NETS
Hunter-gatherer groups in the Central African rainforest ate small animals of all kinds, particularly De Brazza monkeys, which were pursued with bows and arrows, then trapped in cunningly laid nets. The hunters drove troops of monkeys into the nets, where they were speared.

De Brazza monkey

NUBIAN TEMPLE
In the 8th century BC, the worship of the Egyptian sun-god Amun, or Amun Ra, was revived at Jebel Barkal in Nubia by rulers of the Nubian kingdom, which arose around 750 BC with its capital at Napata. A substantial new temple at the foot of the great rocky massif at Jebel Barkal was built on top of the one begun in the New Kingdom period (1550-1070 BC), when Egypt controlled the area. The layout of the new temple, with its pylons (gateway towers), courtyards, and pillared hall, echoed Egyptian designs, and it remained in use for many centuries. Much of the work was done during the reign of the Nubian king Piankhy, around 751-716 BC. Jebel Barkal became the ideological center of the Nubian state, and was to remain so even after the capital was transferred from Napata to Meroë in 600 BC.

TECHNOLOGY & INNOVATION

ARCTIC POTTERY

Simple pottery had appeared in the North American Arctic as part of the Arctic small tool tradition, introduced into Alaska by Siberian groups. Although it bears similarities to contemporary ceramics of eastern North America, this Denbigh pottery, named after Cape Denbigh on Norton Sound, did not spread outside northern Alaska, mainly because it would have been impractical for mobile caribou-hunting communities to carry heavy, fragile ceramics.

Denbigh pottery fragment, Alaska

DUG-OUT CANOES

The remains of a series of log boats found in northern Vietnam dating to the 8th century BC are the earliest direct evidence of boat building in Southeast Asia. These dug-out canoes, the largest of which is almost 15 feet long, were hollowed out of tree trunks. They had been used as coffins for the burial of wealthy or important individuals, accompanied by bronze weapons and buckets and, in one, a painted wooden box. Boat building was not a new skill, however – people sailed to Australia around 55,000 years ago and to the western Pacific islands around 1600 BC, but no evidence remains of these earlier boats.

INDO-ARYAN TAKEOVER

Rapid population growth in the fertile Ganges Valley was due as much to the adoption of rice cultivation as to the use of iron tools for forest clearance. The language and culture of the Indo-Aryans had been gradually adopted throughout the region: although their numbers were probably small, their military superiority allowed them to dominate the peaceful indigenous population. The great Indian epic, *Mahabharata*, gives the illusion of a pure Indo-Aryan population in the Ganges Valley. Invaders settled in small agricultural and herding villages, which grew into the kingdoms whose feuding is chronicled in the *Mahabharata*.

SHIPBUILDING

Advances in shipbuilding enabled Greek sailors to trade widely during the 8th century BC and to establish a series of colonies on the Mediterranean and Black Sea coasts. (The *Odyssey*, Homer's account of Odysseus's epic sea voyage, was written at this time.) Their vessels relied principally on the power of sails, but used oars in calm weather and for greater maneuverability in battle.

Rows of oarsmen

Painted pot showing a warship, Greece

WEAPONS OF IRON

Iron tools and weapons were exotic and highly prized curiosities in Egypt until around 800 BC, when they first came into more regular use. They were introduced to North Africa west of Egypt by Phoenician traders from the Levant (the coastal strip of Syria, Lebanon, and Israel) at about the same time. It was many centuries before iron became a utilitarian metal, used in the fields and households as well as in battle.

Iron spearhead, Egypt

ART & RITUAL

POLISHED BEADS

Produced by a painstaking process of grinding and polishing, these bird-shaped beads were among the distinctive artistic achievements of the Poverty Point people of what is now Louisiana and Mississippi. Raw materials like feldspar, amethyst, quartz, jasper, and limonite were acquired through long-distance trade. These beads are 1 to 2¼ inches long.

Red jasper beads, Mississippi

DECORATED CHARIOTS

In the 8th century BC, war chariots, each with two caparisoned horses, were sometimes buried in pits in Chinese royal tombs. These wooden vehicles had bronze fittings such as axle caps; beads, cowries, and bronze plaques were hung from the harness; and the horses wore decorated bronze jingles, frontlets, and face masks, testifying to the high rank of their owner.

Bronze horse jingle, China

FUNERARY PRACTICES

Built in the 8th century BC, the Tomb of Midas at Gordion is among the most spectacular tombs dating to this period in the Middle East. Ordinary citizens were more likely to be buried in a communal or family tomb, or individually beneath the floors of houses. The poor were provided with only a humble pottery vessel to help them on their way, but royalty were buried with great quantities of jewelry and other valuables, as shown by the richly furnished tombs of the late 8th-century BC Assyrian queens discovered recently at Nimrud in Iraq.

OLYMPIC GAMES

Religious games, which combined athletic contests and festivals, were held every four years at the important Greek sanctuaries of Delphi and Olympia. Tradition maintains that the first Olympic Games were held in 776 BC, and votive figurines from this period and earlier have been found at the site.

Votive bronze horse, Olympia, Greece

MUMMY CASES

By 800 BC, the portrait on Egyptian coffin lids was increasingly replaced by painted scenes showing the deceased making offerings to the gods. On the underside of the lid, it became common to paint extracts from the *Book of the Dead*, the collection of spells designed to protect the deceased on the journey to the afterlife. The coffins were made of narrow pegged planks plastered and painted to give a smooth finish. Only the wealthiest individuals and royalty could afford gilded decoration.

Painted mummy case and detail, Egypt

700 - 600 BC

FOOD & ENVIRONMENT

SHELTER & ARCHITECTURE

AMERICAS

EARLY GARDENING

The growth of permanent villages in southeastern North America was linked to the cultivation of several native plants, including squash, knotweed lamb's quarter, marsh elder, and sunflower. At first, little effort was put into gardening, and plant cultivation was no more than a minor supplement to hunting and gathering. But eventually these plants and others from Mesoamerica became the food base for increasingly complex societies.

Early North American garden

TOWN PLANNING

Monte Negro, a site in the Mixteca region of Oaxaca in southern Mexico, developed during this period from a highland agricultural village into an organized town with planned streets and various public buildings. Archaeological discoveries of high and low status goods clearly indicate the existence of social classes.

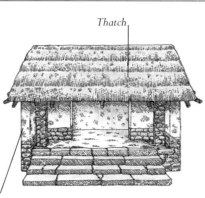

Thatch

Whitewashed walls

Dwelling, Monte Negro, Mexico

EAST ASIA & AUSTRALASIA

TOOLS FOR CULTIVATION

In China, the potential for mass production of bronze agricultural implements was never realized. The expense of casting bronze and its association with power and ancestor worship made it inappropriate for daily use, and until the introduction of iron, cultivation depended on wooden or stone implements, such as the wooden-bladed plow.

Man with wooden plow, China

CITY PLANS

Cities in China were surrounded by massive perimeter walls of rammed earth. The area within was divided into the "inner" and "outer" cities. The inner city, enclosing palace buildings and temples, occupied the northern part of the site; the outer city in the southern part consisted of residential and industrial areas and commercial streets where goods were sold. The cities had elaborate drainage systems with underground terra-cotta pipes. This use of double- or, later, multiple-walled enclosures became the standard pattern for Chinese cities for the next 2,500 years.

MIDDLE EAST & SOUTH ASIA

ASSYRIAN AGRONOMY

Behind its great cities and imperialism, the Assyrian Empire remained, in the 7th century BC, very largely a rural society. Peasant farmers drafted into service formed the bulk of the conquering Assyrian armies. The plains of northern Mesopotamia at the heart of the empire were fertile arable lands, and provided the grain crops that were essential to support the growing cities of Nimrud and Nineveh. The provinces of the empire were required to provide contributions of food as part of their tax obligation; these were probably used to feed locally based imperial garrisons, since it would have been prohibitively expensive to transport consignments of bulky foodstuffs over long distances by land.

COURTYARD PALACE

The Assyrian king Sennacherib (reigned 704-681 BC) built a palace at Nineveh on the River Tigris, which he claimed had no rival. The throne room lay between two courtyards, the outer one for administration, the inner one housing the royal apartments. Colonnaded columns were supported on vast bull- and lion-shaped bronze bases.

Stone relief showing palace walls, Nineveh, Iraq

EUROPE

TRADE PRODUCTS

The establishment of overseas colonies by the Greeks was caused partly by lack of space in the Greek homeland as the population increased. The culture and diet of the colonists influenced their non-Greek neighbors, giving them a taste for wine and perfume, in which a brisk, lucrative trade soon developed.

Typical linear painted decoration

Greek wine cup and perfume jar, Cumae, Italy

RELIGIOUS ARCHITECTURE

Around 700 BC, a major change took place in the design of temples in Greece. Before this, temples had been small, simple buildings of stone or mud brick with a steeply pitched roof covered with tiles or thatch. Only at the entrance were more elaborate arrangements attempted, such as a porch supported by columns. After 700 BC, the temples were raised on a plinth, and a wooden colonnade that continued around all four sides was added. Columns of stone began to replace the earlier wooden ones from around 600 BC.

AFRICA

DEPENDENCE ON FISH

Marine foods were very important to communities in the southwestern Cape region of southern Africa. Enormous shell middens (mounds of discarded debris) have been found at coastal settlement sites such as Eland's Bay. Reliance on marine food was at its greatest during the 1st millennium BC; in later centuries terrestrial foods became increasingly important. The analysis of skeletons of the period has revealed that women had a greater intake of terrestrial foods than men; this may reflect the fact that women were responsible for gathering plant foods, and men for fishing, and that both sexes consumed some of their food as they foraged.

HOUSE STYLES

Egyptian workers lived in small mud-brick houses built in rows, often back-to-back. Typically, an entrance passage led to a central room from which doorways opened onto smaller chambers. Nobles lived in much larger, opulent dwellings with many rooms and courtyards that presented blank walls to the outside world.

Home of a wealthy family, Egypt

TECHNOLOGY & INNOVATION

PERUVIAN GOLDWORKING
Metallurgy developed early on the northern coast of Peru, where gold was hammered into sheets and decorated using the repoussé method, whereby a design is embossed by hammering the metal out from behind. Made in the dominant Chavín artistic style, this ear ornament, found near Chiclayo, is one of the earliest examples of goldworking in the Americas.

Gold ear ornament, Peru

EARLIEST COINAGE
Increased trade in China led to the introduction of a bronze coinage that, unlike cowries, could be mass-produced. The first coins were spade- or hoe-shaped with a hollow shaft and were often marked with a place name. Later regional variations included knife-shaped coins and round coins with a hole in the center.

Bronze knife-shaped coin, China

Bronze spade-shaped coin, China

TEXTILE MANUFACTURE
The manufacture of textiles was of great importance in the ancient world, especially in Mesopotamia, where the export of cloth paid for the import of resources that did not occur naturally on the alluvial plains of its great rivers. The earliest evidence for textile manufacture is in the form of fragments of linen or flax dating back as far as 8000 BC. In the early 7th century BC, the Assyrian king Sennacherib boasted in correspondence with other rulers that he had planted a wool-bearing tree in his garden: this novelty has since been identified as a cotton plant, which had originally been cultivated in India several thousand years earlier.

Inscribed perfume jar, Corinth, Greece   *Greek inscription*

EARLIEST GREEK SCRIPT
The Greeks adopted the use of an alphabet from the Phoenicians in the 8th century BC, perhaps from a desire to record the epic poems of Homer and Hesiod. The oldest surviving texts are short inscriptions from the 7th century BC. This perfume jar bears expressions of regard from an admirer (or possibly several admirers) addressed to a Corinthian lady, to whom the jar was presumably a gift.

WORKING IN GOLD
This gold pectoral (chest ornament) in the shape of a falcon with outstretched wings represents the solar deity Horus, protector of the Egyptian pharaohs. Ornaments like this were commonly worn by members of royal families during the New Kingdom (1550-1070 BC) and Late Dynastic (712-332 BC) periods, and demonstrate the skill and sophistication of early Egyptian goldsmiths.

Gold falcon pectoral, Egypt

ART & RITUAL

JADE ARTIFACTS
Olmec jade artifacts are found throughout Mesoamerica – some have been found as far away as Costa Rica. At the Olmec capital of La Venta in southern Mexico, jade celts (small axlike objects) were ritually arranged in caches between 900 and 600 BC, probably as offerings. The blue jade, spoon-shaped pendant has a stylized lizardlike form that is typically Olmec.

Olmec jade celt, La Venta, Mexico   **Blue jade pendant, Valley of Mexico**

POTTERY FOR BURIALS
The cemetery of Non Nok Tha in northeastern Thailand entered its final phase around 700 BC, after almost 2,000 years of use. At this time a new type of pottery vessel appeared in the graves, with a red-colored surface and flat base. The burial rites of this period involved placing shellfish shells, and several pottery vessels containing offerings of fish, around the head of the deceased. A few graves also contained metal tools and ornaments. Archaeologists still do not know what such rituals signified.

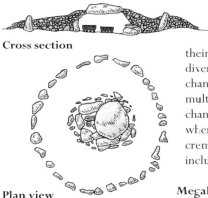

Cross section

Plan view

MEGALITHIC GRAVES
Iron Age pastoralists and farmers of southern India are known chiefly from their impressive burials, which came in a wide diversity of forms: megalithic cists (burial chambers) and dolmens, pits with stone slabs, multi-legged "bathtub" sarcophagi, rock-cut chambers, and later, massive urnfields (areas where pottery urns containing remains, usually cremated, were buried). Grave goods might include bronzes and even exquisite goldwork.

Megalithic grave, southern India

VOTIVE FIGURINES
Thousands of small lead figurines from the 7th century BC were found at the sanctuary of the goddess Artemis Orthia at Sparta in Greece. Mass-produced they were probably bought by visitors to the shrine, who left them there as offerings. Some portray Artemis herself; others represent warriors, horses, and stags.

Votive figurine, Sparta, Greece

PLEASURE-LOVING GODDESS
Bastet, the cat goddess of ancient Egypt, was the protector of pregnant women. She was also a pleasure-loving goddess, the patroness of music and dancing, who protected people against disease and demons. A vast cemetery of mummified cats was established at her city of Bubastis in the Nile Delta, and she was the focus of a very popular cult in the 7th century BC, continuing to be worshiped until Roman times. Her annual festival at Bubastis was the scene of great revelry.

Cat goddess, Egypt

600-500 BC

FOOD & ENVIRONMENT

SHELTER & ARCHITECTURE

AMERICAS

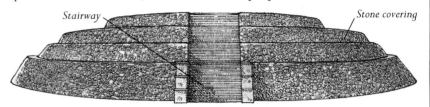

VERSATILE TURTLES
In the dry lands of southern Texas, hunter-gatherers made use of a wide variety of animal species to supplement their diet of roots, berries, and seeds. Turtle remains found in Mule Ears Cave, Texas, indicate that the flesh was scooped out and eaten, leaving the shell intact for use as a container.

Box turtle shell

STONE TEMPLE PLATFORMS
At this time a settlement of about 20,000 people, Cuicuilco was the site of the first ceremonial architecture in the Basin of Mexico. A truncated oval platform made of adobe (mud and straw) was enlarged in later centuries to form a four-tiered round pyramid 260 feet in diameter and 88 feet high, entirely covered with stone.

Temple platform, Cuicuilco, Mexico

Stairway

Stone covering

EAST ASIA & AUSTRALASIA

FARMING WITH IRON TOOLS
Once the Chinese had discovered how to smelt iron from iron ore, they developed an industry that was to revolutionize agriculture. From the 6th century BC, cast-iron sickles, knives, hoes, and cutting edges for spades were made in ceramic molds. Iron was far less expensive than bronze, and foundries were set up to mass-produce these implements. Grain cultivation was transformed by the introduction of the ox-drawn iron plow (the iron blades made the plow too heavy for a person to pull). The power of draft animals was greatly increased when the cumbersome neck yoke was replaced with a breast-strap harness and cart shafts.

STONE CIRCLES
Japanese stone circles consisted of medium-sized stones laid end to end to form a ring. Relatively modest in scale, some circles have an upright stone or an oval pit at the center. The purpose of the stone circles is still unclear, but they may have been built as minor cult-places by small village communities.

Stone circle, Manza, Japan

Plan view

Side view

MIDDLE EAST & SOUTH ASIA

WATER MANAGEMENT
Although the river valleys of the Fertile Crescent could provide immense agricultural yields, the soil in other parts of the Middle East was less productive. In these regions, water and soil management were vital, and dams were constructed both for water storage and to retain soil that would otherwise be eroded by runoff. One of the most famous is that at Marib in Yemen, thought to have been built in the 6th century BC.

Characteristic Ionic scroll shape

Carved column capital, Temple of Artemis, Ephesus, Turkey

TEMPLE OF ARTEMIS
Prosperous Greek cities on the western coast of Anatolia were producing some of the finest examples of classical sculpture and architecture. The Temple of Artemis at Ephesus in Turkey, numbered among the Seven Wonders of the World, was built by Croesus, King of Lydia (reigned 560-546 BC) in about 550 BC. It was rebuilt to the same plan in the 4th century BC.

EUROPE

GRAIN IMPORTS
Greek colonies in some regions became major agricultural producers, sometimes growing sufficient surplus to store and sell to other Greek cities in times of famine or food shortage. The colony of Metapontum in southern Italy was especially famous for its barley, and recorded the fact on its coins.

Silver coin showing stalk of barley, Metapontum, Italy

COLONNADED TEMPLE
The classical style in architecture developed in Greece and the Aegean in the 6th century BC. Temples began to be built of stone to a standard plan: a stepped plinth supported a continuous colonnade of fluted columns, within which stood a sanctuary building containing a statue of the temple's patron god or goddess.

Carved frieze

Temple of Apollo, Corinth, Greece

AFRICA

STAPLE GRAINS
The introduction of grain agriculture into sub-Saharan Africa depended on the domestication of wild sorghum and millet, both of which thrive in a regular summer rainy season. It is not known exactly when sorghum and millet were first domesticated in Africa, but they were certainly grown in what is now the Sudan and western African Sahel by around 500 BC. Both are hardy grains, easy to store and tolerant of a wide range of climatic conditions, including the occasional dry year. For these reasons, sorghum and millet became the dietary staples of the tropical farmer. Their cultivation was to spread widely throughout sub-Saharan Africa with the movement of Bantu-speaking peoples in later centuries.

Cross section of pyramid, Nuri, Nubia

Rubble core

NUBIAN PYRAMIDS
The royal Nubian cemetery at Nuri contains the tombs of 53 queens and 19 kings, dating to around 700-300 BC. In the center stands the great pyramid of King Taharqa (c.690-624 BC), with later royal pyramids to the southeast. These finely stepped structures are smaller at the base and taller than the classic Egyptian pyramid.

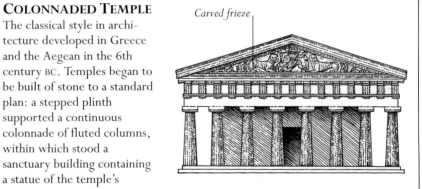

Sandstone brick facing

Sandstone tomb

Stepped ramp

TECHNOLOGY & INNOVATION

ART & RITUAL

HAMMERED GOLD
The most important and sophisticated gold technology in the Americas is found in Colombia. The cultures that developed this technology in its highest forms were the Sinu, the Tairona, and the Quimbaya peoples. This small figurine is an excellent example of modeled and hammered goldwork.

Sinu gold figurine, Colombia

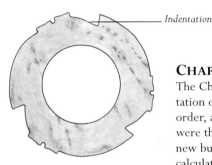

Indentation

CHARTING THE STARS
The Chinese believed that if their physical orientation on earth corresponded with the heavenly order, all would be right on earth. Astronomers were thus consulted frequently, before planning a new building, burial, or even tree planting. To calculate the position of stars and planets, a stone disk was placed on a sighting tube so that the disk's indentations aligned with the constellations.

Steatite circumpolar template, China

EARLY COINS
The first gold and silver coins of fixed weight stamped with the mark of the issuing authority were made around 600 BC in Lydia, Anatolia. Early Indian coinage was inspired by this innovation, which arrived via Persia, but it had its own very distinctive style, consisting of silver bars or disks on which symbols were punched, representing the place and authority of their issue.

Early coin, India

Silver ingot, Nush-i Jan, Iran

FIRST EUROPEAN COINS
The people of Aegina, an important Greek island trading city, were quick to see the advantages of the coinage being used in Asia Minor and, in around 560 BC, began to issue their own coins. These simple pieces of silver with a stamped design on one face were the first European currency. Double-faced coins soon followed, and the idea spread to neighboring cities in Greece, and later to Italy and westward.

Early silver coins from Athens and Corinth, Greece

IRON TOOLS
Around 600 BC ironworking spread up the Nile from Egypt to reach Meroë, which became the capital of the Nubian kingdom during this century. Soon large quantities of iron were being worked around the outskirts of the city, giving rise to huge mounds of slag and other debris, which can still be seen today. Iron was used to make weapons as well as everyday objects such as hoes, axes, and adzes.

Iron hoe, Meroë, Sudan

FIRST BALL COURTS
The ritual ball game, a characteristic feature of Mesoamerican societies, most probably originated in the highlands of western Mexico around 1500 BC. But many archaeologists believe that the earliest formal ball-court precincts are those at the Olmec centers of San Lorenzo and La Venta, dating to around 600 BC. Ceramic figurines found in excavations at San Lorenzo with a variety of headgear and protective clothing appear to be ball players.

The colossal heads so emblematic of Olmec civilization are also believed by many to be ball players, since they are always helmeted. The game was played between two teams on a rectangular court with a ball made of solid rubber. It was more closely related to ritual than to sport, since in some instances members of one team or the other were sacrificed.

GRAVE GOODS
In the steppes of southern Siberia, a society of warlike horse-riding herders had arisen by 600 BC. Tribal leaders were buried in timber chambers beneath large burial mounds, together with bronze weapons and sophisticated gold ornaments. These often featured highly stylized animal motifs, such as a stag's head — probably reflecting the nomads' shamanistic beliefs, in which animal spirits were revered. The gold may have come from the southern Urals, or from panning in Siberian rivers. Gold and gold artifacts may also have been plundered or acquired through trade; evidence suggests that Greek craftsmen were commissioned to make certain items.

NEW BELIEFS
The Buddha, born Siddhartha Gautama (c.563-483 BC), and Mahavira (c.599-527 BC), the founder of Jainism, were religious reformers in an age of warring states in northern India. The Buddha's teaching of the Middle Way — the path of moderation leading to *nirvana* (enlightenment) — was to become the basis of one of the world's greatest religions.

A *Bodhisattva* (enlightened one), India

BLACK-AND-RED POTTERY
The Athenians used the black-figure technique, in which the decoration was executed in fine black paint on a reddish background. Around 530 BC, this gave way to the red-figure style: the whole pot was first covered in black paint, then the decoration was created by carefully scraping away areas of paint to allow the underlying red pottery to show through.

TERRA-COTTA FIGURINES
Most of the Nok terra-cotta figurines found during tin-mining operations near Jos in northern Nigeria represent humans. Some are life-size, usually with elaborate hairstyles and holelike eyes; careful attention was paid to poses, individual features and deformities, and jewelry. The Nok culture itself developed around 500 BC and flourished for about 1,000 years.

Nok terra-cotta head, Nigeria, West Africa

THE OLMEC OF MEXICO

33,000 BC

Less than a century ago, the existence of one of the greatest ancient civilizations – the Olmec – was largely unsuspected. But in 1939 a Smithsonian archaeologist, Matthew W. Stirling, began excavating in southern Veracruz, Mexico. Although Stirling's spectacular finds were artistically and technologically advanced, he believed they were the product of a very early civilization – perhaps the Mesoamerican "mother culture." Decades later, after much excavation and the advent of radiocarbon dating, Stirling's original insight was verified. Between 1500 and 1200 BC, the most significant culture in Mesoamerica emerged in this lowland swamp region. Without the benefit of draft animals, the wheel, or iron tools, the Olmec produced monumental sculpture, elaborate ceremonial centers, and complex water management systems, requiring the organization of time, materials, and labor on a grand scale. A rich artistic tradition suggests that many specialized trades coexisted within a complex, stratified society.

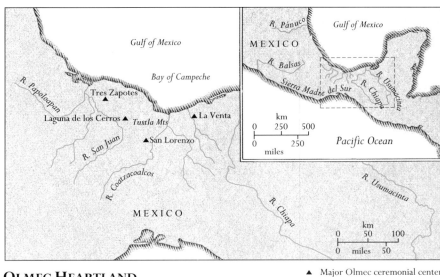

OLMEC HEARTLAND

▲ Major Olmec ceremonial center

The Olmec culture developed and flourished within a well-defined region on Mexico's Gulf Coast. In a swampy river floodplain near the Tuxtla Mountains, the Olmec founded several large ceremonial centers, later to be overgrown by dense tropical jungle.

RITUAL PRESERVED IN STONE *below and right*

Among the earliest and finest lapidary artists in the Americas, the Olmec carved objects from many stones, but were particularly fond of a dark blue jade. An enormous variety of figurines, masks, ornaments, and implements was made, many as offerings to the gods. The group of 16 figures found at La Venta in 1955 (*see below*) is particularly striking. These figurines were arranged as if involved in some ritual meeting, within an enclosure of jade celts, possibly representing the basalt columns that enclose La Venta's ceremonial court. The figures have typically Olmec downturned mouths and almond-shaped eyes, and shaved heads deformed by binding in infancy. At some point the carefully buried scene was uncovered, perhaps rearranged or checked, then reburied, to lie undisturbed for more than 2,000 years.

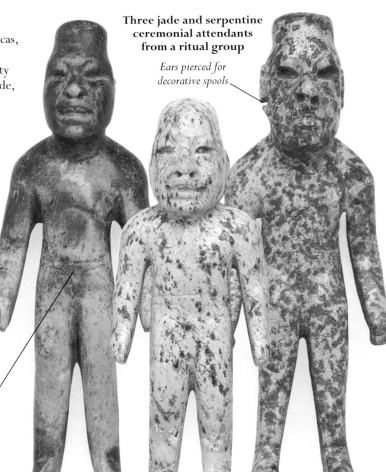

Three jade and serpentine ceremonial attendants from a ritual group

Ears pierced for decorative spools

Largest figures are 7⅛ inches tall

Traces of red ocher

Simple loincloth worn by all figures

Ritual group of jade, granite, and serpentine figures

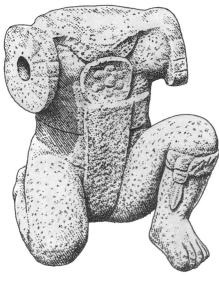

BALLPLAYER IN BASALT *above*

A highly naturalistic, slightly larger-than-life-size basalt sculpture found at San Lorenzo depicts an important personage, perhaps a ruler, dressed as a ballplayer with the wide protective belt often seen in representations of the game and its players. He wears knee bands and a round pendant – probably representing a convex polished pyrite mirror – suspended from a wide band around his neck. The ratcheted shoulder sockets may indicate that the figure once had movable arms.

CERAMIC GRAVE GOODS *right*

Mesoamericans often buried their dead beneath the floors of houses. At Tlatilco, in the Basin of Mexico, hundreds of burials were found dating to 1100-800 BC. Many graves yielded vessels with Olmec designs and hollow, white-slipped ceramic baby figures. These are realistic in form and gesture, although their faces have typically Olmec features. Some wear caps similar to the "helmets" of the colossal Olmec heads.

Olmec baby, Las Bocas, Mexico

TLATILCO CYLINDER STAMP *below*

This large, hollow ceramic cylinder stamp was probably used, in the Mesoamerican tradition, for body decoration and perhaps for imprinting designs on textiles. The highly stylized figure, which is deeply carved into the

Cylinder stamp

Traces of red paint

cylinder, may be representative of a dragon, caiman, or serpent, with classically Olmec motifs such as the cleft head and flame-shaped eyebrows.

Design produced when stamp is rolled

OLMEC INFLUENCE

Portable objects of Olmec manufacture, such as pottery vessels, figures, stamps, and jade and serpentine carvings, are found from the Valley of Mexico in the north to as far south as Costa Rica. Some archaeologists question the notion of contact through trade or other means, believing that artistic motifs long characterized as Olmec may, in fact, just be local versions of symbols common to all Mesoamericans. However, much of what is emblematic of Mesoamerica, such as numerous deities, myths, temple-pyramids, and jadeworking, certainly appears to be Olmec in origin.

Small bust carved in rare blue jade

FEMALE PORTRAIT *left*
This bust is one of only a few remaining Olmec portraits of women, with the unusual feature of finely incised hair. (Male figures are generally bald or helmeted.) Although it is less than 3 inches high, the figure has the same impassive expression and monumental quality of the colossal Olmec head below.

IMPRESSIVE MONUMENTS *below*
Colossal heads carved from single basalt blocks are among the most striking Olmec monuments. The first was discovered and described in 1862; four in all have since been found surrounding La Venta, and eight at San Lorenzo. The one below is the most famous, and also the largest, at 9 feet in height. Called *el Rey* (the King) by native people in the region of San Lorenzo, it depicts a corpulent man with strong, broad features, wearing large tubular ear spools and distinctive, helmetlike headgear fastened with a band tied at the back in a stylized knot.

Cleft head and "flame" eyebrows are classic Olmec dragon features

Downturned mouth, typical of Olmec human depictions

THE DRAGON GOD *above*
Probably one of the earliest and, considering its ubiquity, most important deity in the Olmec pantheon is the dragon, a mythical creature whose features combine elements of serpents, caimans, eagles, jaguars, and humans. Here it is carved on a ceremonial jade ax head.

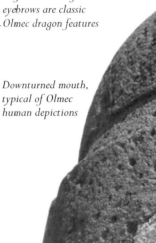

BASALT VOTIVE AX *above*
Votive axes are an Olmec ceremonial form. Often quite large, the one above is 9½ inches tall. Usually carved in basalt, they are quite rare, with only 20 known to exist. This ax is a stylized depiction of the Olmec dragon, also known as God 1.

PART THREE

500 BC

— TO —

AD 800

The balance between hunting and gathering, village farming, and urbanized states continued to change as large cities developed in Mesoamerica and South America. Eurasia came to be dominated by a series of powerful empires, while some of the remotest Pacific islands were colonized by Polynesian sailors. In an age of global trade contacts, world religions were born and rapidly established far-reaching spheres of influence.

Detail of painted decoration on Mayan ceramic jar, with a stylized depiction of a human, Honduras, 8th-10th centuries AD

CHAPTER 12
AN AGE OF EXPANSION
500 - 200 BC

Democracy is born in classical Greece

China's first emperor initiates the construction of the Great Wall

The Zapotecs embark on a millennium-long domination of the Oaxaca region of Mexico

Ashoka consolidates the power of the Mauryan Empire in South Asia

The Bantu of West Africa begin their southward migration

During the 5th century BC the growth of long-distance trade resulted in increasing intercontinental contacts – for example, between Persia and the Mediterranean, and western Europe and India. China became a massive unified state in the 4th century BC. Around the same time, the spread of ironworking from North Africa led to the clearance of larger tracts of land for farming, which in turn led to a quest for fresh land in the southern part of the continent. These new links between distant communities, albeit limited in scale, brought cultural and economic interaction and laid the foundations for the routes along which world religions such as Buddhism and Christianity were later spread.

Key figures

The 6th and 5th centuries BC are often referred to as the Axial Age, because of the number of key figures living at this time who profoundly influenced later generations. They included Confucius in China; Buddha and Mahavira (founder of Jainism) in India; and Pythagoras, Socrates, Plato, and Aristotle in Greece. The 5th century BC was the age of classical ideals in Greece, with its cultural and political center at Athens. The philosopher Socrates taught that virtue was gained through self-knowledge and also developed an original theory of the soul. In 399 BC Socrates was indicted on charges of impiety towards the gods of Athens and, condemned to death, he committed suicide by drinking hemlock.

Characteristic bearded head of Zeus

War chariot pulled by a team of four horses

ZEUS, KING OF THE GODS
Platonic philosophy respected much of traditional Greek religion, and the pantheon of gods headed by Zeus, here portrayed driving a chariot, was still venerated.

The birth of democracy

Athens was the foremost power in a land of autonomous city-states, which were sometimes bound by alliances, but often at war with each other. The status of Athens was enhanced by the rebuilding, on a grand scale, of the religious buildings of the Acropolis, including the famous Parthenon temple. Athens and Attica, the region surrounding it, were also the birthplace of the democratic system of government, in which power rested in the hands of a popular assembly of citizens drawn from separate regional demes (constituencies).

Despite being the source of many liberal ideals, however, Athens had a grimmer side: its economy, like that of many contemporary Greek cities, depended on the vast number of slaves who worked on the land and in the silver mines, the city's richest assets.

Conquering zeal

The driving expansionist ambition of Alexander the Great, a young Macedonian king, inspired him to conquer vast areas of Europe and Asia, including the mighty Persian Empire. This he did with only modest forces. The Persian Empire had reached its height under Darius I (522-486 BC) and enjoyed great power and prosperity for over a century.

SHAMANISM IN NORTH AMERICA
This stone tube, in the shape of the bill of a shoveler duck, was used by shamans of the Adena culture for the ritual withdrawal of invasive spirits from sick individuals.

By 332 BC, however, it had been so weakened by rebellion and war that it fell to Alexander. Alexander's campaigns brought him victory from the borders of India to Egypt, where a new Greek ruling dynasty was established after his death by Ptolemy I Soter (or "Savior"), one of his generals. The Ptolemies adopted and assimilated many of the traditional customs of the Egyptian pharaohs and continued to rule Egypt until the late 1st century BC.

Fragmentation and unification
China had been unified until 770 BC, after which it fragmented. The following 550 years – the Warring States period – were marked by continual struggle. By 300 BC seven large states had formed, but within a century, Qin Shi Huangdi, ruler of the western state of Qin, reunited the whole of China under his rule to become, in 221 BC, its first emperor. To protect against

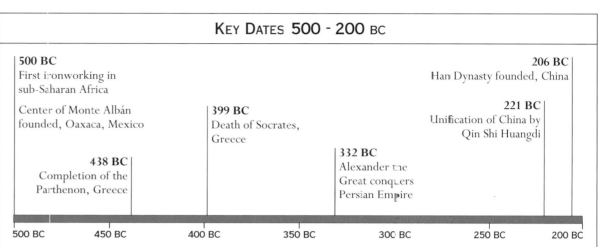

KEY DATES 500 - 200 BC		
500 BC First ironworking in sub-Saharan Africa		**206 BC** Han Dynasty founded, China
500 BC Center of Monte Albán founded, Oaxaca, Mexico	**399 BC** Death of Socrates, Greece	**221 BC** Unification of China by Qin Shi Huangdi
438 BC Completion of the Parthenon, Greece	**332 BC** Alexander the Great conquers Persian Empire	

500 BC   450 BC   400 BC   350 BC   300 BC   250 BC   200 BC

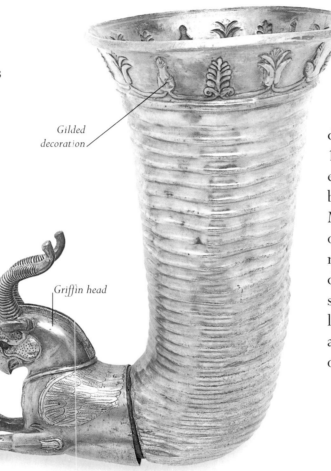

Gilded decoration

Griffin head

DISPLAYS OF WEALTH
The vast wealth of the Persian Empire found expression in splendid palaces and rich tableware. This silver-gilt drinking horn is typical of the 5th century BC.

Zapotec culture
Around 500 BC, competition between elites led to the founding of Monte Albán in Mexico's Oaxaca region. Monte Albán became the capital of the Zapotec people, and the city dominated surrounding regions for over 1,000 years. The earliest attestable evidence of writing in the Americas has been found on public stone monuments at Monte Albán. This writing took the form of hieroglyphs recording the names of rulers, their conquests, and rituals. Their deeds were recorded using a calendrical system of interlocked cycles of varying lengths of time. Writing in the Americas, as in some other parts of the world, originated as an instrument of state power.

NATURALISTIC CERAMICS
This monkey sculpture from Esmeraldas, Ecuador, dates to around 500 BC. The decoration was painted after firing, a method possibly introduced from Mesoamerica.

raids by central Asian nomads, Qin Shi Huangdi built the Great Wall, which incorporated parts of earlier fortifications.
Qin Shi Huangdi was buried in a huge mausoleum that took 700,000 conscripted laborers 35 years to build. Those artisans who worked on the tomb's internal construction were walled up within it. Qin Shi Huangdi's harsh rule left bitter memories, and on his death China was torn apart by revolt. However, central control was soon re-imposed by the Han Dynasty (206 BC-AD 220), and a period of unparalleled cultural and economic prosperity ensued.

Metal-plated armor modeled in clay

Heavy cloth tunic modeled in clay

EMPEROR'S ARMY
Qin Shi Huangdi's tomb at Xian was surrounded by burial pits containing thousands of life-size terra-cotta models of soldiers.

500 - 200 BC

South Asian empire

The cities of northern India that had arisen during the 6th century BC were divided among 16 small states. A power struggle resulted in victory for the kingdom of Magadha in the lower Ganges Valley. With its capital at Pataliputra (modern Patna), Magadha became the core of the Mauryan Empire, the first in South Asia. The greatest Mauryan emperor, Ashoka (reigned 297-232 BC), extended his rule over most of modern India and Pakistan. Magadha was also the birthplace, in the late 6th century BC, of Siddhartha Gautama, the Buddha. Ashoka was a convert to Buddhism, which soon gained the status of a major religion.

Nonurban societies

Urban civilizations covered only a fraction of the world in 500 BC. Other kinds of society could be found in Africa south of the Sahara, in Europe and the Eurasian steppes, in Australia, and the forests of Southeast Asia. Many of these societies underwent major changes in this period. In Africa, the gradual spread of ironworking technology resulted in improved weapons and agricultural tools. This was also a time of expansion for the Bantu peoples, whose homeland probably lay in West Africa near the Niger River delta. By the 5th century BC they had reached the Great Lakes region of East Africa, cultivating millet and herding sheep, goats, and cattle, which were an important indicator of wealth. From this area Bantu farmers began the agricultural colonization of southern Africa and by AD 500 they had reached the Cape.

Rural communities in Southeast Asia left few remains, but much is known of their way of life from representational art on ritual objects, including bronze drums found throughout the mainland and islands. By 200 BC, farming villages in the fertile river valleys had begun to fuse into larger political units, forming the basis of the first Southeast Asian kingdoms.

Northern life

In temperate Europe, the people of Iron Age communities (who were called Celts by the Greeks and Romans) created a distinctive artistic style, seen in wine goblets, sword scabbards, and richly decorated ornaments such as gold torcs (neck rings) made for the use of their warrior elite. Celtic societies were tribal, living mainly in small farmstead villages, but withdrawing to fortified hilltop enclosures in times of danger.

The cooler, wetter climate of this period particularly affected the small-scale Germanic farming communities of northern Germany and Scandinavia, where peat bogs grew at the expense of farmland. The bogs provided excellent conditions for preserving ritual deposits, such as metalwork and human sacrifices, placed in the bogs as divine offerings.

To the east, on the Eurasian steppes, societies of horse-riding nomadic herders were well established by 500 BC, often traveling vast distances as they herded sheep and cattle between pastures. The remarkable remains in frozen tombs at Pazyryk in Siberia vividly illustrate the life of these people.

AMERICAS

REGIONAL DIVERSITY

An increase in the population and growing socio-political complexity in Ecuador during the period 500 BC-AD 100 are reflected in the development of regional ceramic styles known as Bahía, Tolita, Jama Coaque, Jambeli, Tiaone, Guangala, Tejar, and Daule. Typical of Bahía ceramics are sophisticated cast and molded sculptures, which principally represent standing or seated human figures, sometimes with painted decoration. This figurine portrays a woman holding a child.

Bahía ceramic figurine, Ecuador

Region possessing unique ceramic style ≡

AFRICA

SPREAD OF IRONWORKING

Ironworking spread into sub-Saharan Africa down trade routes from North Africa during the 1st millennium BC. Nomadic cattle herders, whose chariots are depicted in their rock art, may have helped to spread this technology. By 500 BC, the Nok people were smelting iron ore with charcoal in pit-furnaces at Nsukka and Taruga in modern Nigeria. Ironworking reached West Africa just as it was becoming common in towns in the Nile Valley as far south as Meroë in Nubia. Later in the 5th century BC, ironworking spread from West Africa to the area west of Lake Victoria in East Africa.

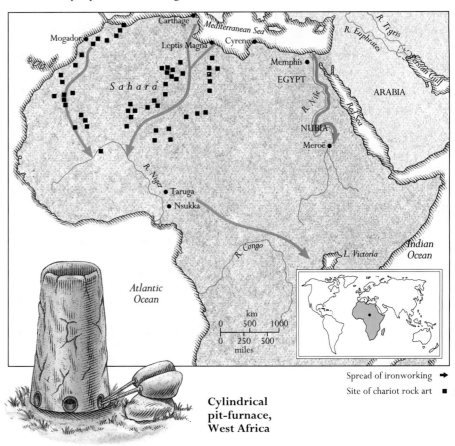

Cylindrical pit-furnace, West Africa

Spread of ironworking ➔
Site of chariot rock art ■

EUROPE

CELTIC ART STYLE

The peoples of central and western Europe were referred to collectively as Celts by Greek and Roman writers. Divided into a number of different tribes and nations, they shared a distinctive decorative art style, which was characterized by abstract curvilinear designs, including tightly coiled spirals and motifs incorporating lotus petals, palmettes, tendrils, and the heads or bodies of mythical animals. Most of the surviving examples of Celtic art are ornaments for personal use such as gold and bronze torcs (neck rings) and bracelets, vessels, and weapons such as decorated sword scabbards or this bronze shield with decorative inlays of colored glass, which was found in the River Thames at Battersea in London, England.

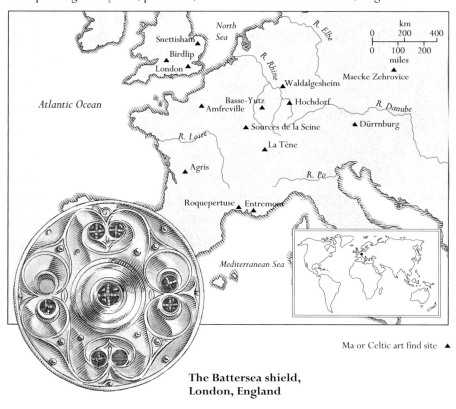

Major Celtic art find site ▲

The Battersea shield, London, England

EAST ASIA & AUSTRALASIA

DONG SON DRUMS

Trading contacts between the mainland and islands of Southeast Asia in the last centuries BC are well illustrated by the wide distribution of Dong Son ceremonial bronze drums, named after the site of Dong Son in Vietnam. They were produced in Au Lac, an early Vietnamese kingdom with its capital at Co Loa in the Red River valley. Characterized by geometric or figurative decorative friezes, they were often buried as grave goods. A large drum found at Co Loa contained no fewer than 100 bronze plowshares.

■ Dong Son drum find site

Dong Son drum, Vietnam

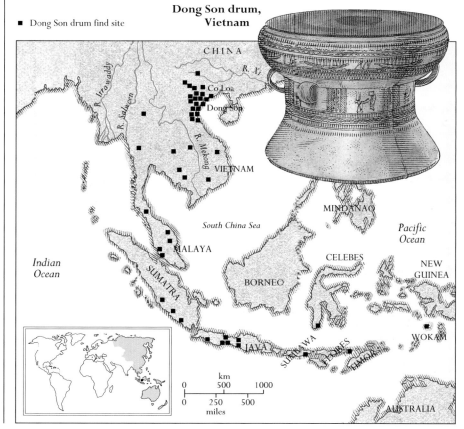

MIDDLE EAST & SOUTH ASIA

ROUTE OF ALEXANDER

Son of the ruler of Macedon in northern Greece, Alexander the Great (356-323 BC) conquered the Persian Empire and destroyed its capital, Persepolis (in modern Iran). Alexander's campaigns took him as far as Tashkent in modern Uzbekistan, to Kashmir, and across the Indus River. Many Greek cities were founded in the wake of these campaigns. After Alexander died in Babylon, his empire soon fragmented, although the kingdom of Macedon remained dominant in Greece.

Roman mosaic detail showing Alexander, House of the Faun, Pompeii, Italy

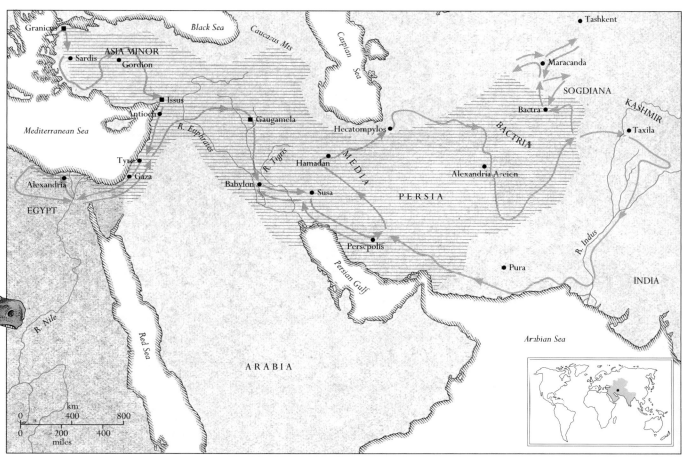

Battle site ■

Extent of Persian Empire ≣

Route of Alexander ➡

500 - 400 BC

FOOD & ENVIRONMENT	SHELTER & ARCHITECTURE

AMERICAS

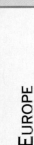

SMOKING EQUIPMENT

This bear-effigy pipe and "napkin-ring" tube from Tennessee may both have been used for smoking a variety of materials (although not, at this period, tobacco), probably in a ritual context. The tube might alternatively have been used by shamans in treating illnesses – a healing method still practiced in several regions of the modern world.

Tube and pipe, Tennessee

SUBLIME STONEWORK

The beauty and sophistication of the stonework — sculpture, stelae, columns, tombstones, and obelisks carved to represent mythological themes — carried out over the centuries at the Chavín de Huantar temple now made it the pinnacle of Andean architectural achievement.

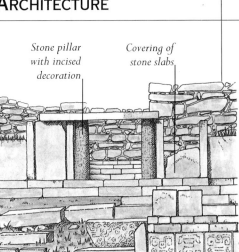

Stone pillar with incised decoration   *Covering of stone slabs*

Chavín de Huantar ruins, Peru

EAST ASIA & AUSTRALASIA

CANNABIS SMOKING

Tombs dating to the 5th century BC at Pazyryk in the Siberian Altai Mountains yield evidence that cannabis smoke was inhaled within the felt tents of nomadic herdsmen. Charcoal-filled bronze braziers have been found with leather bags of hemp seeds. When thrown on the smoldering coals, the seeds released intoxicating smoke.

Brazier from a grave, Pazyryk, Siberia

DECORATED FELTS

The Siberian nomads whose rulers were buried at Pazyryk lived in felt-covered tents that resembled the modern Mongolian yurt. Although they could quickly be dismantled when the occupants wished to move on to new pastures, these tents were by no means makeshift shelters, but were comfortable and colorful homes. The felts were richly decorated with appliquéd geometric designs and scenes depicting the exploits of horsemen. They were sometimes hung on tomb walls.

MIDDLE EAST & SOUTH ASIA

ANCIENT DRESS

Stone reliefs on a ceremonial stairway at Persepolis in Iran show the ecological diversity of the vast Persian Empire (550-331 BC) by the differences in clothing of the peoples depicted. Those from the hot plains wear loose, full-length robes, while the horsemen of the cold mountains wear trousers, tunics, and cloaks.

Detail, stone relief, Persepolis, Iran

PERSIAN ECLECTICISM

The Persians built in a bold, eclectic style using the architectural traditions of their defeated subjects: columned halls from Media in western Iran, reliefs from Mesopotamia, Greek stoneworking techniques, Egyptian doorways, and rock-cut tombs from mountainous Urartu (on the borders of modern Turkey and Armenia). The rock-cut tomb of the Persian ruler Darius I (522-486 BC) re-creates a facade of the palace at the Persian capital, Persepolis.

Rock-cut tomb of Darius I, Persepolis, Iran

EUROPE

DRINKING PARTIES

The symposium, or wine-drinking party, was a popular entertainment among the wealthier classes in 5th-century BC Athens. Wine was diluted with two or three parts water to one part wine and drunk from cups of pottery or precious metal. Courtesans were the only women allowed to attend these events.

Cushioned couch

Red-figure vase with symposium scene, Athens, Greece

NEW STYLES AND MATERIALS

As Greek merchants from the Mediterranean and Black Sea colonies brought new styles of sculpture and architecture to the peoples with whom they traded, local rulers adopted Mediterranean styles as a means of impressing their neighbors. For example, at the Heuneburg in southern Germany, in around 500 BC, a Celtic chieftain had a mud-brick fortification wall of the Mediterranean type built along one side of his hillfort. Since mud brick was a totally unsuitable building material for a wet European climate, only the stone foundations of the building still survive.

AFRICA

HUNTING IN THE DESERT

By 500 BC the Sahara had become almost as dry as it is today. Few people now ventured into the desert, although pockets of vegetation and game animals survived in the central Saharan uplands. The Greek historian Herodotus, writing in about 440 BC, tells of the peoples then living at the Sahara's northern limits. These included the Garamantes, who used two- and four-horsed chariots for desert hunting expeditions. The level areas surrounding the uplands and the major Saharan *wadis* (watercourses that are dry except in the rainy season) would have been ideal chariot country, and paintings of chariots are found in rock shelters in these areas.

MEROITIC CAPITAL

Meroë, in Nubia, had become the capital of the Nubian kingdom by the 6th century BC. By 500 BC, it was a city of mud-brick houses centered in a complex of royal temples surrounded by cemeteries of pyramid-tombs. The principal temple was dedicated to the Egyptian sun-god Amun, and consisted of a series of columned halls and courtyards enclosed within a substantial mud-brick wall. Much of the temple was built of mud brick, but sandstone was used for columns and doorways. Although building styles owe much to Egyptian influence, Meroë became increasingly independent of its powerful neighbor, with Egyptian hieroglyphs being abandoned in favor of an indigenous Meroitic script.

TECHNOLOGY & INNOVATION

EARLY CALENDAR

Although there are finds of carved symbols dating to around 600 BC, the earliest known text in the Americas was carved around 400 BC on a monolith, now in three pieces, erected in the Zapotec city of Monte Albán in Oaxaca, Mexico. Zapotec script is largely undeciphered, but appears to use a native system of writing and calendrical notation.

Fragmented monolith with Zapotec script, Monte Albán, Mexico

PORTABLE CARTS

The peoples of the Central Asian steppe used ingeniously constructed wheeled vehicles to carry heavy belongings as they moved between pastures. When they struck camp, the upper part of the wagon could simply be lifted off and set up as a tent. Where they met rough ground, the entire wagon could be dismantled into pieces small enough to be carried by packhorse.

Wooden wagon from grave, Pazyryk, Siberia

MASTER GOLDSMITHS

Throughout the Persian Empire, gold was used for coins and fashioned into artifacts. Many pieces were destined for tombs and for palace and temple treasuries. It is thought that the Oxus Treasure, discovered in the Oxus River near where it merges into the Aral Sea, was part of a temple hoard accumulated between 500 and 200 BC. The treasure's magnificent pieces of jewelry and ornamentation display a mastery of precious metalworking.

Gold armlet, Oxus Treasure, Uzbekistan

MILITARY SEA POWER

Sea power was vital to Greek conflicts of the 5th century BC — first an abortive Persian invasion, then lengthy struggles between Athens and Sparta. The key warship was the trireme, a lightweight vessel with three banks of oars giving great speed and maneuverability, and a powerful ram.

Lower deck
Oarsman
Leather grommet to protect oar
Deck rail

Cutaway of model trireme

UTILITARIAN TOOLS

Ironworking had spread to West Africa by the 5th century BC, when the Nok people at Taruga in Nigeria are known to have smelted iron using shallow pit furnaces with cylindrical clay walls. They produced arrowheads, knives, spearheads, axes, and hoe blades — enabling the tropical forest to be cleared more efficiently. This basic iron technology was soon widely adopted all over West Africa.

ART & RITUAL

RITUAL MUMMIFICATION

The isolated Paracas culture (500-1 BC) along the southern coast of Peru was noted for the wealth of paraphernalia used in human burials. The burial bundles were wrapped with dozens of woven and embroidered pieces of cloth. Embroidered robes and false heads were part of the wrapping ritual.

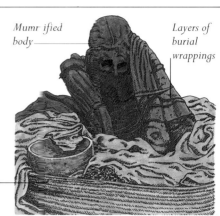

Mummified body

Layers of burial wrappings

Basketry coffin

Paracas mummy, Peru

CONFUCIAN MORALITY

The teachings of Confucius (551-479 BC) were to form the basis of one of the most powerful political philosophies in history, used by the scholar administrations of the Chinese Empire to maintain obedience, social cohesion, and equilibrium. Confucius taught that social well-being depended on assigned roles in a society based on reciprocal obligations. As with children and their parents, the subjects' duty to their ruler was balanced by the ruler's moral duty to the subjects. The emphasis on morality acquired by education created the Chinese ideal of the "scholar gentleman."

Gold plaque showing priest with *barsom*, Uzbekistan

FIRE WORSHIPERS

The ancient Persians worshiped fire. Their magi (priests), who may have been drawn from the nation of Media in western Iran, carried a bundle of twigs, called the *barsom* or *baresman*, as shown on this gold plaque found in the Oxus River. The twigs were used to feed the sacred fire. Persian religion had much in common with the Brahmanism of India, including an intoxicating drink called *soma*.

CREATING NEW STYLES

Bronze wine flagons found at Basse-Yutz in France show how Celtic artisans took ideas from Mediterranean countries and combined them in their own distinctive style. The shape of this flagon is Etruscan (from the part of northern Italy that is now Tuscany), but the inlay of coral and enamel, and the handle in the form of an animal, are purely Celtic.

Wine flagon, Basse-Yutz, France

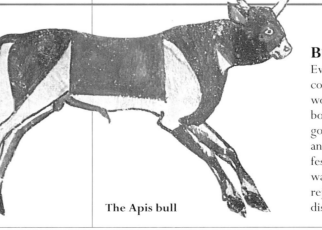

The Apis bull

BULLS AS ORACLES

Even under Persian rule, Egyptian ritual continued unabated. The sacred Apis bull worshiped at Memphis was believed to be born of a virgin cow, impregnated by the god Ptah. It was paraded in golden raiment and served as an oracle at the god's festivals. When the Apis bull died, there was general mourning for 70 days, then rejoicing when his successor (revealed by distinctive color markings) was found.

400-300 BC

FOOD & ENVIRONMENT

SHELTER & ARCHITECTURE

AMERICAS

AGRICULTURAL TOOLS
Digging sticks date from the beginnings of North American horticulture, in around 1000 BC. In the southwest, pointed sticks were probably used for planting seeds or digging tuberous roots. These later spatulate examples, dating to AD 1000-1200, were probably used to loosen soil before planting.

Digging sticks, Moqui Canyon, Utah

EARLY PYRAMID
The Maya, originally migrants from North America, gradually settled, then came to dominate, a huge area of Mesoamerica. Their civilization was known for writing, astronomy, mathematical computations, and fine art and architecture. Like other Mesoamerican cultures, the Maya built on top of existing buildings. This early pyramid, dating to around 400 BC, was found beneath a later one. Even fine stucco masks on a stairway were well preserved.

Pyramid, Uaxactun, Guatemala

EAST ASIA & AUSTRALASIA

EATING WITH CHOPSTICKS
The use of chopsticks, which had hitherto been reserved as a privilege of the rulers of the Shang Dynasty, became common in China in these centuries. This simple but efficient way of eating, ideally suited to the Chinese tradition of serving food already cut into morsels, spread rapidly throughout most of Asia.

Wooden chopsticks and bowl

BUILDINGS DEPICTED
Ceremonial drums decorated with scenes of daily life have provided insights into the buildings in Southeast Asian villages. Houses were raised on stilts, with decorated end posts and soaring gables. The large bronze drums, named after the site of Dong Son in northern Vietnam, were produced for local leaders in the last few centuries BC. Buildings similar to those shown on the drums are still seen in the region; the Toba Batak tribe of Sumatra, for example, continue to build magnificent meeting houses with tall thatched roofs rising to horned gables at either end.

MIDDLE EAST & SOUTH ASIA

NEW CROP VARIETIES
Increased contact between western Asia and India following the Persian conquest of the Indus in around 500 BC led not only to increased trade in Indian goods throughout the Persian Empire, but also to the introduction of new varieties of crops. Cotton (first recorded in the Middle East by the Assyrian king Sennacherib around 700 BC) became more widely cultivated. Rice, though as yet uncommon in the Middle East, was certainly grown in Bactria, north of India, and in Babylonia by the 4th century BC. It seems likely that Indian ebony, sugarcane, and the banana were also introduced at this time. Indian elephants played a prominent role in the armies of the Persians and Greeks.

STATELY TOMB
Mausollos, King of Caria in southwestern Turkey (reigned 377-353 BC), was buried in a magnificent tomb that is numbered among the Seven Wonders of the World. The towering edifice of gleaming white marble, decorated by the most noted sculptors, became the model for many elaborate tombs, to be known thereafter as mausoleums.

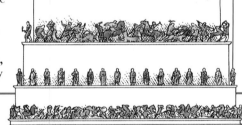

The Mausoleum, Halicarnassus, Turkey

EUROPE

TABLEWARE AS ORNAMENT
A set of bronze vessels from a 4th-century BC tomb at Bolsena in northern Italy illustrates the elaborate and costly tableware used by wealthy families. Wine was poured from the jug into the bowl, mixed with water, then ladled into individual cups.

Etruscan bronze wine bowl, jug, and ladle, northern Italy

OPEN-AIR THEATERS
Theaters were built at the center of many Greek cities, and were used for the staging of plays, public meetings, and religious ceremonies. One of the best preserved examples is that at Epidauros, which was large enough to accommodate 14,000 spectators. The acoustics of these open-air theaters were outstanding and are lasting testimonies to the skill and ingenuity of the architects who designed them.

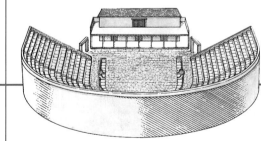

Theater, Epidauros, Greece

AFRICA

MILK IN THE DIET
The Bantu-speaking cattle herders who began to migrate from West Africa into eastern and southern Africa brought with them an ability to digest milk that was not shared by the existing hunter-gatherer peoples of these regions. Milk contains lactose, a substance that adults in many human populations have difficulty digesting. The problem is caused by a lack of lactase, an enzyme that is present in babies and allows them to digest their mothers' milk, but is normally lost by the time a person reaches adulthood. Over the last few thousand years, the populations of Europe, the Middle East, and certain parts of North America have developed the ability to digest milk by retaining lactase into later life. In other parts of the world, such as East Asia, or Africa south of the Sahara before the arrival of the Bantu, this ability was absent; milk played little part in the traditional diet.

CARTHAGE REDEVELOPED
The city of Carthage, which began life as a Phoenician trading colony on the North African coast, quickly rose to prominence as one of the largest and most successful commercial centers of the Mediterranean. During the 4th century BC, the entire layout of the city was revised. An extensive new area of grid-plan streets was built, and a pair of elaborate man-made harbors was created. One of these was circular and reserved for use by the powerful Carthaginian navy; the larger, rectangular harbor was designed for ordinary merchant shipping. The whole city was enclosed and protected by massive city walls.

| TECHNOLOGY & INNOVATION | ART & RITUAL |

ANCIENT SURGERY

Trephination, a method by which sections of skull were removed with a sawlike instrument, was employed in Peru to treat head injuries, migraine headaches, and seizures. Surgeons cut away portions of the skull to relieve pressure caused by depression fractures from falls or blows, and then closed the wound. Some of the earliest trephined skulls date to around 400 BC. Skulls like these, with two holes or more, show that patients sometimes survived more than one trephination.

Surgical hole

Trephined skull, Peru

HUNTER-GATHERER ROCK ART

Elaborate decorated anthropomorphic figures, ceremonial and supernatural in appearance, are part of the North American Barrier Canyon rock-art style. The figures measure from a few inches to over 6 feet in height and are often crowded together in rows. Large, hollow-looking eyes are usually their only facial features; faces often appear decorated and masklike.

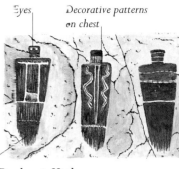

Eyes *Decorative patterns on chest*

Characteristic brush-like base

Rock art, Utah

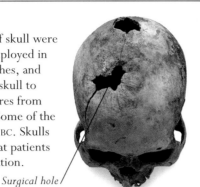

Bronze silver-inlaid finial for a halberd shaft, China

METAL INLAYS

Originally reserved solely for objects of ceremonial use, inlays of precious metals — copper, gold, and silver — became popular decoration in China for more utilitarian objects such as this

finial for a halberd (long-handled dagger ax). This new decorative technique largely usurped the earlier, thousand-year-old tradition of inlaying bronze with precious stones.

NOMADIC ART

Bronze and metal objects from China's northwestern border regions are dominated by stylized animal motifs, reflecting the importance of animals to the nomadic peoples of these areas. They also show, in both their style and

manufacture, influences from peoples farther west. A cloth impression on the reverse of this buckle shows that it was cast in a mold reinforced with fabric, a technique not used in central China.

Silver belt buckle, Ordos region, China

NETWORK OF ROADS

In the vast Persian Empire (550-331 BC), good communications were vital, and a system of roads with regular way stations was established so that those on state business could travel quickly and safely throughout the empire. By the 4th century BC, however, security was a problem, and even the king had to pay protection money to ensure safe passage in dangerous mountain regions.

Gold chariot model, Uzbekistan

DIFFERENT FAITHS

The Persian Empire was still powerful during the first half of this century. Within it were many peoples following different faiths, from Indians who thought it wrong to kill any living

creature to Greeks who believed in pure reason. It was the policy of the Persian kings to tolerate and even to support other faiths; they were worshiped as gods in Egypt, helped the Jews rebuild their temple in Jerusalem, and celebrated the festival of the god Marduk in Babylon. The Persians themselves had strong beliefs. Persian inscriptions stress the supremacy of their god Ahuramazda and the importance of personal morality in the struggle between good and evil.

NEW POTTERY TECHNIQUES

Celtic craftsmen made important advances in pottery manufacture, importing new techniques such as the potter's wheel from the Mediterranean world. A decorative pattern of curving spirals is typical of Celtic La Tène art of this period — a distinctive style named after a site in Switzerland. La Tène art is widely found throughout western and central Europe.

Painted urn, Prunay, France

SOCRATIC DIALOGUES

The Athenian Socrates (469-399 BC) pioneered the new philosophy of Classical Greece. His method of inquiry, using question and answer, was recorded in the famous *Dialogues* by his pupil Plato (427-347 BC). Plato systematized and developed Socratic thought, and in around 380 BC founded the Academy at Athens, which dominated philosophical study until late Roman times.

Roman copy of Greek statue of Socrates

POISONED ARROWS

Early African iron technology produced improved weapons for the hunt, still an important food source long after farming began. Ironsmiths held a privileged place in African society and were surrounded by a mystique of power. Light, iron-tipped arrows, often with barbs, were especially effective against antelope. Vegetable poisons smeared on the tip slowed down wounded prey.

Iron-tipped arrowhead, Africa

RULER AS PHARAOH

When Alexander the Great conquered Egypt in 332 BC, he adopted many of the customs and privileges traditional to Egyptian pharaohs. He sacrificed

publicly to the sacred Apis bull and ordered the restoration of the great temples of Amun at Luxor and Karnak in Upper Egypt. He also traveled across 600 miles of desert to visit the oracle of the god Ammon at the Siwa oasis. By conforming to tradition, Alexander gained the acquiescence of the Egyptian people in his conquest and governance of the land, a policy followed by his successors, the kings of the Ptolemaic dynasty founded by Ptolemy, one of Alexander's generals.

300-200 BC

FOOD & ENVIRONMENT

SHELTER & ARCHITECTURE

AMERICAS

WOVEN SANDALS
The earliest Anasazi people of southwestern North America wore sandals. These at first had square toes and heels, but styles changed frequently; slightly later, sandals were made with rounded toes. The weave could be a twill, producing a chevron design; a plait, producing a checkered pattern, or a wicker technique, producing the over-under weave on these sandals, which are in a style seen from around 200 BC.

Sandals, Cottonwood Canyon, Utah

URBAN CENTER
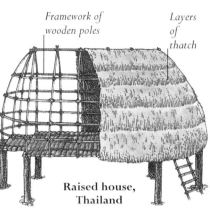
Teotihuacan in Mexico was the earliest large and densely settled urban center in the Americas. It was unique in developing the apartment house as the standard residential unit. The city contained more than 2,000 apartment compounds containing many residential rooms arranged around patios with kitchens and workshops.

City plan, Teotihuacan, Mexico

■ Temples   ▢ Apartments   ▢ Open patios

EAST ASIA & AUSTRALASIA

BUFFALO IN HARNESS

Evidence from Ban Chiang in Thailand shows that the water buffalo was first used here as a plow animal in the last few centuries BC. Although costly to maintain, it was quickly appreciated by the early rice farmers of Southeast Asia, who had previously relied on human muscle power to cultivate their fields. The water buffalo soon became the traditional plow animal of this region.

Water buffalo

HOUSES ON STILTS
Archaeological remains of houses in Southeast Asia are rare. What remains there are indicate that house styles changed little over the centuries. At Nong Chae Sao in southern Thailand, patterns of postholes are the only evidence of early houses. The posts supported living floors raised 6-10 feet above ground and reached by ladder. A framework of wooden poles covered in thatch kept out the monsoon rains.

Framework of wooden poles *Layers of thatch*

Raised house, Thailand

MIDDLE EAST & SOUTH ASIA

AGRICULTURAL TECHNIQUES
Plow agriculture was by now commonplace in many regions of southern India and on the island of Sri Lanka. Agricultural productivity was also greatly increased by the development of a variety of irrigation techniques. Most spectacular of these were the vast reservoirs and complex sluice gates built during the last few centuries BC in Sri Lanka's Dry Zone, notably at Anuradhapura.

Iron blade from a plow, Wurragaon, India

GREEKS IN ASIA
After Alexander the Great (reigned 326-323 BC) had conquered the Persian Empire, the Greek settlers who inherited his Middle Eastern domains brought with them their own classical culture. The eclectic style of Persian architecture did not survive in these Hellenistic times, although column bases at Ai Khanum (a Greek city on the Oxus River) and in the temple on the island of Failaka in the Persian Gulf are derived from those at Persepolis. Greek cities were founded throughout the Middle East, among them Antioch in Syria, founded by Seleucus, one of Alexander's generals who established the Seleucid Dynasty (312-64 BC). These cities were built according to the Greek model, with a regular rectangular street plan, agoras (marketplaces), temples, and theaters.

EUROPE

PRISON CONDITIONS
Analysis of the stomach contents of Tollund Man, a 2,200-year-old garroted body found remarkably well preserved in a Danish peat bog, showed that his last meal had been a gruel of cultivated barley and flax. Unusually, quantities of weed seeds were found within the gruel; although fields at the time were infested with weeds, sieving or some other method was usually used to eliminate them from the crop. Tollund Man's poor-quality fare may indicate that he passed his last days as a prisoner, perhaps kept alive with kitchen sweepings before his death.

EARLY SPORTS CENTERS
Greek sports complexes became increasingly elaborate during the 3rd and 2nd centuries BC. At Olympia, home of the Olympic Games, the Great Gymnasium and Palaestra (athletics hall) were rebuilt in around 200 BC. They provided a covered running track and wrestling ground where Olympic athletes could practice in bad weather, together with washrooms and social amenities.

Gymnasium *Palaestra*

Model of sports complex, Olympia, Greece

AFRICA

NEW HUNTING GROUNDS
As Bantu cattle herders moved south, earlier communities of hunter-gatherers withdrew into such remote areas as the dense tropical forests or the deserts of the southwest. Their technology was little changed by contact with the iron-using newcomers. The bow and arrow remained the principal hunting weapon, and an effective one: razor-sharp bone or wooden arrowheads on detachable foreshafts enabled the hunters to take even large animals like giraffes.

Modern bow and arrow, Kalahari region, Africa

PRINCIPAL SETTLEMENT
The settlement of Jenne-jeno on the inland Niger Delta in modern Mali was founded around 250 BC as a small farming village. Though small, it may have been the principal settlement of the region, and from its beginnings was an active ironworking center. Other crafts such as pottery production were practiced in villages nearby. Jenne-jeno soon outstripped its neighbors, and by AD 800 had developed into one of West Africa's first urban centers.

TECHNOLOGY & INNOVATION

TEXTILE TECHNIQUES

The Andean region has a long tradition of textile production, which by this time had reached a very high level of specialization. The Paracas people of southern Peru were particularly skillful embroiderers, using advanced techniques unknown elsewhere and a distinctive combination of colors and design motifs. The materials used were cotton and wool.

Paracas embroidery (inset) and detail, Peru

UNIFIED COUNTRY

Qin Shi Huangdi, first emperor of China in 221-210 BC, consolidated his unification of the country by creating a highly centralized administration based on military force. He secured the frontiers by joining separate sections of fortifications to form the Great Wall, and linked the provinces to the capital, Xianyang, through a network of tree-lined roads. Qin Shi Huangdi tried to impose uniformity of thought by standardizing script, weights, and measures, and by forbidding the teaching of the classics and burning classical books.

NEW SCRIPTS

In the Middle East the old cuneiform script, composed of wedge-shaped marks, had given way by the 3rd century BC to new alphabetic scripts, Aramaic and Greek. At about the same time in the Indian subcontinent, the needs of trade combined with western influences led to the development of the Brahmi script, ancestor to most modern Indian scripts. The first Brahmi inscriptions appear on monuments of the 3rd-century BC emperor Ashoka.

Clay tablet inscribed with Greek letters in an unknown language, Iraq

CLINKER-BUILT BOATS

The earliest examples of the clinker-built type of boat date from around 300 BC; one has been found deposited as an offering in a peat bog at Hjortspring, Denmark. The technique involved overlapping each plank of the hull over the one below to form a shell, then inserting an internal frame to give rigidity. The 62-foot Hjortspring boat was powered by oars.

FIRST LIGHTHOUSE

The new city of Alexandria founded by Alexander soon developed into a major trading port. To overcome the navigational hazards of the featureless, low-lying Egyptian coast, a great lighthouse, the Pharos of Alexandria, was built between 297 and 280 BC. The 425-foot-high marble tower had a fire in its base; its light was reflected out to sea by bronze mirrors. It was counted among the Seven Wonders of the World.

Mosaic, Pharos of Alexandria, Egypt

ART & RITUAL

CERAMIC SCULPTURE

The Jama Coaque culture (500 BC-AD 500) of coastal Ecuador is particularly known for human figurines modeled in clay, with well-defined physical traits and the scarce use of paint. They almost always wear headgear and jewelry. Here, a priestess is depicted wearing a ritual headdress, necklace, and bracelets, indicating her high status.

Jama Coaque figurine, Ecuador

UNDERGROUND ARMY

The first Chinese emperor, Qin Shi Huangdi, designed his own tomb, one of the greatest ever built. A vast underground palace with bejeweled roofs and rivers of flowing mercury, it attempted to recreate the magnificence of his empire. Thousands of life-size terra-cotta warriors with real weapons "guarded" the approach to the tomb.

Terra-cotta warriors, tomb of Qin Shi Huangdi, Shaanxi, China

BUDDHIST CONVERT

The Mauryan emperor Ashoka (reigned 272-232 BC) ruled over most of the Indian subcontinent. Eight years after his accession, he underwent a spiritual crisis of remorse at the slaughter of war and converted to Buddhism. The religion spread throughout his empire and into neighboring regions. Among works dedicated to the Buddha were a series of pillars with decorated capitals, which Ashoka commanded to be set up at locations of key importance in the Buddha's life story.

Ashokan decorated capital, Sarnath, India

HUMAN SACRIFICE

Ritual sacrifice in northern Europe at this time is indicated by the "bog body" of Tollund Man found in Denmark. Not only is his 2,200-year-old corpse remarkably preserved, but so too is a leather noose around his neck, with which he was garroted. Since other evidence suggests he was kept captive before his death, his role as a sacrificial offering was probably an unwilling one.

Head of Tollund Man, Denmark

FIRST LIBRARY BUILT

The founder of the Ptolemaic Dynasty in Egypt, Ptolemy I Soter (reigned 304-282 BC) established a Shrine of the Muses within his palace complex at Alexandria. Integral to this was the Great Library, in which most of the writings of classical antiquity were stored. It grew steadily in size from the 3rd century BC; during the Roman period, its contents numbered almost half a million papyrus rolls. Under the patronage of the Ptolemies, Alexandria became one of the greatest centers of Hellenistic culture, and the greatest center of learning in the western world. It was noted for the study of medicine, geography, and mathematics. Much of the new building work was funded by taxing the Egyptian people.

THE ART OF CLASSICAL GREECE

33,000 BC

Greek culture during the classical period (5th–4th centuries BC) was one of the richest and most innovative in European history, with key developments both in the visual arts and in drama, literature, and philosophy. Although the Greek homeland was politically fragmented into a series of independent city-states, the ancient Greeks nonetheless retained a strong sense of cultural identity that was reinforced by institutions such as the quadrennial Olympic Games, in which all Greeks were eligible to compete. In the 5th century BC, Athens became the cultural center of a Greek world that stretched from the Black Sea to the western Mediterranean. New styles of sculpture and architecture developed to encapsulate ideals of proportion, balance, and harmony. Even in minor arts, such as pottery painting, a new level of elegance was reached, and red-figure ware from Attica, the region around Athens, became widely fashionable during the 5th and 4th centuries BC.

CLASSICAL GREECE
The main centers of the Greek world during the classical period were the city-states of Greece and Aegean Turkey, and the colonies of southern Italy and Sicily. Sea travel linked all these areas to colonies of the western Mediterranean and the Black Sea.

Hand once held a thunderbolt

Eyes originally inlaid with colored glass and ivory

JEWELRY
Wealthy Greek women wore earrings of gold embellished with filigree and enamel decoration. Semiprecious gems were also expertly carved to make seal-stones, small engraved gemstones used for signing documents.

Boat-shaped earrings

DECORATIVE ARTS
Greek craftsmen mastered a wide range of skills and techniques. They sculpted statues in bronze, gold, and marble, and produced fine gold and silver tableware in addition to their distinctive painted pottery. Many of these objects were decorated with figured scenes, drawn from Greek mythology, religion, history, or everyday life.

OLYMPIAN ZEUS
The bronze statue recovered from an ancient shipwreck off Cape Artemisium in southern Greece is one of the most striking examples of classical sculpture. Dating from the mid-5th century BC, it depicts Zeus, king of the gods, hurling a thunderbolt. The eyes were originally inlaid with glass, ivory, and colored stone, the lips probably tinted with copper. Statues such as this were cast, usually in several sections, by the lost-wax technique, in which intricate shapes were first modeled in wax, then a clay mold was made around the wax model. As the clay was fired, the wax melted away, leaving a void that was filled with molten bronze.

PAINTED POTTERY
The most famous Greek pottery was produced at workshops in Attica during the 6th and 5th centuries BC. There were two principal types: black-figure (with scenes painted in black on a red background) and red-figure, invented at Athens in about 530 BC, in which the background was painted in black, leaving the scene itself in red. The Athenian red-figure technique was widely copied, especially in the Greek colonies of southern Italy.

Black-painted figures on red clay

WORKING WITH GOLD AND IVORY
The most sumptuous Greek sculptures were the statues of gold and ivory made for major shrines. At Olympia, a sanctuary of Zeus, a sculptor's workshop was discovered, in which were found bone tools, used to shape gold drapery and terra-cotta molds that were used to cast colored glass into clothing.

Black-figure amphora

Naturalistic form created by skilled casting

Red-figure plate

Fragments of terra-cotta mold

Central figure left in red

Black glaze over red clay

Bronze statue of Zeus, Cape Artemisium

Bone tools

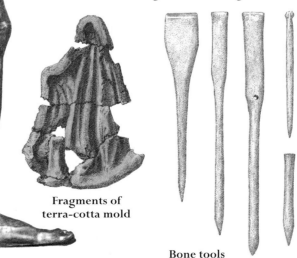

DORIC COLUMN

The Doric column had an undecorated "cushion" or rounded capital. The gently tapering columns were made of carefully joined stone drums and carved with decorative fluting.

COLUMNS AND CAPITALS

Greek temples of the 5th century BC were built in either the Doric or Ionic style, named after Greek dialects. Originally, both were translations of carved woodwork into stone. The Doric style was common on the mainland, while the Ionic was popular in the Greek cities of Aegean Turkey. A third style, Corinthian, came into use at the end of the century.

CORINTHIAN STYLE

The Corinthian style substituted a capital shaped like an upturned bell decorated with carved acanthus leaves. It became the leading architectural style in the Roman Empire.

Decorated abacus supports lintel

IONIC CAPITAL

Characterized by scroll-like appendages, the Ionic capital was probably inspired by curving fronds of foliage. The columns were fluted like those of the Doric style, but were taller and more slender. One of the earliest Ionic temples was that of the goddess Artemis at Ephesus, built around 560 BC and regarded by the Greeks as one of the Seven Wonders of the World.

Echinus (convex molding) with egg-and-dart pattern

Decorative spiral volutes

CARVED CARYATIDS

Another temple, the Erechtheion, stands near the Parthenon on the Acropolis. The Erechtheion has two porches, one with a roof supported by caryatids, carved standing figures of women in long drapery.

SHRINE TO ATHENA

The Parthenon was built on the Acropolis as a shrine to Athena when her city, Athens, was at the height of its power in the mid-5th century BC. The style chosen was Doric, and only the finest materials and sculptors were employed in its construction. Work began in 447 BC and the

final details – carving and painting of the sculptural decoration – were completed in 432 BC. Despite being badly damaged by an explosion in AD 1687, when the Turks used it as a gunpowder storage site, the Parthenon remains one of the most eloquent statements of Greek architectural ideals.

Reconstruction of the Parthenon

Marble roof tiles

Metopes (carved stone panels) show sack of Troy

Outer colonnade

Cutaway section of inner frieze shows Panathenaic religious procession

Main entrance

CULT STATUE

Within the Parthenon stood the great cult statue of Athena, completed by Pheidias, the leading Greek sculptor of his day, around 438 BC. The gold and ivory statue was over 36 feet high.

DECORATIVE THEMES

The carved decoration of the Parthenon portrayed themes of special significance to the citizens of 5th-century BC Athens. The principal frieze depicted the great quadrennial procession in honor of the goddess Athena, while the triangular pediment above the west front depicted the contest between Athena and Poseidon, god of the sea, for control of Attica.

Reconstruction of eastern front of the Parthenon, showing the birth of Athena

Rising sun

Poseidon

Departing moon

Hephaestus strikes Zeus's head with an ax

Zeus, from whose head Athena springs

Athena, fully formed

Metopes show mythological battle of gods and giants

CHAPTER 13
IMPERIAL REALMS
200 BC - AD 200

Europe and the Mediterranean fall under the rule of Rome

Unified China prospers under the Han Dynasty

Flourishing trade routes link Europe, the Middle East, India, Southeast Asia, and China

Irrigation systems and geometric mounds built in North America

The Moche Empire arises in coastal Peru

These centuries were the great age of empire-builders: the Romans in the West, the Parthians in the Middle East, and the Han rulers in China. These three empires accounted for more than half the total world population, with some 50 million people each. Global population had risen to perhaps 250 million by the start of the Christian era — less than a tenth of the present world population, but a massive increase over that of 1,000 years earlier. A rich archaeological legacy and many written documents from this time reveal a wealth of detail about the lives of ordinary people.

Imperial Rome

The rise of Rome owed much to its disciplined army and pragmatic diplomacy, and by 100 BC Rome dominated the Mediterranean. Successful generals such as Julius Caesar further extended Rome's control during the 1st century BC, paving the way for the first Roman emperor, Julius Caesar's adopted son Octavian (later called Augustus), who overthrew the republican government in 27 BC.

Imperial rule brought relative peace and prosperity. Magnificent public buildings were built and towns were linked by an extensive network of roads. At sites such as Pompeii in Italy, much of the detail is astonishingly modern: streets lined with shops, mills, and bakeries, and walls painted with graffiti promoting election candidates or forthcoming entertainments.

Asian sovereignty

The Han Empire of China (206 BC-AD 220) also maintained an effective central administration. The Great Wall was a stable and secure frontier that allowed trade and agriculture to flourish. Populous cities were connected by roads and canals. The

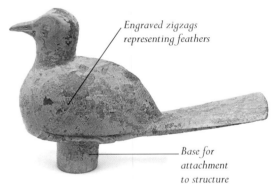

Engraved zigzags representing feathers

Base for attachment to structure

HAN DOVE FINIAL
Cities in Han China often had tall towers with finials in the shape of birds, such as this bronze dove, on the roofs. Finials were believed to attract benign spirits.

wealthy and powerful were buried in richly furnished tombs, with models of musicians and attendants as well as fine examples of contemporary crafts — lacquer bowls, silk hangings and clothing, and writing on bamboo or on the newly invented paper. Craftsmen also furthered the ancient art of bronzeworking, making ritual vessels, tomb models, and ornaments.

Between Han China and the Roman Empire lay other powerful states: the Parthian Empire (240 BC-AD 226), which dominated Persia and Mesopotamia, and the Buddhist kingdoms of northern India. Land and sea routes brought all these states into contact with one another and trade flourished. The Romans imported frankincense from Arabia and Somalia, spices from Southeast Asia, and silk from China. Much trading was done by sea, but after military expeditions against the warlike steppe nomads in the 1st century BC, the Chinese

ROMAN EMPEROR
Lucius Verus, depicted here in a bronze bust, was the adopted heir of the emperor Antoninus Pius. He ruled jointly with Marcus Aurelius from AD 161 to AD 169.

IMPORTED STONE FOR LUXURY ITEMS
This Roman cup is carved from fluorspar imported from the Persian Gulf. The stone is seldom found in pieces large enough to carve, so such vessels were rare and expensive.

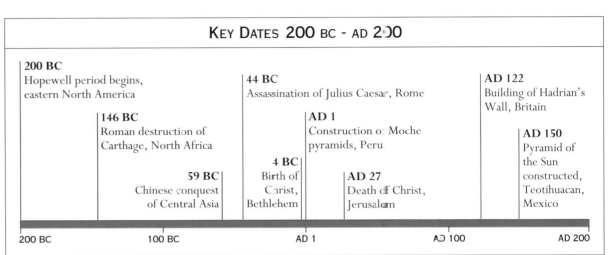

KEY DATES 200 BC - AD 200

200 BC
Hopewell period begins, eastern North America

146 BC
Roman destruction of Carthage, North Africa

59 BC
Chinese conquest of Central Asia

44 BC
Assassination of Julius Caesar, Rome

AD 1
Construction of Moche pyramids, Peru

4 BC
Birth of Christ, Bethlehem

AD 27
Death of Christ, Jerusalem

AD 122
Building of Hadrian's Wall, Britain

AD 150
Pyramid of the Sun constructed, Teotihuacan, Mexico

| 200 BC | 100 BC | AD 1 | AD 100 | AD 200 |

gained control of much of Central Asia and opened up the lucrative overland Silk Roads through to Persia and the markets of the Middle East.

South and Southeast Asia benefited from the prospects for trade that these contacts offered. In South Asia, richly decorated stupas (dome-shaped Buddhist monuments containing burials or relics) were built in the main cities. Only in southern India did Hinduism remain the main religion.

Smaller-scale communities
On the fringes of China, the influence of the Han Empire was significant. Independent kingdoms began to develop in northern Vietnam, Korea, and Japan. Local rivalry between competing clans in Japan led to the establishment of the Yamato State (AD 200-1185). Southeast Asia became a region of small states, each connected to the others by trade and diplomacy and drawing power from shifting ties of loyalty.

Australia lay beyond the reach of these developments, and Aboriginal groups continued the way of life that had served them well for centuries. In the Pacific islands, a new phase of expansion and colonization began around 150 BC, when Polynesian settlers from the islands of Tonga and Samoa moved as far west as Tahiti and the Society Islands.

Incised hand

HOPEWELL HAND
Incised with a stylized human hand, this stone disk was found in a Hopewellian burial mound in eastern North America; its significance is unknown.

Egyptian hieroglyphic script

Grooves representing date

TUXTLA STATUETTE
Found in Veracruz, Mexico, this statuette carved from nephrite with columns of incised glyphs dates to AD 162.

North Africa came under Roman control during the 2nd and 1st centuries BC. Carthage and Egypt were reduced to the status of Roman provinces. One of the most famous of all Egyptian artifacts, the Rosetta Stone, is from the Ptolemaic period (323-30 BC). It proved invaluable to 19th-century Egyptologists because it is inscribed with parallel texts in Greek and Egyptian writing, thus providing the vital key to deciphering hieroglyphs. The defeat and death of Cleopatra, queen of Egypt, in 30 BC ended the Ptolemaic Dynasty, which had ruled Egypt since the death of Alexander the Great.

THE ROSETTA STONE
Three scripts – hieroglyphic, demotic (another Egyptian script), and Greek – record the coronation in 196 BC of Ptolemy V, king of Egypt.

200 BC - AD 200

Meroë and sub-Saharan Africa

The kingdom of Meroë proved a powerful neighbor on the southern border of Egypt, and was never conquered by Rome. In sub-Saharan Africa, Bantu farmers and herders from the Great Lakes region began to move south into lands occupied by hunter-gatherers; some scenes in rock art by these latter groups depict them hunting Bantu domestic cattle. As the Bantu took control of more and more land, the hunters were increasingly restricted to the south and southwest of the continent, where some adopted a herding way of life. Hunter-gatherer groups still thrived in the equatorial tropical forests, where farming and herding were not viable.

American temple-pyramids

During the centuries from 200 BC to AD 200 Mesoamerica was dominated by two cities – Monte Albán in the Oaxaca Valley in western Mexico, and Teotihuacan in eastern Mexico. Monte Albán may have been the first city in the Americas, but the biggest was Teotihuacan, which by the end of the 2nd century AD had a population of around 40,000 inhabitants, more than twice the number at Monte Albán. A great center of trade and craftsmanship, Teotihuacan was a planned city with some 2,000 apartments and 500 craft workshops.

In South America, the Moche people of coastal Peru were devoting much energy to the building of temple-pyramids. The greatest is the Pyramid of the Sun in the Moche Valley, a flat-topped temple-pyramid of 143 million sun-dried bricks, completed early in the 1st century AD. Together with its smaller companion, the Pyramid of the Moon, it marked the heart of the Moche Empire (1st-8th centuries AD), which extended over 250 miles along the coast of Peru. The Moche were accomplished workers of copper, gold, and silver, and produced some of the world's finest painted pottery.

Lines and mounds

No less significant were the achievements of the Nazca peoples, who lived in a confederation of chiefdoms in the desert region of southern Peru. Experts in irrigation agriculture, the Nazca dug long underground tunnels that carried water to specially made tanks. However, they are most famous for the immense figurative outlines they created on the desert earth, the significance of which remains a mystery.

In eastern North America, the monumental mounds built in these centuries were the work of the Hopewell people, who lived in small communities and practised a combination of farming, and hunting and gathering. Some mounds began as modest tombs but grew larger as new burials were added. Most spectacular were the vast geometric mounds in the shape of square and round enclosures, and long parallel embankments. There were also sophisticated societies in southwestern North America, notably the Hohokam people, who dug canals and ditches to irrigate their fields. These communal works of mounds and canals are among the most remarkable early achievements of native North Americans.

AMERICAS

≡ Approximate extent of Hohokam culture

IRRIGATION CANALS

The economy of Snaketown, a settlement of the Hohokam people, who were the ancestors of the modern Papago and Pima Native American groups, was based on as much as 75,000 acres of irrigated farmland flanking the Gila River in Arizona. Water was transported by 300 miles of hand-dug canals and hundreds of miles more of subsidiary ditches. The earliest canals were wide and shallow, in contrast to later ones, which were dug much deeper, possibly to reduce the amount of water lost through evaporation. These sophisticated irrigation works illustrate how well the Hohokam adapted to the conditions of their semi-arid desert environment.

Shallow bed of early canal

Deeper bed of later canal

Cross section of canal showing early and later designs, Snaketown, Arizona

NAZCA LINES

The Nazca Lines, dating to between 200 BC and AD 200, are a series of enormous stylized pictures created in the desert along Peru's southern coast. Made by removing the brown surface stones to reveal the lighter ground beneath, some pictures are the outlines of creatures such as hummingbirds, monkeys and spiders; others are simply pairs of parallel lines, some as long as 12 miles. The significance of the lines has remained a mystery to the present day: they may be related to astronomy, representing star formations; alternatively, they may be iconographic – symbolizing, or ritually associated with, the gods of the landscape. No one knows why the lines and the figures they depict were built to take on recognizable form when seen from a great height.

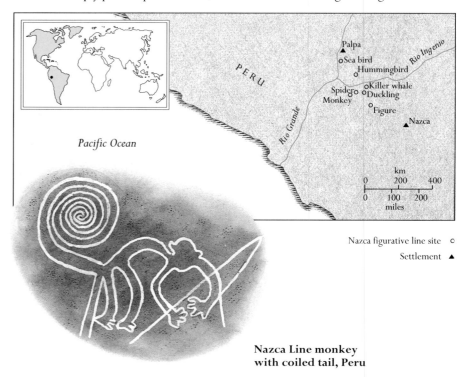

Nazca figurative line site ○

Settlement ▲

Nazca Line monkey with coiled tail, Peru

EUROPE

ROMAN EMPIRE

At its height in the 2nd century AD, the Roman Empire stretched from Armenia to the Atlantic. Frontiers were protected by forts, and sometimes long walls; the most famous was Hadrian's Wall in northern England, named after the emperor who built it in around AD 122. Roads linked frontier regions and provinces to the heart of the empire, enabling the rapid transfer of troops and supplies. The richest provinces were those around the Mediterranean, and major cities such as Carthage and Alexandria lay on its shores. The empire was split into an eastern half where Greek was spoken – this later became the Byzantine Empire – and a western half where Latin prevailed. Rome's rule in the west collapsed in the 5th century AD, when Germanic invaders occupied former Roman provinces.

Statue of the Roman Emperor Augustus, Prima Porta, Italy

≡ Maximum extent of Roman Empire in the 2nd century AD

▲ Major Roman city

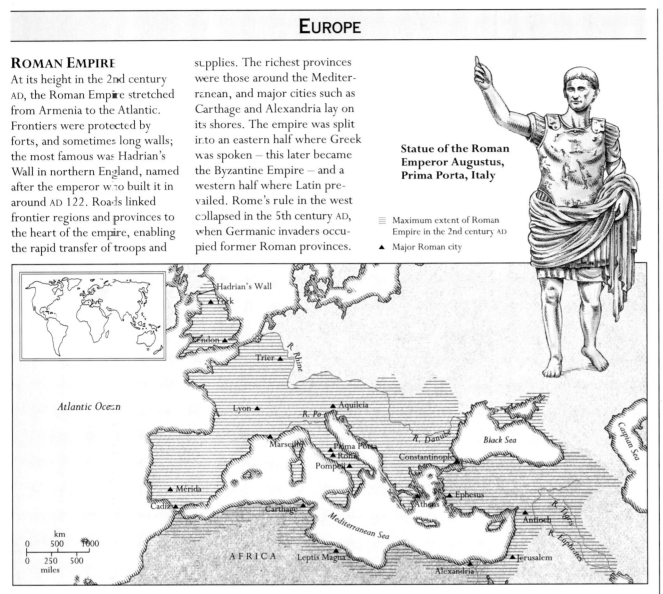

MIDDLE EAST & SOUTH ASIA

INCENSE TRADE

During the 1st millennium BC the markets for aromatic gums – frankincense in Egypt and Mesopotamia, and myrrh throughout the eastern Mediterranean and Middle East – prompted the rise of the incense states of Qataban, Hadhramaut and Sabaea (Sheba) in what is now the Yemen, Ma'in in western Saudi Arabia, and Nabatea in Jordan. Most major towns in these states were fortified against attack by neighboring states. Each state traditionally controlled sections of the land routes along which frankincense and myrrh were traded from their major harvesting areas north to Petra, and tolls were levied accordingly. However, in the early centuries AD, growing sea trade increased the power of those states in control of the main ports of Qana, Samhar, Mundus, Eudaemon Arabia (modern Aden), and Muza, and especially that of Axum in Ethiopia, which dominated the Red Sea trade routes.

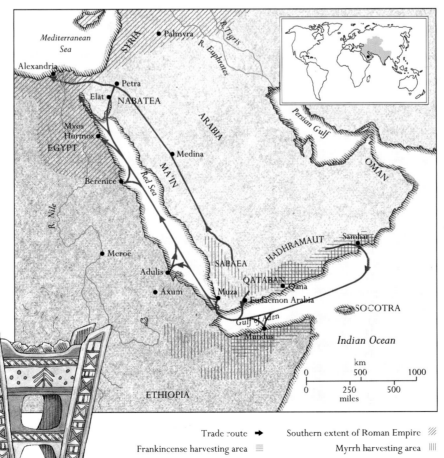

Incense burner, Oman

Trade route ➔   Southern extent of Roman Empire ▨

Frankincense harvesting area ≡   Myrrh harvesting area ▥

EAST ASIA & AUSTRALASIA

HAN EMPIRE

The Han Empire (206 BC-AD 220) covered most of modern China and extended into Korea and Vietnam. The center of government was in the north, first at Chang'an (modern Xian) during the Early Han period (206 BC-AD 2) and at Luoyang during the Later Han period (AD 25-220). A census taken in AD 2 gave a total population for the empire of 57 million, making it the most populous state of its day. The majority lived in the north; the capital at Chang'an alone had 250,000 inhabitants. Grain was shipped to Chang'an along a 77½-mile-long canal connected to the Yellow River. For the purposes of government the Han Empire was divided into some 1,500 administrative districts or commanderies, each centered in a walled town. There were also a number of subject kingdoms, such as the kingdom of Changsha in central China, with its capital at Mawangdui.

≡ Approximate extent of Han Empire

-- Canal

○ Capital city

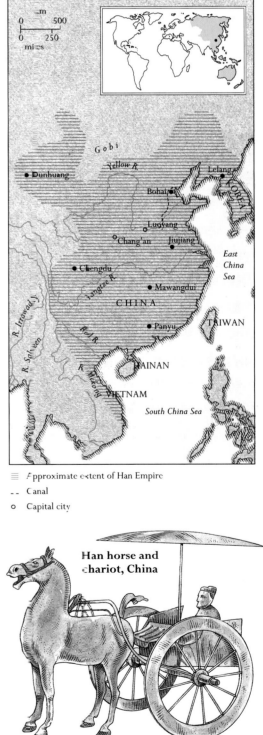

Han horse and chariot, China

200 - 100 BC

FOOD & ENVIRONMENT

SHELTER & ARCHITECTURE

AMERICAS

FOOD STORAGE
Hopewell communities (200 BC-AD 400) were based in Illinois and the Ohio Valley in eastern North America and had widespread trade contacts and cultural influence. Pottery from Louisiana 400 miles to the south, dating to around 100 BC, is remarkably similar to contemporary Hopewell pottery found in Illinois, showing the extent of Hopewell influence. Ceramic containers were used for storage, transportation, and cooking.

Pottery vessel, Marksville site, Louisiana

MONUMENTAL TEMPLES
The Formative period in the Andes (so called because it provided the basis for later complex societies) began around 1000 BC. It was dominated by theocratic societies who constructed ceremonial centers consisting of numerous temples and sacred enclosures. Toward the close of this era around 200 BC, architectural forms became less elaborate and the decorative motifs less complicated. Principal constructions were now modest buildings situated on platforms enclosed by cloisters and decorated with simple stone ornamentation. In some cases, the traditional U shape was conserved, such as in Layzon at Cajamarca in the northern highlands of Peru. These modest shrines were constructed alongside or above the ruins of older temples.

EAST ASIA & AUSTRALASIA

LACQUER TABLEWARE
Lacquer vessels found in a tomb at Mawangdui in central China show the tableware used by the upper classes in the empire during the Early Han period (206 BC-AD 2). Placed on a tray, these bowls were full of food when originally buried, and were accompanied by a bamboo skewer and chopsticks. The deceased, who died around 150 BC, was the wife of the prime minister of the subject kingdom of Changsha.

Lacquer tableware, Mawangdui, China

IMPERIAL CAPITAL
China had been unified in 221 BC by the Qin Dynasty, which was supplanted by the Han Dynasty in 206 BC. Growing prosperity during the Early Han period was reflected in the scale and magnificence of the imperial capital, Chang'an (modern Xian). The outer walls of the city had a circumference of 15 miles. The city itself was built according to a grid plan, and each of its 12 gates and three-laned avenues had identical measurements. The southern part of the city contained vast and splendid palaces and an armory; the northern part was divided into more than 100 industrial and residential districts. Outside the city walls were temples, burial areas, and huge parks landscaped with artificial lakes and mountains that were filled with rare plants and animals for hunting.

MIDDLE EAST & SOUTH ASIA

HORSE-BREEDING
The Parthian Empire (240 BC-AD 226) covered Mesopotamia and Persia. The Parthians of northern Persia were legendary horsemen who bred "blood-sweating" horses in the highlands of the Iranian plateau. These horses were prized for their size and strength, and were much in demand as cavalry mounts as far away as China. They grazed on alfalfa, whose Latin name, *Medicago sativa*, is derived from the region of Media in western Iran. In the late 2nd century BC, alfalfa seeds were exported to China to be grown as fodder for the horses imported by that country.

COMMISSIONED MONUMENTS
Among the many impressive monuments left by the Hellenistic rulers of Anatolia and Syria and their subject kings in the Middle East was the altar at Pergamon in Mysia, western Anatolia, which was commissioned by King Eumenes II (197-159 BC) in the mid-2nd century BC. The flamboyant sculptural reliefs decorating the altar are typical of contemporary Greek art.

Detail of altar, Pergamon, Anatolia

EUROPE

TRANSPORTING GOODS
Large pottery vessels known as amphoras were a characteristic feature of Roman sea trade during the 2nd and 1st centuries BC. Used mainly for transporting wine and olive oil, many amphoras bore an owner's stamp, allowing suppliers of particular areas to be identified. For example, amphoras from Cosa in northwestern Italy stamped with the name "Sestius" were exported mainly to southern France and the Rhône Valley.

Roman amphora

LUXURIOUS TOWNHOUSES
The House of the Vetii at Pompeii in southern Italy was a typical luxurious Roman townhouse. At its center was an atrium (courtyard or hall), with living and reception rooms at the front and a large ornamental garden at the rear.

Colonnaded atrium

House of the Vetii, Pompeii, Italy

AFRICA

REVITALIZING ASH
The spread of farming through much of tropical Africa at this time saw dramatic changes in local agricultural practices. Relying on wooden digging sticks and iron axes and hoes, most tropical farming groups used these implements to clear areas of forest to create farmland, felling trees and clearing undergrowth that were burned just before the onset of the rainy season. The resulting ash was then hoed into the ground to revitalize the soil with nutrients and minerals before the grain was sown.

CULT TEMPLE
From ancient times, Dendera in Upper Egypt was the cult center of the cow-goddess, Hathor. Construction of the Temple of Hathor was begun by kings of the Ptolemaic Dynasty (323-30 BC), and was completed in the Roman period. The capitals of its massive columns are in the form of Hathor heads. On the roof of the temple, the union of Hathor with Ra, the sun-god, was ritually reenacted.

Temple of Hathor, Dendera, Egypt

TECHNOLOGY & INNOVATION

MUSICAL SKILLS

Wind instruments were highly developed and advanced in the Andes. Made from a variety of materials – hollow cane, bone, or clay – they were used to provide musical accompaniment to rituals, feasts, and warfare. Several different types of instruments were used, especially single-pipe flutes, two-pipe flutes, and panpipes with five to ten pipes (the musical scale had five notes). This panpipe belongs to the Nazca culture, which flourished in southern Peru from 200 BC-AD 300.

Ceramic panpipe, Peru

AERODYNAMIC PRINCIPLES

In tropical northern Australia, a stencil that may date to the 2nd century BC was painted on the wall of a rock shelter in what is now Kakadu National Park. It illustrates one aspect of contemporary hunting technology – the boomerang – that had been used for at least 8,000 years by Australian Aborigines who had discovered the aerodynamic qualities of certain types of hunting stick.

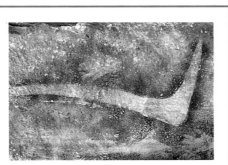

Boomerang stencil, Kakadu National Park, Australia

SILK ROADS

Coin of Mithradates II

During the reign of King Mithradates II of Parthia (124-87 BC), an envoy of the Chinese emperor arrived in Parthia to meet the king. He returned to China bearing gifts of ostrich eggs and conjurers. This meeting was followed in 106 BC by the first trading caravan between the Parthian Empire and China. The principal commodities were silk from China and horses from Iran. The establishment of the Silk Roads heralded the exchange of goods, ideas, and technology between East Asia and the West.

INVENTION OF CONCRETE

The use of concrete revolutionized Roman building and civil engineering from this period onward. One of the first major buildings constructed entirely from concrete was the Porticus Aemilia, a large market hall built on the banks of the Tiber River in Rome in 193 BC. One major advantage of concrete was that it hardened underwater, enabling ambitious harbor installations in Mediterranean ports, including Caesarea in Israel and Thapsus in Tunisia. The ingredients of Roman concrete were rubble and liquid mortar containing volcanic dust, with a protective cover of irregular stones.

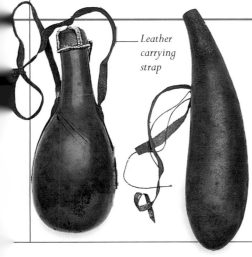

Leather carrying strap

GOURD CONTAINERS

As Africans came to depend more heavily on cattle and agriculture, they developed containers for carrying water or milk, and for storing grain and beer. These were made from dried and hollowed-out gourds, which were durable and easily carried at the waist or slung in a fiber net.

Gourds used as containers, East Africa

ART & RITUAL

HUNTING ART AND MAGIC

To appease the spirits that were thought to control a hunter's success, early Alaskan Eskimos (Inuit) placed images of these spirits on their weapons and clothing. This hat ornament, incised with an intricate curvilinear design known as the Old Bering Sea style, was carved when the style was at its peak. It is in the shape of a predatory spirit that was believed to help guide the hunter's harpoon. Hat ornaments carved with similar beasts continued to be used by Inuit into the 20th century.

Ivory hat ornament, Alaska

COMMEMORATIVE SCULPTURE

The earliest datable stone tomb monument from China commemorates an important victory for the Chinese, when a young general, Huo Qubing, led the cavalry on a campaign to secure a strategic section of one of the Silk Roads. During this period, trade between China and the West became well established along these routes through Central Asia. The routes were secured by successful Chinese military campaigns that doubled the size of the empire, extending its territory to the south and, above all, to the west.

TERRA-COTTA ART

In India, the 2nd century BC saw the flourishing of a long-established terra-cotta folk art, which often portrayed female figures. This plaque, from Tamluk in the Ganges delta, represents a *yakshi* (benign nature spirit) and reflects the dress and hairdressing of the period. Folk art like this was the inspiration for the first stone sculpture in India.

Terra-cotta plaque, Tamluk, India

DECORATED GLASSWARE

The growing opulence of Roman Italy during this period is reflected by the use of expensive glassware by aristocratic households. This bowl, found at Canosa in the south, is an excellent example. The floral design in gold leaf is pressed between two layers of glass fused together at the rim.

Gold leaf design

Glass bowl, Canosa, Italy

CARTHAGINIAN ARTS

The city of Carthage on the Gulf of Tunis in North Africa was founded by Phoenician colonists from the Middle East in the 9th century BC. The styles of sculpture and metalwork in the city owed much to their Phoenician origins, as shown by this limestone stela from the 3rd or 2nd century BC. Carthage was sacked by the Romans in 146 BC, but was re-founded as a Roman city a century later.

Limestone stela, Carthage, North Africa

100 BC - AD 1

FOOD & ENVIRONMENT

SHELTER & ARCHITECTURE

AMERICAS

HUNTING BAGS

The men of the earliest Anasazi culture in southwestern North America wore woven tunic shirts and sandals, and may have used skin bags to carry personal belongings, possibly hunting gear. The bags were unpainted and adorned only with the animals' limbs or tails, which were customarily left intact.

Animal-skin bags, Graham Canyon, Utah

RITUAL MOUNDS

The Hopewell people of eastern North America constructed massive earthworks as ritual and community centers. Among the most impressive of these is the Liberty mound group, which consists of 14 mounds and is located near Chillicothe, Ohio. Some of these earthen monuments formed large geometric arrangements of conjoined circles and squares. Others were used for burial of the dead. Within the burial mounds there were often one or more large rectangular buildings, probably intended to house the remains of important ancestors. Some of these individuals were cremated. Sometimes an entire building was burned and a mound erected over the top.

EAST ASIA & AUSTRALASIA

BUSY KITCHENS

Chinese tombs from the Early Han period (206 BC-AD 2) provide much evidence for the variety and importance of food in Chinese life. Kitchen scenes appear in murals, and figures are depicted plucking and skinning, chopping, preserving, and cooking meat, fish, and fowl. According to Chinese beliefs, a supply of food continued to be important after death, as did other worldly goods. Gifts buried with the dead included bamboo slips with recipes written on them, jars and bags full of dried foods, and even model stoves laden with cooking pots and spatulas.

BRICKS AND TILES

In China, terra-cotta bricks and tiles were increasingly used for palaces and tombs. Large, hollow, rectangular bricks were used for walls, while wedge-shaped bricks were slotted together to create vaults in tombs. Tongue-and-groove bricks were also used. The external surfaces of both bricks and tiles were decorated with impressed patterns or painted scenes.

Impressed brick from a tomb, China

MIDDLE EAST & SOUTH ASIA

INCENSE TRADE

Camel caravans traveled across the deserts of Arabia bringing aromatic gums and resins of balsam, frankincense, and myrrh to the cities of the eastern Mediterranean and Middle East. This trade had started in the early 1st millennium BC, when incense was used in temple rituals, notably in Egypt and Mesopotamia. The custom grew in importance during the last few centuries BC, when small stone altars for burning incense became common.

Altar for burning incense, Saudi Arabia

Holy of Holies

Herod's Temple, Jerusalem, Israel

NEW TEMPLE AT JERUSALEM

Herod the Great was appointed king of Judaea by the Roman senate in 37 BC. He built a new temple at Jerusalem and supported strict observance of Jewish law in Palestine. The core of the temple, the Holy of Holies, stood within a massive colonnaded sanctuary. Parts of the outer wall survive today, notably the famous section on the west side known as the Wailing Wall.

EUROPE

COOKING UTENSILS

Roman kitchens contained metal saucepans and strainers, wooden spoons, and pottery pastry molds. Mortars were used for the preparation of pastes and powders, and glass bottles and pottery amphoras were used to store wine and food.

Roman bronze strainer, Pompeii, Italy

TEMPLE DESIGN

The design of Roman temples owed much to ideas taken from the Greek world, although there were considerable stylistic variations in different parts of the empire. In the east, grandiose temple complexes with elaborate carved decoration were built, while temples in western provinces were simpler and less ornate. The best preserved western temple is the Maison Carrée at Nîmes in southern France, built in 16 BC. It has a deep porch on the facade supported by fluted columns but, unlike most Greek temples, has no freestanding colonnade around the sides and rear.

AFRICA

CATTLE DISEASE

Most herding communities in sub-Saharan Africa kept small short-horned breeds of cattle, but supplemented their diets with hunting and agriculture. Cattle-herding was risky, because epidemics of rinderpest (a severe, infectious disease affecting cattle) and other diseases frequently wiped out entire herds, and because the tsetse fly, whose bite can be fatal to cattle, infested large areas of savanna woodland in sub-Saharan regions.

MOSAIC DECORATIONS

Alexandria, on Egypt's Mediterranean coast, became a center of innovative visual arts in the 1st century BC, especially in the realm of mosaics and frescoes. Copies and imitations were created in Roman Italy, where Egyptian scenes and Alexandrian styles became fashionable in the villas of wealthy aristocrats.

Detail of mosaic "The Inundation of the Nile," Palestrina, Italy

TECHNOLOGY & INNOVATION

EARLY CALENDAR

One of the earliest dated monuments in the Gulf Coast region of Mexico, this stela has an Olmec mask carved on one side and a calendrical inscription on the other, which corresponds to 31 BC in our own calendar. A forerunner of later Mesoamerican calendars, the Olmec calendar used stylized pictographs to denote numbers: a shell for zero, a dot for one, and a bar for five. Numbers of 20 and more were indicated by changing the position of the pictograph.

Fragments of stela, Tres Zapotes, Veracruz, Mexico

SALT MINING

The production of salt in China was under state supervision after the 7th century BC. In the early 2nd century BC, 34 agencies were set up to control salt production, and in 119 BC the salt and iron mines were declared state monopolies. Both rock salt deposits and subterranean brine reservoirs were exploited. Reliefs on bricks from tombs of this period show how the brine was extracted from wells drilled to a depth of more than 1,900 feet. Ropes with buckets attached at intervals were lowered into the wells using winding gear and pulley systems. The buckets collected the brine, which was then piped out and evaporated in large boiling pans.

IVORYWORKING

Found at Nisa, an early capital of the Parthian Empire (240 BC-AD 226) in what is now southern Turkmenistan, this horn-shaped rhyton (drinking cup) of the 2nd or 1st century BC was made of ivory that had been imported from India. It is decorated with a deer head peculiar to Parthian nomadic art and illustrates the skill with which Parthian craftsmen worked exotic materials.

Ivory rhyton, Nisa, Turkmenistan

Diagram of astronomical calculator, Greece

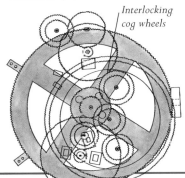

Interlocking cog wheels

CHARTING THE HEAVENS

The most sophisticated piece of mechanical engineering known from the ancient world is a now fragmentary astronomical calculator used to compute the changing positions of heavenly bodies. It was found at the site of a shipwreck near the Greek island of Antikythera and dates to around 80 BC. The concept of differential gearing (this device had 31 interlocking wheels) was not rediscovered until the late 16th century.

HERDERS' TOOLS

Around 2,000 years ago, the hunter-gatherers of Namibia and the Cape Province of South Africa began to shift to a herding way of life, obtaining domestic sheep and cattle from their Bantu neighbors. They relied on bone, wood, and flaked stone for their tools, later adopting the use of pottery vessels. These people were the ancestors of the Khoi Khoi encountered by Portuguese explorers in the late 15th century.

ART & RITUAL

PERSONAL ORNAMENTS

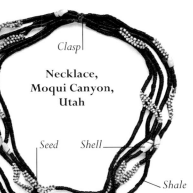

Clasp

Necklace, Moqui Canyon, Utah

Seed *Shell*

Shale

Necklaces were popular among the women of southwestern North America in the 1st century BC. Clasps were often made by securing a loop over a knot or toggle. This five-strand necklace of grey shale, white seeds, and Olivella shell imported from the Pacific coast, is longer and more elaborate than most. It was stored in a small weft-twine bag.

MAGICAL MIRRORS

According to Chinese belief, mirrors provided protection from evil spirits and also revealed spirits that were otherwise hidden. Mirrors were decorated with auspicious spirit-beings and patterns with astronomical meaning that may have enabled the owners to orient themselves in relation to the heavens. Mirrors from the Han Dynasty (206 BC-AD 220) were often inscribed with a date and the names of the maker and owner.

Bronze mirror, China

STONE SCULPTURE

In the late 1st century BC, four monumental stone gateways were added to the Great Stupa at Sanchi in central India, a sacred building founded by the emperor Ashoka in the 3rd century BC. They were embellished with sculptures showing scenes from the life of Buddha and figures from contemporary folklore. Voluptuous female tree-spirits formed brackets supporting the lower bars of the gateways. These spirits represented fertility and the abundance of nature.

Stone gateway bracket, Sanchi, central India

CELTIC TORQUES

Torques (neck rings) had great significance, perhaps as talismans, for the Celtic peoples of northwestern Europe. Many were made in precious metals such as gold or electrum (an alloy of gold and silver). This 1st-century BC electrum torque is one of the most impressive surviving examples: Roman writers described the British queen Boudicca, formidable ruler of the Iceni tribe of East Anglia, wearing a torque such as this when riding into battle.

Torque, Snettisham, Norfolk, England

ROMAN CULTURE

As Roman influence spread up the Nile, and Egypt became a prosperous province of the empire, Roman art styles were diffused farther up the river. This bronze head of the Emperor Augustus is typical of the style of this period. It was found at Meroë, capital of the independent kingdom of Nubia (c.600 BC-400 AD), which was never conquered by the Romans. Its discovery there illustrates how Roman cultural influences spread beyond the frontiers of the empire.

Bronze head of the Emperor Augustus, Meroë, Nubia

AD 1-100

FOOD & ENVIRONMENT

SHELTER & ARCHITECTURE

AMERICAS

HUNTING AND SNARING
The Basketmaker people of south-western North America hunted large animals with atlatls (spear-throwers) and trapped small animals with nets and snares. Snares were set along trails used by small mammals, where birds alighted under bushes, or near grassy areas with food. Fine strings formed a slip noose, tied to the snares' many pegs, that would close around the birds. Much larger nets were used to enmesh rabbits.

Twine

Bird snare, Moqui Canyon, Utah

TEMPLE-PYRAMIDS
During the 1st century AD, the urban center of Teotihuacan in the Valley of Mexico expanded to become a vast metropolis. Its two largest structures – the Pyramids of the Moon and the Sun – were completed at the northern and eastern edges of the city's main avenue, the Street of the Dead. The city controlled the production and distribution of obsidian (a volcanic rock prized for making weapons, tools, and ornaments) throughout Mesoamerica, and embraced entire neighborhoods of foreign merchants and specialized craftsmen.

EAST ASIA & AUSTRALASIA

NEW FARMING METHODS
In China during the Later Han period (AD 25-220), the energies of everyone, from the emperor (who made sacrifices for good harvests and issued the calendar regulating the farming year) to the peasants, were concentrated on improving food production. Yields were increased by innovations such as seed drills, which allowed regular distribution of seeds in a furrow. More efficient plows pulled by two oxen were introduced, as were harrows for breaking up soil, mechanical grain-milling devices with trip hammers, winnowing machines with rotary fans, and winch-and-pulley systems for irrigation.

TOWERS AND PAVILIONS
Contemporary poems, tomb reliefs, and models all point to the popularity of tall towers in Han China (206 BC-AD 220). One of the towers in the capital, Chang'an, was reputedly 374 feet high. The towers were built as look-out posts or pavilions, often with glittering bronze roofs surmounted by birds. These were believed to attract immortal spirit-beings who might help the living achieve immortality.

Moat

Han pottery tomb model of a watchtower with moat, China

MIDDLE EAST & SOUTH ASIA

IMPORTED PEPPER
Exports from southern India to Rome were mainly luxuries such as fine cloth, jewels, and spices, including peppercorns. Great quantities of peppercorns (probably used in cooking to disguise the taste of bad meat) were stored in warehouses at Ostia, the port serving Rome. In payment, Indian suppliers received large numbers of gold coins, which were used as bullion. This trade became such a drain upon the Roman economy that the emperor Nero (AD 37-68) banned the import of pepper.

DESERT TEMPLE
Petra – the desert capital of the Nabataean kingdom in Jordan, which was absorbed into the Roman Empire in AD 106 – has some of the world's most impressive rock-cut architecture. Tombs and temples were hewn into the sandstone cliffs around the city. Roman influences inspired facades such as that of the Deir temple, built in the 1st century AD. As with the other desert cities, Palmyra and Hatra, Petra's wealth came from trade.

Deir temple, Petra, Jordan

EUROPE

PRESERVED FOODS
In AD 79, the volcanic eruption of Mount Vesuvius in southern Italy buried the Roman cities of Pompeii and Herculaneum. Under the ash, remains of food were preserved, including bowls of carbonized figs, prunes, olives, and barley grains. Complete meals with meat, fish, eggs, bread, and nuts were left untouched on tables, hurriedly abandoned by their owners as they fled to safety. Remains of various kinds of food were also found in shops, and in the bakery of Modestus the ovens still contained loaves of bread.

Grapes and fig

CIVIL ENGINEERING
The Romans were expert civil engineers whose skill is reflected in the aqueducts that they built to supply their cities with water. Many survive, such as the Pont du Gard, dating to AD 14, which served Nîmes in southern France. With three tiers of arches and a height of 172 feet, it is one of the tallest and best preserved.

Pont du Gard, Nîmes, France

AFRICA

DOG BURIALS
Dogs had been domesticated in Egypt by around 6000 BC, and were common throughout the African continent by AD 100. They were used for hunting and kept as domestic pets. Dog burials dating to the 1st century AD have been found in farming villages in the Nubian desert, which suggests that dogs had a special place in their owners' affections.

MEROITIC TEMPLE
The Lion Temple was one of a series of temples at Naga in Nubia. Its architecture was heavily influenced by Egyptian styles, although it lay within the independent kingdom of Meroë south of Roman Egypt. It was built by King Netekamani and Queen Amanitare around AD 1 and dedicated to the lion-god Apedemek. All three are depicted in temple reliefs.

Lion Temple, Naga, Nubia

TECHNOLOGY & INNOVATION

BABY CARRIERS

In southwestern North America, babies of the earliest Anasazi families were carried on light, flexible cradle boards, like the one shown here. These were padded with juniper bark, hides, or other soft material to cushion the baby's head. Later (after AD 700), Anasazi peoples caused the backs of the babies' heads to be flattened by fastening the swaddled infant to a stiff wooden cradle board with a broad woven sash or cradle band around the head.

Cradle board, Moqui Canyon, Utah

PAPER AND INK

In China, paper was made from hemp waste or old rags, and fragments dating to the 2nd century BC have been found in northern and northwestern China. The earliest known hemp paper with writing dates to the beginning of the 1st century AD. Solid ink was rubbed on to an inkstone with water, then a brush was used to apply the resulting liquid ink.

Lump of solid ink

Bronze inkstone, China

MONSOON WIND SYSTEM

An understanding of the monsoon wind system, and the rapid route it facilitated, provided the impetus that led to the beginning of Roman trade with southern India and Sri Lanka during the 1st century AD. This trade was supposedly initiated when a Greek merchant, Hippalus, was accidentally blown off course on a journey around western Arabia. Rome soon established trading links and even trading stations like that at Arikamedu on the east coast of southern India, as several finds of Roman pottery testify.

GLASS TECHNOLOGY

The Portland Vase, named after the Duke of Portland who bought it in AD 1745, is the finest surviving specimen of Roman glassware. It dates to the early 1st century AD. and was made by dipping a core of dark blue glass into a vat of molten white glass. The white glass was then carefully cut away to leave only the finely carved figures against a dark blue background. The work would have taken several months and was probably done by a skilled jeweler.

Portland Vase

LIGHTING FIRES

Farmers and hunter-gatherers throughout Africa probably used fire drills to light fires, much as the San hunter-gatherers of the Kalahari Desert in southwestern Africa do today. The technique involves rotating a hardwood drill in a small hollow in a short length of softwood, and adding fine dry grass and leaves as the wood begins to smoke.

Hardwood rotates in hole made in softwood

Hollow for tip of drill

Modern San fire-lighting drills, Africa

ART & RITUAL

WARLIKE ICONOGRAPHY

Iconography from the Nazca culture, in southern Peru, depicts anthropomorphic characters with their tongues sticking out, vomiting blood, and their hands ready to trap or catch. One of these painted figures, known as the "strangler," is associated with local mythology. In other images, figures hold trophy heads, possibly of other spirits.

Nazca bowl depicting the "strangler," coastal Peru

TOMB CHAMBERS

Vertical pit-graves, entered from above, were replaced in China during this period by horizontal tombs consisting of two or three brick- or stone-built chambers, dug into a hillside and entered through a sloping passage. The larger tombs were detailed imitations of everyday mansions, the walls decorated with mythical beings or naturalistic scenes from the life of the deceased. Horses and carriages were placed inside some tomb chambers, although the practice of substituting clay models for real objects was widespread by this time. Tomb models of houses granaries, and pigsties, and figurines of animals and people, provide valuable and fascinating information about daily life in China.

DEAD SEA SCROLLS

At the time of Christ there were several Jewish sects. One of these, the Essenes, may have written the Dead Sea Scrolls, a collection of documents that includes the earliest surviving examples of books of the Bible. There are also sectarian writings, copies of most of the Hebrew sacred canon, and commentaries on prophets such as Isaiah. They date from the 3rd century BC to AD 64, although most were written in the 1st century AD.

Dead Sea Scroll, Qumran, Jordan

CHARIOT RACING

Athletic games were an important element in Roman public festivals, and all important cities possessed an amphitheater and a stadium, or racetrack. Chariot races were a regular entertainment and were often represented in art, while gladiatorial contests and combat between men and wild animals satisfied the popular taste for violence and bloodshed.

Glass beaker depicting chariot race, Colchester, England

SPIRITUAL POWERS

In all African farming societies at this time, there were close links between the living and their ancestors, and between the ancestors and the land. The ancestors were the guardians of fertile soils and brought rain to parched land. Individuals who interceded between the people and their ancestors were gifted spirit mediums who assumed positions of considerable authority. It was they who gauged public opinion and used their skills to effect cures and bring rain. Sometimes they became powerful chiefs, presiding over important trade routes and great shrines.

AD 100-200

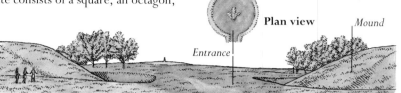

FOOD & ENVIRONMENT	SHELTER & ARCHITECTURE

AMERICAS

VARIED DIET

The traditional mainstay of the Mesoamerican diet was a trio of plants often grown together — corn, beans, and squash. Mesoamericans also grew chilies, avocados, and amaranth along with a wide variety of other fruits and vegetables. Among the few domesticated animals were turkeys, Muscovy ducks, and hairless dogs, three principal protein sources. Insects were also of value — the bee for its honey and the cochineal beetle for making dye.

GEOMETRIC EARTHWORKS

A site at Newark in Ohio displays a 1235-acre arrangement of mounds in geometric patterns, built between 100 BC and AD 400 by the Hopewell people of eastern North America. The site consists of a square, an octagon, circles, and ovals, connected by several sets of walls. By sighting along or through mound center points, angles, and lines, a record of lunar events could be maintained.

Newark Mounds, Ohio

Plan view *Mound*

Entrance

EAST ASIA & AUSTRALASIA

COOKING POTS

The two most common cooking pots used in China during this period were three-legged cauldrons for boiling and stewing, and steamers for preparing grain and vegetables. Their basic forms date back to very early times, and similar vessels are still used. Most were made of clay, although iron and bronze examples have been found in the tombs of wealthy people.

Bronze food steamer, China

EARLY STONE MONUMENTS

Stone towers that mark the approach to important tombs of the Later Han period (AD 25-220), such as this one in Sichuan, are among the earliest surviving surface constructions in China. Their carved decorative reliefs provide valuable information about contemporary life and beliefs, depicting banquets, hunts and processions, and historical and legendary scenes chosen for their moral lessons.

Stone tower, Fan Min tomb, Sichuan, China

MIDDLE EAST & SOUTH ASIA

WATER SUPPLY

During the early centuries AD, new water supply methods were introduced in the Middle East. The Nabataeans, whose kingdom in the western Arabian desert was absorbed into the Roman Empire in AD 106, constructed an innovative network of dams and cisterns to catch enough of the sparse rainfall to supply their capital at Petra. In other regions, pots attached to a long loop of rope were suspended on pulleys over wells or rivers; wheels with buckets attached to their rims also came into use. *Qanats* (underground canals), which tapped water reserves, were also built in Iran at this time.

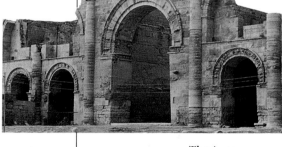

The *iwan* (vault collapsed), Hatra, Iraq

VAULTED CHAMBERS

The most characteristic feature of the architecture that supplanted Greek styles in Iran and Iraq is the *iwan*, an open-ended, barrel-vaulted hall made of baked brick. One of the best early examples is the vaulted *iwan* at Hatra in Iraq, which dates to around AD 150 but has since collapsed. A formal plan of four *iwans,* one on each side of a central courtyard, became the standard formula in later times for mosques, palaces, and schools.

EUROPE

ROMAN DIET

At Vindolanda, on Hadrian's Wall in northern England, a find of letters and documents provides unique insight into life at a Roman frontier outpost around AD 100. Some of the documents are official records listing the foods available for the garrison stationed there. There is mention of wheat and barley, wine and beer, fish sauce and spices, and pork and venison. In one of the letters, addressed to an officer named Lucius, the writer says he has received a gift of 40 oysters. Oyster and mussel shells have been found at Vindolanda, although they were probably a delicacy rather than a staple.

Arch of Trajan, Ancona, Italy

TRIUMPHAL ARCHES

The triumphal arch was an imposing symbol of Roman rule throughout the empire. Some arches were erected by emperors to commemorate particular achievements, others to celebrate an imperial visit. All were decorated with columns, relief carvings, and statues or wreaths of gilded bronze. The arch at Ancona on the Adriatic coast of Italy was built in AD 115 in honor of the emperor Trajan, who had ordered the construction of the harbor there.

AFRICA

FEEDING THE PEOPLE

Beneficent Roman emperors such as Marcus Aurelius (reigned AD 161-180) encouraged wealthy citizens to establish charitable funds to support and feed the poor. An inscription from this emperor's reign records how one Publius Licinius Papirianus, a citizen of Cirta Sicca in Numidia (roughly equivalent to modern Algeria), donated 1,200,000 sesterces so that 300 boys and 200 girls could be supported on the interest.

Bust of Marcus Aurelius, Cyrene, North Africa

ROMAN CITIES

The Roman cities of North Africa grew to considerable size during the 2nd century AD. Some ancient settlements, such as Leptis Magna, were embellished with impressive public buildings and colonnaded streets. Others, like Thamugadi, were newly founded at this time and constructed according to a rigid chessboard plan.

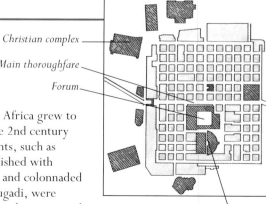

Christian complex

Main thoroughfare

Forum

City plan, Thamugadi, North Africa *Theater*

TECHNOLOGY & INNOVATION

POTTERY CONTAINERS
As societies in the Woodland Period (1000 BC-AD 800) of eastern North America developed sedentary villages based on horticulture, there was less need to transport containers over long distances, as their nomadic predecessors had done. The chief disadvantages of pottery – weight and fragility – became less important, and its advantages could now be fully exploited. This vessel from the Renner site in Missouri dates to between 100 BC and AD 300.

**Pottery vessel,
Renner site,
Missouri**

DETECTING EARTHQUAKES
In AD 132, the Chinese scientist and mathematician Chang Heng invented the world's first seismograph. Installed in Luoyang, the Later Han capital, it was shaped like a wine jar and contained a pendulum with eight mobile arms. The end of each arm was formed in the shape of a dragon holding a ball in its mouth. When the seismograph was shaken, a catch mechanism in the arm pointing in the direction of the earthquake released the ball, alerting the central government to earthquakes in distant provinces.

MORTAR AND PLASTER
In the early centuries AD, the use of quick-drying lime and gypsum mortars and plasters became widespread throughout the Middle East, probably due to the Roman conquest of the area. Mortar facilitated the construction of vaults and domes, and stucco was used to decorate buildings. At Ashur and Qaleh-i Yazdigird – two sites in northern Mesopotamia within the Parthian Empire (240 BC-AD 226) – carved and molded stucco painted with elaborate designs was used to cover facades and walls.

MILITARY ORGANIZATION
The backbone of the Roman army was the highly trained legionary soldier. He wore body armor and a helmet, and his weapons were a javelin and short stabbing sword. Around 80 to 100 soldiers were organized into "centuries," with 60 centuries making up a full legion of some 5,000 troops supported by ancillary staff.

**Bronze figurine
of Roman legionnaire, Italy**

COPPERSMITHS
In the early centuries AD, the working of iron and copper began to spread into southern Africa from the Lake Victoria region of East Africa, as Bantu farmers and herders migrated south. Copper was used by rural craftsmen to make jewelry, such as bracelets, beads, small razors, and pendants.

Copper armlet and bracelet, East Africa

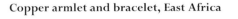

ART & RITUAL

ELABORATE GRAVE GOODS
The Hopewell peoples in Ohio and Illinois traveled great distances in search of rare materials to make ritual and burial items. Reel-shaped gorgets (neck ornaments), like this example from the Naples Mound, Illinois, were made of copper imported from the Great Lakes area, and were often placed on the chests of the dead buried there.

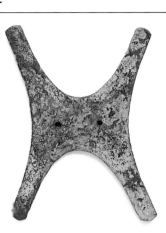

**Hopewell copper gorget,
Naples Mound, Illinois**

ARTISTIC REALISM
In three-dimensional sculpture of the 2nd century AD, Chinese sculptors deliberately concentrated on catching the nature of their subject, rather than aiming for an exact representation. Subjects like this magnificent flying horse were fashioned with simple flowing lines and little surface decoration.

*Fluid line
suggests movement*

Bronze flying horse, Gansu, China

CENTERS OF BUDDHIST ART
Early Buddhist art in India depicted events in the Buddha's life only symbolically, but in the 2nd century AD representations of him in human form began to appear. Two major schools of Buddhist art emerged: Mathura in central India, with its roots in native folk art, and Gandhara in modern northwestern Pakistan, which was influenced by Greco-Roman art styles.

Buddha teaching, Gandhara, Pakistan

BURIAL PRACTICES
Prosperous Romans of the 2nd century AD had their ashes preserved in carved marble cinerary urns, which were placed in niches in family vaults. Cremation continued to be the dominant rite (as it had been in Rome since earliest times), although towards the end of the 2nd century AD the new practice of interment became established.

PORTRAITURE
Citizens of Roman Egypt perpetuated the ritual of mummification. Many mummy cases bore detailed portraits of their owners, painted with colored wax on wood panels. Similar portraits may have hung in the homes of the deceased, before being strapped to the mummy after death. The style of the portraits is purely Greco-Roman, although Egyptian religious beliefs continued to flourish.

**Roman portrait for a
mummy case, Egypt**

URBAN LIFE IN EPHESUS

For many people in Roman times, the city in which they lived was a source of pride and civic loyalty. Civic administration was highly organized, and taxes were collected by the municipality to provide essential utilities such as water supply and drainage. Most cities were governed by local magistrates, even when, as in provincial cities such as Ephesus, ultimate control lay in the hands of the Roman authorities. Civic identity was often associated with patron deities, and temples dedicated to them were conspicuous in the urban landscape. The site of Ephesus, first settled in the 10th century BC, grew to become the capital of the Roman province of Asia, which covered most of modern western Turkey. The city had a population of over 100,000 and was described by the Greek geographer Strabo, writing in the 1st century BC, as a major commercial center. Ephesus was also the focus of a local fertility goddess identified with the Greek goddess Artemis.

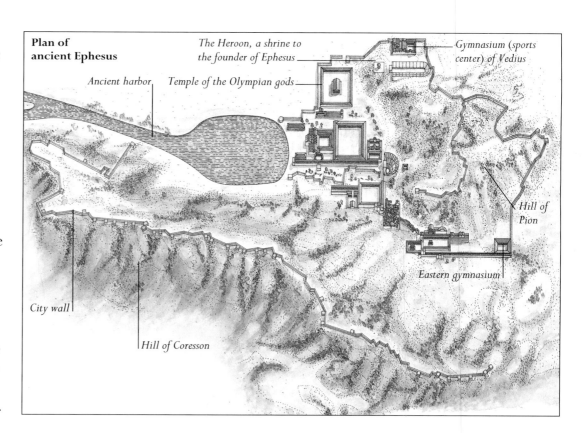

Plan of ancient Ephesus

The Heroon, a shrine to the founder of Ephesus

Gymnasium (sports center) of Vedius

Ancient harbor

Temple of the Olympian gods

Hill of Pion

Eastern gymnasium

City wall

Hill of Coresson

CIVIC BUILDINGS

Unlike some Greek and Roman cities, Ephesus was not laid out in a strictly defined grid plan but fitted in to the natural topography of the Coresson and Pion hills overlooking the harbor. However, the principal public buildings, on the west side of Pion, were constructed on the same alignment, running southwest to northeast. The harbor itself was linked to the sea by a channel, but both have since silted up, and the modern coastline now lies 2½ miles

to the west of the site. All the typical features of a prosperous Roman city can be found at Ephesus: colonnaded shopping streets and marble-paved avenues, a town hall and council chamber, a stadium for sporting events, a theater for spectacles, temples, fountains, public baths and latrines, a brothel, and agoras (marketplaces) for trading. The spaces around these civic structures were occupied by private houses, ranging from luxurious villas to the more modest dwellings of ordinary citizens.

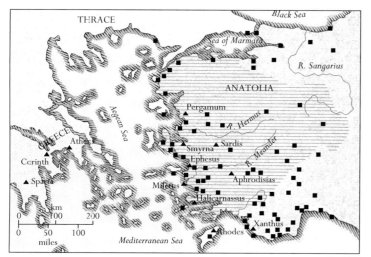

THRACE
Black Sea
Sea of Marmara
R. Sangarius
ANATOLIA
Pergamum
R. Hermus
Smyrna
Sardis
Ephesus
R. Meander
Miletus
Aphrodisias
Halicarnassus
GREECE
Athens
Corinth
Sparta
Aegean Sea
km
0   100   200
0   50   100
miles
Rhodes
Xanthus
Mediterranean Sea

≡ Extent of Roman province of Asia   ▲ City   ■ Town

PROSPEROUS CITIES
The coastal cities of the Roman province of Asia, which covered most of modern western Turkey, were among the most prosperous in the empire. Most of their impressive extant ruins date to Roman times. The entire region was served by a comprehensive road system.

CEREMONIAL APPROACH *left*
Ephesus was a thriving port, and important visitors would have arrived at the city by sea. For this reason the street leading from the harbor to the heart of the city acted as a ceremonial approach. Originally 1,649 feet long and 36 feet wide, the harbor street was flanked by shops under roofed colonnades. Ceremonial gateways were located at either end, and street lighting was provided at night.

PATRON DEITY *right*
Artemis was the patron deity of Ephesus, but she was in essence an Anatolian fertility goddess — very different from the Artemis (goddess of hunting and the moon) mentioned in Greek texts. Ephesian silversmiths sold replicas of this many-breasted cult statue of Artemis to pilgrims visiting her temple. To the east of the city lay the Temple of Artemis, one of the Seven Wonders of the World.

CITY CENTER *below*

The ancient site of Ephesus, near the modern town of Selçuk on Turkey's Aegean coast, began to be excavated by archaeologists as early as AD 1869, and the work continues today. The majestic ruins of the buildings at the heart of the city, most of which date to the Roman period, are among the finest in the region, enabling archaeologists to piece together a comprehensive image of the public face of a prosperous Roman city.

Plan view of the center of ancient Ephesus

PUBLIC LATRINES *above*

Near the center of Ephesus was a public latrine, with space for more than 40 occupants. The seats were cut from marble slabs ranged around four sides of the rectangular room. In the middle was a pool and air shaft. Waste was removed by a continuous flow of water running in the drain beneath the latrines.

LIBRARY OF CELSUS *above*

The library of Celsus occupied a prominent position next to the agora. Its facade survives today and is one of the most magnificent ruins at Ephesus. Documents, in the form of scrolls, were stored in niches in the inner walls of the building. The library was built for public use around AD 117 as a memorial to Tiberius Julius Celsus Polemaeanus, a Roman governor of Asia who was buried in an apse at the rear of the building.

HADRIAN'S TEMPLE *above*

Situated in the street of the Curetes (priests of Artemis) opposite the residences of some of Ephesus's wealthiest citizens, this small, richly ornamented temple was dedicated to the emperor Hadrian, the people of Ephesus, and the goddess Artemis in around AD 118.

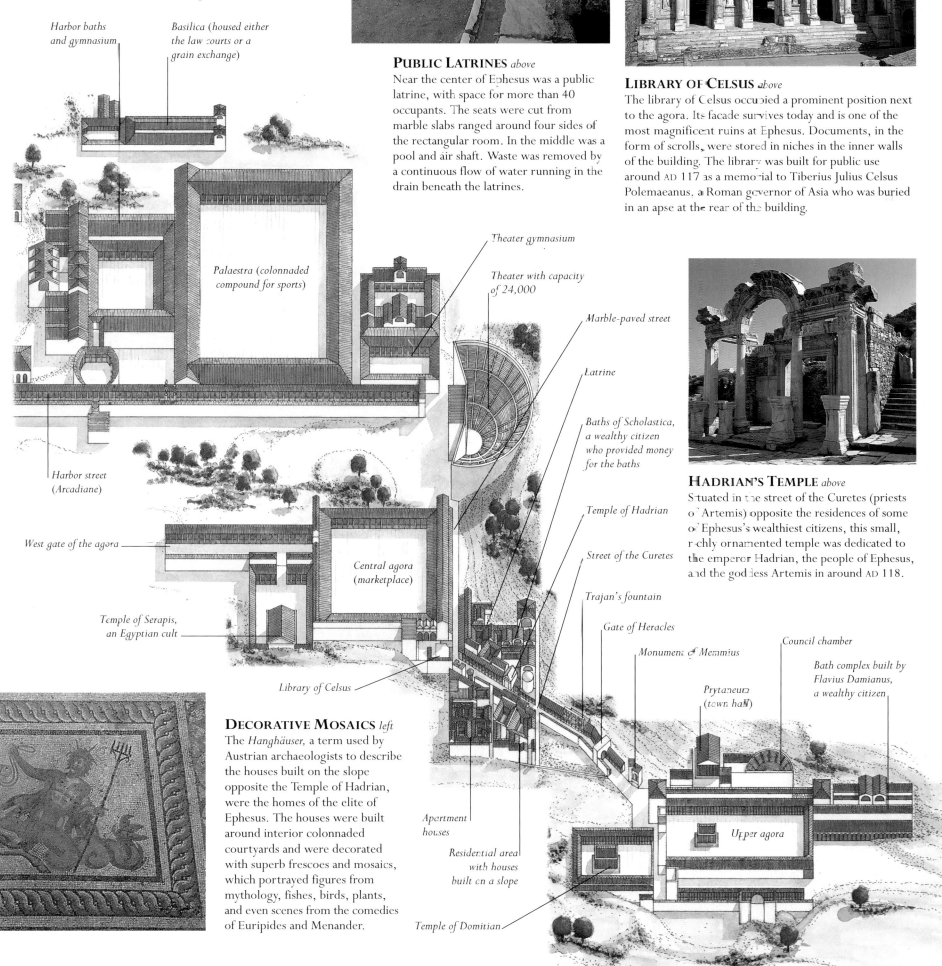

Harbor baths and gymnasium

Basilica (housed either the law courts or a grain exchange)

Palaestra (colonnaded compound for sports)

Theater gymnasium

Theater with capacity of 24,000

Marble-paved street

Latrine

Baths of Scholastica, a wealthy citizen who provided money for the baths

Harbor street (Arcadiane)

Temple of Hadrian

West gate of the agora

Street of the Curetes

Central agora (marketplace)

Trajan's fountain

Gate of Heracles

Monument of Memmius

Council chamber

Temple of Serapis, an Egyptian cult

Prytaneum (town hall)

Bath complex built by Flavius Damianus, a wealthy citizen

Library of Celsus

Apartment houses

Upper agora

Residential area with houses built on a slope

Temple of Domitian

DECORATIVE MOSAICS *left*

The *Hanghäuser*, a term used by Austrian archaeologists to describe the houses built on the slope opposite the Temple of Hadrian, were the homes of the elite of Ephesus. The houses were built around interior colonnaded courtyards and were decorated with superb frescoes and mosaics, which portrayed figures from mythology, fishes, birds, plants, and even scenes from the comedies of Euripides and Menander.

200 BC

CHAPTER 14
THE STRUGGLE FOR POWER
AD 200 - 600

Mayan city-states proliferate in southern Mesoamerica

Colonists reach Easter Island, the remotest island in the Pacific

The Byzantine Empire is born in the east while Roman rule collapses in Europe

The Yamato state is established in Japan

Buddhist and Hindu arts enjoy a Golden Age in India

The centuries from AD 200 to 600 were the great age of Mesoamerican civilizations. In Mexico, the Zapotecs held sway in the Oaxaca region; Mayan city-states were established in southern Mesoamerica; the population of the city of Teotihuacan expanded, possibly reaching 200,000. In South America, the Moche civilization (1st-8th centuries AD) in coastal Peru reached its height and the Tiahuanaco Empire was founded in the Andes. But in other parts of the world, great empires were crumbling: in China, the Han Dynasty was overthown; the Parthians were ousted in the Middle East; and Roman western Europe came under the control of Germanic rulers.

The setting for one of the greatest human achievements of these centuries was not the heart of a kingdom or empire, but the Pacific islands. Polynesians settled Easter Island, the remotest of the Polynesian islands, ending an epic phase of colonization and laying the basis of one of the most distinctive island cultures the world has ever known.

Mayan city-states
By the 3rd century AD, the Mayan lords of southern Mesoamerica presided over as many as 50 independent city-states. Among the most important were Tikal, Copán, Palenque, and Uaxactun. The Maya were an extraordinarily inventive and highly refined people. They developed a complex writing system that has only

recently been deciphered, and which was the most sophisticated in Mesoamerica. Expert astronomers, the Maya also devised counting and calendrical systems that employed the concept of zero nearly 1,000 years before it was understood in Europe.

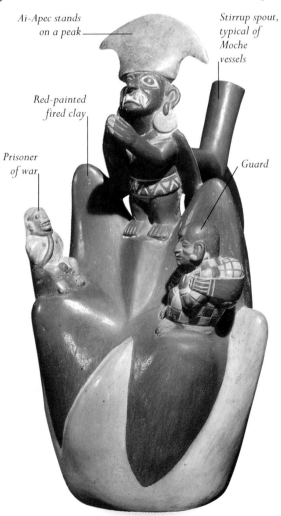

Ai-Apec stands on a peak

Red-painted fired clay

Prisoner of war

Stirrup spout, typical of Moche vessels

Guard

MOCHE PRIEST-WARRIOR
Ai-Apec, the personification of the priest-warrior elite of Peruvian Moche society, is depicted on this stirrup-spouted ceramic jar alongside a captive and a guard.

Mayan craftsmen were accomplished stone carvers and artists, creating elaborate bas-reliefs and brightly painted frescoes on the walls of pyramid-temples, tombs, palaces, and other public structures. Such scenes traditionally show rulers or captives, often engaged in ritual activities. Another characteristic Mayan decorative form used on buildings was the roof comb. The Maya also invented the corbelled arch, which afforded them a variety of new structural possibilities.

Indeed, monumental architecture was an important feature of Mayan culture. The city of Tikal, for example, had five large pyramids up to 230 feet high, which covered rulers' graves and overlooked enormous open plazas. Tikal was the dominant Mayan city in the 3rd and 4th centuries AD, and its population of some 50,000 people was supported by the intensive farming of maize, beans, and squash.

Engraved decoration

MESOAMERICAN BALL GAME
Made in the 5th century AD in Veracruz, Mexico, this carved stone *yugo* (yoke) is a model of a protective device worn on one hip by players in the ritual ball game.

BYZANTINE ARTISTRY
Byzantine craftsmen excelled in the carving of ivory panels, used for caskets, shrines, and as book covers. Christian themes were the most common subjects.

South American cultures

In the arid coastal lands of Peru, elaborate irrigation systems kept the Moche state flourishing in these centuries, when it reached the height of its power and sophistication. One of the most famous archaeological finds of recent years was at the Moche site of Sipán, where the richly furnished graves of the Moche elite were found in pyramid-tombs. They were buried around AD 290, accompanied by attendants, and their bodies and clothes were adorned with gold and silver jewelry inlaid with shell and turquoise.

A third civilization arose in the Andean highlands, centered in the ancient city of Tiahuanaco. This was a city of great public buildings – temples, courts, and palaces –

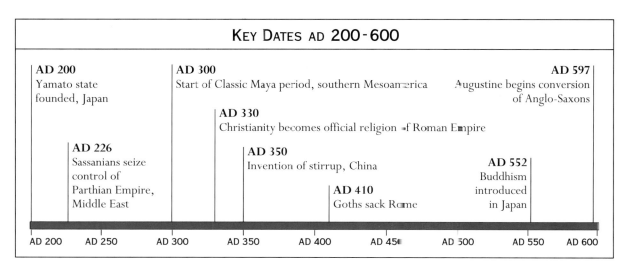

richly decorated with relief carvings covered in gold. At its height, Tiahuanaco had a population of 40,000 people, and was a center of religious pilgrimage for the whole Andean region.

Collapse of empires

For the empires of Rome and China, the 3rd century AD was a time of weakness and decline. Han China broke up into independent states in AD 220, and in the mid-3rd century AD Rome was plunged into crisis by a series of invasions, notably by the Persians in the east.

The Roman Empire survived, although a new capital, Constantinople (modern Istanbul), was founded in AD 330. The most significant change of this period was

ROCK-CUT BUDDHA
The Buddhist cave temples at Longmen in northern central China contained enormous statues of Buddha carved into the rock. The figure shown here is 53 feet tall.

the adoption, in the 4th century AD, of Christianity as the official imperial religion. Fresh incursions in the 5th century AD brought the western provinces under the rule of Germanic invaders: the Goths in Italy and Iberia, Franks in Gaul, and Anglo-Saxons in Britain. Some were bands of marauders taking advantage of the opportunities for plunder offered by the weakness of Roman rule; others, such as the Anglo-Saxons, who came from Jutland in Denmark and adjacent areas of northern Germany, were larger groups seeking new lands to settle.

The retrenched eastern Roman Empire, known from this period onward as the Byzantine Empire (after Byzantium, the old name for Constantinople), retained and consolidated power in the prosperous eastern Mediterranean provinces.

SASSANIAN SILVERWARE
Sumptuous silver dishes of the Sassanian Empire often show the Sassanian king hunting lions, a favorite royal pastime.

AD 200-600

Christianity in Africa

Christianity also spread to northeastern Africa during these centuries, first to the Roman province of Egypt, but soon afterwards to the Sudan and Ethiopia. In Egypt, communities of Christians, known as Copts, developed distinctive traditions of textile and manuscript decoration. In Ethiopia, the kingdom of Axum, a newly emergent state with a powerful Red Sea fleet, became Christian in the 4th century AD. Ethiopia remained Christian into the 20th century, despite the fact that all its immediate neighbors are Islamic nations. Further south, Bantu farmers and herders began their migration into southern Africa, settling in small villages of circular huts grouped for protection within *kraals* (stockades).

Eastern states and empires

In the Middle East, the Sassanians defeated their Parthian overlords in AD 226 and inherited their vast territories. The Sassanian Empire held sway until AD 642, and was marked by fine craftsmanship, notably its silverware, and the building of luxurious palaces and splendid gardens. To support these lavish projects the Sassanian emperors levied harsh taxes and sought to increase agricultural productivity by ambitious government irrigation schemes. The Sassanians engaged in intermittent warfare against steppe nomads to the north and their Byzantine neighbors to the west.

New states were also founded during this period in Korea and Japan. The Japanese Yamato state (AD 200-1185), based in the Osaka region, soon extended its control over almost all of Honshu. In the north, indigenous ethnic groups such as the Ainu of Hokkaido retained their autonomy and traditional way of life. The large mounded tombs of the rulers were a significant feature of these states. As in China, the tombs of the first Japanese emperors were protected by and furnished with terra-cotta figures, known as *haniwa*.

Buddhism and Hinduism

The tradition of mounded tombs ceased when the Japanese rulers converted to Buddhism in the 6th century AD; energies were redirected into the building of Buddhist temples. Major Buddhist shrines were also created or embellished in China during this period. Famous among these are cave sanctuaries such as those at Longmen.

Buddhism also continued to play a major role in South Asia, especially in northern India and Sri Lanka. The valleys of Afghanistan were rich in Buddhist temples and monasteries; in the Bamiyan Valley, a gigantic Buddha figure was carved in the cliff face. Elsewhere in India, particularly in lands ruled by the Gupta Dynasty (4th-6th centuries AD), which included the whole of the Ganges Valley and large areas of western India, political stability and generous patronage allowed both Buddhist and Hindu arts to flourish. However, Buddhism gradually lost ground there to Hinduism, which was adopted by the Guptas and survived, despite the downfall of Gupta rule, to become the dominant religion of peninsular India.

AMERICAS

TEOTIHUACAN'S INFLUENCE

The influence of the great metropolis of Teotihuacan was felt throughout Mesoamerica, and is clearly demonstrated by the presence of its ceramic wares, art, and architectural styles in centers hundreds of miles away – for example, at the Mayan cities of Tikal and Kaminaljuyú to the south. A particular feature of Teotihuacan architecture is the combination of *talud* (sloping wall) and *tablero* (vertical panel) in the construction of pyramidal temple-platforms. Pyramids from regions of central and southern Mexico to Guatemala and Honduras exhibit these characteristic elements. All structures were covered with a layer of stucco and then painted.

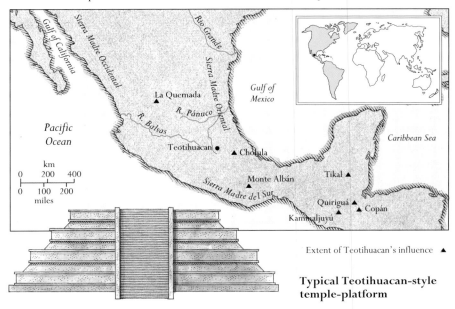

Extent of Teotihuacan's influence ▲

Typical Teotihuacan-style temple-platform

AFRICA

SPREAD OF THE BANTU

From 500 BC, Bantu-speaking farmers moved southward through much of tropical Africa from their homeland in eastern West Africa. Moving south in two waves, they introduced agriculture, herding, and ironworking to areas inhabited by hunter-gatherers. An eastern wave passed along the northern edge of the Central African rainforest, then southward through the savanna, crossing the Zambezi and Limpopo rivers in southern Africa by AD 200. In the west, Bantu spread southward around the same time across modern Angola and into central Botswana, where they mingled with the Bantu in the east.

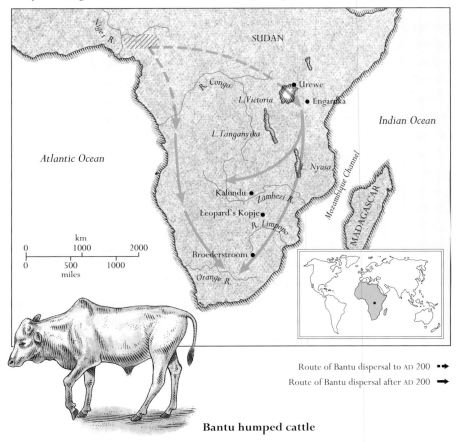

Route of Bantu dispersal to AD 200 ➡
Route of Bantu dispersal after AD 200 ➡

Bantu humped cattle

EUROPE

COLLAPSE OF ROMAN RULE

By the end of the 4th century AD the Roman Empire was no longer able to resist pressures from peoples along its frontiers. In the western Roman provinces, Germanic tribes such as the Franks, Saxons, and Alemanni began to take control. The remains of their distinctive dress ornaments, such as cruciform brooches and other unique items like glass claw beakers allow areas in which they settled to be identified. Northern Gaul and the Rhineland were settled by Franks, while Britain was settled by groups of Angles, Saxons, Jutes, and Frisians from northern Europe, particularly Jutland in modern Denmark. These people crossed the North Sea in their small oar-powered ships. By the end of the 5th century AD, families of Anglo-Saxon warrior-chiefs controlled virtually the whole of modern England, which was divided into a number of separate kingdoms.

Cruciform brooch find area
Boat burial site ▲
Movement of people ➡

Anglo-Saxon cruciform brooch, Cambridgeshire, England

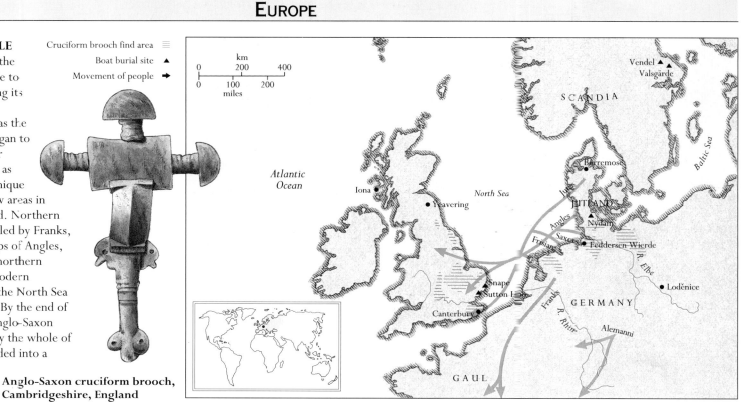

MIDDLE EAST & SOUTH ASIA

BUDDHISM UNDER THE GUPTAS

Before being eclipsed by Hinduism, Buddhism reached its zenith in India under the Gupta Dynasty (4th-6th centuries AD). The Guptas, their heartland in the kingdom of Magadha, ruled an empire that at its height covered most of northern, central and western India. Mahayana Buddhism was the major sect, its ideological center at Nalanda in the north. Buddhist arts flourished: sculpture at Sarnath and Mathura; stupas (dome-shaped monuments housing burials or relics) at Amaravati and Nagarjunakonda; and rock-cut cave-temples at Ajanta and Ellora. In addition to the facades and interiors of these temples, those at Ajanta bore superb paintings illustrating events from the Buddha's life.

Maximum extent of Gupta Empire ‖‖‖
Gupta heartland ▦

Gupta period bronze Buddha

EAST ASIA & AUSTRALASIA

KINGDOMS IN THE FAR EAST

In the 3rd and 4th centuries AD, native kingdoms arose in Korea and Japan. The principal Korean kingdoms were Koguryo, Shilla, and Paekche, their capitals at Pyongyang, Kyongju, and Puyo. Near each capital was a cemetery of mounded tombs where rulers were buried. The Shilla kingdom took control of all the Korean peninsula in AD 668. Mound cemeteries are also found near early centers of the Yamato state in Japan, such as the imperial residence at Asuka-Itabuki, but these are distinguished by their keyhole shape, moats, and the presence of terra-cotta *haniwa* (tomb models). Some *haniwa* depict warriors who helped to extend Yamato control over most of Japan from AD 300-700.

Terra-cotta *haniwa* (tomb model) of an armored warrior, Japan

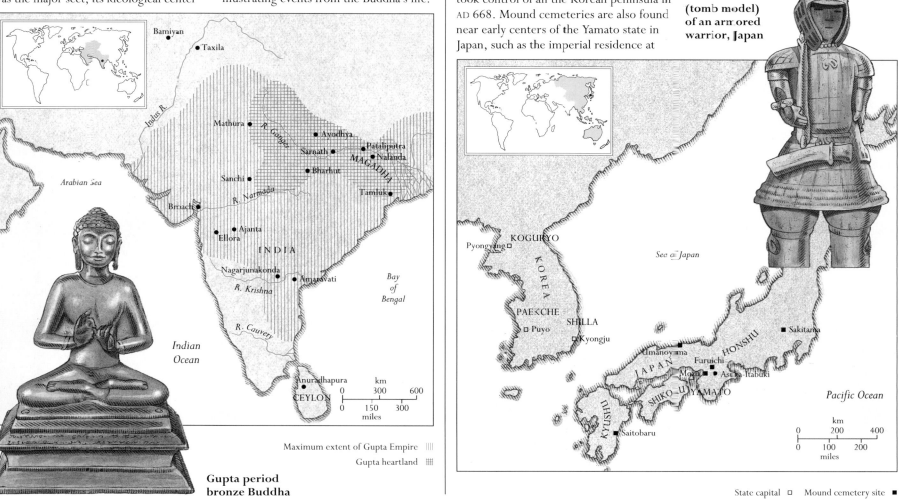

State capital ▫   Mound cemetery site ■

AD 200-300

FOOD & ENVIRONMENT	SHELTER & ARCHITECTURE

AMERICAS

MARKETPLACE TRADING

The urban center at Monte Albán in Oaxaca, southern central Mexico, brought many changes to the lives of the Zapotecs. A denser, more numerous population and larger farms with diversified crops contributed to create a regional market system coordinated at Monte Albán. Women played important roles in the system, both as sellers and buyers.

Ceramic head of Zapotec woman, Oaxaca, Mexico

ROUND DWELLINGS

River valleys were a focus for small scattered villages in southeastern North America. Dwellings at Icehouse Bottom, Tennessee, were circular, made of poles and thatch, and large enough to accommodate about 20 individuals – an extended family, or several small families. The inhabitants cultivated some native plants, but their diet depended more on hunting and the gathering of wild plants.

Icehouse Bottom village, Tennessee

Pole

Thatch

Sunflowers

EAST ASIA & AUSTRALASIA

TEA CULTIVATION

Wild tea plants were first domesticated in southwestern China, possibly as early as the 1st century AD. By the 3rd century AD the formal cultivation of tea had spread to subtropical areas south of the Yangtze River. Initially used mainly for its medicinal qualities, tea did not become popular as a drink until the 10th century AD. Tea still has a host of applications in Chinese medicine today; taken chiefly as a stimulant and digestive remedy, it is also thought to lower blood pressure and cholesterol levels.

RIVERBANK VILLAGES

In Japan, by the 3rd century AD, even nomadic fishing people were adopting a sedentary way of life in agricultural communities. These were small villages that were usually built on natural terraces overlooking rivers. They conformed to a pattern, with separate areas for houses, middens (mounds of discarded shells and other domestic debris), and burial plots.

Wooden granaries raised on stilts, with A-shaped roofs and overhanging eaves, protected the crop from damage by flooding or rodents. Agriculture was organized on a communal basis, with elaborate irrigation systems for watering the fields.

MIDDLE EAST & SOUTH ASIA

MEDICINAL HERBS

Important treatises on Indian Ayurvedic medicine (*ayur* meaning "life," *veda* meaning "knowledge") were written around this time. The emphasis was on maintaining an equilibrium in the body between the humors (influential elements such as fire and water). This was achieved by diet, moderate living, and herbal remedies still in use today, using such ingredients as cinnamon, licorice, turmeric, saffron, and aloes.

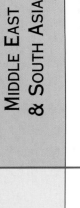

Tombstone fragment, Germany

ARCHED SQUINCH

In the Middle East, the squinch was devised during this period to enable circular domes to be constructed on square buildings. Squinches are half-domes built across the corners of a chamber, transforming the square into an octagon on top of which a dome can more easily be set. The earliest known squinches are in the palace at Gor (Firuzabad in modern Iran), built in the first half of the 3rd century AD by Ardashir, the first king of the Sassanian Empire (AD 226-642). Later Islamic architects devoted much energy and thought to furthering design techniques for squinches.

Arched squinch

Octagonal base for dome

Plan of square chamber with squinches

EUROPE

SHIPPING GOODS

In the Roman world, bulk goods such as grain or wine were transported by water wherever possible. It was more economical to ship a cargo from Spain to the Levant than to transport it 60 miles inland. Most large cities of the Roman Empire were therefore on or near a seacoast or navigable river. This 3rd-century AD tombstone from Neumagen, Germany, shows a Mosel river barge laden with wine.

FORTIFIED CITIES

In the 3rd century AD, powerful fortifications of walls and gates were built to defend Roman cities previously unprotected against barbarian invasion. The Porta Nigra ("Black Gate") at Augusta Treverorum (modern Trier), close to the Roman frontier between Gaul and Germany, was an impressive example of one of these structures, with tiers of arched windows and decorative columns.

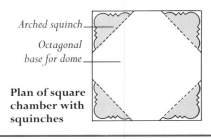

Model of the Porta Nigra, Trier, Germany

AFRICA

INCREASED PRODUCTIVITY

Septimius Severus was born in the city of Leptis Magna (in modern Libya). Rising to become Roman emperor from AD 193 to 211, he reformed imperial government in North Africa, increased agricultural production and annexed large areas of interior Tripolitania (northwestern Libya). The wealth of the area came largely from the production of wheat and olive oil, some of which was exported to supply the larger cities of the empire such as Rome.

Coin of the emperor Septimius Severus

DURABLE DWELLINGS

Builders in the grasslands of southern Africa used many soft and hard woods. The fibrous qualities of grasses, reeds, and long strips of bark were used in a range of durable houses, from temporary shelters to residences for chiefs. Building often began with a circular floor of puddled clay (clay mixed with water to create a level surface), sometimes smeared with cow dung. Then a framework of closely set saplings was constructed, covered with layers of anthill clay. Huts were roofed with a conical or domed framework of poles, covered with thatch overlapping the eaves. Such dwellings could stand for 15 years or more.

TECHNOLOGY & INNOVATION

ASTRONOMICAL OBSERVATORY

The people of Mesoamerica were ardent observers of the heavens. Charting the movement of the planets assisted them in calendrical calculations as well as in planning the orientation of their buildings. In the great urban center of Monte Albán, on top of a leveled mountain, all the buildings are oriented south-to-north except one, an arrow-shaped structure thought to have been an observatory.

Possible observatory, Monte Albán, Oaxaca, Mexico

WHEELBARROWS

During the 3rd century AD, the invention of the wheelbarrow in China allowed workers to transport much heavier loads. This rubbing, taken from the wall of a tomb, shows a large wheel with a barrow attached on each side. Although less maneuverable than the modern design, it allowed a greater weight (over 300 pounds) to be pushed.

Tomb rubbing of a wheelbarrow, China

ARMORED CAVALRY

Both the Parthians and the Sassanians who succeeded them in AD 226 benefited (particularly in battles against Roman forces) from the use of heavily armored cavalry, a phenomenon previously little known in the Middle East. This drawing, which was scratched onto stone, dates to the 2nd or 3rd century AD, and portrays a cavalry soldier charging.

Cavalry soldier, Dura Europos, Mesopotamia

GERMANIC IRON TECHNOLOGY

While the Roman Empire was flourishing in southern and western Europe, Germanic peoples beyond the frontier were becoming increasingly proficient at ironworking. At Lysa Gora in southern Poland, iron was produced on an industrial scale in smelting furnaces. Iron was used for agricultural equipment such as plows and sickles, as well as for weapons. Germanic weapons began to rival Roman ones in quality. Germanic warriors rarely wore body armor or helmets like the Romans, and they continued to rely on spears rather than swords as their principal weapons.

— *Bolt for securing iron blade*

IRON TOOLS

In the early centuries AD, Bantu farmers reached the southernmost regions of Africa and introduced basic iron tools which they used to work with the varied natural resources of their environment. They developed axes mounted in wooden handles for clearing wood and; hoes for farming more efficiently than with the wooden digging sticks of earlier periods; and adzes for shaving bark off poles for fences, huts, and ladders.

Iron adze, southern Africa

ART & RITUAL

RITUAL BATTLE ART

The Moche people of Peru produced iconography that celebrated everyday life and broadcast their success in war. The motifs are largely associated with human sacrifice and other battle rituals. Ceramics and mural paintings show scenes of naked prisoners who have ropes around their necks or are being beheaded.

Moche prisoner figure, Peru

BRONZE BELLS

Japanese craftsmen found artistic inspiration in Chinese and Korean bronzes, but often melted down imported wares to make distinctive national ceremonial objects such as daggers, swords, and clapperless bells. *Dotaku* bells are characteristic of this period of Japanese bronze art. Their manufacture was centralized in large work-shops, reflecting the growing status of specialized craftsmen.

Bronze *dotaku* bell, Japan

DIVINE INVESTITURE

Ardashir, first king of the Sassanian Empire, commissioned this relief at Naqsh-i Rustam (now in southwestern Iran) to portray his investiture by the god Ahuramazda. On the left, Ardashir's horse tramples Artabanus, king of the defeated Parthians, while Ahuramazda's horse stands triumphantly over the stricken demon Ahriman.

King Ardashir

Rock relief, Naqsh-i Rustam, Iran

BURIED TREASURE

In AD 256, the Roman province of Gaul was temporarily overrun for three or four years by Germanic invaders who had breached the Rhine frontier. Wealthy Roman families, especially those living in country villas, reacted by burying their valuables for safe-keeping. A complete silver dinner service that was never reclaimed, found at Chaource in northeastern France, attests to the skill of Roman silversmiths.

Silver plate, Chaource, France

Emperor Septimius Severus standing in chariot

PROBLEMS OF PERSPECTIVE

Roman artists never resolved the problem of perspective. This relief from a triumphal arch (erected in AD 203 at Leptis Magna) shows a compromise; the emperor and his atten-dants are presented frontally while the horses and chariot face right. The relative crudeness of the carving shows that the great days of Roman sculpture were past.

Carved relief, arch of Septimius Severus, Leptis Magna, North Africa

AD 300 - 400

FOOD & ENVIRONMENT

AMERICAS

REMAKING THE LAND

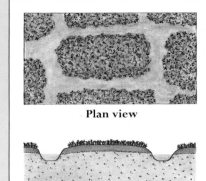

Plan view

Cross section   **Raised field, northern Belize**

Evidence for the elaborate raised field systems built by the Maya has been discovered beneath the jungle of the Yucatán peninsula. At swamp edges and along rivers, the Maya laboriously excavated water channels to build raised soil platforms, which were well watered but safe from flooding. These fertile fields could support several crops a year.

EAST ASIA & AUSTRALASIA

FARMYARD ANIMALS

Tomb figurines reflect the continuing importance of domesticated animals in Chinese society. Intensive grain production left no room for animal grazing, so the main sources of meat were pigs and chickens raised in the courtyards of peasant houses and fed on domestic waste, and fish bred in irrigation ponds.

Chicken emerging from coop

Tomb figurine of chicken in a coop, China

MIDDLE EAST & SOUTH ASIA

SHIPS OF THE DESERT

Camel caravans played a vital role in the economy of the Middle East during the first millennium AD, carrying much of the overland trade essential for the prosperity of western Asia. Both the dromedary (the one-humped camel of Arabia) and the Bactrian camel (the two-humped camel of Central Asia) had been domesticated since before 2000 BC. The camel could graze the marginal pastureland at the edges of the deserts, and by the 4th century AD, camel-herding nomads had become a powerful force in Arabia.

EUROPE

IRON TIPS FOR PLOWING

Most Roman agricultural tools were remarkably similar to those still used in Europe in the 19th century AD. The Roman plow, however, was more like its early predecessor, lacking a moldboard (curved blade) to turn the furrow, although it did by this time have an iron coulter (tip), which cut through the ground more effectively.

Iron coulter from Roman plow

AFRICA

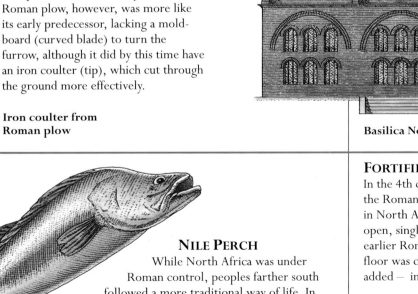

NILE PERCH

While North Africa was under Roman control, peoples farther south followed a more traditional way of life. In the Nile Valley, a vital staple was the Nile perch, a fish of enormous size that was caught with nets or lines. Much of the catch was dried in the sun and stored for later use.

Nile perch

SHELTER & ARCHITECTURE

PLACE OF THE GODS

Teotihuacan, by this time the largest and most populous city of the Americas, covered more than 8 square miles and at its height sustained a population of at least 120,000 and possibly more than 200,000. Around 1,000 years later, the Aztecs were to name the ruined metropolis the Place of the Gods.

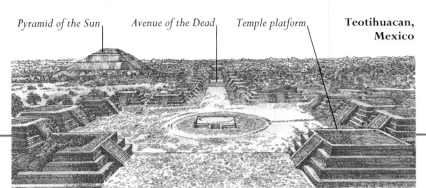

Pyramid of the Sun   *Avenue of the Dead*   *Temple platform*   **Teotihuacan, Mexico**

OVERHANGING EAVES

In Japan, although few traces survive of houses dating to the Kofun period (c. AD 300-700), tomb models and engravings on bronze bells provide clues to their construction. They were built around four posts embedded in the ground, with an upper framework supporting a central raised roof section. Their long overhanging eaves remained a distinctive feature of later Japanese architecture.

FORTIFIED FIRE TEMPLE

One of the most important Zoroastrian fire temples of the Sassanian period (AD 226-642) was at Shiz (modern Takht-i Sulaiman, in the mountains of western Iran). The religious complex, which housed

Site of the fire temple, Takht-i Sulaiman, Iran

the *Atur Gushnasp* (sacred fire of the warriors), was constructed around a deep lake at the top of a hill, and surrounded by a fortified wall.

PUBLIC BUILDINGS

The largest Roman buildings were the basilicas and bath complexes, designed for general social and commercial activity. The Basilica Nova was the last great public building constructed in the Forum at Rome, around 315 AD. It was also the largest, with brick vaults rising 115 feet above the marble floor. However, soon after its completion, Emperor Constantine the Great moved the imperial capital to Constantinople (modern Istanbul).

Basilica Nova, Rome

FORTIFIED VILLAS

In the 4th century AD, villas built by the Roman owners of country estates in North Africa were unlike the more open, single-storied villas typical of earlier Roman times. The ground floor was closed in, and towers were added — in effect, fortifications that transformed the villa into a castle in the event of hostilities. Landowners were increasingly expected to provide their tenants with this protection.

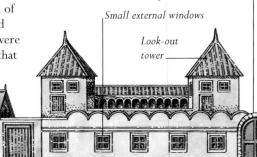

Small external windows

Look-out tower

Red tiled roof

Roman villa, North Africa

Technology & Innovation

Mass Production
Ceramic funerary urns were produced on a prolific scale by the Zapotecs of Monte Albán, Mexico. During this time, a period of intense building, important tombs at Monte Albán were filled with large assortments of elaborate urns. The urns were embellished with decorative elements, which were stamped out from molds in a kind of early assembly line.

Zapotec funerary urn, Monte Albán, Oaxaca, Mexico

Stirrups
The use of stirrups gave riders perfect control of their mounts. A rudimentary form of rope stirrup appears to have been used in northwestern India in the late 2nd century BC, but the first true stirrups known are metal-sheathed wooden examples from Wanbaoting in northeastern China, dating to around AD 350.

Tomb figure of horse and rider, China

Parchment Books
The increased use of parchment (animal skin prepared for writing) may have led to the adoption of the codex, or book, since parchment was less suitable than papyrus for scrolls. In a codex, both sides of each page could be written on. The 4th-century *Codex Sinaiticus* was a Bible inscribed with ink on parchment in Greek capitals.

Page from the *Codex Sinaiticus*, St. Catherine's Monastery, Sinai

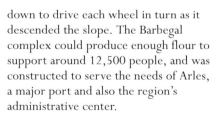

Watermills
The Romans depended on mills that were powered by water or animals to grind grain. The watermill constructed on a hillside at Barbegal in southern France had 16 separate waterwheels, each turning a pair of millstones. No other Roman watermill was as large as this, and most had only a single wheel. An aqueduct carried the water to the top of the hill, from where it flowed down to drive each wheel in turn as it descended the slope. The Barbegal complex could produce enough flour to support around 12,500 people, and was constructed to serve the needs of Arles, a major port and also the region's administrative center.

African Coinage
Axum in northeastern Ethiopia was a major trading kingdom from the 4th to 8th centuries AD. Gold and bronze coins were minted there, at first with the king's name and titles in Greek, later in Ethiopic script. The technology used to mint the coins was a sophisticated technique of the eastern Roman Empire.

Bronze coin with inscription in Greek, Axum, Ethiopia

Art & Ritual

Jade Artifacts
Jade or greenstone pendants, their upper part a stylized human figure and lower half shaped like a celt, are typical of pre-Columbian Costa Rica. This figure is shown in a formal pose, with his hands crossed in front of him, and wearing a headdress and earpieces. He is clearly an important personage – perhaps a chief or priest.

Ceremonial jade pendant, Nicoya, Costa Rica

Buddhist Shrines
Although Buddhism reached China in the 1st century AD, it did not become popular until the early 4th century, when northern China came under the control of Buddhist rulers. The earliest large Buddhist center was Dunhuang, at Gansu, a border town on the trade routes from India and Central Asia. Missionaries and monks built the first great Chinese Buddhist shrine complex in a series of caves at Gansu. It housed almost 500 shrines decorated with painted clay sculptures and murals.

Supreme Trinity
Hinduism, an evolved form of Brahmanism, began to attract more followers in India during the early centuries AD. This was a time during which orthodox Brahmanism suffered a major setback from the spread of Jainism, and still more from Buddhism, new creeds that attacked ritual and pantheism. As Hindu belief gradually usurped its predecessor, large numbers of deities described in the *Vedas*, the most ancient sacred Sanskrit writings of orthodox Brahmanism, were eclipsed by the supreme Hindu trinity of Brahma "the creator," Vishnu "the preserver", and Shiva "the purifying destroyer."

Christian Empire
Christianity became the official religion of the Roman Empire in the 4th century AD under the emperor Constantine the Great (ruled AD 306-337). Christian symbols became increasingly common on sculpture and tableware; silver spoons from the Mildenhall treasure carry the Chi-Rho emblem, formed from the first two Greek letters of the name Christ.

Late Roman silver spoons, Mildenhall, Cambridgeshire, England

Monasticism
The monastic life that became so influential in medieval Europe originated in Egypt, where a wealthy young Christian named Antony renounced social life and retreated to the desert to do spiritual battle with the devil. By the time of his death in AD 356, desert monasteries had been established throughout Egypt.

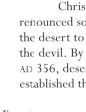

Bronze cross, Egypt

AD 400 - 500

200 BC

FOOD & ENVIRONMENT

SHELTER & ARCHITECTURE

AMERICAS

LAKE FISHING
On the margins of Lake Cahuilla, California, thousands of stone fish weirs mark the changing shoreline between this period and AD 1400. The water levels at Lake Cahuilla and other lakes in the Great Basin fluctuate, rising or falling by as much as 6 feet each year. Shallow water at the lake edges offered brief opportunities for fishing by dip-netting at the apex of fish weirs. Each weir is a pair of 6- to 10-foot rock alignments that partly encloses a triangular area of lake shallows, with a shallow-water opening less than 20 inches wide. Razorback suckers (*Xyrauchen texanus*) may have been trapped when they entered the weirs seeking shallow water in which to spawn.

MAYAN ARCH
The corbeled arch used by Mesoamerican architects is sometimes called the "false" arch because it lacks a key stone, consisting instead of horizontally overlapping stones that reach an apex. The arch is built up from the walls, necessarily massive to support it, to produce the long narrow rooms that characterized lowland Mayan architecture throughout the Classic period (*c.* AD 300-900).

Cross section, Temple of the Cross, Palenque, Mexico

EAST ASIA & AUSTRALASIA

TASMANIAN DIET
At West Point, on the cold, windswept western coast of Tasmania, a band of about 40 individuals camped for several months each summer around this time, living in dome-shaped huts. Evidence from this "village" midden (mound of discarded debris) indicates that seals and shellfish, both rich sources of energy, provided 90 percent of their diet. Other foods were sea birds, lizards, wallabies, and other smaller marsupials but, curiously, no fish.

West Point midden, Tasmania, Australia

KEYHOLE TOMBS
In Japan, the Yamato state (AD 200-1185), centered on the area of Kinai in southeastern Honshu, entered what is known as the "tumulus period," typified by huge tombs shaped like keyholes and surrounded by moats. Stone burial chambers lay within the mounds, and on the surface stood large terra-cotta *haniwa* (tomb models), placed like a fence around the grave.

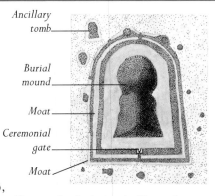

Ancillary tomb
Burial mound
Moat
Ceremonial gate
Moat

Yamato keyhole tomb, Mazu, Japan

MIDDLE EAST & SOUTH ASIA

HUNTING PARKS AND GARDENS
In the Middle East, cool shady gardens had been created and valued for many centuries. During the Sassanian period (AD 226-642), formal gardens were laid out in geometric patterns with ornamental pools. The Sassanians also constructed hunting parks where the king and nobles enjoyed the pleasures of the chase. A royal boar hunt of the Sassanian period is depicted in a relief carved on a rock face at Taq-i Bustan in western Iran.

Stone relief of royal hunt, Taq-i Bustan, Iran

BUDDHIST MONASTERIES
Monastery-building spread through Asia together with Buddhism. One of the best known monasteries was at Takht-i-Bahi, on a rocky hill in Pakistan overlooking the Peshawar Plain. Before its destruction in the late 5th century AD by Huns from Central Asia, it consisted of two principal courtyards. The northern courtyard contained monks' dwellings, the southern the monastery's principal stupa (a dome-shaped Buddhist monument containing burials or relics). In a central courtyard stood smaller stupas and gigantic stucco images of the Buddha.

EUROPE

RISE OF LOCAL LORDS
The fall of the Roman Empire in western Europe took place against a background of gradual economic change dating back to the the 2nd century AD. Birthrates declined, productivity fell, and oppressive taxation led many poorer farmers to seek the protection of powerful local landlords. City life also entered a period of slow decline, especially in the northwestern provinces. In Britain, the major Roman cities were largely abandoned after the 4th century AD. As the machinery of Roman rule crumbled, cash taxes due to central government were replaced by payments in kind to local lords, mainly in the form of agricultural produce but sometimes as free labor.

ARCHITECTURAL TRANSITION
The transition from Roman to medieval architecture is well illustrated by the church of St. Martin at Tours in western France, built around AD 470. The hall-like columned nave was based on a typical Roman basilica; its bell tower for summoning the faithful to prayer was a new feature.

St. Martin, Tours, France

AFRICA

DOMESTICATION OF RICE
African rice (*Oryza glaberrima*) was domesticated from a wild relative, probably in the Niger Delta of West Africa, by the 3rd century BC. The crop soon became a staple. It was grown, as it still is today, in seasonally flooded areas where the farmers planted crops in the fertile land created by rising and falling river waters. The high productivity of African rice and other crops helped the emergence of the first West African towns in the 5th century AD, notably at Jenne-jeno on an island in the River Niger in Mali.

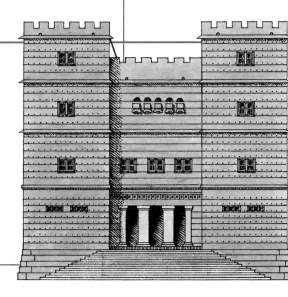

CASTELLATED PALACE
The rulers of the powerful trading kingdom of Axum in northeastern Ethiopia built fine palaces, such as the one at Enda Mikael. The castlelike edifice was 88 feet square, its walls alternately recessed and projecting. Four corner towers with battlements rose from the projections, and a great flight of steps led to a spacious entrance divided by square pillars.

Axumite palace, Enda Mikael, Ethiopia

TECHNOLOGY & INNOVATION

COCHINEAL DYE
The reddish-purple dye derived from the cochineal insect was an important Mesoamerican trade and tribute item. It was especially highly valued by the Zapotecs of Oaxaca, who used it in the manufacture of textiles. The insect was (and still is) "farmed" in large numbers on the leaves of the nopal cactus.

Cochineal insects, dyed fibers, and fabric

LETHAL WEAPON
The composite bow, which was developed during this period by nomadic tribes in northern and Central Asia, was one of the most powerful weapons in existence at this time. Made of thin strips of wood that were then laminated with layers of animal sinew, it was bent to form a curve before the bowstring was attached, thus giving it double the tension and power of ordinary bows of a similar weight

Tomb mural of nomad with composite bow, Gansu, China

CIVIL SERVICE
The rulers of the Sassanian Empire in Persia and Mesopotamia developed a complex machinery of government that reached its height during the 5th and 6th centuries AD. An extensive civil service, divided into separate departments responsible for matters such as justice and finance, carried out the dictates of the kings. Seals, such as this one dating to AD 420, were used as symbols of administrative authority.

Seal and impression of the Sassanian chief storekeeper, Vehdin-Shapur

IRON NAILS FOR BOATS
The western Germanic Anglo-Saxon peoples sailed across the North Sea and colonized England during the 5th century AD. They developed the use of iron nails to hold the timbers of their boats together, replacing the earlier tied or sewn construction. A boat found preserved in a peat bog at Nydam in southern Denmark was made from 11 long pieces of timber (a keel and 10 side planks), with room for a crew of 30 oarsmen sitting on thwarts (cross-benches). The Nydam boat, 75 feet long and 10 feet wide, could only have left the inlets and coastal waters to attempt a sea crossing in good weather, but larger seagoing boats would have been of similar design.

CAPARISON FOR HORSES
The Nobatian kingdom, centered in Faras, replaced the kingdom of Meroë in Lower Nubia. Nobatia was famous for its cavalry. Harness trappings were decorated, and fully caparisoned horses were often buried with dead rulers. Horsemen fought in chain mail, using lances and swords.

Nobatian leather tackle, Sudan

ART & RITUAL

HUNTING ART AND RITUAL
Bering Sea Eskimos (Inuit) used "winged" objects at the butt end of harpoons to counterbalance the weight of the heavy ivory harpoon heads. These objects also had a spiritual function. They were carved with images of helping-spirits in artistic designs. By using beautiful and artfully crafted tools and weapons, the hunter sought to please the spirits of prey animals and make them more willing to be captured.

Carved ivory winged object, Point Hope, Alaska

TOMB MODELS
The earliest Japanese *haniwa* (tomb models) were hollow clay cylinders or jars placed around the tops of burial mounds. These were soon replaced by elaborate models, up to 5 feet high, that provided ritual protection for the deceased. Some were in the form of human figures from all walks of life, including armored warriors, farmers, musicians, and mothers and babies.

Female *haniwa*, Japan

POPULAR RELIGION
Persia was a melting pot of religions at this time. Christianity, which had become the official religion of the Roman Empire in the previous century, was practiced alongside the Persian state religion Zoroastrianism. In addition to these major religions there were many other local, populist faiths. Evidence of such beliefs is provided by small bowls inscribed with magical incantations in Aramaic, Syriac, or Hebrew, found buried beneath the floors of Mesopotamian houses.

Inscription in Aramaic

Incantation bowl, Iraq

CHRISTIANIZATION OF ART
The Byzantine (eastern Roman) Empire continued to hold sway in Greece, the Balkans, the Middle East, and Egypt throughout the 5th century AD. Classical art, however, was gradually being replaced by a more medieval style. Many art objects of the time, such as this ivory panel dating to AD 420, were connected with Christian themes or the Church.

Byzantine ivory panel with Crucifixion scene

ROYAL BURIAL
Non-Christian burial rites continued to prevail in parts of the Sudan well into the 5th century AD. A royal tomb at Ballana, near the Second Nile Cataract, lay under a large mound, inside which a sloping passage led to a series of brick rooms around a small court. The king lay in the chamber nearest the entrance on a canopied wooden bier, wearing full regalia, iron weapons at hand. A male slave and an ox lay nearby. The sacrificed queen was in a separate chamber with her slaves. Other rooms contained gold and silver vessels, and other valuable offerings. The owner's horses, camels, grooms, and a number of soldiers were found sacrificed and buried in the courtyard outside the royal burial chamber.

AD 500-600

FOOD & ENVIRONMENT

SHELTER & ARCHITECTURE

AMERICAS

MAIZE

Maize was the most important crop in southwestern North America at this time. There were many varieties, but those that matured quickly and needed little water were especially valued and developed through selective breeding. Resistance to fungal infections may also have been developed, since finds of cobs showing possible symptoms, such as these "popped" kernels, are rare.

Corncob, Cottonwood Canyon, Kane County, Utah

PRE-PUEBLO PITHOUSES

The Anasazi of southwestern North America began to build more robust pithouses and to expand their design, adding an antechamber. Each pithouse had a central hearth and an opening to

let out smoke. The Anasazi grouped their dwellings more closely together. The new houses took more time and energy to construct than their predecessors, but they lasted longer and required less wood fuel for heating.

Ante-chamber

Opening for ventilation

Central hearth

Cross section, pithouse, Colorado

EAST ASIA & AUSTRALASIA

FOOD OFFERINGS

Japanese *haniwa* (tomb models) of this period included not only human and animal figures, but also model platters and bowls, which were based on those that would have been in everyday use. The model platters and bowls were placed inside tombs and were intended to be used by the deceased in the next world. This platter with bowls dates to around the mid-6th century AD.

Haniwa **platter with bowls, Japan**

BUDDHIST PAGODAS

Chinese Buddhist temple precincts during this period were enhanced by the inclusion of a purely Indian Buddhist feature, the freestanding pagoda. Pagodas, built to enshrine precious relics, were multistory towers of stone, brick, or wood, and could be square, round, or many-sided. The pagoda at the Song Yue temple in Henan in northern central

China dates to AD 523, and is the country's earliest surviving brick building. Hollow and twelve-sided, it is Indian in style. Most pagodas were modified with features from earlier Chinese wooden towers or pavilions, such as successive stories of diminishing size. Each story had projecting eaves supported by roof brackets.

MIDDLE EAST & SOUTH ASIA

AMBITIOUS CANAL PROJECT

King Khusrau Anushirvan (AD 531-578) reorganized the administration of the Sassanian Empire, which covered Mesopotamia and Persia. He calculated the agricultural potential of the land, and introduced a new taxation system based on average

yields, combined with a head tax on men aged between 20 and 50. Khusrau may have been responsible for part of the ambitious Nahrawan canal system, which took water from the Tigris River to irrigate the dry lands east of the Sassanian capital at Ctesiphon (in modern Iraq). A significant feat of agricultural engineering, more than 200 miles long, the Nahrawan Canal remained in use for over 500 years.

PALACE ARCH

Ctesiphon, in modern Iraq, was the capital of the Sassanian Empire. Its only surviving building is the Arch of Ctesiphon, with its 115-foot-high *iwan* (baked-brick vaulted hall). The arch originally formed one side of a palace courtyard

with another *iwan* facing it. It is thought to date to the reign of King Khusrau Anushirvan (AD 531-578).

Arch of Ctesiphon, Iraq

EUROPE

OUTBREAK OF PLAGUE

Plague ravaged southern Europe in the 6th century AD. The first outbreak reached Constantinople (modern Istanbul) from Ethiopia in the spring of AD 542, soon spreading to Italy and west as far as Britain. Three further epidemics, in which thousands of people died in both urban and rural areas, followed before the end of the century. The scale of depopulation allowed peoples from beyond the boundaries of the Byzantine Empire, such as the Slavs in the Balkans and the Lombards in Italy, to take over deserted lands virtually unopposed.

Central dome

BYZANTINE DOME

The most striking example of Byzantine architecture is the Haghia Sophia mosque at Constantinople, built originally as a church between AD 532 and 563, during the reign of the Emperor Justinian. Its revolutionary design included a 184-foot-high central dome.

Haghia Sophia, Istanbul, Turkey

AFRICA

IMPORTANCE OF CAMELS

Introduced to Egypt in the 6th or 7th century BC by Assyrian or Persian invaders, camels replaced horses as the principal means of desert transport in North Africa. By AD 500, paintings of camels were common in Saharan rock shelters; camel caravans were later important in the spread of Islam up the Nile into West Africa.

Saharan camel caravan

CHRISTIAN ARCHITECTURE

The first official Christian mission in Nubia was established in AD 543, although churches had been built there from the early 5th century AD, for example at Faras, capital of the Nobatian kingdom in Lower Nubia (modern northern Sudan). This church had rested on a stone foundation and had followed a Byzantine plan, with an apse (vaulted recess) at its eastern end. However, by the time the missionaries arrived, the church had been partly demolished and converted into a pagan ruler's palace. As Christianity again became officially established in Nubia, this very site was to become the foundation of a major cathedral in later centuries.

TECHNOLOGY & INNOVATION

WHEELED TOYS

The peoples of Mesoamerica understood the concept of the wheel, but they appear never to have made use of it except in the manufacture of toys with which to amuse their children. In the absence of any draft animals, such as oxen, wheeled vehicles would not have been of any great use. This toy, dating to AD 500, represents either a deer or a dog.

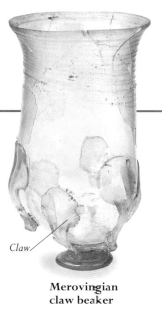

Wheeled toy, Tres Zapotes, Mexico

Tomb model horse, Japan

HORSE-RIDING ELITE

Superior mobility and fighting techniques enabled horse-riding warriors from Korea to seize power in Japan; contemporary Japanese tombs are filled with Korean-style metal horse trappings. The consequent rise of a horse-riding aristocracy in Japan is seen in the large numbers of model horses and mounted figures in tomb mounds.

SILK TEXTILES

The weaving of silk was an important industry in Persia during the Sassanian period (AD 226-642). In earlier times, when the production of silk was a Chinese monopoly, raw and woven silk was imported from China by land or sea. During the 6th century AD, however, the cultivation of silkworms spread west from China, and the Sassanians began to produce their own material. The silk textiles they wove were highly valued and soon became an important and widely traded luxury export, especially in Europe.

INNOVATIVE GLASS DESIGN

The Rhineland, an important center of glass manufacture under the Romans, continued to produce high-quality glassware for its new Merovingian masters (a Frankish dynasty that ruled Gaul and western Germany from around AD 500 to 750). A popular new product was the claw beaker, so called because of its shape, which was exported to France, Britain, and other parts of northern Europe.

Claw

Merovingian claw beaker

SMALL-SCALE MINING

By the 6th century AD, iron was being produced in such quantities in southern and eastern Africa that stone tools had largely fallen into disuse, even for everyday farming. Small-scale mining was practiced to obtain sufficient supplies of the metal. Where they were locally available, copper and gold were also being worked, and copper too was sometimes mined. The massive mines in the Zambian copper belt may have been in use at this time.

ART & RITUAL

MEMORIAL PLAQUE

At Monte Albán in southern Mexico, the Zapotec culture reached its apogee between AD 400 and 600. The scene carved on this stone slab, showing an older couple involved in a ritual thought to be in remembrance of a deceased family member, suggests that ancestor veneration was important in Zapotec society.

Carved stone plaque, Monte Albán, Mexico

ROYAL JEWELRY

By the 6th century AD, three native kingdoms dominated Korea: Koguryo in the north, and Paekche and Shilla in the south. Their rulers were buried in elaborate brick-built chambers beneath enormous mounds, accompanied by royal regalia and jewelry. In Shilla, the metalworking traditions of a nomadic past were kept alive, as shown by these granulated gold earrings, which are similar to objects found in northern Asia.

Detailed goldwork

Shilla gold earrings, South Korea

RELIGIOUS CULTS

As Hinduism evolved in India during the 6th and 7th centuries AD, Brahmanism (the worship of Brahma, "the creator") waned in popularity, while cults devoted to the deities Shiva and Vishnu emerged. Fertility, represented in particular by the *lingam* (phallus), played a major role in the worship of Shiva. These cults, along with various folk religions such as the worship of nature-spirits, appealed strongly to the masses, but were also patronized by emperors of the Gupta Dynasty who ruled northern India, and areas of central and western India, from the 4th to 6th centuries AD.

WARRIOR TRADITIONS

In AD 568 the Lombards, Germanic invaders from north of the Alps, established a kingdom in northern Italy, which had previously been within the boundaries of the Byzantine Empire. Drinking horns, like this Lombardic glass example, were an important element of Germanic warrior tradition. They were used in the great feasts that warrior lords hosted to reward their followers. So close was the bond between chieftain and retainer that warriors often chose to die with honor in battle if their lord was killed.

Lombardic drinking horn, Italy

COPTIC ART

The term "Coptic" is derived from an Arabic word meaning "Egyptian," and has been used to describe the Christianized people of Egypt from late Roman times to the present day. It also describes their language, which has its roots in Ancient Egyptian but incorporated many words borrowed from the Greek. During the 6th century AD, the Copts developed a distinctive art style based on the Greco-Roman classical tradition. Its most characteristic artifacts were painted religious icons and decorative wall-hangings.

Coptic wall-hanging, Egypt

COLONIZATION OF THE PACIFIC

200 BC

The scattered islands of Polynesia were one of the last regions of the world to be colonized. Sailors first set foot on the west Polynesian islands of Tonga and Samoa around 1500 BC, but 2,000 years elapsed before they reached Easter Island, the most isolated of the Pacific islands. Over the centuries, Polynesian communities grew and prospered, developing rich oral traditions, impressive stone monuments, and elaborate wood carvings. At first they depended largely on food from the sea or local wild plants. As the populations grew, they came to rely increasingly on cultivated plants, eventually building elaborate systems of terraced fields on some islands in order to expand the area of productive land. Control over the island societies became concentrated in the hands of hereditary chiefs, who were frequently at war with each other. These chiefs were thought to be imbued with *mana*, a Polynesian concept of a mystical life force, believed to be seated in the head, and associated with high social status and ritual power.

POLYNESIAN COLONIZATION *below right*
The origins of the Polynesians can be traced back through their language and genetic links to the early peoples of eastern New Guinea and the adjacent islands. The major phase of Pacific island colonization began around 3,500 years ago with the settlement of Tonga and Samoa. By 100 BC colonists had spread east to Tahiti, and it was from here, at the heart of Polynesia, that they embarked on breathtaking voyages of colonization: to Hawaii, Easter Island, and New Zealand. Crossing vast expanses of ocean in their tiny craft, these Polynesians are justly ranked among the greatest navigators in history.

3000 BC: limit of human settlement

150 BC: route of colonization

AD 400: route of colonization

AD 950: route of colonization

AD 1000: route of colonization

Area of Lapita ware
▲ Lapita find site

Tahitian outrigger canoe

Feather pennant

Balance board

Seating for second mast

Coconut palm leaf matting

Raised stern

Boom

Outrigger

Smaller balance board

PHILIPPINES

MICRONESIA

SUMATRA

BORNEO

JAVA

NEW GUINEA

ELOAUA

SOLOMON ISLANDS

MELANESIA

VANUA

Indian   Ocean

AUSTRALIA

NEW CALEDONIA

Darling R.

Breadfruit

Coconut

Yam

Sweet potato

Taros   **Bananas**

Coconut-shell container

BOAT BUILDING *above*
The Polynesians were expert navigators and boat builders. The classic vessel was the outrigger canoe, with a long narrow hull built of wooden side-planks sewn on to a dug-out tree-trunk base. An outrigger, a balancing piece of wood attached to the hull by means of slender arms, helped stabilize the canoe. Canoes of this kind were ideal for inshore sailing or short voyages, but for longer journeys across open sea, larger twin-hulled vessels were used. Both types could be paddled or sail-powered. An impressive knowledge of the skies, winds, and ocean currents guided the voyagers.

PACIFIC STAPLES *right*
Polynesian communities depended for everyday food on marine resources and cultivated plants. The most important plant was taro, a nutritious root crop, although yams and sweet potato were also grown, and coconut, banana, and breadfruit were of great importance. The small shrub *Piper methysticum* had a special place in Polynesian life, as its root was used to make *kava*, an intoxicating drink which had a major role in many Polynesian ceremonies.

VERSATILE COCONUT PALM *right*
The coconut palm was especially valuable to the Polynesian islanders because of the diverse uses for its various parts. Its trunk could be used for house posts and bridges, its leaves for roofing. Once the edible meat and milk had been removed, the shell could serve as a container or be crushed to provide a tough fiber for making ropes and cords.

Carved decoration

AD 200-600

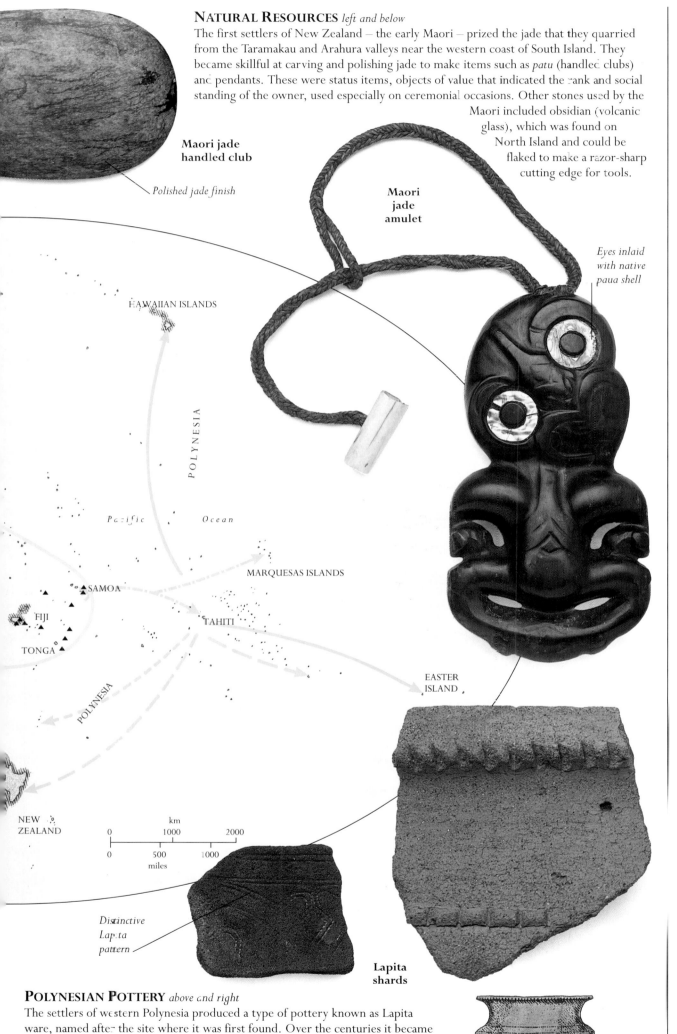

NATURAL RESOURCES *left and below*

The first settlers of New Zealand – the early Maori – prized the jade that they quarried from the Taramakau and Arahura valleys near the western coast of South Island. They became skillful at carving and polishing jade to make items such as *patu* (handled clubs) and pendants. These were status items, objects of value that indicated the rank and social standing of the owner, used especially on ceremonial occasions. Other stones used by the Maori included obsidian (volcanic glass), which was found on North Island and could be flaked to make a razor-sharp cutting edge for tools.

Maori jade handled club

Polished jade finish

Maori jade amulet

Eyes inlaid with native paua shell

ISLAND ENVIRONMENT

The islands settled by the Polynesian navigators varied widely in their shape and setting. Most lie within the tropics and had a rich natural environment which was used to full advantage by the early colonists. The results were not always beneficial. On Easter Island, human exploitation ultimately destroyed much of the natural vegetation and created a degraded and impoverished environment.

Chilean wine palm
(*Jubaea chilensis*)

FOREST CLEARANCE *above*

Easter Island today is bare and treeless. When Polynesian mariners arrived there around AD 500, however, they found an island covered in forest dominated by the Chilean wine palm. Some centuries later, the settlers had begun to clear the forest, using palm trunks as levers and rollers in the transport and erection of the famous Easter Island statues. This process led to soil erosion and environmental deterioration. When the first Europeans visited the island in the 18th century, they found a treeless landscape and a population suffering from food shortages.

FEATHERS

Polynesians used brightly colored feathers to decorate their chiefs' clothes. Most splendid were cloaks from Hawaii incorporating thousands of red and yellow feathers from Birds of Paradise and other tropical species.

Count Raggi's Bird of Paradise

Distinctive Lapita pattern

Lapita shards

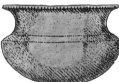

Reconstruction of Lapita pot

POLYNESIAN POTTERY *above and right*

The settlers of western Polynesia produced a type of pottery known as Lapita ware, named after the site where it was first found. Over the centuries it became increasingly uncommon, until by around AD 100, pottery was no longer made on any of the Polynesian islands. Perhaps it was no longer needed, given the availability of containers such as gourds and coconut shells. Its disappearance may also be related to changing cooking practices – boiling food in pottery vessels was abandoned in favor of baking in underground earth-ovens.

CHAPTER 15
THE RISE OF ISLAM
AD 600 - 800

Freak weather phenomena accelerate the collapse of Moche civilization in Peru

The first pueblos are built by the Anasazi people in southwestern North America

Tang Dynasty rules China in a time of unprecedented prosperity

Islam spreads rapidly throughout the Middle East and North Africa

Holy Roman Empire is established in western Europe

In the Old World, this period was characterized by religious developments, with the dominance of Christianity in most of Europe, the growing popularity of Hinduism and Buddhism in Southeast Asia, and the dramatic expansion of Islam in the Middle East and North Africa.

In North America, the first pueblos were built in the southwest, while in South America the Huari state was founded in the Andean highlands. But for other established cultures, it was a time of crisis.

Fall of civilizations in Mesoamerica

Around AD 650, the great metropolis of Teotihuacan in central Mexico began to lose its dominion over most of Meso-america, and by AD 750 it lay in ruins, burned and abandoned. Many historians and archaeologists believe that the fall of Teotihuacan was a cataclysmic event for Mesoamerica; certainly the effects were widely felt throughout the region.

Mayan culture in southern Mesoamerica thrived in the 7th century AD, but after the fall of Teotihuacan, it was also in decline by the end of the 8th century AD. Along with internal upheaval and external threats from neighboring states, the demands of a larger population were causing forest destruction and soil depletion. Unable to alter the course of events, lowland Mayan culture collapsed in the 9th century AD, leaving only the northern fringes to carry on the Mayan cultural tradition.

Climatic disasters in South America

Environmental factors also hastened the demise of the Moche of Peru. A prolonged and catastrophic drought (AD 562-94) was followed, a century later, by a great earth-quake. Periodic climatic disruption caused by unusual sea-current movements – a phenomenon known as *El Niño* (the Child) – accelerated the downfall: torrential rains caused extensive floods along the coast, followed by sandstorms that ruined once-fertile fields. By AD 700, in addition to this climatic adversity, the Moche were overwhelmed by the Huari state, which established its own cultural influence in the central Andes. The effects of *El Niño* were also occasionally felt inland in the Amazon Basin, where severe droughts affected the manioc crops of farming communities.

MAYAN INCENSE BURNER
Decorated with images of the sun god, this ceramic vessel was used to burn incense in rituals.

Finely worked sheet gold

Inlaid precious stone

UKRAINIAN GOLDWORK
Trans-Asian caravan routes met the Byzantine trading networks of the Mediterranean and Black Sea, allowing long-distance exchange of items such as these earrings.

KEY DATES AD 600-800

AD 618
Rise of Tang Dynasty, China

AD 632
Death of Prophet
Muhammad, Arabia

AD 642
Sassanian Empire
falls to Islamic armies,
Middle East

AD 700
Start of first Pueblo period,
southwestern North America

Collapse of Moche
civilization, Peru

AD 711
Islamic armies
invade southern
Spain

AD 750
Teotihuacan
abandoned, Mexico

AD 800
Charlemagne crowned
emperor at Rome

AD 600   AD 650   AD 700   AD 750   AD 800

THE SPREAD OF ISLAM
One in a series illustrating Islamic history, this miniature shows the migration of Arabs into conquered lands.

Southwestern villages

In North America, established peoples in the semidesert region of the southwest – the Hohokam, Mogollon, and Anasazi – began building on a larger scale. The Hohokam created elaborate irrigation systems, while the Anasazi, and perhaps the Mogollon, began to construct pueblos – substantial stone or adobe towns. The Pueblo period is defined by prehistorians as starting around AD 700. There is evidence of contact between the peoples of the southwest and Mesoamerica. Courts for playing the ritual ballgame – of great importance in Mesoamerican societies – were built at larger settlements in the Hohokam area. The maize grown by southwestern peoples was also a Mesoamerican introduction.

East Asian cultures

Buddhism had reached Japan from India in the 6th century AD, and its spread was now helped by the country's rulers, who were recent converts. Resources shifted from the building of massive mounded tombs to the construction of Buddhist temples with elegant timber halls and tall, slim pagodas. At Nara, near modern Osaka, a new capital city was laid out on a grid-plan model derived from contemporary China. Revenue for this project was gathered in taxes. After several centuries of instability, China entered a new period of prosperity with

the ascendancy of the Tang Dynasty (AD 618-906). The imperial capital, Chang'an, became the greatest city of its day, with a population of more than one million people. Silver dishes, decorated silks, and ceramic models, including the famous Tang horses, bear witness to the

*Rich caparison
and ornaments*

CHINESE HORSE MODEL
A love of horses is manifest in the glazed terra-cotta tomb models of the Tang era. Other models depict court dignitaries, merchants, and diplomats.

NUBIAN ART
Friezes and frescoes in the cathedral at Faras were clearly influenced by Byzantine art.

opulence and refinement of courtly life. Tang rulers extended Chinese territories to the northwest, penetrating deep into Central Asia, where they took control of large sections of the Silk Roads; this allowed contacts with the West to be re-established.

Indian religions

The Gupta Dynasty (4th-6th centuries AD) encouraged relative autonomy in the Indian towns and regions it controlled, so that by the 6th and 7th centuries AD, India had split into a number of separate kingdoms. The 8th century AD saw a further flowering of Hindu art, while major scholarly advances were made in the study of mathematics and astronomy. Buddhism remained dominant in Sri Lanka. Alongside Buddhism and Hinduism, new populist cults were gaining ground – one of the most important was Tantrism, a cult with its origins in ancient fertility beliefs. Tantric elements were absorbed into both Buddhism and Hinduism.

Further east, new kingdoms were forming in Southeast Asia, strongly influenced in their culture and institutions by Indian models and often adopting the Indian script, Sanskrit. Indian traders established contacts with many parts of Southeast Asia in the search for gold, spices, and other valuables. Buddhism and Hinduism soon spread to both the mainland and islands along these trade routes, and hybrid forms of the two religions were firmly rooted throughout the region by the 7th century AD.

AD 600-800

200 BC

The spread of Islam

The term Islam means resignation – that is, resignation to the will of God as expressed in the sacred book, the Koran, which contains the revelations made to Islam's founder, Muhammad (AD 570-632), an Arabian merchant. After some initial hostility, Islam soon attracted many followers, uniting peoples of different backgrounds in a common religious cause. In AD 642, Islamic armies overthrew the Sassanian Empire in the Middle East, and by AD 680 they had taken Armenia, North Africa, and Syria from the Byzantines. By AD 750, the Islamic Empire extended from southern Spain to Pakistan and Central Asia. It was governed by the caliphs, the first of whom resided in Medina; under the Umayyad Dynasty (AD 661-750) the capital moved to Damascus in Syria; then in AD 762, under the succeeding Abbasid Dynasty, to Baghdad.

In the West, the 7th and 8th centuries AD marked a low point in the fortunes of the Byzantine Empire. Prosperous eastern provinces, including Syria and Egypt, were taken over by Islamic rulers, and in the Balkans, attacks by Slavic peoples caused great disruption. Yet Constantinople survived, and was to remain a major Christian center for another 800 years.

Christianity in northern Europe

In Europe, new kingdoms assimilated elements of Germanic social organization and features surviving from the late Roman Empire, including Christianity and the use of Latin for official documents. Lavish pagan burials gave way to more modest Christian practices, and a new style of architecture – Romanesque – was developed for churches and palaces.

The most powerful Christian realm north of the Alps was the Frankish kingdom, which by the 7th century AD covered all of present-day France. Under its most illustrious ruler, Charlemagne, or Charles the Great (AD 742-814), it absorbed extensive non-Christian territories east of the Rhine, building churches and missions in an effort to convert the local people. By the end of Charlemagne's reign, his kingdom included most of Germany, Austria, Switzerland, and Italy. A pious ruler and a patron of the arts, Charlemagne was proclaimed emperor of the new Holy Roman Empire in AD 800.

African kingdoms

Christianity also thrived in northeastern Africa, notably in the kingdoms of Nubia in the Sudan and Axum in Ethiopia. These states were cut off from the rest of the Christian world by the advance of Islam across North Africa. Christian rulers built churches on the Byzantine model, decorating the interiors with religious frescoes. Nubia remained Christian until overrun by Egyptian Muslims in the 13th century AD.

Major changes in West Africa occurred in small communities in the Niger Delta region, which became more interdependent, exchanging goods and services, and building contacts with Islamic merchants from north of the Sahara. These early bases for urban life were to lead to the rise of the first large trading cities in the region.

AMERICAS

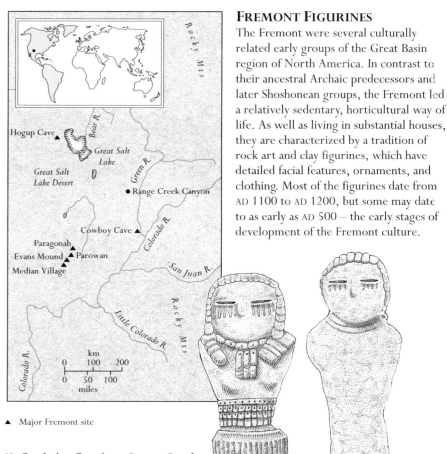

▲ Major Fremont site

Unfired clay figurines, Range Creek Canyon, Green River, Utah

FREMONT FIGURINES

The Fremont were several culturally related early groups of the Great Basin region of North America. In contrast to their ancestral Archaic predecessors and later Shoshonean groups, the Fremont led a relatively sedentary, horticultural way of life. As well as living in substantial houses, they are characterized by a tradition of rock art and clay figurines, which have detailed facial features, ornaments, and clothing. Most of the figurines date from AD 1100 to AD 1200, but some may date to as early as AD 500 – the early stages of development of the Fremont culture.

RITUAL BALL GAME

The ritual ball game was played on fields, often formal masonry courts, with two opposing teams using a solid rubber ball. Individual players wore protective clothing, because the ball could only be hit with the hips, thighs, or elbows. Having existed since the 1st millennium BC, the game became widespread throughout Mesoamerica between AD 300 and AD 900, with several hundred formal courts identified. By AD 600, ball courts began to appear in southwestern North America. Their builders were influenced by contacts with Mesoamerican cultures. The ball game was also common in the Caribbean by this date.

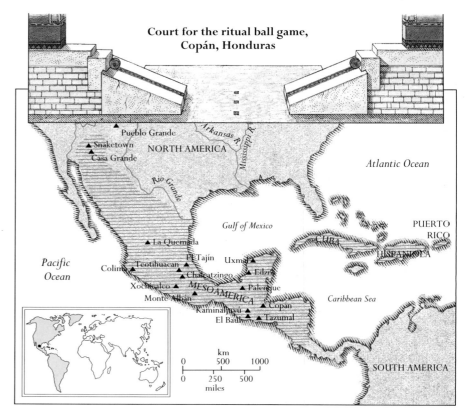

Court for the ritual ball game, Copán, Honduras

Site with ball court ▲   Distribution of ball courts ≡

EUROPE

CAROLINGIAN EMPIRE

The Frankish rulers who took over the former Roman province of Gaul in the 5th century AD consolidated and expanded their power in western Europe from their heartland, the kingdom of Austrasia. By the time of the coronation of the Frankish ruler Charlemagne (AD 742-814) at Rome in AD 800, the kingdom of Lombardy in northern Italy, and much of Germany, had been absorbed into what now became the Holy Roman, or Carolingian, Empire. Carolingian military might depended heavily on armored cavalry, which derived great benefit from the introduction of the stirrup into Europe in the 8th century AD. The Carolingian Empire fragmented in the 9th and 10th centuries AD, and central royal authority over local rulers declined.

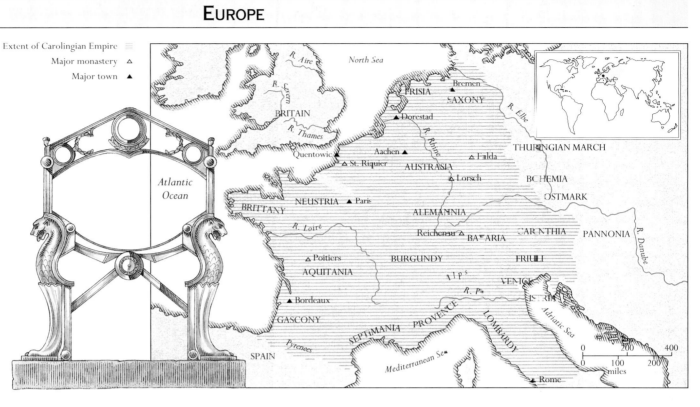

Extent of Carolingian Empire ▤
Major monastery △
Major town ▲

Gold throne of a Frankish king, Paris, France

MIDDLE EAST & SOUTH ASIA

ISLAMIC CONQUESTS

The armies rallied by Muhammad (AD 570-632) captured Mecca in AD 630, and invaded the area of modern Israel and Jordan in AD 633-4. The Sassanian

Empire, which covered Mesopotamia and Persia, was defeated in AD 642. Egypt was invaded in AD 642, and North Africa in AD 643. Islamic expansion into Central Asia resulted in the fall of Tashkent in AD 751; Spain was invaded in AD 711. The Islamic Empire was settled by Muslims, and new towns and mosques were founded, including the Dome of the Rock in Jerusalem, built in AD 691. In AD 750 expansion ceased, and a period of consolidation followed under the Abbasid caliphs, rulers until the 11th century AD.

Dome of the Rock, Jerusalem, Israel

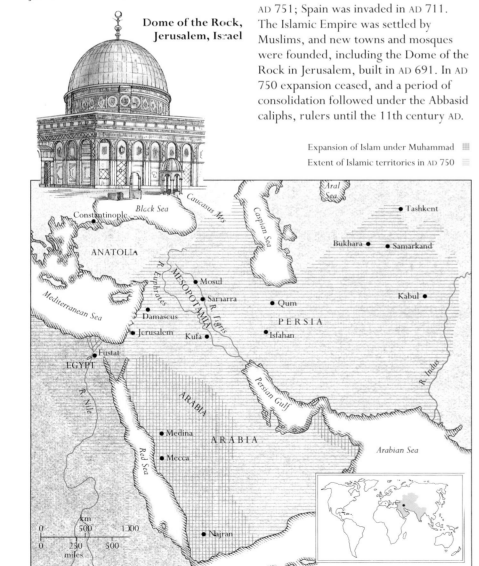

Expansion of Islam under Muhammad ▦
Extent of Islamic territories in AD 750 ▤

EAST ASIA & AUSTRALASIA

TANG CHINA

The Tang Dynasty (AD 618-906) ruled China from capitals at Chang'an and Luoyang. More canals were built to connect these cities with the rich grain-producing lands of the Yangtze River valley. In a series of military campaigns between AD 660 and AD 680, the Tang emperors extended their control as far as

the Tarim Basin in Central Asia. This gave them control over many of the Silk Roads that linked China to Persia and the Mediterranean. The peoples who lived in these regions were great horsemen, engendering in the Tang elite a love of horsemanship, especially polo. Tang influence also extended east beyond the imperial frontier to Japan and Korea.

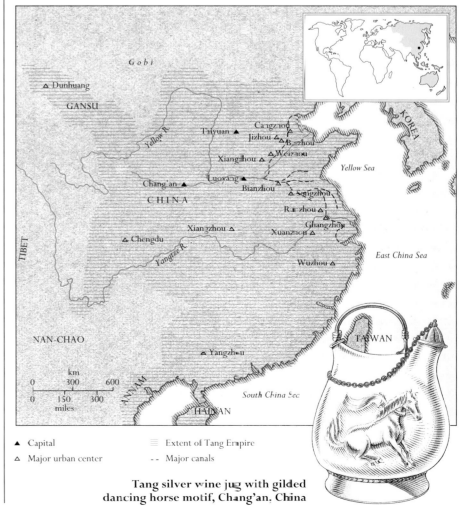

▲ Capital
△ Major urban center
▤ Extent of Tang Empire
-- Major canals

Tang silver wine jug with gilded dancing horse motif, Chang'an, China

AD 600-700

FOOD & ENVIRONMENT	SHELTER & ARCHITECTURE

AMERICAS

DEER HUNTING

The tropical rainforest of Central America abounds with wildlife. From earliest times humans hunted deer for meat and for hide to make clothing. This naturalistically rendered figure of a fawn is incorporated in the body of a ceramic vessel dating to the 7th century AD. The vessel may have had a ceremonial use.

Effigy vessel, Comayagua River region, Honduras

CEREMONIAL TEMPLES

Palenque in southern Mexico, in the midst of the Chiapas jungle, was a superb Classic Mayan (AD 300-900) ceremonial center with many distinctive temples. This building, the Temple of the Inscriptions, stands on top of the tomb of Pacal (meaning Shield), one of the Lords of Palenque, who died in AD 683.

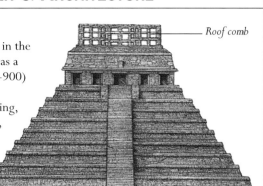
Roof comb

Temple of the Inscriptions, Palenque, Mexico

EAST ASIA & AUSTRALASIA

GRAND CANAL

China was reunified by the Sui Dynasty (AD 581-618), bringing to an end the long period of instability that followed the demise of the Han Dynasty in AD 220. Economic stability led to a population explosion, which was concentrated around the rice-growing fields of the Yangtze Valley rather than the dry wheat and millet lands of central and northern China. In order to transport southern-grown crops west and north to the capital cities of Chang'an and Luoyang, the first Grand Canal was built. It took more than five million laborers 34 years (AD 584-618) to complete.

BUDDHIST TEMPLES

Although Buddhism arrived in Japan by way of Korea in the 6th century AD, Japanese temple building was soon strongly influenced by direct contact with China. The earliest surviving Buddhist temple is that of Horyu-ji at Nara (near modern Osaka), built between AD 607 and 670. Constructed mainly of timber, it included typical Chinese features: a pagoda, terraces, stone column bases, and a tiled roof.

Main Hall, Horyu-ji temple, Japan

MIDDLE EAST & SOUTH ASIA

LAND GRANTS

The feudalism that had developed in India's "Golden Age" during the Gupta period (AD 320-500) continued with their successors, particularly Harsha (AD 590-647), the firm but benevolent ruler of an empire that covered most of northern India. Harsha had little interest in building a centralized state under royal authority, so villages, towns, and districts tended to be self-governing and relatively independent. This trend was promoted by the growing practice of paying government officials with grants of land instead of salaries.

Seal recording a land grant, Gujarat, India

FIRST MOSQUES

The *haram* (sacred places) of pre-Islamic Arabia had been simple structures or unmarked desert sanctuaries. However, the nature of Islamic religious observance required more formal places of worship. The model for early mosques was adapted from the Prophet Muhammad's house at Medina in western Arabia, in which he delivered sermons and recited prayers. It had a rectangular mud-brick courtyard with verandas on the northern and southern sides, and nine private rooms along the eastern wall. The southern wall faced Mecca, the direction of prayer. The southern veranda, built of palm-trunk columns and roofed with palm branches, was extended to provide more shade. Sermons were delivered from a *minbar* (pulpit). This plan was replicated in mosques in the military camps of Basra (AD 635), Kufa (AD 637), and Wasit (AD 702), and in later hypostyle (columned hall) mosques.

EUROPE

SILVER CUTLERY

The Germanic rulers of early medieval Europe treasured finely crafted tableware, as shown by these silver spoons from a ship burial at Sutton Hoo in Suffolk, England. The spoons were probably made by Byzantine craftsmen in the eastern Mediterranean and were found, together with other Byzantine tableware, in the grave of an Anglo-Saxon king who died around AD 625.

Silver spoons, Sutton Hoo, Suffolk, England

NORTHERN COMMUNITIES

Germanic villages of the 7th century AD in northern Europe consisted of groups of timber longhouses. These could be up to 130 feet long and were divided internally into a number of rooms, some used for eating and sleeping, others for grain or for livestock. Down the long axis of the house ran pairs of substantial wooden posts that supported a steeply sloping reed-thatched roof. In Britain, by contrast, ordinary Anglo-Saxon settlers lived in small rectangular houses, with barns constructed as separate buildings nearby. Their rulers, however, constructed large timber-framed halls in which they could feast and entertain their warriors and retainers.

AFRICA

BARK CLOTH

In tropical areas of Africa where palm trees abounded, bark cloth was of great importance. It was used to make large mats and ceremonial garments, often given as symbolic gifts. Bark cloth makers pounded the net-like fiber to produce a soft, lustrous cloth that was often decorated with elaborate designs.

THATCHED HUTS

The early Bantu farmers of southern Africa lived in conical thatched huts, grouped into villages. The floors were of anthill or other clay, mixed with water and laid straight onto the ground, and often smoothed over with cattle dung.

Wooden frame
Thatch
Plastered clay interior

Bantu dwelling, southern Africa

TECHNOLOGY & INNOVATION

COTTON HANK AND SEEDS

In lowland southwestern North America, cotton was grown as early as AD 200. By AD 900 it was traded to the upland southwest, where this hank, remarkable for the regular thickness of the yarn, was found in an AD 1100 cliff dwelling. The seeds discovered with the hank indicate that the cotton was probably grown locally.

Cotton hank, Moqui Canyon, Utah

SILVER COINS

Traders from India brought new ideas and practices to Southeast Asia during the early centuries AD, including the adoption of the Indian script, Sanskrit, and the use of coins. The early silver coins issued by the Pyu rulers of Burma were closely based on Indian models in their manufacture, size, shape, and designs.

Pyu coins, Burma

ISLAMIC COINAGE

The growing economic power of the Islamic Empire in the Middle East led to the minting, in AD 696 and 698, of official gold and silver coins by the fifth caliph of the Umayyad Dynasty, Abd al-Malik (reigned AD 685-705). Whereas earlier mintings had copied Byzantine and Sassanian Persian figural designs, merely adding the Islamic profession of faith, the new coins had only Arabic inscriptions and verses from the Koran (the holy book of Islam) and set the standard for Islamic coinage for many centuries.

Figural gold dinar of the caliph Abd al-Malik

INTRICATE DECORATION

Ornate shoulder-clasps from the Sutton Hoo ship burial in Suffolk, England, are masterpieces of 7th-century Germanic craftsmanship. They are gold, inlaid with panels of garnet and *millefiori* (created from fused glass strands, or threads, of different colors), and were designed to secure a cape or cloak.

Shoulder-clasps, Suffolk, England

Inlaid garnet

MASTER STONEMASONS

The Axumite kingdom in Ethiopia was noted for sophisticated building skills; its engineers were able to quarry and move granite monoliths and other stonework over astonishing distances. Their masons were expert at dressing stone, as shown by still-standing monuments erected to commemorate their rulers.

Granite stela, Axum, Ethiopia

ART & RITUAL

POLYCHROME POTTERY

This finely crafted bowl from a Honduran burial mound shows the decorative bands and paired figures characteristic of Mayan ceramics. Its distinctive painting technique and stylized human and animal forms are regional variations typical of the southernmost Mayan states during the Classic period (AD 300-900).

Ceramic bowl with polychrome decoration, Lake Yojoa, Honduras

INDIAN INFLUENCES

Buddhism spread to Southeast Asia along the trade routes from India, and was firmly established there by the early 7th century AD. Early representations of the Buddha, such as this head from Thailand, show that Southeast Asian artists imitated Indian models in their smoothness of line and serenity of expression.

Bronze head of the Buddha, Thailand

THE KORAN

The Koran is held in Islam to be the infallible word of Allah (God), revealed to the Prophet Muhammad in his 40th year (AD 610) in a series of dreams and visions. It emphasizes the Day of Judgment and the promise of life after death and accepts the Old and New Testaments as revealed by Allah but does not recognize Jesus as the son of God. The Koranic revelations were memorized by Muhammad's early followers, and in AD 651, 19 years after his death, an authorized Arabic text was prepared.

Byzantine necklace of gold and precious stones

OPULENCE

The splendid ornaments made for Germanic rulers of western and northern Europe at this time find their eastern counterpart in the jewelry of the Byzantine Empire. Gold and precious stones were often used for religious objects such as crosses and reliquaries, but wealthy Byzantines also had valuable personal jewelry.

CARVED STOOLS

Wooden stools created by the peoples of sub-Saharan West Africa ranged in style from the strictly utilitarian to elaborately carved symbols of power.

Chief's wooden stool (contemporary example), West Africa

AD 700-750

FOOD & ENVIRONMENT	SHELTER & ARCHITECTURE

AMERICAS

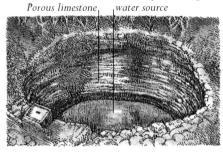

Naturally occurring water source
Porous limestone

Sacred well, Chichén Itzá, Yucatán, Mexico

SACRED WELL
Many Mayan ceremonial centers in the Yucatán peninsula of Mexico flourished around *cenotes* (natural wells), which were their principal source of water. The Yucatán peninsula is a porous limestone shelf with little surface water, honeycombed with underground rivers. The large and important site of Chichén Itzá contained a number of wells; the one shown here was considered sacred.

DESERT VILLAGES
In the low desert of the Great Basin in southwestern North America, the Anasazi people constructed their villages. While the overall population density in the area was lower in comparison to that in the upland southwest, some Great Basin sites – such as Lost City and Evans Mound in Nevada – are extremely large.

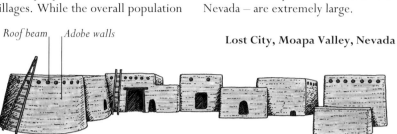

Roof beam *Adobe walls*

Lost City, Moapa Valley, Nevada

EAST ASIA & AUSTRALASIA

LAND REFORM
Good administration in China under the Tang Dynasty (AD 618-906) reduced the power of wealthy landowners by allotting land to peasants in return for tax payments and 20 days unpaid labor. This encouraged the opening of new lands in the fertile south. Tomb figurines reflect the resultant agricultural prosperity.

Tang tomb model of a buffalo cart, China

SHRINES AND STATUES
Early Polynesian temples consisted of rubble platforms, sometimes supporting one or more stone pillars or carved wooden figures. On Easter Island these shrines were called *ahu* and were built only two or three centuries after the first colonists arrived. The oldest, Ahu Tahai, built around AD 700, was a narrow flat-topped platform; a crudely carved statue of scoria (red volcanic stone) may have stood upon it. It was the forerunner of the distinctive rows of giant statues that began to be erected on the island around AD 1000. Like them, Ahu Tahai was probably built as a shrine to the founders, or ancestors, of the community.

MIDDLE EAST & SOUTH ASIA

BUDDHIST MONASTERIES
The great city of Anuradhapura was the capital of Sri Lanka for over 1,000 years; it was embellished by successive monarchs with Buddhist monasteries dominated by enormous stupas (dome-shaped monuments containing burials or relics). One of the largest, the Abhayagiri stupa, was almost 400 feet tall. In the 8th century King Mahinda II added a multistory chapter house at its foot, decorated with fine stone reliefs.

Elephant and rider relief, Abhayagiri stupa, Sri Lanka

AGRICULTURAL DECLINE
In the Levant, olive growing was abandoned when the Christian population was driven out by the expanding Islamic Empire. Depending on local conditions, the new Arab settlers generally favored intensive wheat growing and animal husbandry. The introduction here of nomadic herding, and the neglect of the irrigation system that had supplied the olive groves, led to massive soil erosion.

EUROPE

FARM IMPLEMENTS
The Anglo-Saxon farmer used a range of tools to work the land and harvest crops. A heavy ox-drawn plow first turned the earth, and the harrow prepared the ground for sowing. Iron billhooks were used for pruning, wooden spades shod with iron were used for digging, and crops were harvested with iron scythes and sickles.

Anglo-Saxon iron agricultural tools, Hurbuck, England

Palace of the Exarchs, Ravenna, Italy

BYZANTINE STRONGHOLD
The Palace of the Exarchs, or governors, at Ravenna in northeastern Italy was the center from which Byzantine rulers struggled to retain a precarious hold on parts of Italy until the 8th century AD. Its brick facade displayed classical Roman features, such as round-headed arches and slender columns. Classical Roman tradition continued to thrive in southern Europe even after the Germanic invasions.

AFRICA

MAKING BEER
Throughout sub-Saharan Africa, beer was used to fulfill social obligations, to reciprocate for help given (perhaps for such communal work as house-building), to pay debts, offer hospitality, and celebrate such occasions as marriages. It was made not from barley but from millet and sorghum, soaked in water in closed containers and allowed to ferment. The resulting brew was then diluted to make beverages of varying potency.

FRESCOED CATHEDRAL
The greatest 8th-century church in Africa was the rebuilt cathedral at Faras in Christian Nubia. It was built on the site of a 5th-century church, but on an altogether more impressive scale, with a nave flanked by four aisles. Rebuilding began in AD 707, and the walls were soon covered with a series of frescoes depicting kings, saints, and religious scenes.

St. Anne fresco, Faras, Nubia

TECHNOLOGY & INNOVATION

MINING

Hafted sledges, or hammerstones, were used in mining. This example, which dates to between AD 700 and 1100, was discovered in a salt mine where it had been stored with sandals, a net bag, and salt rocks. Turquoise was also widely mined in southwestern North America and was an important item in trading with Mexico.

Unworked turquoise

Hafted hammerstone from a salt cave, Nevada

JAPANESE TAXATION

Major reforms in Japan during the Nara period (AD 710-84) brought the whole country under a centralized bureaucratic government. Chinese-style administrative and taxation systems were adopted. Taxes were generally paid in agricultural produce and textiles, or in unpaid labor or military service. Thousands of tax tallies, which were tied on to goods in transit, record the nature and origin of government receipts.

Tax tallies, Japan

ADVANCED MATHEMATICS

Indian mathematics and astronomy, already highly developed by the scholar Aryabhata in the late 5th century AD. advanced further with the works of such 7th- and 8th-century scholars as Brahmagupta and Lalla. Geometry and trigonometry were studied, but it was particularly in the field of algebra that Indian mathematicians excelled, using the decimal place and the concept of zero to make important deductions.

Indian mathematicians and astronomers accurately calculated the value of pi (π) and the length of the solar year. Later Indian astronomers tended to modify these scientific approaches, bringing them in line with the beliefs of tradition and religion.

IMPERIAL SILKS

Silkworms were reputedly first smuggled out from China in the hollow of a monk's staff in AD 554, but the finest Byzantine silks belong to the 8th century AD and later. Imperial looms were set up at Constantinople (modern Istanbul), and weaving became a tightly controlled profession. Silk was often woven in panels, then stitched together to form a hanging or garment.

Panel of Byzantine silk from a tunic sleeve

IVORY HUNTERS

African farmers hunted elephants for their ivory, much prized for prestigious ornaments. They trapped the huge beasts in deep pits dug along their trails, or speared them in the heart or soft underbelly with large, iron-bladed spears. African elephant ivory was widely traded, and supplies even reached Constantinople (modern Istanbul), where delicately carved ivory plaques were produced.

Elephant spear with iron head, Africa

ART & RITUAL

MOCHE MURAL ART

On the northern coast of Peru, the Moche culture had developed a rich tradition of mural painting by this time. The Moche decorated their temples and public buildings with delicate drawings, principally scenes of war and depictions of their priest-warriors. The figure in this illustration is a warrior involved in a triumphal ritual.

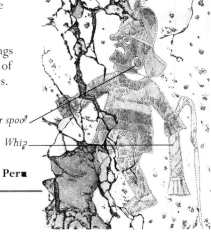

Golden ear spool

Whip

Moche mural, Peru

CEREMONIAL POTTERY

Like Japan, Korea (which had been united in AD 668 under the Shilla kingdom) borrowed from Chinese culture and institutions, particularly architecture and Buddhist sculpture. In pottery, however, it preserved and developed a distinctive indigenous style, reflected in this typically Korean glazed pot with decorative perforation, possibly a ceremonial item.

Shilla glazed pot, Korea

PRAYERS TO MECCA

Under the Umayyad caliph al-Walid I (reigned AD 705-15), the concave *mihrab*, the niche in a mosque that marks the direction of prayer, was adopted as a memorial to the place where Muhammad (died AD 632) had stood to deliver sermons in his house at Medina. Concave *mihrabs* had previously been forbidden because they were considered too similar to statue niches in Christian churches. The first concave *mihrab*, which replaced a block of stone, was in the Mosque of Medina, rebuilt in AD 707-9 to replace the simple mosque of the prophet Muhammad. The second was at Fustat in Cairo, and the third at Damascus. The *mihrab* remains the focal point of all mosques.

Front detail, the Franks Casket, England

DECORATIVE TRENDS

The Franks Casket, of carved whalebone, illustrates the gradual blending of pagan and Christian ideas in Anglo-Saxon England. The Adoration of the Magi and the pagan legend of Wayland the Smith are shown on the front; on one end are the twins Romulus and Remus, and on the back, the capture of Jerusalem by the Romans in AD 70.

ROCK PAINTING

Rock art is widespread throughout eastern and southern Africa. Hunter-gatherers painted scenes of humans and animals, including antelopes and wildebeest. By the beginning of the 8th century AD, these hunter-gatherers had been driven back to southwestern South Africa by the migration of the Bantu. This rock art is from Cedarberg Mountains, West Cape.

Rock art, South Africa

AD 750-800

FOOD & ENVIRONMENT	SHELTER & ARCHITECTURE

AMERICAS

COMMUNAL STORAGE

Central to the success of farming villages in the midwestern region of North America was the storing of crops, like maize, for later communal sharing. At the Range site in Illinois (AD 300-1400) evidence dating to *c.* AD 800 shows that large storage pits could be used and managed by an entire community. In this small village, four large pits were found dug around a pole in a central plaza.

Soil cap — *Maize* — *Squash* —

Cross section, crop storage pit, Illinois

TEMPLE STONEWORK

The Mayan center of Uxmal, meaning "three times built," stands in the Puuc foothills of northern Yucatán. This detail of a 19th-century painting by the artist and explorer Frederick Catherwood shows the extraordinary stonework of the facade of the Temple of the Magician, which sits on top of a unique, curved-walled, oval pyramid.

Detail of a painting showing the Temple of the Magician, Mexico

EAST ASIA & AUSTRALASIA

CULTIVATED FOOD CROPS

Early Polynesian colonists relied heavily on seafood, but they also brought with them both the tradition of plant cultivation and a number of domesticated species from Southeast Asia. They were soon growing these in garden plots throughout the Polynesian islands. The most important food plants were the tubers taro and yam, and three major tree crops — banana, breadfruit, and coconut.

WOODEN TEMPLES

The hall of the Nanchan Temple in Shaanxi province, built in AD 782, is the earliest surviving wooden structure in China. It was one of the few temples to escape destruction when thousands of complexes were destroyed in AD 845 by imperial order in an attempt to halt the growing power of Buddhism.

Main hall, Nanchan Temple, China

MIDDLE EAST & SOUTH ASIA

LAND GRANTS

In 8th-century India, grants of land were often recorded on copper plates, sometimes strung on a copper ring. One surviving example records a land grant to a Brahman priest in AD 753 by King Nandi-varman of the Pallava Dynasty, which ruled on the western coast of peninsular India from the early 4th to the late 9th century AD. The details were inscribed in Tamil (a language spoken in southern India and Sri Lanka), and defined the four boundaries of a village and its surrounding fields, which were the subject of the grant. The copper plates gave the right to draw water from nearby tanks and rivers to irrigate the land and specified in detail the normal agricultural taxation, including a share of figs, corn, cotton, and rice, from which the recipient was exempt.

HEWN FROM THE ROCK

Hindu rock-cut architecture reached new heights at Ellora in northern India with the entirely freestanding Kailasanatha complex. The main temple is flanked by rock-hewn shrines, all elaborately decorated with carvings, especially of the god Shiva.

Kailasanatha temple, Ellora, northern India

EUROPE

FOOD FOR TRADING PORTS

Emporia, or trading centers, sprang up on the coasts of northwestern Europe, at places such as Dorestad in the Netherlands and Hamwic (modern Southampton) in England. Most meat supplies were obtained by driving cattle to the emporium, then butchering them there. At a few of the centers, meat arrived already butchered. The introduction of the deep-water drift net ensured plentiful supplies of herring.

Romanesque arch

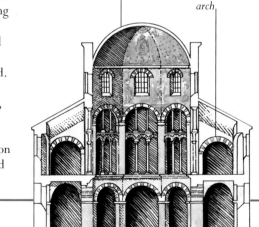

PALACE COMPLEX

At Aachen (formerly Aix-la-Chapelle) in north-western Germany between AD 792 and AD 805 the Frankish ruler Charlemagne constructed an elaborate palace complex to serve as the center of the newly founded Carolingian, or Holy Roman, Empire. The buildings were Romanesque — modeled on Roman lines — and much of the stone was scavenged from Roman ruins. The centerpiece of the complex was a great octagonal church, the so-called Palatine Chapel.

Cross section of Palatine Chapel, Aachen, Germany

AFRICA

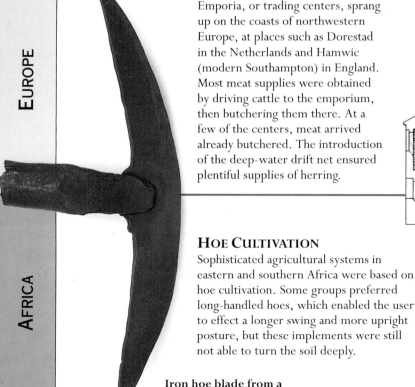

HOE CULTIVATION

Sophisticated agricultural systems in eastern and southern Africa were based on hoe cultivation. Some groups preferred long-handled hoes, which enabled the user to effect a longer swing and more upright posture, but these implements were still not able to turn the soil deeply.

Iron hoe blade from a long-handled hoe, East Africa

TRADITIONAL MATERIALS

Mud bricks and clay mixed with water were the most widely used building material, not only in the arid parts of Africa, but also in the wetter areas of the east and south. Mud bricks were an excellent insulating material, keeping the interiors of the huts cool in summer and warm in winter. They were manufactured in simple wooden molds, then dried in the hot sun, a technique used by the Egyptians for more than 3,000 years. Puddled anthill clay served to make hard floors for huts and formed a durable plaster for grain bins and walls. When protected by thatched roofs from rain, such clay structures could last a generation — or until their timber supports were consumed by termites.

TECHNOLOGY & INNOVATION

WORKING IN IVORY

The emerging Punuk culture in Alaska replaced the ivory engraving of earlier periods with sculptural techniques. This ivory figurine seems to be a fertility charm, but may also have been used as a dressing-up doll to teach young girls to sew. The drum handle with a shaman's face shows considerable skill in its fine detail. Drums were used ceremonially; played by shamans, their "voices" became the vehicle by which the shaman's soul was transported.

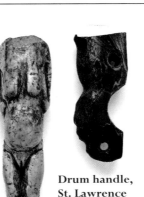

Ivory figurine of a pregnant woman, Punuk Island, Alaska

Drum handle, St. Lawrence Island, Alaska

PRINTING AND PAPER

By the second half of the 8th century AD, the era to which this paper fragment dates, the Chinese system of woodblock printing (which also spread to Japan and Korea) was being used to "mass-produce" Buddhist and Daoist texts, with as many as 15,000 copies made from a single block. Chinese paper-manufacturing techniques spread west, reaching Samarkand, an important trading center on the Silk Roads in Central Asia, around AD 751, and replacing the use of papyrus and parchment.

Fragment of woodblock-printed paper, Chang'an, China

MECHANICAL INVENTIONS

In AD 750 the caliphs of the Umayyad Dynasty (AD 661-750) were succeeded by the Abbasids (AD 750-1258) as rulers of the Islamic Empire in the Middle East. Under the Abbasids, who founded a new Islamic capital, the city of Baghdad, in AD 762, the empire entered a new phase in which science, industry, and the arts predominated. A mechanical model of a horseman who could raise and lower his lance was a typically inventive Abbasid device. It stood on top of the Green Dome at the center of Baghdad.

NOBLEMAN'S HELMET

Society in early medieval Europe was still geared to warfare, as this late 8th-century helmet found at Coppergate, York, illustrates. It is a finely made piece of armor, with sturdy iron cap and hingepieces, and a fringe of chain mail at the back to protect the wearer's neck. Molded brass strips, one of them inscribed with a Christian prayer, show that the helmet was the equipment of a wealthy lord.

The York helmet, England

NUBIAN IMPORTS

Discoveries in Christian Nubia of many imported artifacts, including glassware, gold jewelry, and religious pieces such as this finely worked silver cross, show the rich and varied culture enjoyed by Nubian leaders through their trade contacts.

Silver cross, found in Nubia

ART & RITUAL

ROCK ART

Rock art of the Fremont (people of the Fremont River region in Utah) features human figures, some of which are nearly life-size, with detailed facial features, ornaments, and carefully depicted clothing. Many have enlarged hands and feet. Geometric patterns are important to the designs, as are decorated disks with human legs that are known as "shield figures." The Fremont figures may have shamanistic or ritual significance. Some, with ornate headdresses or snakes, suggest ritual. The inaccessible locations of many rock art panels (many are high on cliff faces where artists must have worked very close to the panels in precarious positions) also suggest ritual or ceremonial importance.

Side view

Overhead view

GOLD AND SILVER

In Tang China (AD 618-906), a market in luxury goods led to the growth of a sophisticated industry in the working of precious metals. Lacking an indigenous tradition, Chinese craftsmen adopted foreign forms (mainly from Persia), decorated with Chinese motifs derived from painting, lacquerwork, and Buddhist reliquaries.

Tang silver cup, China

TANTRIC INFLUENCES

Hinduism gained ground in India in the 8th and 9th centuries AD, particularly as a result of its adoption by major rulers such as the Rashtrakutas of the south.

Buddhism, however, was in decline over much of the subcontinent, surviving only in the east and on Sri Lanka (although it remained strong overseas). The Hindu upsurge was influenced by Tantrism which, with its roots in ancient fertility cults and female deities, encouraged the appearance of female consorts for the male Hindu deities, Shiva and Vishnu.

ICONOCLASM

During the 8th century AD, Constantinople (modern Istanbul) was in the the grip of iconoclasm. Representation of divine or saintly personages in religious art was officially prohibited, a clear sign of underlying Islamic influences. The prohibition extended to coins, on which the head of Christ, usually on the reverse face, was replaced by a plain cross. The emperors themselves continued to be portrayed on the front, or obverse side, however, as shown by this coin issued by the usurper-empress Irene (reigned AD 797-802), who had deposed and blinded her son Constantine VI.

Gold solidus of the Empress Irene, Constantinople (modern Istanbul)

MASKS AND MYTH

African craftsmen developed great expertise in carving wooden masks and sculptures. Masks, like this contemporary example from Zambia, were a creative expression of traditions associated with dance, myth, and ritual. Such masks still play an important part in rituals in many parts of the continent.

Carved wooden mask (contemporary), Zambia

TEMPLE-PYRAMIDS

The construction of ceremonial pyramid complexes was widespread in Mesoamerica and South America. Pyramids varied greatly in size, shape, and finish. Many were surmounted by temple buildings or situated above tombs. Among the most magnificent were those built in southern Mexico by the people of the Mayan culture, which reached its height between the 3rd and 9th centuries AD; and those built on the north coast of Peru by the Moche people (1st to 8th centuries AD). Mayan pyramids were built of stone; those in Peru were made mainly of adobe bricks.

PYRAMID DESIGN

There were many regional variations in pyramid design. In Mesoamerica, pyramids took the form of lofty truncated cones incorporating external stairs or terraces, smooth steep slopes or towers, or a combination of these elements. In Peru, pyramids consisted either of truncated cones or two or three tiers with a platform at the top. All pyramids were originally rendered with plaster and decorated with murals.

LIMESTONE SHELL *below*
The oval-shaped Temple of the Magician is the principal pyramid at the Mayan site of Uxmal in the Yucatán. Limestone slabs were placed over a rubble core. A stairway on the west side leads to the temple chamber at the top.

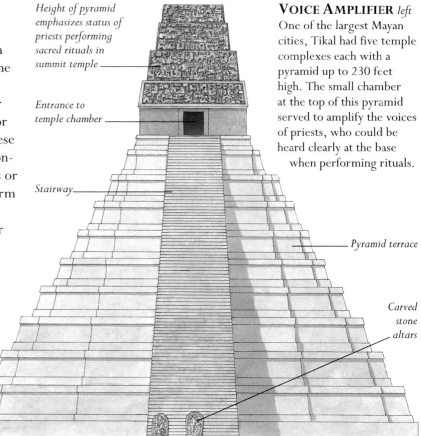

Height of pyramid emphasizes status of priests performing sacred rituals in summit temple

Entrance to temple chamber

Stairway

VOICE AMPLIFIER *left*
One of the largest Mayan cities, Tikal had five temple complexes each with a pyramid up to 230 feet high. The small chamber at the top of this pyramid served to amplify the voices of priests, who could be heard clearly at the base when performing rituals.

Pyramid terrace

Carved stone altars

Reconstruction of the Pyramid of the Giant Jaguar, Tikal, Guatemala

TEMPLE-PYRAMID SITES *above*
The principal pyramid sites in Mesoamerica are located in central Mexico, the Oaxaca region of Mexico, the Yucatán Peninsula, Guatemala, and Honduras.

▲ Major pyramid site

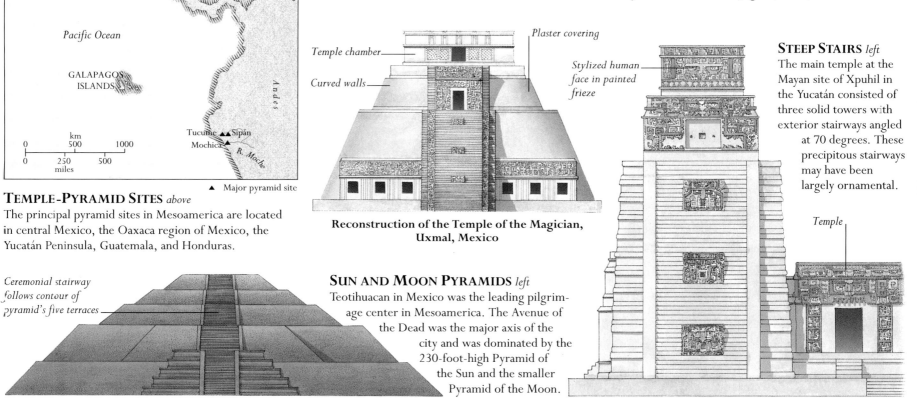

Temple chamber

Curved walls

Plaster covering

Reconstruction of the Temple of the Magician, Uxmal, Mexico

Stylized human face in painted frieze

STEEP STAIRS *left*
The main temple at the Mayan site of Xpuhil in the Yucatán consisted of three solid towers with exterior stairways angled at 70 degrees. These precipitous stairways may have been largely ornamental.

Temple

SUN AND MOON PYRAMIDS *left*
Teotihuacan in Mexico was the leading pilgrimage center in Mesoamerica. The Avenue of the Dead was the major axis of the city and was dominated by the 230-foot-high Pyramid of the Sun and the smaller Pyramid of the Moon.

Ceremonial stairway follows contour of pyramid's five terraces

Reconstruction of the Pyramid of the Sun, Teotihuacan, Mexico

Reconstruction of one tower of the main pyramid, Xpuhil, Mexico

CONSTRUCTION METHOD

The Moche people built their pyramids using adobe bricks. Construction work was done in groups under the guidance of specialists. Marks stamped on the bricks appear to identify separate work parties involved in the process. The pyramid walls were built up in brick courses and the space between them was filled with rubble.

1 Soil and water were mixed with straw to prepare adobe. The resulting mulch was then trodden by foot to achieve the correct texture.

2 Adobe was molded in wooden frames and baked in the sun. Separate work parties were assigned to prepare the adobe and make the bricks.

3 Dried adobe bricks were carried to the construction site either by hand or on wooden frames covered with fiber-woven netting.

4 Bricks were laid in courses by specialist bricklayers, who were assisted by workers, following traditional techniques.

AD 600-800

RELIGIOUS CENTER

The two most important pyramid complexes built by the Moche people in the Moche Valley on the north coast of Peru are the Huaca del Sol and Huaca de la Luna. Together they formed the religious and administrative center of the Moche state. Both complexes are rectangular and face each other across a large level area, or plaza, which was used as a cemetery. The Huaca del Sol faces north and is the largest and most impressive pyramid in the Moche Valley. The south-facing Huaca de la Luna is only half the size of the Huaca del Sol and is decorated with colorful murals. The Huaca del Sol complex measures 748 feet long by 446 feet wide. It was laid out in a series of terraces and the pyramid itself was originally 164 feet high. It was ascended by a ramp 295 feet long and 20 feet wide.

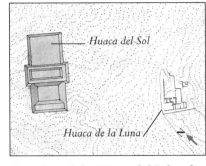

Plan view of the Huaca del Sol and Huaca de la Luna, showing their relative positions

SYMBOL OF STATUS

The deity Ai-Apec personified the Moche priest-warrior elite. The staff indicates his status, and his eyes and teeth are of inlaid shell and mother-of-pearl. Priest-warrior tombs are found in temple complexes.

Reconstruction of the Huaca del Sol, Moche Valley, Peru

Carved representation of Ai-Apec, Viru Valley tomb, Peru

HUACA DEL SOL *above*

On the uppermost platform of the Huaca del Sol are the remains of other structures. The lower part appears to have been used as a burial area.

BRICK COURSES *right*

The bricks at the base of the Huaca del Sol were laid in slanted courses, while those above were laid horizontally. Mud mortar was used as the cementing agent.

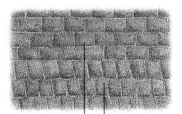

Horizontal course | Slanted course

PRIEST-WARRIOR'S TOMB

This Moche tomb in the Viru Valley in northern Peru contained the body of a priest-warrior and such grave goods as staffs, which symbolized the status of the deceased, and pottery vessels.

DECORATED POTTERY *left*

The Moche people were skilled in the production of ceramic stirrup-spouted vessels and open dishes. These were decorated with brown line drawings on a cream background. The drawings depict scenes of hunting, warfare, feasts, and other aspects of daily life.

MURAL PAINTING *below*

The Moche people developed a tradition of spectacular painted murals with which they adorned important buildings such as the Huaca de la Luna. Many murals depicted war scenes, painted in red, yellow, blue-green, and white.

Fighting warrior

Stirrup-spouted pot, Moche Valley, Peru

Mural with Moche symbols, Huaca de la Luna, Moche Valley, Peru

LORDS OF SIPAN

The burials in the Huaca Rejada pyramid complex, discovered in 1987 at the Moche site of Sipán in the Lambayeque region of northern Peru, are the richest found to date in the Americas. The wealth of grave goods discovered in the five tombs that were excavated testifies to the prosperity of the Moche elite. Many of the goods were made of gold and silver. Two of the tombs are those of priest-warriors – the Lord of Sipán and the Old Lord of Sipán.

GOLD SPIDER *left*

Adorning the remains of the Old Lord of Sipán was a necklace of gold spiders, each on its own circular web and with a human face on its back. These disks were symbols of the Old Lord's royal status.

Gold necklace disk, Sipán, Peru

BURIAL UNEARTHED

The grave goods buried in the tombs at Sipán included ceramics and objects made of gold, silver, turquoise, lapis lazuli, and shell. The corpses were laid to rest on their backs and were dressed in tunics adorned with gold and silver disks and plates. Jewelry included ear spools, nose ornaments, bracelets, necklaces, and breastplates. Many corpses were buried in tombs decorated with painted murals and inlaid metal. Male and female attendants were also sacrificed.

DIVINE SYMBOLS *right*

These tarnished silver heads, complete with inlaid eyes and fangs made from shell, were part of a necklace – one of many necklaces covering the chest and midriff of the Old Lord of Sipán. Gold anthropomorphic heads were also included in the burial. The heads may symbolize divine powers.

Spider's web

Inlaid tarnished silver heads, Sipán, Peru

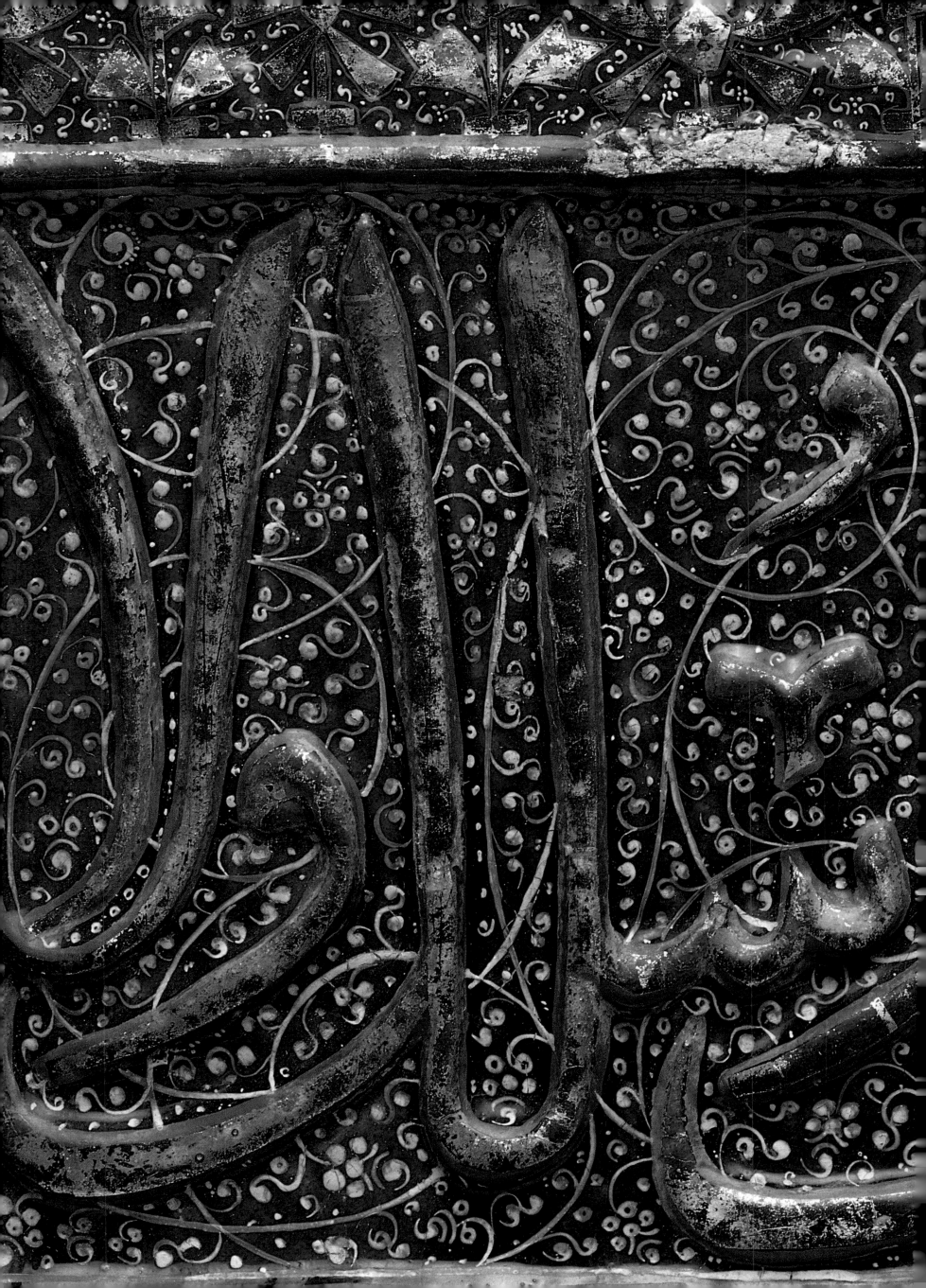

PART FOUR

AD 800

TO

AD 1500

Long-distance trade links brought diverse cultures in different parts of the world into ever closer contact during this period. Camel caravans plied the Saharan routes, linking African empires to the Mediterranean cities, while Chinese navigators sailed the Indian Ocean to reach the coast of East Africa and European explorers arrived in America. Contact brought material wealth for some, but catastrophe for others, as the new arrivals claimed the land for themselves and indigenous cultures disappeared.

Detail of molded tile with Arabic inscription, from a frieze in a mausoleum, northwestern Iran, c. AD 1300

CHAPTER 16
THRIVING ECONOMIES
AD 800-1000

Expansion of Chimu and Toltec states in Peru and Mexico

Small trading kingdoms arise in the West African forest zone

The Chola Dynasty dominates southern India

Islamic culture thrives despite political fragmentation in the Islamic Empire

Viking traders and raiders active in northern and western Europe

New societies evolved in East and West Africa and on the mainland and islands of Southeast Asia between AD 800 and AD 1000. In the Americas, the Moche culture was succeeded by that of the Chimu people on Peru's northern coast, and the Toltecs established and expanded their power in Mexico. In the Mississippi Valley in southeastern North America, new centers such as Cahokia and Moundville rose to prominence, and the foundations of their platform mounds were laid. In the southwest, the pueblo builders of Chaco Canyon – the Anasazi – built ever larger pueblos, some containing more than 800 rooms. Meanwhile, Viking traders and colonizers were altering the political map of northern and western Europe, and some reached as far west as Iceland, Greenland, and Newfoundland.

Successive cultures in the Americas

The Chimu people were the cultural descendants of the Moche and were responsible for building extensive sunken gardens and irrigation canals to feed the burgeoning population of their capital, Chanchan, on the northern coast of Peru.

The Toltecs' rise to power in central Mexico occurred after the fall of Teotihuacan in AD 750; after AD 900 their capital, Tula, became a major center. By means of expansionist military campaigns, the Toltecs established extensive trading networks in the following two centuries.

Toltec cultural influence spread throughout Mesoamerica. Around AD 1000, Toltec architectural features such as colonnaded courts and altars supported by sculpted figures appeared at Chichén Itzá, a late Mayan city in the Yucatán. Tula itself was aggrandized with monuments, including a pyramid dedicated to the planet Venus and adorned with huge basalt columns carved in the likeness of Toltec warriors. The city also seems to have been a distribution center for Mayan ceramics and other items from as far south as Costa Rica.

African trading towns

Developments in sub-Saharan Africa in the 9th century AD were largely due to an expansion in trade. Colonies such as Manda were established on the East

MAYAN VESSEL
Found in El Salvador, this cylindrical ceramic vessel dates to around AD 800 and is decorated with repeated pairs of monkeys. Its purpose may have been ceremonial.

Aperture producing whistling sound

Typical stirrup spout

WHISTLING JAR
Peoples of the southern coast of Peru included jars like this among their grave goods. If filled with water, the jars made a whistling sound when blown through the spout.

Bronze knotted rope

Stand

CHIEF'S BURIAL
Among the grave goods of a chief buried at Igbo Ukwu, West Africa, in the 9th century AD was this bronze water pot decorated with bronze knotted rope.

KEY DATES AD 800 - 1000

AD 800 Rise of kingdom of Ghana in West Africa

AD 802 Khmer state founded in Cambodia

AD 814 Death of Charlemagne

AD 836 Abbasid caliphs transfer their capital from Baghdad to Samarra

AD 1000
First Viking settlement on Newfoundland

Beginning of Toltec influence at late Mayan city of Chichén Itzá

AD 950
Rise of Chimu state in Peru

| AD 800 | AD 850 | AD 900 | AD 950 | AD 1000 |

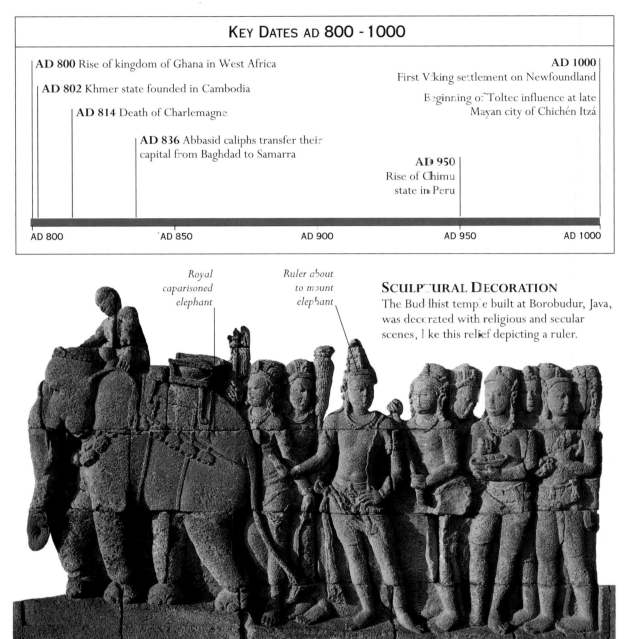

Royal caparisoned elephant

Ruler about to mount elephant

SCULPTURAL DECORATION
The Buddhist temple built at Borobudur, Java, was decorated with religious and secular scenes, like this relief depicting a ruler.

African coast by Arab merchants, who prospered by shipping products from the African interior to markets in the Middle East. Merchant colonies were also founded in West Africa at existing towns such as Kumbi Saleh, Timbuktu, and Jenne-jeno. Luxury goods such as gold and ivory were purchased in these places and transported north across the Sahara by camel caravan. It was in this part of Africa that the ancient kingdom of Ghana emerged around AD 800, the first in a series of powerful states that were to dominate the region for several centuries.

Coiled serpent motif

Inlaid silver studs

ANGLO-SAXON JEWELRY
These Anglo-Saxon silver brooches from Galway were made in Ireland during the 8th and 9th centuries AD.

Farther south, in the West African forest zone, small kingdoms arose that profited from these trade links. The ruler of one such kingdom was buried in full ceremonial attire in a timber-lined tomb at Igbo Ukwu in modern Nigeria. The grave goods included beaded armlets and objects of copper and bronze, reflecting both the dead man's status and the refinement of contemporary indigenous African crafts.

Southeast Asian settlers arrived on the island of Madagascar late in the 1st millennium AD. There are traces of human occupation on the island 1,000 years earlier, but substantial permanent settlements developed only during this period. In reaching such a distant island, these navigators rivaled the exploits of Polynesian sailors who first reached New Zealand at about the same time.

In Australia, by contrast, Aboriginal culture developed without significant contact with non-Australian peoples until the 18th century AD. Within the continent, however, there was active long-distance trade in valuable commodities such as shell pendants and stone axes.

Southeast Asian states
The states that arose in Southeast Asia in the centuries before AD 1000 comprised fluctuating tracts of territory centered in the court of a supreme overlord. They included the kingdoms of Champa in Vietnam and Pagan in Burma, kingdoms centered on Prambanan and Borobudur in Java, and the Khmer state in the Angkor region of southwestern Cambodia. The rise of these states owed much to influences from India, transmitted mainly by Indian traders who had traveled throughout the area since the early centuries AD.

AD 800 -1000

Royal temples

In the Khmer state, a series of temples and royal temple-mausoleums was constructed over a period of more than five centuries, beginning with the Bakong temple-pyramid of King Indravarman I (AD 877-89). Associated with the temples were massive rectangular tanks, which represented the lakes around the mythical Himalayan home of the Hindu gods. They also served a practical purpose as irrigation reservoirs.

Competing religions

Throughout Southeast Asia, Buddhist and Hindu temples were built – evidence of a religious tolerance unthinkable in India at the time. Hinduism was now the dominant religion in peninsular India while Buddhism remained strong in parts of the north and in Sri Lanka. Of all the regional dynasties in India, the Cholas (mid 9th-12th centuries AD) in the south enjoyed the greatest sphere of control, establishing extensive trade links with Southeast Asia and China.

Buddhism played an important role in China and Japan, and some of the most interesting early writings from the 9th century AD are Buddhist scriptures from the caves of the Buddhist shrine at Dunhuang in northwestern China. Wall paintings at Dunhuang and in the aristocratic tombs of central and northern China also depict secular images as well as scenes from the life of the Buddha, offering a glimpse into daily life during the later Tang period in the 9th century AD.

Abbasid decline

During the 9th century AD, the Islamic Abbasid caliphs still ruled an empire stretching from Pakistan to North Africa. However, the power of local dynasties was gradually increasing; already by AD 800 the provinces of southern Spain and Morocco had seceded as separate states. A strong measure of cultural uniformity survived nonetheless; this was one of the greatest periods of Islamic arts and scholarship.

Vikings and Byzantines

While the Byzantine Empire was undergoing a cultural and political renaissance in the 10th century AD, the early medieval kingdoms of western Europe were hampered by internal dissent. The principal political entity in western Europe, the Carolingian, or Holy Roman, Empire, began to fragment soon after the death of Charlemagne (AD 742-814), as his grandsons fought among themselves. By the end of the 9th century AD the empire had split into two kingdoms, a Frankish state in the east, forerunner of modern Germany, and in the west the kingdom of France. Throughout the 9th and 10th centuries AD these kingdoms, along with the Anglo-Saxon and Celtic kingdoms of the British Isles, suffered at the hands of Viking raiders from Scandinavia. King Alfred the Great (AD 871-99) managed to retain independence in Wessex, one of the former Anglo-Saxon kingdoms of England, and his successors in the 10th century AD went on to establish a unified kingdom in England.

AMERICAS

TOLTEC MILITARISM

By AD 1000 the influence of the Toltecs had spread over a large region of Mesoamerica. Their capital was at Tula, in the modern state of Hidalgo, Mexico. The Toltecs expanded their domain by wars of conquest, but trade was fundamental to the spread of their influence. Pottery from Mayan regions to the south and as far away as Costa Rica has been found at Tula. At Casas Grandes in northern Mexico, finds of Toltec goods are a further indication of Tula's extensive trade networks. After the fall of Tula in AD 1160, the Toltecs migrated to the Yucatán peninsula and parts of Central America.

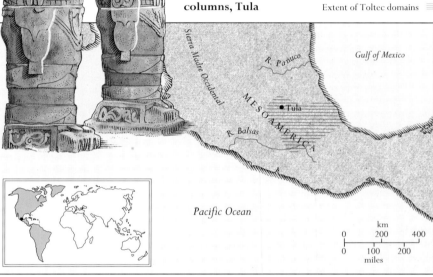

Toltec warrior columns, Tula

Extent of Toltec domains

AFRICA

SETTLEMENT OF MADAGASCAR

The island of Madagascar, off Africa's southeastern coast, was settled by voyagers from Southeast Asia in the late 1st millennium AD. Southeast Asian influences in Malagasy culture are more dominant than those of mainland Africa. Bantu settlers who arrived later from the mainland introduced cattle herding and ironworking. The first Southeast Asian settlers arrived in outrigger canoes, bringing crops like bananas, plantains, and papayas. These crops may later have been carried from Madagascar to the mainland, perhaps via Zanzibar – where there is evidence of contact. They soon became vital staples as far away as West Africa.

➜ Arrival of Southeast Asian settlers

▲ Early island settlement

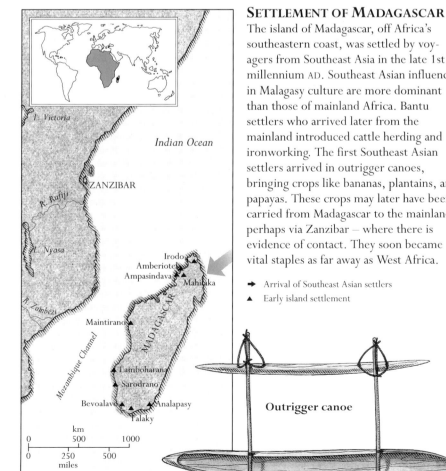

Outrigger canoe

EUROPE

VIKING TRADE ROUTES

The Vikings were merchants, traders, and colonists, who used their skill in seamanship to open up extensive new trading routes along the coasts of western Europe and east toward Constantinople (modern Istanbul) in the 8th and 9th centuries AD. A number of trading towns were founded by the Vikings, such as Dublin in Ireland. Viking farmers migrated as far as Iceland, Greenland, and Newfoundland. The Vikings were also pirates, deriving much wealth from plunder, notably of the rich Christian monasteries in northern Britain. The Vikings dominated northwestern Europe during the 9th and 10th centuries AD, and played a major role in the development of a state centered in Kiev.

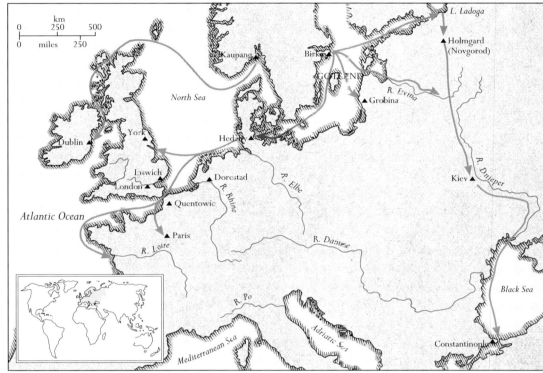

Viking merchant vessel

Major Viking trade route ➡
Important trading center ▲

MIDDLE EAST & SOUTH ASIA

INDIAN DYNASTIES

Southern India in the 9th and 10th centuries AD was locked into a struggle for supremacy between rival dynasties: the Pallavas, Pandyas, and Cholas. The Cholas conquered the Pallavas in AD 897, and the Pandyas were defeated in the early 10th century AD. The Cholas soon dominated all of southern India and invaded northern Sri Lanka under Rajaraja I (AD 985-1014).

Rajaraja's son conquered lands as far away as the Maldive Islands and Sumatra in the early 11th century AD, consolidating Chola naval strength. The Cholas had sea trade links with the states of Southeast Asia and China. The period of Chola rule is also famous for the prolific building of Hindu stone temples, and for stone and bronze sculptures, such as this four-headed manifestation of the god Brahma.

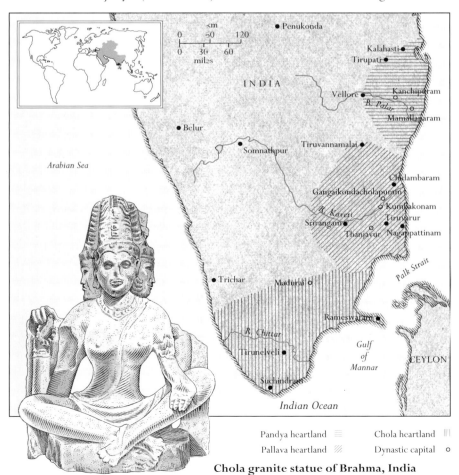

Pandya heartland ☰   Chola heartland ▥
Pallava heartland ▨   Dynastic capital ○

Chola granite statue of Brahma, India

EAST ASIA & AUSTRALASIA

INTERNAL TRADE IN AUSTRALIA

Australian Aborigines had developed networks of exchange and trade routes over considerable distances by AD 1000. Such items as pendants made of mother-of-pearl or baler shell, incised with geometric designs and used in sorcery and sacred rituals, were distributed 2,500 miles across the continent. Stone axes, pituri (native tobacco), and ocher, which was used for body decoration and cave painting, were traded up to 500 miles, in exchange for opossum-skin cloaks, spear shafts, and spinifex (Australian grass) resin to cement stone tools such as spearpoints into wooden handles. Australia's first exports (from Cape York north to the Torres Strait islands) were bone-tipped spears and spear-throwers for fighting and fishing for dugongs (sea cows).

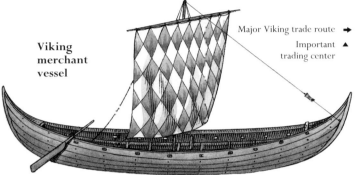

Shell pendant, Northern Territory, Australia

Major trade route for shell pendants ➡

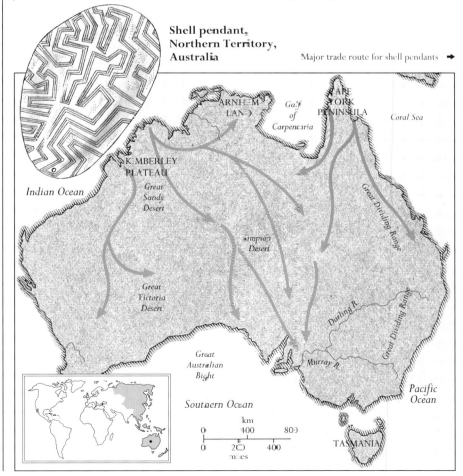

AD 800-850

200 BC

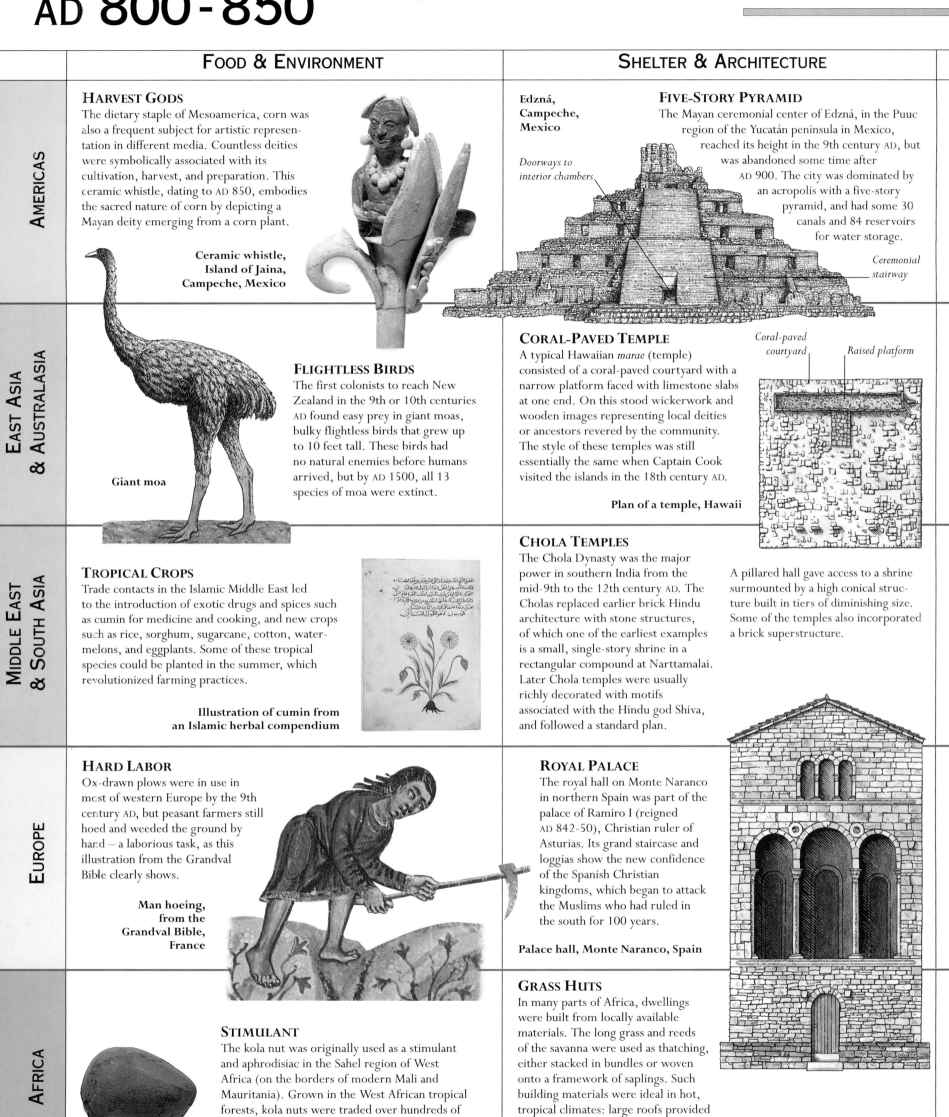

FOOD & ENVIRONMENT

HARVEST GODS
The dietary staple of Mesoamerica, corn was also a frequent subject for artistic representation in different media. Countless deities were symbolically associated with its cultivation, harvest, and preparation. This ceramic whistle, dating to AD 850, embodies the sacred nature of corn by depicting a Mayan deity emerging from a corn plant.

Ceramic whistle, Island of Jaina, Campeche, Mexico

FLIGHTLESS BIRDS
The first colonists to reach New Zealand in the 9th or 10th centuries AD found easy prey in giant moas, bulky flightless birds that grew up to 10 feet tall. These birds had no natural enemies before humans arrived, but by AD 1500, all 13 species of moa were extinct.

Giant moa

TROPICAL CROPS
Trade contacts in the Islamic Middle East led to the introduction of exotic drugs and spices such as cumin for medicine and cooking, and new crops such as rice, sorghum, sugarcane, cotton, watermelons, and eggplants. Some of these tropical species could be planted in the summer, which revolutionized farming practices.

Illustration of cumin from an Islamic herbal compendium

HARD LABOR
Ox-drawn plows were in use in most of western Europe by the 9th century AD, but peasant farmers still hoed and weeded the ground by hand – a laborious task, as this illustration from the Grandval Bible clearly shows.

Man hoeing, from the Grandval Bible, France

STIMULANT
The kola nut was originally used as a stimulant and aphrodisiac in the Sahel region of West Africa (on the borders of modern Mali and Mauritania). Grown in the West African tropical forests, kola nuts were traded over hundreds of miles, wrapped in damp leaves and repacked every five days. The nut's intensely bitter taste relieved thirst on hot days. It was the only stimulant not outlawed under Islamic law.

Kola nut

SHELTER & ARCHITECTURE

FIVE-STORY PYRAMID
Edzná, Campeche, Mexico

The Mayan ceremonial center of Edzná, in the Puuc region of the Yucatán peninsula in Mexico, reached its height in the 9th century AD, but was abandoned some time after AD 900. The city was dominated by an acropolis with a five-story pyramid, and had some 30 canals and 84 reservoirs for water storage.

Doorways to interior chambers

Ceremonial stairway

CORAL-PAVED TEMPLE
A typical Hawaiian *marae* (temple) consisted of a coral-paved courtyard with a narrow platform faced with limestone slabs at one end. On this stood wickerwork and wooden images representing local deities or ancestors revered by the community. The style of these temples was still essentially the same when Captain Cook visited the islands in the 18th century AD.

Plan of a temple, Hawaii

Coral-paved courtyard   *Raised platform*

CHOLA TEMPLES
The Chola Dynasty was the major power in southern India from the mid-9th to the 12th century AD. The Cholas replaced earlier brick Hindu architecture with stone structures, of which one of the earliest examples is a small, single-story shrine in a rectangular compound at Narttamalai. Later Chola temples were usually richly decorated with motifs associated with the Hindu god Shiva, and followed a standard plan.

A pillared hall gave access to a shrine surmounted by a high conical structure built in tiers of diminishing size. Some of the temples also incorporated a brick superstructure.

ROYAL PALACE
The royal hall on Monte Naranco in northern Spain was part of the palace of Ramiro I (reigned AD 842-50), Christian ruler of Asturias. Its grand staircase and loggias show the new confidence of the Spanish Christian kingdoms, which began to attack the Muslims who had ruled in the south for 100 years.

Palace hall, Monte Naranco, Spain

GRASS HUTS
In many parts of Africa, dwellings were built from locally available materials. The long grass and reeds of the savanna were used as thatching, either stacked in bundles or woven onto a framework of saplings. Such building materials were ideal in hot, tropical climates: large roofs provided shade and thin grass walls afforded privacy and protection from mosquitoes, while allowing ventilation.

Side labels
AMERICAS
EAST ASIA & AUSTRALASIA
MIDDLE EAST & SOUTH ASIA
EUROPE
AFRICA

TECHNOLOGY & INNOVATION

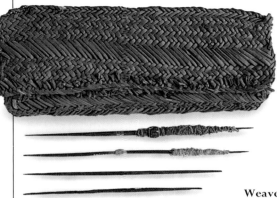

TEXTILE TOOLS
In Andean cultures, women weavers kept their wooden tools in wicker baskets, which were often included among the weavers' burial offerings, complete with their set of tools. This practice illustrates the importance of textile production in Andean societies.

Weaver's basket and tools, Peru

GUNPOWDER
A warning issued in the 9th century AD by Chinese alchemists provides the earliest evidence for the invention of an explosive compound: they advised that anyone mixing the elements saltpeter, sulfur, and charcoal risked producing an explosion, and burning his beard. The alchemists had invented gunpowder, although an exact formula of its ingredients was not printed until AD 1044. Early Chinese fireworks, such as the firecrackers used from earliest times to dispel evil spirits, did not use gunpowder; they were made from hollow segments of bamboo blocked at both ends, which exploded when thrown into a fire.

SCHOLARLY RESEARCH
The caliphs of the Abbasid Dynasty (AD 750-1258), Iraq-based rulers of the Islamic Empire, encouraged the study of astronomy, mathematics, geometry, and engineering, since this research aided trade and navigation. Research led to the refinement of the astrolabe, a navigational tool originally invented by the Greeks. This example dates to the 14th century AD.

Islamic astrolabe

Coin of Charlemagne, France

FRANKISH COINAGE
The Holy Roman emperor Charlemagne (AD 768-814) reformed the Frankish coinage, establishing 12 silver denarii to the gold solidus, and 20 solidi to the pound. These ratios survived in Britain until the introduction of decimal coinage in 1971. Under Charlemagne's successors, inflation forced the weight of the denarius down from 0.06 oz to 0.045 oz under King Charles the Bald (AD 840-77).

Coin of Charles the Bald, France

AFRICAN TRADE
During the 9th century AD, African communities hundreds of miles apart were in regular contact with one another, trading essential commodities like grain and prestige goods such as ivory and copper ingots. These trade networks, linking forest and savanna, became the basis for larger-scale trade in later times, as insatiable demand for African gold, ivory, and slaves stimulated commerce across the Sahara and the Indian Ocean. The availability of exotic raw materials led to the development of new technologies, such as lost-wax casting, in many regions of East and West Africa.

ART & RITUAL

ZOOMORPHIC EFFIGY VESSEL
This ceramic animal effigy vessel takes the form of a stylized puma or jaguar. The jar is decorated with painted geometric motifs using a resist technique: the lighter areas had a resin or wax applied so that the pigment would not adhere to those areas. Little is known about the cultures from the area where this vessel was found.

Effigy pot, Tungarahua, Ecuador

IMPERIAL FASHIONS
The cosmopolitan nature of the Tang Empire (AD 618-906) in China is reflected in tomb murals and figurines. Princes adopted Turkish attire, with boots and felt hats; women hunted and played polo in European-style men's clothing (coats with lapels and wide-brimmed hats), or wore high-waisted dresses with plunging necklines. In the early 9th century AD it was fashionable to be plump, and tomb figurines include voluptuous women in diaphanous robes, with elaborate hairstyles fastened with jewels.

ARABESQUES
Much sculptural decoration in the Middle East was derived from classical art. However, at the new Abbasid capital of Samarra in northern Iraq (founded AD 836), a beveled style of decoration derived from Central Asian woodwork evolved. With its characteristics of endless repetition and visual abstraction, it represented the purest and earliest form of the arabesque and was executed in wood, stucco, and other materials.

Carved teak panel, Samarra, Iraq

GATES OF VALHALLA
On the island of Gotland in Sweden, carved picture stones were erected as memorials to dead Viking warriors. They show battles, longships, and such mythological elements as a warrior's entrance into Valhalla, where slain heroes dwelt in bliss for eternity. On this stone, a dead warrior arrives at the gates of Valhalla on the eight-legged horse Sleipner and is greeted by a valkyrie, a minor goddess, who holds out a drinking horn to him.

Picture stone, Gotland, Sweden

ELEGANT GLASSWARE
Finely worked glass vessels were produced in North Africa during the early Islamic period, especially in the rich provinces of Egypt and Ifriqiyah (modern Tunisia). Many were designed as mosque lamps, but others were intended to adorn the tables of wealthy and discriminating patrons. Among those for the table were round-based bowls, decorated with delicately painted friezes of floral or geometric motifs.

Painted glass bowl, North Africa

AD 850-900

FOOD & ENVIRONMENT	SHELTER & ARCHITECTURE

AMERICAS

TRADE AND EXCHANGE

The Toltecs in Meso-america began to trade with the Anasazi and Hohokam peoples of south-western North America, through Casas Grandes in northern Mexico. Porters were used to transport the goods, since there were no draft animals or wheeled vehicles.

Codex showing porter, Mesoamerica

WINTER HUNTING CAMPS

From around AD 900, people moved from permanent villages in the forests of eastern Oklahoma into the western prairie for winter hunting. Dwellings at their short-term winter camps were probably round, dome-shaped, thatched structures about 16 feet in diameter.

Smoke hole

Winter dwelling, Drumming Sauna site, Oklahoma

EAST ASIA & AUSTRALASIA

NUTRITIOUS MOTHS

Bogong moths were an important source of summer food for Aborigines living in the Australian Alps in the southeastern part of the continent.

Each spring, millions of moths migrated to the area to spend four months dormant on the rocky summits. The Aborigines scraped them off the rock and roasted them. The moths, with abdomens the size of peanuts, had an oily, nutty taste, and were high in protein. They were consumed in large numbers when tribes came together for initiation ceremonies, marriages, and trade.

Bogong moth

TEMPLE CALENDAR

At the heart of Angkor, the royal capital founded by Yasovarman, ruler of the Cambodian Khmer kingdom from AD 889 to AD 910, stood the Bakheng, the king's own temple-mausoleum. Erected in a walled enclosure encircled by a wide moat, the Bakheng was designed to embody a complex cosmic symbolism: perfectly symmetrical, its seven levels represented seven heavens. On each of its four sides were 27 towers, representing the number of days in the lunar cycle, while on each of the seven terraces stood 12 towers, symbolizing the months of the year or the 12-year cycle of the planet Jupiter.

MIDDLE EAST & SOUTH ASIA

NORTH-SOUTH DIVIDE

Feudalism developed a strong grip in northern India in the 9th century AD. The peasants responsible for food produc-tion were treated like serfs, unable to leave the land. Local landowners were responsible for raising taxes to pay the central royal administration; otherwise they were largely autonomous. Towns became rare, trade declined, and villages were generally self-sufficient, with the majority of the population working on the land. In southern India, however, internal and overseas trade flourished: Arabs and Jews managed maritime trade with the west, while on the eastern coast, the Chola state sent its own ships overseas to the states of Southeast Asia and to China.

SPIRAL MINARET

The largest mosque in the Islamic Empire, known as the Great Mosque, was built by the Abbasid caliph al-Mutawakkil (AD 847-61) at Samarra, the Abbasid capital in central Iraq. Outside the north wall of the mosque proper stood a spiral minaret, which had an external staircase leading to a small throne room at the top.

Spiral staircase

Spiral minaret of the Great Mosque, Samarra, Iraq

EUROPE

CROP ROTATION

Farming in northwestern Europe underwent several important changes during the Viking period. One of these was the cultivation of rye, a cereal that flourished even in the cold, wet climate of southern Scandinavia. It gave much more reliable yields than wheat or barley, which had previously been the staple crops. Another funda-mental change was the adoption of the three-field system, in which farmland was divided into three blocks: one for sowing winter crops, the second for sowing spring crops, while the third was left fallow. Crops were rotated each year, allowing the fields to regain some of their fertility every third year. The improved yields led to the adoption of this system in many other parts of northwestern Europe during the 9th and 10th centuries AD.

ROMANESQUE CHURCHES

Romanesque church, Corvey, Germany

Impressive churches in the Romanesque style were built in France and Germany during the 9th century. They were the first truly great buildings in these regions since the collapse of the Roman Empire over 400 years earlier. A common feature of the period was the construction of a massive tower complex at the western end of the church, like that at Corvey, on the River Weser in Germany.

AFRICA

BANANA TRADE

Bananas were introduced to tropical East Africa from Southeast Asia via Madagascar (modern Malagasy Republic) about 2,000 years ago. The banana trade was one of the bases for the development of the first towns on the East African coast, which appeared in the 9th century AD, and it continued to be the focus of commerce across the Indian Ocean in later centuries.

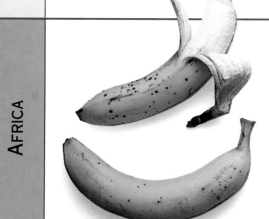

Bananas

MUD-BRICK TOWN

Jenne-jeno, at the southern edge of the Niger Delta in West Africa, had a population of between 5,000 and 10,000 people in the centuries pre-ceding AD 1000. The city wall, built of circular mud bricks, was up to 36 feet wide and extended for about 1 mile, enclosing houses both round and square in plan. Jenne-jeno was the largest of more than 40 mud-brick settlements within a radius of 15 miles. Their inhabitants depended on fishing and rice growing, and main-tained trade contacts along the Niger River, with gold and salt traders from the Sahara and, increasingly, with Islamic merchants from the north.

TECHNOLOGY & INNOVATION

JADE AMULETS

Masklike headdress

Apple-green jade from Guatemala and southern Mexico was prized by the Maya, who often carved amulets conforming to the shape of the stone. Those shown here date to AD 900; one depicts a ruler in typical seated pose, the other represents the head of a noble or priest wearing a masklike headdress.

Maya jade carvings, Mexico

EARLIEST PRINTED BOOK

The earliest known complete wood-block printed book with wood-cut illustration is the *Diamond Sutra*, printed in China in AD 868. Made from seven rolls of paper pasted together, and over 16 feet long in all, it was double-folded into book form. Both the frontispiece and the calligraphy reflect highly advanced wood-cutting and printing techniques.

Frontispiece from the *Diamond Sutra*, Dunhuang, Gansu, China

LUSTER DECORATION

Inspired by imports from China, rapid progress was made in decorating ceramics in the Middle East. An important development was the addition of decorative luster (an extremely thin metallic film); this became a typical feature of Middle Eastern ceramics.

Bowl with painted luster decoration, Samarra, Iraq

IRON SWORDS

Viking warriors used iron swords of exceptional quality, and although some were made in Scandinavia, the best were fashioned by swordsmiths in England or the Rhineland in Germany. Generally, sword blades were double-edged with slightly blunted tips. Some were inlaid and had richly decorated hilts. Used for slashing rather than thrusting at the enemy, swords were carried in decorated scabbards.

Viking sword blade

MEASURING THE FLOOD

The Islamic governors of Egypt, who were appointed by the caliphate in Samarra, central Iraq, built a new nilometer in AD 861 to measure the height of the annual Nile flood. It was built on Roda, an island in the Nile near the heart of modern Cairo, and was designed by the mathematician Ahmad ibn-Muhammad. The device consisted of a square stone-lined pit, connected by tunnels to the river. At the center of the pit stood a graduated column, which served as a marker to determine the height of the flood. This structure was the latest of the nilometers built by successive Egyptian governments for tax assessment. The higher the flood, the more land was inundated and made suitable for cultivation, and the greater the government tax revenue.

ART & RITUAL

SYMBOLS OF STATUS

Chiefs in Honduras carried ceremonial stone axes as symbols of status and prowess in warfare. This ceramic bust, possibly of a chief, shows a small stone ax being carried over one shoulder. The ax is typical of those used throughout Central America at this time.

Ceramic bust, Honduras

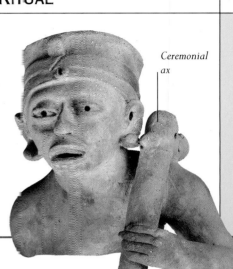

Ceremonial ax

ACT OF DEVOTION

Large-scale tanks and reservoirs were a prominent feature of early Cambodian temple complexes. In the powerful Khmer kingdom centered in Angkor, the pattern for later generations was set by King Indravarman I (AD 877-89), who built a rectangular tank known as the Indratataka, which was 2 miles long and over half a mile wide. This gigantic structure was 150 times larger than any reservoir previously built and held an estimated 300 million cubic feet of water. While some of the water was probably used for irrigation and domestic needs in the vicinity, the purpose of the Indratataka was also religio-symbolic — representing the mountain lakes around the mythical Himalayan home of the Hindu gods. The construction of this tank was not only a great feat of engineering, but also an act of devotion.

WOOD CARVING

Most early Indian art and architecture has vanished, since it was executed in perishable materials such as wood, textiles, and bark. Due to exceptional conditions, some pieces have been preserved, such as this decorated wooden column base from Smats Cave in the northern state of Kashmir.

Wooden column base, Smats Cave, Kashmir

ANGLO-SAXON MASTERPIECE

A masterpiece of Anglo-Saxon artistry, the Alfred Jewel bears the enameled figure of a man, which shows clearly through the polished surface of rock crystal. The jewel takes its name from an inscription on the gold frame, which is written in Old English and reads "Alfred had me made." It may indeed have belonged to Alfred the Great, King of Wessex in southern England from AD 871 to 899.

The Alfred Jewel, England

Bronze altar stand, Igbo Ukwu, Nigeria

Filigree decoration

BURIED BRONZES

An 8th- or 9th-century burial at Igbo Ukwu, Nigeria, testifies to the wealth of the local elite. The deceased dignitary was dressed in full ceremonial regalia and was accompanied by at least five sacrificed attendants, as well as superb bronzes, including altar stands adorned with filigree decoration.

AD 900-950

FOOD & ENVIRONMENT	SHELTER & ARCHITECTURE

AMERICAS

SOIL CONSERVATION

Soil erosion in the Andes was and still is the worst enemy of agriculture in the region. By denuding the land of moisture and fertility, erosion prevented the cultivation of key crops such as peanuts. To keep erosion in check, farming communities developed various strategies for soil conservation, such as the construction of terraced and ridged fields, and crop rotation.

Peanuts in cloth, Peru

MOUND COMPLEX

The most complex settlement in eastern North America was the Toltec site in central Arkansas. It derives its name from a 19th-century AD misattribution to the Toltec of Mexico, but it was actually built by people of the Plum Bayou culture. An important religious center, the site consisted of several burial and platform mounds and a large embankment, which acted as a fortification. It was abandoned around AD 900.

Embankment
Mound
Pit

Plan, the Toltec site, Arkansas

EAST ASIA & AUSTRALASIA

AGRICULTURAL TAXATION

In Cambodia, the maintenance of the Khmer kingdom and army depended on food supplied by peasant farmers. This was delivered through a system of taxation that, in the absence of coinage, involved payments in kind. In order to provide this, farmers had to produce a substantial surplus in addition to their own needs. In the immediate vicinity of Angkor, the Khmer royal capital, this was made easier by the extraordinary natural productivity of the lowland area around the Tonle Sap lake. The lake flooded each year, and it was possible to raise as many as three or four crops of rice annually on the fertile silt left when the waters receded. Government officials assessed the quality of land holdings and recorded them in land registers, which they used as a basis for calculating taxes due in rice and other crops.

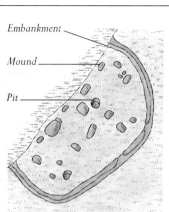

PAGODAS

The mixed architectural origins of the Chinese pagoda are reflected in two dominant styles. Some pagodas, like the one shown here, followed an Indian Buddhist prototype: these hollow stone buildings were decorated with Buddhist motifs. Others, derived from the ancient tradition of Chinese watchtowers, were multistory constructions of brick or stone, with a central staircase and corridors leading to windows and doors on each floor.

Pagoda, Qixia temple, Nanjing, Jiangsu, China

MIDDLE EAST & SOUTH ASIA

INVESTING IN LAND

In favorable environments, such as the fertile plains of Mesopotamia, agriculture was an attractive means of earning revenue from the investment of capital, and an alternative to the more common forms of investment in trade and mercantile ventures. It became a particularly attractive investment in Mesopotamia between AD 886 and AD 893, when maritime trade was disrupted by a rebellion of slaves in southern Iraq. New estates were established from Iran to the Mediterranean coast to produce crops that required capital investment for their success, including rice, sugarcane, and cotton. The appearance of discursive books on agronomy, such as the *Kitab al-filaha al-Nabatiyya* (*Nabataean Agriculture*) written by Ibn Wahshiyya in Iraq in AD 904, was symptomatic of this trend toward a more profit-conscious agricultural economy.

ISLAMIC MAUSOLEUMS

Mausoleums began to appear in the Middle East in the 10th century. They were most popular in Egypt, but their appeal reached as far east as the area of Central Asia ruled by the Samanid Dynasty from AD 874-979, who had their capital at Bukhara in Uzbekistan.

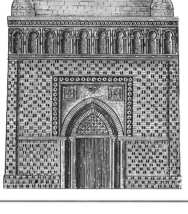

Samanid mausoleum, Bukhara, Uzbekistan

EUROPE

Pine branch

FOREST CLEARANCE

By the 10th century AD, the economy of western Europe gradually began to recover after years of unsettled conditions caused by barbarian raids. This is reflected at Dunum in northwestern Germany, where large areas of mixed woodland were cleared to make room for new villages.

LOCAL BUILDING MATERIALS

Viking houses varied in design and building material, depending on what was locally available. This house from the Viking town of Hedeby in northern Germany was of timber frame construction with walls of wattle and daub. The external posts sloped outwards to give extra support to the walls and the pitched roof, which was covered with reed thatch.

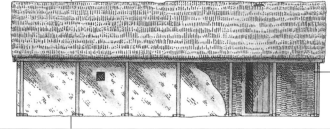

External posts

Viking house, Hedeby, Germany

AFRICA

DAIRY FARMERS

Cattle were vitally important to the early farming cultures that flourished on the grasslands of the Central African plateau. Milk played an important part in the diet and was collected and stored in bag-shaped pots with turned-out rims. These may have been modeled on leather prototypes.

Milk vessel, Central Africa

CATTLE ENCLOSURES

The early farmers of southern Africa lived in an environment where lions and other predators were a constant threat. In the 10th century they began to erect oval cattle enclosures, such as that at Leopard's Kopje in Zimbabwe, topping the rough stone walls with thorny brush to keep out intruders. Such enclosures were the predecessors of more elaborate stone architecture in later centuries.

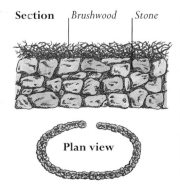

Section *Brushwood* *Stone*

Plan view

Cattle enclosure, Leopard's Kopje, Zimbabwe

| TECHNOLOGY & INNOVATION | ART & RITUAL |

TOOL MANUFACTURE

Grooved abraders made of stone were used to shape and smooth arrow shafts or sharpen awls. Abraders were usually portable items, although sometimes they were hewn from the bedrock. This portable example, notable for its symmetry and fine workmanship, comes from the Mimbres Valley in New Mexico and probably dates to the early 10th century AD, when the valley inhabitants were also producing striking decorated ceramics.

Arrow-shaft smoother, Mimbres Valley, New Mexico

OFFERING TABLES

Ceramic offering tables from the Chiriqui region of Panama in Central America are similar to wooden tables found in layers of volcanic deposits in the region. The wooden tables, often carved from a single tree, frequently take the form of stylized animal figures that are reminiscent of those portrayed in goldwork from Veraguas in Panama.

Ceramic offering table, Chiriqui, Panama

SPREAD OF WRITING

The Koreans adopted the Chinese script by the 7th century AD, and later exported it to Japan. During the 10th century AD, in the Khitan, a kingdom on China's northeastern frontier, a writing system was devised. It was based on 3,000 Chinese characters modified for the Khitan language. In AD 1036, the Mongolians followed suit. Chinese characters, however, were designed for an uninflected language and were unsuited to multisyllabic languages with complicated grammar. In time these hybrids were abandoned: the Koreans invented a new alphabet, and the Mongolians adopted an alphabetic system derived from Aramaic.

POLYNESIAN RELIGION

Religious beliefs in Polynesia varied from island to island, and sometimes even between different communities on a single island. In eastern Polynesia, the four principal deities were Tangaroa (connected with the sea), Rongo (god of war), Tu (associated with farming) and Tane (god of forests and procreation). Religion permeated almost every area of Polynesian craftsmanship, and many craft specialists, including woodcarvers and canoe-builders, were also priests.

ARABIC ALPHABET

Derived from earlier Semitic alphabets, the Arabic script had been in use at Mecca since before the time of Muhammad. Several flowing styles of Arabic writing had developed under the impetus of recording the Koran, and these multiplied dramatically in the 10th century. Abu Ali Ibn Muqlah, a vizier who served under the caliphs in Baghdad and died in AD 940, devised geometric principles for the six major scripts, a system that has been followed ever since.

PERSONAL DEVOTION

Throughout India, Hindu devotional cults (those focusing on one deity to the exclusion of others) were becoming more popular. In the north, cults devoted to Vishnu and his various incarnations, notably Krishna, were prevalent. In southern India, the god Shiva was the main object of devotion. Increasing rigidity in Brahman orthodoxy, combined with greater emphasis on caste purity, made devotional cults most appealing to those of lower caste.

Bronze statue of Vishnu, India

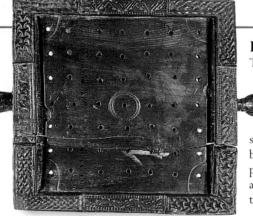

BOARD GAMES

This wooden game board found in Ireland was probably made in the Isle of Man during the 10th century AD. The holes were for small playing pieces of wood, bone, or ivory. The board game played may have resembled "fox and geese," in which players seek to corner their opponents.

Game board, Ballinderry, Ireland

PAGANS AND CHRISTIANS

In the early 10th century AD, the Viking kings of Denmark and Sweden continued to be buried under large burial mounds in the pagan tradition, despite the advances that Christianity had been making in both kingdoms. At Jelling, the Danish capital, two large mounds stood on either side of a Christian church. One was the resting place of the pagan king Gorm the Old (reigned c. AD 940-950). The other is a cenotaph mound with no actual burial, which was built by Gorm's son and successor, Harald Bluetooth (reigned c. AD 950-84), who had converted to Christianity. Harald had his parents' bodies removed from their burial mound and reinterred in the church where he himself was also eventually buried.

SALT TRADE

Salt was an essential commodity for African farmers, whose diet was made up predominantly of carbohydrates. They made salt by boiling reeds and grasses, but preferred it in cake form. Sources of cake salt were rare and therefore of great economic value. Cake salt was traded from the Sahara south to the Sahel (on the borders of modern Mali and Mauritania) and tropical West Africa, in exchange for gold, ivory, and kola nuts. With the arrival of camels from Arabia in the 1st millennium AD, the volume of the salt trade rose dramatically.

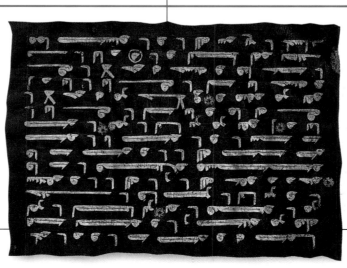

DECORATIVE WRITING

Named after the holy city of Kufa in southern Iraq, Kufic script was a decorative version of Arabic that came into widespread use in North Africa during the 10th century AD. It was specifically designed for ornamental use on panels carved with geometric decoration or in manuscripts like this, where the script is of gold leaf. Its angularity made Kufic script easier to carve than the usual flowing script.

Leaf from a Koran in Kufic script, Tunisia

AD 950 - 1000

FOOD & ENVIRONMENT

SHELTER & ARCHITECTURE

AMERICAS

CLIMATIC DISRUPTION

Every so often, fishing along the Pacific coastline of Peru was disrupted by severe climatic disturbances lasting from a few months to several years. These were caused by warm currents affecting the coast, which destroyed cold-water marine fauna. This climatic phenomenon is known as *El Niño* (the child).

Fishing net, coastal Peru

HIGHLAND CAPITAL

Marcahuamachuco, a powerful highland capital in Peru's northern sierra, was a center of regional commerce and interaction. Its inhabitants developed specialized architecture

Rectangular enclosure, Marcahuamachuco, Peru

for public and private use. They built rectangular enclosures for housing and round *colcas* (storage houses) for food. The city was also fortified with walls to protect against raids by warring groups such as the Cuismancu.

— Stone walls

— Doorway

EAST ASIA & AUSTRALASIA

TEA DRINKING

Tea became a popular drink in China in the 10th century AD, having been confined to the privileged classes for several centuries. Its production and distribution came under government control, but it retained its prestigious status, and great importance was attached to the quality of leaves and the design and workmanship of the vessels in which it was served.

Tea leaves

ISLAND HOUSES

The inhabitants of Easter Island, the easternmost of the Polynesian islands, lived in square or rectangular houses, sometimes with a curb of stones at the base. The superstructure was probably a framework of wooden poles, bent over and tied together to form a crude vault. This was covered with reeds or grass thatching. Most settlements consisted of two or three such houses with associated fields and modest, crudely built ritual platforms and

pavements, the domestic equivalent of the *ahu* (ceremonial stone shrine platform). Despite the small size of individual settlements, some parts of Easter Island were densely populated; in one area, no fewer than 400 house foundations have been found, dating to between AD 800 and AD 1300.

MIDDLE EAST & SOUTH ASIA

RISE OF FEUDALISM

The powerful Abbasid Empire, which had dominated the Middle East for 200 years, began to decline in the 10th century AD, ushering in a period of instability and agricultural disruption. In Syria and Iraq, Bedouin nomads from the desert began to threaten settled populations, especially those living in scattered rural communities, many of whom fled. Flight from the countryside was matched by the depopulation of towns

such as Basra, Kufa, Wasit, and Mosul, and urban breakdown led to the spread of epidemics. The situation worsened in the second half of the 10th century AD: a new dynasty, which had seized control in AD 945, introduced a feudal land tenure system to pay its troops. The recipients of these lands incurred no financial obligations, and there was no investment. Exhausted land was exchanged for new estates and irrigation systems fell into disuse.

COMPLEX SQUINCH

The earliest complex squinch (a half-dome built across a corner to support a larger dome) is in a mausoleum at Tim, near Samarkand in Uzbekistan, Central Asia. Successor to the Iranian squinch, the squinch at Tim was divided into *muqarnas* (smaller elements), to distribute weight more evenly.

Bottom of dome

Exterior of squinch arch

Exterior corner

***Muqarnas* squinch, Tim, Uzbekistan**

EUROPE

EXOTIC CROPS

The spread of the Islamic Empire across North Africa (by AD 680) and into Spain (by AD 800) brought many new vegetables and fruits to southern Europe. In the 10th and 11th centuries AD, spinach, eggplants, rice, and melons, all of South Asian origin, made their first appearance in the Mediterranean, along with new tree crops such as lemons, oranges, and mangoes.

Orange, lemon, and mango

TOWER REFUGES

Slender towers around 100 feet high were built in Ireland during the period of the Viking raids, the finest of them during the 10th and 11th centuries AD. They were built next to churches and monasteries as refuges and as repositories for church valuables. The doors were set well above ground level and could be reached only by a retractable ladder.

— *Door reached by retractable ladder*

Round tower, Glendalough, Ireland

AFRICA

COCONUT PRODUCTS

Coconuts were an important resource for East African coastal communities. Introduced to the region from Southeast Asia a few centuries earlier, by AD 1000 they were being used for making wine. The palm provided tough fiber for making matting and ship's ropes, and for caulking the hulls of dhows.

Coconuts

Lozi chief's enclosure, Zambia

Plan view

Side view

CHIEFS' RESIDENCES

As previously egalitarian societies evolved into chiefdoms in southern Africa around AD 1000, leaders began to distance themselves from their subjects, living in virtual seclusion inside high-walled enclosures of grass, mud, or stone. Here the chief dispensed justice and presided over important ceremonies. A similar enclosure is still inhabited by the Litunga, paramount chief of the Lozi people of western Zambia.

TECHNOLOGY & INNOVATION

STONE EFFIGIES

Made from a dense brown stone, this carving, which resembles a duck, was made in Puerto Rico and dates to between AD 950 and AD 1500. It may have been used as the head of a war club or as a symbol of status. Traces of paint show that the head and wings were colored blue and the body white.

Eye

Wing

Bird effigy, Puerto Rico

STONE QUARRIES

The stone quarries in the Rano Raraku volcanic crater at the center of Easter Island were first worked in the 10th or 11th century AD. Over the following 700 years, about 1,000 of the famous Easter Island statues were made from the yellow-brown volcanic stone. As no metal tools were available, the carvers had to rely on hammers made of basalt. The statues were carved at the quarry, then lowered down the slope of the volcano using a system of ropes attached to wooden scaffolding that was fixed to the rock near the crater rim.

Quarry, Rano Raraku, Easter Island

EDUCATIONAL CENTER

Buddhism continued to flourish in eastern India while on the wane in other parts of the country. Buddhist monasteries, such as the one at Nalanda near Patna, had long acted as major economic and cultural focal points, as well as being centers of learning with libraries of religious texts and theological instruction provided by monks. During the 10th century AD, the monastery at Nalanda was restored and extended, and it eventually became the major educational center for the whole of northern India.

ROYAL MINT

Coinage in Anglo-Saxon England during the 10th century AD was tightly controlled by the state, which issued coins from mints in only a handful of major towns. Apart from the coins themselves, which usually bear the name of the town in which they were made, coin dies and trial strikings on lead strip have also been found.

Coin die and trial piece, York, England

WEAVING

Cotton was grown in low-lying river valleys in eastern and southern Africa. It was woven into coarse cloth on basic looms; the weavers used pieces of broken pottery for spindle weights, grinding them into disks and perforating them through the center. The cotton was often dyed, and weavers produced multicolored patterns, usually of geometric design. Weaving was especially important on the East African coast, but the highest-quality fabrics still continued to be imported from the Middle East.

ART & RITUAL

POLYCHROME POTTERY

Together with its three bird-shaped legs, the shape, motifs, and many colors of this vessel from the island of Ometepe are typical of pottery made across a large area of Nicaragua and Costa Rica at this time. The artistic style was strongly influenced by trade contacts with centers of Mayan civilization to the north.

Polychrome vessel, Nicaragua

GLAZED STONEWARE

The production of stoneware fired at extremely high temperatures reached its peak in the Yue kilns in central China. Made from very fine clay, these elegant vessels had a thin silvery-green glaze and were either plain or adorned with incised decoration. They were prized for their durability and exported to the Philippines, Indonesia, the Persian Gulf, and Egypt.

Yue ware jug and vase, China

BRONZE FIGURINES

Portable bronze images of deities, such as this bronze of Shiva, were produced on a lavish scale in both eastern and southern India for display in processions during religious festivals. The figurines were produced by the lost-wax technique. Bronzes from the north were hollow, but those made under the auspices of the Chola Dynasty (9th-12th centuries AD) in the south were solid-cast, which gives some indication of the immense wealth that existed in the region.

Chola bronze figurine of Shiva, southern India

BYZANTINE ART

The 10th century AD was a great era of Byzantine art, as Byzantine cultural influences began to spread northward into Slavic lands, a process fostered by trade and marriage alliances. The influence of Byzantine art also spread west along trade routes to Venice. St. Mark's Basilica was rebuilt there in the 11th century AD and decorated with Byzantine-style gilded mosaics like this example, which shows Noah intoxicated after the Flood.

Gilded mosaic, St. Mark's Basilica, Venice, Italy

CLAY FIGURINES

The people of Zimbabwe fashioned stylized figurines of animals and humans in clay. Some may have served as children's toys, but others were probably fertility symbols, used in planting and harvesting rituals and in rainmaking ceremonies. Similar figurines were made at the same time by people living north of the Zambezi River and in South Africa. A tradition of wood-carving also existed, probably for creating figurines and elaborate ceremonial masks.

PUEBLO VILLAGES

The deserts and high-altitude forests of southwestern North America might appear to be unlikely, if not impossible, environments for the growth of agricultural societies hundreds of years before the invention of such modern necessities as electric pumps and deep wells. Yet, by AD 700, small blocks of adjoining rooms became the first pueblos – a term used by 16th-century Spanish explorers to describe the large apartment villages they encountered. By AD 1000 many pueblos consisted of 200 rooms or more. One of the most spectacular groups of pueblos was in Chaco Canyon, northwestern New Mexico. Several large buildings, each containing hundreds of rooms, were constructed along a small stream. The success of each of these pueblos depended on water control. Methods used to conserve and funnel rain to the fields involved the intensive use of dams and irrigation systems.

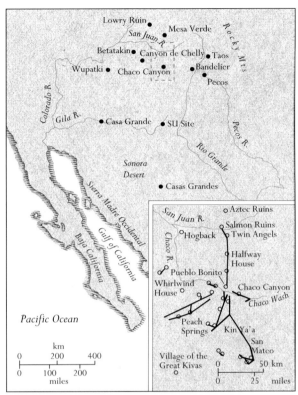

— Road system   ○ Site of Chaco regional system

PUEBLO SITES *left*
Important sites of the different southwestern cultures are found in the region that encompasses Arizona, New Mexico, southern Utah, Colorado, and northern Sonora and Chihuahua in Mexico. A remarkable road network was built in north-western New Mexico (*inset map*) between AD 900 and 1140, with its hub at Chaco Canyon. The roads extended for hundreds of miles across desert and canyon lands. In the absence of pack animals other than dogs, and given the relatively sparse foot traffic, it is still a mystery why the roads were up to 33 feet wide, running in straight lines for many miles.

MULTISTORIED GREAT HOUSES *below*
In the Sonora Desert around the modern city of Phoenix, Arizona, people of the Hohokam culture (which dates from AD 1 to 1450) built pithouse villages and later (by AD 1300) multistoried buildings. These "Great Houses" reflect architectural influences from northern Arizona where large, multiroom buildings were common. Casa Grande is the only Great House still standing.

MASONRY STYLES *below*
Some of the finest stonework in North America was used in the construction of the pueblos in Chaco Canyon. The intricate placement of small stones on the exterior of the wall is all the more remarkable since the walls were not meant to be seen, but were covered with a layer of plaster.

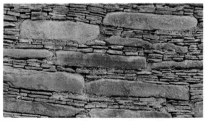

Masonry using stones of similar size

Masonry using large and small stones

Reconstruction of Pueblo Bonito, New Mexico

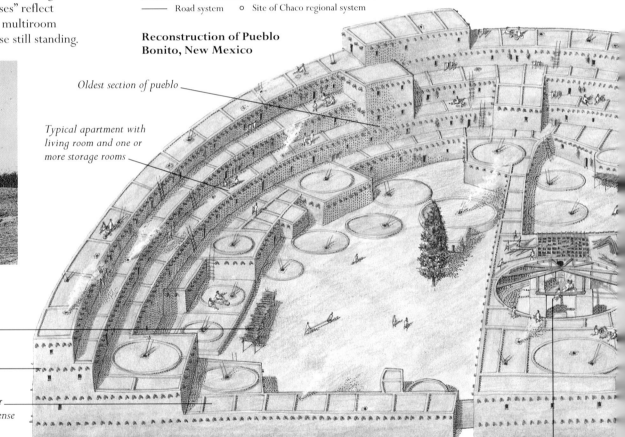

Oldest section of pueblo

Typical apartment with living room and one or more storage rooms

Arbor to provide shaded outdoor work space

Protruding pine-beam floor support

Continuous perimeter wall for effective defense

Great Kiva under construction

STONE AND MORTAR *below*
The walls of Pueblo Bonito were made of stone and mud mortar. The floors and roofs were made of beams and cross-beams covered by layers of bark, willow mats, and a final layer of soil. Construction methods changed little, although later rooms were more carefully laid out with greater attention paid to wall and roof details.

Cross section showing floor and wall

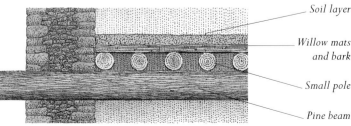

Soil layer

Willow mats and bark

Small pole

Pine beam

VILLAGE LIFE IN PUEBLO BONITO *above and right*
One of the largest and most complex pueblos, Pueblo Bonito was built between AD 900 and 1150 and may have been an administrative or religious center. The close-knit agricultural community that lived here paid careful attention to changes in the weather. Fields were tended while domestic chores were performed on the pueblo's terraces. Household activities included grinding and storing maize and other crops, preparing meals, manufacturing pottery, weaving, hauling water, and tending the children. Woven throughout the pattern of daily life was a spirituality that bound the community together. Rituals were performed in the *kivas*, or ceremonial rooms (*right*), the people asking the gods for rain to safeguard crops and ensure prosperity. *Kivas* also functioned as meeting places and were used as workplaces by weavers.

AD 800-1000

CRAFTS AND TRADE

In addition to carrying on with everyday household and farming chores, the pueblo people were a community of artisans. They worked with many types of locally available materials and the more exotic materials that could only be acquired through long-distance trade. At Pueblo Bonito in Chaco Canyon, artisans worked with many different materials: among them, various fibers for weaving, clay for pottery, bone, shell, wood, lignite (a type of coal), and many types of stone. Turquoise was especially important because it was highly valued in Mexico and the pueblos could trade it for tropical bird feathers and other exotic items from the south.

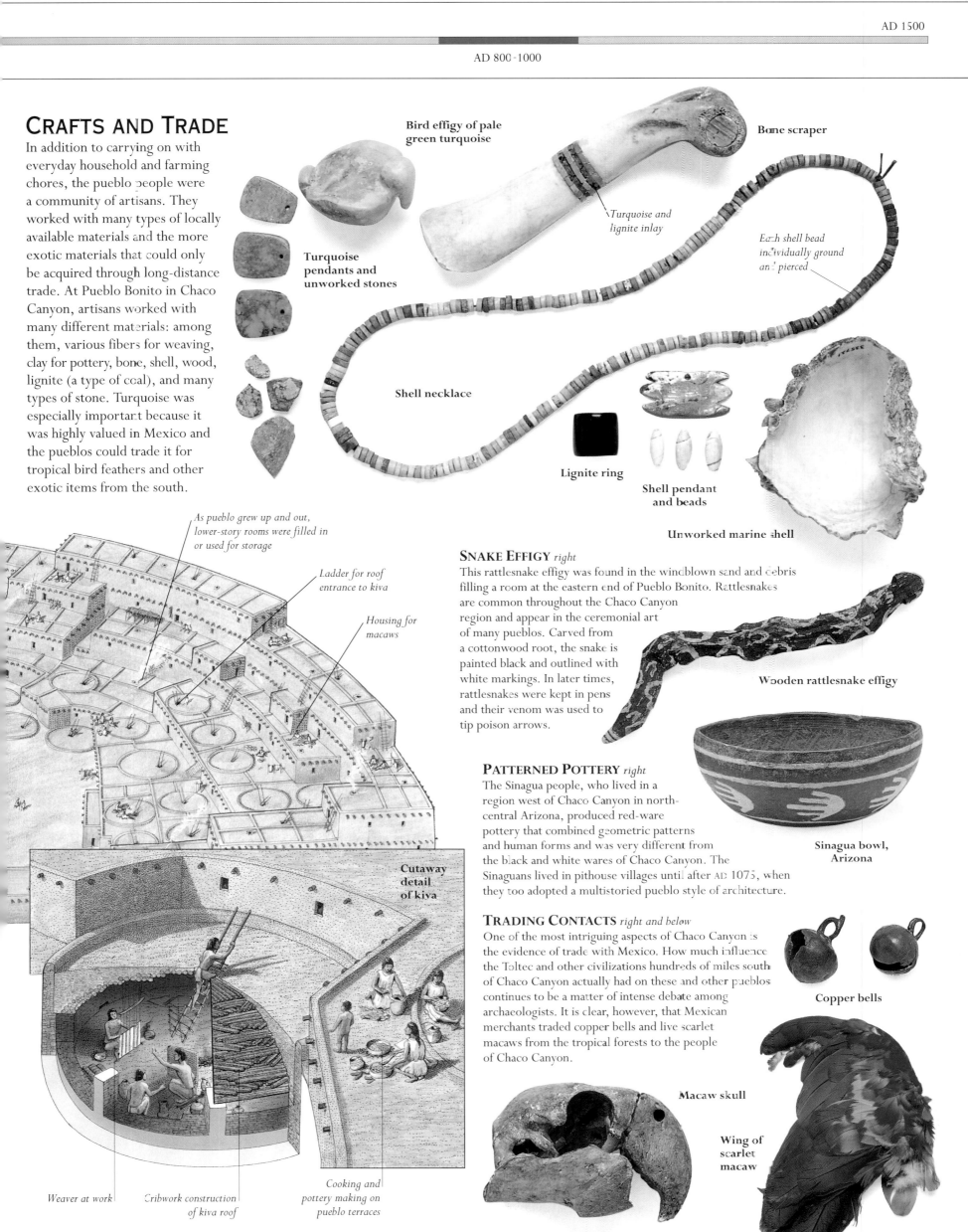

Bird effigy of pale green turquoise

Bone scraper

Turquoise and lignite inlay

Each shell bead individually ground and pierced

Turquoise pendants and unworked stones

Shell necklace

Lignite ring

Shell pendant and beads

Unworked marine shell

As pueblo grew up and out, lower-story rooms were filled in or used for storage

Ladder for roof entrance to kiva

Housing for macaws

Cutaway detail of kiva

Weaver at work

Cribwork construction of kiva roof

Cooking and pottery making on pueblo terraces

SNAKE EFFIGY *right*

This rattlesnake effigy was found in the windblown sand and debris filling a room at the eastern end of Pueblo Bonito. Rattlesnakes are common throughout the Chaco Canyon region and appear in the ceremonial art of many pueblos. Carved from a cottonwood root, the snake is painted black and outlined with white markings. In later times, rattlesnakes were kept in pens and their venom was used to tip poison arrows.

Wooden rattlesnake effigy

PATTERNED POTTERY *right*

The Sinagua people, who lived in a region west of Chaco Canyon in north-central Arizona, produced red-ware pottery that combined geometric patterns and human forms and was very different from the black and white wares of Chaco Canyon. The Sinaguans lived in pithouse villages until after AD 1075, when they too adopted a multistoried pueblo style of architecture.

Sinagua bowl, Arizona

TRADING CONTACTS *right and below*

One of the most intriguing aspects of Chaco Canyon is the evidence of trade with Mexico. How much influence the Toltec and other civilizations hundreds of miles south of Chaco Canyon actually had on these and other pueblos continues to be a matter of intense debate among archaeologists. It is clear, however, that Mexican merchants traded copper bells and live scarlet macaws from the tropical forests to the people of Chaco Canyon.

Copper bells

Macaw skull

Wing of scarlet macaw

CHAPTER 17
CONQUESTS & CRUSADES
AD 1000-1250

Crusaders capture Jerusalem and establish Christian kingdoms in the Levant

Early kingdoms of Southeast Asia reach the height of their power

Large towns develop in eastern North America

Mongols invade and take control of the Middle East and China

Trading kingdoms prosper in West Africa

The 11th and 12th centuries AD were periods of major new developments in many parts of the world. In the Pacific, the inhabitants of Easter Island began to erect the stone statues for which the island is famous. Elsewhere, impressive religious buildings were constructed – Gothic cathedrals in western Europe and Hindu-Buddhist temples in Southeast Asia. South of the Sahara in West Africa, prosperous trading kingdoms arose, connected by caravan routes with the Islamic states of coastal North Africa. In eastern North America, large towns were built, characterized by ceremonial platform and burial mounds.

Christian architecture

In Europe during the 12th and 13th centuries AD, power was divided between secular barons and ecclesiastical dignitaries such as bishops and abbots. Cathedrals and monastic churches testified to the strength of religious authority. By AD 1100, the Romanesque style of architecture was giving way to the Gothic style, in which load-bearing was concentrated in piers and flying buttresses. The spaces between the piers were filled by magnificent stained-glass windows. Monasteries proliferated and many monastic orders, including the Cluniacs and Cistercians, were founded. The wealth needed to build the cathedrals

BIBLICAL STORIES
The stained-glass windows of Gothic cathedrals, like this example from Chartres Cathedral, France, depict biblical stories and scenes from the lives of saints.

rich and powerful on the profits of trade with the Middle East. It was with the help of these cities that an army of Crusaders, fired with religious zeal to recover the Holy Places from Muslims, invaded the Levant (the coastal strip of Syria, Lebanon, and Israel) and captured Jerusalem in AD 1099. The Crusaders, mostly lords and retainers from western Europe, founded a series of states in the Levant, building castles and cathedrals. The foremost of these states was the Christian kingdom of Jerusalem, which survived until AD 1291, although the city of Jerusalem itself was retaken in AD 1187 by the armies of the Muslim hero, Saladin.

of western Europe came largely from agriculture, although trade and manufacturing were on the rise and walled towns of prosperous merchant communities were well established in many regions. In southern Europe, commerce played a more prominent role, with Italian cities such as Pisa and Venice growing immensely

SCULPTURAL DECORATION
Stone sculptures of *nagas* (mythical Hindu beasts that are half-human, half-serpent) are among the many sculptures adorning the temple of Angkor Wat in Cambodia.

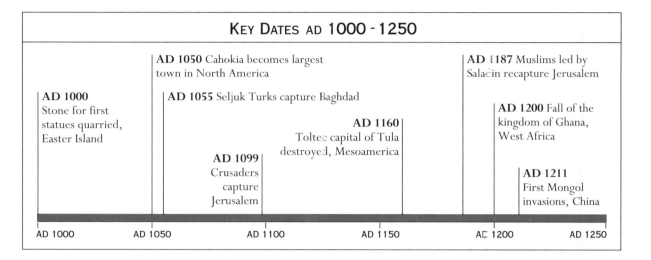

AD 1000 Stone for first statues quarried, Easter Island

AD 1050 Cahokia becomes largest town in North America

AD 1055 Seljuk Turks capture Baghdad

AD 1099 Crusaders capture Jerusalem

AD 1160 Toltec capital of Tula destroyed, Mesoamerica

AD 1187 Muslims led by Saladin recapture Jerusalem

AD 1200 Fall of the kingdom of Ghana, West Africa

AD 1211 First Mongol invasions, China

AD 1000   AD 1050   AD 1100   AD 1150   AD 1200   AD 1250

ANIMAL SYMBOLISM

Found in Georgia, this pot is decorated with a rattlesnake with falcon wings and deer antlers – Mississippian symbols for the underworld, the sky, and the earth.

Extensive kingdoms

The early kingdoms of Southeast Asia reached their height between the 11th and 13th centuries AD. Ever larger and more splendid Hindu-Buddhist temples were built at major centers, including Pagan in Burma and Angkor, capital of the Khmer kingdom in Cambodia. The Angkor temples are decorated with carved stone relief-friezes showing armies locked in combat and hostile flotillas of boats driven back by Khmer soldiers on the Mekong River and other scenes showing royal feasts and ceremonies.

Growth and demise of cultures

The largest of the towns that arose in the Mississippi Valley in central North America was Cahokia, with a population of around 10,000 people. A series of ceremonial mounds and plazas stood in the center of the town. Other mounds were used for the burials of the local elite. In southwestern North America the Chaco Canyon pueblos reached their peak, then declined in the mid-12th century AD. The amount of dependable farmland in the region was reduced from AD 1050 due to fluctuating patterns of rainfall. As populations in some areas decreased, settlements like the cliff-dwellings of Mesa Verde continued to grow. From AD 1250, however, diminished water supplies caused large areas of the southwest to be abandoned.

In Mexico, Tula – the Toltec capital – was burned at the end of the 12th century AD, and looted by successive groups.

Despite this, the city continued to be occupied until the 16th century AD. In the Oaxaca region around AD 1000, the Mixtec culture mingled with the Zapotecs, appropriating their buildings and tombs. Founding a major center at Tilantongo, the Mixtecs became expert metalworkers and ceramists. Meanwhile on Peru's northern coast, the Chimu people built grand centers and extended their capital, Chanchan.

Rise of hierarchical societies

On the Pacific islands, populations grew and new types of society emerged. Temple-platforms were extended, notably on Easter Island, where stone for the island's statues was first quarried around AD 1000. Projects like these required cohesive labor, indicating that Polynesian island societies were becoming more complex and hierarchical and that power lay in the hands of a lineage of chiefs.

Circle of punched dots represents an ear spool

FUNERARY MASKS

The Chimu people on Peru's northern coast produced large gold and silver laminate masks, which they used as funerary masks to cover the faces of mummified bodies.

CERAMIC CENTER

Kashan in western Iran became a major center of ceramic production in Seljuk times. This bowl is an example of the lustrous polychrome-glazed ware produced there.

213

AD 1000-1250

Successive conquerors

In the Middle East, the period from AD 1000 to AD 1250 was marked by Crusader invasions from the west and disruption by Turks and Muslims from the northeast. In the 11th century AD the Seljuk Turks, who came from what is now Turkmenistan in Central Asia, conquered Mesopotamia and Iran. This was a time of great mathematicians and astronomers, including Omar Khayyám, and of major architectural innovations such as the development of the cylindrical minaret, which soon became a distinctive feature of Islamic cities. The Seljuks lost control of the Middle East in the 13th century AD, overwhelmed by nomadic Mongols under Genghis Khan. Population and prosperity gradually declined as irrigation systems were neglected and peasants fled the land. In the east, the Mongols also conquered China, bringing to an end the rule of the Song Dynasty (AD 960-1279).

Militaristic society and political diversity

In Japan, a militaristic society held sway during these centuries, based on powerful *daimyos* (warrior lords) bound by ties of allegiance to a *shogun* (overlord). The *mikado* (emperor) retained little real power. Japanese *samurai* (warriors) fought with long swords of finely tempered steel and adhered to a rigid code of honor known as *bushido*.

In South Asia, this period was one of religious and political diversity. Buddhism remained dominant in Sri Lanka, where the state capital was moved from Anuradhapura to Polonnaruwa. In peninsular India, the Hindu Chola Dynasty (mid 9th-12th centuries AD) retained power in the south, but in the north Turkish rulers from Afghanistan, recently converted to Islam, began to wrest control from local *rajahs* (kings) in the 11th century AD, a process that culminated in the establishment of the Islamic Delhi sultanate in the early 13th century AD. Architects working for the new regime developed artistic and architectural styles that successfully combined traditional Islamic and Indian features.

Lucrative trading routes

In East Africa, the Islamic towns along the coast continued to flourish, exchanging goods from the African interior for merchandise from the Middle East, India, and China. North Africa was fragmented into a number of smaller kingdoms ruled by local dynasties after the demise of the united Islamic Empire of the 8th and 9th centuries AD. From North Africa trade routes passed southward over the Sahara to important trading centres including Gao, Timbuktu, Jenne-jeno, and Kumbi Saleh. These towns formed the core of the savanna empires of Ghana (8th-11th centuries AD), then Mali (12th-14th centuries AD), which grew rich by supplying Islamic merchants with gold and other products from the kingdoms of the West African forest zone to the south, including Benin and Ife in what is now Nigeria. It was the wealth to be gained from these lucrative trade routes that later led Portuguese navigators to undertake their first major voyages.

AMERICAS

NORTH AMERICAN TOWNS

Built over several hundred years from AD 1050, the settlement at Cahokia, in a fertile valley near the confluence of the Mississippi, Missouri, and Illinois rivers, was the largest of all the early settlements north of Mexico. One feature of the site was a circular arrangement of huge cypress posts near the central precinct. Referred to by archaeologists as Woodhenge, the logs making up the 137-yard-diameter circle were placed in such a way as to create an observatory in which celestial sighting lines could be traced. Over the next 300 years Cahokia continued to grow and by AD 1250 over 120 mounds had been constructed, which served as temple-platforms or burial mounds.

Woodhenge, Cahokia, Illinois

Settlement and ceremonial center ■

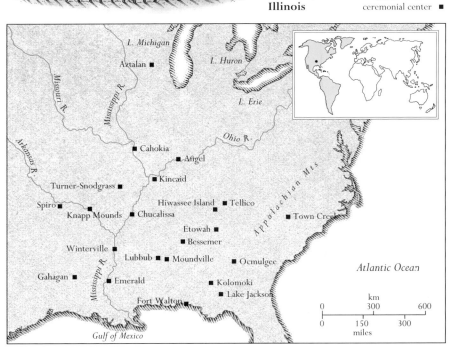

TRADING CENTER

Between the 11th and 14th centuries AD Casas Grandes was a major trading center in what is now northern Mexico. The town served the area including southwestern North America and northern Mexico. In its construction, Casas Grandes bears similarities to earlier pueblos of the region. However, there were also ceremonial mounds, a Mesoamerican-style ritual ball court, specialized work areas, storerooms, and many bird pens to house macaws imported from tropical regions to the south. Macaw feathers were highly prized and used for personal adornment.

Area with trading center sponsored by Mesoamerican *pochteca* (long-distance merchants)

Scarlet macaw

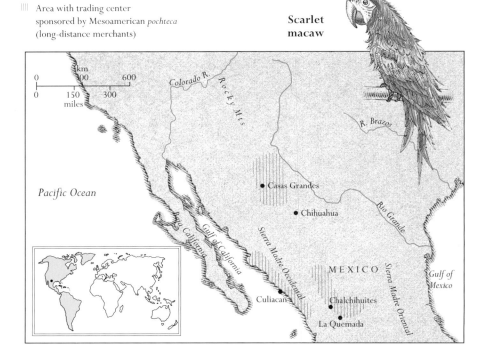

EUROPE

CHRISTIAN WESTERN EUROPE

During the 11th and 12th centuries AD, as western Europe became more stable and prosperous due to increased trade and agriculture, resources became available for church-building on a grand scale. Among the greatest churches in the Romanesque style, characterized by the round-headed arch and the barrel vault, were those along the pilgrimage routes leading to major shrines and those constructed in large monastery complexes such as the church at Cluny in eastern France, built between AD 1086 and AD 1121. Throughout western Europe during this period there was a shared religious culture, based on allegiance to the Pope in Rome, and clerics, pilgrims, and scholars were able to pass relatively easily from one kingdom or principality to another.

Major Romanesque church △
Center of pilgrimage ▲

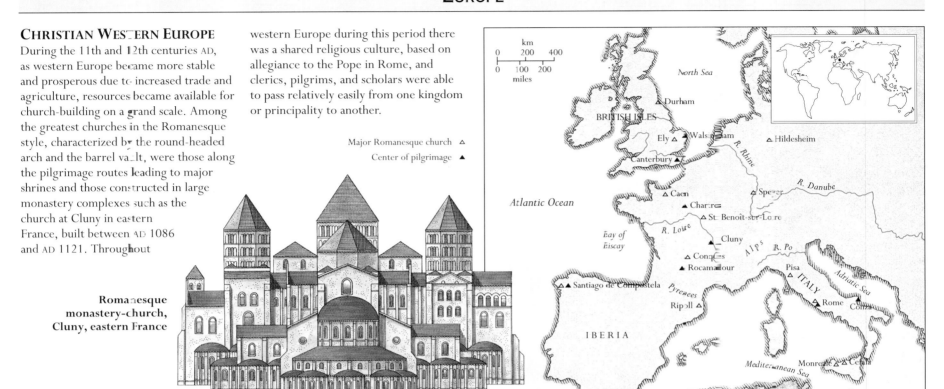

Romanesque monastery-church, Cluny, eastern France

AFRICA

WEST AFRICAN TRADING STATES

The ancient kingdom of Ghana was the first major state in sub-Saharan West Africa, its towns acting as trading stations between the interior of West Africa and the Islamic north. Ghana fell in AD 1200 and was succeeded by the empire of Mali, which ruled subject lands as far west as the Atlantic coast. In about AD 1340, Sonni Ali of Songhay defeated Mali and built an empire that stretched from Lake Chad to Timbuktu. Meanwhile, important trading centres such as Ife, on the edge of the West African rainforest in what is now Nigeria, were gaining in power. Benin, founded in the 11th or 12th centuries AD, became the richest Nigerian forest kingdom. Its economy, like that of Ife, was largely based on slave trading, and its bronze art echoed Ife styles.

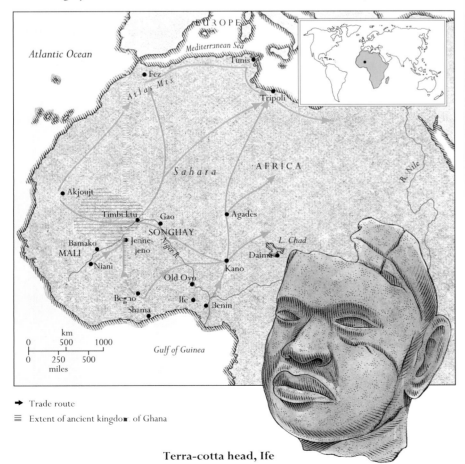

→ Trade route
≡ Extent of ancient kingdom of Ghana

Terra-cotta head, Ife

EAST ASIA & AUSTRALASIA

REGIONAL POWERS

In the 11th and 12th centuries AD, mainland Southeast Asia was divided into a number of states that were often at war with one another. The most famous was the Khmer kingdom, centered in Angkor and covering most of modern Cambodia, including the fertile lands of the lower Mekong Valley. To the northwest were the kingdoms of Thailand, and beyond them the empire of Pagan in modern Burma. On the eastern side of the mainland in Vietnam, the major power was the kingdom of Dai Viet, which in the 13th and 14th centuries AD absorbed the Champa kingdom to the south. All these states are famous for fine Hindu-Buddhist sculpture and temples.

▨ Approximate extent of Khmer kingdom
▥ Approximate extent of Thai kingdoms
▧ Approximate extent of Pagan kingdom
▨ Approximate extent of Dai Viet kingdom
░ Approximate extent of Champa kingdom
■ Major political center

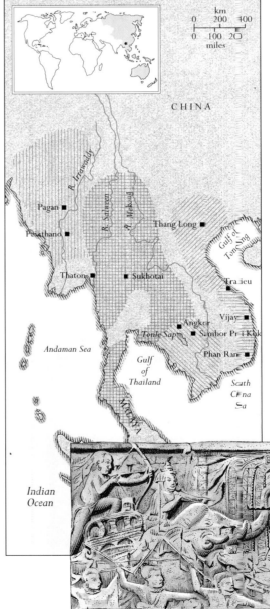

Bas-relief showing Khmer and Champa warriors, Angkor Wat, Angkor, Cambodia

AD 1000-1050

200 BC

FOOD & ENVIRONMENT

AMERICAS

Corn kernels

Prickly pear seeds

Pumpkin seeds

Squash stem

Red beans

Walnut shell

PLANT FOODS
Through expert control of water resources, farmers in southwestern North America were able to grow crops such as maize, beans, squash, and pumpkin. They also gathered wild plant foods, including prickly pears and walnuts. These 11th-century AD food remains were found at Chaco Canyon in New Mexico.

EAST ASIA & AUSTRALASIA

SHIFTING CULTIVATION
Early agriculture in Polynesia was generally based on shifting cultivation; small plots were cleared by burning and used for two or three years until their natural fertility waned. They were then left fallow for 15 years or so before being cleared again. Farming took place mainly on coastal strips of low-lying ground; root crops and tubers rather than seed crops were typically grown, and tree crops such as coconuts were also important.

MIDDLE EAST & SOUTH ASIA

MAJOR LANDOWNERS
In southern India, Hindu temples were at the heart of economic and social life. They were the major institutional landowners, gaining revenue from land donated by secular landowners, from the villages they owned, and from investment and usury. This bronze image shows Candi Kesvara, the treasurer of one such temple in the Chola Empire (mid 9th-12th centuries AD), who lived in the early 11th century AD.

Chola bronze of Candi Kesvara, southern India

EUROPE

BYZANTINE TAXATION
Prosperous farmers, who paid taxes in coin to the government, were the backbone of the Byzantine Empire (AD 330-1453). The major consideration in evaluating wealth and taxation was the capacity to plow, and individual farmers were assessed differently according to whether they owned a pair of plow oxen, a single ox, or none at all. The simple scratch plow was still widely used in the Byzantine Empire, since not turning the soil helped to preserve moisture levels. By the 11th century AD, farmers were increasingly coming under the control of powerful local lords and the great Byzantine monasteries such as Mount Athos, situated on one of the three prongs of the Chalcidice peninsula in Macedonia, northern Greece.

AFRICA

LION HUNTING
The spread of agriculture into southern Africa, and the continuing growth of towns in West and East Africa, reduced the amount of virgin land. In most parts of Africa, however, large expanses of untamed bush still existed, and wild animals continued to be a threat to livestock. Lion hunting was a dangerous, prestigious activity associated with initiation rites, and lion teeth and skins were important symbols of chieftainship.

Lion, Africa

SHELTER & ARCHITECTURE

CLIFF STAIRS
A series of roads was built in the early 11th century AD to connect towns in and around Chaco Canyon, New Mexico. Built by clearing rubble, the roads sometimes had paved surfaces and curbs. Some were 30 feet wide and often completely straight, sometimes scaling cliff faces with stairways cut into the rock. This rock stairway is near the ruined town of Chetro Ketl.

Stairs cut into rock

Rock stairway, New Mexico

ARCHITECTURAL UNIT
The basic unit of architecture in Song China (AD 960-1279), as in earlier centuries, was a building within a walled enclosure. In large complexes this unit was repeated many times, with a series of interconnecting court-yards on a north-south axis enclosing halls of increasing splendor. These buildings had timber superstructures, which were flexible in wind and earthquakes – not designed to last, but easy to replace in the original style. The color and choice of materials depended on the rank of the occupants. Colors were status-related – imperial palaces had white marble terraces, red wooden columns, polychrome ceilings, windows, and doors, and yellow-tiled roofs. Lesser royalty were permitted to use green tiles, whereas commoners were restricted to gray tiles.

TOMB TOWERS
Funerary towers became popular in Iran during the 11th and 12th centuries AD. The most spectacular example is the 167-foot-high Gunbad-i Qabus in northeastern Iran. Built of brick in a star-shaped design in AD 1006-7, it was intended to house the coffin of Prince Qabus ibn Vashmgir, an Islamic convert from Zoroastrianism.

Gunbad-i Qabus tomb tower, northeastern Iran

Romanesque church, Ripoll, Spain

ROMANESQUE STYLE
Settled conditions in western Europe after Viking and Magyar attacks in the 10th century AD led to a revival in church architecture in the early 11th century AD. The Romanesque style spread from France to Spain and Germany.

Roman arches

TWIN CITY
An Arab geographer writing around the middle of the 11th century AD described the capital of the early kingdom of Ghana in West Africa (in what is now part of Mauritania) as a "twin" city. The area for the Muslim population covered about 2 sq miles, and had no fewer than 12 mosques; the other part, the indigenous king's town, was 6 miles away, and consisted of a royal palace surrounded by domed houses within an enclosure wall. The remains at Kumbi Saleh are those of the Islamic merchants' city rather than the king's town, which has not yet been located. Merchants lived in two-story houses, using the ground floor to store goods. Humbler, densely packed dwellings and a marketplace occupied the lower part of the town.

TECHNOLOGY & INNOVATION

HISTORICAL TEXT

The manuscript known as the Codex Nuttall is an early example of Mixtec pictographic writing. It records the genealogy and history of the first and second ruling dynasties of Tilantongo, a center of the Mixtec culture in Oaxaca, Mexico.

Detail depicting the ruler Eight-Deer Tiger Claw, Mixtec Codex, Mexico

MOVABLE TYPE

The earliest movable type for printing was invented in China between AD 1041 and AD 1048. It consisted of individual characters made of clay, which could be fixed onto an iron-framed plate. The clay characters were reusable, but the method was painstaking. It was replaced in the 13th century AD by a wooden-type process, which used over 30,000 wooden pieces. The characters were sorted according to a rhyming system and stored in revolving cases.

Modern reproduction of movable type, China

PREMIUM IRONWORK

India enjoyed an international reputation for the quality of its iron and steel. By the 11th century AD, it was producing rare and costly swords, which were damascened (decoratively inlaid with other metals such as gold and silver), and in demand worldwide. Iron beams were also being used in construction by this time, notably in the building of temples in the Orissa region of eastern India. Iron and steel production was small-scale and simple, but highly efficient. The Indian technique of producing steel, by carefully manipulating the proportions of iron ore and charcoal in the furnace, took a fraction of the time required by contemporary European steelmaking processes, which demanded several hours of reheating and hammering after the initial casting of the iron.

NAVIGATIONAL DEVICES

It was with simple navigational devices such as weather vanes that Viking sailors embarked on their great voyages of settlement and exploration to Iceland, Greenland, and North America during the 10th and 11th centuries AD. This weather vane from Heggen in Norway was probably attached to the prow of a Viking ship. Streamers tied through the holes on its lower edge would have indicated the direction and strength of the wind.

Weather vane, Heggen, Norway

LAKEWORTHY CRAFT

The lakes of East Africa are stormy and unpredictable, requiring the use of craft more substantial than dug-out canoes. The fishing people around Lake Victoria (the largest lake in Africa, bordering on modern Kenya, Tanzania, and Uganda) developed double-ended canoes with no prow or stern. Planks were fastened with fiber lashings onto a long keel hollowed out from a single tree. Powered by up to 20 seated paddlers, boats of this kind have probably been in use for at least the past 1,000 years.

ART & RITUAL

ZOOMORPHIC ART

Ceramics in the style known as Parita Polychrome are highly individualistic and found at only a few sites in Panama. Bird-effigy pedestal bowls, like this one from Herrera, usually depict vultures and are naturalistically modeled and brightly painted in red, black, and purple. Other effigy vessels show fish, turtles, and frogs.

Ceramic pedestal bowl, Herrera, Panama

FOOT-BINDING

The decline in the status of women in the cities of Song China, where their work was needed less than in the countryside, was accelerated by the introduction of foot-binding. The custom was to bind the feet of young girls with cloth bandages so that they would grow up having small "lily" feet. Small feet were considered erotic and prestigious. The practice of foot-binding continued among the Chinese upper classes until the 20th century.

ILLUSTRATED BOOKS

Despite being mentioned in Iranian texts, no illustrated books survive from before the 11th century AD. The illustrations in one of the first, al-Sufi's *Book of Fixed Stars* (painted AD 1009-10), were drawn from classical representations on a celestial globe. The desire to render the positions of stars accurately ensured the survival of this genre until the 16th century AD.

Constellation Andromeda, *Book of Fixed Stars*, Iran

RUNIC SCRIPT

The Vikings borrowed the practice of writing from France and Britain where Latin script was in use, but developed their own script, with characters known as runes. This runic inscription, from the stone sarcophagus of a Viking settler in London, reads "Ginna and Toki had this stone set up." Runic script used by Viking communities in Scandinavia and the British Isles was gradually replaced by Latin script during the 11th and 12th centuries AD.

Runic inscription on Viking sarcophagus, London, England

CHURCH ART

Christian churches in Ethiopia were decorated with brightly colored frescoes and hangings from at least as early as the 9th century AD. Separated from the rest of Christendom by Islamic Egypt and the Levant (the coastal strip of Syria, Lebanon, and Israel), Ethiopian artisans developed their own individual style, reflected in the production of textiles such as this altar cloth woven with geometric designs.

Altar cloth, Ethiopia

AD 1050 - 1100

FOOD & ENVIRONMENT

SHELTER & ARCHITECTURE

AMERICAS

RABBIT HUNTING
In many areas of western North America, rabbits were a major protein source. Hunters used long nets into which the rabbits were driven. They also used a variety of snares and throwing sticks — boomerang-shaped weapons, like these examples found in Arizona and Utah.

Hunters' throwing sticks, Utah and Arizona

MASONRY STYLES
Each Chacoan pueblo, however distant from Chaco Canyon, New Mexico, had a planned layout. Large sections were laid out before walls were erected. Masonry walls had a rubble core thickest in the lower stories, enabling them to support heavy upper stories. This wall at the Aztec Ruins site was built between AD 1088 and AD 1093 and was covered with mud plaster.

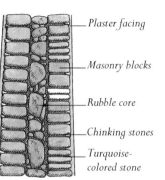

- Plaster facing
- Masonry blocks
- Rubble core
- Chinking stones
- Turquoise-colored stone

Cross section, wall, Aztec Ruins, New Mexico

EAST ASIA & AUSTRALASIA

DISTANT ORIGINS
The sweet potato was an early staple crop in Polynesia and was grown on the Cook Islands by AD 1050. This plant is native to South America, and it is unclear how it reached the Pacific islands, since there are no signs of any maritime contact. The distance from Easter Island, the easternmost Polynesian island, to the Chilean coast is around 2,015 miles.

Sweet potato

Stupa of the Ananda temple, Pagan, Burma

TEMPLE STUPA
The site of the ancient city of Pagan in Burma has remains of no fewer than 5,000 stupas (dome-shaped Buddhist monuments containing burials or relics), built between the 10th and 14th centuries AD. The most famous stupa is that of the Ananda temple, dedicated in AD 1090 — a massive structure with a towering central *sikhara* (spire).

MIDDLE EAST & SOUTH ASIA

East by AD 1092. The Seljuk sultan seized power from the caliph in Baghdad, who became solely a religious figure. The Seljuks formed part of a massive migration of Turkish-speaking nomads that continued until the 12th century AD. The reasons for this migration remain unclear, but the unsettled conditions led to agrarian neglect and a decrease in population. The collapse of irrigation and sewage systems caused disease, which was often followed by famine.

FAMINE AND PESTILENCE
The Seljuk Turks crossed the Oxus River from Turkmenistan in Central Asia soon after AD 1030, capturing Baghdad in AD 1055 and establishing control over the whole of the Middle

CYLINDRICAL MINARETS
The early minarets of Islamic western Asia were rectangular stepped towers. These were superseded around AD

Detail of brickwork from cylindrical minaret, Damghan, Iran

1050, when the tall cylindrical tower minaret was developed in Iran. This form was probably first used to commemorate victories or political events. Minarets built at a distance from settlements may have been used as beacons to mark important caravan routes or oases.

EUROPE

HERBAL REMEDIES
Throughout the Middle Ages in Europe, herbal remedies played a leading role in medicine. This page, showing the plants common teasel and yellow bugle, is from the *Winchester Herbal*, an 11th-century manuscript from Hampshire, England. It is a translation from Latin of an herbal, or guide to the medicinal uses of plants, by the Roman writer Apuleius.

Common teasel and yellow bugle, *Winchester Herbal*, Hampshire, England

EPITOME OF ROMANESQUE
One of the greatest Romanesque cathedrals was Speyer Cathedral in the German Rhineland, built between AD 1040 and AD 1082. The cathedral still stands, but in modified form. The nave was 240 feet long and 114 feet high (to the crown of the vault), and there were four tiered towers near the corners of the building; the design embodied simplicity and balance.

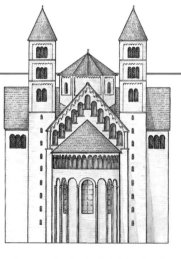

Speyer Cathedral, Rhineland, Germany

AFRICA

HIPPO HUNTING
The Arab writer al-Bakri provides a vivid account of life in the Middle Niger Valley in his *Description of North Africa*, written in AD 1067. The local inhabitants, he records, had many cattle but no sheep or goats. They did, however, hunt the *cafou* (hippopotamus), which al-Bakri describes as an aquatic animal the size of an elephant. The hunters were armed with short metal harpoons with long cords attached, which they hurled in large numbers at the chosen beast. The dead hippo sank to the river bottom, from where the hunters hauled it out with the cords. The flesh of the hippopotamus was cooked and eaten, and the skin used to make a special kind of whip known locally as a *ceryafa*.

MOUNTAIN PALACES
During the 11th century AD, local North African rulers built themselves fortified mountain palaces. One of the largest was the Dar al-Bahr (Palace of the Lake) in Algeria, a sprawling complex of courtyards, reception rooms, and a mosque. An important feature of the complex was the strong defensive al-Manar tower, which contained living rooms on its upper floor and a low-vaulted prison or storeroom in the basement.

Cross section, al-Manar tower, Algeria

TECHNOLOGY & INNOVATION

MIMBRES POTTERY
Potters of the Mimbres Valley in New Mexico produced black-on-white ceramics, which were common grave goods from about AD 900-1200. Most examples, including this bowl, have "kill" holes in their bases, making them useless for practical purposes. Some were painted for mortuary use, a practice unique in southwestern North America at this time.

Mimbres bowl with fishing scene, Mimbres Valley, New Mexico

OCEAN COMMERCE

Improved navigational equipment, the continuing expansion of Islam, and the unprecedented prosperity of Song China (AD 960-1279) combined to spur the first great era of oceanic commerce. China's contacts with the West were now largely maritime, often conducted through Islamic Arab ambassadors.

Statue of an Arab ambassador, northern China

ADVANCES IN SCHOLARSHIP
Under the early Seljuk sultans in the Middle East, advances were made in mathematics, geometry, and astronomy. A leading scholar of the late 11th century AD was Omar Khayyám, who was commissioned by Sultan Malik Shah to develop a new calendar. This ran from the day of the spring equinox in AD 1079. Khayyám developed a theory of irrational numbers (those that have no finite form, such as the number pi [π], which is the ratio of the circumference of a circle to its diameter) and also calculated a systematic method for solving cubic equations.

Norman cavalrymen, Bayeux Tapestry, France

NORMAN CAVALRY
An authentic picture of warfare in the late 11th century AD is provided by the Bayeux Tapestry, which depicts the Norman invasion of Britain and the Battle of Hastings in AD 1066. The Normans (Vikings who had settled in Normandy, France) relied heavily on their cavalry in battle, devising new and effective tactics. They wore long tunics of chain mail and simple helmets with noseguards, carried long tapering shields, and fought with spears.

COPPER CURRENCY
Copper rings were used as currency in parts of West Africa during the late 11th century AD. Most of the copper originated from mines at Igli in Morocco, North Africa, because local supplies were unable to meet the demand. The copper was initially smelted into bars and traded south across the Sahara by camel caravans. Archaeological confirmation of this trade was unearthed in the western Sahara in 1964, when a hoard of more than 2,000 copper bars was discovered buried in the desert sand. They dated to the late 11th or 12th centuries AD. The bars were approximately 29 inches in length, each weighing about 1 lb, and were wrapped in matting in bundles of 100. The owner must have buried them for safekeeping, and then either failed to return or was unable to find them again in the desolate terrain.

ART & RITUAL

COPPER BELLS

Eyelet

Made using the lost-wax technique, copper bells were used as earrings and as ornaments on necklaces, headdresses and belts. They were made from copper ore mined in the Mexican states of Jalisco and Nayarit and were traded north, to Chihuahua in northern Mexico, where these examples were found, and to southwestern North America. The bells usually had eyelets at the top for attachment.

Copper bells, Chihuahua, Mexico

BUDDHIST SHRINES
The Ananda temple complex and other Buddhist shrines and monuments at the ancient city of Pagan in central Burma are richly decorated with carved stone reliefs and statues. The reliefs depict scenes from the life of the Buddha and stories from the previous incarnations preceding his enlightenment. Both the style of carving and subject matter were derived from northern Indian traditions.

LORD OF THE DANCE
A popular theme of bronze sculpture in southern India under the Chola Dynasty (mid 9th-12th centuries AD) was that of Shiva Nataraja, the Lord of the Dance. Shiva dances to destroy and recreate the universe; he is often portrayed dancing on the back of a dwarf, a symbolic figure representing human ignorance.

Chola bronze of Shiva Nataraja, India

PILGRIMAGE ROUTES
A new Christian fervor began to sweep western Europe at the end of the 11th century AD. Lords and commoners alike flocked to take part in pilgrimages to famous shrines, such as St. Peter and St. Paul in Rome and St. James at Santiago de Compostela in northwestern Spain. Pilgrimage routes became arteries of trade and cultural interchange based on shared religious belief, giving western Europe an international character unparalleled in more recent centuries. Innovations in art and architecture followed and internationally recognized schools of learning began to develop in Paris, France, and Bologna, Italy. From these schools, the first universities in Europe developed in the 12th century AD.

COPTIC INFLUENCES
Under the Islamic Fatimid Dynasty in the 11th century AD, Egypt was a great center of artistry in glassware, ceramics, textiles, bronze, and rock crystal. Distinctive products included luster-ware vessels, traded between Egypt and the Middle East. Despite the fact that Islam forbade any representations of the human form in art, some of these vessels were adorned with human figures, because Coptic Christian influences remained strong in Egypt.

Fatimid luster-ware bowl, Egypt

AD 1100 - 1150

FOOD & ENVIRONMENT

SHELTER & ARCHITECTURE

AMERICAS

INTENSIVE AGRICULTURE

The people of the Chimu culture, which flourished on the north coast of Peru, practiced intensive agriculture, often using military force to seize new territory with agricultural potential. With the help of huge and elaborately constructed irrigation systems, they grew a great variety of foodstuffs. Chimu pottery was made in the shape of fruits, vegetables, and other foods.

Chimu pottery in the shape of vegetables, Peru

GREAT CITY

The largest city in the Americas at this time was probably Chanchan, capital of the Chimu people on Peru's north coast. Covering almost 990 acres, the city was divided into huge compounds with spacious plazas and burial platforms. The city was originally surrounded by fields irrigated by the Moche River.

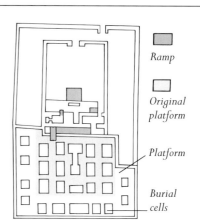

Ramp

Original platform

Platform

Burial cells

Plan view, Huaca Las Avispas burial platform, Chanchan, Peru

EAST ASIA & AUSTRALASIA

WATER MANAGEMENT

The Khmer Kingdom in Cambodia reached its height in the 12th century AD. To support the population of the capital, Angkor, management of water supplies was crucial. Reservoir tanks and moats were built by rulers such as Suryavarman II (AD 1113-50), allowing more land to be cultivated. Together, natural water resources and irrigation tanks at Angkor would have allowed the annual production of 126,000 tons of rice, sufficient to feed 600,000 people.

TEMPLE-MAUSOLEUM

The height of religious architecture in the Khmer Kingdom in Cambodia is represented by Angkor Wat, the great temple-mausoleum built by King Suryavarman II. Covering almost 495 acres, the temple is dominated by five sandstone towers in the shape of lotus buds — the largest of them is 213 feet tall.

Angkor Wat temple-mausoleum, Angkor, Cambodia

MIDDLE EAST & SOUTH ASIA

ARTIFICIAL LAKES

Irrigation and water control were important throughout the Indian subcontinent since earliest times. Irrigation systems ranged from wells and the simple but effective tanks, or reservoirs, dotted over southern India to the massive artificial lakes of Sri Lanka, which had complex dams and sluice gates. The largest and most magnificent of these reservoirs, the

Parakrama Samudra (Sea of Parakrama), was constructed in the 12th century AD. Elaborate constructions were also associated with the domestic water supply; among the finest are the impressive Gujarati step-wells, elegantly carved structures on a number of levels leading down to the water. Elsewhere, wells and ghats (bathing places) often had substantial stone steps leading down to the water.

THE FOUR-IWAN PLAN

In the early 12th century AD, the four-iwan courtyard plan was adopted in Iran. This consisted of four open-ended, barrel-vaulted halls facing each other, one on each side of a courtyard. The plan is exemplified in the Jami Mosque at Zavareh, constructed in AD 1136. The plan became standard for mosques, palaces, caravanserais (inns built to accommodate camel caravans), and madrasa (religious colleges).

Cross section, Jami Mosque, Zavareh, Iran

EUROPE

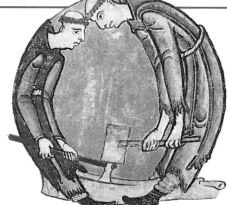

LAND CLEARANCE

Monasteries of the Cistercian order, founded at Citeaux, France, in AD 1098, played a crucial role in land clearance in western Europe. Between AD 1098 and AD 1150, more than 300 monasteries were founded in remote marshy and forested environments.

Manuscript detail showing Cistercian monks splitting a tree trunk

MOTTE-AND-BAILEY CASTLES

Many motte-and-bailey castles were built in northern Europe during the

Motte

Timber guard tower

Bridge and gate

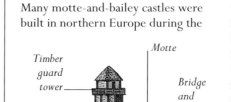

11th and 12th centuries AD. The motte was a mound with a timber tower at its summit and palisade at its base; the bailey, or defensive enclosure, protected the tower and other buildings. Castles like this could be built quickly in regions with territorial disputes, such as the eastern frontier of Germany, where Germans and Slavs were engaged in regular warfare.

Motte-and-bailey castle, Elmendorf, Germany

AFRICA

PRINCIPAL CROPS

West African peoples in the 12th century AD cultivated a variety of food plants. In the savanna region south of the Sahara, sorghum was the staple, although onions, gourds, and watermelons were also grown, along with millet and African rice in some areas. In sharp contrast, the principal crops in the forest zone to the south were not grains but tubers and tree crops such as yams, oil palms, and kola nuts.

Watermelon plant

NEW ISLAMIC STYLES

Elaborate Islamic architectural styles came into fashion in North Africa during the 12th century AD and are exemplified in the Kutubiya Mosque in Marrakesh, Morocco. The mosque was built by the Almohads, an indigenous Islamic sect that conquered the Maghreb region (encompassing the Atlas Mountains and coastal plains of Morocco, Tunisia, and Algeria) in

the 12th century AD. The square minaret tower is more than 196 feet high, and decorated with arches and niches. The vast prayer hall has 17 naves, and the whole mosque is adorned with cupolas and domes. This tradition of mosque architecture also spread across the Sahara, where it was executed in mud brick rather than stone.

TECHNOLOGY & INNOVATION

ANDEAN WEAVING
In spite of the simplicity of the tools used, textile weaving in the Andes was highly developed. Sophisticated tapestry, gauze, and drawn-thread work was produced on two-pole looms, using wool and cotton in combination.

Textile fragment, Andes

PAPER MONEY
The demands of commerce in Song China (AD 960-1279) could no longer be met with heavy copper coins, so official agencies were established for issuing paper money. "Flying money," or credit vouchers, had already been introduced in the 9th century AD, but now money vouchers of different denominations were printed. Valid for three years, they were subject to conditions similar to modern banking restrictions. Government bureaus also issued exchange certificates which could be converted to copper coinage by provincial producers of monopoly products like salt and tea.

SGRAFFITO-WARE POTTERY
Developed by Islamic potters from the 9th century AD onward, the manufacture of sgraffito-ware glazed pottery reached its peak at this time. The name sgraffito comes from the Italian *sgraffire*, to scratch. The technique involved covering an earthen vessel with a white slip, or coating, before firing, then scratching designs through it. Green and brown lead glazes were also applied before firing.

Lead-glazed sgraffito-ware bowl

ADMINISTRATIVE RECORDS
The many written documents that have survived from the medieval kingdoms of western Europe in the 12th century AD testify to the growing complexity of bureaucratic administration. Substantial collections of royal and ecclesiastical records detail expenditure and receipts and were written on sheepskin or parchment using a stylus. Styli were usually made of bone with a metal tip, but some were made entirely of metal.

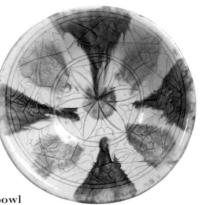

WOOLEN GARMENTS
In the Sahara and western Sudan, garments woven from sheep's wool from the Maghreb grasslands of North Africa were highly prized for their quality and warmth. Lengths of wool were woven on looms set on the ground, then sewn together into robes and traded across the desert.

Sleeve of a modern woolen garment, North Africa

ART & RITUAL

GAME OF SKILL
Variations of the game of *chunkee* were played throughout much of North America by this time. *Chunkee* involved rolling a stone disk along a path while other players attempted to strike it with a spear. On this engraved shell, a figure clad in ceremonial regalia bends down to release the stone.

Chunkee stone held in hand

Engraved shell, Kentucky

PORCELAIN VESSELS
The development of Korean pottery, which had always maintained its own distinctive style, reached a peak between the 10th and 12th centuries AD with celadon porcelain, like this example in the shape of an eight-petaled cup on an inverted lotus. The technique was derived from a Chinese tradition: vessels were fired in a reducing atmosphere (poor in oxygen), which resulted in a semitransparent, jade-colored glaze of the finest quality.

Celadon cup and stand, Korea

FEMALE DEITIES
From the 7th century AD, Buddhism in India had been increasingly affected by influences from Tantrism (a magical fertility cult), which led to the male saints of the Buddhist pantheon being given female consorts known as *taras* (savioresses). Initially, Tara was a consort of the Bodhisattva Avalokiteshvar. The title Bodhisattva denotes a divine being who, although deserving of *nirvana* (the state of absolute blessedness), stays on the plane of mortals to help them to salvation. By the 12th century AD, Tara herself had become a revered Bodhisattva.

Bodhisattva Tara, India

SCULPTED PORTALS
Churches built at this time in central and eastern France were decorated with masonry sculptures. Many depicted biblical scenes. The most splendid creations were panels over the main doors at the western end of these churches. A popular theme of such portals was the Last Judgment, showing Christ as arbiter between the blessed and the damned.

Last Judgment portal, Vézelay, France

CEREMONIAL HORNS
The settlements established by Islamic merchants and traders along the East African coast developed their own special regalia and ceremonial equipment during this period. From Lamu, Kenya, in the north, to Sofala, Mozambique, in the south, side-blown horns came to be used on ceremonial occasions such as processions or formal gatherings. Fashioned from elephant tusks and often inlaid with gold or other precious metals, they were still used for ceremonial purposes until recent times.

Modern side-blown horn, Lamu, Kenya

AD 1150 - 1200

FOOD & ENVIRONMENT

SHELTER & ARCHITECTURE

AMERICAS

POTTERY TRADING
Between AD 1150 and AD 1300, the economy of Casas Grandes in Mexico depended on trade as well as on local resources. Turquoise and other stones, macaws, feathers, and pottery were all traded. Distinctive ceramics from the Casas Grandes region were taken as far south as Teotihuacan in southern Mexico and north to villages in southwestern North America.

Effigy jar, Casas Grandes, Mexico

TEMPLE-PLATFORMS
The Tarascan kingdom in western Mexico had its center at Lake Patzcuaro, in the modern state of Michoacán. Around AD 1000 the Tarascans began to build a huge base for five *yacatas* (terraced temple-platforms) on a mountain slope at Tzintzuntzan. The residence of the Tarascan priest-king, who was also considered a god, was located near the platform.

Temple-platform, Tzintzuntzan, Mexico

EAST ASIA & AUSTRALASIA

TERRACED RICE PADDIES
In Southeast Asia, terraced fields were constructed at around this time to extend agriculture on to otherwise unusable hillsides. They were sometimes combined with irrigation networks that allowed the terraces to be flooded at certain times of the year, so that rice could be grown. Although extremely laborious to build and maintain, terraced rice paddies such as these at Luzon in the Philippines enabled large populations to be supported even in mountainous regions.

Terraced rice paddies, Luzon, Philippines

FORTIFIED MANOR HOUSES
The 12th century AD was a period of political fragmentation in Japan, with increased power going to the *samurai* (local lords). These were members of a warrior elite, who built *yakata* (fortified manor houses) on their estates. The buildings were constructed with a raised timber floor, timber frame superstructure, and thatched roof. The typical *yakata* consisted of a group of such structures, including food stores, stables, and living quarters, all clustered inside an enclosure protected by an earth bank, a timber fence, and a moat. The *yakata* provided a measure of security for their owners.

MIDDLE EAST & SOUTH ASIA

ISLAMIC STYLES
The conquest of much of northern India by Turk and Afghan rulers in the 12th century AD introduced Islamic styles of architecture to the region. An outstanding example is the Qutb Minar, a minaret with decorated balconies built to commemorate the conquest of Delhi in AD 1193 by the Afghan Qutb-ud-Din Aybak.

Qutb Minar, Delhi, India

SELJUK HERDING
Large regions of Iran were never suitable for intensive settled farming. The nomadic way of life, which depended to a great extent on sheep, predominated in many parts of the Seljuk realm in the 12th century AD. Tribal custom demanded that all visitors be fed, and some Seljuk sultans had sheep slaughtered each day to feed both court members and the poor. Evidence for the continuing nomadic reliance on sheep can be found in state documents which refer to the Sultan as the "shepherd of his people."

EUROPE

MEDIEVAL SANITATION
Sanitation in medieval Europe was rudimentary. In towns, most houses had a yard at the back where hut-like wooden privies stood over timber-lined cesspits. By building these privies at a distance from the houses, a measure of hygiene was introduced, but water wells were often dug only a few yards away. Effluent was also discharged into rivers, which were used as a source of drinking water. Only monasteries and houses of wealthy lords had stone-lined sewers.

STAVE CHURCHES
In those parts of Europe that were still heavily forested, early churches were built of timber. Borgund is the location of the oldest surviving Norwegian stave church, a building constructed entirely of wood with tall timbers, or staves, supporting a tiered roof. These tall structures are masterpieces of woodworking technology, with braces, trusses, and cross beams ingeniously arranged to ensure stability.

Stave church, Borgund, Norway

AFRICA

LEGUMES FOR PROTEIN
An important source of protein, common beans (*Phaseolus vulgaris*) were a vital staple crop of farmers cultivating the tropical savanna woodlands of East and southern Africa. Beans were hardy and drought resistant and were frequently planted as a secondary crop in fields already used for millet or sorghum.

Engraving of a common bean plant

LOCALIZED ADAPTATIONS
The spread of Islam to West Africa brought new architectural styles from North Africa. These, however, had to be modified to suit local conditions, since fired brick and stone were not available. Mud was the primary building material, although mud-brick structures were not as durable as stone. Wooden poles, sticking out from the walls and minarets, supported spiral staircases and interior roofs. Ceilings were low, and thick walls kept the interior cool. Such buildings were constantly rebuilt as the mud walls crumbled.

TECHNOLOGY & INNOVATION

Andean unku, Peru

EVERYDAY WEAR

Andean peoples produced beautiful woven items and high-quality cotton and wool clothing. This shirt has short sleeves and a V-neck and is patterned with geometric motifs. It is called an *unku* and was intended for everyday wear. For feasts and rituals, Andean people wore clothing of a higher quality.

Detail

LACQUER INLAY

Metalworkers in Korea developed skillful techniques of inlaying silver wire and mother-of-pearl on lacquer. From the late 12th century AD onward, inlaid boxes like this were made for storing Buddhist sutras (collections of doctrinal writings), and were prized for their high quality by the Chinese imperial court.

Lacquer sutra box inlaid with mother-of-pearl, Korea

FRIT-BODIED CERAMICS

Originating in Ancient Egypt, frit (a hard composite of silica and glass) was used to make beads. The use of frit for the manufacture of ceramics designed to imitate imported Chinese white porcelain may also have developed in Egypt, probably in the late 11th or early 12th centuries AD. However, frit ceramics were produced most widely in the Middle East, notably at Raqqa in Syria and later at Kashan in Iran. The almost perfect match between frit-bodied ceramics and the glaze applied to them made the surfaces ideal for overglaze decoration in luster (an extremely thin metallic film) or polychrome enamels, both of which required a second firing. The first dated frit ceramics with luster and polychrome enamel decoration are from Iran and date to AD 1179-86.

HARNESSING THE WIND

The windmill with vertical sails was invented in Europe in the late 12th century AD — the earliest references are found in manuscripts from England and northern France. By AD 1300, windmills were a typical feature of the European landscape, allowing natural forces to be harnessed for milling grain into flour, especially where there was no running water available nearby to drive a traditional watermill.

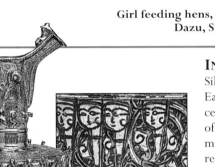

Windmill illustrated in the Luttrell Psalter, England

POTTERY EXPERIMENTATION

The pottery technology of Bantu farmers and herders living in settled villages in southern Africa gradually became more refined. Potters experimented with exterior polishes and thinner-sided vessels. They crafted shallow bowls and bag-shaped pots with black graphite surfaces and cord-impressed decoration. They mixed in mica (lustrous rock-forming minerals) to temper their clays and developed painted designs, sometimes using red ocher to make deep red-colored vessels. These ceramics were made without the use of the wheel, the potter building up long coils of wet clay. The finished pots and bowls were fired in open, fast-burning brush hearths.

ART & RITUAL

CERAMIC SCULPTURE

The Chancay culture (AD 1000-1400) on Peru's central coast is known particularly for its woven gauze and light-colored ceramics. Chancay ceramists specialized in the production of standing human statuettes, usually couples. Typical features include almond-shaped eyes, a cap on the head, and horizontal outstretched arms.

Chancay figurines, Peru

BUDDHIST SCULPTURE

The sculpture at the Buddhist complex at Dazu in China portrays the life of the Buddha and includes scenes from Chinese daily life. This statue of a girl feeding hens, which dates to between AD 1179 and AD 1249, retains the natural simplicity of traditional Chinese sculpture.

Girl feeding hens, Baodingshan, Dazu, Sichuan, China

INLAID METALWORK

Silver vessels had been in use in the Middle East since around AD 300. In the 12th century AD, however, owing to a shortage of silver and demand from urban mercantile consumers, they began to be replaced by brass and bronze vessels inlaid with copper, silver, and gold. These pieces quickly gained popularity after AD 1150.

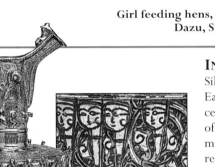

Brass ewer with a decorative inlaid silver inscription and detail (*above*)

ARISTOCRATIC PASTIME

The ancient game of chess reputedly originated in India. By the 12th century AD it had become a favorite pastime among the aristocracy throughout Europe, much to the disapproval of clerics, who deemed it frivolous and distracting from spiritual life. The kings, queens, bishops, knights, and pawns (foot soldiers) testify to the strict hierarchy of medieval society.

Walrus-ivory chess piece, Lewis, Scotland

DECORATED DOORS

Domestic architecture in the coastal towns of East Africa often presented a drab external appearance, for the rich kept a low profile, preferring to lavish money on the interiors of their homes. Carved wooden doors were a traditional means of revealing the status of the occupants, as seen in this door detail from Lamu in Kenya.

Detail, traditional carved door, Lamu, Kenya

AD 1200 - 1250

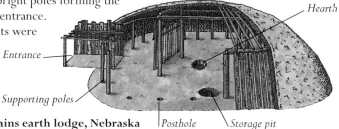
200 BC

FOOD & ENVIRONMENT	SHELTER & ARCHITECTURE

AMERICAS

JUNGLE FAUNA

Chiefdoms and small states that existed in the jungles of Costa Rica reflected the diverse fauna of the region in the design of their pottery. This tripod vessel is thought to be a bird effigy, although insects are painted around the top and the bird itself incorporates feline characteristics.

Bird-effigy vessel, Costa Rica

PLAINS HOUSES

The dwellings of people living in the central plains of North America were usually square and built of upright poles forming the walls and entrance. Storage pits were often dug into the floor. A thick layer of soil covered the exterior of the houses, which served as protection against the elements.

Hearth

Entrance

Supporting poles

Cutaway, Plains earth lodge, Nebraska *Posthole* *Storage pit*

EAST ASIA & AUSTRALASIA

NOMADIC DIET

The vast deserts, mountains, and grasslands of Mongolian Central Asia were ill-suited to cultivation. Nomadic groups kept herds of sheep and supplemented their diet with a little fish and game. These horsemen had a great liking for koumiss (fermented mares' milk). Sheep provided meat, milk, wool, skins for clothing and tents, and bones to make basic implements. Camels were used as long-distance draft animals.

Nomadic groups traveled seasonally, from lowland pastures in winter to mountain valleys in summer. Control of grazing lands was in the hands of individual clans or tribes, and territorial disputes among them often led to localized warfare.

YURTS

The nomadic groups of Mongolian Central Asia lived in yurts (circular portable tents), as they still do today. Yurts were made with a lattice framework of wooden poles, covered with skins or thick felts anchored with ropes. Inside, thick, brightly colored woven rugs covered the ground. The entire structure could be dismantled very quickly.

Felt covering

Framework of wooden poles

Cutaway, yurt, Mongolia

MIDDLE EAST & SOUTH ASIA

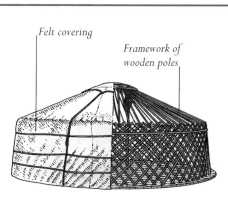

Indigo textile fragment, Gujarat, India

FIBERS AND DYES

Cotton was a major crop in India and the principal source of textile fiber. Different regions made specialized kinds of cloth, from coarse cotton to fine muslins. Dyes such as indigo were derived from plants, and several different dyeing techniques were in use by the time of the Delhi sultanate (from c. AD 1200).

MILITARY FORTIFICATIONS

The citadel of Aleppo in northern Syria was a key Islamic stronghold in the Middle East at the time of the Crusades and was heavily refortified in AD 1211. Its defenses included a masonry *glacis* (sloping rampart), but the principal feature was a massive rectangular gate-tower, reached by a narrow, tall-arched bridge. Within the tower the entrance passage bent right and left, with gates and portcullises at several points for additional security. The Crusaders also built powerful fortresses to maintain their control of the Levant (the coastal strip of Syria, Lebanon, and Israel), the most impressive being Krak des Chevaliers in northern Syria.

EUROPE

HERBAL TREATMENT

During the Middle Ages medical practitioners relied on the writings of Greek and Roman physicians. Herbal remedies were prepared by physicians, as this medical treatise dating to AD 1240 illustrates, and surgery was also occasionally performed. By the 13th century AD, autopsies were undertaken on unsuccessfully treated patients in an attempt to improve medical knowledge.

Detail from a medical treatise showing the preparation of herbal remedies

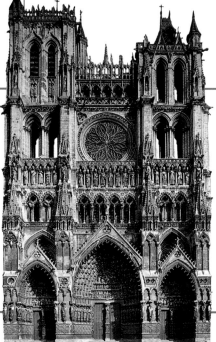

GOTHIC CATHEDRALS

A series of great cathedrals was built in northern France during the early 13th century AD, reflecting the wealth of the region and the prestige of the Church. These were in the new Gothic style, with soaring ribbed vaults, flying buttresses, and carved turrets and canopies. Large stained-glass windows with tracery (ribbed-stone patterns) transformed the interiors into a blaze of color.

Amiens Cathedral, France

AFRICA

PLAGUE RATS

The disease-spreading plague rat migrated from North Africa into the interior, having been introduced by Islamic trading ships from the Middle East as early as the 9th century AD. Other rodents such as the cane rat had been eaten by farmers in sub-Saharan Africa since early times.

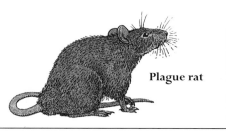

Plague rat

ROCK-HEWN CHURCHES

In the early 13th century AD, the highlands of Ethiopia were ruled by the Zagwe emperor, Lalibela. A Christian, he built 11 rock-cut subterranean churches at his capital Roha (later renamed Lalibela), including the cross-shaped Beit Giorgis (Church of St. George). These remain important places of pilgrimage today.

Rock-cut Beit Giorgis (Church of St. George), Lalibela, Ethiopia

TECHNOLOGY & INNOVATION

MONOLITHIC AXES

Large axes were used as status symbols by chieftains in eastern North America. This fine-grained sandstone ax from Georgia was probably used as an emblem of prowess in warfare and reflects the stoneworking expertise of the craftsmen of the Mississippian period (AD 1000-1500). The handle is carved with designs associated with contemporary chiefly religion.

Carved stone ax and detail, Georgia

NORTH-SOUTH AXIS

At the Bay of Fires in northeastern Tasmania, a 183-foot-long line of 93 flat stones was laid out in around AD 1220 and was the setting for initiation ceremonies in which teenage boys were instructed in Aboriginal teachings. The stones, oriented along a north-south axis at right angles to the east-west passage of the sun, may indicate that the Aborigines followed complex rules in planning sacred sites.

**Bay of Fires
stone arrangement,
Tasmania, Australia**

CERAMIC PROCESSES

Middle Eastern ceramists, especially in Iran, continued to diversify. By AD 1215 they were producing large technically demanding items such as entire ceramic tomb covers and ceramic *mihrabs* (niches in mosques). Innovations included the blue-and-black painted underglaze decoration.

**Bowl with underglaze decoration
in blue, black, and turquoise, Iran**

MAGNETIC COMPASS

European invasion of the Levant during the Crusades in the 12th and 13th centuries AD, and the active commerce between Italian cities such as Genoa, Venice, and Pisa and the Middle East, brought oriental innovations to medieval Europe. One of the most important was the magnetic compass. This had been invented in China in the 12th century AD, and soon spread westward. As early as AD 1218, a French manuscript describes it as essential for navigation at sea, and by AD 1225 it was being used in places as remote as Iceland. The novelty of the compass was that it allowed navigators to plot an accurate course when the sky was obscured by mist or bad weather – a common problem in northern Europe.

EXOTIC TRADE GOODS

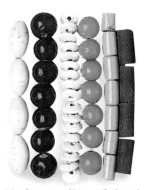

East African coastal towns such as Kilwa (on an island off the coast of southern Tanzania) and Gedi owed their prosperity to the insatiable demand in the Middle East for gold, ivory, and other African raw materials. Foreign merchants traded all manner of exotic goods for this merchandise, including strings of brightly colored glass beads, which were highly valued in the far interior.

Modern replicas of glass beads, East Africa

ART & RITUAL

BURIAL OFFERINGS

Funerary offerings and equipment from the Peruvian coast were very opulent during this period. Owing to the region's dry climate, many items have been well preserved. Found in a burial at Huarmey, on the north-central coast of Peru, this figurine made out of cotton yarn was placed with the mummified remains of a person. Such figurines served to protect the dead and were also used in healing rituals by shamans (healers).

Funerary figurine, Peru

ARTISTIC CENTER

Japanese art flourished under the ruling aristocratic clans. At the capital of the Minamoto clan, Kamakura, on the Pacific coast of Honshu, a vast bronze statue of the Buddha was erected in the mid-13th century AD and has remained a national treasure ever since.

**The Great Buddha, Kamakura,
Honshu, Japan**

TEMPLE CARVINGS

Religious festivals in India involved processions, as they do today, in which the image of a deity was drawn along in a decorated *ratha* (chariot). At Konarak, in the eastern state of Orissa, a temple was built in the early 13th century AD in the form of a *ratha*. Dedicated to Surya, the sun-god, it may have represented the sun's journey. Among the elaborate carvings in the now ruined temple are 12 pairs of wheels that represent the signs of the zodiac.

RELICS AND RELIQUARIES

Religious relics were greatly revered in medieval Europe, and much popular superstition surrounded them. They were often kept in special, lavishly decorated receptacles known as reliquaries. This head-shaped reliquary from Basel Cathedral, Switzerland, contained relics of St. Eustace (an early Roman Christian martyr), and was made in the early 13th century AD of gilded silver and semiprecious stones.

**Reliquary of St. Eustace,
Basel, Switzerland**

TERRA-COTTA ART

Ife, the sacred town of the Yoruba people in Nigeria, was heir to ancient art traditions that dated back to the time of the Nok terra-cottas over 1,000 years earlier. Most Ife sculptures were terra-cotta heads, but the Yoruba also made heads in bronze. The imposing sculptures of 13th century AD and later are evidence of emerging social stratification, since facial striations denoted status.

**Terra-cotta head of a man
with facial striations, Ife, Nigeria**

EAST AFRICAN TRADE

The coast of East Africa was part of a wider Indian Ocean world from as early as 100 BC. The monsoon winds that link the Red Sea with Arabia and India made the East African coast accessible to Arab sailors and merchants, who founded trading settlements there from the 9th century AD. The Arabs settled among the local African farmers and fishermen, and Swahili culture – a mix of African and Islamic traditions – was born. The coastal towns exported gold, ivory, mangrove poles, iron ore, copper, elephant tusks, tortoise shells, and slaves from the interior in exchange for cloth, cowrie shells, glass beads, porcelain vessels, glassware, and iron swords. Gold was especially in demand, much of it coming from the gold-rich Zimbabwe plateau.

SOURCE OF WEALTH

Africans exported precious raw materials such as gold and ivory in exchange for imported goods that were highly valued in the interior. The gold and ivory trade provided wealth to people who had previously depended on unpredictable farming environments for their livelihood. Human labor was another commodity offered by African chiefs: slaves were exported to Arabia as servants, and to build canals in the Persian Gulf.

Elephant tusk

IVORY FOR CARVING
Unlike Indian ivory, African elephant tusks are soft and easily carved. In China and India they were much in demand, especially for making intricate carved jewelry. Africans themselves prized tusks as symbols of chieftainship.

Gold nugget

EXTRACTING GOLD
African miners extracted gold by panning for nuggets in streams and by mining surface outcrops with narrow shafts that followed the gold-bearing seams. Gold was traded as dust stored in porcupine quills, as nuggets, and as strings of small beads. It was also hammered into thin sheets.

Celadon porcelain flask

Deteriorated glaze

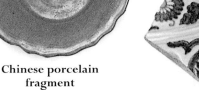

Chinese porcelain fragment

CHINESE IMPORTS
Porcelain vessels were imported from China in large quantities. This Chinese celadon (green-glazed) porcelain flask was found in the Husuni Kubwa palace at Kilwa, an Islamic trading town on an island off the southern coast of Tanzania. Such vessels were prized imports, because they could be stacked and transported easily, and were popular with chiefs as symbols of wealth and status. Both celadon wares and Ming blue-and-white vessels have been found in excavations on the coast and deep in the southeastern African interior, showing the strong trade networks between the coastal towns and inland settlements.

Ming blue-and-white porcelain fragments

INDIAN OCEAN TRADE ROUTES
An extensive system of trade routes linked the East African coast and the Red Sea with Arabia, the Persian Gulf, the Malabar Coast of India, and beyond toward China. Oceangoing dhows sailed from Islamic trading settlements at Chibuene, Sofala, Kilwa, Gedi, Malindi, Manda, and Shanga. They voyaged up the coast of Somalia and Ethiopia and across the Indian Ocean using the monsoon winds. On the fertile interior plateaus between the Zambezi and Limpopo rivers, further land trade networks were established between Bantu-speaking tribal centers. Great Zimbabwe, Chumnungwa, and Manekweni were three of over 100 territorial capitals of the Shona people, located at 43-mile intervals.

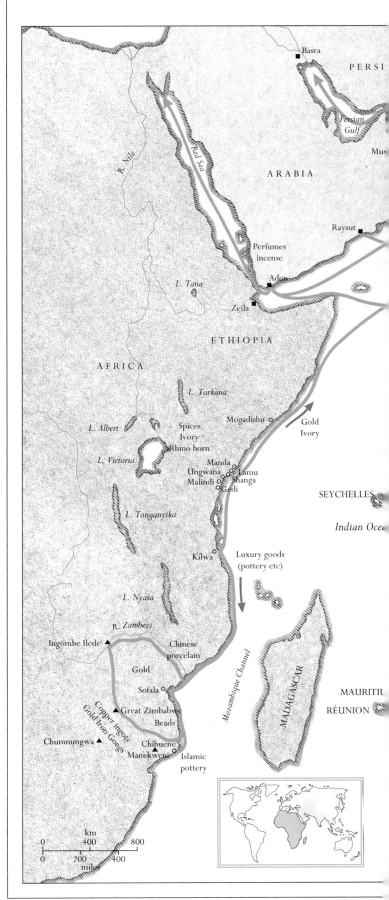

TRADING CENTERS

Manda was the most prosperous early trading town founded by Arab merchants on the East African coast. It was succeeded in the 13th century AD by Kilwa, which became a major transshipment station and trading center. Mosques and palaces were built in these Islamic towns. Major African centers in the interior were typically focused around stone-walled enclosures like that at Great Zimbabwe, the largest of over 100 territorial capitals that controlled the trade in local gold supplies.

Elliptical Building, Great Zimbabwe, East Africa

SHONA CAPITAL

Great Zimbabwe was the religious and trading capital of the Bantu-speaking Shona people, who lived on a plateau south of the Zambezi River. The chiefs, who controlled a society of royal families and commoners, lived in the Elliptical Building (*right*), a compound with high dry-stone walls. A small valley with hamlets and stone cattle enclosures separated the Elliptical Building from the Hill Ruin, where stone walls enclosed small shrines and compounds associated with ancestor cults and rainmaking ceremonies. Ritual soapstone pillars found at the site are carved with birds that may represent tribal ancestor-figures. The pillars were originally positioned along the top of the walls of the Elliptical Building.

Cast of a soapstone pillar with bird carving, Great Zimbabwe, East Africa

ISLAMIC TOMB

Gedi was a walled coastal town occupied by Swahili merchants and fishermen from the 13th century AD. Wealthy Islamic merchants lived in substantial houses and were buried in coral cement tombs, usually adorned with Chinese porcelain bowls embedded in them.

Coral cement tomb, Gedi, East Africa

SULTAN'S PALACE *above*

Kilwa was dominated by the Husuni Kubwa palace and a large mosque with a barrel-vaulted, domed roof. Overlooking the harbor, the palace was the sultan's residence, but with its storerooms, audience courts, and bathing pool, it was also a warehouse and meeting place for traders.

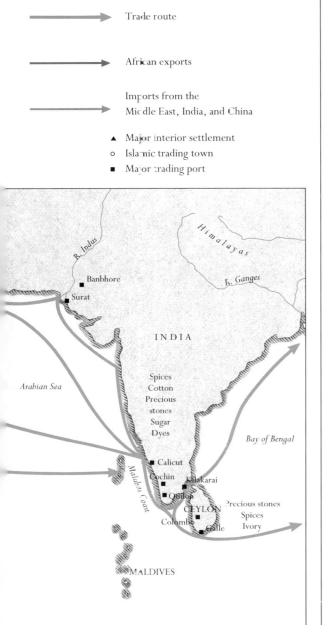

Arabian Sea

INDIA

Spices
Cotton
Precious stones
Sugar
Dyes

Bay of Bengal

Calicut
Cochin
Kilakarai
Quilon
CEYLON
Precious stones
Spices
Ivory
Colombo
Galle

MALDIVES

TRADING VESSELS *below*

Lateen-sailed dhows were developed by Arab sailors over 2,000 years ago. The large, triangular sails, suspended at 45 degrees to the mast, would have added considerable speed when running before the monsoon winds. By AD 500, ocean-going dhows were sailing direct from India to East Africa. Smaller dhows linked remote coastal towns with trading ports.

Lateen-sailed dhow

RODRIGUES

Skeleton surrounded by burial goods, Central Africa

GRAVE GOODS

The Kisalian people of Central Africa were Bantu-speaking fishermen and traders. Grave goods found in Kisalian burials dating to the 12th century AD include fine clay pots, iron bells, and anvils. The Kisalian people traded dried lake fish for copper from the Zambian copper belt to the south, but the presence of glass beads and cowrie shells in burials shows that they were in contact with the coastal trading towns, indicating the extent of trade into the interior.

CHAPTER 18
CONTACT & DIVERSITY
AD 1250-1500

The European Renaissance begins in Italy

The Aztec and Inca Empires prevail in Mesoamerica and Peru

Mongol rule is overthrown in China and the Ming Dynasty established

Ottoman Turks capture Constantinople and establish their rule in the Middle East

Trading states flourish in West and East Africa

By the 14th and 15th centuries AD, each region of the world had developed its own distinctive cultural identity, manifest in religion, society, and the arts. The ever larger scale of regional states and civilizations was also accompanied by growing international links, which brought relatively isolated cultures into contact with each other. Not all these new long-distance contacts were beneficial, however, as the spread of epidemic disease proved.

VIOLENCE IN EARLY AMERICAN ART
The figure on this copper plate from Georgia brandishes a war club and severed human head.

In AD 1346, bubonic plague began to ravage the Crimea and Asia Minor. A few months later, Genoese merchant ships carried infected rats to Messina in Sicily. By AD 1348 the disease was rampant in Italy and soon spread throughout Europe, killing a third of the population. Epidemics recurred regularly in Europe over the next 300 years. Surprisingly, this was the back-drop against which the Renaissance was set in the 14th century AD. Originating in Italy, the Renaissance was characterized by a new interest in the classical cultures of Greece and Rome, scientific discovery, and novel political ideas that combined with rapid economic growth to reform society.

Royal crest of Richard II

INTERCONTINENTAL TRADE
Found at Kumasi in West Africa, this bronze ewer was traded to Africa from England. It was made in the reign of Richard II (AD 1377-99).

AZTEC GODDESS
The Aztec goddess Chalchiuhtlicue is shown emerging from the jaws of the Earth Monster on this carved relief.

CHINESE PORCELAIN
Blue-and-white porcelain characteristic of Ming China was exported as far away as Europe and East Africa.

Stylized clouds   *Stylized peony motif*

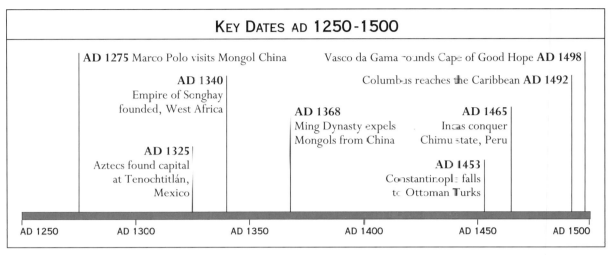

KEY DATES AD 1250-1500

AD 1275 Marco Polo visits Mongol China

Vasco da Gama rounds Cape of Good Hope **AD 1498**

AD 1340
Empire of Songhay founded, West Africa

Columbus reaches the Caribbean **AD 1492**

AD 1368
Ming Dynasty expels Mongols from China

AD 1465
Incas conquer Chimu state, Peru

AD 1325
Aztecs found capital at Tenochtitlán, Mexico

AD 1453
Constantinople falls to Ottoman Turks

AD 1250   AD 1300   AD 1350   AD 1400   AD 1450   AD 1500

Trading cultures of Africa

In sub-Saharan West Africa, a number of autonomous states were flourishing: Benin and Ife in the forest zone and the empires of Mali, then Songhay, in the savanna to the north. Trans-Saharan trade continued to be a major economic force in these lands. One important commodity was slaves; this trade had long been fostered by Arab merchants, who bought slaves for export to North Africa and the Middle East. North Africa was still occupied by prosperous Islamic communities, as it had been since the 7th century AD. The arrival of the Portuguese on the southern coast of West Africa in the 15th century AD opened up new markets, encouraging further slave raids by indigenous merchants. Trade was also crucial in East Africa, where the Islamic coastal towns and gold-producing inland states maintained their prosperity. Further south, Bantu farmers and herders had occupied most of southern Africa, except the southwest, where indigenous peoples lived a hunter-gatherer way of life on the fringes of the Kalahari Desert.

Aztecs and Incas

The Aztec Empire arose in Mesoamerica in the 14th century AD, gradually growing in power and influence. The Aztecs, or Mexica as they called themselves, were one of several ethnic groups who settled in the Valley of Mexico. Founding their capital, Tenochtitlán, on a lake-island in AD 1325, they dominated much of modern Mexico in less than a century. Conquered regions were required to pay tribute in services and goods, which funded further conquest and growing trade networks. By AD 1500, the city of Tenochtitlán was large and

Red hat focuses viewer's eye on perspective vanishing point

Brick courses follow line of perspective

Shadow cast by peacock increases sense of depth and realism

Bars on window resemble grid device used by artists to calculate perspective

Realistic stone step invites viewer into the scene

MASTERY OF PERSPECTIVE
Painted in egg tempera and oil in AD 1486 by the Italian Carlo Crivelli, *The Annunciation, with Saint Emidius* shows the mastery of perspective achieved by artists of the European Renaissance.

powerful, covering an area of 20 square miles and linked to the mainland by a series of causeways. Warfare, an important aspect of Aztec life, was used to acquire territory and to gain captives for use in rituals involving human sacrifice. In a history rewritten to extol their glory, the Aztecs claimed to have sacrificed 80,000 prisoners at the dedication, in AD 1487, of the Great Temple at Tenochtitlán, in order to appease their sun god, Huitzilopochtli.

The great South American realm of the 14th and 15th centuries AD was the Inca Empire. This extended from a heartland around the capital, Cuzco, in the Peruvian Andes north to the borders of modern Colombia and south as far as Chile and Argentina. At its greatest around AD 1500, the empire was approximately 2,175 miles long with 14,000 miles of roads. It was highly organized, with tax levies of food and goods kept in centralized warehouses.

AD 1250-1500

200 BC

Mongol and Ming

In the Far East, the great regional power, China, had been invaded earlier in the 13th century AD by the Mongols under Genghis Khan. His successors, notably Kubilai Khan (AD 1260-94), extended Mongol rule to southern China and parts of Southeast Asia. The splendors of the Mongol court under Kubilai were recorded by the Venetian traveler Marco Polo, who arrived in China in AD 1275. Kubilai's successors were less able rulers, and native Chinese resistance to their foreign overlords steadily increased until AD 1368, when the Mongols were finally overthrown and the Ming Dynasty (AD 1368-1644) was established. China soon regained many of its past glories – the Ming capital, Peking, became the largest and most populous city on earth.

Asian empires

India in this period was divided into Muslim kingdoms and sultanates in the north and Hindu kingdoms in the south. In the mid-15th century AD the southern kingdoms came under the control of the Vijayanagara Empire, based in the Krishna Valley. The imperial capital, Vijayanagara (modern Hampi), was a vast city with splendid royal residences and temples.

In Southeast Asia, new kingdoms in Burma, Thailand, and Cambodia succeeded the empires of Pagan and the Khmer, which collapsed during the 13th century AD. The most important of the new states were the Thai kingdoms, notably Ayutthaya, and Ava and other kingdoms in Burma. In the region's islands, Muslim sultanates were established at strategic trading points such as Malacca in southern Malaysia.

The impetus for discovery

The major development in western Asia was the rise of the Ottoman Turks. The Ottoman Empire began as a minor Islamic principality in modern western Turkey, but soon its control extended over most of Asia Minor and the Balkans. The Byzantine capital, Constantinople, eventually fell to the Ottomans in AD 1453, to be renamed Istanbul. Ottoman rule closed Middle Eastern ports to Europeans, thereby blocking long-distance trade routes to the East. This was one factor behind the European quest for new sea routes to the east via the southern tip of Africa and west across the Atlantic. The drawing together of diverse cultures gathered pace at the very end of the 15th century AD, with the voyages of the Portuguese navigators Bartolomeu Dias and Vasco da Gama to southern Africa and the Indian Ocean, and Columbus's first voyage to the Caribbean. Over the course of a mere 80 years, from AD 1440 to AD 1520, European explorers established sea routes that embraced almost the whole world within a vast trading system. For many regions, European contact was to be a catastrophe, as it was accompanied by the exploitation of native peoples and by diseases, notably smallpox, which decimated populations with no immunity. The result was an immense toll of human suffering and a loss of cultural diversity. But it also laid the foundations of the modern world.

EUROPEAN EXPLORERS

The European voyages of exploration of the 15th and 16th centuries AD were motivated by the prospect for economic gain and were made possible by advances in shipbuilding. The vessels used by these early navigators were three-masted caravels, with stout hulls and a combination of square sails and lateen-rigged sails (angled at 45 degrees to the mast). These allowed the vessels to make progress in a wide range of wind conditions and made vessels highly maneuverable. Exploration was stimulated by the high prices that East Asian products such as silk and spices fetched in European markets. The ports of the eastern Mediterranean were blocked by the expansion of the Ottoman Empire in the 15th century AD, forcing European merchants to seek alternative routes. The Portuguese initiated the process by exploring the West African coast in the 1430s, and in AD 1498 they rounded the Cape of Good Hope to sail east into the Indian Ocean. In AD 1492, Columbus tried to reach East Asia by sailing west across the Atlantic, but instead encountered the Caribbean islands. The eastern and western routes were linked by Magellan and Elcano in AD 1522 when they made the first circumnavigation of the globe.

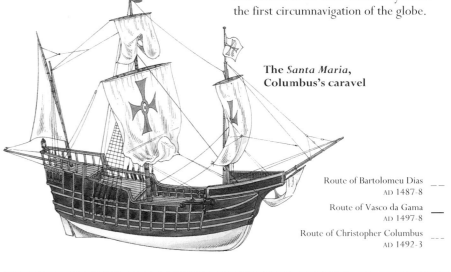

The *Santa Maria*,
Columbus's caravel

Route of Bartolomeu Dias
AD 1487-8

Route of Vasco da Gama
AD 1497-8

Route of Christopher Columbus
AD 1492-3

AMERICAS

THE AZTEC EMPIRE

At its height, the Aztec Empire (14th-16th centuries AD), with its capital at Tenochtitlan, dominated much of modern Mexico. Aztec society was divided into nobility, warriors, commoners, and slaves. The Aztecs either invaded and colonized territories or simply made areas safe for their merchants who, along with tribute collectors, supplied the capital with a constant flow of luxury goods. However, the Aztecs never exercised complete control; to the north, the Tarascan people built forts to defend against their imperialistic neighbors, and the smaller Tlaxcalan and Mixtec states to the south managed to remain independent.

|||| Extent of territories paying tribute to the Aztecs

▦ Center of Aztec foreign trade

**Terra-cotta
Aztec warrior,
Templo Mayor,
Mexico City**

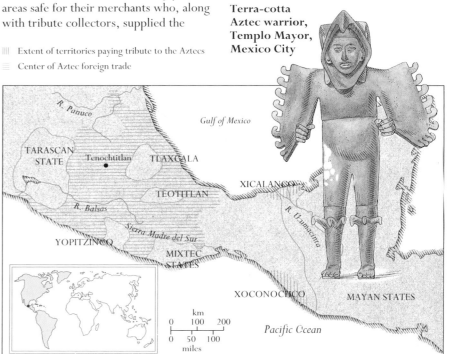

R. Pánuco

Gulf of Mexico

TARASCAN
STATE   Tenochtitlan   TLAXCALA

TEOTITLAN

XICALANGO

R. Balsas

Sierra Madre del Sur

YOPITZINCO

MIXTEC
STATES

R. Uzumacinta

XOCONOCHCO   MAYAN STATES

km
0   100   200

0   50   100
miles

Pacific Ocean

VOYAGES OF EXPLORATION

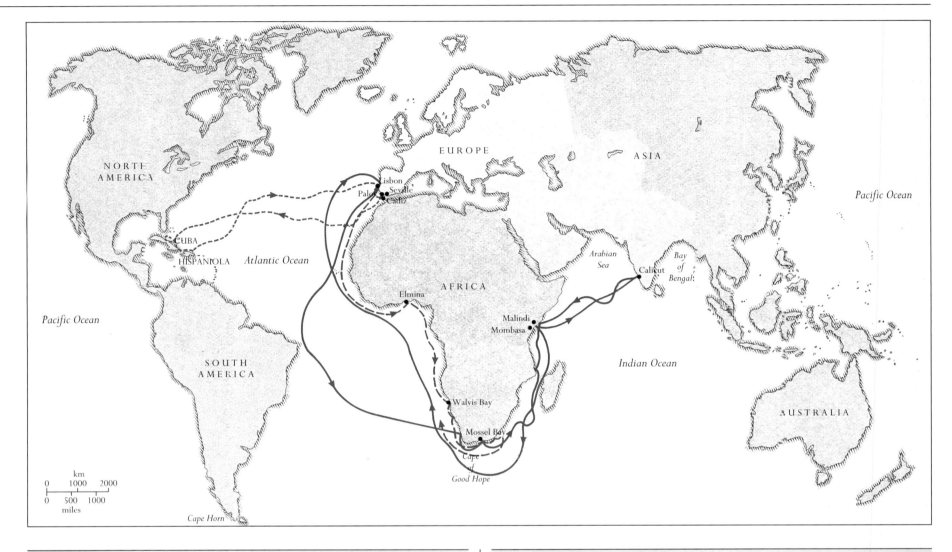

EAST ASIA

MING CHINA

After a century of Yuan (Mongol) rule, China once more came under the control of native rulers, the Ming, in AD 1368. The Ming emperors rebuilt the Chinese economy and made Peking their capital, embellishing the city with parks and palaces. They also encouraged exports, relying mainly on foreign merchants. Characteristic Ming products such as blue-and-white porcelain and enamel wares were highly sought after overseas, soon reaching Africa and Europe, and Central America via the Philippines from the 1560s.

Extent of Ming Empire

Ming red lacquer tray, China

AUSTRALASIA

MAORI NEW ZEALAND

New Zealand, one of the largest Polynesian island groups, was probably the last to be colonized. Settlement was concentrated on the North Island, and it is here that most of the early Maori sites are found. During the 14th century AD, increasing population led to inter-group rivalries, which stimulated the construction of *pas* (fortified settlements). Many original *pas* were still in use at the time of European contact in the late 18th century AD, when the native population numbered around 250,000. However, large parts of the South Island, especially the rugged western coast, were still only sparsely settled.

Fortified settlement ▲

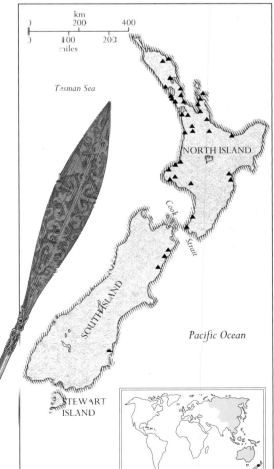

Decorated wooden paddle, New Zealand

AD 1250-1300

| FOOD & ENVIRONMENT | SHELTER & ARCHITECTURE |

AMERICAS

SUITABLE CLOTHING

Among the artifacts found at the mound site of Spiro in Oklahoma were marine shells from the Gulf of Mexico some 700 miles away. The shells were incised with decorative engravings, many of which depict figures wearing clothes well adapted to the variable climate of the region. The engraving on this shell, which dates to between AD 1100 and AD 1300, shows a figure dressed in a tunic and wide, banded belt. The most common depictions are of individuals wearing loincloths.

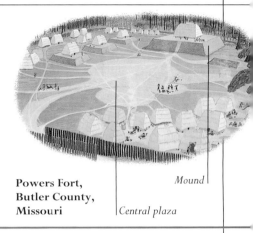

Engraved shell, Oklahoma

MOUND CENTER

Powers Fort (c. AD 1300) was a small ceremonial center situated in the Mississippi Valley in southeastern North America. The site covered an area of 12 acres within its fortified walls and was laid out around a central plaza and four adjacent mounds. The settlement acted as the focal point for a local community whose members largely lived in villages and farmsteads in the surrounding countryside.

Powers Fort, Butler County, Missouri

Mound

Central plaza

EAST ASIA & AUSTRALASIA

FAMINE CROP

Originally domesticated in Africa, sorghum was introduced into southwestern China from the Middle East via India. Like soy, it was an excellent famine crop, giving good yields on land too poor for wheat or millet. The grain could be used for human consumption or animal fodder and for making alcohol. The discarded stalks were burnt as fuel.

Sorghum plant

MONGOL CAPITAL

China was conquered and reunified by Kubilai Khan (AD 1215-94), who became the first emperor of the Yuan (Mongol) Dynasty (AD 1279-1368). His new capital, Dadu (modern Peking), which so impressed the Venetian traveler Marco Polo, was built according to classical Chinese plans. The emperor's palace in the southern part of the capital was surrounded by an imperial city that included parks with artificial lakes and

hills. The eastern and western parts were occupied by temples, while the northern area was divided into shop-lined avenues and smaller lanes for houses, each with a spacious court-yard. Drainage systems were laid before each section was built, and a canal network connected the Grand Canal to the artificial lakes in the imperial city, so that produce could be transported there directly.

MIDDLE EAST & SOUTH ASIA

AGRICULTURAL DECLINE

The Mongol conquest of Iran and Mesopotamia in AD 1258 had a devastating effect on the region's agriculture. The nomadic economy of the Mongols was suited to rolling grassland, where horses, sheep, and camels could graze. Consequently, much arable land reverted to grazing under the Mongols, and many peasant farmers were forced to flee. Neglect of the land and the consequent collapse of irrigation systems led to a decline in agricultural wealth in most areas of the Middle East.

PORTABLE TENTS

The Mongol rulers of the Middle East continued their nomadic life in Iran even after they had assumed the role of sultans. Eyewitnesses described their royal camp as a moving city; some of the yurts (felt tents) were so big that carts were used to transport them. There were huge reception tents, separate quarters for women, royal apartments, and even portable shrines and temples.

EUROPE

WINE TRADE

In the later Middle Ages, maritime trade flourished along the coasts of Atlantic Europe. One major traded commodity was wine. Wealthy people in England drank wine, most of which was imported from the region of Bordeaux in southwestern France. This trade was at its height from the 13th to the 15th centuries AD, when Bordeaux was under English rule. Many Bordeaux wine jugs have been excavated at medieval English towns.

Wine jug, Bordeaux, France

WATERFRONT PALACES

Many cities in Italy became rich as a result of the growth of Mediterranean trade in the 13th century AD. The wealth of Venice was reflected in the waterfront palaces lining its canals. The ground floors typically had a colonnade through which goods could be unloaded, and business was carried out in a great hall flanked by stores and offices. Facades with elegant windows were designed to display the status of the owner.

Palazzo Ca' Da Mosto, Venice, Italy

AFRICA

FOREST PROVISIONS

The peoples of the West African forest kingdoms grew staple crops like yams, oil palms, kola nuts, akee fruits, and gourds. Yams and oil palms provided carbohydrates, fat, and vitamin A. African rice was a staple at the fringes of the forest. Mele-gueta pepper (*Aframomum melegueta*), the so-called "grains of paradise" native to West Africa, was highly prized as a spice and traded widely.

Melegueta peppercorns

MOSQUES AND PALACES

The construction of new mosques and palaces in the Islamic coastal towns of East Africa during the 13th and 14th centuries AD reflected the growing wealth and sophistication of these trading colonies. The mosque of Fakhr al Din in Mogadishu, Somalia, was built around AD 1269, its domes constructed with coral concrete (concrete made with pulverized coral rather than sand). A complex system of timber beams divided the roof into

nine bays, the central bay having a tall, plain dome. Other features were a decorated octagonal vault located above the main entrance and a marble *mihrab* (niche), which pointed in the direction of Mecca and was probably made in northern India, illustrating well-developed trading links across the Indian Ocean.

TECHNOLOGY & INNOVATION

BOWS AND ARROWS

Excavated from the Craig Mound at Spiro, Oklahoma, were neatly arranged piles of small projectile points. They are the only remaining parts of what were once quivers full of arrows. The use of the bow and arrow was widespread in both North and South America. Although arrow points are found throughout the continent, there is little evidence as to the nature of the bows that were used. In some regions, however, bows are depicted in rock carvings, and at the Spiro mounds, bows and arrows were engraved on conch shells, which were acquired through trade from the Gulf of Mexico. These shell engravings indicate that bows were generally about three-quarters the height of the archers.

Modern *tachi* (slashing sword) and sheath, Japan

SLASHING SWORDS

Japanese swordsmiths reached their greatest technical excellence during the Kamakura period (AD 1185-1333), forging long *tachi* (slashing swords) that were sharp enough to remove a human head at a single stroke. Such was the significance of these weapons that the forging of them was bound up with ritual sanctions. The swordsmith was required to be both celibate and vegetarian, like a Buddhist monk, and to don courtly robes during the production process, in itself a religious act.

SPINNING AND WEAVING

The *charkha* (spinning wheel) typifies traditional Indian industry, which has always combined relatively basic technology with great efficiency. The *charkha* was introduced into Europe from India around AD 1200, and the horizontal loom, which had a framework of string or wire to separate the yarn threads, by AD 1300.

European women using a horizontal loom

CHAIN MAIL

Mounted European knights fought in complete suits of chain mail and heavy iron helmets with narrow eye slits. A decorated surcoat was also essential for recognition in the heat of battle. This extraordinary 13th-century copper aquamanile (water jug) in the form of a fully caparisoned knight, from Hexham in northern England, would once have stood on a nobleman's table. Originally there was a lance in the knight's right hand and a shield on his left arm.

Copper aquamanile, Hexham, England

CENTER OF CRAFTSMANSHIP

The town of Benin, in the forest region of what is now Nigeria, was the most important of many walled settlements founded by the Edo people. Benin controlled river trade routes to the north and the coast and was a center of fine craftsmanship, with artisans skilled in ironwork, woodwork, leather and beadwork, and ivory-carving.

Carved ivory bracelet, Benin, Nigeria

ART & RITUAL

FUNERARY FIGURINE

Mortuary ceremonies in midwestern North America in the 13th century AD involved small ritual figurines. Found in a mound at Spiro, Oklahoma, this cross-legged figurine is carved in a naturalistic style from cedar wood. Figurines like this are rarely found in the eastern woodlands, as wood is seldom preserved.

Cedar-wood figurine, Oklahoma

RELIGIOUS TOLERANCE

China under the first Yuan emperor, Kubilai Khan, enjoyed a high degree of religious tolerance. Kubilai recruited his administration from all faiths, and Buddhist, Daoist, and Confucian temples, Christian churches, and Muslim mosques were all tax-exempt. He also awarded the leading Tibetan Buddhist monk spiritual authority over the entire empire, in return for acknowledging Kubilai's temporal supremacy in China.

Luster tile with Chinese dragon decoration, Iran

DECORATIVE SYMBOLS

Under Ghazan Khan (reigned AD 1295-1304), who was subordinate to the Mongol emperor Kubilai Khan, Islam was adopted as the state religion of Iran. Many of the Mongol elite, however, retained their Buddhist beliefs and continued to use Chinese decorative symbols, such as the dragon and the phoenix, which were restricted to court use until AD 1300.

ORIGINS OF THE LUTE

The classical lute, which came into widespread use throughout Europe in the later Middle Ages, was based on an Arab prototype, the *al-'ud*. This was adopted in the 13th century AD by the Christians of northern Spain from their Islamic Moorish neighbors in the south.

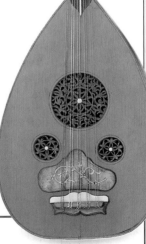

Contemporary Moroccan *al-'ud*

SOAPSTONE FIGURES

At the site of Great Zimbabwe, near the Sabi River in modern Zimbabwe, a number of anthropomorphic soapstone figures have been found. The figures represent birds and humans and are decorated with geometric patterns. They were probably used in rituals and date to a period before the greatest construction phase at the site during the 14th and 15th centuries AD.

Cast of soapstone bird figure, Great Zimbabwe, Zimbabwe

AD 1300 - 1350

FOOD & ENVIRONMENT

SHELTER & ARCHITECTURE

AMERICAS

FLOATING GARDENS
The Aztecs constructed *chinampas* (artificial garden plots) in the form of rectangular islands in the swamps and shallow lakes surrounding their capital Tenochtitlán, in the Valley of Mexico. While *chinampa* agriculture may have begun as early as 1000 BC, it was the Aztecs who, during the 14th and 15th centuries AD, developed it into the most intensive form of garden cultivation in Mesoamerica.

MOSAIC STONEWORK
The ancient ceremonial center of Mitla, in Mexico's Oaxaca region, was taken over by the Mixtec people at about this time. The Mixtecs applied ornamental stonework to the walls of existing structures, including brightly painted geometric mosaics reminiscent of Mixtec pictographic writing and ceramics.

Mixtec stonework, Mitla, Mexico

EAST ASIA & AUSTRALASIA

Yam

POND FIELDS
In the 14th century AD, terraced field systems were constructed on several of the eastern Polynesian islands, in an effort to produce more food to support a growing population. Pond fields were built on the terraces, and irrigation systems devised so that water flowed down the slopes from plot to plot. These were designed for the cultivation of taro, a nutritious tuber that flourishes in waterlogged ground. On western Polynesian islands such as Tonga, the principal crop was yam, a plant suited to dry, well-drained ground – making terraced irrigation unnecessary.

FORTIFIED REFUGES
Fortifications began to be built in New Zealand in the 14th century AD, especially on the more heavily populated North Island. They testify to the endemic warfare that characterized Maori society at this time. Known as *pas*, they display a variety of defensive arrangements: some were built on steep hillside terraces, defended only against attack from below, while others were located on promontories with a ditch across the neck, making them more secure. The most elaborate *pas* had an entire circuit of banks and ditches. At all sites, the earthwork defenses were enhanced by the construction of wooden barriers and raised timber fighting galleries. Some *pas* may have been permanently occupied – there are remains of houses and storage pits at many sites – but most were probably intended as refuges in times of danger.

MIDDLE EAST & SOUTH ASIA

REFORMS IN LAND TENURE
Around AD 1300 there was a temporary halt in the continuing decline of agriculture in the Middle East under Mongol rule. Rashid al-Din, chief minister to the Mongol ruler Ghazan Khan (reigned AD 1295-1304), lessened the burden of taxes, stopped the billeting of troops on citizens, and reformed the system of land tenure.

Manuscript detail showing peasant farmers and a Mongol, Iran

DOMED TOMB
The Mongol rulers of the Middle East chose to settle in what is now Azerbaijan. Their capital, Sultaniyya, was built by Oljaitu Khan in AD 1306. Oljaitu planned that it should become a pilgrimage center to rival Mecca and Jerusalem, and with this in mind he built the Gunbad-i Oljaitu, an impressive tomb intended to house the remains of the martyr Ali, Muhammad's son-in-law and founder of the Islamic Shi'ite sect. The tomb echoes the Dome of the Rock in Jerusalem in plan.

EUROPE

PEASANTS EVICTED
During the 14th century AD many small villages in northwestern Europe were abandoned. One contributory factor may have been the Black Death of AD 1347-50; another, the economic boom of the previous century, during which land had been farmed more intensively than before in an effort to feed the growing population. Some soils were unable to support such intensive cultivation, and harvests diminished as the natural fertility of the land was exhausted. In England, landlords responded to these changes by converting unprofitable arable land into highly profitable sheep pasture. English wool was prized on the international market, and large stocks were exported to mainland Europe through Calais. Fewer people were needed to manage the flocks and many of the peasant farmers were evicted, abandoning their villages to seek a new life in the towns.

ADMINISTRATIVE PALACES
The prosperous Italian cities of the 14th century AD, including Florence and Siena, were governed by councils of officials drawn from among the citizens themselves. Their civic pride is evident from the construction of impressive palaces designed to house administrative offices and city records, like the Palazzo Vecchio in Florence, built between AD 1299 and AD 1314.

Palazzo Vecchio, Florence, Italy

AFRICA

MEAT FOR ROYAL FEASTS
Cattle were a major source of wealth and food for the elite of southern African communities during the 14th and 15th centuries AD. At the site of Great Zimbabwe, near the Sabi River in modern Zimbabwe, finds of animal bones show that large numbers of surplus male cattle were brought from the surrounding countryside and slaughtered, probably for feasting or sacrifice. The herds would have been moved from place to place throughout the year as new pastures were needed. Ordinary people probably rarely ate meat: their staples were millet, sorghum, and vegetables.

RULER'S PALACE
By the first half of the 14th century AD, the Arab trading town of Kilwa, located on a strategically placed island off the southern coast of Tanzania, acquired a monopoly in the East African gold and ivory trade. The ruler of Kilwa resided in the Husuni Kubwa, a cliff-top palace complex with courtyards, pavilions, and arcades. Its many rooms (well over 100 in number) included an imposing audience chamber, baths and living quarters, and a warehouse complex.

Interior view, Husuni Kubwa palace, Kilwa

TECHNOLOGY & INNOVATION

METAL ALLOYS

By AD 1300, the people of Colombia and Ecuador had developed a variety of techniques for alloying metals. The production of *tumbaga*, an alloy of copper, silver, and gold, was widespread in the region. It was used to make jewelry including pectorals (chest ornaments), bracelets, earrings, and nose rings.

Gold pectoral, Colombia

BARK-CLOTH TEXTILES

The inhabitants of the Pacific islands made extensive use of bark cloth for clothing. The finest material came from the inner bark of the paper mulberry tree, which was cultivated specifically for this purpose. The bark was stripped from the tree, and the inner bark was soaked in water. It was then beaten with a wooden pounder and dried and bleached in the sun. The resulting pieces were felted, pasted, and sewn together.

MUSICAL INNOVATOR

The Indian poet and historian Amir Khusram (AD 1253-1325) was also a great musical innovator to whom the composition of a number of early *ragas* (traditional Indian musical forms) has been attributed. These are the basic rhythmic melodic structure over which a piece of music is improvised. Khusram is also said to be the inventor of the *sitar*, a metal-stringed instrument of the lute family, and the *tabla*, a drum.

Modern *tabla*

Modern *sitar*

SOPHISTICATED WEAPONRY

Although gunpowder was invented in China during the 9th century AD, the first indisputable evidence for the use of cannons is provided by this illustration from a western European manuscript that dates to AD 1326. Clumsy and sometimes unpredictable when they first came into use, cannons nevertheless were to become increasingly important on the battlefields of Europe during the 14th century AD.

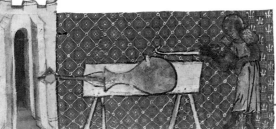

Illustration showing cannon from the *Treatise of Walter of Milemetre*

EXTRACTING GOLD

In the southern African interior, the construction of stone-built enclosures in the 14th and 15th centuries AD was directly related to the increased exploitation of metal deposits, particularly gold. Some gold was extracted by simple mining techniques — narrow pits or shafts sunk into gold-bearing rock seams — but most was probably panned in streams. However, the amount of gold obtained in this region was small compared to the enormous quantities being traded in West Africa. Despite its rarity, gold was buried in the graves of the wealthy elite, usually in the form of gold foil affixed to wooden objects such as clubs or bowls.

ART & RITUAL

EMBROIDERED TEXTILES

Ponchos were worn by the peoples of Peru for special ceremonies and were also used as funerary coverings. The poncho shown here is embroidered with feathers in the Chancay style (AD 1000-1400), characterized by geometric patterns and geometric portrayals of plants, animals, and humans. The central figure here is open-armed and wears large ear spools and a headdress hanging down on both sides of the face.

Poncho, Chancay Valley, Peru

EARLY THEATER

The *No* drama of Japan combines music, singing, dance, and poetry. One of its exponents was the artist Kan-ami (AD 1334-85). Traditional entertainment for the ruling classes, *No* plays were performed on a bare stage, which encouraged the audience to become involved in the action. Actors distanced themselves by wearing masks. *No* drama still survives in Japan today.

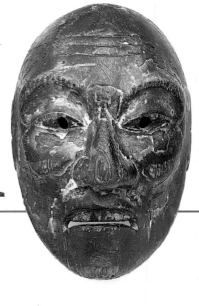

***No* mask, Japan**

MANUSCRIPT ILLUSTRATION

During the reign of the Mongol ruler Oljaitu Khan (AD 1304-16), several illustrated manuscripts were produced at Tabriz in northwestern Iran. Influences from Iraq, Central Asia, and China produced an eclectic style of illustration best exemplified in the *World History* written by Oljaitu's chief minister, Rashid al-Din. Later works include the richly illustrated *Book of Kings*, produced between AD 1330 and AD 1340.

RUDIMENTARY PERSPECTIVE

The Florentine painter Giotto di Bondone (AD 1266-1337) introduced new principles and techniques into European art, most notably the discovery and rudimentary use of perspective, an innovation that gave his paintings an unprecedented three-dimensional quality. His most famous works are the cycles of religious frescoes decorating the twin churches at Assisi in central Italy.

***The Adoration of the Magi* by Giotto di Bondone, Assisi, Italy**

ILLUSTRATED MANUSCRIPTS

In the 14th and 15th centuries AD, Christian artists in Ethiopia began to produce richly decorated Gospel manuscripts. Surviving illustrations depict scenes from the life of Christ, with particular attention being paid to the Passion and Crucifixion.

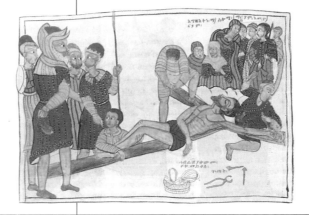

Detail of the Crucifixion, illuminated Gospel manuscript, Ethiopia

AD 1350-1400

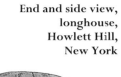

FOOD & ENVIRONMENT	SHELTER & ARCHITECTURE

AMERICAS

DRINKING CHOCOLATE

Cacao beans were highly valued by the Aztec nobility and priesthood. They were the chief ingredient of *chocolatl*, a frothy drink to which cornmeal, spices, or chili were added and which only the elite were permitted to drink. Cacao beans were also used as trading currency. One of the principal sources of cacao was a region known as Soconusco in what is now Guatemala.

Cacao beans in pod

COMMUNAL LONGHOUSES

The Iroquoian peoples of northeastern North America built communal longhouses grouped within a fortification. At the Howlett Hill site, the remains of a longhouse more than 328 feet long were discovered. Built in the 14th century AD, the house had a pole frame covered by sheets of bark. Each family had its own section and hearth within.

End and side view, longhouse, Howlett Hill, New York

EAST ASIA & AUSTRALASIA

COTTON CULTIVATION

By the late 14th century AD, cotton had become the most important fiber crop in China. It had been introduced into the southern and western regions of China from India. The government stimulated cotton cultivation by allowing peasants to use it to pay the tax on textiles, which had previously been paid in silk. Consequently, more silk was available for export to Asia and the West. Cotton became the most common material for clothing, replacing rougher-textured hemp cloth. From cultivation to spinning and weaving, the production of cotton was labor-intensive and was carried out by women, providing an important additional source of agricultural income.

SPLIT-LEVEL HOUSES

Domestic dwellings on the Marquesas Islands in the South Pacific were built on platforms of basalt rock, carefully fitted together without mortar. The superstructure was constructed from a light framework of timber poles, and covered with thatch. Houses were usually split-level, with a slightly raised section at the rear that served as sleeping quarters and a lower front section, which was open like a veranda.

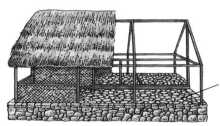

Basalt rock platform

House, Marquesas Islands, South Pacific

MIDDLE EAST & SOUTH ASIA

CINNAMON EXPORTS

In the 14th century AD, political troubles caused the collapse of Sri Lanka's economy, which was based on hydraulic operations including massive artificial reservoirs and irrigation systems. The political center in the dry north-central part of the island shifted to the zone of rain-fed agriculture in the southwest. The importance of trade increased, much of it controlled by mercantile Arabs who settled extensively on the island. One of the island's major exports was cinnamon.

Cinnamon sticks

STYLISTIC COMBINATION

An Indo-Muslim style of architecture developed in northern India in the 14th century AD. Indigenous architects adapted their designs to accommodate Islamic requirements, notably by omitting any figurative representations. At Tuqhluqabad, a Muslim city near Delhi, the tomb built in AD 1368-9 for Khan-i-Jahan Tilangani, prime minister to the sultan Firuz Shah Tuqhluq, retained projecting eaves, a stylistically Hindu feature.

Tomb of Khan-i-Jahan Tilangani, Tuqhluqabad, India

EUROPE

MEDICINE JARS

From the late 14th century AD onward, the shelves of apothecaries in Italy were lined with small pottery jars known as *albarelli*. These contained dry medicines and elixirs to protect against plague, and their cylindrical shape, with slightly curved sides, was based on the hollow sections of bamboo that had traditionally been used to transport drugs and spices from the East.

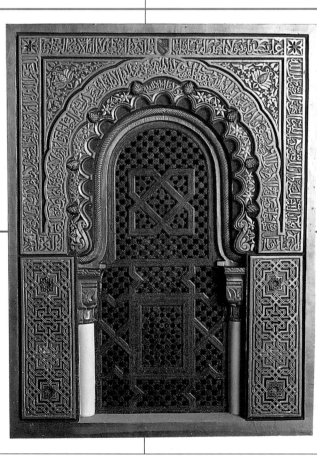

INTERIOR DESIGN

During the 14th century AD, splendid new buildings were constructed at the Alhambra at Granada, the last surviving capital of the Islamic Moorish rulers of southern Spain. Its elaborate interiors are attributed to the reign of Yusuf I (died AD 1354). Moorish architects used carved and painted geometric and Arabesque motifs, incorporating Koranic verses into their designs.

Decorated window, Alhambra, Granada, Spain

AFRICA

IRRIGATED FIELD SYSTEMS

Elaborate irrigated field systems were constructed in parts of the East African Rift Valley during the 14th century AD. Although irrigation had long been practiced in other regions of the world, these fields were the first of their kind in sub-Saharan Africa. The most extensive remains are at Engaruka in northern Tanzania, where water was channeled from streams via stone-lined culverts, and used to irrigate over 7 sq miles of stone-walled fields. The complete range of crops that was cultivated is unknown, but sorghum was one of the most important.

DRY-STONE WALLS

Cattle-herding kingdoms flourished in the southern African interior during the 14th century AD. Stone was the preferred material for major structures, and the evolution of building techniques in stone can be identified from sites such as Great Zimbabwe, near the Sabi River in modern Zimbabwe. Before the construction of free-standing dry-stone walls, which usually had a rubble core, stone walls had been fashioned around naturally occurring outcrops of rock, with dry-stone walling filling any gaps.

TECHNOLOGY & INNOVATION

SPORTS EQUIPMENT

Originating in the Mexican highlands between 1500 BC and 1200 BC, the Mesoamerican ball game eventually spread to the Caribbean. In Puerto Rico, carved stone and wooden belts were worn by the players. This stone belt, which dates to around AD 1350, was probably used in the ceremonies associated with the game.

Stone belt, Puerto Rico

BLUE-AND-WHITE WARE

The government kilns at Jingdezhen in eastern China increased their output of blue-and-white ceramics soon after the Ming Dynasty (AD 1368-1644) was established. This fine porcelain had been developed for markets in the Middle East, but was now produced both for export and for use by the the imperial Ming court.

Blue-and-white ware dish, Jingdezhen, China

GLASSMAKING CENTERS

In the 14th century AD under the Mamluk Dynasty, which ruled Egypt and Syria from AD 1250-1570, glassmaking reached a peak. At Cairo and Damascus, glassware was decorated with polychrome enamels and luster (an extremely thin metallic film), for the most part with Chinese motifs, floral designs, and Koranic inscriptions. Mosque lamps often bore the name and heraldic badge of their donors.

Enameled glass mosque lamp, Syria

MECHANICAL CLOCKS

One indication of the European technological revival in the later Middle Ages was the invention of the mechanical clock, in c. AD 1280. The earliest surviving examples, such as the clock from Wells Cathedral, Somerset, England, date to the late 14th century AD. Such clocks were adopted by monasteries to order their daily schedule.

Workings of Wells Cathedral clock, Science Museum, London, England

STONE-CARVED STOOLS

The craftsmen of the West African forest kingdoms were adept at working with terra-cotta, bronze, and stone. This quartz stool, from the Ashanti region in what is now Ghana, was carved from a single piece of rock and was used by a prominent dignitary or ruler.

Ashanti quartz stool, Ghana

ART & RITUAL

GOD OF SPRING

The Aztec pantheon of gods consisted of more than 200 deities symbolically linked with directions, social groups, days and months, and food and flowers. Xipe Totec, the god of renewal, was associated with spring and the rising sun and was a patron of merchants and artisans working with precious metals and stone. His priests honored him by dressing themselves in the flayed skins of human sacrificial victims. This image of Xipe Totec comes from the Aztec capital, Tenochtitlan.

Xipe Totec, god of spring, Tenochtitlan, Mexico

TOMB SCULPTURE

The classical tradition of Chinese stone sculpture continued during the Ming Dynasty, notably in the "spirit roads" – avenues of stone figures lining the approaches to important tombs. Statues associated with imperial tombs presented a picture of an idealized empire, with figures representing the highest state officials, and animals symbolizing different virtues.

Stone statues of military officials, Imperial Ming Tombs, Beijing, China

ROYAL WORKSHOPS

Born in Kesh in modern Uzbekistan, Timur (AD 1336-1405), also known as Tamerlane, conquered most of the Middle East previously ruled by the Mongols and founded the Timurid Dynasty (AD 1370-1506). At his capital, Samarkand, artisans worked for the royal workshops in an atmosphere of experiment and unlimited financial sponsorship. Huge objects, including cast-bronze cauldrons weighing 2 tons, were produced.

Cast-bronze cauldron made for Timur. Samarkand, Uzbekistan

PILGRIM SOUVENIRS

Pilgrimages to the shrines of important saints remained popular in late medieval Europe. In England, the tomb of St. Thomas à Becket at Canterbury, Kent, was particularly popular. At the instigation of King Henry II, Becket had been assassinated in Canterbury Cathedral in AD 1170. Pilgrims could purchase inexpensive souvenirs of their visit in the form of lead badges depicting events from the saint's last days, including his martyrdom. Such badges have been found at sites throughout Britain.

BRONZE PORTRAITURE

Much of the bronze used by artisans at the Yoruba town of Ife, in western Nigeria, was imported from the Tada region of the Niger River valley directly to the north. Some of the extremely lifelike bronze heads made at Ife are adorned with impressive headdresses, which would have denoted the position of the individual in Yoruba social hierarchy.

Bronze head, Ife, Nigeria

AD 1400 - 1450

200 BC

FOOD & ENVIRONMENT	SHELTER & ARCHITECTURE

AMERICAS

ANIMAL OFFERINGS

Together with agriculture, herding was the basis of the economy of the Inca Empire. Llamas were used for transport and alpacas mainly for wool. Both animals provided meat. These stone figurines, known as *conopas*, date to the 15th century AD and were used as fertility amulets in livestock rituals.

Stone figurines of alpacas, Peru

INCA STONE WALL

Inca architecture is characterized by its megalithic construction and fine masonry. Stone blocks fit together so exactly that not even a thin blade can be inserted between them. Retaining walls were carefully finished, usually with pillow-shaped stones, with trapezoidal openings and niches. Stone was carved using stone chisels and hammers and sand abrasives.

Inca stone wall, Peru

EAST ASIA & AUSTRALASIA

IMPERIAL MENAGERIES

The Chinese imperial collections of strange beasts in menageries or parks owed their existence in part to the belief that certain animals possessed supernatural powers. In the early 15th century AD, Chinese interest in natural history was fanned by the expeditions of the great eunuch admiral Zheng He (AD 1371-1433), who returned from his trips with previously unknown animals. The first giraffe ever seen in China was given an imperial welcome by the Chinese Ming emperor Yongle (reigned AD 1402-24). On later trips, the admiral brought back lions, elephants, rhinos, zebras, and ostriches.

Tiers of decreasing size

TEMPLE OF HEAVEN

The Chinese Ming emperors performed their most important duties at the Temple and Altar of Heaven, which were built between AD 1420 and AD 1430 in Beijing, the Ming capital. The emperors made sacrifices for good harvests and reported to heaven on the state of the empire. The circular temple and altar are both enclosed within a square wall, reflecting the ancient belief in "heaven round, earth square."

Temple of Heaven, Beijing, China

MIDDLE EAST & SOUTH ASIA

INDIAN SERICULTURE

Early Indian silk weavers relied on thread imported from China. By the 15th century AD, however, sericulture was established in Bengal, although the kingdom of Gujarat in western India, which produced the finest silk cloth, continued to use Chinese silk thread. Gujarati silks included *patoli* cloth, in which the silk threads were tie-dyed before being woven.

***Patoli* silk cloth, Gujarat, India**

BLENDING TRADITIONS

The Jami Masjid (Friday Mosque) at Ahmadabad in the kingdom of Gujarat was built by the ruler Ahmad Shah and completed by AD 1424. A blend of native Indian and imported Islamic traditions, it consists of a large courtyard surrounded by a cloister. On the west side lies a massive stone-pillared prayer hall. The perforated screens in the upper stories of the building are typical Gujarati features.

Perforated stone screen, Jami Masjid, Ahmadabad, Gujarat, India

EUROPE

PEASANT REVIVAL

In AD 1450, after more than a century of plague, the population of western Europe had fallen to 65 or 70 percent of its total in AD 1330. The pressure on land, a key feature of the early 14th century AD, was now replaced by a labor shortage. This created favorable conditions for many peasant farmers, because where labor was scarce and fields were abandoned, they were able to persuade landlords to reduce rents or feudal obligations. Attempts to prevent peasants from moving from one estate to another in search of better tenancy agreements were largely ineffective. As a result, by the end of the Middle Ages, western Europe's peasants were freer and more prosperous than ever before.

EARLY RENAISSANCE

Renaissance architecture developed in the cities of northern Italy in the early 15th century AD. One leading exponent, Filippo Brunelleschi (AD 1377-1446), based his designs on Roman construction methods. His masterpiece, the dome of Florence's Gothic cathedral, completed in AD 1446, was a technological triumph.

Il Duomo, Florence, Italy

AFRICA

IMPORTED COTTON CLOTH

Burials dating to the early 15th century AD in the Zambezi Valley provide evidence for the principal materials used for clothing at this time – bark cloth and cotton. Most cotton was made locally, as it had been grown in Africa since at least AD 1200, but especially fine cotton was still imported from India.

Modern garment made of imported Indian cotton, East Africa

COURTYARD HOUSES

During the 15th century AD, palatial houses were built in Cairo, Egypt, reflecting the continuing wealth of this populous and important trading center. These were courtyard houses, built of fine ashlar (straight-edged, stone-block masonry), with splendid wrought-iron window grills and finely carved timber balconies projecting from the upper stories. The life of the household focused on a central courtyard and, for reasons of security and privacy, the houses presented a relatively blank facade to the street, with few doorways or other openings.

TECHNOLOGY & INNOVATION

ACCOUNTING SYSTEM

The Incas did not adopt a writing system until the 16th century AD, but they had a mnemonic accounting system, which used a device called a *quipu*. This consisted of a series of knots tied in cords grouped into bundles. *Quipus* were officially superseded after the Spanish invasion, but are still used today in some traditional communities.

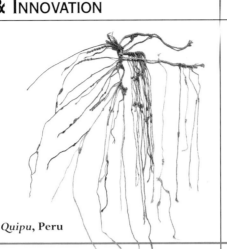

Quipu, Peru

INLAID EYES

Between AD 1000 and AD 1650 *moai* (giant statues) were erected on Easter Island in Polynesia. Each has eye sockets, some of which may have originally been inlaid with artificial eyes. The whites of the eyes were made from white coral inlaid with either red scoria or obsidian, which formed the irises.

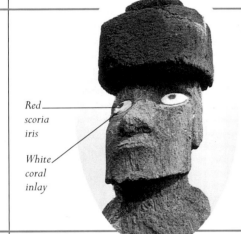

Red scoria iris

White coral inlay

Head of statue, Easter Island

ASTRONOMICAL TABLES

Influenced by a boyhood visit to the observatory (built in AD 1258) at Maragheh, Iran, the Timurid sultan Ulugh Beg (AD 1405-47) built his own observatory in Samarkand, the Timurid capital in modern Uzbekistan, in AD 1420. The observatory was used until at least AD 1511. It consisted of three astronomical instruments built into a round structure: a sextant set within a deep trench to record the movements of the heavenly bodies, a solar clock like a sundial, and a quadrant to calculate angles. A new set of astronomical tables was recorded in the *Zij-i Sultani* (Royal Almanac). Research went on after Ulugh's death under the astronomer Ghiyath al Din and the mathematician Al-Kashi.

SEAFARING EXPLORERS

Portuguese seafarers began to explore the coast of West Africa in the early 15th century AD in small but sophisticated wooden sailing ships known as caravels. These were sturdy enough to withstand Atlantic storms, and their triangular lateen sails (suspended at an angle of 45 degrees to the mast) enabled them to exploit both side and stern winds.

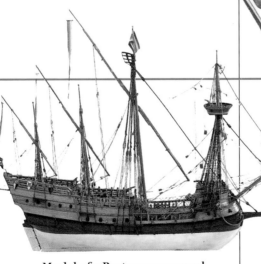

Model of a Portuguese caravel

CRUCIFORM INGOTS

Mined from deposits north and south of the Zambezi River, copper was an important source of wealth in southern Africa during the 15th century AD and was widely traded. Copper ingots found in an early 15th-century burial at Ingombe Ilede in the Zambezi Valley were cast in cruciform molds and could be easily transported by bearers using shoulder sticks.

Copper ingots, Ingombe Ilede, Zambia

ART & RITUAL

FELINE FIGURINE

Measuring 5 inches in height, this feline effigy dating to around AD 1450 is one of many well-preserved wooden artifacts from the waterlogged Cushing site at Key Marco in southwestern Florida. The region was controlled at this time by the Calusa, a people of southern Florida who developed a complex chiefdom based on the use of marine resources. The Key Marco cat is a ritual item, probably symbolizing a spiritual connection between humans and animals.

Feline effigy, Key Marco, Florida

Lozenge motif   *Slot for hand*

Decorated wooden shield, New South Wales, Australia

SYMBOLIC DECORATION

Australian Aborigines used a variety of artifacts made from wood, including boomerangs, spears, spear throwers, clubs, and narrow fighting shields like this example from Braidwood in New South Wales. Shields were often carved with designs incorporating circles, spirals, lozenges, and curvilinear motifs. Similar designs on the inside of skin cloaks signified the wearer's totem (clan symbol), and are also found on *tjuringa* (sacred boards) used in secret rituals.

BLUE-AND-WHITE TILES

Developed in China in the early 14th century AD, blue-and-white porcelain was being imitated at centers of ceramic production in the Middle East by the early 15th century AD. This tile from the mosque of the Ottoman sultan Murad II (reigned AD 1421-51) at Edirne, an Ottoman capital in Balkan Turkey, dates to around AD 1425.

Tile with blue-and-white underglaze decoration, Edirne, northwestern Turkey

INCREASED REALISM

Painting underwent major developments in the 15th century AD, particularly in Italy and northern Europe. A decisive change was the complete mastery of perspective, first achieved in the work of the Florentine painter Masaccio (AD 1401-28). Flemish painters, notably Jan van Eyck, developed a new painting medium — oils. Oils allowed the artist to create a dynamic quality of light that enhanced the exactness of detail derived from Gothic miniaturists and manuscript illuminators.

BRONZE SCULPTURE

It is not known exactly when artisans at Benin, capital of the Edo kingdom in the forest zone of what is now Nigeria, first mastered bronze casting, although it was probably during the 15th century AD. Bronze sculpture was one of many artistic traditions that had spread south from the ancient Yoruba town of Ife, continuing to flourish at Benin under the control of the *oba* (king).

Bronze head, Benin, Nigeria

Elaborate headdress

AD 1450 - 1500

200 BC

FOOD & ENVIRONMENT

SHELTER & ARCHITECTURE

AMERICAS

AZTEC MARKETPLACE
The city of Tlatelolco in Mexico was the sister city of the Aztec capital Tenochtitlán and was the commercial center of the Aztec Empire from the 14th until the early 16th century AD. It was one of the largest trading centers in the Americas. Hundreds of merchants and farmers served tens of thousands of customers daily.

The Great Market, Tlatelolco, Mexico

ISLAND VILLAGES
The Taino people were once widely distributed throughout the Caribbean. On the island of Hispaniola, the larger Taino villages had 1,000 to 2,000 inhabitants, who occupied multi-family dwellings scattered around a plaza. Early Spanish explorers described the houses as round and made of wood with thatched roofs.

Taino house, Hispaniola

EAST ASIA & AUSTRALASIA

TEA CEREMONY
The tea ceremony, which took place in specially designed tea rooms or tea houses, played an important role in Japanese society, with officials appointed to the rank of Grand Tea Master. The ceremony has its origins in gatherings convened to assess the quality of different kinds of tea and the beauty of the objects used in its preparation and serving. Ceremonies came to include an appreciation of many aspects of life, including gardening, architecture, furniture design, calligraphy, history, and religion. Indeed, under the influence of Zen (meditative) Buddhism, the ceremony was an occasion combining the Japanese sense of practical beauty with enjoyment and conversation.

MING STONE TOWERS
In Ming China (AD 1368-1644), those parts of imperial tombs that lay above ground were built to imitate imperial palaces, with splendid halls and courtyards. Many such buildings still stand, as do most of the stone towers guarding the entrances to burial enclosures, like this example built in the 15th century AD.

Stone tomb tower, Beijing, China

MIDDLE EAST & SOUTH ASIA

ROYAL ELEPHANTS
In the mid-15th century AD, the great Hindu Vijayanagara Empire emerged in southern India. The empire was ruled from Vijayanagara ("city of victory"). One building consisted of 11 domed chambers, thought to be the royal elephant stables. Elephants were used for transport and in warfare, although they could prove disastrous in battle, trampling fighters on their own side.

Stone relief, Vijayanagara, India

TIERED PAVILION
One of the finest buildings at Vijayanagara in southern India was the Lotus Mahal, a two-storied pavilion that may have been a royal residence. Built on a stone plinth, the super-structure was made up of nine towers, planned symmetrically to create 13 bays, with one additional bay housing a staircase. The towers had diminishing tiers with projecting eaves to provide shelter from the sun.

Projecting eaves

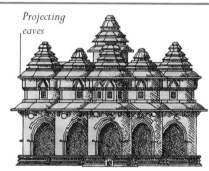

Lotus Mahal, Vijayanagara, southern India

EUROPE

MAJOR EXCHANGE
When Columbus returned to Spain from the New World in AD 1493, he brought with him many native plants including pineapples. This was the beginning of a major exchange of plants and animals between the Old and New Worlds. Within a century of Columbus's voyage, New World crops such as maize, potatoes, and tobacco were commonplace in Europe.

Pineapple

KREMLIN CATHEDRALS
Renaissance styles arrived in Russia when Ivan III (AD 1462-1505), also known as Ivan the Great, first Tsar of all the Russias, hired the Italian architect Aristotle Fioravanti to build a series of cathedrals in the Kremlin. The Cathedral of the Annunciation, built in AD 1484-89, reflects Italianate theories of symmetry and structure.

Cathedral of the Annunciation, Moscow, Russia

AFRICA

SUGARCANE
Spanish adventurers invaded the Canary Islands in AD 1478, and within five years the largest of the islands, Gran Canaria, had been brought under Spanish control. The leader of the invading forces, Pedro de Vera, soon found a way to make a profit from the conquest by introducing the cultivation of sugar-cane. He built his first mill for grinding cane in AD 1484, and forests were felled to make way for sugarcane plantations throughout the islands. The stalks of the cane were ground to extract the juice, which was then boiled until it thickened. Cane sugar from the Canaries and the Americas gradually replaced honey as the principal source of sweetening in the 16th and 17th centuries AD.

PREFABRICATED FORT
The Portuguese arrived on the West African coast in AD 1471. They immediately built a string of forts at strategic points. On the Gold Coast of Ghana, one such fort was São Jorge of the Mine, now called Elmina, which became the main Portuguese trading port in the Gulf of Guinea from AD 1482 onward. Most of the fort was built from locally quarried stone, but some items, such as the shaped-stone surrounds for the doors, gates, and windows, lime mortar and timbers and tiles for the roofs, were all imported ready-made from Portugal.

TECHNOLOGY & INNOVATION

WOODEN THRONE
This *duho* (wooden seat) was used by a Taino chief in the Bahamas as a status symbol. Carved from a single piece of hardwood, it shows a remarkable degree of skill in woodworking using stone tools.

Wooden seat, Bahamas

SILK BROCADE
In Ming China, tapestry and silk-weaving techniques were combined to produce silk brocade, adding to the wide range of silk fabrics already being made in state-run workshops. Brocade garments were often decorated with mythical creatures, which were considered to be lucky.

Ming silk brocade jacket with reconstruction of detail, China

CANNONS AND FIREARMS
Putting an end to more than 1,000 years of Christian rule, the Muslim Ottoman Turks captured the Byzantine capital at Constantinople (modern Istanbul) with the aid of artillery in AD 1453. Often difficult to differentiate from incendiary devices mentioned in written sources, artillery may have been used as early as AD 1204 in North Africa, but its use is first reliably documented in early 14th-century AD manuscript illustrations from western Europe. By AD 1453 the Ottoman Turks had introduced artillery pieces with a bore of 35 in, which fired shot that weighed 600 lb each. These large cannons were used to great effect by the Ottomans in their wars of conquest in the Balkans and the Middle East. Hand weapons such as the arquebus (long-barreled gun) were also being used by the Ottoman army by this time.

MAPS FOR MARINERS
Late medieval European mariners relied on portolan (harbor-finding) charts to navigate the coasts of the Mediterranean and Atlantic Europe. A network of crisscrossing lines on the charts was used to plot a course with the aid of a magnetic compass. The charts were made mainly in Barcelona, Venice, and Genoa. After AD 1450, large areas of West Africa were added to the charts in the wake of Portuguese exploration.

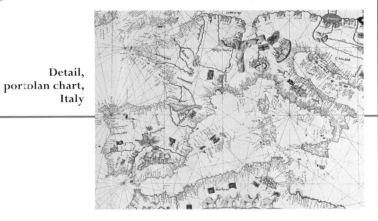

Detail, portolan chart, Italy

MEASURING GOLD
In Akanland, roughly equivalent to modern Ghana, the mining of gold deposits had increased dramatically in the early 15th century AD, due to the arrival of Islamic merchants from the north. The Portuguese reached the area in AD 1471, and gold became a major commodity in their trade with its inhabitants. By AD 1500, a Portuguese weights system replaced the Islamic one used for measuring out the gold.

ART & RITUAL

MASKS AND DOLLS
Miniature masks and heads, commonly found at sites of the Koniag culture (AD 1400-1700) on the Pacific coast of Alaska, appear to depict real people and may have been used in shamanistic healing or other rituals. Such removable heads and masks were used with headless dolls, enabling the dolls' identities to be changed. Dolls allowed children to play-act adult roles and to learn design and sewing skills.

Koniag masks, Kodiak Island, Alaska

RAINMAKING CEREMONIES
In Australia, rock paintings of Ancestral Lightning Beings, such as this one in the Northern Territory, were associated with Aboriginal rainmaking. According to tradition, two brothers fought so violently that they created lightning, brought rain and frogs, then "painted themselves" onto the rock face. Ceremonies involved singing, dancing, and cutting grooves in rocks "to cut the Old Man Rain to make him bleed."

Rock painting of the Lightning Brothers, Australia

HAND OF THE ARTIST
In the Middle East, many early-14th-century miniatures from illuminated manuscripts were painted anonymously, but by the end of the 15th century AD, signed works were more common. The most famous artist was Bihzad (AD 1440-1514), who developed an expressive style, especially in the rendition of everyday scenes. This one shows builders at work and dates to around AD 1494.

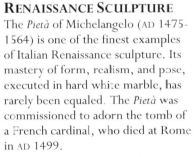

Manuscript illustration by Bihzad, *The building of the legendary castle of Khavarnaq,* **Herat, Afghanistan**

RENAISSANCE SCULPTURE
The *Pietà* of Michelangelo (AD 1475-1564) is one of the finest examples of Italian Renaissance sculpture. Its mastery of form, realism, and pose, executed in hard white marble, has rarely been equaled. The *Pietà* was commissioned to adorn the tomb of a French cardinal, who died at Rome in AD 1499.

Michelangelo's *Pietà*, St. Peter's Basilica, Vatican, Rome

ETHIOPIAN CALENDARS
Two of the three calendars used in parallel throughout the Middle Ages in Ethiopia were based on cycles of 532 years (the so-called "Great Lunar Cycle"). One took the date of the biblical Creation (assumed to be 5500 BC) as its starting point, while the other began from the persecution of Christians by the Roman Emperor Diocletian (AD 284). The third resembled the first but had no cyclical component.

INCA ROADS

The Inca Empire was the largest preindustrial state in the New World, covering, at its height, modern Peru, southern Colombia, Ecuador, Bolivia, northern Chile, and highland Argentina. The Incas themselves were the ruling elite of an ethnically diverse population of around 10 million. The state was highly organized and the Inca emperors administered their territory, called *Tahuantinsuyu* (the Land of the Four Quarters), without a writing system or knowledge of the wheel or iron. The vast road system, fundamental to the empire's success, served a triple function: to transport goods; to exert political and military control over dispersed peoples; and to link the Inca capital, Cuzco, with highland and coastal provinces.

INCA NETWORK *right*

The Incas built around 14,260 miles of roads varying between 6½ and 52 feet in width. *Tampus* (way stations) were located at intervals of 15-25 miles and stop stations every 3-5 miles. Messages were carried by *chasquis* (messenger-runners) in relays of 1-3 miles.

INCA ROAD TODAY *above*

The section of road shown here crosses the west side of Lake Chinchaycocha, south of Pumpu in the central highlands of Peru. It is 20-26 feet wide and is still used today.

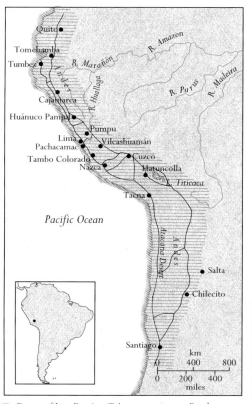

≡ Extent of Inca Empire (*Tahuantinsuyu*) — Road system

EXCHANGE SYSTEM *below*

Since there was no currency in Andean society, a system known as *trueque* was developed for exchanging goods. People from the Andean uplands traded *chuñu* (freeze-dried potato) and *charki* (freeze-dried meat) for lowland and coastal products including salt, fish, maize, cotton, fruits, and beans. Textiles, *chicha* (maize beer), guinea pigs, and ceramics were also traded. Exchange was busiest in the harvest season. Markets also provided good opportunities for social interaction.

Typical Andean market scene

Chuñu (freeze-dried potato)   *Guinea pigs*

Jars containing chicha (maize beer)

THE ROYAL ROUTE *below and right*

As part of the political struggle to consolidate his empire, the Inca emperor visited remote provinces accompanied by members of the royal court. He and the *coya* (queen) were carried in procession on a throne decorated with exotic bird feathers, gold, silver, and precious stones. Young girls specially chosen to serve the state sang and danced, and the soldiers of the royal guard carried the throne. The emperor was considered to be the sacred son of *Inti* (the sun god), consecrating produce and the places he visited. The royal party traveled along official roads, with lanes separated by low stone walls. In desert areas, roads were marked with posts, but those built in mountainous regions ultimately testify to the ingenuity of Inca engineering.

BUILDING A MOUNTAIN ROAD

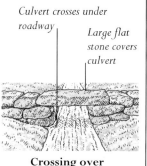

Retaining stone wall supports road

Cross section of mountain road

Culvert crosses under roadway

Large flat stone covers culvert

Crossing over a water channel

ZIGZAG DESIGN *above*

Inca roads generally traversed mountainous terrain in sweeping zigzags. Where a broader road was required, the roadbed was constructed by cutting into the rock surface of the slope and was then buttressed with a stone retaining wall. Many such roads have stood the test of time and are still being used by local traffic.

BUILDING A STEPPED ROAD

Slope of less than 12 degrees, as in coastal valleys   *Rough stone stairway*   *Stepped stairway*

Shallow gradient

Steep highland slope

Major gradient

COPING WITH GRADIENTS *above*

Roads were essential links between highland populations and those of the coastal deserts. Steep slopes presented major but unavoidable obstacles for Inca road builders. The solution was to step the roads according to the gradients of the slopes; on the steepest slopes, small stone steps were embedded in the hillside.

Inca royal procession

Llamas used as pack animals could transport up to 88 lb of goods 22 miles per day

Tampus (way stations) located at regular intervals along the road

Warehouses built at way stations to store luxury goods, food, clothing, and weapons, which were periodically distributed to the local people

Chasquis (messenger-runners) delivered state messages and supplies

Chasqui bag, also used as a cape and blanket

Strombus horn for announcing chasqui's arrival

Throne decorated with black and white royal symbols

Young girls entertained the royal procession with singing and dancing

RIVER CROSSINGS

Inca engineers devised remarkable technologies for crossing rivers. A variety of bridges was developed to cope with different environments, including suspension bridges and pontoon bridges made from floating rafts of reeds. Culverts, drains, and causeways were also constructed where necessary. Suspension bridges often spanned substantial gorges — one over the Apurimac River is 148 feet long. Every suspension bridge had a *chaka-camayoc* (bridge-keeper).

BUILDING A BRIDGE

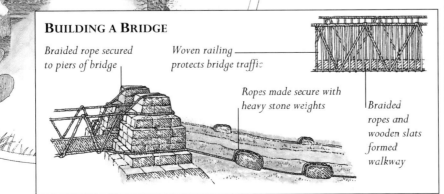

Braided rope secured to piers of bridge

Woven railing protects bridge traffic

Ropes made secure with heavy stone weights

Braided ropes and wooden slats formed walkway

STATE ORGANIZATION

The Inca state had a highly organized army under the direct control of the emperor and his provincial representatives. The military were instrumental in conquering new territories and enforcing government policies, and the extensive road system allowed quick access to those areas of the empire where there was civil unrest or revolt. Soldiers fought in single combat using simple weapons.

RITUAL WEAPONS

Metal mace heads were fashioned in the shape of rings or stars. Integral to Andean culture since ancient times as ritual items, maces were primarily used as weapons by the Incas.

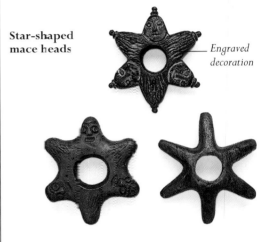

Star-shaped mace heads

Engraved decoration

BOLAS AND SLINGS

Inca soldiers used bolas and slings as weapons, but they were also used for hunting and in rituals. Bolas consisted of three woven strands with stone balls at one end. The strands are known as an *ayllu,* a term also meaning a kindred group, the basic unit of Inca social organization. Slings were made of braid woven from strands of llama wool or natural fiber derived from the agave plant, a type of succulent. They were used in rituals to combat hostile spirits and in ceremonial dances.

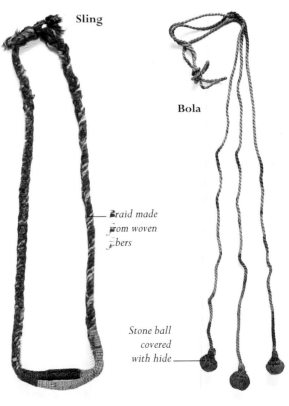

Sling

Bola

Braid made from woven fibers

Stone ball covered with hide

AMERICAS

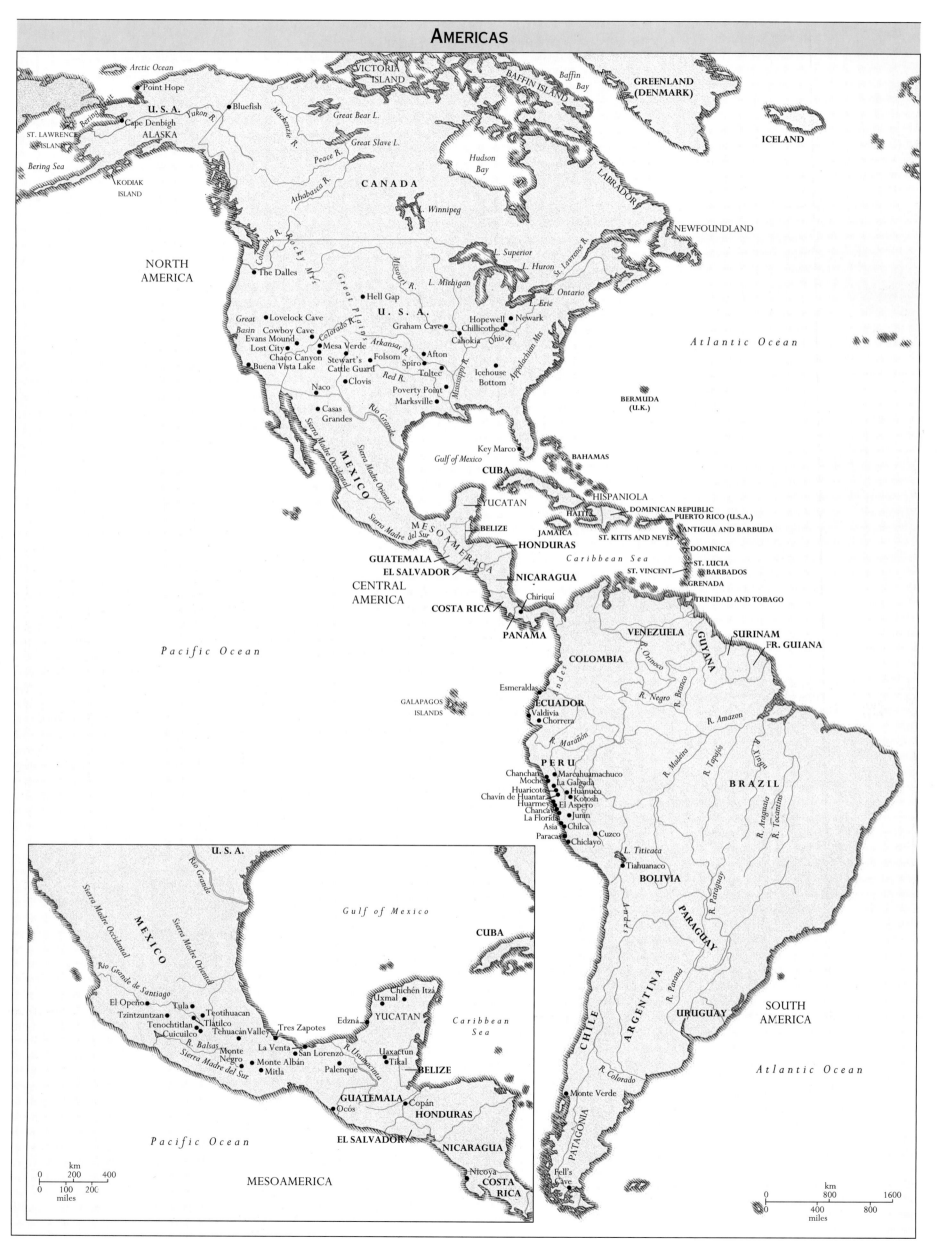

Arctic Ocean
Point Hope
VICTORIA ISLAND
BAFFIN ISLAND
Baffin Bay
GREENLAND (DENMARK)

U.S.A.
Bluefish
Yukon R.
Cape Denbigh
ALASKA
KODIAK ISLAND
ST. LAWRENCE ISLAND
Bering Sea
Bering St.
Mackenzie R.
Great Bear L.
Great Slave L.
Peace R.
Athabasca R.
Hudson Bay
LABRADOR
ICELAND

CANADA
NEWFOUNDLAND

NORTH AMERICA
The Dalles
Columbia R.
Rocky Mts.
L. Winnipeg
L. Superior
L. Huron
St. Lawrence R.
L. Ontario
L. Erie
Atlantic Ocean

Hell Gap
Missouri R.
L. Michigan
Great Plains
Lovelock Cave
Great Basin
Cowboy Cave
Evans Mound
Lost City
Colorado R.
Mesa Verde
Chaco Canyon
Stewart's Cattle Guard
Buena Vista Lake
Naco
Clovis
Casas Grandes
Sierra Madre Occidental
Graham Cave
Arkansas R.
Folsom
Spiro
Red R.
Hopewell
Chillicothe
Newark
Cahokia
Afton
Toltec
Ohio R.
Mississippi R.
Icehouse Bottom
Poverty Point
Marksville
Appalachian Mts.
Rio Grande

BERMUDA (U.K.)

Key Marco
Gulf of Mexico
BAHAMAS
CUBA
HISPANIOLA
HAITI
DOMINICAN REPUBLIC
PUERTO RICO (U.S.A.)
ANTIGUA AND BARBUDA
ST. KITTS AND NEVIS
DOMINICA
ST. LUCIA
BARBADOS
ST. VINCENT
GRENADA
TRINIDAD AND TOBAGO
Caribbean Sea
JAMAICA
YUCATAN
BELIZE
HONDURAS
GUATEMALA
EL SALVADOR
NICARAGUA
MEXICO
Sierra Madre Oriental
MESOAMERICA
Sierra Madre del Sur
CENTRAL AMERICA
COSTA RICA
PANAMA
Chiriquí

Pacific Ocean

GALAPAGOS ISLANDS
VENEZUELA
GUYANA
SURINAM
FR. GUIANA
COLOMBIA
R. Orinoco
Esmeraldas
Andes
ECUADOR
Valdivia
Chorrera
R. Marañón
R. Negro
R. Branco
R. Amazon
BRAZIL
R. Madeira
R. Tapajós
R. Xingu
PERU
Chanchan
Marcahuamachuco
Moche
La Galgada
Huaricoto
Huánuco
Chavín de Huantar
Kotosh
Huarmey
El Aspero
Chancay
Junín
La Florida
Chilca
Asia
Cuzco
Paracas
Chiclayo
L. Titicaca
Tiahuanaco
BOLIVIA
R. Araguaia
R. Tocantins
PARAGUAY
R. Paraguay
CHILE
ARGENTINA
R. Paraná
SOUTH AMERICA
URUGUAY
R. Colorado
Monte Verde
PATAGONIA
Fell's Cave
Atlantic Ocean

Inset: MESOAMERICA

U.S.A.
Rio Grande
Gulf of Mexico
CUBA
MEXICO
Sierra Madre Occidental
Sierra Madre Oriental
Río Grande de Santiago
El Openo
Tula
Tzintzuntzan
Teotihuacan
Tenochtitlan
Tlatilco
Cuicuilco
Tehuacán Valley
R. Balsas
Monte Negro
Sierra Madre del Sur
La Venta
San Lorenzo
Monte Albán
Mitla
Palenque
Tres Zapotes
Edzná
R. Usumacinta
Uaxactún
Tikal
Chichén Itzá
Uxmal
YUCATAN
Caribbean Sea
BELIZE
GUATEMALA
Copán
Ocós
HONDURAS
EL SALVADOR
NICARAGUA
Nicoya
COSTA RICA
Pacific Ocean

km
0   200   400
0   100   200
miles

km
0   800   1600
0   400   800
miles

EAST ASIA & AUSTRALASIA

SIBERIA

R. Lena

R. Amur

L. Baikal

Sea of Okhotsk

SAKHALIN

Bering Strait

Bering Sea

• Pazyryk

MONGOLIA

MANCHURIA

HOKKAIDO

Pacific Ocean

Altai

Gobi

• Dunhuang

Yellow R.

• Longgu

NORTH KOREA

Sea of Japan

HONSHU

• Zhoukoudian • Peking

• Pyongyang

ORDOS

SOUTH KOREA

JAPAN

North China Plain

Anyang

Zhengzhou • Gongxian

Banpo • Erlitou

Xianyang • • Erligang

Chang'an • Luoyang

Lantian

Yellow Sea

Puyo • • Kyongju

Kamakura •

Nara •

Fukui Cave •

Nagasaki •

SHIKOKU

Kamikuroiwa Cave

KYUSHU

CHINA

• Guanghan

• Nanjing

Shanghai •

TIBET

R. Brahmaputra

Himalayas

Yangtze R.

Jingdezhen •

Hemudu •

Mawangdui • Dayangzhou •

East China Sea

R. Ganges

• Changsha

TAIWAN

Red R.

Co Loa •

Phung Nguyen •

HONG KONG (U.K.)

MACAO (PORTUGAL)

R. Irrawaddy

R. Salween

• Fagan

Dong Son •

BURMA • Spirit Cave

LAOS

HAINAN

Gulf of Tonking

Ban Na Di • • Ban Chiang

Non Nok Tha •

THAILAND

VIETNAM

R. Mekong

LUZON

PHILIPPINES

Ban Kao •

Nong Chae Sao •

Angkor •

Kok Phanom Di •

CAMBODIA

Gulf of Thailand

Andaman Sea

South China Sea

MINDANAO

MALAYA

BRUNEI

Celebes Sea

MALAYSIA

• Great Cave

CELEBES

HALMAHERA

Pacific Ocean

SUMATRA

• Malacca

SINGAPORE

BORNEO

SERAM

Bismarck Archipelago

Java Sea

JAVA • INDONESIA

Mojokerto •

Ngandong • • Trinil

Borobudur •

Indian Ocean

FLORES

Banda Sea

NEW GUINEA

PAPUA NEW GUINEA

• Huon Peninsula

SOLOMON ISLANDS

TIMOR

Arafura Sea

Cape York Peninsula

Timor Sea

AUSTRALIA

km
0   500   1000

0   250   500
miles

For Australia and New Zealand
see inset (above).

Inset:

INDONESIA

NEW GUINEA

PAPUA NEW GUINEA

KIRIBATI

SOLOMON ISLANDS

TUVALU

Indian Ocean

Malangangerr •

Kakadu •

ARNHEM LAND

Cape York Peninsula

Quinkan •

SANTA CRUZ ISLANDS

VANUATU

FIJI

Kimberley •

Ingaladdi •

Coral Sea

NEW CALEDONIA (FRANCE)

AUSTRALIA

• Uluru (Ayers Rock)

Great Dividing Range

Pacific Ocean

NORTH ISLAND

• Walga Rock

Panaramitee •

Darling R.

Lake Mungo

Roonka

Great Australian Bight

Fromm's Landing •

Murray R.

NEW ZEALAND

Wyrie Swamp •

Cave Bay Cave •

West Point •

Bass Strait

Tasman Sea

Bay of Fires •

Ahuara Valley •

SOUTH ISLAND

Taramakau Valley

Southern Ocean

TASMANIA

km
0   500   1000

0   250   500
miles

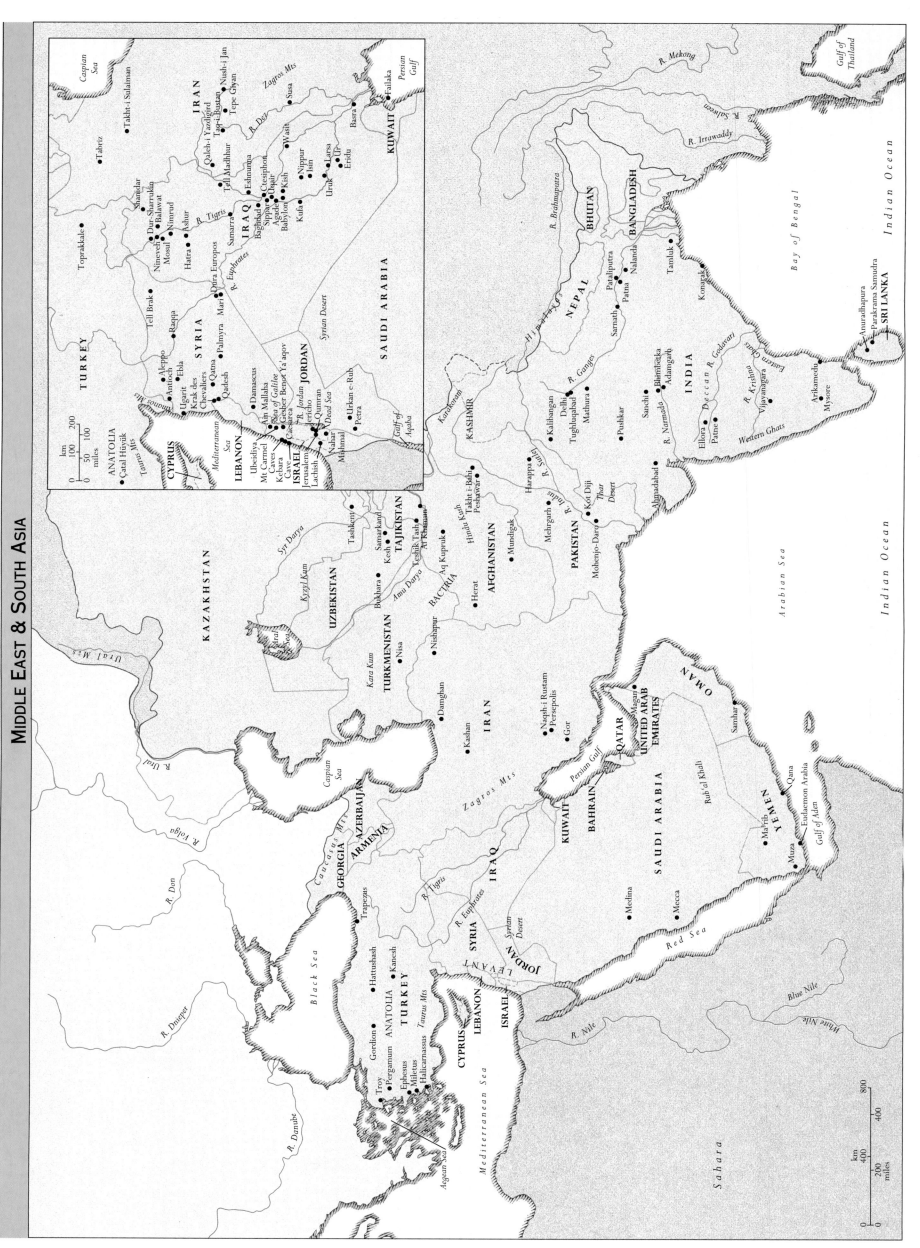

MIDDLE EAST & SOUTH ASIA

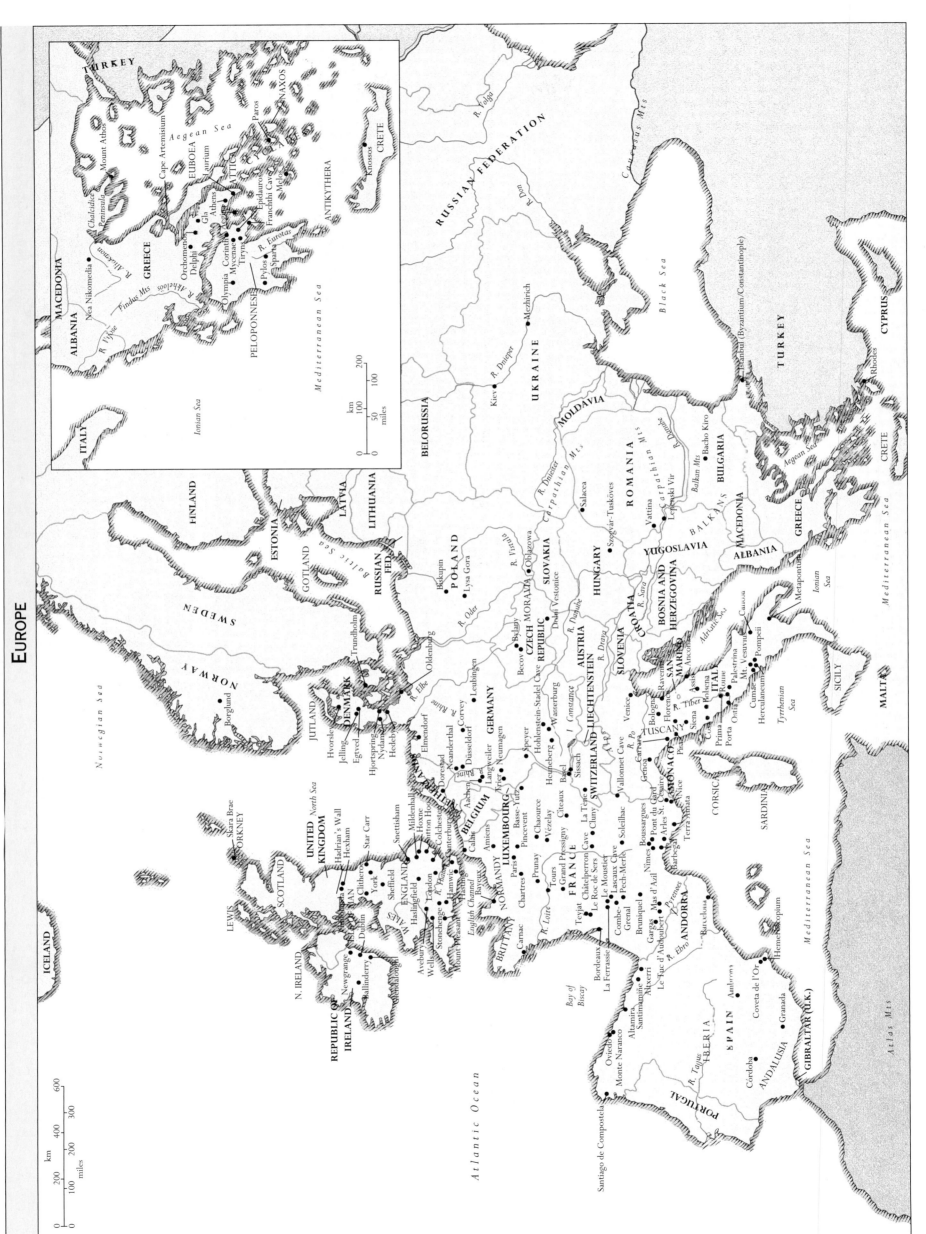

EUROPE

AFRICA

Atlantic Ocean

Black Sea

Gulf of Tunis

Afalou Bou Rhummel
Carthage
Cirta Sicca
Taforalt
Thapsus

MOROCCO
Marrakesh
Igli *Atlas Mts*

TUNISIA
Leptis Magna

Haua Fteah
Cave

Mediterranean Sea

Persian Gulf

**CANARY
ISLANDS**

**GRAN
CANARIA**

ALGERIA

LIBYA

Siwa

EGYPT

WESTERN SAHARA

*Tassili
Massif*

Sahara

Hoggar

Sahara

R. Nile

Red Sea

*Tibesti
Massif*

MAURITANIA

MALI
Timbuktu

NIGER

CHAD

Darfur

Meroë
Khartoum
Naqa

ERITREA

Axum
Mekele
Roha

Gulf of Aden

SENEGAL
Kumbi Saleh

GAMBIA

Sahel

Jenne-jeno

BURKINA

Sahel

Jos

SUDAN

Blue Nile

*Ethiopian
Highlands*

DJIBOUTI

Mundus

GUINEA

**GUINEA-
BISSAU**

**SIERRA
LEONE**

**IVORY
COAST**

GHANA

TOGO

BENIN

Tada

NIGERIA
Taruga

White Nile

ETHIOPIA

SOMALIA

LIBERIA

Elmina

Ife
Benin
Igbo Ukwu
Nsukka

CAMEROON

EQUATORIAL GUINEA

CENTRAL AFRICAN REPUBLIC

Matupi

UGANDA

Mogadishu

KENYA

**SAO TOME
AND PRINCIPE**

GABON

CONGO

R. Congo

R. Kasai

ZAIRE

RWANDA

Ishango

Olgorgesailie

Rift Valley

Gamble's Cave

L. Victoria

Manda
Lamu
Gedi

Kalemba

BURUNDI

Olduvai Gorge

Engaruka

ZANZIBAR

*Indian
Ocean*

L. Tanganyika

Kisese

TANZANIA

ANGOLA

Rift Valley

Kilwa

L. Nyasa

COMOROS

ZAMBIA

R. Zambezi

Ingombe Ilede

MALAWI

MOZAMBIQUE

Mozambique Channel

MADAGASCAR

NAMIBIA

ZIMBABWE

Pomongwe

Leopard's Kopje

Great Zimbabwe

Sofala

BOTSWANA
*Kalahari
Desert*

R. Limpopo

Apollo II

*Atlantic
Ocean*

Orange R.

Taung

SOUTH AFRICA

Orangia

Drakensberg Mts

Border Cave

SWAZILAND

LESOTHO

Eland's Bay Cave
Boomplaas Cave
Klasies River Mouth
Nelson Bay Cave

*Cape of
Good Hope*

Egypt inset

Mediterranean Sea

Alexandria

Nile Delta

Pi-Ramesse
Tanis
Bubastis

Heliopolis
Giza Cairo
Memphis
Saqqara Dahshur
El Lisht
Faiyum Basin Maidum

*Gulf of
Aqaba*

Sinai

Roda

*Gulf of
Suez*

Red Sea

El Amarna

El Badari

EGYPT

Abydos

Dendera
Naqada
Valley of the Kings Thebes
Karnak
Nekhen Luxor
Hieraconpolis Edfu

Sahara

+1st Cataract

R. Nile

Bir Tarfawi

Ballana
Abu Simbel
Buhen Faras
2nd Cataract

SUDAN

Nubian Desert

km
0   200   400
0   100   200
miles

Jebel Barkal Nuri
Napata

km
0   500   1000
0   300   600
miles

INDEX

The structure of the timecharts in *Smithsonian Timelines of the Ancient World* gives direct access to information by time period and, within each time period, by five geographical bands and four themes. To complement this structure, the index gives alphabetical access to many additional themes, from major topics such as agriculture and writing to specific cultures, activities, or artifacts. Where appropriate, locations are also given. In this way, using the book's inbuilt structure, the index guides the reader to starting points for further exploration and comparison.

BIBLIOGRAPHY & ACKNOWLEDGMENTS

AMERICAS

Berdan, Frances F.: *The Aztecs*, University of Oklahoma Press, Norman, 1991
Burger, Richard L.: *Chavin and the Origins of Andean Civilization*, Thames and Hudson, New York, 1992
Cordell, Linda S.: *Prehistory of the Southwest*, Academic Press, New York, 1984
Diehl, Richard A.: *Tula: The Toltec Capital of Ancient Mexico*, Thames and Hudson, London, 1983
Fitzhugh, William W.: *Crossroads of Continents: Cultures of Siberia and Alaska*, Smithsonian Institution Press, Washington, D.C., 1988
Flannery, Kent & **Marcus**, Joyce: *The Cloud People: Divergent Evolution of the Zapotec and Mixtec Civilizations*, Academic Press, New York, 1983
Frison, George: *Prehistoric Hunters of the High Plains* (2nd ed.), Academic Press, New York, 1991
Jennings, Jesse D. (ed.): *Ancient Native Americans*, W. H. Freeman and Company, New York, 1978
Lumbreras, Luis: *The Peoples and Cultures of Ancient Peru*, Smithsonian Institution Press, Washington, D.C., 1974
Marcus, Joyce: *Mesoamerican Writing Systems*, Princeton University Press, Princeton, 1992
Meggers, Betty J.: *Amazonia: Man and Culture in a Counterfeit Paradise*, Aldine Atherton, Arlington Heights, IL, 1971
Milanich, Jerald T. & **Fairbanks**, Charles H.: *Florida Archaeology*, Academic Press, New York, 1980
Morse, Dan F. & **Morse**, Phyllis A.: *Archaeology of the Central Mississippi Valley*, Academic Press, New York, 1983
Moseley, Michael E.: *The Incas and their Ancestors – The Archaeology of Peru*, Thames and Hudson, New York, 1992
Rouse, Irving: *The Tainos: Rise and Decline of the People Who Greeted Columbus*, Yale University Press, New Haven, 1992
Sharer, Robert J. & **Grove**, David D. (eds): *Regional Perspectives on the Olmec*, Cambridge University Press, New York, 1989
Snow, Dean A.: *The Archaeology of New England*, Academic Press, London, 1980
Stone, Doris: *Precolumbian Man Finds Central America*, Peabody Museum Press, Cambridge, 1972
Stuart, George E. & **Stuart**, Gene S.: *Lost Kingdoms of the Maya*, National Geographic Society, Washington, D.C., 1992
Sturtevant, William C. (ed.): *Handbook of North American Indians* (20 vols), Smithsonian Institution Press, Washington, D.C., 1978-1994
Weaver, Muriel Porter: *The Aztecs, Maya, and Their Predecessors – Archaeology of Mesoamerica*, Academic Press, New York, 1993
Wedel, Waldo R.: *Central Plains Prehistory: Holocene Environments and Culture Change in the Republican River Basin*, University of Nebraska Press, Lincoln, 1986
Williams, Stephen: *Fantastic Archaeology: The Wild Side of North American Prehistory*, University of Pennsylvania Press, Philadelphia, 1991

EAST ASIA & AUSTRALASIA

Aikens, C. M. & **Higuchi**, T.: *The Prehistory of Japan*, Academic Press, New York, 1982
Bahn, P. G. & **Flenley**, J.: *Easter Island, Earth Island*, Thames and Hudson, New York, 1992
Bellwood, Peter: *The Polynesians* (2nd ed.), Thames and Hudson, New York, 1992
Flood, Josephine: Archaeology of the Dreamtime: *The Story of Prehistoric Australia and its People*, Yale University Press, New Haven, 1983
Flood, Josephine: *The Riches of Ancient Australia: A Journey into Prehistory*, University of Queensland Press, Brisbane, 1990
Higham, Charles: *The Archaeology of Mainland Southeast Asia*, Cambridge University Press, New York, 1989
Ki-baik, Lee: *A New History of Korea*, Harvard University Press, Cambridge, Mass., 1984
Mulvaney, D. J. & **White**, J. P. (eds.): *Australians: A Historical Library: Australians to 1788*, Fairfax, Syme & Weldon Associates, Sydney, 1987
Nelson, S. M.: *The Archaeology of Korea*, Cambridge University Press, New York, 1993
Paine, Robert & **Soper**, Alexander: *The Art and Architecture of Japan*, Penguin, New York, 1975
Reischauer, Edwin O. & **Fairbank**, Jonathan K.: *A History of East Asian Civilization* (2 vols), Houghton Mifflin, Boston, 1958, 1960
Sickman, Lawrence & **Soper**, Alexander: *The Art and Architecture of China*, Yale University Press, New Haven, 1992
Stanley-Smith, Joan: *Japanese Art*, Thames and Hudson, New York, 1984
Temple, Robert: *The Genius of China*, Simon & Schuster, New York, 1989
Thorne, Alan & **Raymond**, Robert: *Man on the Rim*, Angus & Robertson, Sydney, 1989
Walsh, Grahame L.: *Australia's Greatest Rock Art*, Robert Brown and Associates, New South Wales, 1988
White, J. P. & **O'Connell**, J.: *A Prehistory of Australia, New Guinea and Sahul*, Academic Press, London, 1982

MIDDLE EAST & SOUTH ASIA

Allchin, B. & **Allchin**, R.: *The Rise of Civilization in India and Pakistan*, Cambridge University Press, New York, 1982
Basham, A. L. (ed.): *A Cultural History of India*, Oxford University Press, New York, 1984
Brend, Barbara: *Islamic Art*, Harvard University Press, Cambridge, Mass., 1991
Ettinghausen, Richard & **Grabar**, Oleg: *Pelican History of Art: The Art and Architecture of Islam*, Yale University Press, New Haven, 1992
Harle, J. C.: *The Art and Architecture of the Indian Subcontinent*, Viking Penguin, New York, 1986
Herrmann, G.: *The Iranian Revival*, Elsevier-Phaidon, Oxford, 1977
Huntington, S. L.: *The Art of Ancient India: Buddhist, Hindu, Jain*, Weatherhill, London, 1984
Lewis, B. (ed.): *The Cambridge History of Islam* (2 vols), Cambridge University Press, 1970
Mellaart, J.: *The Neolithic of the Near East*, Thames and Hudson, London and New York, 1975
Michell, George (ed.): *Architecture of the Islamic World: Its Social History and Meaning*, Thames and Hudson, New York, 1984
Pritchard, J. B. (ed.): *The Harper Concise Atlas of the Bible*, HarperCollins, New York, 1991
Roaf, M. D.: *Cultural Atlas of Mesopotamia and the Ancient Near East*, Facts on File, New York, 1990
Safadi, Y. H.: *Islamic Calligraphy*, Thames and Hudson, New York, 1984
Thapar, R.: *A History of India* Vol. 1, Viking Penguin, New York, 1966

EUROPE

Barker, G.: *Prehistoric Farming in Europe*, Cambridge University Press, New York, 1985
Burn, L.: *The British Museum Book of Greek and Roman Art*, British Museum Press, London, 1991
Champion, T., **Gamble**, C., **Shennan**, S. & **Whittle**, A.: *Prehistoric Europe*, Academic Press, New York, 1984
Coles, B. & **Coles**, J.: *People of the Wetlands: Bogs, Bodies and Lake-Dwellers*, Thames and Hudson, New York, 1989
Conant, K. J.: *Carolingian and Romanesque Architecture 800-1200*, Yale University Press, New Haven, 1992
Cornell, T. & **Matthews**, J.: *Atlas of the Roman World*, Facts on File, New York, 1982
Holmes, G. (ed.): *The Oxford Illustrated History of Medieval Europe*, Oxford University Press, New York, 1992
Lawrence, A. W.: *Greek Architecture* (4th ed.), Yale University Press, New Haven, 1992
Levi, P.: *Atlas of the Greek World*, Facts on File, New York, 1981
Nelson, Sarah: *The Archaeology of Korea*, Cambridge University Press, New York, 1992
Renfrew, C.: *Archaeology and Language: The Puzzle of Indo-European Origins*, Cambridge University Press, New York, 1987
Rolle, R.: *The World of the Scythians*, University of California Press, Berkeley, 1990
Todd, M.: *The Northern Barbarians 100 BC-AD 300*, Blackwell Press, Oxford, 1987
White, L.: *Medieval Technology and Social Change*, Oxford University Press, 1962
Whitrow, G. J.: *Time in History*, Oxford University Press, New York, 1989

AFRICA

Connah, Graham: *African Civilizations*, Cambridge University Press, New York, 1987
Fagan, Brian: *Ancient Africa*, Thames and Hudson, New York, 1994
Garlake, Peter: *Great Zimbabwe*, Thames and Hudson, 1973
Kemp, Barry: *Ancient Egypt: Anatomy of a Civilization*, Routledge, Chapman, & Hall, New York, 1989
Oliver, Roland: *The African Experience*, HarperCollins, New York, 1992
Oliver, Roland (6th rev. ed.): *A Short History of Africa*, Facts on File, New York, 1989
Phillipson, David: *African Archaeology*, Cambridge University Press, New York, 1985
Smith, Andrew: *Pastoralism in Africa*, University of Witwatersrand Press, Johannesburg, 1992
Vansina, Jan: *Kingdoms of the Savanna*, University of Wisconsin Press, Madison, 1966
Willett, Frank: *African Art*, Thames and Hudson, New York, 1985

The **Editor-in-Chief** woud like to thank all those who, by advice, information, and support, helped to bring *Smithsonian Timelines* to a successful conclusion. Particular thanks must be reserved for the editorial and design staff at Dorling Kindersley, whose patience and tireless attention to detail were so vital to the whole undertaking.

Dorling Kindersley would like to thank Tim Scott (Design); Nicola Rawson (Design); Mike Snell (Design); Kate Sarluis (Design); Karen Mackley (DTP); Alistair Wardle (DTP-Maps); Milly Trowbridge (Picture Research); Alexa Stace (Editorial/Proofreading); David Harding (Index); Roger Bullen, Andrew Heritage, and Iorwerth Watkins of DK Cartography Division; Dr. Leslie Aiello of University College, London, Anthropology Department; Graham Javes, Paul Gardner, Ivor Kerslake (British Museum); the staff of the Ashmolean Museum.

The Smithsonian Institution is grateful to the staffs of the following Smithsonian museums and offices for their generous support of the *Smithsonian Timelines* project: National Museum of Natural History, National Museum of the American Indian, National Anthropological Archives, Smithsonian Books.
The Smithsonian would particularly like to thank the following individuals at the National Museum of Natural History: Mary Jo Arnoldi, Marcia Bakry, Kathleen Baxter, Anna K. Behrensmeyer, Jennifer Clark, Kristin M. Coxson, Susan B. Crawford, Catherine Creek, Natalie Firnhaber, James B. Griffin, Greta Hansen, Deborah A. Hull-Walski, David R. Hunt, Adrienne Kaeppler, Thomas Killion, James Krakker, Roxy Laybourne, Stephen Loring, Karen Moran, Felicia Pickering, Abelardo Sandoval, Stanwyn G. Shetler, William C. Sturtevant, Robert D. Sullivan, Frank H. Talbot, Vyrtis Thomas, William B. Trousdale, Javier Urcid, Gus Van Beek, John Verano, and Scott L. Wing. The Smithsonian would also like to thank: Timothy G. Baugh, Western Cultural Resource Management, New Mexico; Elizabeth Boone, Dumbarton Oaks; Pete Bostrom, Lithics Casting Lab, Illinois; Carol Callaway, Dumbarton Oaks; Michael Coe, Yale University; Sally Cole; Sharon Dean, National Museum of the American Indian; Thomas Dillehay, University of Kentucky; Richard R. Drass, Oklahoma Archaeological Survey; George Frison, University of Wyoming; Patricia Gallagher, Smithsonian Books; Glen Goode, Texas Department of Transportation; Kelley Hays, Museum of Northern Arizona; Patrick Hogan, University of New Mexico; Janine Jones, National Museum of the American Indian; Margaret Jodry, American University; Randi Korn; Robert Mallouf, Texas State Archaeologist; Juan Mesas, Federal Bureau of Investigation; René Millon, University of Rochester; Dan Morris, University of Arkansas; Pat Olson; Rocky Mountain Bison Company; Frances Rowsell, Smithsonian Books; Inge Schjellerup, National Museet, Denmark; Christine Steiner, Smithsonian Institution; Yoko Sugiura, Universidad Nacional Autonoma de México and Samuel M. Wilson, University of Texas.

ILLUSTRATORS: David Ashby, Will Giles, Gillie Newman, Sandra Pond, Jim Robins.
MAP ILLUSTRATORS: John Woodcock, Kuo Kang Chen.
SPECIAL RECONSTRUCTIONS: Stephen Conlin: pp. 40-41 *Ice Age Cycle*, pp. 92-93 *Uruk Civilization*, pp. 104-5 *Pyramids at Giza*, pp. 114-15 *Alpine Lake Village*, p. 127 *Fu Hao's tomb*, p. 155 *Parthenon* (x 2), pp. 194-95 *Temple-Pyramids*, pp. 210-11 *Pueblo Villages*; Richard Phipps: pp. 58-59 *Cave interior*, pp. 68-69 *Hunting (kill/butcher site)*, pp. 242-43 *Inca Roads*; Stephen Gyapay: pp 168-69 *Ephesus plan views*; Jim Robins: p. 32 *Hominid*, pp. 48-49 *Neanderthal burial*.

PICTURE CREDITS (Key to illustrations)
c = center
b = bottom
r = right
l = left
t = top
Where the location of an image appears as a number in superscript, this signifies its position on a timechart page, according to the diagram (*right*):

1	2
3	4
5	6
7	8
9	10

The publisher would like to thank the following for their kind permission to reproduce the photographs:
Ashmolean Museum, Oxford (Peter Anderson): 74[6] 75[3,5,6] 91[5] 93 *bl* 99[7] 111[6] 113[5] 121[3,5] 134[5] 135[4] 139[6] 151[4] 153[5] 156 *cr* 161[6] 162[4] 165[3] 166[3] 176[3] 179[6] 185 *c* 190[3] 191[4] 196-97 209[4] 221[4] 224[5] 229 *tl* 235[4] 237[5] Except 5 *second from right* 65[6] 89[9] 205[8] 221[5]
British Museum, London (Ivor Kerslake, Peter Hayman, Nick Nicholls, Tom Cochrane): title page 2, 3 *c* 39[7] 45[5,7] 47[5,7] 55[7] 57[5,7,8] 61 *tl, br* 65[7,9] 67[8,9] 70 *cb* 71 *bl* 74[9,10] 75[7,9] 77[9] 79[5] 82-83, 85 *tl, bl* 88[9] 90[9,10] 91[9] 92 *cl, bl* 93 *cl* 94 *c, bl* 95 *cr, cb* 98[5] 99[4,5,6,9,10] 100[5] 101[5,6,7,8,9] 102[5,7] 103[7,9,10] 105 *cr* 106 *cr, cl* 107 *tl* 110[9] 111[5,7,9,10] 112[9] 113[10] 117 *tl, cb, bl* 120[7] 121[7,10] 123[3,4,6,8,9,10] 124[5,9] 125[3] 126-127 127 *tl, bl* 132[5,6,8] 133[5,6,8,10] 134[6] 135[7,8,9,10] 136[6,7,10] 137[3,7,8,9,10] 138[6] 139[5,7,9] 148[7] 149[5,6,8] 150[7] 151[3,5,7,8] 152[7,8,10] 154 *bl, tr* 155 *bl, t* 160[7] 161[7,8,9] 162[5,7] 163[4,8,10] 164[4] 165[7,8,9] 166[9] 167[6,7,9,10] 174[9] 175[8,9] 176[7] 177[3,8,9,10] 179[5,8,9] 181[4,7,8,10] 182 *br* 182-83 *t* 183 *cr, cb* 184 *br* 185 *cb* 188[5,7] 189[3,4,5,7,8,10] 190[6,7] 191[8,9] 192[9] 193[4,8,9,10] 199 *br* 203[5,6,7,10] 205[5,6,7] 207[6] 209[6] 213 *br* 216[5] 217[10] 219[6] 221[6,9,10] 223[3,6,7] 225[5,8,9,10] 227 *tr* 228 *bl* 232[7] 233[7,9,10] 237[5,9,10] 238[9] 239[10]

Ancient Art & Architecture Collection: 154 *c* **Peter Andrews**: 28 *c, cr* 29 *cl* **Archivio Veneziano**: 232[8] **Paul Bahn**: 39[5] 40 *br* 65[4] **Bible Society**: 177[5] **Bibliothèque Municipale, Dijon**: 220[7] **Bibliothèque Nationale, Paris**: 233[5] (Bridgeman Art Library, London) **Bodleian Library, Oxford**: 217[6] 235[7] (Christchurch College) **Bridgeman Art Library**: 183 *br* **British Institute in Eastern Africa, Nairobi**: 226 *bl, br* **British Library**: 185 *tl* 193[3] 202[5,7] 205[3] 218[7] 234[5] 235[10] 241[6] **Jane Callender**: 44[6] **John Carswell**: 239[6] **J. Allan Cash**: 41 *tl* 222[8] **Photo Peter Clayton**: 104 *bl* **Bruce Coleman Limited**: 191[10] (Gerald Cubitt) **Commonwealth Institute**: 30 *bl* **C. M. Dixon**: 116 *b* **Dr Chris Scarre**: 79[10] 91[8] 168 *cb* 169 *tc, tl, cr* 98[8] **E. T. Archive:** 223[7] (Bodleian Library) **Editions La Goélette**: 221[8] **Mary Evans**: 49 *br* **Brian Fagan**: 239[9] **Josephine Flood**: 47[3,4] 54[3] 55[4] 57[4] 61 *m* 71 *cr* 74[4] 77[4] 84 *b* 88[4] 91[4] 100[4] 113[4] 161[3] 178[3] 225[3] 239[4] 241[4] **Sonia Halliday & Laura Lushington**: 212 *c* 168 *bl* 168-169 *b* **Robert Harding**: 104 *cb* (Cairo Museum) 199 *cr* 220[4] 222[3] 223[10] 224[10] 225[4] 227 *cr* 238[6] **John Hillelson Agency**: 190[10] (© Dr Georg Gerster) **Michael Holford**: 125[9] 218[4] 212 *br* 219[7] 224[8] 233[6] 238[8] 241[10] **David Horwell**: 209[3] **Hutchison Library**: 139[10] (National Museum, Jos, Nigeria) 227 *cl* (© Mick Csaky) 235[10] (© Mick Csaky) **The Image Bank**: 234[8] (© G Colliva) **Israel Museum, Jerusalem**: 91[6] 165[6] **Keir Collection, Ham, London**: 219[10] **Jane McIntosh**: 24[5] **Pierre de Maret**: 227 *bl* **Professor Alex Marshak**: 39[8] 43 *tl* 47[10] 48 *bc, br* 55[8] 65[8] **National Gallery**: 229 *cr* **National Museum of Ireland, Dublin**: 207[7] **National Museum of Scotland**: 175[4] 179[4] 180[3] 181[3] **Nationalmuseet, Copenhagen**: 75[8] 113[8] **G. Newlands**: 30 *c* **Novosti Press Agency**: 40 *bl* 163[5] **Ann Paludan**: 153[4] 166[4] 206[4] 223[4] 219[3] 237[4] 240[4] **Dr. David Phillipson**: 46[10] 71 *tl* 79[9] **Photo R.N.M., France**: 59 *bl* (Musée des Antiquités Nationales) 103[6] (Louvre) **Josephine Powell, Rome**: 216[6] **Dr. Michael Roaf**: 148[5,6] 164[6] 166[6] 175[6] 176[6] 204[6] 218[6] **Dr. Robert Rodden**: 77[7,8] **Roemer-Pelizaeus-Museum, Hildesheim**: 149[10] **Ann Ronan Collection**: 218[3] **Royal Geographical Society**: 241[7] (Bridgeman Art Library, London) **Royal Ontario Museum**: 155 *cr* **Scala, Florence**: 92 *c* (Iraq Museum, Baghdad) 152[9] 209[8] 235[8] **Bill Schopf**: 20 *tl, tc, tr* 21 *tl* **Science Museum, London**: 237[7] **Professor Thurstan Shaw**: 199 *tl* **Andrew Sibbald**: 160[6] **Tony Stone Worldwide**: 240[8] **Christopher Tadgell**: 236[6] **Paul Taylor**: 21 *cb* 23 *cl* 25 *cr* 27 *c* **J. Thackeray**: 30 *cb* **Ann Thackeray**: 54[10] **Trinity College, Cambridge**: 224[7] **Frank Valla**: 54[6] **Jean Vertut**: 16-17 51 *tl* 58 *bl, tr, tl, cr, br* **Victoria & Albert Museum**: 238[5] **Werner Forman Archive**: 89[10] 91[10] 141 *r* 153[8] 203[8] 207[10] 227 *ct* **York Archaeological Trust**: 209[7] **York Castle Museum**: 193[7].

ADDITIONAL PHOTOGRAPHY BY: University Museum of Archaeology and Anthropology, Cambridge; Pitt-Rivers Museum, Oxford; British Museum (Natural History) – Harry Taylor, Colin Keates; Philip Dowell, Dave King, Steve Gorton, Karl Shone, Andrew McRobb, Kim Taylor, Nina M. de Garis Davies, Stephen Oliver, Matthew Ward, Jerry Young, Martin Norris.

SMITHSONIAN INSTITUTION PICTURE CREDITS
National Museum of Natural History: Except as noted below, all photography of artifacts from the National Museum of Natural History was taken by Mark Gulezian/QuickSilver Photographers for reproduction in the Americas band and in the following features: pp. 32-33 *Olduvai Gorge*; pp. 68-69 *The Big-Game Hunters*; pp. 114-15 *Alpine Lake Villages*; pp. 140-41 *The Olmec of Mexico* (except p. 141 *r*); pp. 194-95 *Temple-Pyramids*; pp. 210-11 *Pueblo Villages*; pp. 242-43 *Inca Roads*. Also pp. 43 *b* 60 *r, c* 70 *r* 85 *c, r* 94 *b* 95 *t* 107 *c, b* 117 *r* 128 *l* 142-43 145 *t, bl* 157 *r, c* 170 *r* 184 *l* 198 *l, r* 213 *t* 228 *t*. Additional Smithsonian photography taken especially for *Smithsonian Timelines* by Mark Gulezian/QuickSilver Photographers appears on the following pages: p. 3 *l, r* p. 5 *far right* p. 6 *second from right* p. 8 *cl, cr* p. 10 *c, first from right* p. 11 *far right* p. 12 *far left, cr* p. 13 *far right*. Additional photography from the National Museum of Natural History: 240[1] Photo Chip Clark, Mural McKay Studios 213 *t* Photo Harold Dougherty 139[1] 223[1] 225[1] Photo Victor Krantz.
National Museum of the American Indian: 123[1] Photo David Heald 128 *r* Photo Karen Furth 137[1] Photo Karen Furth 153[2] Photo David Heald 170[1] Photo David Heald 191[1] Photo Pamela Dewey 203[2] Photo David Heald 205[2] Photo Pamela Dewey 214 *c* Photo Pamela Dewey 228 *r* Photo David Heald 235[2] Photo David Heald 237[2] Photo David Heald.
The Smithsonian would also like to thank the following for their kind permission to reproduce photographs: © **Walter Alva,** Bruning Museum, Lambayeque, Peru: 195 *t, tr, bl, bc, br*; **Dumbarton Oaks Research Library and Collections**, Washington, D.C.: 141 *t* 202 *l*; **Dr. Clifford Evans**: 195 *t, tr*; **Kenneth Garrett**: 68 *l*; **Margaret Jodry**, Rocky Mountain Bison Company: 68 *t*; **Jordan Archaeological Museum**, Department of Antiquities, Amman, Jordan: 81 *c*; **Dr. Ramiro Matos**: 242 *tl*; **National Anthropological Archives**, Smithsonian Institution, Robert Heizer: 140 *lc*; **National Anthropological Archives**, Cosmos Mindeleff: 210 *lt*; **Dr. Richard B. Potts**: 32 *t* 33; **Dr. J. Daniel Rogers**: 210 *bl*; © **Scientific American**, René Millon: 152[2]; **Smithsonian Books**, Smithsonian Institution, photo by Mark Gulezian, painting by John Douglass: 232[2]; **Utah Museum of Natural History**, University of Utah: 77[2]; **Dr. Melinda Zeder**: 81 *t*.